PERSONALITY THEORIES

A GUIDE TO HUMAN NATURE

SECOND EDITION

NICHOLAS S. DiCAPRIO

JOHN CARROLL UNIVERSITY

HOLT, RINEHART AND WINSTON

Fort Worth   Chicago   San Francisco

Philadelphia   Montreal   Toronto   London   Sydney   Tokyo

Library of Congress Cataloging in Publication Data

DiCaprio, Nicholas S.
  Personality theories.

  Bibliography: p. 544
  Includes index.
  1. Personality. I. Title.
BF698.D52   1983   155.2   82-15745

ISBN 0-03-059094-9

Address Editorial correspondence to:
301 Commerce Street
Fort Worth, TX 76102

Holt, Rinehart and Winston, Inc.
The Dryden Press
Saunders College Publishing

PREFACE

Some of the objectives that inspired the first edition are continued in this revision. One of them is to highlight the rich and vital thinking of the major personality theorists and the implications of their views and research for practical problems of living. Each theory may be identified by one or more distinctive themes which embody the continual concerns of humanity. We have drawn from the thinking and research of highly trained and sensitive experts in personality and behavior science. The most powerful constructs and postulates of each theory are elaborated extensively, and the substance of each theory is displayed to best advantage by the format we have established. Again, we may use the analogy of memorable themes from a symphony or of outstanding arias of an opera to bring out the notion of the powerful explanatory constructs and postulates of the theories of personality. Our insights into human nature are expanded and deepened by means of the theories of personality.

This revision stresses the functional aspect of the major theories of personality. The theories are viewed as functional tools that should aid us in describing, understanding, predicting, and changing human personality and behavior; that is, they constitute a guide to human nature, the subtitle of this edition. From the perspective of this text, the value of a theory of personality depends upon the purpose we demand of it. For example, one theory may serve better as a guide to therapy than as a guide to research. The theories may be judged in terms of their usefulness as guides, with the understanding that they vary considerably in the possible uses we may expect of them.

One important function of theories of personality is as a *guide to observation* of behavior and data collection. The theories should tell us what to look for and how to interpret what we observe. The treatment of each theory in this book directs the user in selecting the behaviors that are most distinctive and characteristic of the person being studied. Each theory has its own perspective, its own particular area of focus. A theory may stress behaviors that reveal principles of development, learning, motivation, conflict, or fulfillment.

We may also use theories of personality as *guides to prediction*, or the generation of hypotheses to be tested empirically. A section of each chapter treats the theories as guides to research. The scientific value of a theory depends upon its capacity to generate testable hypotheses. Although this is not the only criterion for determining the value of a theory, it is certainly one of the most critical.

Another important application of the theories of personality is as *guides to therapy* or counseling. Most of the personality theorists discussed in this text were or are also personality or behavior therapists. They have developed theories to account for what they were observing and to guide them in restoring healthy functioning and growth. As a guide to therapy or counseling, a theory should specify the potential causes of abnormalities. It should also reveal the nature of ideal personality and living. For each of the major theorists, these topics are treated in sections entitled Views on Abnormality and Views on Ideal Personality and Living.

As discussed in the sections on Guides to Living, another important function of some of the theories of personality is their potential for personal application. Some of the theories can help us to understand better our problems and portray for us ideals to promote effective living. Several of the theories specify quite explicitly the attributes of fulfillment and the good life, for example: Allport's criteria of maturity, Rogers' fully functioning person, Maslow's self-actualized living, and Fromm's productive orientation. Some of the theories even offer suggestions for attaining the ideal state they portray.

In the first edition we sought to highlight the distinctive focus of each theory by dividing the book into key topics of personality study: development, motivation, learning, conflict, and fulfillment. The theories were examined from the standpoint of their contributions to one or another of these major topic areas. In this edition the theories are organized according to broader conceptions of humans, which we have termed *models of human nature*. The purpose of the change of emphasis is to view more globally the various theories of personality.

Theories of personality have certain similarities in that they have some common attributes, so that several may be grouped under a single category, which we call a model of human nature. A general model is defined by certain characteristics, for example, assigning a major role to unconscious motivation; thus, theories that have this aspect in common may be grouped under the same model. Following the first chapter dealing with the nature and uses of theories of personality we have grouped the theories under four models:

1. The psychodynamic model stresses unconscious motivation as the major determining factor in human life. The spokesmen for this position are Freud, Jung, and Murray.
2. The ego-social model stresses the powerful role of the social and cultural environment in the development of the personality, and especially the growing ego, which is also assigned a major controlling force in personality. The representatives of this school are Erikson, Adler, and Horney.
3. The humanistic-existential model concentrates on attributes and problems associated with the condition of being human. The theories of Allport, Rogers, Maslow, and Fromm are presented as prototypes of this model.
4. The behavioristic model stresses objectivity in definition, observation, and measurement of variables. The *radical behaviorists*—for example, Watson and Skinner, concentrate on environmental determinants of behavior and reject personality variables. The *cognitive behaviorists*—for example, Bandura, Rotter, Ellis, and Mischel—accept intervening variables, with specific emphasis on cognition.

One advantage of grouping theories under more general models of human nature is that similarities and differences among the various groupings and within each model group may be clearly highlighted. Another advantage is that the order of presentation also points out the historical progression from the early theories of Freud and Jung to the current cognitive behavioristic theories.

To further highlight the distinctive themes of each theory, a standard format of topical headings has been followed when feasible. The headings represent the basic issues of personality study. The same topics are discussed for each theory under the following headings: (1) Biography and Historical Perspective, (2) Basic Constructs and Postulates, (3) Views on Abnormality, (4) Views on Ideal Personality and Living, (5) Critical Evaluation, (6) Guides to Research, (7) Guides to Living, (8) Summary, (9) Glossary, (10) Suggested Readings.

Distinctive features of the present text include greatly expanded summaries, glossaries in which related terms are grouped as an aid to study, and suggested readings with brief overviews. The general organization of the book, along with the standard format of each chapter, has been designed to promote mastery of the many theories of personality surveyed.

ACKNOWLEDGMENTS

This revision was greatly enriched by the work, thought, and personal support of several people who are important to me. I owe a special debt of gratitude to Joyce McConnell for her sustained effort through many dreary and routine tasks. She was a model student assistant. Bernice Kiley, who typed the manuscript, devoted many long afternoons to proofreading the manuscript. Margaret Minshall worked diligently on all phases of the project from the very beginning. Cynthia Downing reviewed most of the chapters and supplied valuable notes. Ada Harrison was always ready to record material as needed. Mirian Keresman, secretary, took care of many odds and ends which were invaluable to the completion of the project.

I owe a special debt of gratitude to the Committee on Research of John Carroll University for reducing my teaching schedule so that I could work on the revision. I also want to thank Dr. Elizabeth Swenson, of the Psychology Department, who gave me priority in scheduling classes.

Finally, I wish to thank the following reviewers for their helpful suggestions: Dr. Leon Teft, of Bridgeport University; Dr. Richard Beattie, of Mississippi State University; Professor John Vogels, of Baldwin Wallace College; Professor Brian Yates, of American University; Professor Robert Williams, of William Jewel College; Professor Donald Bowers, of Community College of Philadelphia; Professor Rodger Fink, of Towson State University; and Dr. James Megas, of Pan American University.

Cleveland, Ohio   *Nicholas S. DiCaprio*
December 1982

CONTENTS

NATURE AND USES OF PERSONALITY THEORIES

INTRODUCTION

In studying another person or ourselves, we may apply knowledge about perception, learning, motivation, and development, but we need to find a way of *characterizing* the distinctive quality of the particular individual, what G. W. Allport (1961) termed "patterned individuality." Each person is certainly like every other person in some ways and quite similar to a number of people; nevertheless, if we follow Murray's idea (1938), each person has his or her own particular identity and style of life. We are quick to sense when someone we know is not himself or herself. The major task of the student of personality is to *characterize* the individual's behavior. To put it simply, we should be able to form a model of a person so that the characteristics of the model parallel the actual characteristics and processes that take place in the person who is being represented. Studying the model should enable us to learn about the person it represents. Model means representation; thus, we can have a model of a single person or a model that depicts human nature.

Our curiosity need seems to impel us to strive to understand things, people, and events. We analyze and synthesize, compare and contrast, seek to know constituents and total contexts and meaning. We wish to form mental representations of things and the laws that govern them. Our symbolic representations may simply consist of images or ideas or of more complex forms such as hypotheses and assumptions, or we may strive for comprehensive representations that are termed models. A model of humans is a conceptual portrayal of human nature. It serves both as a summary of the ways in which we view the nature of humans and also as a potential guide for understanding the makeup and operating principles of an individual's personality and behavior.

CAUSES OF BEHAVIOR

What are the various causes of behavior? One way to conceptualize the determinants of behavior is to categorize them as (1) genetic, (2) organismic, (3) environmental-situational, and (4) personality variables.

Genetic Causes

HEREDITY

Our behavior is certainly influenced by our inheritance. The most obvious example is our sex. We inherit a specific constitutional makeup that greatly influences the lifestyles we might develop. A person who is tall and thin will have to face a world that is quite different from the one faced by a person who is short and fat even when the environmental circumstances appear to be quite similar. A bad mood may be due to an individual's hormones rather than to bad thoughts or unpleasant experiences. Certain abilities seem to be largely inherited; thus you may have inherited the body structure and muscular equipment characteristic of an athlete. A professional football player is generally quite different in physique from a professional basketball player. A sense of rhythm, tonal sensitivity, and timing, all of which appear to be inborn talents, would make a musical career more feasible for one person than for another. Though difficult to assess, hereditary factors surely are a major cause of behavior.

There is no question that we are born with certain native equipment and that we have potentialities and predispositions to grow in certain directions. Striking resemblances between parents and offspring are found in many variables. But in humans the role of learning is so great and the possible directions that behavior can take are so plastic that it is difficult to parcel out the direct influence of heredity. Nevertheless, we do know that genetic factors are major determinants of behavior.

The biological basis of behavior, which is so pervasively influenced by heredity, is the major determinant of behavior for William Sheldon (1954). Sheldon relates constitutional makeup (one's bodybuild) to enduring temperamental traits. He divides people into three types: the endomorph, who is short and fat; the mesomorph, who is muscular and broad; and the ectomorph, who is tall and thin. Each type can be described by a set of characteristics: for example, the endomorph is comfort-loving and congenial, the mesomorph is energetic and assertive, and the ectomorph is secretive and shy. Sheldon does make allowance in his system for variations in body types and temperament. The key point here is that biology is the major determinant of an individual's personality and behavior according to Sheldon. This is an extreme position that oversimplifies the determinants of behavior.

Organismic Causes

Behavior is greatly influenced by physiological, biochemical, and other organismic determinants. Our moods, our capacity to carry on sustained work, our emotional reactivity, even our intelligence — practically everything that goes on in personality is influenced in important ways by organismic causes (Arnold, 1970). We could not understand the causes of behavior without considering the organismic influences. The fact remains that although behavior is influenced by organismic determinants and though some of the most enduring aspects of personality have a biochemical basis, for the personality psychologist the *major determinants of behavior are personality and situational variables.* We cannot, however, ignore the biological aspect of behavior (Raush et al., 1959).

If a person is experiencing an intense emotion, this will be reflected in marked changes in the body such as changes in skin chemistry, dryness of the mouth, stomach cramps, and heart palpitations. But the body can certainly influence the personality: fatigue can cause depression, irritability, and listlessness. A toothache or other physical ailment may temporarily incapacitate a person, so that the only major concern is relief. We should always be alert for the possibility that organic factors are the cause of behavior. Typically, several causes are active, and organic ones may be a part of the picture. Some people must always deal with chronic physical conditions such as indigestion, low energy level, chronic arthritis, backache, recurrent headaches, and general nervousness.

Environmental-Situational Causes

The physical and cultural environment plays a widespread and continuous role in determining the form and operations of behavior. We need only to think of the pervasive influence of learning upon every facet of life. We are born into a culture, and it imposes all sorts of demands and pressures. The culture not only presents us with the problems we are to solve but also prescribes the acceptable solutions that are available to us. So important are environmental and situational causes that some psychologists, notably the learning theorists, have given preponderant weight to them.

We are constantly bombarded by stimuli. A friend makes a cutting remark, and we are not quite sure how to respond. An unexpected bill comes through the mail, and we are not sure that we can pay it. While driving to work, someone cuts in front of us and causes an accident. Certain things may be more upsetting than others. We may feel uncomfortable in social situations and thus avoid them.

One way to study personality is to identify *situations* that produce *responses*. For example, we may discover that we get upset when someone does not see things the way we do. When something seems logical and perfectly reasonable, we may feel that others should see it our way. Knowing this situation-response relationship provides useful information about ourselves or others.

We can learn much about a person by identifying situations and stimuli that produce changes in behavior and experience. As we know someone better, we can be quite specific concerning the types of responses that will occur in particular situations. We may be quite certain that Mary would be especially pleased by a surprise party or that John gets extremely angry when he does not occupy the center of attention. One situation after another sets off specific chains of thoughts, feelings, and desires. Our responses to these situations may become habitual, so that we behave in characteristic ways; for example, we may be depressed on rainy days or typically nervous just before taking a test.

The behaviorists were very much impressed by this basic psychological approach; they believed that we did not need to rely on anything except the relationship between situations and responses. This general model has been termed the S–R approach because it reduces all explanations of behavior to stimuli or situations and responses. Both are observable and measurable; thus we need not have recourse to personality variables, which are unobservable.

Personality Variables

PERSONALITY

We have seen that our behavior is influenced by our heredity, by the condition of our body, and by stimuli and situations; but there is more. Our personality itself is a major source of behavior. If we neglect personality variables, we would not be capable of obtaining a complete picture of the causes of behavior. A friend may greet us every time we encounter him or her, but on a particular occasion totally ignore us. The present behavior is not simply the outcome of the immediate situation but is influenced by a contemporary state of mind. Perhaps our friend may have been told that we said something critical about him or her. If the person had just received a failing grade, behavior might also be different from what is typical. As the social behaviorists claim, a particular behavior depends upon the total context of factors that are active in any given moment, many of which are within the personality itself (person variables). A certain event may cause one man to be upset, whereas his friend is not affected in the least. The two people respond differently because they have different personality make-ups. We may accept the assumption that personality is a something that is describable, that grows and changes, and that has working principles which can be known. We will study various theories of personality to learn about the components, dynamics, and development of personality.

When we do not know the structure and working principles of a thing, we may begin by guessing. We seek to understand the causes of behavior. If we cannot account for behavior by means of external causes, we may look to personality variables, such as sentiments, drives, and anxieties. These must be inferred from behavior if we hope to be successful in depicting personality. If Jim always resigns when he is about to be promoted, there are a number of personality factors that may be causing this peculiar behavior. It might be a sense of inferiority that will not allow Jim to experience success in anything. It could be a profound fear of failure that holds Jim back from taking any responsibilities he believes he can't handle. The explanation could even be what personality scientists call masochism, an insidious tendency toward self-destruction.

Whichever explanation we accept, it is necessary that there be other evidence, other manifestations of the particular personality variable we have assumed or postulated as the cause of the behavior. Thus, we can see that personality factors that are tentatively proposed as explanations must be verified in other behaviors.

Lest the reader get the wrong impression, a caution should be noted regarding personality factors. As Mischel (1973b) argues, personality variables are not to be viewed as automatic dispositions that control behavior but rather as determinants that are greatly influenced and modified by situations. Even a slight change in a situation could cause a radical alteration in behavior; for example, a man who is stern with his family may be a jokester with his office staff.

Any proposed personality variable, such as suspiciousness, accounts for more than just the present behaviors. This variable existed in the past and may continue into the future. Thus, ample opportunity for validation of this suspiciousness is possible. The point is a basic principle of personality study: if we know something about another person, his or her past, present, and future will be revealed to some extent because personality has stability, and personal identity does not easily change (Kelly, 1955). We might sum this up by saying that any proposed variable must be verified.

To sum up: Personality theorists do not deny the significant influence of the varied behavior determinants; rather, they deal with their effect on the makeup and functioning of personality. Thus, the environment influences personality; the biological determinants affect personality functioning; heredity fixes the limits of personality development.

DEFINITION OF PERSONALITY

Core and Peripheral Components of Identity

The term *personality* is used in many ways. It may refer to all there is to know about a person or to what is unique about someone or to what is typical of a person. The popular meaning includes traits like social appeal and attractiveness to others. But, from a scientific point of view, we all have a personality. It is simply our individual *psychological nature*. For the sake of simplicity, we may think of personality as an individual's

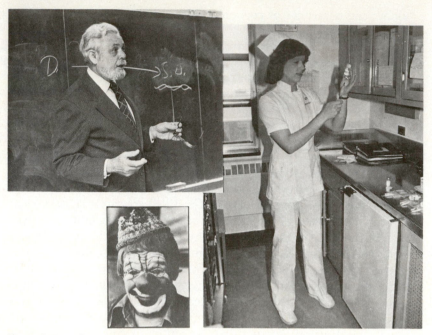

Photo credits: *upper* © Frank Siteman 1980/Stock, Boston; *lower* Anestis Diakopoulos/Stock, Boston; *right* Danbury Hospital/ © Russ Kinne Photo Researchers, Inc.

A major aspect of personality development is the establishment of one's personal identity, which is expressed and defined by the roles one assumes.

personal identity. Identity has a number of components, some of which are more central than others: central components define the person whereas peripheral components are limited and subject to change. As we become acquainted with someone, we acquire knowledge of his or her her core identity.

We know that some things about personality are more central, more enduring, and more characteristic and also that other things are simply peripheral. Consider the following peripheral characteristics:

- Mary likes coffee rather than tea.
- She prefers sugar and cream rather than black coffee.
- She takes baths, not showers.

Such statements reveal very little of significance about Mary. We could catalog hundreds, perhaps thousands, of similar statements and would still not have a clear picture of the person that Mary is. Contrast the preceding descriptive statements with the following, which reveal central aspects of Mary's identity:

- Mary is frequently selfish in her dealings with others.
- Mary is a poor loser and not a very good sport in any competitive game.
- Mary gets easily depressed when things do not go her way.
- Mary submits readily to authority.

A core aspect of personal identity is analogous to a constant in an equation (in this case, the personality equation). It almost always must be considered in the evaluation process. A theory of the person would have to include this factor. Its absence would constitute a significant difference in personal identity. If personal integrity is an essential component of your identity, it would cut across much of what you do. In making decisions, in social contacts, and in practically everything you do, personal integrity would play a part. In the same way, such a pervasive factor as intelligence certainly must play a part in most of what you do—your thoughts, judgments, perceptions. Having greater or lesser intelligence would certainly make a big difference in total functioning. Such core determinants of personal identity as having or not having a sense of humor, respect for others, civic-mindedness, and so forth make a difference in overall functioning. In attempting to become acquainted with yourself and others, you should always clearly distinguish between core and peripheral aspects of personal identity.

Another way to think of the notion of personal identity is to consider instances when a person does not seem to be himself or herself. When an essential ingredient of identity is missing or is changed significantly, we observe that the person seems different; that is, he is not behaving in a characteristic manner according to our model of this person. For example, an old school friend may seem different to us because she has become more serious and sober. A temporary change of identity may occur during a serious illness. We say of such a person, "He is not his normal self."

OUR OWN THEORY OF PERSONALITY

We form *images or conceptions* of people, including ourselves. These conceptions may be only approximately correct and, certainly, quite incomplete. A particular trait may be overweighted, and we might overlook many important qualities (Kelly, 1955). What we find depends upon a theory of personality, either our own or someone else's. We may think of people in terms of rather limited categories: they are bright or dull, generous or stingy, attractive or unattractive, pleasing or not pleasing to us. Our particular theory of personality guides us in observing the behavior of ourselves and others and helps us to interpret what we observe. It includes certain assumptions about the nature of humans, such as that all people are selfish or that people are really out to hurt us if they can or that everyone wants to be at the top. We also have our own interpretation of what is desirable and undesirable behavior. One person may value competitiveness and judge another or himself (or herself) by the amount of this dimension displayed. A second person may value considerateness of others and judge himself (or herself) and others accordingly. People tend to be quite categorical in their judgments: their thinking runs along lines of either/or without allowing for intermediate states. They describe others with single terms, for example, a grouch, a nice guy, a real sport, a passivist.

Suppose that you are dining at a restaurant, and at the next table is a young couple with two children. There is much commotion as the children and parents argue over the choice of food. While waiting for the order to be filled, the children become restless

Radical changes are occurring in the models we form of the other sex.

Bruce Roberts/Rapho, Photo Researchers

and quarrelsome. The younger child gets out of his chair and starts running down the aisle between the tables. Immediately the older child begins chasing him, and a real show ensues. All this creates quite a stir among the patrons, several of whom also have children of the same age who are seated quietly at their tables. The young parents are carrying on an animated conversation, apparently unconcerned about the disturbance caused by their children. Several of the patrons are evidently upset, and one of them calls for the waitress and makes a complaint. Still the young couple show no sign of displeasure with their children, who are getting noisier by the minute.

An analysis of this situation will bring out the concept of theories of personality. The patrons who were disturbed apparently had a model of a child that established a certain behavior as acceptable and other behaviors as unacceptable for a child in a restaurant setting. Furthermore, their disapproval of the parents' behavior was also based on a theory. Not everyone in the restaurant was disturbed; thus, it may be concluded that people vary considerably in the theories of people they bring into a situation. Both the children and their parents were judged according to preexisting concepts and norms of conduct. It appeared that some of the patrons were more disturbed by the behavior of the parents than by that of their children. Each person had rather specific models that served as a framework or guide, permitting observations to be categorized, evaluated, and synthesized. This is what we call the beginnings of a theory of personality.

Assumptions Underlying Our Views of Human Nature

As we have noted, our views of human nature are guided by hidden assumptions that serve as the ground rules of our judgments. Identifying these assumptions can help us to broaden our own theory of personality. Consider your position on the following questions:

1. In what ways do you think that people are equal?
2. On what bases do you respect people? How much weight do you give to status, age, wealth, roles, titles, appearance, type of background?
3. Do you believe that some people are more developed as humans than others? What does it mean to be human?
4. Where do you stand on accepting differences among people? Do you believe that people of certain races are not as human as you are? Could you fall in love with someone of another race?
5. How much freedom do you think you have in shaping your own life? Over what aspects of your life do you have control? Consider the same question from the standpoint of the past. How much stress would you place on your heredity, your family history, early childhood experiences in shaping your life? What aspects of your environment continue to control your behavior? What things and people restrict your behaviors and choices of action?
6. What causes evil in people? Do you think that some people are by nature antisocial, destructive, and violent and that some people are good, moral, sociable, and appealing? Where does the evil in people come from: human nature, our early experiences, current frustrations, deficiencies in development?
7. What are your views on personality and behavior change? Do you believe that you have will power? Do you think that you can change almost everything about yourself if you really set yourself to doing so? Do you believe that marriage changes most people? How much influence in shaping your life are these factors: learning, hurtful and pleasant experiences, other people, professional counselors and therapists?
8. What are the driving forces behind your behavior? Are you motivated more by your past, your present, or your intended future?
9. Do you believe that you have an unconscious mind? If so, how can you find out what is in it? Where did it come from?
10. What are the causes of your behavior? organism? environment? heredity? history? personality? Is one of these causes more influential at one time than at another?
11. Where do your feelings about yourself originate?

Theories Vary in Comprehensiveness

Our own models are usually limited in scope, often being only a general image or concept. We may have formed a single concept to encompass an entire class of people, a racial or religious group, for example, that allows for no individual differences in evaluation. A single category is used to stereotype all the members of the class whereas the individuality of the various members may not even be sensed.

Consider a child growing up in a traditional American middle-class home. If the child is a boy, he will have a model of husband and fatherhood that includes such attributes as head-of-household, breadwinner, authority figure, disciplinarian, final arbiter, or dominant figure. His model of wife will include such concepts as cook and homemaker, feminine submissiveness, nurse and comforting person, and similar feminine roles. His models of the respective roles of the sexes will have a significant influence on much of his behavior. (Here we are using the term *model* to stand for a mini theory of personality.) If such a child grows up and marries a woman who does not have similar models, there certainly will be considerable friction. If his experiences alter his models as he assimilates the changed roles of men and women, his marital life is likely to be successful. Narrow and inflexible models of friendship, of vocational success, of parental roles, and all other aspects of life will produce frustration and conflict. Our models become like prejudices once they are consolidated.

THEORIES AS MODELS

What Is a Model?

As a beginning step toward understanding the meaning of a theory of personality, we will use the analogy of a theory as a model. In simplest terms, a model depicts or represents something. A globe is a model that depicts the location and features of specific areas of our planet. A statue is a model. A child builds a model airplane or ship. An architect may draw a model of a house that has not yet been constructed, and it may serve as a guide in the construction of the house. The model depicts the layout of rooms, the location and specification of fixtures, and even the specific characteristics of the materials of construction. We can use the model to learn about the heating system, the plumbing system, storage areas, sleeping areas, or any other aspect of the home. If the model is elaborated in much detail, we can learn about specific operations. The more complete the model, the better is the picture we may attain. Similarly, a model of personality depicts the components of an individual's identity. The model may tell us what structures or enduring features to look for, the operating principles or personality dynamics, and what constitutes normal growth and fulfillment.

One point about personality models should be kept in mind: personality models are *postulated*. The personality model is derived from inference, hunches, and imagination. To put it simply, it is a guess about the makeup and operations of personality. The usefulness of a model depends upon its validity, namely, the correspondence between itself and what it represents. Validity must be established and not simply assumed. Most of the personality theories discussed in this book are crude models of human nature that have received little or no validation according to the strictures of scientific criteria. The personality scientist uses his or her experiences and knowledge of existing principles as the foundation for his or her proposed model, but, ultimately, the model proposed is the personality scientist's own construction as Kelly (1955) points out. By means of models of personality, we will attempt to understand what happens within personality when it is growing and functioning normally or abnormally.

What Is a Theory of Personality?

A theory of personality is a characterization of personality that is based on observation, intuitive hunches, rational considerations, and the discoveries of experimental research. We naturally desire to put our knowledge into some type of orderly system, as in the case of a map that depicts the major features of a geographical area. The map may be used to obtain a total picture of the layout and other geographical features of the area. This would be difficult to obtain by personal travel and observation.

We do not have a theory of personality that is as exact as a map. Our characterizations or theories of personality are more like portraits. A portrait is one person's interpretation of what is being depicted. It must bear some resemblance to the subject who is being portrayed in order to be considered a work of art. Sometimes there may be too much emphasis on certain features, and thus the picture is somewhat distorted. We should, therefore, be aware of the basic assumptions of the various theories of personality we will be considering because, like portraits, they too may be one-sided or distorted in other ways.

Scientists also seek to formulate models of what they are attempting to study, particularly when the object is highly complex or not yet observable, like the atom. Their models may in actuality be more like portraits than a real map, but they cannot in principle take the liberties that the artist does; thus, their real aim is to create a "map."

What we term personality cannot be observed directly. We certainly can learn about it from our own personal experience. It surely can be influenced by external stimuli, and it can be known through its effects, observable behavior; thus, we can attempt to form a theory of its makeup and working principles. We might also study the nature of its growth and how to bring about change and certain desirable ends. The theory we form to interpret our findings can also be used to make predictions about what behavior we might expect under given conditions. This is what is meant by the practical use of a theory of personality: It can be used to help us in testing new observations by experimentation and personal experience. This is exactly what the physicist does with the model of the atom.

A theory of personality serves as a model that informs us about the nature of humans. Many of the theories of personality were formulated by professional psychotherapists for the purpose of helping them to picture the components and working principles of the personality, which they hoped to restore to health. The theory was useful if it helped them understand what went wrong in the development or functioning of personality. The theory might specify what should be ideal development and functioning for people. The therapist needed an understanding of the causes of abnormal behavior and also some idea of what constituted normal or ideal behavior in order to bring about change.

We will deal with theories of personality that are more complex than single categories or concepts. The theories of the personality scientists have many terms and working principles that should enable us to describe, explain, predict, and influence the behavior of a wide range of people. In the restaurant example, we spoke of models of children. A comprehensive theory of personality should be able to account for wide experiences among people and encompass many possible models.

Why So Many Theories of Personality?

The question of whether there could be a single, all-embracing theory of personality that would render all existing theories obsolete has been taken up by Professor Leon Levy (1970). Given the nature of a theory as an interlocking system of postulates, principles, and definitions that explain and predict behavior in general and the behavior of the individual in particular, Levy takes the position that *no single theory could accomplish such a task*. He maintains the following:

> It is unlikely that a single comprehensive theory of personality could ever be formulated to account for all the phenomena within the domain of personality. There are surely relationships between many of these phenomena, but there is no reason to believe that they are all governed by a single set of principles, and that they could all be encompassed by a single theory of personality. Nor is there any reason why the field of personality would not be well served by the formulation of a number of personality theories (in contrast to theories of personality) each concerned with accounting for a limited range of phenomena within the domain of personality. This indeed appears to be what has been happening, and it seems both strategically and scientifically sound [Levy, 1970, p. 440].

It soon will become obvious to you that there is no all-encompassing theory of personality, and perhaps, as Levy believes, there never will be. The various theories of personality have a "range of convenience" (Kelly, 1955), which means that *they apply best to certain aspects of personality*. For instance, Erikson's theorizing focuses upon the *development* of personality. Murray's theorizing concentrates on *motivation*. Freud dealt a great deal with *conflict*. The focus of each theory is well defined, and each theorist offers his (or her) most valuable insights in a particular area of personality study.

The theories of personality we will discuss differ on basic issues regarding the nature of people — for example, the degree to which the environment is stressed over the forces within the personality, the place given to the nonrational and irrational in people, the highest potentials that are possible, the type of training that should be undertaken, the role of self and will, and many other important dimensions that make a real difference in our approach to life.

THEORIES AS GUIDES TO HUMAN NATURE

We can judge the usefulness of a theory of personality by its capacity to describe, explain, predict, and change personality. A particular theory may be more adequate in meeting these objectives than others. One theory may be more descriptive and explanatory for one type of problem or personality makeup than another. Furthermore, it is possible to personalize a theory and use its constructs and postulates for self-understanding and self-improvement.

Guides to Description

Just as we have a physical identity, we also have a personal identity by which we are known. One attempts to obtain a picture or conceptual model of a person. For example, try to think of the ways you would describe a friend, your teacher, the family doctor, an older sister, and yourself.

Just as certain terms are used to describe appearance, such as tall, short, light-skinned, good figure, so also terms are needed to describe personality makeup. To describe means "to name" or "to label." A particular form of description involves classifying things or people into categories.

One way to arrive at descriptive terms is to think of common verbal nouns such as walking, talking, eating, singing, loving. Such terms are descriptive at the level of observable behavior, but there are also terms that attempt to describe more central aspects of personality. A frequently used category of personality description is the *trait concept*. There are literally hundreds of trait terms to describe all aspects of personality. Consider such traits as generosity, cleanliness, stinginess, conservativism, radicalism, revolutionism. Certain behaviors are expressive of a trait; that is, many different behaviors have the common element of generosity, for example, giving and sharing. In describing personality, we have a great advantage when we can identify descriptive units such as traits that exhibit the natural patterns in personality makeup. We understand more completely the makeup of personality by knowing such units and labeling them properly. The patterning may be still more complexly organized into types. Thus a type is expressed by several traits that have one or more common elements.

From the foregoing, it should be obvious that we need descriptive terms that can depict the patterning that personality makeup displays. By way of an example of the different levels of patterning, we might consider the personality of an introvert. An introvert is characterized by such traits as withdrawing from social participation, self-preoccupation, focusing of interest inward on ideas rather than on people, valuing inner experience more than external contacts. Each of the traits that describe the introverted orientation is expressed in quite specific behaviors, so that, for instance, we might designate certain behaviors as avoiding people and engaging in solitary activities. A good theory of personality should provide concepts that can adequately depict the different levels of complexity and patterning in personality and, furthermore, be broad enough in scope to encompass the wide diversity of personality types.

Guides to Explanation

To explain means "to identify causes" or to "make sense" of something. We know a young couple who seemed to have an unusually good relationship, but we just learned that they are getting a divorce. Why do marital partners have so much trouble getting along? Why is there so much strife in the world? On a personal level, too, we are frequently puzzled by our lack of understanding. Why is it that we make friends easily and cannot keep them very long? We might wish to be more poised and emotionally controlled in social relationships, but we find ourselves getting tense and too eager to please. When we say that we are looking for explanations, the scientist would say that we are looking for causes or active conditions. Whereas description answers the "what" question, explanation answers the "why" question.

External causes. As we have noted, the principal causes of behavior may be external in the immediate setting or in the personality makeup itself. Although the instigating cause or condition is external, the total effect on behavior involves personality factors. For instance, just a stranger in a small town might arouse fear and suspicion. In this instance, external and internal causes are operating. Our trait of suspiciousness was set off by an external event. On the other hand, the personality factor may be so powerful as to be the major instigator of behavior, as when a lonely person seeks out companionship or a talkative one seeks out a willing listener. Satisfactory explanations must involve both types of causes in order to be complete, but one explanation may be dominant. Consider the following propositions: A child is having problems in school *because* he is not accepted by other children. A young woman is frustrated *because* no eligible suitor is available in her immediate circumstances. A man is extremely resentful *because* he was passed up for a promotion. The term "because" in these propositions denotes a causal relationship between one event and another. To explain means to discover this causal connection.

Internal causes. The three propositions just listed express causal relationships between external situations or stimuli and behaviors. In the following statements, the primary causes are personality dimensions: Susan will not accept a date *because* she is convinced that she will fail to impress. John will usually submit to the will of others *because* he is afraid of being rejected by them. Jack approaches only unattractive girls *because* he does not want to risk being turned down. The source of the difficulty in each case is a personality factor that is probably abnormal.

One more point about explanation is salient. We collectively and individually have a strong motivation to explain what is observed. So powerful is this desire that when factual explanations are not available, tentative ones are invented. Returning to our example of the couple that is getting a divorce, it is very natural to seek an explanation. Our explanations will vary in validity according to the amount of supporting evidence. Theories of personality provide tentative internal determinants based on the experience and knowledge of a personality scientist and, typically, a personality therapist. Typical constructs that personality psychologists use to designate the causes of behavior are needs, traits, types, roles, intentions, sentiments, habits, dispositions, tendencies, trends, ego functions, thoughts, images, and desires.

Correlational approach. We may distinguish between the *causal* approach and the *correlational* approach as a means of explaining. We have considered the causal approach: relating behavior to environmental causes, to historical causes, to biological causes, to personality causes, to conscious or unconscious determinants. However, we may observe that certain behaviors are found together. A person who conforms to the demands of others may also be submissive and shy. One who feels dominant in relation to others may also be high on extroversion. Because personality has *organization* and *structure*, we can discover the factors that are correlated. Explanation frequently takes the form of identifying the network of interacting or coacting personality variables (Cronback, 1957).

Guides to Hypotheses and Prediction

One of our greatest assets is the ability to anticipate the future. We know that, on the Fourth of July in certain places, it is much more likely to be warm and sunny than cold and snowy. We know this, not through some special intuition or divine revelation, but through knowledge of repeated previous instances. On the individual level, the ability to anticipate and prepare for the unknown future is a significant aspect of effective living. We can prepare adequately to the extent that our predictions are valid.

But predictions that scientists make differ markedly from the ordinary notion of prediction. Scientists make predictions on the basis of their knowledge of causes and effects, conditions and consequences, and variables that predict other variables through correlation.

There are many pseudosciences that purport to make predictions. The fortune-teller, the tea-leaf reader, the diviner who uses cards—all prognosticate future events without any particular evidence to draw from. At times the prediction is correct by chance, but sometimes the diviner uses subtle cues about the person to make a prediction and thus is using the legitimate methods of science, perhaps without realizing it. Most of the time, though, the predictions are simply guesses. Scientists do not deny the possibility of prediction of the future based on personal gifts, but they do not accept this method as one of their scientific tools. Then in what sense does prediction play a part in science, and how can models of personality be used to make prediction in a scientific sense?

One useful function of a theory is prediction. A theory should allow the user to predict events or relationships, which may then be tested or verified by observation and experiment. Explanation is usually easier than prediction because theories contain general principles that can be stretched or interpreted to cover almost any behavior (Holt, 1962). It is much easier to explain phenomena after they have taken place than to predict them.

Freud observed rather frequently that his adult patients displayed a childish quality in certain areas of their lives. He finally concluded that these childish trends were fixations of desires and motives blocked or frustrated in early life. He proposed a principle to account for or explain this phenomenon: Frustrated needs or desires of childhood remain in unaltered form throughout life. This principle seems to explain his repeated observations, but there are other ways of accounting for the same thing. What is needed is an experimental test of the postulate. We might think of an application of

Michael Weisbrot and Family/Stock, Boston

A fortune teller bases his or her predictions on an untested system. The therapist uses a conceptual model of personality to draw inferences.

this principle in a contrived situation. We might, for example, predict that children who have received strict oral training will chew tasteless gum significantly longer than a matched group who have not been orally frustrated. We would have to define and measure "oral frustration" operationally in order to select our two groups. If the experiment were carried out and the hypothesis received confirmation, we would have to conclude that Freud's postulate about childhood frustration is a useful guide from which to make predictions. Usually, one confirmation of a hypothesis drawn from a theory is not sufficient to establish a postulate as a principle of behavior. Many hypotheses must be derived and repeatedly tested. Probably the best test of a theory is its capacity for suggesting hypotheses that are confirmed. Hall and Lindzey summarize the predictive uses of a personality theory as follows:

> First, and most important, it leads to the collection of *observation of relevant empirical relations not yet observed.* The theory should lead to a systematic expansion of knowledge concerning the phenomena of interest and this expansion ideally should be mediated or stimulated by the derivation from the theory of specific empirical propositions (statements, hypotheses, predictions) that are subject to empirical test. In a central sense, the core of any science lies in the discovery of stable empirical relationships between events or variables. The function of a theory is to further this process in a systematic manner. The theory can be seen as a kind of proposition mill grinding out related empirical statements which

can then be confirmed or rejected in the light of suitably controlled empirical data [Hall and Lindzey, 1970, p. 12].[1]

Another point about prediction: If we have confidence in a theory (confidence in a theory is gained through repeated confirmation of hypotheses derived from it), we can make predictions rather than ask questions. Instead of posing the question, "I wonder what would happen if I do such and such," we may make a presumption: "I'll bet that if I do such and such, I will get the results that the theory proposes." Prediction requires principles that have been demonstrated to have some validity. The first stages of science begin with questions, but as empirical knowledge is accumulated and useful theories are developed, predictions become possible. If we learn how to use rewards to influence behavior, we may specify the behaviors that will occur under the rewarding conditions set up by the experimenter.

Erikson proposes that there are eight stages of life and that each requires that the ego accomplish a certain task: for instance, a sense of trust, a sense of autonomy, of initiative, or of identity. The researcher might draw some inferences about each of the stages and test them. He or she might identify those individuals who have not attained the goal set for a particular stage and might study what happens to the ego accomplishments under stress. Allport proposed seven aspects of the development of the self, and again we might draw inferences that could be tested experimentally. Rotter suggests that those who believe that they have control of their circumstances behave quite differently from those who believe that control is external to them. Much research has been generated by this proposal. A scientifically useful theory will stimulate research through its postulates. From a persoanl point of view a useful theory will actually engender self-knowledge and knowledge of others, as well as promote the art of living.

The distinction between asking a question and proposing a hypothesis may illustrate the valid use of a theory to make predictions. We begin by posing questions. When we meet someone for the first time, we pose many questions that we hope will be answered: Do I like him? Does he like me? Would he enjoy a party or music or sports? As we acquire knowledge, we begin to propose hypotheses: I know that he will enjoy a surprise birthday party. I know that she was hurt by that remark. I'll bet that they will not like that restaurant. Before we can propose hypotheses, which should be understood as predictions in this context, we need considerable supporting evidence or a sound model of personality. A hypothesis is an affirmative statement of a relationship between two or more events. If a model of personality truly depicts the makeup and dynamics of an individual personality, then we can use it as a means of making predictions, proposing hypotheses. Consider the difference in approach between asking the question, "I wonder what would happen if . . .?" and proposing the hypothesis, "I'll bet this would happen if . . ."

Guides to Application

As knowledge is accumulated, it may be used for practical ends. One of the outcomes of science is technology. Application of knowledge for practical purposes may be harm-

---

[1]*Theories of Personality*, 2d ed., by C. S. Hall and G. Lindzey. Copyright © 1970 by John Wiley & Sons, Inc. Reprinted by permission of John Wiley & Sons, Inc.

ful or useful. Knowing about the makeup and working principles of a thing usually enables us to apply this knowledge to produce specified changes. The personality theories provide us with knowledge of our nature; thus, they can be used to guide us in bringing about changes. We have noted that many of the theories were proposed by therapists who deal professionally with influencing or changing personality.

A theory may indicate what is normal and abnormal. It provides goals of therapy and also reveals the things that must be done to attain the goals.

BEHAVIOR AND PERSONALITY CONTROL

A highly regarded formula for living is "Know, and then do." We are able to produce specified effects if we have appropriate knowledge. The history of discovery is replete with examples of the relationship between knowledge and real-life application. Robert J. Oppenheimer (1956), the famous physicist who helped to invent the atomic bomb, pointed out the terrible implications that the application of knowledge could have in controlling human behavior. The advances in behavior technology have rivaled the dangerous consequences of physical technology. Knowledge gained from the esoteric concerns of scientists has often led to technological advances that have had practical significance in solving human problems. Thus, behavior control is today effectively applied in a wide range of professions. Teachers use knowledge of personality to foster learning in their students; marriage counselors use specialized techniques and knowledge of human behavior to promote insights in couples who are having marital difficulties; the psychotherapist and the behavior therapist use psychological principles to modify behavior in people who are suffering from personality disturbances. As principles of behavior are acquired, this control potential will increase, a factor that could present problems if behavior modification is abused (Lefcourt, 1973).

We may now consider behavior control from the standpoint of the explanatory causes that we discussed previously. Consider the control of behavior through environmental manipulation. In many different settings, from the classroom to the mental hospital, from the prison to the work setting, the behavior of different types of people of all ages has been and is being controlled by the use of rewards and punishments. Many of the same principles of behavior control that have been used with animals are found to be successful with humans. Consider the possibility of controlling biological causes of behavior. A great deal of control has already been acheived through tranquilizing and psychoactive drugs. The possibility of altering genetic abnormalities is just beginning to open up. With respect to personality factors, the whole basis of counseling and psychotherapy is the ability to control or change intrapsychic variables such as self-image, attitudes, motives, and cognitions. A traditional therapist attempts to broaden his or her patients' insights into their abnormal behavior so that they are motivated to change their approach to life. The assumption is that changing the intrapsychic causes will alter behavior. Both conscious and unconscious determinants of behavior can be influenced or controlled.

The control of behavior has also been achieved by the behaviorists, who stress objective measurement of variables and stimuli. The behavior modifiers and behavior therapists seek to control the controllers of behavior. The radical behaviorists focus on the external determinants of behavior: the stimuli that instigate behavior and the consequences that sustain or block it. The newer brands of behaviorists, the cognitive and social-learning theorists, focus on both external and internal causes of behavior, but they strive for operational definitions of variables in order to promote greater precision in changing and controlling behavior. The postulates of their theories are used to guide them in conducting functional analyses of target behaviors and identifying the active causes that need to be changed.

GUIDES TO LIVING

What can theories of personality do for those of us who simply want to improve our lives? They should help us to a better understanding of ourselves and of those with whom we associate. Furthermore, many of the theories offer us a view of humans in their ideal state. A theory may explicitly or implicitly characterize the model of the good life. In this sense, a particular personality theory offers us a guide to living. It provides the goals of personality growth and functioning we should strive to attain. Several of the theories deal almost exclusively with ideal human existence. Many of the personality theorists were also personality therapists; thus, they were concerned with the restoration of healthy growth and functioning. Frequently, they theorized about the abnormal conditions of their patients and also about the ends that they sought to attain with the therapeutic concepts and techniques they employed. Knowing both the ideal states for human beings and the means of accomplishing these should assist us in living more effectively and in perfecting our own capabilities. We can attempt to accomplish these ends by applying the concepts and techniques proposed by the personality theorists presented in this book.

Some of the same things that others can do to control behavior we can do for ourselves. We do have a certain amount of control over our environment: We have some vocational freedom or choice in the location of a home or liberty in selecting companions. Through personal efforts we may gain increased environmental control. We can take advantage of discoveries in the biological sciences to promote our health. But probably the greatest control we have is over our own personality variables. Many people have demonstrated that they can quit smoking or lose weight effectively or get hard jobs done and, in general, take charge of their lives. We can alter our knowledge, our desires, our emotional reactions, even our interpretation of the past. And through the personality theories presented in this text, we can increase this self-control by learning about ourselves.

In the model of a human being proposed by B. F. Skinner (1953), we are given working principles that help us manage better our own behavior, as well as that of others. Skinner identifies the determinants of behavior in his theory that can be manipulated to control behavior of others and ourselves. The terms of his theory should guide those who wish to modify behavior. Without his theory, which is greatly supported by research, we would be on a trial-and-error level. Skinner (1953) holds that producing favorable consequences and avoiding or escaping unpleasant ones is the major motivation of living. Medieval philosophers stressed the development of will power as the best means of self-control; but will power, if such a process exists, frequently proves inadequate. We can support will power by controlling both the stimuli that instigate behavior and also the consequences produced by our own behavior. By using such stimulus controls, we are abetting will power just as we might lift a heavy weight with brute strength alone or use a lever and fulcrum device to supplement our own strength. We can control stimuli that instigate behavior by making certain that such stimuli do not occur as when a dieter wards off temptation by not keeping fattening foods around the house. Furthermore, we can control the consequences of our own behavior by administering rewards and punishments to ourselves for specific behavior. Such techniques are receiving much experimental attention today (Goldiamond 1965; Mahoney 1977).

Uses of Personality Theories — *provides knowledge of human nature + guides*

Let us see how personality theories may actually be used to guide us in studying behavior. Consider the following situation: Suppose you are given the assignment of interviewing someone for an hour in order to "get to know" the person as thoroughly as possible. You are pretty much limited to interview procedures; you cannot use drugs or place the individual under severe stress. What types of information would you seek? What types of information would tell you most about the interviewee? There are a variety of possibilities open to you, not all equally valid and useful in yielding information. You may soon feel at a loss as to how to select the proper approach. Let us consider some of your options.

Is it better to study the person as she now is, or would it be more profitable to study her past? Since everyone has plans to a greater or lesser degree, would it be helpful in your diagnosis to learn about these? Everyone copes with stress, and it may prove valuable to identify the particular ways in which this person deals with frustrations, disappointments, failures, and threats to the ego. Everyone has needs, and these determine many behaviors; thus, it would seem that a knowledge of needs would be the best way of getting to know a person. Everyone is forced to play out certain roles, and maybe you had better focus on your subject's knowledge of roles, performance of roles, and conflicts among various roles. It should be possible to identify a person's major traits, and this approach might give you what you are seeking. The answer is not easy, and you cannot use all these approaches. It may have occurred to you that some of the approaches include others: the trait and role approach—and perhaps the need approach—could accomplish the same result by different avenues. Again, a theory of personality will serve as a guide.

COMPONENTS OF A THEORY

In discussing the components of personality theories, we will use four cognitive representations: concepts, constructs, principles, and postulates. All have in common the attribute of summarizing. They are derived from the observation of many behaviors and experiences. We will consider the nature of these cognitive devices and give some illustrations of each.

Concepts and Constructs

The difference between a concept and a construct is degree of evidence. *Constructs are proposed concepts,* concepts that have a hypothetical status. We have the ability to understand and conceptualize the things around us and also the things that are occurring within ourselves. We can accomplish this because we are capable of forming mental representations of things, people, and events. We can look at something and form an image or idea of it. Such mental representations can be preserved and later recalled. We have the amazing faculty to form concepts and other mental symbols that stand for many situations, events, and qualities. We express our mental representations in words and phrases. We have thousands of these to name our mental representations. This amazing ability to picture to ourselves the things of our world gives us a great potential for understanding.

One of the most fundamental human needs is to make events of our world intelligible. We see the manifestation of this need in a child in the persistent effort to name objects. The story is told of the amazing deaf and blind child, Helen Keller, who expressed her desires in the form of gestures prior to the learning of words. If she wanted a drink of water, she would depict the act of drinking water from a glass. When she finally learned that objects and events could be named by words, she was so excited that she begged her teacher-companion to teach her all the names of familiar things in her young life. It was a significant step in the life of this handicapped child. Her world took on an entirely new aspect. Her scope of comprehension was dramatically increased because she was able to use her natural ability to symbolize or cognitively represent the things of her world.

One of our most important concerns is understanding human behavior, our own and others. Just as we can form mental representations of external events, we can use this capacity to understand experience and behavior. We observe behavior and our own experiences, and we assign verbal labels to them. We have many terms for many of our behaviors and experiences, and we use these to obtain a picture or conceptual model of a person.

Personality scientists propose constructs to represent many behaviors that pertain to personal identity. Once we understand the meaning of a construct, we can apply it to behaviors that previously appeared unrelated. Further, having a construct predisposes us to look for certain behaviors that might otherwise be overlooked.

To arrive at a new concept or construct requires imagination, creativity, keen insight, and a high level of intelligence; but to benefit from someone else's creation requires little more than understanding its meaning.

The following quotation from Nordby and Hall gives an excellent summary of the nature of concepts and constructs and their value to those who use them. (Bear in mind that constructs are tentative concepts.)

> . . . The development of a concept is an immensely exciting and aesthetically pleasing mental activity, for to form a concept is an attempt to impose order, coherence, and meaning on the myriad, and often chaotic sense impressions, memories, and random thoughts that pass relentlessly through our minds. A concept is the product of contemplation and a concept invites contemplation. Science, art, philosophy, religion represent the highest mani-

festations of man's need and aspiration to discover harmonious order in the universe. To find unity in diversity is a very human enterprise . . . [1974, p.6].

Suppose we have two friends: one works hard to gain our attention whereas the other seems not to care. How can we account for the difference? One way is to propose a construct of *need for affiliation* (need to be with people) and hypothesize that one friend has a greater need than the other. We look for other manifestations of the need in order to explain behavior that we could not otherwise explain. Of course, someone else might suggest a different construct: perhaps one friend seeks our attention because he is more insecure than the other. This alternative explanation could be further tested, and it might account for the difference in the behaviors of the two friends better than the first construct.

We can see that although personality constructs are initially used to explain isolated actions, they must be verified in other behaviors. Any proposed construct, such as a trait of generosity, accounts for past and present behaviors and also predicts future behavior. This fact allows ample opportunity for validation of the hypothesis. If one knows something about another person, his or her past, present, and future will be revealed to some extent because personality variables have stability.

Principles and Postulates

When concepts are brought into relationship with one another, a more complex type of representation, *the principle*, is formed. Principles are cognitive devices that depict uniformity and lawfulness among variables. The ability to form cognitive representations and to combine and connect such representations into principles provides us with phenomenal potential to deal with our internal and external circumstances. *Principles that are assumed to be true* (not fully established) are *postulates*. Postulates account for empirical generalizations and deal with the operation of personality variables. Empirical generalizations summarize relationships that exist between and among observable variables. Postulates acquire more and more the status of explanatory principles of personality as they are repeatedly confirmed through empirical observations. Theories of personality are constructed from constructs and postulates, and their purpose is to help us deal with certain phenomena, namely, the structure and dynamics of personality. Just as constructs become concepts by empirical validation, so may postulates become principles through repeated validation.

What we have termed empirical generalizations summarize what has been discovered through observation and experiment. There is frequently considerable agreement regarding the validity of empirical generalizations: anxiety produces distortions in perception; repression blocks thinking; conflict interferes with action; behavior is acquired through imitation; and so on. As we have noted, to account for or explain empirical generalizations, we need postulates. Postulates are the proposed principles that represent the determinants within the personality. Empirical generalizations are proposed principles of behavior, as contrasted with postulates, which are proposed principles of personality.

As we have said, a postulate is a proposed or tentative principle. Though less validated than an empirical principle, it may be considered as a working principle and points to potential, causal factors. Having a principle of behavior, whether it is established empirically or based on the experience and creative intuition of a personality scientist (postulate), tells us what to look for in personality. Many of the theories contain postulates that can be applied in individual form to all people. These postulates tell us about ourselves and others. It should be kept in mind that postulates require validation in order to attain the status of principles of behavior.

We might examine a postulate taken from Professor Gordon Allport (1961). Allport offers a model of the mature person. One of this postulates is that the mature person is motivated more by intentions than basic drives. The mature person expends most of his or her energy working toward well-defined goals. His or her present behavior is future-oriented, and he or she has a priority of values and is attempting to achieve them in actual behavior. The mature person obviously has basic drives, but these are not obsessive; rather they are put in their proper perspective in his or her life. Allport's postulate describes and explains the differences in behavior between the mature and immature person. Although this principle is simply a proposal, it is based on a great deal of experience. It should fit our own experiences with mature people.

THEORIES AS CONCEPTUAL PICTURES

In this section we will develop the following proposition: *Theories of personality are personal interpretations of our individual and common psychological nature* and *are not established principles or laws of behavior.*

As we have noted, a theory of personality may be viewed as a "conceptual picture" of personality. Like any other picture, a personality theory should capture the essence of what it represents. If it does, we ought to be able to learn about personality from the theory that represents or pictures it. There must be a correspondence between elements of the picture (theory) and the actual determinants of our nature. But just as a painting communicates the view of the painter, so a representation of anything as complex as personality is not simply an exact copy. A personality theorist gives us a portrait, a conceptual picture that is his or her own invention and embodies his or her interpretation of personality. Another theorist depicting the same subject matter could alter the perspective. Yet if the picture is too one-sided or distorted in other ways, its usefulness as a scientific tool is reduced. Some believe that Freud's extreme stress on sexuality as a motivational force in personality is an example of a distorted picture of us.

It should be noted that a theory not only prescribes what is salient in personality from one expert's point of view, but it also prevents the user from seeking fruitless alternatives. It keeps him from making errors and wasting time and effort. Hall and Lindzey describe this function of a theory as follows:

> Another function which a theory should serve is that of *preventing the observer from being dazzled by the full-blown complexity of natural or concrete events.* The theory is a set of blinders and it tells its wearer that it is unnecessary for him to worry about all the

aspects of the event he is studying. To the untrained observer any reasonably complex behavioral event seems to offer countless different possible means for analysing or describing the event and indeed it does. The theory permits the observer to go about abstracting from the natural complexity in a systematic and efficient manner. Abstract and simplify he will, whether he uses a theory or not, but if he does not follow the guidelines of an explicit theory the principles determining his view will be hidden in implicit assumptions and attitudes of which he is unaware. The theory specifies to the user a limited number of more or less definite dimensions, variables, or parameters which are of crucial importance. The other aspects of the situation can to a certain extent be overlooked from the point of view of this problem. A useful theory will detail rather explicit instructions as to the kinds of data that should be collected in connection with a particular problem. Consequently, as might be expected, individuals occupying drastically different theoretical positions may study the same empirical event and share little in the way of common observations [Hall and Lindzey, 1970, p. 14].[2]

Theories Represent Types of People

This author proposes the hypothesis that each of the outstanding theories of personality depicts some portion of the population and describes that segment better than other models do. That is to say, each model reflects not only the personality of the theorist who proposes it, but also the people who resemble the theorist. This view assumes that people can be grouped or typed according to similarities—an assumption that does, in fact, receive both empirical and experiential support (Peterson, 1965). If the hypothesis is correct, we should be able to select a theory of personality that fits us—one that describes, explains, and predicts our behavior better than the others. We may use the theory to help us identify explicitly the goals of fulfillment, of maturity, of self-actualization, or of whatever the theorist designates as the ideal personality.

Many (but not all) personality theories propose a number of types of people. Usually, there are several abnormal types and at least one that is considered normal or even ideal for humans. The types, of course, reflect the biases of the theorist, and we find wide differences in what is considered both abnormal and ideal. Yet, as the sections of this text demonstrate, there are classes of theories, and within each class there is considerable resemblance. Again, the author's hypothesis about individual differences in the applicability of the theories is relevant; if the theories depict different types of people, the ideals of personality development and functioning should also vary. We will encounter such ideal types as the genital personality, the fully functioning personality, the self-actualized personality, the mature personality, the productive personality, and the individuated personality. In some of the theories, we will need to draw out personality types because they are not detailed.

Total Theory Versus Eclectic Approach

We might pose this question, How can we use theoretical concepts to explain behavior? We can take two viewpoints on this issue: We can attempt to *rely exclusively on a*

---

[2]*Theories of Personality*, 2d ed., by C. S. Hall and G. Lindzey. Copyright © 1970 by John Wiley & Sons, Inc. Reprinted by permission of John Wiley & Sons, Inc.

single theory and use all of its components and their complex interrelations to explain what we observe. An example of this approach is to take a comprehensive theory, such as Freud's, and explain what we observe within the framework of that theory. The second approach is to *use principles from all the theories, using each concept to do a specific job.* This approach is termed *eclectic:* it involves taking the best from each theory, or taking what is needed from each. There are some serious disadvantages and limitations to the practice of using theoretical principles without considering their whole context.

It will be recalled that ideally a theory of personality is a network of interlocking, logically coherent postulates representing actual processes of personality. The theory is a model of personality, so that we can learn about personality through the study of the model. To understand the nature of a theory of personality, we should understand two basic principles of behavior: that behavior is *multidimensional* and that behavior is *multidetermined.* To say that behavior is multidimensional means simply that there are always several behaviors happening at the same time — weighing opposing tendencies, considering the consequences of behavior, choosing between alternatives. We must take account of all these behaviors if we wish to understand or explain a given cross section of behavior. A theory must provide principles to help accomplish this task, and usually a single principle is insufficient. To say that behavior is multidetermined means simply that several causes are responsible for a given cross section of behavior. Again, more than one theoretical principle is usually required to provide an adequate explanation. Using a single postulate limits the "explanatory power" of the theory.

Rather than grasp a total theory of personality, you will probably follow the eclectic approach: you will acquire constructs and postulates from the various theories. Such constructs and postulates can be useful in describing, explaining, and predicting our own behavior and that of others. It will be recalled that the theoretical principles were meant to be functional by those who proposed them. The student of personality should be better off with them than without them.

A CAUTION REGARDING PERSONALITY THEORIES

We have been considering some of the ways in which personality has been represented. Each theory will confront the student with new terms to master. Keeping some of the following principles and suggestions in mind may assist you in understanding and remembering the various theories.

1. A theory is a functional tool that should help you to describe, explain, and predict behavior. Without the theory you would have difficulty deciding what to look for in yourself and others. Remember, we all have a theory of personality, whether we know it or not.

2. Theories of personality are conceptual portraits of human psychological nature. Each theorist gives us a different portrait. Usually, the theorist focuses on a particular aspect of personality and of living, such as development, motivation, conflict, fulfillment; thus, the theory is at its best when it is applied in the manner in which the theorist used it.

3. Postulates taken from a theory can be used to describe, explain, and predict behavior, but single postulates are usually insufficient for the task. Because personality is *multidimensional* and *multidetermined*, the postulates that represent it must also be *multifaceted*. The operations of the components of personality simply cannot be brought together under one postulate. All the components of a theory should be employed for the greatest scope of coverage.

4. Theories of personality reflect the personality makeup of the theorists who formulated them. They also may be applied to specific types of people who resemble the theorists.

5. Many theories provide an ideal model or type of personality as well as non-ideal types. The theory tells us what a well-developed and fully functioning person is. It also tells us what happens when the requirements for ideal development and functioning are not met. Some theories are not specific in detailing this information, but often it can be derived from the theory.

6. Theories usually provide statements about human nature in general as well as the ways of living of real people that we encounter.

7. Theories of personality often consider what is characteristic of a person as well as what is distinctive.

8. The theory may provide for a comparison among people, and it may also account for the particular complex of variables within a single individual. Both types of data are essential for a complete knowledge of personality makeup and functioning.

We have said that a personality model is one person's construction. We may become fascinated by the apparent explanatory power of a model, but we should not be content with knowledge that is only theoretical. Ultimately, we seek laws of personality. One of our greatest personality theorists, C. G. Jung, offers us the following observations concerning the allurement of theory. (Note: model and theory are used interchangeably in this context):

> Theories in psychology are the very devil. It is true we need certain points-of-view for their orienting and heuristic guiding value, but they should be regarded as mere auxiliary concepts that can be laid aside at any time. We still know so very little about the psyche that it is positively grotesque to think we are far enough advanced to frame general theories. We have not even established the empirical extent of the psyche's phenomenology [total range of our experiences[1]]. How then can we dream of general theories? No doubt theory is the best cloak for lack of experience and ignorance, but the consequences are depressing. They are a bigotedness, superficiality, and scientific sectarianism [1953, Vol. 17, p. 7].

Many theories of personality have a commonsense appeal because they appear to summarize and account for real-life experiences. Theories vary in this dimension, of course. When we are following a theory, we are selectively construing events from someone's viewpoint. Like those who follow a political candidate, we become subject to all the tricks and shortcomings of a system—overemphasis, omissions, stretched

---

[1]Author's note.

interpretations, and partisanship. As an enthusiastic adherent of the theory, we become its victim and may be guilty of the above-mentioned shortcomings. But identification with a scientific theory has some advantages for science as well: scientific research is hard work, and the inspiration gained from a theory can provide the motivation to undertake research to support the theory. If the research is properly executed, it makes a contribution to science, whether or not it supports the theory from which it was derived. We have already noted the benefits of theories of personality with respect to describing, explaining, predicting, and controlling behavior.

Knowledge of theories of personality can aid us in deciding the ideals for healthy personality and the good life. The major theories usually specify what goes wrong in personality when it is abnormal—insecurity, lack of self-expression, unresolved unconscious conflicts, faulty expectancies, distorted perception. They also specify the goals of full development and living—inner peace, gratifying needs comfortably, expressing self fully, keeping tension to a minimum, using skills efficiently, or being all that we can be.

In discussing the constructs and postulates of the theories of personality, we will use the terminology and meaning as the theorists used and intended them. For example, the term *alienation* for Horney meant loss of contact with the real self whereas, for Fromm, it meant a sense of estrangement. The term *neurosis* is frequently used as a diagnostic category by some of our theorists although in the latest issue of the *Diagnostic and Statistical Manual* of the American Psychiatric Association (1980), *neurosis* is not accepted as a definable illness. In place of the general category, specific types of pathologies traditionally designated as neuroses have been delineated.

SUMMARY

1. A theory of personality serves both as a summary of the theorist's view of human nature in general and as a guide for understanding an individual case.

2. The determinants of behavior are genetic, organismic, environmental-situational, and personality variables. The personality psychologist is primarily interested in environmental and personality variables.

3. Personality has stability; it does not easily change. It refers to our personal identity and has core (central) and peripheral (secondary) characteristics.

4. Our views of human nature are guided by hidden assumptions that serve as ground rules for our judgments and form the basis of our own personality theory.

5. Theories of personality are personal interpretations of the person's individual and common psychological nature and are not established principles or laws of behavior.

6. We can judge the usefulness of a theory of personality by its capacity to describe, explain, predict, and change personality. Theories may be thought of as guides to human nature: guides to data collection and interpretation, guides to hypotheses and research, guides to personal application, and guides to counseling and therapy. Probably the best scientific test of a theory is its capacity for suggesting hypotheses that may be confirmed. The value of theories can also be judged in terms of their usefulness as guides to human nature.

7. Theories may be understood as models in that they are representations. A model or theory of personality depicts the components and operations of an individual's personality. One purpose of theories of personality is to help us determine what happens when personality is functioning normally or abnormally. There are many theories of personality because human nature is complex and because it can be conceptualized in so many different ways. Each theory tends to focus on a specific aspect of human nature and neglects others. The all-encompassing theory has not been formulated.

8. Theories are made up of constructs and postulates. Constructs are hypothetical concepts, and postulates are hypothetical or tentative principles. A concept is a cognitive representation of specific behaviors. A principle is made up of several concepts that embody lawful relationships.

9. We may use the constructs and postulates of a single theory as a guide to understanding, predicting, and changing behavior, or we may follow the eclectic approach and use constructs and postulates from a variety of theories.

GLOSSARY

Approaches to personality: Methods of identifying determinants.

    Causal approach: The characterization of behavior in cause-and-effect terms; one event occurs as a result of another event.

    Correlational approach: A means of explaining behavior in which a cluster of characteristics is identified. Correlated variables covary. Correlation is not causation.

Cognitive representations in personality theories: Symbolic components of the theories.

    Concepts: Cognitive representations that impose unity; cognitive representations that summarize many behaviors having something in common.

    Constructs: Proposed concepts; major components of theories of personality.

    Terms: Verbal expressions of concepts and constructs.

    Principles: Generalizations that summarize lawful relationships.

    Postulates: Principles that are assumed to be true; major components of theories of personality.

    Empirical generalization: A proposed principle of behavior based on experimentation, (for example, the principle of reinforcement), which more and more approximates a principle of behavior as it is repeatedly verified.

    Propositions: Verbal expressions of principles and postulates.

Components of personality: Enduring structures of personality.

    Core characteristics: That which defines the person; the central, enduring characteristic traits that influence large segments of behavior.

    Peripheral characteristics: Limited determinants of behavior that are subject to change; preferences and aversions.

Determinants of behavior: Causes of behavior.

    Genetic: Inheritance of a specific constitutional makeup and potentialities that influence behavior.

    Organismic: The biological aspects of behavior.

    Environmental-situational: Situations and stimuli that produce changes in behavior and experience.

    Personality variables: Factors within the personality itself that influence behavior.

Theory of personality: A conceptual portrayal of human nature that characterizes a person's behavior, including images or concepts of people.

    Eclectic approach: Selective use of constructs and postulates from various theories to suit individual requirements.

    Single theory approach: Construing the phenomena of personality from the framework of a total theory.

    Model: A representational device used to portray anything complex.

Model of humans: Synonym for theory of personality. A conceptual representation of human nature; also general categories in which theories may be classified, for example, psychodynamic model.

Patterned individuality: The unique configuration of characteristics that constitute individuality (Allport).

Range of convenience: The specific focus of a theory; aspect of personality that is best explained by the theory (Kelly).

Traits: A frequently used category of personality description in which single terms such as generosity, cleanliness, stinginess, or radicalism are used to describe characteristics or features of personality and behavior (Allport).

SUGGESTED READINGS

Cattell, R. B. *Personality: A Systematic Theoretical and Factual Study.* New York: McGraw-Hill, 1950.

Cattell's factor analytic approach to personality is elaborated; it is an example of the nomothetic approach to personality, which emphasizes trait dimensions on which people may be assessed.

Nye, R. *Three Views of Man: Perspectives from Sigmund Freud, B. F. Skinner, and Carl Rogers.* Monterey, Calif: Brooks/Cole, 1975.

Illustrating the notion that a theory is grounded in the basic assumptions of the theorist concerning human nature, this book presents the three points of view most prevalent in modern personality theory.

Peterson, D. R. *"The Scope and Generality of Verbally Defined Personality Factors,"* *Psychological Review*, 72:48–59, 1965.

Peterson presents both empirical and experimental support for the notion that human beings can be grouped according to similarities.

Rychlak, J. *A Philosophy of Science for Personality Theory.* Boston: Houghton Mifflin, 1968.

The author considers fundamental issues relevant to personality theorizing and research.

Skinner, B. F. *Science and Human Behavior.* New York: Macmillan, 1953.

Skinner's description of the determinants of behavior from a behavioristic point of view; his most comprehensive statement on personality; an example of the ideographic approach to personality study.

PSYCHODYNAMIC MODEL

If we would assemble the fifteen personality theorists we will be considering in this text, we would find that they would disagree on many issues. We might also find that many of the disagreements are only in terminology and that there is considerable agreement about the makeup and operating principles of personality and behavior. Furthermore, we would find that our theorists would tend to cluster in small groups. It turns out that personality theories have enough similarities to be grouped into classes. Several theories resemble each other enough in basic orientation for us to be able to fit them into a broader model of humanity. Thus, we might speak of the psychodynamic model, the ego-social model, the humanistic-existential model, and the behavioristic model. We would find disagreement even within each model group, as in the case of Freud, Jung, and Murray, whose theories we have categorized as the psychodynamic model. Yet in their basic orientation to human nature they have more in common with each other than with the other models, such as the behavioristic or the humanistic-existential models. For example, a common feature of the psychodynamic theories is that they tend to stress unconscious motives and conflicts and use indirect assessment procedures such as projective tests and the word association test to uncover such unconscious content.

Freud and Jung clearly identified themselves as *depth psychologists* because they dealt with the nature and operating principles of unconscious layers of the psyche. Murray also has accepted the pervasive role of the unconscious and makes use of Freud's divisions of the personality: id, ego, and superego. The term *psychodynamic* also denotes the active nature of personality. The causes of behavior for Freud, Jung, and Murray are primarily internal: the dynamic (motivational-emotional) forces. These driving forces are predominantly unconscious. Perhaps Murray's formulations do not stress the unconscious quite as much as do those of Freud and Jung, but he is sympathetic to this emphasis.

The medieval philosophers were impressed with human rationality and the role of consciousness in directing behavior, and they defined humans as the rational animals. The British associationists and faculty psychologists were also impressed with the content of the mind or consciousness. The early experimental psychologists, particularly the structuralist school, viewed the purpose of scientific psychology as being the discovery of conscious elements and compounds. They were interested in the structures of consciousness. They left out both the unconscious aspects of the mind and the motivational and emotional forces that set the mental apparatus into action. It became quite apparent to personality investigators such as Freud and Jung that there was much more to the mind than faculties and conscious content, such as ideas, images, and feelings. To them, and Murray as well, the mysteries of the mind could be unraveled only by plumbing the deepest recesses, the hidden forces that make people behave in strange ways at times. Humans, the rational animals, are more conspicuous by their irrationality in that they are more influenced by unconscious dynamic forces, personal motivations, and emotions, than by rationality. For the psychodynamic theorists, *conscious activity and behavior* were largely determined by *unconscious motives and conflicts.*

Freud came to believe that the unconscious portion of the psyche was always active and that we experience its influence most directly in dreams. Dreams reveal the operating principles of unconscious processes. However, according to Freud the unconscious is most convincingly revealed in cases of psychopathology—unexplained anxieties, irrational wishes and urges, phobias and compulsions, faulty ideas and unexplainable physical ailments. But Freud also believed that the operations of the unconscious exert a pervasive influence over conscious experience and behavior all the time. We all experience the operation of the unconscious by slips of speech, lapses in memory, unaccountable losses of our possessions, and even in self-defeating behaviors such as saying the wrong thing at the wrong time, doing harm to people we love, and resisting authority inappropriately.

Jung went still further than Freud in studying the unconscious by postulating the existence of an inherited collective unconscious. Freud held that the unconscious was accumulated during one's lifetime. Jung accepted the existence of the personal unconscious but viewed the collective unconscious with its archetypes as exerting a profound influence on both conscious experiences and behavior. He traced the manifestations of this collective unconscious in the most obscure forms of human expression—mythology, the symptoms of the insane, primitive art forms, symbolic rituals, and the occult. He sought to discover the very foundation of the psyche itself to appreciate the origins of our most basic strivings and aspirations.

Jung, Murray, and, to some extent, Freud found that the unconscious is not all bad. It can be beneficial for us because from it can come our most creative ideas and images and the spontaneous solutions of our most pressing problems. We may be either in harmony or in conflict with our unconscious, our three psychodynamic theorists maintain.

Murray is probably the most explicit theorist with regard to the motivational base of personality. He certainly recognizes the interactive aspect of personality and situations, but he posits needs as the basic driving forces in personality. He is more specific than any of the others about the number of viscerogenic and psychogenic needs.

Choosing between the powerful force of the environment and the dynamic force of motivation, our first three theorists would select the motivational-emotional forces in our nature. As we shall see, our three psychodynamic theorists reacted against the one-sided character of earlier philosophical traditions that overemphasized consciousness and rationality in humans, but they themselves became one-sided in overemphasizing the unconscious and the irrational in man.

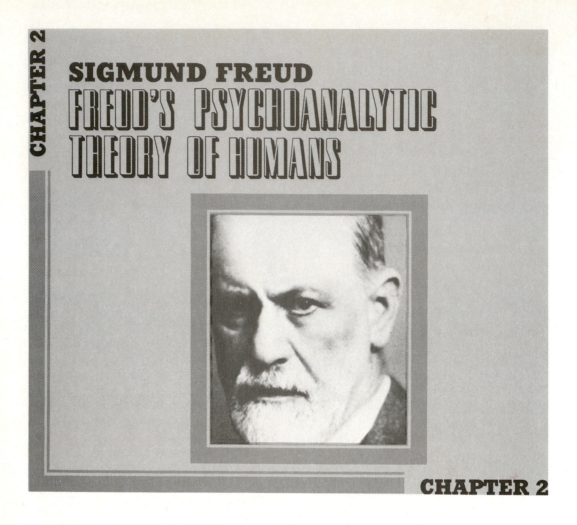

SIGMUND FREUD
FREUD'S PSYCHOANALYTIC THEORY OF HUMANS

BIOGRAPHY AND HISTORICAL PERSPECTIVE

Sigmund Freud was born in Freiberg, Moravia, in 1856, but lived most of his life (eighty years) in Vienna. He died in 1939 in London, where he had fled from the Nazis. Because he was Jewish and because he held views that were offensive to the Hitlerian regime, his life was threatened.

Freud wrote extensively of his investigations into the dynamics of the human psyche. He learned from his patients about the operations of the mind. Beginning in 1897 and continuing throughout his life, he also conducted a self-analysis the last half hour of each day. Freud trained as a physician, specializing in neurology, not because he wanted to practice medicine but because he wanted to learn about the scientific approach to humans. He graduated from medical school in 1881 and became a research associate of a professor of physiology. It was a job that did not pay well; thus Freud eventually began private practice, specializing in the treatment of neurotic disorders.

As a branch of medicine, psychiatry was in its infancy in Freud's day, and, in fact, Freud made significant contributions to the field over a span of fifty years as a practitioner. Jung, one of Freud's early disciples, credited Freud with introducing psychology into psychiatry. By this Jung meant that Freud called attention to the intensive study of the individual case. For the most part, the early psychiatrists were concerned with describing and classifying mental and nervous illness. Freud sought to understand the dynamics or causes of psychopathology within the patient's life rather than simply to categorize symptoms.

Freud made significant advances in the understanding and treatment of the functional (psychogenic) disorders, those in which no organic basis could be demonstrated. He used hypnosis early in his career both as an analytic procedure and as a means of implanting curative suggestions.

Freud learned a great deal about the unconscious from his association with Joseph Breuer, a physician who was treating hysterical illness. Hysteria was a general category that referred to a host of strange symptoms such as psychological blindness or deafness, mutism, various paralyses of the limbs, sensitivities, and anesthesias. Such symptoms appeared to be organic in nature, but their origins were psychological. Their understanding and treatment required knowledge of the dynamics of the psyche, and in this area Freud made significant discoveries. Freud credited Breuer for the development of the cathartic procedure, the so-called "talking cure" of hysteria. This treatment procedure involved having the patient discuss a particular symptom while under hypnosis. There seemed to be immediate relief following the procedure, but the symptom might reappear if the patient underwent a trying episode. Furthermore, the method was limited to those people who could be hypnotized into a trancelike state, a condition that many patients could not achieve. Freud tried a variety of other techniques and eventually developed his famous psychoanalytic methods of free association, dream analysis, the *overcoming of resistance*, and the *resolution of the transference phenomenon*.

Free association required the patient to say whatever came to mind in the course of discussing symptoms or relating historical events. By this method Freud discovered the operation of repression as the cause of hidden sources of anxiety. Unconscious conflicts or desires caused the symptoms. It became necessary to uncover the repression. Dream analysis provided an important means to get to unconscious material. Freud viewed the dream as the embodiment of a wish or a conflict. The dream was the "royal road to the unconscious." Resistance to free associating became for Freud an indication that significant unconscious material was being approached. The resistance had to be overcome. Freud found that the relationship between himself and the patient also became important in the therapy as the patient would transfer to him attitudes and feelings of an earlier period. Dealing with these potent emotional reactions was necessary in bringing about a change in orientation to people. We have hardly done justice to the therapeutic techniques and theory that Freud developed, but our concern in this chapter is with the theory of personality that Freud derived from his therapeutic efforts.

Freud was a medical psychologist who was attempting to understand and treat what we today would call personality and behavior problems. The science of psychology was just getting under way as a viable discipline, but it had little to offer Freud. Psychologists were academics whose major purpose was to prove that mental phenomena were lawful and could be studied just as other objects of nature. The early psychologists sought to study the laws of conscious states. Problems confronting the practitioner had no interest for these early mind-scientists. They studied the senses, perception, learning, concept formation; and only much later, largely as a challenge from Freud's work, did they deal with abnormal behavior. Clinical psychology, the field that would have been of interest to Freud, formally started only during and after World War II.

In 1900, Freud published *The Interpretation of Dreams.* This book laid the foundations of his approach to psychology. As we have noted, while the psychology of his day studied the normal person's conscious mind, Freud probed the deeper layers, the unconscious, which he believed contained the hidden sources of the symptoms he was observing in his patients. His *Psychopathology of Everyday Life* was published in 1901. In this book, Freud demonstrated numerous instances of pathological behavior in normal people, including examples from his own life. He came to believe that the same processes occurred in normal and abnormal behavior; what is considered normal is a matter of degree of abnormality. With the publication of three works on infantile sexuality in 1905, he shocked the Viennese physicians with his psychosexual theory of development. He spent the rest of his life embellishing and revising his psychoanalytic theory into two main thrusts: developmental and interactive. The interactive approach deals with motivation, conflict, and the structures of personality. The developmental aspect deals with the course of development, the unfolding of the sex instincts, and the formation of character types. From Freud's point of view, one may study personality from the standpoint of its formation and growth or from the interactions of its components.

An overview of the organization of this chapter should enable the reader to retain better the material. The chapter began with a brief biography and historical perspective. The next section entitled "Basic Constructs and Postulates," includes Freud's views on the levels of awareness; the structures of the psyche and their interactions; and the operating principles of the three components, the id, the ego, and the superego. The next section contains Freud's views on the psychosexual stages of development. Freud's views on abnormality from the standpoint of faulty development and the structures of personality follow. The next section deals with Freud's views on ideal personality and living: again from the developmental and structural points of view. This is followed by a critical evaluation of Freud's views and their historical and scientific impact. Then there is a section on Freud's theoretical ideas as guides to research and another section dealing with them as guides to living. The chapter concludes with a summary, a glossary, and suggested readings. This format is generally followed for all the theorists, although there are some variations.

BASIC CONSTRUCTS AND POSTULATES

Levels of Consciousness: Conscious, Preconscious, and Unconscious

Freud heard about the work with hypnosis of the great neurologist Charcot in Paris. After receiving a grant from the University of Vienna, Freud spent several months observing the French doctors using hypnosis with neurotic patients. He was so greatly impressed by their demonstrations that his abiding interest in the study of the unconscious was inspired by what he observed. The phenomenon of posthypnotic amnesia, for instance, puzzled him. A patient in a deep hypnotic trance would recall the events that took place in a previous hypnotic state, but he would be unable to recall the same events in the waking state. Then there was the phenomenon of posthypnotic suggestion: the patient would carry out a suggestion given during the hypnotic state even several days later, yet there was lack of awareness of the cause of his behavior. Furthermore, many of the symptoms that are commonly observed among hysterics could be induced by suggestion while an individual was in the hypnotic state. Deeply impressed by these phenomena, Freud began his medical treatment of hysteria by using hypnosis. Although he eventually abandoned the use of hypnosis and replaced it with his own psychoanalytic therapy, his interest in the dynamics of the unconscious, kindled by his early work with hypnosis, continued throughout his professional life.

One of the cornerstones of Freud's system of concepts was his strong belief in the division of the psyche into different layers that at times oppose each other. What a person experiences consciously is only a small portion of his mental life and may, in fact, be a distortion of the true motives that exist unconsciously. Conflicting motives may create so much frustration for a person that they are excluded from awareness but continue to function unconsciously to influence behavior.

Obviously, we do not experience everything we know at every moment; actually, momentary awareness constitutes a minute part of total possible recall and current stimulation. Thus, Freud distinguished between the conscious and the preconscious systems on the one hand and the unconscious on the other (see Table 2-1). Consciousness is the awareness that occurs as a result of external stimulation or the revival of inner experiences or both in some combination. The preconscious consists of latent memories, which can be brought to consciousness deliberately or which arise through association with current experiences. The largest and most significant realm of the mind is the unconscious system. In fact, Freud defined psychoanalysis as the *science of the uncon-*

TABLE 2-1. LEVELS OF CONSCIOUSNESS

Conscious	Preconscious	Unconscious
Awareness as a result of external stimulation or revived inner experiences	Latent memory arising spontaneously and deliberately or through association with current stimulation	Mental storehouse of past
Present moment of awareness	Between conscious and unconscious	Not bound by moral obligation or restriction
Awareness of identity	Filters between the conscious and unconscious	Ordinarily inaccessible

scious. Although the unconscious system is not experienced directly, it has profound effects on the contents and operation of conscious and preconscious activity.

MEANING OF THE UNCONSCIOUS

A great deal of controversy centers around the notion of the unconscious. Because Freud stressed its place in personality so strongly and because his reputation is so outstanding, the topic deserves serious consideration. It should be pointed out, however, that Freud was not the first to recognize the unconscious, nor was he the only one to explore its operations. As a matter of fact, Carl G. Jung gave still more weight to the unconscious than Freud and viewed it as playing a greater part in personality. Jung's views, nevertheless, are not as popular and widely known as Freud's.

One of Freud's earliest insights into the dynamics of motivation was that abnormal behaviors could be caused and sustained by hurtful early experiences that had apparently been forgotten. (This peculiar kind of forgetting he later termed repression.) The unpleasant experience was alive in the unconscious realm of the psyche and caused disturbances in consciousness and behavior. A wife or husband might have unaccountable difficulty with the sexual aspects of marriage as a consequence of a traumatic sexual experience in childhood.

In general, there are two meanings of unconscious: (1) unconscious as *unawareness* and (2) unconscious as a *layer of the psyche* (Freud, 1933). This distinction requires some elaboration. A man may have the habit of biting his lower lip when he is under stress, but not realize it until someone calls the matter to his attention. His mannerism could be considered unconscious in the first sense; his behavior lacks the quality of awareness. In like manner, a child may defy his teacher for a reason that the child does not know, but to the trained observer the explanation for the defiance may be obvious: the child does not receive the attention he wants by ordinary compliance with regulations; thus, he resorts to other measures. The purpose of his behavior is outside his awareness; the behavior may be said to be governed by motives of which he is momentarily unaware. He may come to understand his behavior if it is explained to him or if he spontaneously recognizes his motivation.

The first meaning of unconscious mental processes seems to lessen the mystery that the second meaning creates. According to this first view, there is no independent layer of mental activity that is inaccessible, only a lack of full awareness. Freud probably would have accepted the phenomena covered by the foregoing explanation, but he could have pointed to some striking but common experiences that he believed prove the existence of an unconscious mind that is independent of the conscious one.

EVIDENCE FOR THE EXISTENCE OF THE UNCONSCIOUS MIND

According to Freud (1917a), the unconscious has a life of its own. Among other things, it is made up of basic psychobiological urges that oppose conscious motives and thus produce the major conflicts of life. Freud held that we have unconscious thinking, unconscious wishes, and unconscious conflicts that may directly affect our behavior.

They exert a great deal of influence upon conscious and preconscious mental activity. If the man who habitually bites his lip continues to do so even after he is made aware of his mannerism, the *meaning or purpose* of the habit is unconscious. Ordinarily, he cannot discover this meaning or purpose. The example thus becomes an instance of the operation of the unconscious in the second sense: as an independent layer or level of the psyche having a life of its own.

Another source of evidence for the existence of the unconscious is "forgetting," which serves an obvious purpose. A person may completely "forget" an appointment until it is too late to meet it. Without using a great deal of analysis, it can be shown to the person that the "forgetting" deliberately kept her from the appointment because it was an unpleasant or threatening event (Glucksberg and King, 1967). The fact that the person later remembers the appointment indicates that the "forgetting" was only temporary—and hence not really forgetting, but *repression*. Missing the appointment, of course, does not really solve anything; hence we would suspect that the desires that were active to block the recall were not conscious and, therefore, were unconscious. The behavior of the person was in the service of an unconscious desire rather than a conscious one.

Freud traced the strange symptoms he observed in his patients to repression of early traumatic experiences. He came to believe that the ego was too weak to cope with the painful experience; it, therefore, excluded the threatening material from consciousness and placed it in the unconscious. But rather than being forgotten, the memory, the repression, created tension and became the basis of symptoms. Medicine had discovered the bacterial cause of several important infectious diseases. Repression was for Freud an analogous psychic agent that exerted toxic effects over conscious activity as well as behavior. The repressed material needed to be uncovered through psychoanalytic techniques.

To clarify the nature of repression further, Freud used the analogy of a burglar who breaks into a home, but is then ejected by the family. They hold the door shut to keep the burglar out. They cannot rest comfortably, however, because they fear that he is still menacing their home. The fear persists for a long period. The repression obliterates the awareness of the painful experience, but the person experiences anxiety because the material is dynamically active in the unconscious, ever threatening to break into the ego.

A variety of similar situations seem to point to the operation of unconscious motives and thoughts. Slips of speech (errors that express what the person really feels or believes) are also difficult to explain without invoking the concept of unconscious motives (Freud, 1901). Usually what the person has said turns out to represent true feelings that may have gone unrecognized because they were unacceptable to the person.

Certain accidents may be the outcome of unconscious wishes to hurt ourselves. The person who is "accident prone" (the victim of many accidents) is a good example of the operation of an unconscious self-destructive wish. Quite often there is an inconsistency in the person's behavior. He might be quite observant and cautious with respect to certain activities, but totally unreceptive and reckless in regard to others. Such discrepancies would be difficult to explain without assuming the operation of unconscious wishes. We can often detect unconscious motives, Freud believed, from observation of apparently careless behavior.

Freud pointed out the operation of unconscious motives in an unsuspected place: criminality. Commonly the criminal experiences guilt or remorse after the commission of a crime, but the occurrence of guilt before the crime, although not directly felt, may operate to lead the person to commit the crime as a form of self-punishment. In other words, the offender may commit the crime because he or she unconsciously wants to be punished. This strange interpretation needs to be demonstrated, of course, in any particular case. Freud pointed out that some criminals completely disregard precautions.

Some people neglect matters of health in such a way as to suggest the operation of an unconscious desire to hurt themselves. An overweight person who has a serious heart condition may continue to overeat despite repeated warnings from his or her physician. Many people (even well-informed and otherwise responsible persons) go on smoking cigarettes despite overwhelming evidence of the harmfulness of this habit (Wolitzky, 1967).

For Freud, the most convincing evidence of the existence of the unconscious as an independent layer of the psyche were personality disorders. He held strongly to the principle of *psychic determinism*—that any psychological event has an adequate explanation or cause. Antecedent conditions must account fully for the event. With respect to symptoms, the application of this principle means that symptoms are explainable; they do not just happen. Furthermore, they have meaning for the person; they serve a purpose. If the purpose is not consciously apprehended, then the symptom is serving an unconscious motive of which the person is unaware.

Freud (1925a) arrived at the notion that symptoms serve, or stem from, the unconscious through cases similar to the following. A young woman came in for treatment complaining that she was unable to do her work at home because of paralysis of one arm. (A medical examination revealed no organic cause that could explain the mysterious symptom.) She was caring for her invalid father, who was a widower and had no one else to care for him. Because she would not forsake this obligation, her fiancé broke their engagement, and soon afterward the paralysis developed. Since there was no apparent physical weakness or conscious motivation causing the symptom, Freud came to the unorthodox conclusion that the symptom must be serving an unconscious motive—avoidance of her conflict.

In this case, we can readily perceive the operation of strong conflicts between powerful unconscious motives. The young woman could not deal with her conflicts consciously; thus, she resorted to unconscious solutions that really were quite irrational because they did not solve her problems. She neither helped her father in his time of need, nor did she resolve her own difficulties. She wanted marriage and freedom and in the end failed miserably at satisfying her needs. She tried to solve her problems in a primitive way by getting sick herself. Admittedly, she was in a difficult situation, but her solution, which was largely unconscious, gave her only some relief from her conflicts and did not resolve them.

One point that Freud (1933) made is that when a conscious motive or conflict is made unconscious, *it is preserved* and continues to affect behavior as if it were conscious. If a person cannot discover the cause of his or her symptoms, presumably there is no way of eliminating them. Whatever maintains the symptoms continues to operate because the person cannot identify the cause.

The Structure of Personality: Id, Ego, and Superego

Freud conceived of the personality as made up of warring systems that are continually in conflict with one another. The id represents the psychobiological urges or the lower self; the ego represents the conscious agent or controlling self; the superego is the moral and social aspect of personality or the higher self. Each system strives to dominate the personality as much as possible. The id would do away with considerations of reality and morality and tensions associated with needs; the ego strives to be rational and realistic; the superego seeks to eliminate impulses and to strive for moralistic or idealistic goals. But there is no doing away with any of the basic components of the personality. The only solution is for the ego to take over the personality and allow some expression

Photo credits: *upper* and *lower* Robert V. Eckert Jr./EKM-Nepenthe; *right* Timothy Eagan 1982/Woodfin Camp & Associates

I am three: the lower self, the controlling self, the higher self.

TABLE 2-2. COMPONENTS OF PERSONALITY

Id	Ego	Superego
Is the primitive part of the psyche	Is the "I" (self)	Has two functions: conscience and ego ideal
Comprised of inherited psychobiological instincts	Serves and controls the id	Is moral or cultural component of personality
Source of psychic energy	Administers the personality	
"True psychic reality"	Uses the psychological faculties	Is primitive in the neurotic
Operates according to the pleasure principle; reduces tension	Distinguishes between objective and subjective	Strives for moralistic and perfectionistic ends
Controls reflex action and is characterized by primary process thinking	Obeys the reality principle	Promotes self-control
Is totally unconscious	Characterized by secondary process thinking	Inhibits impulses of the id
	Is conscious, preconscious, and unconscious	Is both preconscious and unconscious
	Mediates between the id and the superego, and deals with the external	Opposes the id and ego

to both the self-seeking motives of the individual and the social and moral restrictions imposed by external forces. We will discuss the component systems that Freud proposed as well as the interrelationships among them (see Table 2-2).

THE ID

The id is difficult to describe because we do not have direct access to it. It may be thought of as the most primitive part of the psyche, the *original personality*. It is the storehouse of psychic energy. It represents the psychological counterpart of biological needs: for every biological need there is a corresponding urge in the id that becomes active when the need does (Freud, 1933). As the need for food increases in intensity, for instance, the wish for food, which takes place in the id, also increases in intensity. At some point the intensity of the id urge is great enough to be experienced in the ego as a conscious desire, unless there is some force that opposes the desire. Thus the total process begins with a biological need that is experienced in the id (but not consciously because the id is totally unconscious). The desire for food becomes consciously felt in the ego when the need in the body is of sufficient intensity.

To obtain an appreciation of the operation of the id, consider what happens when one is sleeping. During sleep, even though the operations of the ego and consciousness are greatly reduced, there is considerable activity (Webb and Agnew, 1973). The biological functions are active, though at a diminished level. The person moves about much more than we would expect. He digests his food and may actually become hungry enough to be awakened. If the skin becomes irritated by being in one place too long, the person changes position — all without awakening. The tension associated with the irritation is translated into movement without mediation of the ego or consciousness. The same thing may happen with an irritation of the throat or nostrils: the person coughs or sneezes without the intervention of the ego. Thus it may be seen that the id may actually control bodily activity directly, but it may also be active enough to disturb the ego during sleep, as when a person wakes up hungry. The point here is that the id is or may be active all the time. One of its main functions is to communicate tensions, which it cannot discharge directly into the ego, which is more capable of discharging them. The id contains wishes and controls certain reflex activities.

The id is an important part of the unconscious. But the unconscious includes also repressed ideas, impressions, and desires. Such material must be held in check by counterforces from the ego.

The id may be experienced as an unwanted impulse that intrudes into consciousness at the most unwelcome times. Impulses related to sex and aggression are commonly the most troublesome. The young man who is trying to concentrate on the lecture cannot get his mind off the red-haired girl in the front row. He may feel so tense and restless that he cannot keep his mind on the lecture. He may become angry to the point where he loses control and says things he never intended to utter. No effort by the ego at suppression will be effective against the power of the id impulses. Anger may be expressed in the form of sarcasm or even as wit. Yet no matter how the impulses are given outlet, according to Freud, the id is the main driving force in personality.

The pleasure principle and primary process thinking.   The id is governed by the *pleasure principle* and *primary process thinking*.

The *pleasure principle* embodies the idea that the most basic motivation of humans is the pursuit of pleasure, primarily through the reduction of basic drives. Freud (1917b) believed that this principle governs the activities of the id. The id impels the person to seek immediate relief from tension whenever it arises. Tension arises when needs are active and is reduced when they are gratified. Relief of tension was considered by Freud to be the major source of pleasure; thus, the absence of need tension was in a sense the highest form of human existence for him. Later in life he came to the conclusion that some tensions are pleasurable and constitute a source of motivations, as when a person enjoys sensual experiences and activity for their own sake. When the id dominates the ego, the pleasure principle reigns at the expense of realistic and moralistic considerations.

By *primary process thinking*, Freud (1900) meant thinking that is fantastic, illogical, wish-fulfilling. Such thinking is induced by strong unfulfilled motives of the id. Primary process thinking is the first, or earliest, form of thinking. Primary process thinking is highly personal, or autistic. It does not follow the rules of logic, reality, or common sense. When the ego is under the influence of the id, as when a person is sexually motivated, primary process thinking may replace realistic thinking, which is the proper function of the ego. The ego may then construct a world of fantasy. The ordinary limitations of reality are suspended. Dreaming is an example of primary process thinking. Objects may substitute for people, or a part may stand for the whole. In a dream, cutting a person's hair may symbolize the act of killing him. Killing a bear may symbolize the killing of a person's father or the wish to do so.

It should be noted that the pleasure principle and primary process thinking take place in the ego but are induced by the id. When the id urges are strong, the proper activities of the ego are preempted by primary process thinking and the pleasure principle.

Why the id?   We might question why Freud proposed the existence of the id, which was supposed to intervene between the biological needs and the rest of the personality. Why should motives be experienced first by the id and then consciously in the ego? The answer is that Freud observed repeatedly a discrepancy between conscious and unconscious motivation. What a person might give as conscious motives for a particular behavior did not adequately account for the behavior. Different motives, which were apparently unconscious, were behind the behavior. An example is a father who repeatedly claims that he loves his son, yet punishes the boy severely for even trivial matters. To Freud, it made more sense to infer that the father unconsciously resents having a son. The real motivation, which is unacceptable to the father, has been disguised or transformed into a motive that is reasonable.

To understand Freud's notion of the relation between the ego and the id, one should bear in mind that the ego is the servant of the id, although at the same time it must administer the total personality. However, the ego enjoys the gratifications of the id motives. The nonthreatening id wishes are experienced directly by the ego, but others are disguised so as to be acceptable to the ever-watchful superego and the power of external authority. A portion of the ego, the unconscious segment, is an ally of the id and brings about the disguises before they are experienced in the conscious part of the ego.

The *derivative* motive experienced in the conscious portion of the ego may have little resemblance to the *root* motive in the id. Motives that are especially disapproved by society (and by the superego when it develops) produce motive derivatives that are made acceptable to self and society. Freud (1930) held that the frustration of such disapproved motives as sex and aggression is an important cause of people's highest achievement, both on an individual and a cultural level. Having to find new and better outlets for forbidden motives, people develop and vigorously utilize the power of the ego. However, if the derivative motives take the form of ego defenses and primary process thinking, personality growth and functioning are faulty and abnormal.

THE EGO

The ego is the administrator of the personality. It is what is ordinarily experienced as the subject and object of action—the "I" or self. Its main function is to take care of need satisfaction. The ego stems from the activity of the higher centers of the brain. Freud believed that a portion of the id becomes differentiated into a distinct part of the personality, the ego. All of the psychological faculties (such as perception, memory, judgment, reasoning, problem solving, decision making) are at the disposal of the ego. The ego can come to know and learn about the external world. Unlike the id, it is constantly in touch with the outside environment (Freud, 1933). The growing child must learn to obey the reality principle and engage in secondary process (correct and logical) thinking. The ego grows in strength by drawing energy from the id. It does this by investing energy in object choices, interests, and activities. As the ego grows, the id weakens. Freud describes the problems of the growing ego in the following manner:

> Instinctual demands from within operate as "traumas" no less than excitations from the external world, especially if they are met halfway by certain dispositions. The helpless ego fends off these *problems* by attempts at flight (by repressions), which turn out later to be *ineffective*, and which *involve permanent hindrances to further development.*
> . . . In a few short years *the little primitive creature must grow* into a civilized human being; he must pass *through an immensely long stretch of human cultural development in an almost uncannily abbreviated form.* This is made possible by hereditary disposition: but it can scarcely ever be achieved without the additional help of education, of parental influence, which, as a precursor of the superego, restricts the activity of the ego by means of prohibitions and punishments and facilitates or compels the setting-up of repressions [1949, pp. 83–84].

The reality principle and secondary process thinking. The ego operates according to the reality principle and by means of secondary process thinking. By the reality principle, Freud meant that the ego must take into account all pertinent facts in the process of satisfying needs. Often tension must be endured while an appropriate course of action is worked out. There are always obstacles and hindrances that have to be surmounted or overcome. Since direct pleasure seeking usually is not possible, there is continual conflict between the pleasure principle of the id and the operation of the reality principle of the ego. But the ego does, in fact, have the capabilities of securing need gratification: thus, the reality principle gets better results. The reality principle is supported by secondary process thinking. By secondary process thinking Freud meant thinking that is valid. The person must perceive correctly, follow the rules of logic, and learn natural laws. He or she must be in touch with the real world. Secondary process thinking conflicts with primary process thinking, and often primary process thinking wins out because it requires less effort and produces immediate relief from unbearable tensions. In the end, secondary process thinking alone serves the reality principle, which, in turn, must be obeyed if the person is to survive (Freud, 1920a).

Conflicts between the id and ego. We might picture the relationship between the id and the ego in this manner: the id is like a very successful but not very bright heir of a large fortune. With all his wealth, he has many wild and impractical desires. He wants to buy a boat and is talked into buying a luxury liner. He decides that he likes baseball, so he buys a whole team. These actions get him into serious debt. Finally, he hires a very knowledgeable business manager. The business manager is like the ego, whose job it is to hold back the irrational id. The witless heir has the resources, but the manager must put them to good use. His job is to satisfy the desires of his boss without making him bankrupt or provoking his anger. The ego works in behalf of the id. When the id says: "I want it, and I want it right now," the ego replies: "I'll try to get it for you. Give me a chance to work out a plan. Will you accept a substitute, or would you be willing to take less than what you asked for?"

THE SUPEREGO

Freud uses the term *superego* to designate the moral ideal aspect of the self. At times, he treats the superego as if it were the "better" self. When you are following your conscience or pursuing ideals, the superego is dominating the ego. Thus, being moralistic or perfectionistic competes with being realistic or pleasure-seeking. The term *superego* can mean the better ego. If you keep this view of the superego in mind, the id is the lower self, the ego is the controlling self, and the superego is the higher self. This view of the superego allows it to be preconscious in that through conscious probing you can identify the principle or precept that is being violated. After going to a movie rather than studying for the evening, a student may feel guilty because she should have been studying. She can certainly bring to consciousness the reasons why she should have been studying rather than going to the movie.

Freud also used the term *superego* to designate an unconscious region of the mind that contained precepts learned early in life. The superego is formed in childhood when the child perceives his or her parents as being godlike beings. The conscience and ideals that are introjected are highly moralistic or idealistic. *To introject* means "to make something an integral part of yourself." The child takes over the superego of the parents rather than their actual behavior. The superego thus exerts impossible moral and idealistic demands upon the ego. It is not enough for the ego to be moral; it must be moral and perfect.

The superego consists of two important aspects of the personality: the *conscience* and the *ego ideal* (Freud, 1933). The conscience represents the *cultural prohibitions* (the "don'ts"), and the ego ideal the *positive prescriptions* (the "do's"), both of which are internalized. The superego is the moral or cultural representative within personality. The ego must not only take rational steps to satisfy the demands of the id and at the same time meet the requirements of the external world, but it must also obey the prescriptions or requirements of the superego. Only certain modes of meeting needs are acceptable to the superego; even though a variety of means of meeting needs are permitted by the culture, the superego does not necessarily tolerate all of them. Dancing, for instance, is permitted by the culture as a means of bringing young persons together, but it is not acceptable to members of some religions. In this case, the superego blocks a channel of need satisfaction that is open to the ego: the conflict is within the person rather than between the person and his or her environment.

Many of the do's and don'ts that guide behavior are matters of secondary process thinking and the reality principle. The mature person gradually takes over the precepts of the superego conscience and exposes them to the scrutiny of the ego. In other words, if development is normal, the controlling force in personality becomes more and more the ego. *Conscience becomes more and more conscious.* This point will have more meaning as we explore the functions of the superego further.

Like the id, part of the superego is unconscious although it can produce conscious effects in the ego, such as guilt, remorse, and anxiety. It operates by forcing upon the ego certain prescriptions, such as "never think about sexual matters; never get angry at one's parents; never be selfish; never be unloving." The person who harbors a strict superego is usually unable to verbalize its prescriptions but is nevertheless influenced by them. Just as the command of the superego is unconscious, so the reason behind the command is equally unknown to the person.

An example of the operation of the superego may make this last point clear. A man feels driven to work hard, and he does, in fact, work many hours and is merciless with himself. Although he is on a vacation that he rightly deserves, he feels ill at ease, tense, and restless. He cannot give any reasonable explanation for these feelings. He finds peace only when he is back at work. For a large segment of Western culture, there is a taboo against pleasure. This has now been superseded by a taboo against low achievement and inferior status. To engage in recreation is to take time away from striving for success.

In brief, the primitive superego conscience says, "Thou shalt not," but it does not tell why not; just as a child is told to do something without knowing why, so the superego issues its commands without giving an explanation. A second point is relevant regarding the strictness of the superego. You must work all the time or be generous and thoughtful all the time or never have an immoral thought and the like. However, in the mature adult, the dictates of the superego conscience are ordinarily moderated or even disregarded altogether from time to time. In other words, the person learns how to adapt his or her code of values to his or her needs and circumstances. A person usually works hard but occasionally deviates from this requirement and allows himself or herself some relaxation and fun.

The formation of the superego is greatly fostered by the child's identification with the parent of the same sex (Bronfenbrenner, 1960). Identification means making the characteristics of the parents an integral part of the personality. The little boy worships and admires his father, whom he perceives as a more perfect specimen of manhood than he is himself. He models his behavior after his father's in hopes of becoming the wonderful person he imagines his father to be. In every respect his father is superior to him. To be like father means to have what father has. His image of his father is glamorous, not marred by unfavorable comparisons.

The little girl also views herself as greatly inferior to her mother. Mother is a much more perfect specimen of womanhood. The little girl takes her mother as a model and identifies with her by taking on her characteristics.

Since parents can withdraw their love and punish the child, a part of the identification involves the internalization of this parental authority. A part of the ego, the dictates of the parents, later enters the realm of the superego by splitting off from the ego and becoming unconscious. In this role, the superego judges and prescribes the rules of conduct that the ego must follow in its work of meeting the demands of the id. Thus, the ego has to contend not only with the pressures of the id and the requirements of reality, but also with the demands of the superego, which constantly monitors it. Just as the child fears the authority of the parents because of their power over him or her, so the superego as the psychic representative of the parent is also feared because of its power. Violating the commands of the superego brings upon the ego guilt, anxiety, self-depreciation, and the desire for punishment.

Resolution of the Oedipus complex.   According to Freud (1924b), a significant factor in the development of the superego is the manner in which the Oedipus complex is resolved. The Oedipus complex involves the romantic attraction of the child for the parent of the opposite sex. At the same time, the parent of the same sex is both feared and loved. As a consequence of the fear, the child gives up the attachment and rivalry and instead identifies with the parent of the same sex. The child learns to be a member or his or her own sex by identification with the parent of the same sex. The identification process is greatly affected by the resolution of the Oedipus complex, in Freud's view, which is discussed more fully later in this chapter under the heading "Oedipus Complex in the Phallic Stage." The identification is much more intense than the early identification occurring before the Oedipus complex, which is supposed to manifest itself between three and five years of age. Important changes take place in the superego conscience and ego ideal if the resolution of the Oedipus complex is normal. Basic attitudes are formed: attitudes toward authorities, toward members of the same and opposite sex, toward acceptance of the roles that the culture prescribes, and many others. Failure to resolve the Oedipus complex may result in the carry-over of the early conflicts and attitudes to other significant people, a factor that hinders the process of socialization.

DEVELOPMENT OF PERSONALITY

Fixations and Trait Formation

While attempting to understand and treat the personality disturbances, Freud was struck by the frequency with which he found a certain childish quality in his patients (Freud, 1925a). Intellectual endowment or attainment seemed to have little to do with the appearance of the primitive trends: even his bright patients displayed childish traits when he got to know them. A highly intelligent, well-educated woman, apparently mature and poised in early meetings, would soon manifest emotional reactions and childlike needs that seemed to be totally out of character. The repeated occurrence of these phenomena perplexed Freud very much and led him to the hypothesis that such trends were *fixations* from earlier life that the patient had not outgrown. The inconsistent elements could be explained as partial blocking deficiencies or exaggerations of specific personality traits rather than as complete stunting since the patient was an adult in many respects. Certain traits and reactions from an earlier life period, normally replaced by more mature traits and reactions, continued to be active in personality, usually producing a disruptive effect. Freud finally came to the conclusion that the *childish trends became permanent features* of the adult's personality. One could trace large segments of behavior to them: the choice of mate, vocational preferences, recreational interests and activities, even such pathological traits as compulsive orderliness, promptness, extreme optimism, and the like.

ARRESTMENT OF GROWTH

What could cause an arrestment of growth so early in life? Freud came to the conclusion that there are two basic causes: *excessive frustration* and *excessive indulgence* (Freud, 1917b). If the child's needs are either frustrated too much or indulged too much, a particular aspect of his or her personality is totally stunted or hindered in some degree. An excessive need might be created as the result of the stunting of growth; this process Freud termed *fixation* (Freud, 1917b). He referred to fixations as *infantilisms*, which are childish trends in the personality.

Given this view of the formation of personality, we can see how Freud could place so much stress on the early years of life, the so-called formative years when the foundations of personality are laid down. Every personality psychologist accepts the significant influence of the early years, during which the most basic learning takes place, but Freud went one step beyond; he held that the structure of personality was permanently set through the child's experiences, particularly his or her frustrations and pleasures. Traits formed during this period are quite resistant to change. In fact, as the child develops, many conditions increase the growth and potency of the early traits: selectivity of perception, sheer repetition, fear of change, unwillingness to give up certain pleasures, and so on.

Parents and other authorities have the serious responsibility to help the child learn the important lessons of living without receiving either too much indulgence or too much frustration during the training process. They must work for the child's welfare so that he or she can take over his or her own life, a process that occurs gradually over many years. You do not have to stretch the imagination to see how a particular mode of living, created by the behavior of the parents toward their child, might become habitual. During the first year of life, when the receptive mode of dealing with the world is dominant, an overindulgent parent could produce a fixation of that mode in the child. If the child is given little opportunity to experience frustration or to learn gradually to use his or her own resources to secure what he or she wants—if everything is given to the child without any conditions—such a child will probably acquire a deeply ingrained dependent and receptive orientation to life. He or she may develop a strong habit of expecting things to be given to or done for him or her.

Regions of the Body and Stages of Development

Freud proposed the novel hypothesis that stages of personality development were caused by, or at least were associated with, the prominence at different times of various regions of the body, such as the mouth, the anus, and the genitals (Frued, 1905). Specific pleasures and frustration result from the needs associated with specific regions of the body. In the process of satisfying his or her needs, the child encounters the significant people in his or her life and experiences healthy gratification or frustration or indulgence.

CHARACTER TYPES

Fixation at a particular stage of development produces what Freud (1925b) calls a character type, which is manifested through a syndrome of traits. A character type may be interpreted as an abnormal personality type. A syndrome of traits is a particular pattern of interrelated traits. We may speak, for instance, of the oral character type and also of oral traits. Freud held that regions of the body, such as the mouth, become focal points for the development of personality. There are even specific varieties of oral character types, depending upon when the fixation occurred during the oral stage.

WHY PSYCHOSEXUAL STAGES OF DEVELOPMENT

Freud termed his stages of development psychosexual because he assigned a significant role to the sexual instincts in the formation and development of personality (Freud, 1917a). For Freud, the best way to understand the meaning of sexuality, particularly in infancy and childhood, is to equate it with any *sensual pleasure*.

The development of personality consists of the growth or unfolding of the sexual instincts. At first these instincts are separate, but gradually they become integrated and focused in the mature sexual act.

On the basis of the particular zones of the body that become the focuses of sexual pleasure, Freud delineated four psychosexual stages of development: oral, anal, phallic, and genital. Between the phallic and genital stages is a latency period that is not a psychosexual stage of development (Freud, 1917b). The first year and a half is the oral stage; from eighteen months to about three and a half years is the anal stage; from age three to five or six is the phallic stage; from six to twelve is the latency period. Finally, at puberty, the child reaches the genital stage, which will continue through adulthood. Maturity of personality is attained with full genitality.

For our purposes, the point to keep in mind is that during childhood, *certain regions of the body take on*, at a particular time, *a prominent psychological significance*, and each region comes to be the source of new pleasures and new conflicts. What happens, with respect to both the pleasures and the conflicts, molds the personality. Much of the early learning of the child is prompted by needs associated with the major zones of the body, and such learning relates significantly to the art of living and to the manner of meeting these needs.

The oral stage (oral personality types). During the first year of postnatal life, the major source of pleasure-seeking and, at the same time, of conflict and frustration is the mouth. The child's enjoyment of sucking, chewing, biting, and vocalizing is soon restricted by those who care for him or her (Freud, 1905). The child's mother becomes upset when he or she sucks the thumb or bites into toys or vocalizes instead of going to sleep or plays with food by spitting it out instead of eating it. The child is

Fixation results in the persistence of a particular pleasure-producing behavior.

© R. S. Uzzell III 1980/Woodfin Camp & Associates

expected to conform to his or her mother's demands concerning oral activities and to move gradually in the direction of oral self-management. He or she is criticized and punished for failure to conform and is praised and rewarded for conforming. Again, the child's independence is proscribed, so that he or she must operate within certain limits — that is, eat three meals a day and at the times when the rest of the family eats and also follow the same manners they follow. It should be noted that during the oral stage, the child is not motivated by pleasures of other zones of the body. He or she is not at all concerned with excretory functions, nor do the genitals occupy his or her interests; only oral activities are prominent.

During the oral period, the child first encounters the power of authority in his or her life, an authority that limits pleasure-seeking activities. As we noted earlier, Freud believed that the manner in which the needs are satisfied or frustrated determines the formation of specific traits that mold the personality in particular ways. Such generalized traits as pessimism or optimism, determination or submission, are engendered by *the interaction of child-rearing practices and the constitutional makeup of the child*. Freud believed that no matter how complex or intelligent or educated the person becomes, the general orientation, established early in life, is always manifest.

The oral character types experience disturbances in receiving and taking. Faulty receiving may take the form of passive dependence whereas faulty taking may result in manipulativeness, envy, and avarice.

Oral traits. Freud and several of his followers have detailed some other traits of the oral character (Maddi, 1972). They are presented in bipolar form, with the right end of the continuum suggesting the product of fixation due to frustration; and the left, the result of fixation due to indulgence. Neither extreme promotes optimal functioning, and if an extreme form of the trait is a dominant force, it constitutes a persistent pathological trend, a factor that hinders development and functioning. An intermediate position on the continuum, incorporating some elements of the two extremes in moderate form, promotes healthy growth and functioning. The pairs are these (Maddi, 1972, p. 271):

optimism	pessimism
gullibility	suspiciousness
manipulativeness	passivity
admiration	envy
cockiness	self-belittlement

The anal stage (anal personality types). Freud designated the second major stage of personality development the *anal stage* (Freud, 1949). You may find this a curious, almost bizarre, label, but his purpose was to highlight dramatically the major source of concern and activity for the child. While oral needs continue to be active, by this time the child has worked out some of the problems associated with the oral period. Certainly, the oral concerns are not as prominent in this next stage as they were previously; anal concerns take over. The anal stage extends from about eighteen months to about three and one half years, roughly the period of toilet training. The child seems actually to derive pleasure from the buildup, retention, and expulsion of fecal matter, pursuits that soon bring him or her into conflict with the authorities in his or her life. Again the fixation principle is applied: overindulgence or excessive frustration of needs in the process of toilet training may produce lasting traits of personality.

Depending upon whether there is too much adult frustration or indulgence of the child, the traits that develop may reflect *compliance*, *overcompliance*, or *defiance*. During the anal period, the child is learning some basic orientations to life, namely, holding on to things and letting them go (Adelson and Redmond, 1958); these orientations may become distorted or exaggerated into obstinacy, compulsive orderliness, stinginess, or untempered generosity. Consider how the personality trait of overvaluing one's accomplishments is formed. A mother who tends to overvalue what her child produces anally will probably overvalue any other accomplishment even though it is quite miniscule. Her overvaluing may continue for a long period. The child may come to overvalue all his or her activities if the mother, in her zeal to motivate the child to perform, fusses excessively over what he or she does. It is the overvaluation of anal products, however, that initially engenders the personality trait, according to Freud. At the other extreme, a mother may delight in trapping or tricking her child by catching him or her at the right time or in simply keeping him or her to the task until performance is accomplished. Such practices may engender traits of depression, psychological emptiness and loss, and insecurity. These traits may manifest themselves in excessive hoarding or accumulating or in compulsive trends.

Anal traits.   Several bipolar traits have been identified as anal traits by psychoanalysts. All have their origins during the anal period, and all express, in one way or another, the tendencies of giving or withholding. To repeat, anal traits may be understood in terms of compliance, overcompliance, or defiance. The extreme forms of the traits are abnormalities, whereas moderate degrees of the traits are productive of healthy growth and fuctioning. An individual may possess a trait that is so all-encompassing that he or she is identified by it, as was noted with the oral types (Maddi, 1972, p. 273).

stinginess	overgenerosity
constrictedness	expansiveness
stubbornness	acquiescence
orderliness	messiness
rigid punctuality	tardiness
meticulousness	dirtiness
precision	vagueness

All these anal traits apply to a greater or lesser degree to everyone because they are necessary for meeting the requirements of living in a social group.

The phallic stage (phallic personality types).   The phallic stage occurs from about three to five or six years of age. The genital organs become a prominent source of pleasure during this period. Curiosity about the body may begin much earlier; the child at some point encounters the hands and feet with amazement. He or she may even discover the genital organs quite early, but they do not become objects of concern and interest until the phallic period, when the tensions and pleasures of this zone of the body are much more intense. The child now begins to notice and comment upon the differences between men and women — that boys and girls dress differently (Thompson and Beutler, 1971); his or her concern increases significantly if anatomical differences are noticed. The child becomes more curious about sexual dissimilarities as he or she begins to experience sexual tensions. But this curiosity is quite diffuse because the child does not yet know, unless he or she observes directly, the actual differences between the male and female sex organs.

In the phallic stage Freud believed that the source of stimulation for the boy was the penis and for the girl the clitoris rather than the total sex organ. The stimulation is autoerotic in that it involves the individual alone. In the genital stage sexual stimulation centers about heterosexual activities, and in the girl the clitoris is superseded by the vagina. The phallic stage involves self-stimulation, whereas the genital stage involves heterosexual concerns.

Oedipus complex.   One of Freud's most controversial proposals is the Oedipus complex, with its accompanying castration anxiety (Freud, 1924b). Its intricacy permits only the briefest discussion here. Taken from the Greek myth of Oedipus Rex, who unknowingly slew his father and married his mother, the complex refers to the sexual attachment that a boy purportedly develops for his mother during the phallic stage. At the same time, the boy views his father as a rival for his mother's affection. Mixed or ambivalent attitudes exist toward the father, who on the one hand is feared because he can remove the offending organ, the source of castration anxiety, and on the other is respected and revered as a model of manhood, superior to the child. If development is normal, the child gives up his amorous desires for his mother and strives instead to take on the masculine role by patterning himself after his father. His affection toward his mother then loses its sexual aspect. By accepting the father's masculinity, the boy's superego undergoes its final development and embraces a positive ego ideal. But if either parent creates too much frustration or overindulges the child by not providing appropriate training and knowledge during this crucial period, serious fixations with long-term consequences may occur. The child may fail to accept the masculine role, or his conscience may be stunted. He may have difficulty relating to women his own age, being comfortable only with older women. He may overvalue his sexual prowess and assume an arrogant, egotistic attitude in his dealings with women of any age. Other traits that may develop during this period are discussed in a later section.

Electra complex.   During this period, the little girl undergoes a similar process, the Electra complex, but with some important differences (Freud, 1905). Freud believed that a little girl takes her father as a sex object and views her mother as a rival. It should be remembered that her sexual interests and feelings are still quite rudimentary, by no means having the intensity or directedness of the emotional and physical love that characterizes the sexual drive of an adult. If a girl discovers that she lacks a penis, the relationship with her mother is further complicated because she blames her for the loss. At the same time, she also loves her mother and a conflict ensues that, unlike the Oedipus complex in a boy, is never completely resolved — a condition that Freud held had profound effects on the emotional life of a woman and the development of her superego. The major pathological trait developed at this stage is "penis envy," undervaluing the feminine role and overvaluing the masculine. Freud believed that he traced many disturbances in female sexual functions, such as frigidity and dysmenorrhea, to the conflicts of the phallic stage. As with a boy, mishandling of the training during this period will engender pathological trends in the personality of a growing girl.

Traits of the phallic stage.   During the phallic stage the child's circle of contacts gradually widens to include significant people outside the family: playmates, teachers, police, clergy, and many more. The child must learn to take a place with other children, to give in at times to the demands of others, and to assert his or her own claims when others threaten to violate his or her rights. As might be expected, the traits that develop during this stage are related to the nature of the child's growth and to the types of problems and lessons that are to be learned. In both normal and abnormal form, they involve *self-assertion*, *self-feelings*, and *relationships with others*. There is also the dimension of narcissism versus object involvement: the degree to which interest and energy are invested in the self or in other people and things (Freud, 1904). The traits in the following list are some of the outstanding ones developed during the phallic period (Maddi, 1972, p. 276):

vanity	self-hatred
pride	humility

blind courage	timidity
brashness	bashfulness
gregariousness	isolationism
stylishness	plainness
flirtatiousness	avoidance of heterosexuality
chastity	promiscuity
gaiety	sadness

If development during this period is normal, that is, if there is a proper balance between gratification and control, with neither too much frustration nor overindulgence, the child should acquire a moderate degree of both aspects of the trait dimensions. The pairs of traits are in balance if both tendencies are present. For example, a certain amount of dissatisfaction with one's self is a prerequisite for self-improvement; at the same time, a good measure of self-regard offsets the negative effects of self-dis-

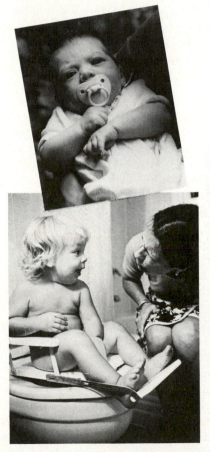

Photo credits: *upper* © Erika Stone; *lower* © Ray Ellis/Rapho Photo Researchers, Inc.; *right* Fredrik D. Bodin/Stock, Boston

The foundation of personality is established early in life.

satisfaction and, in fact, also contributes to self-improvement through a sense of pride. Consider some other traits of this period that are in proper balance. In relations with others, a person will be neither overly haughty nor unduly self-effacing. He or she will yield and conform to the expectations of others for the sake of harmony, but will protect his or her rights when they are threatened. The person will strike a balance between unrealistic and hopeless perseverance at a task on the one hand and fearful and premature withdrawal on the other. He or she will be neither so other-directed as to reckon worth through the appraisal of others nor so self-sufficient as to deny social needs and obligations.

The latency period.   The period from approximately six to twelve years, during which preparations for the next important stage gradually take place, was named by Freud the latency period. Freud maintained that this period involves the consolidation and elaboration of previously acquired traits and skills, with nothing dynamically new emerging (Freud, 1949). The child continues to grow quite rapidly, but the growth patterns follow the lines established in earlier stages. Significant new interests and needs await the marked physiological, psychological, and social changes occuring during adolescence, when new sources of pleasure, hence new conflicts and frustrations, come to the fore. Thus, Freud had little to say about the latency period. It did not represent a genuine psychosexual stage.

The genital stage (genital personality types).   The genital stage begins with puberty and constitutes the last significant period of personality development. The term *genital* may be somewhat puzzling; it derives from the outstanding feature of this period as Freud saw it, the emergence and full unification and development of the sexual instincts. In the earlier psychosexual stages, certain zones of the body are the loci of sexual tensions and pleasures. Some confusion may arise concerning the difference between the pregenital phallic stage and the genital stage itself because the sex organs are involved in both. In the phallic stage, sexuality is primitive and rudimentary, primarily self-centered, whereas in the genital stage, sexuality attains maturity and becomes heterosexual. Each zone is autonomous, but, with the maturation of sexual instincts, the genital organ becomes the major source of sexual tensions and pleasures, and the other organs are ancillary.

Genitality, in a narrow sense, involves sexual potency and orgasm. Various disturbances in both of these aspects of sexual functioning accompany psychological disorders, and Freud frequently found such disturbances in his patients. But genitality, in a broader sense, is more than sexual potency. For a man, it means competence and mastery in a wide range of activities: vocational, recreational, and social. Many abilities and traits are needed for potency, as Freud saw it. Genitality in a woman also involves more than orgastic potency; she must be capable of standing on her own feet, of reponsiveness to men, and of capability in certain feminine attributes such as emotional warmth, motherly concern, and creativity. We must conclude, therefore, that to Freud genitality was masculinity and femininity fully developed, an equivalent to what others have called personal maturity. We perceive an individual who has these genital traits and abilities as living effectively, even without reference to the Freudian personality theory.

What things occur in the adolescent period to produce new pleasures and new frustrations? Sexual interests increase markedly in vigor and intensity and are focused on members of the opposite sex; there are new problems that result directly from the increased role of sex. The adolescent finds social disapproval and the prohibitions of his or her own conscience conflicting with intense heterosexual desires. There is also the fear of pregnancy and the still prevalent view that premarital intercourse is an unacceptable way of dealing with sex. In a sense, the genital stage fosters not new traits but rather the full integration and utilization of earlier traits; however, the ability to work and to love becomes sharpened and highly focused. If a person is to develop successfully in the genital stage, the traits acquired in previous stages must be present in the proper proportion and form. Any fixations in development will hinder subsequent growth; thus, each stage builds upon the preceding ones. As the number of traits increases, there is an integration of the new and the old. Difficulties in one stage predispose the individual to have still greater difficulties in subsequent stages.

To sum up, immaturity, according to Freud, is characterized by the uneven development of certain traits: mature in some, less mature in others, and highly immature in still others. Maturity, then, is the harmonious blending and balance of all the pregenital traits properly developed. See Table 2-3 for a summary of the characteristics of Freud's psychosexual stages of development.

VIEWS ON ABNORMALITY

Pleasure Versus Reality

Freud believed that people are pleasure-seeking creatures at bottom. Everything people do represents an avoidance of pain or an attempt to generate pleasure. Reality is accepted only because of necessity, and a conflict between the pleasure and the reality principles is always present.

One of the main tasks of life is the "taming of the id" (Freud, 1933). If the ego did not limit the id, the person would always act selfishly and without regard for the rights of others. In fact, given only the id, survival could not take place. During infancy and childhood (when each person is strongly dominated by the id), those responsible for children do not expect them to manage their own impulses; rather, the expression of the id is controlled by external authorities. A parent does not permit a two-year-old to take charge of the money that he or she is given as a gift, nor does the parent allow the child to make decisions for himself or herself regarding matters of daily living. The child is judged with the view that the ego has not yet taken over his or her personality.

As children grow older, more and more is expected of them. They are held accountable for impulse control. If they display anger toward their parents, they may be punished whereas such behavior was not punished during an earlier period of their lives. When something is not available, older children are expected to accept that fact

TABLE 2-3. CHARACTERISTICS OF FREUD'S PSYCHOSEXUAL STAGES OF DEVELOPMENT

Age	Stage	Source of Pleasure	Traits
First 18 months	Oral	Mouth, lips, and tongue: sucking, chewing, eating, biting, vocalizing	Optimism — Pessimism Impatience Envy Aggressiveness
18 months to 3½ years	Anal	Anus: retention-expulsion control, toilet training, cleanliness	Stinginess Obstinacy Compulsive orderliness } anal retentive Meticulousness Cruelty Destruction } anal expulsive Messiness
3 to 5 or 6 years	Phallic-Oedipal	Genital organs: body curiosity about self and others	Relatedness with others Assertiveness Self-regard Gregariousness Chastity
6 to 12 years	Latency	Sensory-motor: pleasure from knowledge, skill, building, peer group interactions	Differentiation (elaboration of prelatency traits) Social learning Conscience development
Puberty	Genital	Heterosexual contacts and productiveness	Harmonious blending of pregenital traits (fullest capacity for love and work)

and not to cry about it. Gradually, but inevitably, they must take over the management of their impulses. The id always presses for gratification and pleasure, but the ego must face the harshness of reality and the consequences of unlimited and untempered gratification.

Conflicts Caused by the Superego

The conscience and ego ideal, which comprise the superego, add a new dimension to personality that creates many conflicts. Not only must the ego contend with id impulses and external forces, but it must also follow codes of conduct that rigidly limit the means of satisfying needs. The impulses and the superego are directly opposed. In some instances, the superego so controls the ego that most avenues of gratification are blocked. Thus we ourselves may hinder our possibilities of need gratification even more than the external world does. The superego may torment us mercilessly, set goals that cannot be attained, and produce guilt and feelings of unworthiness in the process. Unless we lessen the tyranny of the conscience and the unreality of the ego ideal, we will experience severe restrictions in every aspect of life. This necessary process can best be accomplished by strengthening the ego.

The superego, nonetheless, is a necessary condition for societal living. Given the nature of the id and ego, there is the necessity of a restraining force within personality because external controls would not suffice to promote group life. The law of the jungle would hold, and "might makes right" would be the dominant principle of action. The human race quite likely would have become extinct in this state. The superego, with the conscience and ego ideal, exerts a restraining force over the id-dominated ego. It assists the external forces of authority to promote societal living and the best climate for the fulfillment of the individual. However, Freud believed (1930) that even with all the controls, both external and internal, individual fulfillment is still more of a dream than a reality.

Freud did not have great regard for the average person. He believed that most people never arrive at an adequate balance between impulse and control. Personality development, he believed, was usually one-sided. For most people, the impulses are dominant and must be held in check by persistent pressures from outside. Without the power of the law and even more subtle pressures such as the presence of superiors, heroes, customs, and tradition, life would be impossible; people would destroy themselves. On the other hand, there are many who suffer all their lives from a rigid, primitive, self-limiting superego that constantly torments them. They carry around a heavy load of guilt and self-depreciation. Their impulses are kept under strict control and restriction. They lack spontaneity, freedom to grow in accordance with their individual natures, and, in general, fall far short of living a fulfilling life. There are those who have an overglamorous ego ideal and go through life chasing after rainbows and impossible dreams. They strive after the unattainable and in the process overlook what they have. The outcome is disillusionment and cynicism (Freud, 1930). Freud believed that the best solution is a balance among the opposing forces of personality.

Anxiety

In attempting to get to the root of anxiety and for the purpose of describing its true nature, Freud (1936) proposed that the earliest and most powerful source of anxiety was birth itself. The fetus in the uterine environment enjoys a high degree of protection from external stimuli. With birth the environment changes radically, and the infant is open to a great variety of experiences, some of which are overwhelming. In such instances he or she feels small and helpless, unable to change the disturbing event. The experience of anxiety, in situations where the individual cannot cope with the stress, is a reawakening to some degree of this original form of anxiety.

Freud distinguished three types of anxiety: objective, neurotic, and moral. Each involves an unpleasant emotional state.

OBJECTIVE ANXIETY

For Freud (1933), objective anxiety was equivalent to fear. A real threat or actual danger is involved in objective anxiety. There is something definite that is the cause of the fear. If not too intense, the fear serves to stimulate the individual to some kind of action. The unpleasant emotional reaction is often a warning that there is a threat of danger.

NEUROTIC ANXIETY

In *neurotic anxiety*, the ego is afraid of the id rather than of the external world. The fear thus arises from forces within the personality. The anxiety is produced by the threat of an id impulse breaking through the defenses that the ego has erected to keep it repressed. The fear is not so much of the impulses, but the consequences that impulse gratification may produce. The ego senses the danger before it actually occurs and experiences anxiety. The anxiety, of course, may assist the ego in dealing with the dangerous impulse. It intensifies the efforts of the ego to hold the impulse in check (Freud, 1933). This fear is diffuse and is experienced as dread.

MORAL ANXIETY

Moral anxiety is caused by the superego. It is felt as guilt, self-depreciation, the desire for punishment, and some forms of depression. The ego experiences a sense of unworthiness, and this is often a chronic state. The more primitive and rigid the superego, the greater the intensity of the anxiety feelings (Freud, 1933).

Many people carry around an excess amount of guilt. They fret constantly over their worthiness and effectiveness. This overconcern about personal adequacy is given the name of insecurity. The insecure person suffers from a superego that has not been tempered in its severity. Either the superego conscience or the ego ideal or both continue in their primitive state and rage against the impulses of the id. As a consequence, the person suffers moral anxiety. He or she finds the management of his or her impulses a terrible ordeal and cannot deal with them because the restrictions against them are totally unyielding.

THE EGO AND ANXIETY

It should be remembered that the three types of anxiety are experienced by the ego. Whether the anxiety is caused by (1) an impulse from the id that threatens to overwhelm the ego, (2) the superego, through its conscience, condemning the ego for thinking about or actually giving into the id impulses, (3) the ego ideal condemning ego as evil, or (4) the overwhelming stress from the external environment, the fact remains that the ego is the victim.

The ego cannot remain passive when it experiences anxiety, irrespective of the type. In the case of objective anxiety, the cause of fear may be dealt with directly. The person may attempt to perceive the situation correctly, evaluate possible alternative solutions, and make a decision to follow a particular line of action. When an individual carries out a plan, more often than not the problem is solved, and the anxiety associated with it passes. Anxiety as a *warning signal* serves the important function of preparing the person for appropriate coping or avoidance behavior. Sometimes appropriate action is not possible, and the anxiety continues to rage. In such instances, the ego employs defense mechanisms, which deal *directly with the anxiety* rather than with the situation that produces it. In neurotic and moral anxiety, the danger is from within the personality. The ego usually has more difficulty dealing in a rational manner with these forms of anxiety, and much of its defensive strategy may be used to protect against the powers of these forces.

Ego Defense Mechanisms

Freud had much to say about the important role of defense mechanisms as a means of dealing with the difficult situations that the ego confronts. The portion of the ego that is unconscious—and thus not so tightly constrained by the requirements of reality—acts to distort, disguise, and deny motives, perceptions, and other psychological contents. The ego develops strategies by which it protects itself against the oppressive forces of the id, superego, and external reality. It may simply deny any expression to the impulses of the id, or it may disregard external realities, or it may block out conscience. In any case, the consequences will be undesirable. The conscious ego is often not aware of the deception. The major purpose of ego defense mechanisms is to reduce anxiety. In some instances a defense mechanism may also bolster the ego, but most of the strategies are protective. The defense mechanisms reduce anxiety most effectively when they operate unconsciously. You could not deliberately decide to excuse yourself from an obligation without experiencing guilt feelings; but if you did so unconsciously, the guilt would not occur. The mechanisms are learned: a person is not born with them. Blaming others is discovered by a child to be a means of avoiding the anxiety of being caught. Thus, it may become an established strategy for dealing with anxiety.

Defense is accomplished by two means: self-deception and reality distortion. Through self-deception, you may deny or minimize certain unpleasant truths that you do not want to face. Through reality distortion you may alter events to suit your wishes. If the real events are not what you desire, they may simply be altered by overlooking certain aspects, by distorting some parts, and by a variety of other techniques for making over what is actually present. It should be kept in mind that defense mechanisms are like painkillers: they reduce the pain of anxiety, but they do not accomplish anything in the way of resolving the conflict or solving the disturbing problem. Painkillers can be useful as temporary aids over rough spots, but if they are used in excess, they can so warp the personality as to cause permanent damage. Then, too, defense is costly. If you assume, as Freud did, that the amount of psychic energy is limited, then whatever energy is used for defense must decrease the amount available for more fruitful functions. A rigid, defensive, guarded person is usually so busy and occupied with his or her difficulties that he or she does not have much time or energy for anything else.

REPRESSION

Repression is one of Freud's key defense mechanisms and is probably an element in all the ego defense mechanisms. It refers to an *unconscious exclusion* of threatening material that is performed by the ego. As we noted earlier, Freud viewed the ego as being weak and defensive against the powerful forces of the id, the superego, and the external world. Overwhelmed by threat and conflict, the ego resorts to repression as a protective device. The repression accomplishes the purpose of reducing anxiety by removing the emotionally charged material from awareness, but obviously the problem is not solved. In fact, the repression itself is not really a type of forgetting. The threatening material remains dynamically active in the unconscious and ever threatens to break through the defenses of the ego; thus, the ego must tie up part of its energy blocking the repressed material. Then too, the repression is often replaced by a symptom such as a compulsion, which constitutes a disturbance in the ego. Repressed material has peculiar effects on behavior and consciousness, as we have noted earlier, and must be uncovered in order to alleviate its toxic effects. One of the major tasks of psychoanalysis is to *free* the patient from repression, so that the ego is free from restrictions and can use its energies for realistic problem solving.

RATIONALIZATION

Rationalization means justification of one's behavior or desires. To rationalize is not to think rationally as the term implies, but rather to make conduct appear rational. If there is a conflict between an impulse and the conscience, then one might either rationalize away the restriction of conscience or deny the impulse; thus, the conflict is lessened or eliminated altogether. If a young person has a strong desire to engage in forms of lovemaking that violate his or her moral code, that person may weaken the force of conscience by a rationalization — for example, "everybody is doing it; it can't be so bad." The rationalization may succeed in lessening the force of conscience sufficiently to allow the person to give way to the impulse. Many conflicts are resolved in this manner: one of the opposing forces is weakened by rationalization.

What is unacceptable behavior in others may be made quite acceptable to yourself by a bit of rationalizing. If another takes an unfair advantage, that person is a cheat; but if I do so, I may conclude that it is a matter of "good business practice." A fault in another makes him or her unworthy of my friendship, but a fault in me makes me "only human." We use rationalization to dress up the flaws in ourselves.

PROJECTION

People are projecting when they fail to see their own shortcomings, but instead perceive them in others. The mechanism of projection causes a person to ascribe falsely his or her own qualities to someone else. The gossip says more about himself or herself than about the person he or she is maligning. People who feel a great deal of hostility toward others may through projection ascribe the hostility to the others. Paradoxically, we are quick to see and condemn our own weaknesses in others (Putney and Putney, 1964). By doing so, we draw attention from our own failings.

REACTION-FORMATION

In reaction-formation, a motive that conflicts with the ego ideal or a dictate of conscience is blocked by a conscious motive that is opposite in character. The conscious motives and feelings are diametrically opposed to the unconscious motives and feelings. Before the motive reaches consciousness, it has been converted to its opposite. For instance, a husband who despises the power his wife exerts over him may consciously feel solicitous about her health. In reaction-formation, root motives in the unconscious become disguised as derivative motives in the ego, which are acceptable to both the ego and the superego.

Since the conscious motives and emotions are disguises, real feelings occasionally come to the surface explosively. More typically, the real motives and feelings find devious outlets that are acceptable to the censoring powers. A man who never forgets his wife's "important days" always manages to get her things that she does not want. He might bring her candy when she is on a diet or buy her flowers that remind her of funerals.

DISPLACEMENT

If a man is irritable with his family because he harbors a hatred of his boss that cannot be openly expressed, his behavior toward his family may be described as a displacement. The mechanism of displacement involves substituting an available outlet of need gratification for one that is blocked.

There is probably no other mechanism that hinders social relationships as much as displacement. A popular song says: "You Always Hurt the One You Love"; we hurt the ones we love because they happen to be the ones we are near. We often take out our frustrations, bad moods, and anger on others unknowingly. Tension is an everpresent part of living, and the handling of tension is one of the major tasks of growing up.

Some people use others to play out their emotions. Their inner moods are directly reflected in their behavior: if they are in a good mood, then all is well; but if they are in a bad mood, all around them must suffer. The ones who suffer most are those who are victims by virtue of dependence. A child may be tormented by the moodiness of parents who lash out at him or her viciously. In such instances, the behavior of the child may have little to do with the parents' erratic outpouring of venom. There are many mean-spirited people full of resentment and hatred who use subordinates as targets for their hostile emotions.

SUBLIMATION

Sublimation refers to a displacement that is socially and personally acceptable. The object that is selected to satisfy the forbidden motive is a substitute, but it and the means of securing it are tolerable and even commendable (Freud, 1920b). A man who hates a rival cannot attack him directly because the law and his own conscience prevent him, but he can channel the energy that the hostile impulse arouses into acceptable activities and, in the end, accomplish the same objective. For instance, he may gain superiority over his opponent in some achievement: earning power or marrying a more attractive wife. The point is that there are usually acceptable or harmless outlets, even for unacceptable motives.

Sublimations vary in degree of usefulness. Freud greatly emphasized the role of sublimation in healthy living. He believed that people should seek the best possible sublimation for their needs. A man who has lost his own children may dedicate his life to Boy Scout work or to helping wayward boys. A woman who did not marry may

Photo credits: *upper right* Foldes/Monkmeyer Press Photo Service; *lower left* © Josephus Daniels 1975/Photo Researchers, Inc.

The ego must control, not deny, the animal within.

find great satisfaction in her work as a nurse. She may be extremely dedicated and care for her patients far beyond the call of duty. Her patients become substitutes for children and a husband. But other sublimating activities that a lonely woman might adopt are of questionable value, even though they are socially and personally acceptable. She might sublimate her desire to have children in caring for a pet poodle as if it were an infant. She might make clothing for it, bathe it often, and arrange to have it sleep in a special bed in her room at night. Or she might collect stuffed animals as a hobby, spending a great deal of time caring for them, reading about them, and obtaining them.

Whether or not the theory of sublimation is valid as Freud proposed it, there is something of value that everyone can learn from it. Whenever there is frustration, there seems to be a buildup of tension, even more than one would expect. The manner in which the tension is utilized makes a great deal of difference in personality functioning. It may be directed toward hostile, aggressive ends; or it may be squandered in self-pity, worry, depression, and other maladaptive behaviors; or it may be used to promote rational activity. An angry person can accomplish a great deal if his or her anger is properly channeled. Emotions can add extra force to motivation. Thus what for many is a disturbance can be a source of great productivity for others.

TABLE 2-4. IDENTIFYING CHARACTERISTICS OF COMMON DEFENSE MECHANISMS

Defense Mechanism	Identifying Characteristic
Denial	Refusing to accept reality
Fantasy	Imaginary achievements, magical need gratification
Rationalization	Making behavior appear rational
Projection	Seeing one's faults in others
Repression	Preventing painful or dangerous thoughts from entering consciousness
Reaction-formation	Concealing a motive or feeling by consciously experiencing the opposite
Regression	Reacting to stress by immature behavior and using earlier habits
Identification	Unconsciously copying the characteristics of another
Compensation	Making up for an inferiority by pretending superiority in a different way
Overcompensation	Attempting to excel in one's weakest area
Displacement	Finding a substitute outlet for aggression
Intellectualization	Dealing with a painful situation only on an intellectual level
Sublimation	Finding harmless outlets for tension associated with frustrated needs
	Finding refined cultural outlets for primitive impulses

We have been discussing Freud's views on abnormality from the interactive point of view, that is, from the standpoint of the three structures of personality. The weak ego may be overwhelmed by the id, by the superego, or by stresses from the external world. If the id is the dominant feature of the personality, the person is impulsive, selfish, and unsocialized. If the superego is the dominant force in the personality, the person may be morally rigid, inhibited, anxiety-ridden, and perfectionistic. If the ego completely dominates, the person may be highly intellectual and may disregard the emotional and moral aspects of living.

Faulty Personality Formation

Freud also considered abnormality from the standpoint of the formation and growth of personality. It will be recalled that character types are formed as a result of fixations early in childhood. Frustrated or indulged needs are the basis of the formation of character types, which are defined by trait syndromes. The fixated needs also direct the person to object-choices that occupy an important place in the person's life.

Character types should be thought of as character disorders. Character disorders are distortions in personality formation and growth. The distortion may take the form of an exaggeration, a deficiency, or an imbalance of traits. The total personality may be organized about a particular trait, such as passive-dependence, suspiciousness, or aggressiveness. In these cases, the outstanding trait is so dominant in the personality that it plays a determining role in much of what the person does.

Freud delineated various character types, which are to be taken as abnormal personalities. Examples of such types are the oral passive-dependent type, the oral aggressive type, the anal retentive type, and the anal expulsive type. These various disorders reflect immaturities, inadequacies, inappropriate exaggerations, and, in general, a lopsided personality formation. A character disorder is a failure in ego development and predisposes a person to develop faulty adaptive and coping mechanisms. A person with a character disorder is vulnerable to stress to a much greater degree than is a normal person who has a well-developed ego. A weak personality structure collapses under stress. Character disorders may deteriorate into psychotic or neurotic disorders under stress conditions. A passive-dependent person may develop schizophrenia under stress that a normal person could handle.

We have probably all encountered one of the anal character types described by Freud. It is manifested by three highly pathological traits: stubbornness, stinginess, and orderliness. Trait clusters are also found in people who are normal, but they are not disruptive. Excess or deficiency of a trait can throw off the entire balance and orientation of a personality.

One more point is salient here: The bipolar traits that are listed in Table 2-5 are the names of abnormal traits associated with the stages of development in Freud's schema. Each pair is to be considered as the extremes of a continuum, and they are pathological. Oral optimism is to be taken as a Pollyanna hopefulness without any basis in fact. Oral pessimism is a chronic and widespread gloom that colors the person's perceptions of events. In Freud's view, the normal person should possess a moderate degree

TABLE 2-5. TRAITS OF PSYCHOSEXUAL STAGES OF DEVELOPMENT

	Abnormal	Normal	Abnormal Zero (Absence of Trait)	Normal	Abnormal
Oral	optimism	(←		→)	pessimism
Traits	gullibility	(		)	suspiciousness
	manipulativeness	(		)	passivity
	admiration	(		)	envy
	cockiness	(		)	self-belittlement
Anal	stinginess	(		)	overgenerosity
Traits	constrictedness	(		)	expansiveness
	stubbornness	(		)	acquiescence
	orderliness	(		)	messiness
	rigid punctuality	(		)	tardiness
	meticulousness	(		)	dirtiness
	precision	(		)	vagueness
Phallic	vanity	(		)	self-hate
Traits	pride	(		)	humility
	blind courage	(		)	timidity
	brashness	(		)	bashfulness
	gregariousness	(		)	isolationism
	stylishness	(		)	plainness
	flirtatiousness	(		)	avoidance of heterosexuality
	promiscuity	(		)	chastity
	gaiety	(		)	sadness
Genital	sentimental love	(		)	indiscriminate hate
Traits	compulsive work	(		)	inability to work

The ideal personality should possess each of the above pairs of traits to a moderate degree. There must be a proper balance between opposing traits. Lack of balance among the traits constitutes a less than ideal personality. Abnormality in personality may be determined in three ways: (1) possession of a trait to an extreme degree, (2) lack of the trait altogether, (3) imbalance between pairs of traits.

of both aspects of a bipolar trait dimension. The hopeful-trusting person needs a little suspiciousness and fear to function well.

VIEWS ON IDEAL PERSONALITY AND LIVING

The Ego as Mediator

The ego must constantly contend with three powerful forces: the *external environment*, the *id*, and the *superego*. Both the external demands and the id impulses are ever present and increase with age. Somehow the ego must attempt to moderate the three competing forces. In the process it may become helpless and confused, especially if the external demands and the id impulses are diametrically opposed. The ego may experience anxiety or *psychic pain*. If the superego is moderated in its expectations of the ego, the outlets of the ego are more directly what the id motives require. On the other hand, if the id impulses and the superego demands are equally powerful, the ego resorts to defense mechanisms and primary process thinking rather than to secondary process thinking and problem solving.

The Synthesizing Functions of the Ego

Given the nature of personality as Freud saw it, certain questions regarding its growth and functioning are in order. How can the ego reconcile the opposing forces within personality? What can society do, and what can the individual do for himself, to help the ego in its tasks? Can child-rearing play an important part since so much of the foundation of personality, according to Freud, is established during childhood? Can one who has experienced an unhealthy childhood do anything to rectify the damage? The following discussion about the healthy ego will not attempt to cover all these questions, but it aims to suggest some ideas that can aid people to deal with them.

An important point to bear in mind is the principle of the conservation of energy, which Freud (1920a) believed applied to psychic energy as it does, of course, to physical energy. The principle holds simply that energy can be transformed, but it cannot be created or destroyed. The amount of psychic energy at any period of life is constant; what is used up in one kind of activity limits what is available for others. Therefore, if the ego develops and becomes dominant, it takes over the energy from the id and superego. These are weakened and more easily managed by the ego. It should be noted that, in the ideal personality, the ego is the largest system, and both the superego and the id are accessible to awareness.

HOW CAN THE EGO MASTER THE ID AND THE SUPEREGO?

Consider the superego first: the reasons behind much of what we do ordinarily are not known to us. We are "creatures of habit"; thus, many activities continue long after the need that they served is no longer active. Habitual behavior is not usually accompanied by rational evaluation. One way of making the superego conscious is to examine from time to time one's basic values, aspirations, and standards of right and wrong conduct. Many people find that their beliefs begin to change as they examine them. The normal person certainly alters his superego as he or she grows up. The normal person learns when to follow rules and when not to and reexamines the role of authorities in his life. Many of his or her fictional dreams and hopes are toned down. He or she learns to make many adjustments and compromises with the superego. Both the superego conscience and the ego ideal more and more become functions of the ego. The normal person comes to know what he or she wants and what steps must be taken to attain his or her objectives. Such a person is also clearer about what is right and wrong. All this, of course, is a matter of degree: not all of us come to terms with our superego, and many people carry its primitive form with them for life. Here again the expression "Knowledge is power" applies. *Knowledge of the superego conquers the superego.*

Children can be taught the habit of examining their assumptions and values as a matter of course. If children are given increasing freedom to make decisions and to evaluate courses of action for themselves, the ego gradually takes over. The opposite of this is an authoritarian approach, in which the parents make all the decisions for the child. The superego, by taking over the role of the parents, may also keep the ego under control and subservient. Even a very young child can be given some freedom of choice in the color of clothing, the type of food for meals, the time for a party. Giving the child an explanation of the reasons behind parental decisions also lessens the absolute force behind authority. The child should come to recognize that rules and laws make sense when you understand them. Authority for its own sake is the poorest basis for rules or laws. The parents' reasoning with the child should be on a graded basis, of course.

With respect to the id, Freud (1933) made the statement that "where the id is, the ego should be." He also on many occasions indicated that the main task of psychoanalysis is making the unconscious conscious. One of Freud's most important objectives was to free the person from repressions that he believed limited the functions of the ego. Bringing repressed material to consciousness would enable the secondary process thinking of the ego to work out realistic solutions. Correct awareness of impulses was also essential for healthy ego functioning. Knowledge of impulses does not eliminate them or reduce their strength in the same way that knowledge of the superego weakens its power.

But knowledge of impulses can aid in bringing the impulses under the reality principle and secondary process thinking of the ego. If we know our impulses and experience them without distortion, there is great probability that we can do something in the way of satisfying them. Incidentally, with all of his emphasis on sex, Freud did not advocate free expression; he believed that the purpose of sex is procreation and that its pleasure is incidental, and he made this point quite clearly. But disguised outlets for sex are dangerous to personality development and functioning. We must come to know our impulses before we can do anything to master them. Expression that is outside of awareness and not under voluntary control is potentially damaging and limits the effectiveness of the ego in obtaining gratification of needs. Every culture provides some acceptable outlets for potentially dangerous impulses. Often the person must meet certain requirements, such as marriage, as a means of satisfying the sexual outlet, and during the period of preparation tension is inevitable. However, life is made up of compromises and displacements, sublimations, and even denial. The well-adjusted person has learned to moderate desires, to conform to the established standards of the community and, in general, "carries his load."

The "perfect act," according to Freud, takes account of all the agencies within personality, as well as the pressures and exacting demands of the external world. Such people may be described as enjoying inner harmony as well as concord between themselves and their environment. Two conflicts, the psychosocial and the intrapsychic, are held at a minimum level. The bywords to personality functioning are moderation, the golden mean, conformity, compromise, and a degree of acceptance of conditions as they exist.

Self-Examination Through Freud's Psychosexual Model

It would seem that if we could identify traits that are essential for effective living and attempt to acquire these traits in the appropriate degree, we would have a model with which to compare our present behavior and toward which we could strive. A promising beginning in this direction is provided by the traits associated with Freud's stages of development. We might look at the various bipolar dimensions, recognizing that each represents a potential problem area. Perhaps some of us cannot be objective enough to view ourselves in such a detached manner; thus, we would not be able to perceive our traits without assistance from a professional therapist. But most of us are aware of many of our traits, both desirable and undesirable.

Consider each of the traits in Table 2-5 with respect to whether it serves or hinders adjustment. For example, consider the bipolar traits of vanity—self-hate. We should possess enough vanity or self-love to withstand assaults to the ego and to strive for autonomy in decision making, but at the same time we should have enough self-hate or self-dissatisfaction to strive for continual improvement. One offsets the other. One without the tempering effect of the other would create problems. Each bipolar trait dimension should be examined from the same point of view: a moderate amount of each component of the bipolar dimension is necessary for optimum functioning.

Two defining attributes that begin to develop during the genital stage and come to fruition with maturity are the ability to love and the ability to work. Each of these requires the healthy development of the traits of the earlier stages of personality growth. According to Freud, to be able to love and work effectively, a person should have the oral trait of optimism but not carefree indifference or recklessness, the anal trait of perseverance but not unyielding obstinacy, the phallic trait of self-confidence, but not blatant brashness and self-overvaluation. A person should be courageous without being callous and insensitive, orderly without being compulsive, sociable without being self-effacing. In short, such a person must possess all the traits of the pregenital and genital stages in moderate amounts. Through work and love, we can best satisfy our most basic and most human needs. Mature people, according to Freud, accommodate themselves to the demands of their culture, do their share to maintain it, and function within its limits: laws, taboos, and standards of conduct. Instead of unlimited self-fulfillment, they satisfy their needs in socially approved ways. Freud's ideal person, then, might be described as a social conformist.

It should be noted that genitality represents a fairly high level of personality growth and functioning, presupposing normal development in all the previous stages, with the major lessons of life learned well. It involves the development and proper balancing of the bipolar traits noted in Table 2-5. The genital person is viewed as a fully developed individual who has resolved, as far as possible, the opposing tendencies in his or her personality. Everyone carries into adulthood some fixations from the past, for ideal child-rearing has not yet been established.

When asked about the objective of psychoanalytic therapy, Freud said that his aim was to replace neurotic misery with the ordinary unhappiness of everyday living. And, we might add, as the misery diminishes, the level of happiness increases.

CRITICAL EVALUATION

Criticisms of Freud

REACTION AGAINST INFANTILE SEXUALITY

Many people, including professional psychologists and psychiatrists, find Freud's ideas on infantile sexuality quite out of touch with reality. It is conceded by some experts that Freud's views apply to a minority of cases in which a family could be described as abnormal. If you consider sexuality in a broad sense, as maleness and femaleness, the picture is clearer. A little girl of three is already a feminine creature, and has a feminine personality that is appealing on some level to her father. The father, in turn, having a masculine personality, is naturally appealing on some level to his daughter. As a matter of fact, the father plays a significant role in helping his daughter become a woman. The same notions also apply to the relationship between a mother and her son; she normally has a special attraction for him and he for her, again based on sex, taken in the broad sense as gender differences.

Each parent plays an important role in the sexual development of the opposite-sexed child because each parent possesses, by virtue of his or her own gender, a particularly direct understanding that the other does not have. The little boy wants to help his mother with the grocery bags because his father does that. The little girl may want to cook for her father because she wishes to imitate her mother, but not necessarily replace her, as Freud maintained. A little girl of four came to her parents' bed one morning and announced boldly as she lay down next to her father that she wanted to go to bed with daddy and that mommy could sleep in the baby's bed. One could be easily misled into a sexual interpretation, and, as a matter of fact, her parents were a bit surprised by what the child had said. Actually, the child was indicating that she, too, wanted to be a grown-up and do what her mother did—to reverse things for once and put her mother in the place of the child. There is no reason to add a sexual component to a phenomenon that can be accounted for by other general principles, perhaps by the principle of identification, according to which the child takes on the qualities of an adult.

OVERSTRESS ON EARLY PERSONALITY FORMATION

Freud has been criticized for his adherence to a strict determinism with respect to personality development and self-improvement. He believed, as do his followers, that the structure of personality is formed and fixed in childhood. The vast changes that take place as a result of learning and maturation are considered a mere elaboration of the earliest themes. Thus, if children are gullible, envious, self-assertive, vain, or compulsive, their characters are not altered by subsequent experiences. Even when they are old enough to perceive the desirability of making changes in their personalities, everything about them has already been formed, including the ego itself. In the Freudian view, personality is fixed from the standpoint of both its structure and the role that the self or ego can take in bringing about changes.

FAILURE TO CONSIDER CHANGES IN ADULT PERSONALITY

A most serious objection to Freud's psychoanalytic theory of development is his lack of interest in the alterations in personality beyond the genital stage. Significant new problems, frustrations, and even needs emerge as a person approaches middle age (Tuddenham, 1959), and still more profound are the changes of old age. Even if we restricted significant developmental dynamics to the unfolding of the sex drive, surely there are important changes that follow upon the diminution or cessation of so important a drive in middle and old age. What happens to the personality of a man or woman when this function begins to wane? With major goals accomplished at the approach of middle age, there is often (as Carl Jung pointed out) a striking reorientation in the form of an intense concern for a meaningful philosophy of life (Jung, 1933). An individual who progresses normally has accomplished much of what he or she set out to do by the age of forty, but the "urge" for life continues. A great deal of energy that was previously utilized for the pursuit of basic needs becomes available for cultural and spiritual pursuits. Some of Freud's followers, notably Erikson (1968), have recognized this shortcoming in his work and have proposed theories to take account of the personality changes following adolescence.

OVEREMPHASIS ON THE UNCONSCIOUS

To many behaviorists, the notion of the unconscious appears to be an evasion of the obligation to explain phenomena that are difficult to explain. The unconscious is purported to be active in every person and at all times, but the evidence is far from conclusive (Erikson, 1960). Those who are inclined to accept the existence of unconscious processes thus modify the position by holding that the normal person is much more conscious of his or her motivations, emotions, and judgments than is the abnormal person, who may lack such knowledge to a remarkable degree.

ARTIFICIAL DIVISION OF PERSONALITY

Many also find the personality structures an artificial breakup of personality that has no value beyond the rather obvious one of conveying the place of conflict in people's lives. As constructs the structures serve no useful purpose in the effort to discover principles of behavior. To simply label phenomena (as is done with concepts such as id, ego, and superego) gives the illusion of explanation, but, in fact, to remain at the level of description constitutes only the premature stage of science. However, many therapists have reported that they find the concepts useful both in diagnosis and treatment. In any case, Freud's ideas on the unconscious and on the structures of personality have been extremely influential in the fields of personality theory and psychotherapy.

OTHER CRITICISMS

Every significant aspect of Freud's theory has been criticized by a well-known author-ity. In addition to the criticisms noted earlier, Freud has been criticized for his pansex-ualism, his stand on the inferior status of women, the internal inconsistencies of his theory, his conception of the death instinct, his tension reduction view of motivation, his methods of investigation, and still others.

Contributions of Freud

COMMONLY ACCEPTED FREUDIAN VIEWS

Freud's views have had a remarkable influence on all facets of Western culture during the past four decades. His ideas have pervaded literature, drama, television, films, edu-cation, child-rearing practices, psychology, and psychiatry. Although many of Freud's views have not been proved valid, they have received wide professional and popular acceptance. It should be illuminating to consider some of the commonplace beliefs that can be directly traceable to Freud.

Many people believe that harmful tension builds up when sexual and aggressive impulses are not expressed freely, yet this has not been conclusively demonstrated. Freud adhered to strictures against free sexual expression, while at the same time he advocated that to frustrate sexual desires would have harmful effects. People have ignored this contradiction in favor of sexual permissiveness.

Another unproved Freudian notion is that repression of sexual and aggressive impulses causes harmful personality and behavioral disorders. It is assumed that ratio-nal control of these impulses is only a partial solution. The common belief is that if people wish to experience inner spontaneity and freedom, basic urges should be acted out.

With respect to abnormal behavior, it is fashionable to blame uncontrollable instincts or the persistent influence of early traumatic experiences for all of our psy-chological ailments. In either case, the individual is the helpless victim of forces that are overwhelming. It is popularly believed that other people or a "bad" environment are the causes of undesirable behavior. As an outcome, deviant behavior must be treated by professionals or by changing the environment—not by the individuals themselves. The effect of these views of human nature is to promote a dangerous type of freedom and to minimize individual responsibility. We must reiterate that these views are untested suppositions, yet they have been accepted as if they were valid principles of behavior.

THE IRRATIONAL IN PEOPLE

Freud worked with patients who suffered from severe personality and behavior disor-ders. The irrational aspects of human nature were quite evident in such people, but Freud concluded that milder forms of the same abnormalities were part of everyone's life. He believed that humans, the rational animals, are more conspicuous by irrationality, disguises, defences, and distortions of reality. The cognitive processes served the motivational-emotional forces of the psyche.

EXPLORER OF THE UNCONSCIOUS

Although not the discoverer of the unconscious, Freud did much in the development of techniques to study its operations. Freud demonstrated quite convincingly that we often act with purposes that are not conscious to us. Behavior may accomplish the very thing we claim that we did not want to do. Freud found that symptoms serve unconscious purposes, and although the victim finds them painful and troublesome, they are needed as protective mechanisms.

STRESS ON THE ANIMAL NATURE OF HUMANS

Freud called attention to the constant struggle between our human nature and our animal nature. We all have a "wild beast" (the id) within us that needs to be civilized. Pleasure-seeking, in all its various forms, is more primary (natural to humans) than reality and ethical considerations. Conflict within the person and between the person and the environment is unavoidable. Inner harmony and total unity of personality are unattainable ideals for humans.

STRESS ON INFANCY AND CHILDHOOD IN PERSONALITY FORMATION

Freud has demonstrated that childhood is not a tranquil or uneventful period, but rather a time when personality is being formed. Traits, defenses, styles of adapting and coping, and general sets are formed early and remain as integral functions of the personality.

DEFENSE MECHANISMS

Freud described the major defense mechanisms. In his therapeutic work, he was confronted daily with instances of defensive distortions. Freud found distortion and disguise frequently in his abnormal patients, but he found many instances of them in normal people, including himself. One could be the victim of defenses without any awareness of the true motivation. Discrepancies between behavior and the reasons given led Freud to distrust consciousness and to assign greater strength to unconscious strivings. He felt that conscious motives are derivatives of unconscious motives; they may be refinements, or the very opposite of unconscious motives.

We all know that there are people who deliberately attempt to deceive us, but Freud proved that people often deceive themselves. Behavior is not always what it seems to be. Freud believed that we might be quite surprised by how petty and selfish our true motives are. Confrontation with our unconscious can be quite frightening and revealing; we have more to fear from the terrors within than the terrors without.

Repressions during the early years of life when the ego is too weak to cope with painful experiences cause long-term disturbances in consciousness and behavior. Symptoms are relieved when the repressions are uncovered.

SYMPTOMS HAVE MEANING

The strange and bizarre symptoms of Freud's patients made sense when he discovered how they helped to deal with the problems of the patients. Symptoms were often compromises and symbolic solutions rather than adequate coping mechanisms. The symptom revealed something about the nature of the problem, Freud believed. But it should be noted that his view that symptoms could not be treated directly because other symptoms would substitute for them has not been supported by clinical research. Work in behavior therapy (Meichenbaum, 1978) has demonstrated convincingly that so-called symptom removal can be affected by behavioristic techniques.

PHYSICAL SYMPTOMS MAY HAVE PSYCHOGENIC ORIGINS

Freud greatly promoted the idea that physical symptoms may have psychogenic origins. Conflicts could be converted into physical symptoms. The physical impairment might serve as a protective escape device, enabling the person to excuse himself or herself from distasteful obligations. Many physical conditions that were attributed to psychogenic causes are now being traced to biochemical dysfunctions, but there is still plenty of room for psychogenic explanations, and Freud deserves the credit for being a pioneer.

OVER- AND UNDERSOCIALIZATION AS A PROBLEM

With the construct of the superego, Freud clearly established a basis for problems in over- and undersocialization. One could suffer as much from a tormenting conscience or ego ideal as from an uncontrollable id. A primitive superego can exert harmful inhibitory influences in personality growth and functioning. Lack of conscience could have wide ramifications with respect to all facets of behavior. Moral and social development was to be considered as important as intellectual growth.

PSYCHOANALYTIC THERAPY

Freud developed psychoanalysis as one of the earliest forms of therapy. It was an alternative to hypnosis for uncovering repressions and retrieving early memories. His brand of therapy continues to be practiced after eighty years, despite many assaults and criticisms. Although Freud held ideas that are surely erroneous, it is reasonable to assume that some of his major ideas about the human psyche are valid, assuring him a prominent place in the history of psychology. If there is ever an all-encompassing theory of the psychological nature of humans, Freud's key ideas would have to be incorporated.

GUIDES TO RESEARCH

Freud's theorizing has certainly been productive in both therapy and research. His therapeutic concepts and procedures have prompted researchers to study personality and behavioral changes. Studies comparing psychoanalytic therapy with other forms have also been conducted (Eysenck, 1952; 1965A; 1966).

Therapeutic effectiveness is difficult to determine. Comparisons of various therapies are also fraught with many problems. The early studies, such as those of Eysenck's, appeared to demonstrate that psychoanalysis was inadequate as a therapeutic procedure. Later studies, however, have been more favorable to psychoanalysis (Bergin, 1971; Korchin, 1976; Meltzoff and Kornreich, 1970). With respect to the general efficacy of psychoanalysis, Liebert and Spiegler observe:

> It is true that some people are helped by psychoanalysis, and this fact raises the issue of the efficiency of the process. "Successful" psychoanalysis often takes years of intensive effort (as often as four or five sessions per week), and it is not at all clear that such an expenditure of time (not to mention money) is worth the results obtained. The great length of time required for psychoanalysis may account in part for reports of favorable outcomes since spontaneous remission rates increase with the passage of time [1974, p. 116].

The research suggested by Freud's theory of personality is mixed in that some studies are favorable to Freud and some are not. Studies relating to the psychosexual stages have demonstrated the partial validity of Freud's descriptions of character types but have not conclusively supported his views of the genesis of the types. Surveying the literature on this point, Kline concludes:

> The major empirical research strategy which has been used to validate the hypothesis of character types involves examining adults' responses to personality inventories to see whether the behaviors

which are postulated to make up each character type actually occur together. For example, do the key anal traits of obstinacy, orderliness, and parsimony occur in the same individuals? Correlational studies of this kind have provided some support for the hypothesis of oral and anal character types although the evidence is substantially stronger for the latter [Kline, 1972, p. 11].

The universality of the Oedipus complex has been seriously challenged by research and cross-cultural observations. The Oedipus complex appears to be found in abnormal home environments in which the parents may encourage competition between the child and the same sexed parent for the affection of the other parent.

With respect to the structures of personality—id, ego, and superego—there is a certain commonsense appeal about them. We can draw upon our own experience for a demonstration of their existence. We can readily experience the various conflicts among the three aspects of self, for example, between impulse and restraint, between a rational-realistic approach and a moral restriction, and between the reality principle and the pleasure principle. Using factor analysis as a means of extracting basic traits derived from a large number of tests, Pawlik and Cattell found three primary factors that resemble Freud's structures of personality: high self-assertion, immature self-centered temperament, and restrained acceptance of external norms. They note the resemblance between Freud's structures of personality and these factors in the following statement: "Although we did not start our studies with any predilections for psychoanalytic theory, it is a striking fact that the psychoanalytic descriptions of Ego, Id, and Superego would fit very well the three major patterns found in this research" (Pawlik and Cattell, 1964, p. 16).

A number of studies have dealt with repression (e.g. D'Zurilla, 1965; Worchel, 1955; Zeller, 1950, 1951), but whether or not the proper Freudian view of repression was dealt with is problematic. Freud considered repression to take place when a highly threatening situation occurred with which the weak ego could not cope. Furthermore, Freud believed that most repressions took place in early childhood, for example, the Oedipus complex. The studies on repression have not dealt with early childhood, and it is highly doubtful that the threat or actual pain involved was of the intensity that Freud had in mind. One of the procedures is to have matched groups of subjects learn the same material. Then the experimental group is subjected to a painful experience such as an electric shock or a test that points up an inferiority. Then both groups are tested for recall. If the control group remembers the material better, the experimenter would attribute the difference in the results to the effects of the painful experience and conclude that the repression was operating to hinder recall. The results of these studies are difficult to interpret. Even when they are positive, it is doubtful that they validate the mechanism of repression. Furthermore, some of the studies show no differences between the experimental and control groups (Holmes, 1972; Holmes and Schallow, 1969).

Another area of research supportive of Freud's concepts is the study of the learning that occurs as a result of identification. Studies dealing with modeling and matching behavior have yielded positive results with respect to the validity of this phenomenon. However, Bandura and his followers do not interpret modeling effects as identification.

It is clear that Freud's views have been highly stimulating to researchers, and many studies have been undertaken under the inspiration of Freud's ideas. Silverman (1976) surveys a number of studies that are supportive of Freudian constructs and postulates. Especially notable is Silverman's own research on the defense mechanisms and the operation of the unconscious. Surveying the empirical research inspired by Freud's theory, Ewen sums up the matter in the following way: "All in all, the research evidence is hardly positive enough to change the mind of a hardened skeptic. Nor is it sufficiently negative to trouble a dedicated psychoanalyst" (1980, p. 66).

GUIDES TO LIVING

FINDING SUITABLE SUBLIMATIONS

Freud believed his investigations demonstrated that early needs become enduring features of the personality. Personality development at first consists primarily of increasing the ways of satisfying these early needs. In primitive form, infantile needs would make civilized life impossible. Their satisfaction requires their sublimation into suitable outlets. The means of need gratification must be socially acceptable as well as acceptable to the self, and thus each individual must find socially and personally acceptable outlets.

In keeping with Freud's notion that needs

may be sublimated, consider some of your deepest desires and the manner in which these might be expressed freely. A person who has a strong need for directing or instructing others will encounter a great deal of frustration if he or she attempts to satisfy this need in his or her personal relationships with friends, but he or she may satisfy it openly as a teacher, guidance counselor, lawyer, judge, or business consultant. A person who is prone to find fault in others may give free expression to this tendency through the profession of literary critic.

REGRESSION AND SELF-KNOWLEDGE

Freud offers us a useful method of identifying our fixated traits through his principle of regres-

sion. Regression is the opposite of sublimation: it generally means reverting to less mature forms of behavior under stress. When frustration is experienced, earlier and more direct forms of need gratification may override and replace current sublimated outlets. Thus, whenever regression takes place, our traits may be experienced in their more primitive form. Observing our reactions to stress can thus be a valuable method of gaining self-knowledge because we will see our personality structures more directly. A talkative person becomes more talkative; a timid person becomes even more timid. An optimist may

resort to magical or unrealistic thinking when he or she cannot solve problems. If we find relief from tension through eating, smoking, or drinking, under stress these activities are intensified. Under extreme pressures, we may even discover traits that we did not previously perceive in ourselves. Many people have reported gaining insights into their deepest motivations during critical times. Selfishness, for instance, is often revealed when survival is in jeopardy.

OPTIMISM-PESSIMISM

Though most of us tend toward either one or the other of these oral traits, some people are generally pessimistic or optimistic, no matter what happens to them. In such instances, we might suspect a strong oral fixation. Consider your own attitudes in this respect; do you feel that the world is a friendly place in which you fit fairly comfortably? Do you regard the future without much fear and expect to obtain your share or more of the good things in life? Do you have a basic sense of faith, hope, and trust that good things and loving people rather than tragedies and unfriendly people will be a part of your existence? Whenever things look bleak, do you find that you can somehow pull yourself together and muster hope for a better tomorrow? If your answer is yes, you exhibit the general trait of oral optimism, the expectation of an eternal flow of good things. Although it would seem that optimism is a highly desirable quality for effec-

tive living, its extreme form may lead to carefree indifference and lack of adequate preparation for potential dangers.

If you find that you are fundamentally dissatisfied with present circumstances and, in fact, have difficulty specifying what you really want, if you view the future as being frightfully uncertain, and if you feel that you are highly vulnerable to a variety of imagined mishaps, then you fit the description of the extreme oral pessimist. This is especially true if you appreciate the fact that your circumstances do not actually warrant a pessimistic attitude. Some other manifestations of pessimism are finding everything difficult—even the simplest undertaking provokes a great deal of fear and anxiety—and always dwelling on the worst aspects of a situation and expecting the worst outcome even though it is the least likely.

PARTICIPATION IN CURING ILLNESS

Freud contended that psychologically disturbed individuals continually relive inappropriate conflicts and faulty emotional responses from their early history. The sufferer is not simply the passive victim of his or her neurosis, but rather actively sustains it. While such people do not desire their illness, they are terribly afraid to make changes. Their current defenses help them to function on a level that they do not like, but

that they cannot give up because they have not worked out better methods of solving their problems. Two basic requisites for personality change are these: (1) you must truly want it, and (2) you must realize that you are the agent that brings it about.

Giving up infantile conflicts and behavior will ultimately secure greater gratification and more satisfying social relationships, but there may be a feeling of helplessness and loss in the transitional state. Here are some practical suggestions. First, be sympathetic with yourself in the struggle to improve. This does not mean self-pity and excusing yourself from hard work. Sympathetic self-understanding means an appreciation of yourself as a combatant in a painful struggle that nevertheless must be waged. Second, reexamining old conflicts may help to dissipate the pent-up emotions that continue to cause current emotional responses. Third, replace inappropriate models of ideal human figures with more realistic ones. You should see important figures differently at each stage of life: the heroes of childhood should be superseded by heroes more helpful to adult living. Fourth, be willing to admit your mistakes. Self-disclosure has many therapeutic effects. If you are fortunate enough to have a sympathetic friend, the process of confession may produce good results. Fifth, self-awareness and self-study will occasionally be punctuated with insights. In this context, the term *insight* means "a clear awareness of truths about oneself." Such experiences are highly conducive to personality improvement and should be used to the best advantage.

Freud (1914) did not picture mature adulthood as a "turned on" state with continual exuberance and happiness, but rather as a never-ending battle with many hurts and sorrows, but also with great moments of joy and satisfaction. Adults must learn to take less than they really want, to work for what they desire, to be willing to suffer for what they most cherish, to take charge of their own lives, and to assume responsibility for their successes and failures. You should strive to meet life head-on and to face the trials and frustrations of living with a sense of inner equanimity. Each person must ultimately stand alone and be the master of his or her own destiny. Truths about yourself and reality are often painful to bear, but self-deception and distortion of reality can lead only to madness and suffering.

SUMMARY

1. Theories of personality resemble each other enough to be grouped into more general categories termed models of humans. Although there is disagreement within each model group, as in the case of Freud, Jung, and Murray, whose theories are categorized under the psychodynamic model, in their basic orientation to human nature they have more in common with each other than with the other models.

2. The causes of behavior and conscious activity for Freud, Jung, and Murray are primarily internal: the dynamic motivational and emotional forces that impel the organism to action. Freud and Jung stressed unconscious determinants, repressed motives, conflicts, and powerful complexes and archetypes.

3. Freud's theorizing may be viewed from a developmental or interactive approach. The interactive approach deals with motivation, conflict, and the structures of personality. The developmental approach considers the course of development through the unfolding of the sex instincts and the formation of character types. We may study personality from the standpoint of its formation and growth or from the interactions of its components.

4. Freud divides the psyche according to levels of consciousness. Consciousness is the awareness that occurs as a result of external stimulation or the revival of inner experience. The preconscious consists of latent memories, which can be brought into consciousness deliberately or which arise through association with current stimulation. Freud viewed the unconscious as the largest portion of the psyche, which has its own operating principles. He defined his brand of psychology as the science of the unconscious. The unconscious may also be viewed as lack of awareness, but this was not what Freud meant by the term.

5. The operation of the unconscious is revealed through dreams, slips of speech, memory lapses, and, most convincingly, by personality and behavior disorders.

6. Freud introduced the mechanism of repression to account for psychological symptoms. It may be described as an exclusion of material from consciousness, an exclusion that is performed unconsciously. When a conscious motive is repressed, it is dynamically active in the unconscious until it is uncovered and worked through. Behavior may reveal the presence of an unconscious motive, the root motive, which is different from the reported motive, the motive derivative. Motivational derivatives are disguises of root motives that exist in the unconscious.

7. Freud viewed the personality as being divided into three warring systems: id, ego, and superego. The id is the most primitive portion of the personality. It is the source of unconscious urges, and it presses the ego to follow the pleasure principle and primary process thinking. The ego is the controlling system, the administrator of the personality. Its most appropriate function is to follow the reality principle by means of secondary process (correct) thinking. The superego is the moral and ethical component of personality. It consists of the conscience and the ego ideal. It is formed through introjection of moral and cultural precepts: prohibitions and ideals. The ego frequently experiences conflict involving pleasure, reality considerations, and moral and cultural standards. The ego attempts to reduce such conflicts and produce harmony within personality.

8. In its role as administrator, the ego is frequently flooded with anxiety. Objective anxiety is realistic fear; neurotic anxiety results from impulses that threaten to overwhelm the ego; moral anxiety is caused by the superego and is felt as guilt, unworthiness, and the desire for punishment. Confronted with anxiety, the ego may either use its abilities to solve problems, or it may engage in defense mechanisms. The purpose of ego defense mechanisms is to reduce anxiety by protecting the ego through self-deception and reality distortion.

9. Freud viewed personality development as the unfolding of the sex instincts. Various zones of the body are the loci of pleasurable stimulation early in life. Freud delineated four stages of psychosexual development: the oral,

the anal, the phallic, and the genital stages. Each psychosexual stage has specific needs and gratifications. Specific character types, consisting of a syndrome of traits, are formed during each stage as a result of the manner in which the needs are gratified or frustrated. Overgratification or excessive frustration causes fixation, which is to be understood as arrestment of growth.

10. The oral stage occurs during the first year and a half and may result in passive-dependent or aggressive oral character types. The oral character types experience disturbances in receiving and taking. The anal stage is from a year and a half to about three and results in the anal-retentive or anal-expulsive types. Anal traits may reflect tendencies toward compliance, overcompliance, or defiance. The phallic stage occupies the years from three to five or six and involves self-feelings and attitudes toward the same and opposite sex. The Oedipus and Electra complexes are critical features of this stage, and their resolution or lack of it has profound effects for later personality growth. The ages from six to twelve are the latency period, which is not a psychosexual stage. The genital stage occurs during adolescence and, if properly traversed, adds the qualities of productive work and love to the ego.

11. Freud deals with abnormality in two ways: by means of developmental failures such as fixations and by exaggerations or deficiencies in one or other of the systems of personality — id, ego, and superego. Abnormality may result from an inadequate ego, so that the id is dominant; or the person may be tormented by an overly strict superego. Neurotic symptoms are forms of defense, used by a weak ego. Faulty character types (exaggerations and deficiencies of specific traits) are Freud's developmental forms of abnormalities.

12. The ego as mediator must harmonize the competing demands of the three systems of personality and cope adequately with the demands of the external world. If the ego becomes dominant, it takes over the energy from the id and superego. The superego may be made a part of the ego by examining one's values, beliefs, and assumptions about right and wrong behaviors. Healthy personality functioning results from freeing ourselves from repressions and finding sublimated outlets for the id impulses. Impulses should be brought under the control of secondary process thinking and the reality principle. One may view the psychosexual stages as contributing vital traits to personality. The various bipolar traits must exist in proper balance in order for personality to function optimally. The healthy and well-functioning personality is capable of productive work and loving relationships.

13. Freud's views have led to research dealing with the effectiveness of psychoanalytic therapy and the testing of the validity of constructs and postulates derived from his personality theory. Early studies question the value of psychoanalytic therapy, but the later studies have been more favorable. Several studies have indicated some validity for Freud's character types. Cross-cultural observations have cast doubt on the universality of the Oedipus complex. Studies dealing with repression are mixed, and many may not be dealing with repression as Freud defined it. One thing is clear: Freud's views have generated a great amount of research.

14. Freud has been criticized for his views on infantile sexuality, overstress on early personality formation, failure to consider changes in personality in adulthood, overemphasis on the unconscious, and artificial division of the personality. Freud has been criticized also for his pansexualism, his stand on the inferiority of women, the internal inconsistencies of his theory, his conception of a death instinct, his tension-reduction view of motivation, and his methods of investigation.

15. The following contributions to psychology are generally attributed to Freud: proponent of the irrational in human nature (disguises, defenses, and distortions); explorer of the unconscious; symptoms serve unconscious purposes; continual conflict between our animal and human nature; pleasure is more powerful than reality or morality; stress on infancy and childhood in personality formation; the elucidation of the major defense mechanisms; behavior is not always what it seems to be; the terrors within are more frightening than the terrors without; symptoms have symbolic meaning; physical symptoms may have psychogenic origins; over- and undersocialization as a result of faulty superego development; the development of one of the first forms of psychotherapy, psychoanalytic therapy.

GLOSSARY

Conscious: To be conscious is to be aware. This awareness occurs as the result of external stimulation or the revival of internal experiences.

Conservation of energy: The view that the amount of psychic energy at any given period is constant. Energy used for one type of activity limits the amount available for other activities. As the ego increases in strength, the superego and id weaken.

Defense mechanisms (protective strategies of the ego): Processes that deal directly with an anxiety rather than with the situation that produces it. Their major purpose is to reduce anxiety, which is accomplished by self-deception and reality distortion. (Refer to Table 2–4 for definitions of major defense mechanisms.)

Derivative motive: Motive that is consciously experienced, a disguise of the root motive, which is unconscious.

Dream analysis: The process of discovering the meaning of a dream through free association. This process also uncovers the unconscious wishes and symbolic meanings in dreams.

Electra complex: Sexual interest of the female child for the father and rivalry with her mother.

Free association: The process of reporting whatever comes to mind in the course of discussing symptoms or relating historical events without trying to be logical or exercising censorship.

Infantilism: A childish trend that is a part of the adult personality caused by fixation.

Oedipus complex: Sexual interest of the male child for the mother, occurring during the phallic stage. When it is resolved properly, the child identifies with the father, and the superego begins to take shape.

Pleasure principle: The view that man's most basic motivation is the pursuit of pleasure.

Preconscious: A level of awareness that consists of latent memories that can be brought to consciousness deliberately or that arise spontaneously.

Primary process thinking: Fantastic, wish-fulfilling, illogical thinking that is induced in the ego by strong unfulfilled motives of the id.

Psychosexual stages of development: Oral, anal, phallic, and genital stages are based on zones of the body, which become the focus of pleasures and frustrations. The stages of personality development during which character types are formed.

Reality principle (the proper function of the ego): The principle that refers to the ego, using its abilities to maintain contact with the environment.

Science of the unconscious: Freud's definition of psychoanalysis.

Secondary process thinking: Thinking that is logical and valid and serves the reality principle. A proper function of the ego.

Structures of personality: Distinctive processes within the personality governed by different operating principles that are responsible for specific behaviors.

> **id** (the lower self): The unconscious portion of the psyche, which is the seat of urges. It presses the ego to follow the pleasure principle and to engage in primary process thinking.
>
> **ego** (the controlling self): The ego is the administrator of the personality and mediates between the person and the environment. Its proper functions are secondary process thinking and following the reality principle.
>
> **superego** (higher self): It embodies moral and cultural ideals and restrictions; made up of conscience and ego-ideal.

Unconscious: There are two meanings: (1) unconscious as unawareness and (2) unconscious as a layer of the psyche. The unconscious has a life of its own with operating principles different from those of consciousness.

SUGGESTED READINGS

Freud, Sigmund. *The Interpretation of Dreams,* 1900. Standard Edition Vol. 5. London: Hogarth 1963.

> Freud always considered this his principal work. It laid the foundation for his new psychology. May be considered as autobiography in disguise.

————. *The Psychopathology of Everday Life.* New York: New American Library, 1901.

> Freud expands his theories to include normal persons. He cites numerous examples of pathological behaviors in everyday life, such as lapses of memory, slips of speech, accident proneness, mistakes, and other similar forms of unconscious behavior in normal people. This is a good second book on Freud.

————. *The Ego and the Id.* London: Hogarth, 1923.

> This brief book presents Freud's earliest ideas on the systems within personality. The relationships between the ego and the id are extensively explored.

————. *Civilization and Its Discontents.* London: Hogarth, 1930.

> In this book Freud discusses the conflicts between the individual and society and also the conflicts within the individual. An enlightening treatment of the superego is included. The book is an excellent supplement to this chapter.

————. *Outline of Psychoanalysis.* New York: Norton, 1938.

This is Freud's last book. It is brief and easier to understand than his other works. It was intended to be an introduction to psychoanalysis for the nonspecialist. It is the best source for a beginner in the study of Freud.

————. *New Introductory Lectures on Psychoanalysis*, 1933. Standard Edition 22. London: Hogarth, 1963.

Intended originally as a supplement to his 1915–1917 lectures, these lectures are a summary of psychoanalysis and an extension of old concepts as well as a presentation of new ones. Important because of its insight into Freud's later thought.

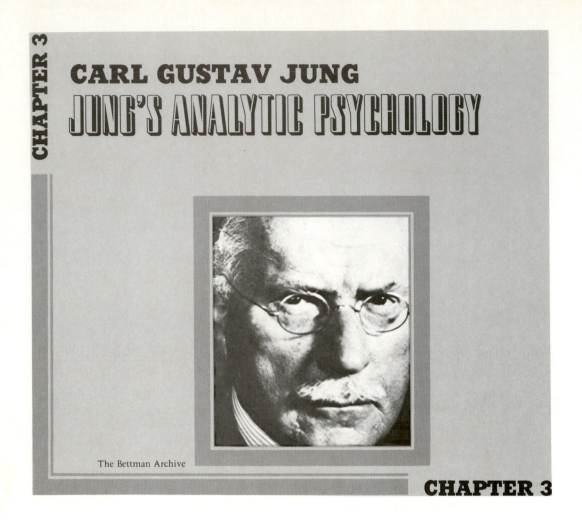

CARL GUSTAV JUNG
JUNG'S ANALYTIC PSYCHOLOGY

The Bettman Archive

BIOGRAPHY AND HISTORICAL PERSPECTIVE

Born in Switzerland in 1875, Carl Gustav Jung was one of the pioneers of modern psychiatry. He made significant contributions to personality theory and psychotherapy, particularly with respect to the role of the unconscious in the life of human beings. Early in his medical career, he was influenced by the ideas of Sigmund Freud and for several years was one of his collaborators. But his interest in the deeper layers of the unconscious—the *collective unconscious*—together with his rejection of the extreme position Freud assigned to sexuality in humans, eventually separated them; as a result, Jung formulated his own school of psychology, *analytical psychology*.

Jung explored many aspects of humans that others had not yet considered. Like Freud, he studied his own dreams, fantasies, experiences, and behaviors. He sought to discover the fundamental origins of the psyche. For more than 60 years he studied his patients. He examined such diverse phenomena as the mythology of primitive people, the religious and ceremonial practices of ancients and moderns, the dreams and fantasies of psychotics, and medieval alchemy. He even investigated the occult: prophetic dreams, mediums, flying saucers, astrology, and extrasensory perception. Although he had been trained in the biological and physical sciences, he was not afraid to tackle things that were apparently outside the science of his day. He died in 1961, working until the very end. His last work was finished just ten days before his death. He presented an extensive account of the genesis of his ideas in his autobiography, *Memories, Dreams, Reflections* (1961). This book may be used as a vehicle to become acquainted with some of Jung's major concepts, as well as his emotional and intellectual development.

One of the recurrent themes in Jung's writings is the loss of contact by people today with the unconscious foundations of their personality. Although Jung certainly had a profound respect for the achievements of science and for the human reasoning capacities that have made them possible, he felt that human beings nevertheless remain an enigma. Many people complain that their lives are empty and meaningless. Much of the wonder and awe that the primitive mind found in the world is missing in contemporary life. Jung believed that people today need explanations, beliefs, and mysteries to make life meaningful.

Jung also introduced the term *individuation* to designate the full differentiation and integration of personality. The individuated person is fully developed and fully functioning—a complete individual. As a person matures, he or she undergoes the process of individuation, during which potentials are fulfilled, experiences expanded, and self-realization is attained. When selfhood is achieved, the ego is recentered as the core of the psyche, a process that involves much learning, self-exploration, and vigorous participation in fulfilling an individual's potentials. To achieve individuation, people must accomplish certain basic tasks in sequence. (A person undergoing Jungian therapy would be aided in dealing with such tasks.) The individual may be informed both about his or her progress and about the direction he or she should follow by changes in the characters and occurrences of his or her dreams and in the events of the environment. One of the basic tasks of the individuation process is the acquisition of self-knowledge. All the components of the personality must be allowed as complete as development and expression as possible (Jung, 1964b). Any one-sided emphasis will produce personality disturbances.

Steps in Jungian Analytic Theory

Self-knowledge begins with an exploration of the *persona*, which for now may be taken simply as the sum total of social roles *(social masks)*. All too frequently we believe that there is nothing more to personality than these social roles. Jung pointed out that masks, although essential for effective living, are not the full personality; indeed, they are not even the most important part.

A further analysis of the personality requires an exploration of the *shadow*. The shadow comprises the undesirable aspects of personality. We are all aware of some of our faults, but many others are kept out of awareness. We cannot become individuated persons unless we learn about these shadow elements. They are a vital part of the personality, and they must be dealt with, either by changing them or by accepting them as part of the self and integrating them into the mainstream of life.

After we become acquainted with our social personality and with our shadow side, we can take the next step, which is to become acquainted with and deal with our opposite-sex qualities. Jung believed that we all have male and female qualities, and these greatly affect all aspects of living, particularly when the opposite sex qualities are not acknowledged and integrated into the ego structure. Jung held that every man has within him an *anima*, Jung's construct for feminine traits and images and that every woman has an *animus*, his construct for masculine traits and images. An individuated man must know his feminine traits and integrate them with the other components of his personality: the ego, the persona, and the shadow. A woman must similarly perceive and integrate her masculine traits. A complete person is a balance of male and female qualities; or, at least, while the male or the female qualities may predominate, they are tempered by the opposite attributes.

As we learn about our social personality, our shadow personality, and our feminine or masculine personality, we are becoming more and more knowledgeable of our unconscious. Our personality is expanding; our awareness is increasing. The early ego is no longer the center of the personality, and the self, which is the recentered ego, emerges as the new center of control. We have become our real selves. We are more in touch with our inner nature and can better meet our *archetypal needs*. *Archetypes* are inborn predispositions that must be satisfied: for instance, to worship power, to relate to members of the opposite sex, to experience a god-image. The individuated person expresses his archetypes in daily affairs.

In addition to the tasks just noted, we should strike a balance between our extroverted and introverted orientations. Furthermore, we should avoid being too intellectual, too sensitive and evaluative, too literal-minded, or too intuitive. The key word is balance among all the systems of personality.

Because of the vital role that personality plays in adaptation and growth, there is much we can learn from Jung's elaborate system of personality constructs and postulates. What are the components of personality, and how do they operate? How are they related to one another? What conditions cause faulty development and other disturbances? What is healthy growth? What should the ideal of personality growth be? Let us now examine the answers to these questions in more detail.

BASIC CONSTRUCTS AND POSTULATES

The Influence of the Unconscious on Consciousness

Much goes on "underneath the surface," and what appear to the individual as conscious thoughts, desires, and emotional responses to specific situations are often the end products of unconscious processes. Ideas and images that cannot be traced to immediate happenings are striking examples of the operation of the unconscious. A person may visualize a scene or draw a picture resembling typical mythological events of which he or she has no knowledge. Jung traced these parallels assiduously. He took dream images and showed their resemblance to images in the Old and New Testaments and a great number of other sources, including primitive religious ceremonies. How can we account for the similarity between the production of a contemporary city dweller and the symbolic expression of people removed by centuries and great distance? Certainly the phenomenon cannot be explained on the basis of the specific contents of consciousness or learning built up in the individual's lifetime.. Usually the person who creates the drawing or the artistic representation or the dream fantasy has no idea of what it signifies. (Jung, 1959a). Such observations led Jung to postulate the existence of a layer of the psyche, the collective unconscious, that could actually produce powerful images and concepts—what Jung termed the archetypes. Jung believed that the contents and operations of the unconscious deserve serious consideration because so much of conscious content and activity is influenced by the unconscious. He proposed the intriguing concept of a collective aspect of the psyche, shared by all people and manifesting itself in behavior, irrespective of culture. What we experience consciously comes from the experience of our senses, our personal unconscious, and the collective unconscious; often conscious contents have no discernible relation to any experiences in the individual's history.

THE TOPOGRAPHY OF THE UNCONSCIOUS

The unconscious layer may be divided into the personal unconscious, with *complexes* as the primary structures, and the collective unconscious, with *archetypes* as the primary structures. The total personality includes all layers of consciousness and unconsciousness.

The personal unconscious and complexes. The personal unconscious is accumulated through individual experiences after birth. For the most part, it consists of unacceptable impulses, wishes, memories that cannot be integrated by the ego, and experiences that have registered psychologically but not consciously. In the broadest sense, the personal unconscious includes all stored impressions, accessible or not. One of the significant components of the personal unconscious is the complex.

A complex may act like a personality within the personality. It may be thought of as a network of thoughts, feelings, and attitudes held together by a nuclear idea or *core disposition* (Jung, 1960). Jung referred to this network of ideas and feelings as the *constellating power* of the complex. Complexes vary in scope and in the extent to which they are a determining force in the personality. Jung (1918) developed a test to identify complexes, known as the *word association test*. He gave his subjects a list of words and asked them to respond with the first word that came to awareness. The nature of the response could reveal something about the nature of the complex. If the *response latency* (the time for the response to occur) was slow, Jung believed that the word was connected with a complex. If the response was *rare* (not the usual response made to the word), again it would indicate the presence of the complex. Jung also used physiological measures, such as changes in heart rate, breathing patterns, and the galvanic skin response as indicators of complexes.

Complexes may be easily aroused by a certain class of stimuli. Many ideas are usually linked together by the core of the complex. For instance, a man may have a woman complex: almost anything can set it off; a great many of his activities are in the service of this complex; no matter what the conversation, he finds a way of getting back to the subject of women. A complex may be so powerful that it resembles a distinct personality that operates outside the control of the ego when it is activated. Even when a person knows that he or she is dominated by a complex, he or she has little control over it. Most often the core is unconscious, and therefore doing something to overcome it is very difficult. A complex disrupts ongoing behavior: people find themselves doing or saying things that they did not intend.

Nature of complexes. As we have noted, Jung held that the core of many important complexes exists in the personal unconscious. In such instances, the ego is being influenced by forces over which it has little control. The person cannot get his or her "mind" off a particular topic. A particular thought or desire is elicited by an ever-widening array of stimuli. As we get to know Jung further, we will discover that the archetypes of the collective unconscious can also be complexes, as in the case of the person who is continually seeking the perfect love object—even after marriage. Negative elements from the shadow aspect of personality can dominate the ego and literally take over the personality. In like manner, we are also aware that certain interests and desires are significant motivating forces in our lives. These are consciously felt and have their origins in the structure of the ego. We can thus identify complexes that have their origin in the ego, the personal unconscious, and in the collective unconscious.

We have been speaking of complexes as if they were always detrimental for us, but there are complexes that can enhance living and contribute to the betterment of humanity. A complex is any powerful driving force, whether positive or negative. The old parish priest whose consuming ambition in his remaining years is to build an impressive church is under the domination of a complex. The harassed parishioners who are weary of fund-raising schemes may feel the force of his complex in a negative way, but the outcome will benefit the parish for a long time to come. An idea or image may take such a powerful hold of a person that it leads to positive action and great accomplishment. Jung believed that many of the world's greatest achievements were the products of all-consuming complexes.

The collective unconscious and archetypes: Archetypes as real images. The collective unconscious consists of latent thought-forms that are inherited by each individual. These thought-forms are archetypes, predispositions to have certain experiences (Jung, 1959a). Such images are not based on our personal life experiences, although they are activated by them; they are found universally. Other human beings with widely varied life experiences at other times and places have had similar images. Just as the mind is tied to sensory inputs, so also the structure of the psyche affects the types of experiences we are capable of having. An archetype is a real image

Strix Pix, David S. Strickler/Monkmeyer Press Photo Service

The child interprets experiences primarily through an archetype.

that a person has. It is a universal thought-form rather than an image that fits a specific person or event. In order to deal adequately with people and events, our archetypal images should be modified to correspond with the nature of those events and people.

As we have noted, Jung (1959a) viewed the archetypes as *predispositions* to have certain experiences. Archetypes do not have a concrete existence. A disposition to believe in a deity is only a potentiality until it is given an actual imaginal form, but, conversely, one must have the disposition before one can have the "God" experience. One can play any combination of tunes on a piano, but it never sounds like an organ. One cannot have experiences for which there is no potentiality: learning depends upon preexisting potentials. One cannot teach a chimpanzee to use speech meaningfully because it does not have the structures necessary for such activity. Even when the structures are present, actual experiences are needed to give the predisposition concrete form. The mother archetype requires an actual mother experience to take a definite shape.

Table 3–1 demonstrates the manner in which a particular concept is formed, as a combination of archetypes and actual experiences.

TABLE 3-1 ROLE OF ARCHETYPES IN EXPERIENCE AND BEHAVIOR

Some General Roles Assigned to Women by Men	One Man's Specific Concept of Woman, Based on His Experiences of the Feminine Role as Nurturant Companion
Temptress	Care from devoted mother
Successful career woman	Solace and comfort when troubled
Nurturant person	Praise for accomplishments
Companion	Physical demonstrations of affection
Lover	Good human relationship with mother
Sexual partner	Mother perceived as perfect woman
	Maternal behavior as ideal feminine quality

Psychologists have long noted the tendency to stereotype and overgeneralize people and events. The image of the family doctor is generalized to all doctors. The stereotype that results when the archetype is activated does not really correspond to any doctor. Where does it come from? It is a generic image or archetype that was formed in our racial past—the experience with healing persons. The perception of one's own mother becomes a stereotype for all mothers. Policemen may be regarded as all alike. The generalizations or stereotypes are subject to modification through learning although stereotypes are remarkably resistant to change, for example, prejudices toward members of the opposite sex, different races, and the like (Stouffer et al., 1949). Jung would explain the tendency to stereotype and overgeneralize in terms of archetypes.

The feminine archetype is easily activated by a woman who makes an impression on a man such as the one referred to in the table. He is likely to find one aspect of woman most attractive and most characteristic of femininity. One who had different experiences with his own mother and sisters would have a different stereotype of women.

What we are saying regarding the formation of archetypes in men also applies to the formation of archetypes in women. The particular archetype of men is activated by early experiences that a girl has had with boys and men, and the archetype may persist into adulthood affecting all her relationships with men.

The collective unconscious and archetypes: Archetypes modified by learning. Jung was quite emphatic about the distinction between preexisting ideas and preexisting idea-forms. Archetypal images or ideas do not simply emerge spontaneously, but rather are aroused by experiences with events in the external world that are fitted into idea-forms. The resulting image or concept is at first an overgeneralized or inadequate representation of the external event. The image depicts more an archetype than the real event. With further learning, the image is modified and more closely approximates the real event. The child eventually comes to perceive significant people as they are. If the learning experiences are abnormal, the concept does not undergo the appropriate change. Thus, the person is dominated by an archetype. He or she may, for example, overvalue authority. In Jung's system, reality orientation is essential to effective living, but archetypes are frequently inappropriate images.

If we observe the course of development of an infant, it becomes quite evident that practically everything the infant does is the product of learning. Except for a few basic reflexes and drives, the original equipment is primarily potential for behavior. Each person inherits tendencies or predispositions for certain types of learning that are characteristic of the species and also unique to that individual. Given no opportunity to learn, the human would remain in a highly primitive state. Several outstanding thinkers, including Aristotle and Locke, argued that the mind is like a wax tablet on which experiences make impressions.

In contrast to Locke and Aristotle, Jung argued that we are born with tendencies to have certain experiences. The brain is a complex organ with its own evolved structures. He believed that *significant human experiences, often repeated, create dispositions to have images of those experiences* and that these dispositions are inherited. Thus, the mind is limited by its own makeup in the number of experiences it can have. We inherit certain latent images that will be activated, or filled in, when we encounter real experiences. For example, think of the perfect mother. There are only a limited number of images that fit the mother — protector, spiritual guide, a witchlike creature, the embodiment of wisdom. Which of these becomes the dominant image depends on actual experiences. One of them will be activated.

The collective unconscious and archetypes: Types of archetypes. The collective unconscious contains latent images of typical human situations — death, birth, femininity, masculinity, growth — and of significant figures — God, the devil, mother, the wise old man. Take another example that further elaborates the nature of archetypes: Our conception of death may be quite varied. One person may see it as complete annihilation and the end of everything. Another conceives of it as a sleeplike state, a transition to immortal life. Death has been depicted as a dark stranger that comes like a thief in the night. How do these images and conceptions originate? They surely depend upon experiences fostered by a person's particular culture. But then there are remarkable cultural and subcultural similarities that need to be explained. Likewise, the image of God varies from person to person: One experiences the deity as a powerful judge who has full control and is to be feared. Another experiences the deity as a providential father who tempers justice with mercy. The world and the psyche of primitive people were dominated with gods and demons. Jung asked where they came from, and his answer was: from the person's collective unconscious. We inherit predispositions to have certain fears — such as fear of the dark, of snakes, or of the devil. These are part of our unconscious potential at birth, and our actual learning experiences will activate these original images.

Certain experiences are easy to have because there is already a predisposition to have them. Jung points out that more archetypes will be activated as our experience broadens. A person who has a very dominant father may perceive all men in authority as tyrants, but having experience with many men in authority increases the number of images that one may use in dealing with authorities.

We may see the operation of archetypes most directly in children. For the child, images of things and people are highly tinged with the fantastic and the magical. The child believes that his or her father is all-powerful or all-knowing. The child stands in awe of the doctor, the policeman, the teacher, the minister. These important figures are not seen as human beings with frailties and shortcomings, but according to archetypal forms — forms that can be found all over the world, both now and in the historical past.

The collective unconscious and archetypes: Archetypes versus correct images. Our images help us to interpret events, but if these images are distorted, either we may fail to see things that are there or we may see things that are not there. The child's images, dominated as they are by archetypes, must be modified so that they correspond to the real events and people in his or her environment. A person who trembles before any authority figure or one who deifies members of the opposite sex will not behave adaptively and effectively because his or her images of these people are distorted. For example, if you misperceive members of the opposite sex, you may actually fall in love with your archetypal image of the person rather than with the real person. This can only lead to serious error. You must always be on guard to check your images against reality. Some people are convinced that practically everyone else is superior and endowed with unusual charm, capabilities, and desirable traits. In these instances the distorted image causes a misinterpretation; it is clear that in a sense, then, an archetype may be seen as a complex, since it can, like a complex, influence the ego.

The archetypal image may so dominate the perceptual and interpretive functions of the ego that it seriously distorts judgment. The father archetype, as we have seen, may distort a man's perception of his boss, primarily through the mechanism of *projection*. He does not really see the boss as the person he is, but adds elements embodied by the father archetype that dominates his own ego. Adaptation to the environment obviously requires perception that approximates real events; thus, real experiences can lessen the power of the primitive archetypes. When the archetypes are properly modified, they assist in the process of perceiving correctly.

The collective unconscious and archetypes: The frustration of archetypes.   Under normal conditions we do not acutely experience the operation of archetypes. As long as our needs are being met and there is harmony between the conscious and unconscious spheres of our psyches, with all aspects of personality given the opportunity to develop and function, we attain individuation and live effectively. But when important activities and requirements are not carried out, the effects of the archetypes are felt as symptoms of illness. Some problems that are widespread in our day may be seen as failures to find adequate expression for archetypes. We are experiencing a loss of trust and faith in our leaders. The government no longer holds its authority for many. The consequence of the lack of a "father" is the sense of meaninglessness that is so common among the young (Keniston, 1965). The father archetype may attach itself to political and philosophical movements that seem to offer a great hope for the future and for individual fulfillment. Thus, though archetypes are most strikingly obvious in those pathological conditions in which they completely take over the psyche, they also underlie the lives of "normal" people.

As we have noted, the archetype should be considered a real image that a person has, not a mysterious and abstract entity. Our images are often strong motive forces and generate much behavior; thus, certain archetypes may be considered as powerful human needs that require some form of gratification. Frustration of these causes serious disturbance in personality and behavior. Consider the many monuments—pyramids, cathedrals, churches, mosques, temples—that have been erected in fear or homage to a deity. These buildings are nonfunctional in any practical sense, but they are expressions of a powerful archetype, a real image in the life of people.

Some examples of powerful archetypes that serve as needs in Jung's view are meaningfulness, belief in something greater than the person, guidance, authority, mothering and fathering, belief in something that makes our lives intelligible. These are similar to Fromm's five basic human needs and Maslow's metaneeds, to be discussed later.

The collective unconscious and archetypes: Symbolic expression of archetypes.　You may obtain an appreciation of the active aspect of archetypes by considering some significant but typical human situations. What would you do to celebrate the birth of a baby? Surely this is an important event in the life of a married couple that warrants some kind of response. How might a community commemorate the death of one of its great leaders? Perhaps a day should be set apart for ceremonies, or a monument should be erected. Jung held that significant events, whether positive or negative, elicit ceremonial and symbolic expressions. Primitive people celebrated important events—drought, famine, a bountiful harvest, the passage of children into adulthood, and the like with symbols and rituals. We also need such rituals in dealing with the same types of events.

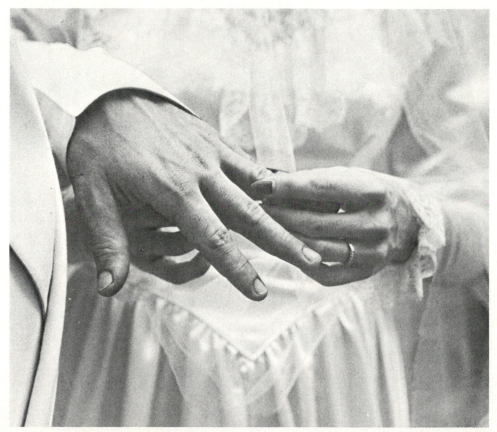

Seghers/Monkmeyer Press Photo Service

Rituals are symbols that give meaning to important events.

The collective unconscious and archetypes: The culture and the collective unconscious.   As we have seen, the most important task of the growing organism is to become an individual. The biggest danger is that of being smothered—both by the requirements of social living, which demand and reward conformity, and by the collective unconscious, which can overwhelm and take over the ego. Individuation means freedom from these oppressive forces. Such freedom can be achieved through a strong ego and a realm of consciousness that includes all significant aspects of the personality.

The environment, by means of the culture, forces the growing child into certain prescribed patterns. Children have little choice in their early years when all their decisions are made for them. When they do acquire the power of decision and judgment, they still must give up their freedom to a great extent in order to keep out of trouble and, more importantly, to meet their needs. It is much easier to conform than to be an individual; thus, most people are swallowed up by their cultures. The ego must also adjust to the pressures of the collective psyche. This means that certain archetypal requirements, which in this context refer to certain basic human needs, must be met. Failure to do so leads to pathology. Whereas the power of the culture is visible, the force of the archetypes is quite invisible. Neither culture nor the archetypes should hold sway. When development is smooth, neither is in command, but rather the ego deals with each satisfactorily.

Certain archetypes are instinctive requirements: they are promptings from within ourselves. Failure to take account of them, like lack of knowledge or attention to external forces, endows them with power over us. The archetypes may take over the ego when they are not being satisfied in behavior. They cannot be ignored without damage to the personality. The ego must master both external and internal forces. Ignoring the demands of the two sources of influence is the surest way to bring about an unhealthy state.

The collective unconscious and archetypes: Some confusing issues regarding archetypes.   Jung repeatedly stressed the notion that archetypes are not inborn preformed ideas or images, but are rather latent idea-forms that require actual experiences to activate them. He viewed the mind as having a limited number of potential categories of images that serve as the vehicles for the perceptions we actually form. Yet he frequently cites examples of fantasies, hallucinations, and drawings of his patients that depict archetypes that do not correspond to any experiences the persons have had. Here we are faced with an apparent contradiction: the existence of iamges that were not formed by the usual sensory and perceptual processes. Are these not examples of preformed ideas that spontaneously emerge into consciousness?

Jung could argue that we can have experiences that have not occurred in our learning history as a result of the use of our own constructive imagination and reasoning processes. Furthermore, we could activate archetypal images through our own cognitive, affective, and conative processes. Suppose you were asked to draw a picture that depicts your mood caused by the loss of a loved one. The image that emerges, which is the inspiration for the drawing, might be an archetype that was never activated previously. Jung could argue that your mood activated an archetypal image just as an encounter with an external event might activate a particular archetype.

Another puzzling view that Jung holds regarding archetypes is that some of them must be active in our lives in order that we may grow and function properly. In this sense, some archetypes are like needs or instincts that must be gratified. We can understand the usual meaning of archetypes as potential images that one may activate through personal life experiences. The particular archetype that emerges depends upon the type of experience one has. For Jung, however, certain archetypes embody essential requirements of our human nature, and thus must be experienced and expressed. If they are not experienced and expressed, we will develop pathological symptoms. Thus, we must identify and find suitable outlets for such archetypes. Summing up the relation of the conscious and unconscious segments of the psyche, Jung says:

> Conscious and unconscious do not make a whole when one of them is suppressed and injured by the other. If they must contend, let it at least be a fair fight with equal rights on both sides. Both are aspects of life. Consciousness should defend its reason and protect itself, and the chaotic life of the unconscious should be given the chance of having its way too — as much of it as we can stand. This means open conflict and open collaboration at once. That, evidently, is the way human life should be. It is the old game of the hammer and anvil: between them the patient iron is forged into an indestructible whole, an "individual" [Jung, 1959, 289].[1]

Compensation

Jung believed that the collective unconscious and the personal unconscious make up for or correct the excesses or omissions of the conscious ego; it is in this sense of a *corrective* that compensation is to be understood in Jung's (1953) usage. The collective unconscious contains the "wisdom of the ages" and is often communicated in dreams and fantasies. The dream reveals the problem as well as the solution. The unconscious serves as a regulatory mechanism to curb the conscious. If you take your role too seriously, you may dream that you are in a destitute and despicable state. The dream serves as a reminder of the overemphasis on the persona. In the waking state, a period of intense emotional activity may be followed by a state of quiescence during which emotional reactivity is deadened. Dreams are frequently compensations for conscious disturbances.

If the conscious aspect is one-sided, as when a man identifies so completely with his persona that he does not look within for anything else, the unconscious will help to correct the defect. In his dreams the man will play an introverted role. The dream actually draws attention to the one-sided slant in his life, and, although he does not necessarily recognize its meaning, it does its work just as a medicine may work to cure an illness, whether we understand how or not.

Jung held that compensation occurs if there is moderate overdevelopment of one component of personality. The unconscious usually works harmoniously with con-

---

[1]*The Archetypes and the Collective Unconscious.*

sciousness by exerting a corrective counterforce. The unconscious ceases to compensate and actually becomes highly destructive if there is an extreme overemphasis on conscious aspects. If we refuse to acknowledge our bad moods, for instance, we may be dominated by them at times.

Whereas the unconscious normally compensates for the one-sided character of the conscious, the intervention of the ego is usually required. Without such intervention, the operation of the unconscious may be insufficient or may become destructive rather than compensatory. When a minority group is not permitted adequate participation in the main stream of activity, it may react in a violent manner. So also portions of the personality that are not acknowledged and given adequate expression by the ego may cause serious disturbance in the functioning of the personality. We need to pay attention to all aspects of our personality makeup, in Jung's view. Forces in the unconscious interfere with the operation of the ego: this is experienced as mild suffering in its moderate form and, in its extreme form, as a total collapse of the personality, possibly culminating in suicide.

The Anima and the Animus

Jung held the controversial notion that we all have both male and female qualities and that the fully developed person of each sex allows the opposite qualities to be integrated into the self and expressed in behavior. The fully developed male expresses his female tendencies, and the fully developed female expresses her male tendencies. This "complete person" has a much broader potential for behavior than the exclusively male or female person.

The *anima* is the feminine aspect of a man whereas the *animus* is the masculine aspect of a woman. Normally, these are suppressed as a result of the effort to express the persona, which causes a one-sided development. The persona embodies appropriate sex-roles as defined by the culture. Jung seems to have used the terms anima and animus in two senses: to denote the masculine or feminine qualities in man or woman and to describe archetypal images of femininity and masculinity. Unlike the sociologists, who make femininity and masculinity cultural products, Jung (1953) held to *clearly delineated traits for the sexes*. Jung's description of the sexes was not intended to be demeaning of either of them. He perceived admirable traits in both. The psychology of man is radically different from the psychology of woman.

Jung's views of masculinity and femininity coincide pretty well with the traditional notions: for example, he saw men as decisive and rational and women as emotional and intuitive: men are seen as aggressive where women are seen as passive (Garai, 1970). Jung held that both sexes possessed both desirable and undesirable qualities. Women exemplify nurturance and orientation to people whereas men at their best are problem solvers and reality-oriented. The point is that each person has the desirable qualities of both sexes in his or her nature, which can be actualized if the personality is fully developed. An overemphasis on the persona for both sexes may impede the normal functioning of the anima or animus, with a resulting loss of vitality, flexibility, and responsiveness.

ANIMA TRAITS AND IMAGES

The anima is Jung's construct that designates both feminine traits and images in a boy. The feminine traits are inherited as part of the genetic potential, and the feminine images are embodied in the archetypes that the child inherits. This same notion applies to the masculine traits and images inherited by a girl. Jung also believed that the anima image that a man may develop (his ideal image of woman) was greatly influenced by early romantic involvements that activated a particular archetype of woman.

In Jung's view (1953), the anima of a man is derived from three sources: (1) the feminine inheritance (some men are by nature more feminine than others), (2) actual experiences with girls and women (of particular importance is the experience with the mother, who is the first source of attachment), and (3) the primordial deposits of the collective unconscious (all the potential images of the roles women have taken in relation to men). The manner in which an individual woman is regarded depends not on her actual qualities alone, but on what is brought to the relationship from these three sources.

According to Jung, the roles in which men have cast women are quite varied and include such images as the harlot, the temptress, the witch, the spiritual guide, the goddess, the nurturing mother, the loving sexual companion, and others. Whether a particular woman appears to a man as a goddess or she-devil or whatever depends upon his early experiences with girls and women. Abnormal experiences can result in the persistence of an archetypal image or a stereotype of women and can create many problems in heterosexual experiences. What we have said here applies also to masculine traits in a woman and to the formation of the image of man in a woman, as we shall see. Jung believed that one should have varied experiences with many persons of the opposite sex in order to prevent a powerful archetype from dominating the ego.

ANIMUS TRAITS AND IMAGES

Much of what has been said about the anima applies also to the animus, or masculine aspect of a woman's personality. Again, by animus Jung refers to masculine traits and images that are part of a woman's nature. Just as a man might project an anima image onto a woman who makes an impression upon him, so also a woman might project her animus image onto a particular man, with the effect of deifying him. The animus considered as traits should complement the feminine ego and persona and add qualities that make her rational and reality-oriented . If the animus traits of a woman are denied or underdeveloped, her personality is adversely affected. She may overidentify with the persona image of femininity that her culture prescribes. It may have other effects, such as making a woman opinionated and encouraging her to rival men. On the other hand, animus traits and images can function to promote healthy living and satisfactory relationships with men. Animus traits can serve to temper the feminine personality traits. But in order to attain this level of maturity, a woman must recognize the animus and give it a hearing. Denial of the opposite traits by a man or woman makes them uncontrollable.

Just as the anima of a man contributes to the images a particular man has of women, the animus of a woman also contributes to the images she has of men. There have been many roles that men have played in the life of women. The particular image depends on early experiences with men and boys—father, brothers, and sweethearts. Once the image of man is formed in the psyche of a girl, it persists as an influence in her dealings with men. She may perceive a man as an adventurer, a seducer, a rapist, a protector, a father image, or as a knight errant who will sweep her off her feet. Any particular man who makes an impression on her is judged according to one of these images. Her relationships with men may be seriously disturbed. She may fall head-over-heels in love with a particular man, only to find that he turns out to be totally different from her first impressions of him. Of course, her first impression was formed primarily under the domination of the masculine archetype. Men and women who have difficulty knowing and responding to the opposite sex usually have not dealt adequately with their archetypes of the other sex and the opposite sex tendencies in their nature. Their response is more appropriate to the universal image than to the real people they encounter. Thus, each person should allow his or her full nature, which includes both masculine and feminine traits, to be expressed, and he or she should also broaden his or her experiences with members of the opposite sex so that he or she forms functional images that depict real people, not archetypes.

MASCULINE VERSUS FEMININE PSYCHOLOGY

Masculine and feminine psychology are distinctly different, Jung believed. The purest form of man (what might be termed "raw masculinity": brutishness, combativeness, savagery) is disagreeable to women and is dangerous. It needs to be tempered by some of the positive emotions of femininity. Likewise, the purest form of womanhood (fickleness, emotional volatility, hypersensitivity to any supposed insult) is unappealing to men and usually creates a neurotic existence for the woman. It must be tempered by the logic and rationality of masculine traits. These *tempering influences* exist in the unconscious and normally do their work unnoticed. But when the anima and animus remain in a primitive state because they are denied expression and integration within the self, they intrude into consciousness and create psychological disturbances. A man may become effeminate; or a woman, overly masculine.

Once again, balance and moderation are the keys. A man must recognize his feminine qualities and accept them as a real part of his personality. A woman must similarly recognize her masculine traits and accept them as a part of her nature. The anima of a man adds a dimension of humanness to his masculine role, and the animus of a woman anchors her persona in rationality and control.

We might ask, Is there an anima type of woman, and is there an animus type of man? Are there women who are especially attractive to men, and likewise are there men who are particularly attractive to women? We all know a man or a woman of whom everyone says, "How could he fall for her, or what could make such a fine young girl fall in love with a good-for-nothing like him?" Even individuals involved in such romantic relationships often recognize their irrationality as well as their own helplessness. They may say, "I know this whole thing is crazy, and my head keeps telling me no, but my heart says yes." What a person sees in the other are extraordinary powers and attributes, not what is objectively there, and this is painfully obvious to those who are not captivated. Projection is at work: qualities are ascribed to the other that are projections of the anima or animus, depending on whether it is a man or a woman who is smitten.

Who are these women who seem by nature to attract anima projections from certain men? Incidentally, these are men who are immature and inexperienced with women. According to Jung (1959a), such women may be described as sphinxlike. They are equivocal and elusive: there is always an intriguing uncertainty about them. They are not an indefinite blur that offers nothing, but have an indefiniteness that seems full of promise. A woman of this kind embodies opposite qualities: she is both old and young, mother and daughter, childlike and yet endowed with an extreme cunning that is disarming to men.

What about the man who is so attractive that he is like dynamite for some women? According to Jung, he is a real master of words—words with a great deal of meaning that also create intrigue by leaving a great deal unsaid. In popular language he might be described as "having a good line." He is one of those who are "misunderstood" or in some manner at odds with their environment; he might be someone from another country. He may create the illusion that he is capable of great self-sacrifice. He is regarded as an undiscovered hero, recognized only by the woman who loves him. These are the men who capture the heart, even though the head says no. We are speaking here of an abnormal involvement on the part of a woman in which her animus (image of the perfect man) is interfering with her correct evaluation of the man with whom she has fallen in love. This same man would impress other women who are not dominated by the same animus image as being artificial and shallow. What Jung seems to be saying about this type of man is that he fits a stereotype that is highly appealing to certain women.

Harmful Aspects of Anima and Animus Traits

As we have noted, Jung believed that both men and women have opposite-sex qualities in their nature. These opposite-sex qualities are opposed to the persona role for each sex. Thus, they are denied and thereby made a part of the shadow. If the process of becoming a fully developed self—the individuation process—is to take place, a man must become aware of and express his anima traits; and a woman, her animus traits. If discovering one's persona or social mask is difficult and if becoming aware of shadow elements is a task of heroic proportions, the discovery and acceptance of the opposite-sex qualities are most difficult of all. These tendencies conflict with our conception of self and are among the most strongly repressed of the shadow qualities. But as we have noted previously, the anima and animus temper the persona and are a vital part of the true nature of the individual. The ego pays much attention to the persona requirements, but until the other aspects are allowed to develop and play a part in the personality, selfhood will not occur. Awareness and expression of the anima or animus is one of the most complicated steps (but an absolutely essential one) in the attainment of the good life, in Jung's view (see Sanford, 1980).

Jung believed that the total person should include both male and female qualities.

Each complements the other and adds vital dimensions to the personality. Jung uses the term *androgyny* to refer to this balanced person. The androgynous person of both sexes is capable of a much broader range of reactions and actions than the person who is primarily dominated by the male or female persona.

STAGES OF DEVELOPMENT OF THE ANIMA AND THE ANIMUS

The anima of a man undergoes changes throughout his life. There are at least four different images of woman, each of which characterizes a man's *growing relationship* with the opposite sex. In the first stage the woman is pictured as sensual, an attractive physical being who can tantalize a man: the sexual aspect is most outstanding. The woman who exemplifies this image is Eve: she was the greatest thing that happened to Adam after his creation. The next stage is that of the romantic woman. Helen of Troy, with "the face that sank a thousand ships," is a good representative of this stage. The woman is idealized and captures a man's passions and love. The sexual component remains quite prominent. The third stage is that of the virgin; woman is depicted as simple, beautiful, warm, innocent, and capable of great love for only one man. In the fourth stage she becomes a spiritual guide—a source of stability, comfort, and wisdom. In normal development, a man's relationship with women follows this course. If a mar-

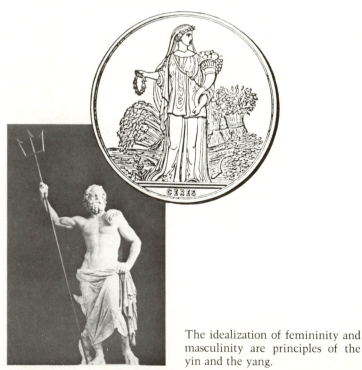

The idealization of femininity and masculinity are principles of the yin and the yang.

The Bettman Archive

riage is successful, the husband acquires a sincere respect for his wife as a person in her own right, and the bonds between them increase on the spiritual level (Jung, 1966, p. 174). By spirtual level, Jung refers to emotions and particularly to emotional needs.

The animus of a woman also goes through four stages, each depicting man in a characteristic masculine role. The first portrays him as powerful, sensual, animalistic, and sexually attractive. This image may be termed the "power man." In the second stage man is depicted as a lover, an attractive gentleman who has power over the woman's emotions; this image is the "romantic man." The third stage is that of the "action man." Man is seen as competent, masterful, authoritarian. Of course, the woman has a role to play in this through her support and encouragement: man has power over her only if she endows him with it. In the fourth stage, man is viewed as "a wise old man." He is the spiritual guide to woman. He gives her support, stability, and inspiration. In a healthy relationship between a man and a woman, the anima of the man complements the animus of the woman; they work harmoniously together, cooperating with their conscious aspects.

You may be assisted in understanding and remembering the meanings of anima and animus by connecting the term *animation* with anima and the term *animosity* with animus. Jung (1933b) often referred to the anima in a man as the soul or spirit. He did not use the term in its religious or metaphysical sense; rather he meant the tender emotions that are associated with femininity. A man who lacks spirit or soul suffers from a disturbance of his anima. The animus implies strength, courage, and aggressiveness. A woman who is capable of animosity can deal actively with the people and things of her environment. Of course, animosity can lead to destructive behavior and can be a source of disturbance in the personality, just as animation can be uncontrolled emotionality.

Table 3–2 depicts the normal and abnormal manifestations of the anima in man and the animus in woman. It should be noted that abnormality in this sense may take the form of a deficiency or excess in required behaviors.

Jung found support for his concepts of the anima and animus in the Chinese principles of the yin and the yang. The yin embodies being receptive, yielding, withdrawing, turning inward, enclosing, containing, giving birth. Yin is nurturing and seductive; it is sensuous and exudes reverence for stillness and beauty. The yang emphasizes the active, outgoing, aggressive, strong, firm, life-giving principles. It is a realistic being-in-the-world. (See Blofeld, 1965.) Specific behaviors are heroism, abstract spirituality, disciplined morality. Yang is reality-oriented and restrictive.

Introversion and Extroversion

PSYCHOLOGICAL TYPES AND FUNCTIONS

Though he did not deny the uniqueness and complexity of each individual, Jung nevertheless felt that people could be categorized into definable types. He proposed two major types or attitudes: introversion and extroversion (Jung, 1933b). Extroverts focus their interest on objects outside themselves; introverts attend more to their inner life, their

TABLE 3-2 ANIMA AND ANIMUS TRAITS

Anima

Normal	Abnormal
Keeps a man in touch with his emotions	Causes a man to be petty and picayune
Helps him to be creative and spontaneous	Makes him cynical and bitter about his lot in life
Makes him more intuitive	Makes him moody and overly concerned with interpersonal matters
Helps him to be sensitive to the needs and feelings of others	Makes him gossipy and intrusive in the affairs of others
Makes him a gentleman in his relationships with both men and women	Makes him effeminate and insecure in social relationships

Animus

Normal	Abnormal
Makes a woman reality-oriented	Makes a woman emotional and irrational
Makes her problem-oriented	Makes her morbidly introspective
Produces a balanced orientation	Produces uncontrolled emotions and fragmentation of the personality
Makes for goal-directed behavior	Causes disorganized and dissociated behaviors
Makes a woman capable of inspiring the anima in a man to be creative	Makes a woman highly opinionated and competitive with men
Helps her to establish a sense of identity and integrity	Makes her attempt to divest a man of his role, causing problems with her sense of feminine identity
Makes her stable	Makes her argumentative, negativistic, moody, irrational
Gives her self-assurance and backbone	Makes her feel inferior and insecure

Like other forms of abnormality, abnormality of the anima and animus may follow a pattern either of excess or of deficiency. The animus in a woman may cause her to castrate men as she attempts to assert her power and independence. Or it may take the form of spinelessness and an inability to be autonomous. The anima in a man may make him overly emotional and sentimental, but it may also result in a bland and shallow personality. Again the element of balance is essential to a healthy personality, according to Jung's view of human beings.

Bear in mind that Jung's constructs of anima and animus refer to the opposite sex traits and images that a person possesses. When these images and traits are functioning properly, they make the individual a complete person.

self. Obviously, such attitudes vary in degree, but an individual tends to organize his or her psychic structures in either one direction or the other.

In addition to the two attitudes, there are various psychological functions that also vary in strength in each person. We might consider these functions as powers or faculties that enable a person to deal with his or her environment. Jung (1933b) named only four: thinking, feeling, sensing, and intuiting. At any single moment we may engage in one or more of these activities. Combining the attitudes and the functions, we may distinguish eight major types of people. Depending upon the priorities of the various functions (which is dominant, which auxiliary, which inferior), there are many, many variations (Mann et al., 1972). There are tests based on Jung's notions of introversion and extroversion and the various functions. The Myers-Briggs Type Indicator assesses a person's standing on Jung's eight major types — the two major attitudes and the four functions associated with each attitude (Myers, 1962).

A word should be said about typologies. Some psychologists, as we have seen, believe that typing human personalities does an injustice to the remarkable individuality of each person. The argument is that the typology forces very different people into a neat category. The type says both too much and too little. It says too much by ascribing all of the attributes of the type to the particular individual, without specifying degree. It says too little because the specific characteristics of the person are not delineated. To say that John and Mary are both introverted does not tell you much about the unique set of traits that constitutes each personality. It should be pointed out that, with present knowledge, thorough description of personality is far beyond the achievement of psychology. Yet one may discern generalities and approximations. There are relatively few styles of houses — Colonial, Tudor, Cape Cod, and the like — but each specific house has its own particular character, size, color, contents, and location. There is no good reason why personalities cannot be examined from the same point of view. The notion of types does not require that all the members be identical, only that there is enough similarity to apply a designation or label.

Jung's two types may be considered from the standpoint of attitudes toward objects: the introvert resists the power of objects and draws life energy away from them and toward himself or herself; the extrovert invests energy in objects and finds greatest value in objects external to himself or herself. The introvert, as a consequence of inward orientation, tends to be shy, quiet, and difficult to know. The extrovert tends to be in touch with the world — open and eager to participate in his or her surroundings. All classes of society have these two characteristic types; whether a person is educated or not, whether a highly gifted musician or a day laborer, does not obliterate the two life orientations. Furthermore, the two types are found in both men and women (Cattell, 1957). Jung believed that the basis must be native biological factors. Extroverts adapt by expanding their contact with the environment; introverts, by making themselves impregnable.

Jung refers to extroverted and introverted attitudes as being natural types, by which he means that people are born with one or the other tendency. A study by Siegelman (1968) challenges this view. He found that type of parenting influenced the development of introverted or extroverted orientations. Specifically, parents who relate to their children with love and acceptance tend to foster extroverted behaviors whereas parents who have cold and negative relationships with their children tend to foster introverted behaviors. It is not clear whether Siegelman was dealing with introversion or shyness, as Jung defined these terms.

There is a natural inclination to think of the extrovert as more "normal" or healthy than the introvert. The reason may be the identification of action with extroversion: in an action-oriented culture, the extrovert seems to fit better. Jung held that the two orientations are *natural* types of humans; to attempt to convert a naturally introverted person to an extrovert usually creates psychophysiological disturbances. A child who is forced into an attitude that is not suited to his or her nature will usually become neurotic. Jung (1933b) believed that just as femininity and masculinity are distinctive qualities, so there are introverts and extroverts, and their respective orientations to life are quite different.

SUPERIOR AND INFERIOR FUNCTIONS

Usually some components of personality are more highly developed, and more energy is employed for their operation than for others. Thus there are *superior and inferior functions.* If a person is an extrovert consciously, his or her introvertive tendencies are inferior and unconscious. We may remind the reader again of a minority that is prevented from full participation in the mainstream of activities. The minority may become destructive and violent as it seeks expression of its rights in an active manner. Inferior functions in the psyche are caused by failure of the ego to pay attention to them. Inferior functions frequently exert a disruptive influence and create tension. Although the extrovertive tendencies are under conscious motivation, there may be intrusion from the unconscious introvertive tendencies. For example, a cooperative extrovert may at times display a childish obstinacy and resist the suggestions of his or her friends. Since the introvert in him or her is not under conscious control, at times it takes on a childish, destructive aspect and constitutes a serious weakness in his or her personality. Recognizing his or her introvertive side and directing attention inward would bring such tendencies under control. A lopsided wheel does not run smoothly. If the dominant conscious orientation is organized around introvertive traits, the extrovertive tendencies are unconscious and also are not under ego control. They, too, may create difficulties for the person when they intrude into the ego. The introvert may strongly desire to be more popular, to be more comfortable with people, and to develop rich friendships. But these motives may be pushed into the background and not given much attention. For example, an introverted professor who always seemed self-sufficient and content with his quiet life apparently longed for companionship. His attempts to relate to others were rather primitive and crude; he was usually left out of things. He was driven to seek companionship with an unsavory crowd and almost ruined his reputation. With them he felt comfortable: he could let his guard down and be more himself. Thus, Jung's idea that undeveloped tendencies are dangerous is applicable to both introversion and extroversion. An individual may be by nature predominantly extroverted or introverted, but allow adequate expression for the opposite attitude in himself or herself. It should be borne in mind that Jung meant by *inferior function* an underdeveloped function, one that has not been integrated into the ego structure. Jung's theory of psychological types is so complex that to develop it extensively would go far beyond the scope of this book. Since the purpose of this chapter is to highlight the individuation process, Jung's idea of one-sided development and disequilibrium will be considered.

To appreciate Jung's notion of the individuation process, one must take into account both the general qualities of introversion and extroversion and the four functions of the psyche: thinking, feeling, sensing, and intuiting. One of these is usually overemphasized and overdeveloped while the others are not expressed adequately. In such instances, people are handicapped because they are not using all their abilities as completely as possible. Extroverted intellectuals may be so intent on making an impression on others that they neglect their own feelings and emotions. Likewise, intuitive introverts may focus so much on their inner life that they lose vital personal contacts. Jung held that there should be full expression of all the functions, so that people fully use what they have. Any one-sided emphasis (being too extroverted or too introverted, being overly intellectual or overly intuitive) hampers normal growth and functioning.

What we have said about superior and inferior functions is also applied by Jung to the major components of personality. For example, an individual may direct most of his or her energy to the development of the ego and the persona and neglect the shadow component, or the conscious aspects may be highly developed, and the unconscious components remain as inferior functions.

The Human Being as Symbol Maker

SYMBOLS AND THEIR FUNCTIONS

One of Jung's most significant contributions to our understanding of human behavior is his emphasis on the role of symbols in human life. We are all familiar with the symbolic nature of language; the words of a language, which of course vary from language to language, stand for or represent things, names, complex relationships, and even situations that do not actually exist, as, for example, a negative number in mathematics. Words and phrases are symbols because they stand for something else; they do not have meaning in themselves but are assigned meaning. A word represents some other thing or person or situation or relationship. The ability to symbolize events is one of the most distinctively human attributes (Werner and Kaplan, 1963).

Nonverbal symbols.   There are many other symbols besides words. Certain gestures and facial expressions, certain customs and rituals, have acquired meaning and serve as symbols: a smile and handclasp to greet a friend, the giving of gifts as tokens of love. Symbols express what may be difficult to communicate in other ways or what cannot be easily expressed, such as the love of a mother for her child, or of a man for his wife, or of people for their homeland. A man sends his beloved flowers, which say things that he could not say as effectively: "I want you to care for me." "I think a lot of you." "Please forgive me — I really did not want to hurt you."

Many people do things that apparently have a great deal of meaning for them

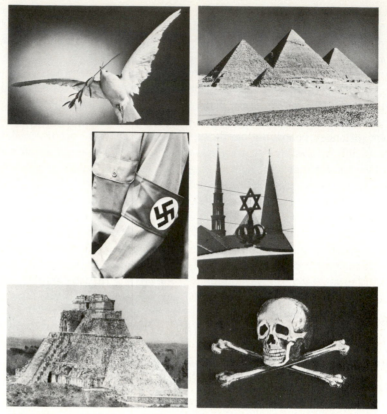

Photo credits: *upper left* The Bettman Archive; *center left* Copyright Leif Skoogfors 1982/Woodfin Camp & Associates; *lower left* Copyright © Beryl Goldberg; *upper right* George Holton/Photo Researchers, Inc.; *center right* © Thomas Hopker 1980/Woodfin Camp & Associates; *lower right* The Bettman Archive

Some archetypes have powerful motivating force.

because they repeat the practices again and again without knowing why. A great many customs have arisen — the Christmas tree, the Easter rabbit, the cap and gown, the wedding ring — and such customs have much meaning, yet those who are touched by these symbols usually cannot give an explanation of their origin. Interference with the exercise of the symbolic activities produces a disturbance: "How can you have a wedding without a wedding ring or a graduation without cap and gown?" A woman may be terribly distressed if she has to forgo a wedding ring even though she recognizes quite clearly that the ring is "just a matter of custom," a frill that she could just as well do without. The ring touches her in some mysterious way that she herself cannot explain. Jung held that symbols and symbolic practices give a meaning to life and are absolutely essential for effective living.

Jung also proposed the challenging idea that we behave first and question later. People have done things for centuries without knowing why they do them. Systems of theology and philosophy followed rather than preceded beliefs and ceremonial practices. Reasoning and consciousness are late evolutionary developments in human psyche. Even in ordinary day-to-day living, we do things first and find explanations later, particularly if we are required to justify our behavior (Johnson, 1968). Symbolic practices, in Jung's view, satisfy essential requirements of our nature. In our effort to be rational and reality-oriented, we often ignore the more primitive requirements of our nature.

Many things are outside the realm of our knowledge — the meaning of life, the necessity of death, birth, pain, and natural disasters. Images of these have led to ceremonies, customs, and a variety of symbols and symbolic practices. Our symbolic practices play an essential part in living and help us to cope with the condition of our existence as humans. To do away with such symbols leaves the mysteries of life without any kind of response. Jung held that this elimination of a proper channel for response is very dangerous and that it is one of the causes of the widespread unhappiness of our time.

Certain rituals and ceremonies have had a remarkable persistence. They have occurred in many diverse places and times throughout human history. Although the practices have varied in specific content, the forms they have taken and the responses of the peoples are often strikingly similar, even when no contact was possible, a factor that precludes imitation.

Symbols give meaning to life.   Beliefs and practices are acknowledged and used by many people, suggesting that they satisfy something important in personality. Jung held that symbols have given people a way of dealing with their problems, a way of making the human condition more bearable and comprehensible. Difficulties such as disease, loss of loved ones, the erratic character of nature, aging, and personal death can all acquire meaning and, therefore, be made more acceptable through religious practices, symbolism, and beliefs. Symbols are the expression or products of archetypes. The symbolic rituals surrounding such experiences as birth, marriage, and death are universal.

A failure to find expression for the archetypes necessarily leaves unsettled certain requirements of living. One needs some form of spiritual life (a set of beliefs to explain the unknowns in life) in order to live fully just as one requires a warm temperature to be comfortable. Life is possible at lower temperatures, but one experiences tension. Lack of gratification of archetypes involves a similar persistence of tension. For primitive people, myths were a mental therapy for suffering and dealing with the unknown, but modern-day humans also have myths — for instance, science will solve everything, or wealth will make us happy, or being beautiful and staying young will make life exciting and interesting. *The impotence of the ordinary person is banished by the power of his or her prayers, rituals, beliefs, and practices* (Jung, 1933).

Symbols produce numinous experiences.   When we isolate ourselves from our archetypal requirements, serious consequences ensue. Becoming more and more conscious and rational has cut us off from our own inner nature; giving up ritualistic practices and beliefs has made our lives less rich. We experience depression, tension, restlessness, and a feeling of alienation. Symbols touch our deepest core tendencies;

they provide for what Jung called *numinous experiences*—experiences that impart spiritual power or special significance to those who are affected by them.

Consider the flag of a country. It stands for the ideals that are cherished by the people. The flag serves as a source of security and strength. It stands for my country, of which I am an important part. My country is greater than I am, and I can find courage and strength from being a part of it. The flag is a concrete physical object that can have considerable meaning. It can become a focal point for the expression of many archetypes. Jung would say that it has a numinous quality. We feel a sense of awe in the presence of nationalistic symbols, such as the flag. We honor them and treat them with great reverence. A great deal of ritual and ceremony surrounds them, creating the numinous tone. When the flag or any symbol loses its numinous quality, then something is lost for the individual, who is left without the support needed. The symbols of people today—wealth, power, prestige, security—have proved unfulfilling and must be replaced, Jung (1964b) believed.

New symbols to replace primitive ones. Symbolic activity may be regarded in two ways: (1) as the product of a need that has been blocked or (2) as one means of satisfying a need. Dancing is symbolic behavior that many psychologists regard as an outlet for frustrated sexual tensions, but it may also express people's longing for freedom, for instance, those dances in which physical contact is not present. Progressive art forms seem to bring to the fore our deepest longings: for wholeness or rebirth or freedom from constraints. They not only are the products of frustrated impulses, but they also point to the solution, to the goals toward which we are striving. The symbol reveals its *origins* on the one hand and demonstrates the *solutions* on the other (Jung, 1917).

The advancement of scientific understanding has changed our relation to our world and in many respects has blocked the expression of significant unconscious tendencies. For instance, for the urban man an empty field may be simply an empty field, but for one who derives his livelihood from the fertile soil, the same field is endowed with mystery and wonder. The responses of the two men are very different: for one the experience touches upon nothing significant whereas the other has a numinous experience, a sense of appreciation of the source of his existence.

According to Jung, we should discover new symbols to replace those that were significant to life during more primitive eras. Although he spoke of the futility of relying on science to solve all of our problems, he did not mean that the discoveries of science and the achievements of technology must necessarily remove the wonder, mystery, and numinosity that characterized human prescientific status. The scientist and technical specialist do not create the laws of nature; they discover and apply them. A scientist did not produce the fact that mercury rises and falls in a tube with changes in temperature; he merely discovered it. The common gadgets of a middle-class home are "miracles of nature" and can produce numinous experiences in those who will take the time to contemplate them. The contemporary automobile is a marvel of scientific achievement that captivates many. One of the pitfalls of modern science is that we may overvalue the power of the scientist and overlook the mysteries he or she is utilizing. Indeed, science may have an almost religious impulse, for as G. Stanley Hall, an early

American psychologist, once said: "It seeks to think God's thoughts after Him" (quoted in Misiak and Sexton, 1966).

What is Jung telling us here? He seems to be saying that we need to sense our deepest needs, which are the products of important archetypes. This means greater participation in the mysteries of life. A person might derive great pleasure from growing things or making things by hand. All aspects of our nature should be permitted expression. We ought to examine the popular view of pleasure and interpret it more personally.

VIEWS ON ABNORMALITY

Jung speaks of abnormality in a number of ways. He generally accepted the notion of abnormality as excess or deficiency of functioning, but he was especially concerned with imbalance among the various components of the personality. We have noted that one-sided development creates tension and uncontrolled aspects of the personality. The inferior functions may take over the operations of the ego and create serious malfunctioning of the adjustive capacities. Jung was insistent that none of the components of the personality be overemphasized at the expense of the other systems. If the persona is too powerful, the person may be like a hollow shell and live a sham existence. If the shadow is dominant, the person may be overly selfish and violent. For example, the shadow aspect of personality is freely expressed in many criminals. If the anima of a man is overemphasized, he may be moody or overly sentimental. If the animus of a woman is not adequately expressed, she may be argumentative and excessively competitive with men. A system of personality may be overemphasized or neglected. Both instances are abnormal. One-sided development causes vital functions to be inaccessible to the ego.

Other forms of abnormality derive from one-sided development of attitudes and functions, according to Jung's schema; thus the extreme extrovert or introvert suffers from lack of development and utilization of the opposite quality and fails to utilize the full potential of which the individual is capable. In like manner, one of the functions may be overemphasized while the others remain in the underdeveloped or inferior status. The superintellectual may neglect his or her feelings; the intuitive-introspective artist may not deal adequately with realistic requirements; the dreamer gets lost in fantasies and speculation and fails to solve his or her problems and to meet his or her needs. Individuation occurs when all aspects of the personality are provided outlets for expression.

Abnormality may result from both realms of the unconcious, the personal and the collective. We have already considered the harmful effects of complexes and archetypes that dominate the ego and interfere with its proper functions. Complexes and archetypes may impair perception and judgment, for example, when a man misperceives the attributes of a woman as a result of his anima image. We have also spoken of archetypes as needs that must be met if we are to develop and function normally. Conditions in our environment must satisfy certain archetypes, or we will experience

© Rick Winsor 1981/Woodfin Camp & Associates

The inflated persona requires attention.

frustration, tension, and lack of fulfillment. Jung believed that we have inborn needs to respond to the mysteries of life. We need to find an outlet for our God archetype to give some meaning to the unknowns of life. We need a mother or a father figure to maintain our stability. We need heroes and respect for power. Such needs are not outgrown, but rather are expressed in different ways throughout life. We need heroes as adults just as we needed heroes as children. Such needs, as noted earlier, are part of our nature, and failure to satisfy them causes abnormality, in Jung's view.

It should be noted that the types of abnormality with which Jung was most concerned were *failures* in adequate *differentiation* and *integration* of the various component systems of personality. By *differentiation*, Jung meant directing attention to developing and utilizing a particular component of the personality. A differentiated persona, for example, means that you have learned and know how to apply social skills effectively. A differentiated anima or animus means that you have identified and permitted opposite-sexed traits assimilation into the self and have made them functional aspects of living. Such differentiations increase the range of reactions and actions of which a person is capable. By *integration*, Jung meant that an individual has achieved unity and balance among the opposing elements of personality, for example, the ego and the shadow, the persona and the anima or animus, the self and the archetypes.

The Persona and Inflation

As we noted in our discussion of the steps in Jungian therapy, an important aspect of individuation is the recognition and dethroning of the persona or social personality, the mask that is worn for the sake of others (Jung, 1953). By dethroning the persona, Jung meant that people should become aware of their social roles and make good use of them rather than being dominated by them or taking them too seriously. In a sense, the persona is the ideal self, but in a social sense rather than from the standpoint of the individual's own ideals. An arrogant, tough, poised air may be the persona a man attempts to express: he believes that he is behaving at his best when he acts in this manner. The persona, of course, is determined largely by cultural expectations: a man is expected to behave in a prescribed manner, and this is different from the expectations placed upon a woman. Doctors have a persona different from that of teachers, and so on.

Jung pointed out that one's profession may contribute materially to the formation of the persona. A man may take on the characteristics of his office. His ego is inflated by the attributes of his status. As a professor, he becomes the stereotype assigned to that profession. At work, his behavior may be tinged with solemnity, pomposity, and an air of great importance. But to those who really know him outside the academic setting, he may be an empty shell with no real substance of his own. In real life, if we strive to fit a self-image that is not ourselves, we suffer the consequences of this sham existence (Pervin, 1968).

The persona, like Freud's superego, regulates and controls behavior to bring about effective adjustment to one's circumstances. Many compromises with individualistic desires and requirements are usually necessary, however. The person who likes his or her persona and shapes his or her entire life in accordance with its ideal (for example, the lawyer who strives to be the best in the world twenty-four hours a day, seven days a week) necessarily gives up much of what is really himself or herself. The cultural model does not perfectly suit any particular individual, and when one takes over the expectations fully, there is usually an extreme quality about the personality. Being an extrovert is an expectation of American culture, but an individual who adopts extroversion as a way of life, especially if this role does not fit his or her real nature, becomes a shallow, artificial, and dwarfed personality. Yet unless we come to know our persona, we cannot become our real self. Understanding the persona and coming to terms with it are necessary steps in the individuation process. Effective personality development and functioning require a balance (see Levinson et al., 1978). The persona roles we adopt should be serviceable: They should help us to meet the social demands of everyday life. We might think of clothing that we wear for a particular occasion and then remove when the circumstances change. It would be abnormal, for instance, for a person to continue to wear formal dress in the privacy of the home. Jung maintained that we need to know our persona in order to make it functional for us.

Harmful Aspects of the Shadow

Jung believed that each person also has a shadow, which is the "evil" aspect of his or her nature (1959a, 1959b). The term itself is quite descriptive: the shadow is the shaded aspect of personality, darkened because we attempt not to recognize it. In its most primitive form, it includes animalistic impulses, for example, cannibalism, incest, destructiveness, utter selfishness. The shadow is in opposition to, and always conflicts with, the persona because it embodies the qualities that are opposite to the social image we are trying to present to the world (Jung, 1959a). "I do not want others to see anything but my best behavior; the shadow is my worst side; therefore it must be covered up as much as possible." In fact, the covering up is usually done so well that the very person is unaware of his or her shadow. Most of us, even those who claim to be objective about themselves, have a good self-opinion (Scott, 1963). Paradoxically, the person with a profound sense of inferiority is overidentifying with his or her persona and is no more aware of his or her shadow than anyone else. We think that we are reasonable and considerate, more than most people anyway. It is extremely rare to find people who know their most undesirable qualities. Yet for the purpose of the individuation process, it is necessary to discover the shadow, to become aware of our negative and animalistic tendencies and desires. We can hardly do anything about improving our development and functioning if we fail to recognize our weaker aspects. Whether we change such qualities or are simply aware of their existence without doing anything about them — from the standpoint of the individuation process — this is certainly preferable to lack of awareness or, what is worse, a false belief that we possess only desirable qualities. Knowing our evil tendencies may give us great power over our personality. A man who tries to deny his feminine qualities — or a woman, her masculine qualities — may at times be victimized by them. We can best manage our personality and behavior if we are aware of them. Generally speaking, what is unknown in ourselves is uncontrollable and potentially dangerous. Jung believed that the shadow imparts dimension to personality: angels may be suitable for heaven but not for earthly existence. An all-perfect being would be unbearable for most of us, for we do recognize our own shortcomings in part and welcome others with theirs.

Much of the shadow is unconscious. Though excluded from the ego, however, the shadow material is, nevertheless, an important aspect of the individual; it should be available to consciousness because it is part of the self, and if we wish to attain selfhood, we must expand the sphere of consciousness to include the attributes of the shadow. A man's feminine attributes and a woman's masculine attributes may be denied and exist as part of the shadow, but complete personality development requires their integration into the self. Usually, the major reason for *repression* is that the material is unacceptable and too threatening to be integrated within the ego and persona. This material can also undergo *projection*. The user of projection not only fails to perceive his or her undesirable qualities but also assigns them to others. "If I can see dishonesty all around me, I can easily overlook it in myself." Consequently, what vague recognition we might have or acquire of our own faults is muddled through the perception of these faults in others. We say in effect, "My little sins are nothing compared to those of my friends." Thus, through repression and projection some very basic material is usually kept unconscious.

Jung believed that repression and projection produce a sense of *moral inferiority*: you feel that you are unworthy or evil, but you cannot put your finger on the reasons for your feelings. The personal unconscious is a kind of dumping place for unwanted aspects of the self. Therapy consists, in part, of bringing the unconscious back to consciousness. This involved for Jung an enlarging of the ego; the ego acquires more strength in the process.

To achieve the fullest personality functioning, however, we must go beyond making the unconscious conscious. All aspects of both the conscious and unconscious areas, including the collective unconscious, must be developed and expressed completely. This involves an expansion of the total personality and a recentering of the ego, which is what Jung means by "the attainment of selfhood." Abnormality results when components of the psyche are not adequately differentiated and integrated into the self.

VIEWS ON IDEAL PERSONALITY AND LIVING

As we have suggested, the individuation process is the full development (differentiation) and growth of the person. It also includes the *unification process*: the integration of the various differentiated components. Given the proper conditions, there is a natural unfolding. Just as a seed needs light and moisture to grow into a particular plant or tree, so also human beings require favorable conditions to become what they can become. With humans, however, there is a difference: the ego must participate if fullness of growth is to be achieved (Jung, 1964b). Growth occurs naturally only in part. A man with a talent for music does not perfect it — or develop it at all — if he does not recognize it and, recognizing it, deliberately work to express and improve it.

One of Jung's students recounts the story of a woman who lamented that she had never done anything worthwhile in her life. She was told about a carpenter who complained to his assistant that a certain large oak tree was not good for anything and that was the reason why the tree had not been cut for lumber. The tree appeared to the carpenter in a dream and chastised him for making the critical remark and pointed out that, if it had been useful as lumber, it would have been cut down long before. The woman was judging her worth according to prevailing cultural standards rather than in a broader perspective. If we gear our lives only to productive skills or compulsive striving for success, we may overlook our inner potentialities. We may force ourselves to become what we are not by nature meant to be. Specific occupational accomplishments are much less important, Jung believed, than realizing our psychobiological potentials.

The Self and the Individuation Process

As we noted earlier, Jung distinguished between the ego and the self. Whereas the ego primarily serves the persona, the self primarily serves the total personality. He referred to the self in two ways: (1) the self as an archetype and (2) the self as a controlling agent. It will be recalled that for Jung the ego is the center of consciousness and is at first greatly affected both by the persona and by the external world. As the person becomes more individuated—that is, as we begin to understand the nature of our persona, our shadow, our anima or animus, and our archetypal requirements—the realm of consciousness is increased to include many areas of the psyche that were previously unconscious. When this occurs, the ego must assimilate and take control of the newly emerging aspects of the psyche. In other words, it must occupy the center of the expanded personality. When this occurs, Jung terms the recentered ego the *self*. Another way of describing this process is to say that the person has attained selfhood.

Figure 3–1 depicts the unindividuated and individuated persons. Notice how much larger is the realm of consciousness for the individuated person.

The self as an archetype is analogous to the notion of self-concept although Jung seemed to endow the self archetype with active powers. As an archetype the self is experienced in dreams in various forms depending upon the degree of individuation the person has attained. Jung used the dreams of his patients as a means of determining the extent to which individuation had been achieved. The self might appear as a child of the same sex who plays a helping role, or it might be a godlike image or a wise old man or woman. Like other archetypes, the self archetype is dependent upon acquired experiences as well as on innate dispositions for its makeup. Jung held that the self archetype could be a constructive force in the attainment of individuation if the person paid attention to the messages of his or her dreams and was receptive to his or her intuitions and inner promptings.

The self may work at cross-purposes with the ego and create discord in the personality. It may actually take over the ego functions and cause the person to behave in antisocial and destructive ways. But Jung believed that it could also serve the personality in a positive way by communicating to the ego the requirements of the unconscious. We must be willing to listen to the self and to become sensitive to its intuitions. Promptings from the self can be extremely valuable in making important life decisions, Jung maintained. Ultimately, the self should be the true center of the personality, but this takes place only when differentiation and integration of all the components are complete. (See Bolen, 1979, for a present-day interpretation of Jung's self concept by a Jungian analyst.)

The Transcendent Function

When selfhood is achieved, the ego has been recentered and becomes the true center of personality. Consciousness has expanded greatly, and the various components of the personality have become fully differentiated. Increased differentiation means that the various aspects of personality are in opposition to one another; thus, there is conflict and tension. The self is confronted with the task of integrating the competing elements. The transcendent function is the *integrating activity of the self* as it manages the personality and deals with the external environment. Jung's concept of the transcendent function is very similar to what Maslow termed the transcendence of dichotomies, which he found to be one of the outstanding characteristics of Maslow's self-actualizing people. It refers to the harmonizing of opposites. In such a state, the individual experiences a sense of unity, of well-being, of harmonious functioning.

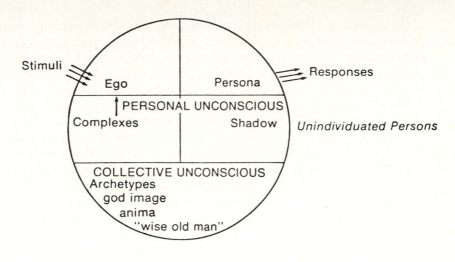

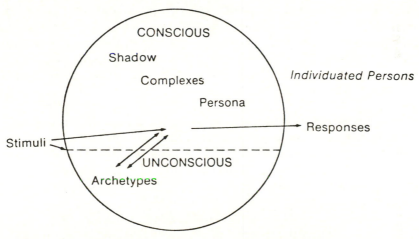

Figure 3-1.
As one's comprehension of persona, shadow, and so forth, increases, the conscious realm expands to incorporate many formerly unconscious areas of the psyche. There is thus a free interchange between the conscious and the unconscious in individuated persons.

The individuated man behaves in a manly manner, yet is not fearful of expressing his emotional nature. The feminine woman maintains her autonomy and self-assurance. She can relate socially without fearing to assert claims and personal interests. She can deal with the demands of the external world without being swallowed by it and with her own inner requirements without becoming self-preoccupied. In short, the transcendent function allows balanced expression of the components of personality (the persona, the shadow, the anima or animus, the self, the archetypes) and the attitudes of introversion and extroversion and the four psychological functions (sensing, feeling, thinking, and intuiting). As personality grows, it becomes more complex. New traits and capabilities increase the adaptive potential of the individual; but these also cause conflicts, as the various systems that make up personality compete. The systems compete with each other for the existing psychic energy. Consider the following oppositions that may develop. The persona attempts to influence the ego by displaying to it the many benefits of social success. On the other hand, the shadow draws the attention of the ego to basic personal strivings — to drive satisfaction and to appetite indulgence. It may flood the ego with negative emotions such as hate, resentment, and antisocial impulses. The anima traits of a man may pressure the ego toward tenderness, creativity, sentimentality, and love; but these compete with his persona. The animus traits of a woman may cause her to question her feminine roles and prompt the ego to compete with men.

These opposing tendencies are natural in humans; thus, it requires a highly developed personality, one in which selfhood has been attained, to resolve the conflicts. As we become fully aware of ourselves, greater control becomes possible. The union of opposites is a high level function of the self. We noted earlier that this transcendent function of the self involves moderation, blending, and creative use of abilities. Opposite traits are turned into complementary traits, and these support rather than compete with one another. Instead of being a fawning, self-degrading employee, you accept yourself as a cooperative worker, but also as a person who is self-assertive and self-respecting. You might display both strength and courage in your everyday dealings, but also have compassion and concern for others. A woman may be femininely appealing, but also self-assured and capable in meeting the requirements of living.

Jung makes an interesting observation with respect to conflicts. A person who has many conflicts with others may be experiencing conflicts within himself or herself — conflicts between his or her own opposing tendencies and traits. A man who is creating a great deal of friction with others may be manifesting his own inner conflict between his persona and anima nature. A woman who cannot get along with her superiors may be reflecting her own conflict between her animus and persona. Her unrecognized masculine tendencies conflict with her feminine identity. In both instances, the union of opposites within will lessen the conflicts without.

CRITICAL EVALUATION

Many of Jung's critics accuse him of being mystical and unscientific. This criticism is valid for some of his ideas, such as synchronicity, but many of his ideas are no more mystical than those of other personality theorists. Jung and his disciples have not done a good job of elucidating their basic concepts; thus, many who criticize the constructs do not really understand them. For example, Jung held that dreams sometimes prognosticate the future, a statement that could easily be misinterpreted as a belief in the preternatural and occult. However, Jung's explanation is quite plausible; he proposed the hypothesis that the unconscious is influenced by external events and may process information in a manner that creates a prediction of a future event through the medium of a dream. Conscious prognostication occurs frequently. Why cannot an analogous process take place unconsciously?

How different are Jung's principal constructs from those of Freud in terms of abstractness and scientific status? Freud defined id, ego, and superego by means of specific behaviors; Jung also defined his concepts of the persona, the shadow, the ego, the self, the anima and animus in terms of specific classes of behaviors. Anima behavior in men and animus behavior in women can be specified. The notions of the anima (within the man) and animus (within the woman) are no more mystical than the notions of the primitive id, or ego, or superego.

If we compare Jung with the other personality theorists on the possibility of attaining the good life, Jung is one of the most optimistic because his individuated person is one who is in a "natural" state. The return to, and expression of, the unconscious is within the power of everyone. Most of the other theorists—Allport, Maslow, Fromm, Rogers—set many conditions for the attainment of the good life. Only the genetically gifted and environmentally favored can become self-actualized, mature, fully functioning, or productive.

Jung did not establish such qualifications for the achievement of individuation. He would agree with the others that the individuated person is rare, but the potential for all of humanity is great. The college professor and the coal miner alike have the potential for individuation, and perhaps Jung might hold even more promise for the coal miner. Personality weaknesses are to a great extent unnatural states, caused by life circumstances that have drawn us from our natural condition. For example, many of our problems are the result of our own intelligence, which Jung believed is a late evolutionary development in humans. Consider the personality disorders associated with alcoholism, with the use of addictive drugs, with the excessive intake of manufactured foods. Modern living conditions are a product of human ingenuity and inventiveness, but the animal in people is being perverted or denied. The diseases (arteriosclerosis, hypertension, obesity) associated with highly seasoned foods, stress, and other conditions of contemporary living are caused directly by people themselves. Is there any parallel in other creatures?

If our consciousness and advanced intelligence have created problems for us, surely the same capabilities can solve them. This is Jung's creed for humankind.

GUIDES TO RESEARCH

HEURISTIC VALUE OF JUNG'S THEORY

Jung's theory is gaining some popularity as a means for interpreting phenomena that are not covered adequately by other theories. Jungian constructs and postulates are used by theologians to account for human spiritual impulses and activities. Belief in the supernatural and ceremonial practices are found universally and appear to have existed throughout human history. To treat religious beliefs and practices as expressions of neurosis or as examples of immature reactions to the unknown, as Freud believed, is a denial of an important requirement of human nature, as Jung sees the matter. Many sincere and scientifically minded theologians and hard-core scientists as well find Jung's views on the nature of spirituality in humans much more valid in accounting for human behavior historically and in contemporary life.

Jung is also gaining popularity among the youth who find the values and practices of Western societies unfulfilling. Jung's emphasis on self-discovery and personal fulfillment is attracting the attention of many thoughtful people. Such important thinkers as Arnold Toynbee, the historian; Philip Wylie, the writer; Lewis Mumford, the essayist and critic; and Paul Radin, the anthropologist, derived inspiration from Carl Jung.

With respect to topics that Jung studied and the novel methods that he employed to sup-port his conclusions, he has not been very influential. A few of his closest disciples are continuing to explore the areas in which Jung pioneered, using his methods, but they have failed to gain much support. It would seem that research psychologists are not yet ready to investigate the kinds of human behavior that were so inspiring to Jung. It is probable that the psychology of the future will investigate the phenomena that Jung discusses in his writings. Unfortunately, Jung's style of writing is one of the major stumbling blocks in communicating his ideas. His disciples have not ameliorated this situation to a great extent.

EMPIRICAL SUPPORT FOR JUNG'S THEORY

It might be instructive to consider some of the methods of investigation that Jung himself employed in studying the phenomena that were the bases of his constructs and postulates. He derived his ideas from many diverse sources. He was a brilliant and widely read scholar, and although he was trained in the sciences and as a physician, he delved into the most abstruse literature.

Hall and Lindzey describe his approach in this fashion:

Jung was both a scholar and a scientist. He found his facts everywhere: in ancient myths and modern fairy tales; in primitive life and modern civilization; in the religions of the Eastern and Western worlds; in alchemy, astrology, mental telepathy, and clairvoyance; in the dreams and visions of normal people; in anthropology, history, literature, and the arts; and in clinical and experimental research. In scores of articles and books, he set forth the empirical data upon which his theories are based. Jung insists that he is more interested in discovering facts than he is in formulating theories. "I have no system; I talk of facts" [personal communication to the authors, 1954; Hall and Lindzey, 1978, p. 140].[2]

Jung studied aspects of behavior that others had ignored. He had his patients depict their fantasies and moods by drawings, paintings, and modeling with clay. He studied their dreams from the standpoint of symbolic and mythological expression. Their characters and themes could reveal the state of development of the psyche. Even the symptoms of his patients could be understood in terms of archetypal expression as the following passage from Fordham reveals:

The existence of the collective unconscious can be inferred in the normal man from the obvious traces of mythological images in his dreams—images of which he had no previous conscious knowledge. It is sometimes difficult to prove that no such knowledge ever existed (one can always say there was the possibility of cryptomnesia), but in certain kinds of mental disorder there is an astonishing development of mythological imagery which could never be accounted for by the individual's own experience.

Jung gives as one example of this the case of a patient in a mental hospital, in whom he was interested in the year 1906. The man was insane and was at times much disturbed, but in his quiet periods he described peculiar visions and produced very

[2]*Theories of Personality*, 3d ed.

unusual symbolic images and ideas. It was not until 1910 that any light was thrown on these symbols, when Jung came across a Greek papyrus which had recently been deciphered and which dealt with similar material. The patient had been committed to a mental hospital some years before the text of the papyrus had appeared, which rules out the possibility of latent learning [1966, pp. 25–26].

The patient reported to Jung that he had seen a vision of the sun with a moving phallus, which he said was the origin of the wind. Jung was convinced that his patient did not have access to the symbolism and mythology that the image depicted. This type of evidence led him to conclude the existence of universal archetypes.

Experimental Study of Complexes

Jung applied the *word association* procedure to study complexes. Patients were given a list of critical words to which they were to respond with the first word or idea that came to mind. Jung examined the nature of their responses, which could reveal the presence of sensitive topics. For example, if there were a long pause before a response was given or if the stimulus word were simply repeated or if the type of response were quite different from the typical one, Jung believed that he was eliciting a complex. He supplemented the psychological procedure by obtaining physiological measures such as changes in breathing patterns and in electrical conductance of the skin, the galvanic skin response. Such physiological measures are used as indicators of emotion.

Study of Occult Phenomena

As we have noted, in attempting to understand and treat the human psyche, Jung followed unorthodox paths of investigation. He even took sojourns to live with and study the life-style and ceremonial practices of several African and American Indian tribes. Believing that the prevailing image of humans as fully conscious and rational beings is incomplete, Jung sought to discover the true nature of humans by delving into primitive symbolic and ritualistic practices and artifacts that reveal hidden facets of human behavior. Everything that people have created as well as their traditional beliefs and practices sheds light on elements of human nature. Thus, Jung was led to study primitive rituals, ceremonial practices, mythology, symbology, alchemy, the occult, astrology, ESP, UFOs, and even mediums. Jung steeped himself in the literature of Hindu religion, Taoism, Eastern philosophy and psychology (both ancient and modern), the Christian and other major religious traditions, and literature from many nations and times. He frequently found archetypal expressions and motifs from these varied sources. He found parallels between the dream productions and the symptoms of his patients with the characters and symbolism of myths of people who lived many centuries ago. Even when Jung dealt with occult phenomena, he did not intend to demonstrate their validity, but rather dealt with them as expressions of the psyche that required explanation. Whether God exists as an ontological fact was not as important to Jung as the psychological fact of a belief in a diety, a phenomenon that requires an explanation.

Jung studied the symbols used by the alchemists to understand the meaning of the strange dreams of his patients. Incidentally, Jung distinguished between big dreams and little dreams. Big dreams contained symbolic expressions of the archetypes and were abstract and mysterious; little dreams were more concerned with people's conscious preoccupations. The similarities he found led Jung to conclude that the same archetypes were being expressed in both dreams and in alchemy. The intentions and goals of the dreamer are portrayed by the same symbols that the alchemists used to depict their objectives. Jung found the same archetypes in a variety of other sources: in ancient and modern religions, in artistic productions of all types, in myths and fairy tales that were prevalent among the people of diverse societies and from different eras.

Jung developed two techniques to study imagery: (1) the *method of dream amplification* by which the individual was encouraged to elaborate the elements of a dream so that many facets of its meaning might emerge. The analyst may help the person to amplify the dream images by contributing knowledge of mythology, symbolism, and historical data. (2) The *method of active imagination* involved having the person react to a conscious image by drawing a picture, by writing poetry, by modeling a form out of clay, or by some other artistic production. The individual is encouraged to concentrate upon the image and to note the changes that take place. The purpose is to gain access to relevant unconscious material. Jung used these methods to draw out the meaning of dream images and fantasies.

Experimental Work Supportive of the Collective Unconscious

Many of Jung's basic constructs and postulates are so abstract that they have not tempted tough-minded experimentalists to translate them into testable form. One of these constructs, the collective unconscious, has generated so much controversy that few behavioral scientists would identify with it. We will briefly review two interesting studies that support the notion of universal mental operations and imagery (the collective unconscious) that Siegel (1980) describes as "the common biological wiring of homosapiens." Siegel experimented with the use of hallucinogenic drugs (drugs that elicit visual imagery in the absence of sensory inputs). His procedure consisted of training subjects to describe in great detail the types of hallucinations they have while under the influence of such drugs as LSD, psilocybin, mescaline, PCP, and marijuana. Prior to the administration of the drugs, the subjects were trained by viewing thousands of slides containing visual forms so that they might identify such forms in the minutest detail after taking the drugs. These forms were based on four types of hallucinations identified by Heinrich Kluver in the 1920s. They are (1) gratings and honeycombs, (2) cobwebs, (3) tunnels and cones, and (4) spirals. He varied the slides according to color, brightness, and symmetry prior to the administration of drugs. He then administered the same drugs to an experimental group and to a control group, who had not had previous training with the slides. He found that the subjects who had the previous sensory training seemed to be much more influenced by their hallucinations than the control subjects because they reported imagery on the average of twenty times per minute vs. five times per minute for the control subjects. Siegel found that in a study of 500 LSD experiences, a high percentage of the subjects reported having similar experiences of simple and complex hallucinations, which led Siegel to conclude that he was studying the fundamental operations of the psyche.

Siegel infers from his experimental research with hallucinogens that

There is a universal common denominator of behavior. It's something similar to what Jung called the collective unconscious, typified by symbols like the mandala. Whether you use that kind of labeling or choose to call it something else, the fact remains that, given an infinite variety of stimulations, the brain seems to respond in finite ways.

Fever delirium, epilepsy, syphilis, photostimulation, sensory deprivation, extreme hunger, cold, or thirst, crystal gazing, swinging in the witch's cradle, hypoglycemia, and a variety of drug intoxications all make the brain respond in patterns that are definable, predictable, and explainable in terms of where they came from and how they were produced [Siegel, 1980 (September), p. 58].

In a nutshell, Siegel trained subjects to be sensitive to images and then gave them drugs known to induce images, so that they could describe them in great detail. Siegel's results showed a remarkable similarity in the types of images reported in the drugged state.

An exercise on dreaming was conducted at Harvard Medical School to teach students what the altered state of psychotic experience is like for the mental patient. "We regularly," said J. Allan Hobson, "experience in our dreams mental states more similar to psychosis than anything a patient, or I, could describe in words."

Hobson said that every symptom of major mental illness is experienced in students' own dreams: disorientation, memory loss, bizarre thoughts, hallucinations, grandiosity, delusions and intense fear, rage and euphoria . . . The dream exercise conveys the 'functional' nature of psychosis—that mental illness is not necessarily caused by an external agent but "by the normal system being disorganized . . ." [*Brain/Mind Bulletin*, June 1, 1981, 6 (10):1].

Hobson also emphasizes the constructive, synthetic aspect of perception represented in dreams. One student likened this facet of the dream experience to "the confabulations, distortions and creativity of art."

The point of both Siegel's research and the Harvard dream exercise is that there is now being identified by experimental research some universal, subjective experiences common to all humans. This was what Jung meant when he proposed the idea of a collective unconscious. Research, similar to the preceding, is necessary to give credibility to Jung's intriguing constructs and postulates.

GUIDES TO LIVING

WORKING TOWARD INDIVIDUATION

Jung held that we can participate in the individuation process by attempting to listen to our unconscious promptings. We should not be afraid to go off alone and simply attend to spontaneous thoughts and feelings. Jung believed that our unconscious contains the wisdom of the ages and that we can draw upon this fund of knowledge if we take note of our dreams, if we let ideas come to us from within, and if, in general, we pay attention to our subjective life. Individuation means an expansion of consciousness, so that all aspects of the psyche are experienced. Certainly, we need to perfect our persona and differentiate it as much as possible in order to deal effectively with our various social relationships.

But our shadow also gives vitality and spontaneity to behavior. We should be aware of and find expression for our impulses and emotions. They are vital forces that give depth to living. The most dangerous forces in our nature are those that are not perceived consciously and that are not under control. As the person attains fullness, the ego gives way to the self, the new center of personality. The self then allows all aspects of the personality expression.

The self can find ways of bringing together the conflicting systems. The shadow and persona represent opposites in personality, but the self can harmonize our roles with our personal desires and feelings. Both aspects may require some moderation, but the result is a sense of wholeness and integration. The opposite-sex traits can also be experienced and expressed in a balanced manner with the shadow and persona. The total blending gets rid of one-sidedness. We have already mentioned the necessity to balance extroversion and introversion and the four functions of thinking, feeling, sensing, and intuiting. Each aspect adds an important dimension to the total personality.

SELF-DISCOVERY

In his autobiography, Jung describes the personality as being vast and mysterious. Our inner world is like the universe. Jung believed that the greatest adventure of life was the exploration of this inner world. The search can be a lifelong project because each period of life is accompanied by many changes in the external environment, but more importantly within the personality itself. We can derive great excitement and joy from being a participant in this growth. One of our most cherished attributes is self-reflection, the ability to observe and contemplate our own inner workings. The greatest joy of life for Jung was self-exploration.

Many people are afraid to look within themselves. All that seems desirable is external—to be entertained, to be doing something exciting, stimulating, and drive-satisfying. However, the individuation process can become evident to us only through self-reflection. As pleasurable as this is in itself, a still greater pleasure is to promote our growth processes actively through the use of all our abilities. Jung himself devoted most of his life to studying the manifestations of the unconscious mind, his own included.

DEALING WITH THE SHADOW

Dealing with the shadow is like dealing with a friend who seems to have qualities that are opposite to yours. The friend deserves a hearing because her views may be just as right and valid as your own. Working with her often lessens the opposition: maybe both of you are seeking the same ends but both are too one-sided in your approach. There is usually more than one way of getting to your destination. The friend needs restriction and opposition if she interferes with your rights, but she needs love and acceptance as well. Getting along means giving and taking on both sides. The shadow is a vital part of the total self; in normal functioning it *complements* the conscious ego rather than opposes it. If it is perceived as evil or weakness, it is because the ego has not been able to bring together the opposites

in personality. But opposition is the very stuff of growth: from contrasts and differences may come a higher synthesis. The *well-rounded person accepts and makes good use of everything that is within him or her; nothing in personality is totally bad; it is merely misused.* The shadow becomes hostile and troublesome only when it is ignored.

We are all conscious of some of our faults, and these are difficult enough to accept or change. Much more so are the unconscious ones. Something of the nature of these qualities may be discovered by considering those things about others that are most distasteful to us. Quite likely these are the very same qualities that we possess but have repressed in ourselves and projected onto others.

DIALOGUE WITH THE ANIMA AND THE ANIMUS

Jung recommended that a man carry on a dialogue with his anima and a woman with her ani-

mus. The anima or animus frequently takes the form of an emotional state—a mood of depression, for example. We may deal with this mood by treating it as if it were an autonomous personality and letting it state its case fully. Jung believed that this dialogue process comes rather easily because the anima or animus causing the disturbance has broken off from the rest of the personality and operates as a separate identity. No criticism should be made until the anima or animus has stated its case completely; then each point can be examined critically and answered until there is a reduction of the emotional intensity. This inner dialogue is advisable, however, only when the anima or animus make themselves felt in moodiness and dissatisfaction, an indication that they are functioning abnormally. Personifying inner components of personality and having a dialogue with them may appear to the reader to be semipsychotic activity, but recent developments among cognitive behaviorists suggest the same procedure, for example, self-monitoring, self-directed imagery, and self-instructional approaches.

Jung personified aspects of the personality. The anima or animus, the shadow, and the self may actually be treated as if they were persons with whom you might carry on a discussion. Let the "selfish me" have its say; do not automatically rule it evil and undesirable. Let the rebellious faction have its opportunity to express itself, and so on. Like other personality theorists, Jung maintained that all aspects of the self are to be integrated and accepted as a part of the personality. Some aspects may be changed, but certainly they must be perceived as being a part of the total system.

DELIBERATELY REACTIVATING ARCHETYPES

Jung made the point that the individuation process is promoted by early recollections. These recollections may reactivate archetypes that are no longer being expressed properly. One may even attempt to activate archetypes deliberately, as when we reexamine our concept of God or of motherhood or of authority. Archetypes take on different forms in the course of life. A reactivation of an archetype can produce dramatic changes in personality, Jung believed. Since archetypal ideas are highly charged emotionally, they can be very disturbing when experienced. Jung says of the process of reactivating archetypes:

> The recollection of infantile memories, and the reproduction of archetypal ways of

psychic behavior, can create a wider horizon and a greater extension of consciousness, on condition that one succeeds in assimilating and integrating in the conscious mind the lost and regained contents. Since they are not neutral, their assimilation will modify the personality, just as they themselves will have to undergo certain alterations. In this part of what is called the individuation process . . . interpretation of symbols plays an important practical role, for the symbols are natural attempts to reconcile and reunite opposites within the psyche [1964b, p. 90].

PERSONIFICATION AND POSSESSION

Jung held that the components of the personality, when not given adequate expression, may act as autonomous agents. In dreams they take the form of characters: for instance, the anima of a man might be embodied as a beautiful woman or one who was disreputable; the shadow might be the stranger; the self might take the form of a helping child. The nature of dream characters and the changes that occur reveal the progress toward individuation. During the waking state, the ego might be taken over by the so-called people within the personality. We might be *possessed* by our shadows. Everyone has observed that a friend is not himself today. This condition makes sense in Jung's notion of ego possession. When my shadow or anima takes over my ego,

I may not know it, but everyone around me certainly does. Those who allow the various faces of their personality to develop and be expressed fully is less likely to be a victim of possession.

REESTABLISHING CONTACT WITH NATURE

In the following passage, Jung seems to be saying that people today have lost contact with the natural phenomena of our world. As a consequence, contemporary life is barren and empty. It lacks the wonder, inspiration, and mystery of an earlier day. The solution is to find adequate outlets for our archetypes. Jung blames modern science for our loss of contact with nature and for the dehumanization of human beings. However, he does not tell us to return to the superstitions of earlier peoples but rather to use the amazing discoveries of science as they should be used—to appreciate nature and to find our place within the wonders of the cosmos:

> As scientific understanding has grown, so our world has become dehumanized. Man feels himself isolated in the cosmos, because he is no longer involved in nature, and has lost his emotional "unconscious identity" with natural phenomena. These have slowly lost their symbolic implications. Thunder is no longer the voice of an angry god; nor is lightning his avenging missile. No river contains a spirit; no tree is the life principle of a man; no snake the embodiment of wisdom; no mountain cave the home of a great demon. No voices now speak to man from stones, plants, and animals; nor does he speak to them, believing that they can hear. His contact with nature has gone, and with it has gone the profound emotional energy that this symbolic connection supplied [1964b, p. 95].

SUMMARY

1. Every human possesses a genetic blueprint that unfolds if the proper conditions are met. The process of becoming a fully differentiated and integrated person is called individuation by Jung. Growth consists of differentiation, fullfillment of potentials, expansion of experiences, and the realization of self. Integration of all the parts of the personality makes it possible for the ego to be recentered as the core of the psyche. It then becomes the self.

2. The psyche is composed of a conscious and an unconscious. The center of consciousness is the ego, which at first primarily serves the persona. The unconscious layer consists of a personal unconscious, with complexes as the major components, and a collective unconscious, with archetypes as primary structures.

3. The personal unconscious contains experiences that have been forgotten, overlooked, or repressed. The collective unconscious is inherited and is a major determinant of the types of experiences that are possible for humans. It contains thought-forms that are known as archetypes.

4. Archetypes are inherited thought-forms that are only predispositions to have certain experiences until they are activated by actual life events. Archetypes are modified by learning. When the archetypes are properly modified, they assist in the process of perceiving correctly. More archetypes will be activated as our experience broadens. An archetypal image may so dominate the perceptual and interpretive functions of the ego that it seriously distorts judgment. Archetypes are to be understood as real images that embody common human experiences and important figures. Some archetypes are so basic to human nature that they act like needs that must be gratified. Common expressions of archetypes are symbols and rituals.

5. The persona may be taken as the sum total of social roles. It is the mask one wears for the sake of others. It reflects an inborn tendency to develop a social personality and may block other essential components of the personality that are opposed to it. A major task of the individuation process is to lessen the ego's preoccupation with the persona.

6. The shadow comprises the undesirable aspects of personality, which are inconsistent with the persona. We cannot become individuated persons unless the shadow elements are brought to awareness and integrated into the self.

7. Jung viewed male and female psychology as being different and held that both sexes, as well, have qualities of the opposite sex in an inferior underdeveloped state. Every man has within his nature an anima, which is Jung's construct for feminine traits and images. The animus refers to masculine traits and images in women. An individuated man must know his feminine traits and integrate them into the self. A woman must similarly perceive and integrate her masculine traits into her self. A complete person has qualities of both sexes, with the opposite sex traits tempering the persona and adding vital dimensions to the personality.

8. Jung distinguishes between attitudes and functions. Attitudes refer to introverted or extroverted orientations, whereas functions (sensing, feeling, thinking and intuiting) refer to the manner in which information is processed. A one-sided orientation is abnormal and leads to superior functions and inferior functions. The superior functions are overemphasized while the inferior functions remain undeveloped and unintegrated into consciousness. The individuated person permits all aspects of the personality to be differentiated and expressed.

9. The self is the center of the expanded personality. The self, which is the recentered ego, emerges as the core of the total personality. One of its major tasks is the transcendent function, which is the harmonizing of opposites.

10. Symbolic expressions are means of dealing with insoluble human problems. They are expressions of archetypes, which enable humans to have experiences that celebrate important events in life. Jung held that to do away with symbolic practices would be dangerous because certain archetypes would thereby be frustrated. Symbols are forms of expression that are distinctly human. Many customs are symbolic expressions. Symbols give meaning to significant human events. Symbolic activity produces numinous experience.

11. The types of abnormality with which Jung was most concerned were failures in differentiation and integration of the personality. Overemphasis on the persona causes the shadow, the anima or animus, and the archetypes to be neglected. These may disrupt the ego by causing tension and inconsistent behavior. In this case, the ego may be possessed by shadow elements. Greater differentiation increases the breadth of reactions and actions of the individual. Integration refers to the harmonizing and unification of opposing aspects of personality. Individuation covers both processes. Jung stressed the idea of balance in personality. Some of the oppositions in personality that must be given recognition are conscious and unconscious; emotional and rational; introversion and extroversion. Imbalance hinders enjoyment and productivity at best and may destroy the personality at worst. Imbalance is one of the chief causes of abnormality; thus, normality is defined as having achieved integration, or unity and balance among opposing elements of personality.

12. Dream imagery and fantasy were studied by Jung through the method of dream amplification and the method of active imagination. The purpose of both is to gain access to relevant unconscious material.

GLOSSARY

Attitudes: The direction of energy flow; the orientation one takes toward the world and self; introversion and extroversion.

   Introversion: The focus of attention on subjective experiences, preoccupation with self rather than external events; a natural orientation to life for many people.

Extroversion: A focus of attention and energy externally; social-orientation and concern with making an impression.

Functions: Ways of interpreting experience. One may be dominant while the others may be inferior (underdeveloped).

Sensing: Provides information about external objects, people, and events, a nonrational function.

Thinking: Involves (interpretation) processing information through cognitive faculties, a rational function.

Feeling: Refers to cognitive evaluation of worth, also a rational function.

Intuition: Refers to hypotheses and hunches about possibilities, a nonrational function.

Individuation: The process of differentiating the various components of personality and bringing them under conscious control of the self, which is the recentered ego; the attainment of selfhood, self-realization, becoming a full individual.

Differentiation: Developing and expressing a component of personality.

Integration: Assimilating the differentiated components into the self.

Transcendent function: A high-level function of the self that attempts to harmonize opposite tendencies within personality, turning conflict into complementation—for example, persona and shadow, and harmonizing opposite sex qualities.

Motivational structures: Dynamic forces within the psyche, especially complexes and archetypes.

Archetypes: Inherited predispositions to have common experiences. Inborn tendency to form certain universal images. The archetypes make up the collective unconscious.

Complex: A network of thoughts, feelings, and attitudes held together by a core disposition, which is highly valued by the individual and is activated by many stimuli, for example, erotic concern.

Numinous experience: A profound experience in the presence of a meaningful symbol; the activation of archetypal material; a spell, similar to Maslow's peak experience.

Symbol: An expression of archetypes; refers to representational expression in many forms such as artistic, religious, and even ritualistic practices.

Structures of personality: Components of the personality that require differentiation and integration into the self.

Ego: Center of consciousness that primarily serves the persona, felt subjectively. The ego performs the adaptive and coping functions of everyday life.

Persona: The social personality or mask worn for the benefit of others and determined largely by cultural expectations.

Shadow: The unacceptable aspects of personality, which are often hidden in our unconscious and which are inconsistent with our social roles or masks. Our opposite sex qualities may be part of the shadow.

Self: Controlling agent in personality when individuation has taken place; core of the whole personality; the integrating force that harmonizes opposites; the recentered ego.

Anima: As archetype is the ideal image that a man has of a woman. Also refers to feminine traits in a man.

Animus: As archetype is the ideal image that a woman has of a man. Also refers to masculine traits in a woman.

The unconscious: Psychical material that is not ordinarily available to the ego, but may influence it.

Personal unconscious: The level of the unconscious mind that is unique to each individual and which contains impulses, wishes, and memories accumulated through his or her experiences, which are not assimilated by the ego.

Collective unconscious: Inherited predispositions, the archetypes. The deepest level of the unconscious common to the human species; the inherited primordial racial past.

SUGGESTED READINGS

Jung, C. G. "An Analysis of the Prelude to a Case of Schizophrenia," in R. F. Hull, trans. *Symbols of Transformation*. New York: Harper & Row, 1962. (Originally published in 1912).

In this book, Jung begins to develop his own version of the unconscious. He argues for the important function of the collective unconscious: the production of symbolic material.

————. *Studies in Word Association*. London: Heinemann, 1918.

The notion of the complex is elaborated, and methods for identifying and measuring the intensity and scope of complexes are detailed.

————. *Psychological Types*. New York: Harcourt Brace Jovanovich, 1933.

In this book, Jung presents the major principles of his school of analytical psychology. He also develops his theory of types (introvert and extrovert) and the four functions (thinking, feeling, sensing, and intuiting).

————. *The Archetypes and the Collective Unconscious* in H. Read et al., eds.; R. F. Hull, trans. *Collected Works of C. G. Jung*, Vol. 9, Part I. New York: Pantheon, 1959.

This is an excellent presentation of Jung's theory of personality, with a discussion of such topics as the persona, the shadow, the anima and animus, the self, and the individuation process.

————. *Man and His Symbols*. New York: Doubleday, 1964.

Written by Jung and several of his most devoted disciples, this book is probably the best introduction to Jungian psychology. Jung designed it for the intelligent layperson.

————. *Memories, Dreams, Reflections* New York: Vantage Books, 1961–1963.

In this book Jung presents his own life story, which he calls his "personal myth." Through Jung's recounting of his subjective experiences, we can understand his work more completely. It is his autobiography.

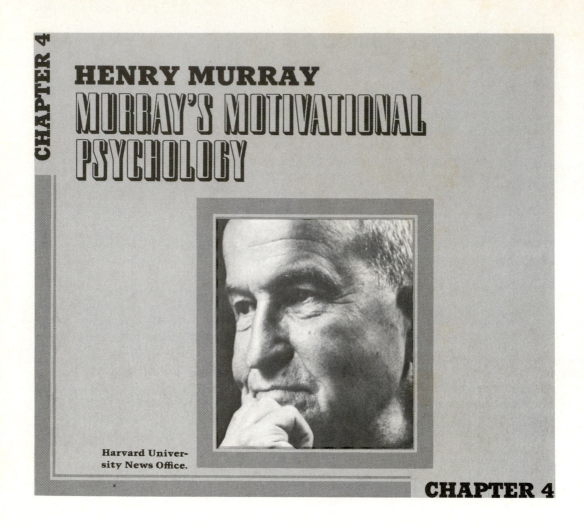

HENRY MURRAY
MURRAY'S MOTIVATIONAL PSYCHOLOGY

Harvard University News Office.

BIOGRAPHY AND HISTORICAL PERSPECTIVE

Henry Murray (1938) coined the term *personology*, which means "the scientific study of the total person." He has introduced a large number of concepts to represent the factors that must be understood in describing, explaining, predicting, and controlling personality phenomena. His concepts encompass the personality, the environment, and the history of the organism. He takes a holistic view of people but at the same time strives for detailed understanding through a meticulous analytic approach. Murray views each person as highly complex and unique and takes into account the totality of determinants. He has a bewildering list of factors from which you can draw to represent a single personality. He is known as a taxonomist—one who classifies and describes phenomena in a given field.

Murray has much in common with the interactionist theorists (Julian B. Rotter and Walter Mischel, for example) who view the environment and the person as mutually shaping each other. Born in New York City in 1893, he graduated from Harvard in 1915 with a degree in history and went on to Columbia in the School of Physicians and Surgeons and received a medical degree in 1919, graduating at the head of his class. He took an M.A. in biology from Columbia in 1920 and did some teaching at Harvard. For two years he trained as a surgeon in New York. He then went to England and studied biochemistry at Cambridge, receiving a Ph.D. in that subject in 1927. Up to this point he had no formal training in psychology or psychiatry, but he reports that as a physician he was highly concerned and curious about the psychogenic causes of his patients' disturbances. He says he had actually visited the haunts of some of his sordid patients and began to learn psychology in the rough from dope addicts, prostitutes, sword swallowers, and gangsters (Murray, 1940). While in Europe in 1925, he visited C. G. Jung, whom he credits with kindling his total involvement in psychology. Murray was trained as a psychoanalyst between 1927 and 1935, when he was head of the new psychological clinic at Harvard.

Many well-known students were trained at the clinic, and a great deal of productive work took place there. *Explorations in Personality*, written by Murray and his collaborators and published in 1938, gives an account of some of the work—an intensive study of a small group of subjects. During World War II, Murray joined the Army Medical Corps and distinguished himself by his work in psychological assessment. He was charged with the task of identifying personnel who could handle secret and dangerous missions. Murray (1943), together with his student Christiana Morgan, developed the well-known Thematic Apperception Test. He also developed tests to screen and select espionage agents during World War II. (see Murray and MacKinnon, 1946). After the war he returned to Harvard and remained there until his retirement in 1962.

A flavor of Murray's formulations can be seen in the following quotation, which highlights his view of human beings:

> I can hardly think myself back to the myopia that once so seriously restricted my view of human nature, so natural has it become for me to receive impressions of wishes, dramas, and assumptions that underlie the acts and talk of everyone I meet. Instead of seeing merely a groomed American in a business suit, travelling to and from his office like a rat in a maze, a predatory ambulating apparatus of reflexes, habit, stereotypes, and slogans, a bundle of consistencies, conformities, and allegiances to this or that institution—a robot in other words—I visualize (just as I visualize the activity of his internal organs) a flow of powerful subjective life, conscious and unconscious; a whispering gallery in which voices echo from the distant past; a gulf stream of fantasies with floating memories of past events, currents of contending complexes, plots and counterplots, hopeful intimations and ideals. To a neurologist such perspectives are absurd, archaic, tender-minded; but in truth they are much closer to the actualities of inner life than are his own neat diagrams of reflex arcs and nerve anastomoses. A personality is a full Congress of orators and pressure-groups, of children, demagogues, communists, isolationists, warmongers, mugwumps, grafters, log-rollers, lobbyists, Caesars and Christs, Machiavellis and Judases, Tories and Promethean revolutionists. And a psychologist who does not know this in himself, whose mind is locked against

the flux of images and feelings, should be encouraged to make friends by being psychoanalyzed, with the various members of his household [1940, pp. 160–161].[1]

Murray expresses his objections to traditional academic psychology in the following statements:

> At first I was taken aback, having vaguely expected that most academic psychologists would be interested in Man functioning in his environment. But not at all: almost everyone was nailed down to some piece of apparatus, measuring a small segment of the nervous system. . . . If my chief aim had been to "work with the greatest scientific precision" I would never have quit electrolytes and gases. I had changed because of a consuming interest in other matters, in problems of motivation and emotion. To try to work these out on human subjects was to become a literary or applied psychologist, a practitioner of mental hygiene, outside and looking in upon the real psychologists who, I concluded, were obsessed by anxious aims to climb the social scale of scientists and join the elect of this day's God at any cost. (1940, p. 154)[2]

We are placing Murray under the category of psychodynamic model because he greatly emphasizes the need approach in the study of the individual. Murray is difficult to categorize because he takes a broad view of humans and formulates constructs and postulates that are compatible with many viewpoints, even humanistic thinking. He is also sympathetic to the ego-social psychologists who will be discussed next, yet he identified himself with the psychoanalytic tradition. Murray was greatly influenced by Jung and gave Freud much credit for his thinking. He assigned a strong role to unconscious motivation and the irrational in humans; thus, we are classifying his formulations under the psychodynamic model.

BASIC CONSTRUCTS AND POSTULATES

The Structures of Personality

Murray was receptive to Freud's division of the personality into three competing systems: id, ego, and superego; but he introduced some major modifications in the roles of the three components. For example, he viewed the id both as the source of basic psychobiological urges that have the purpose of maintaining the organism and also as the origin of creative and growth-promoting urges. He felt that Freud overstressed the tension-reduction aspect of the id and did not give adequate consideration to the constructive and growth-promoting forces that are so evident in living things.

He viewed the ego as being complex rather than being an agent of the id. His emphasis on needs endowed the ego with its own motivations. The ego is certainly a servant of the id at times — particularly when it is weak and easily overwhelmed by the id — but the ego grows in strength as its own needs develop. An intense need for achievement may become the dominant force in one's life. Major conflicts might result

---

[1,2]From H. A. Murray, "What Should Psychologists Do About Psychoanalysis," *Journal of Abnormal Psychology*.

from powerful needs of the ego, which are of greater intensity than the conflicts between the id and the ego stressed by Freud.

With respect to the superego, Murray also made some major changes. Unlike Freud's view, which assigned the major determinants of the formation of the superego to ages three to eight, Murray viewed its development as a long-term process. Murray did not limit the development of the superego to the influence of the home environment and the oedipal conflict. When we acquire values or work them out for ourselves, the superego is undergoing significant modification. Our values, goals, and even the prescriptions of conscience change as we encounter new models and ideals of living. There is similarity between Murray's and Bandura's notions of the influence of heroes, fads and fashions, and cultural models who set standards of conduct.

Evidence for the Existence of Needs

The most tangible aspect of personality is behavior. Surely there can be more agreement on what a person *is* doing (and on the products of behavior) than on *how* or *why* he or she does it. Because behavior is observable and measurable, the most widely accepted definition of psychology is the science of the causes of behavior.

To some psychologists, particularly the behaviorists, the observable causes of behavior are the stimuli that precede and follow behavior. What goes on within the person can only be inferred, not observed directly. "Why use some unobservable thing to explain that which can be observed?" they might argue. Would it not be better to deal with the tangibles alone, since only with them can one hope to get agreement?

Other psychologists have found behavioral explanations in terms of observables inadequate to account for what takes place and equally insufficient for making predictions. Except for relatively simple reflexes, a knowledge of the stimulus does not give us enough information to specify the response that may follow. To say it another way, responses are seldom predictable from a knowledge of the stimulus alone. A man may almost always answer his telephone when it rings, but on a certain day, because he does not want to talk with a certain person, he does not answer. This explanation may fall under the heading of the "history" of the organism; if the man's unwillingness to talk to his friend is known, his unusual behavior in relation to his phone, on this particular day, may be understood. However, the notion of the history of the organism covers so much as to be practically meaningless as a working principle in dealing with behavior. Murray (1959) has sought to develop working concepts for classifying and understanding behavior and its causes, both environmental and intrapsychic. He places a great deal of stress on the personality as a real structure with active forces: needs, abilities, and achievements. Murray thus accepts both situation and person variables as determinants of behavior.

THREE PHASES OF A NEED

The activities of the organism are usually divisible into three classes. There is usually (1) a beginning state (a disequilibrium of some sort), (2) an activity directed to changing the situation, and (3) an end state. Activities that are blocked may be replaced with different activities, but the same end state is sought. This latter point suggests the operation of a force within the personality that continues to act until the end state is attained, no matter which mode of activity is used.

One of the best proofs for the existence of needs is the degree of readiness of the organism to respond to the same stimulus situation at different times. Consider hunger as an example. When you have just eaten, even the most appetizing food may have no appeal because the need has been rendered inactive. Sometimes, however, a person who is not actively hungry may be enticed by the sight and odor of food because the hunger need is in a state of readiness. In the active state, although there is no food present, a hungry person begins seeking it. Thus three states of a need may be distinguished: (1) *an inactive phase*, in which no stimulus will arouse the need, (2) *a readiness phase*, in which only certain stimuli will arouse the need, and (3) an *active state*, in which the need impels the person to seek gratification, even without the presence of an appropriate stimulus.

Although it is true that a person may not be thirsty until he or she passes a drinking fountain or may not be hungry until he or she smells the odor of cooking food, the external instigation of behavior is not the whole of the motivational picture. To show the inadequacy of external causation of behavior, consider the man who strongly desires feminine companionship and actively seeks out the means of meeting appropriate mates. The strong need dominates the psychological environment entirely, and other matters may become subsidiary.

It should be pointed out that success at something may create a need, a factor indicating mutual interaction of internal and external causes. People who find that they have much more of an effect on others than they expected, although they never had a strong need to dominate or influence others, may acquire this need through the easy success of their efforts. Sometimes this is referred to as "tasting blood"; one does not acquire some needs until there is an encounter with a satisfier associated with them (Murray, 1938).

Murray perceives the motivational value of external objects and people by introducing the term *press*, which we will discuss in a later section, but he, nevertheless, emphasizes the dynamic force of *needs*. A specific need may be inferred from observing the repeated occurrence of particular behaviors that have a common objective. A person may reveal the need for companionship (affiliation need) by a variety of behaviors—joining clubs, frequent telephone conversations, development of social skills, frequent statements about liking people. Emotions, too, reveal the presence of a need that is either satisfied or frustrated. The person with an intense affiliative need is enthusiastic and joyful in the presence of certain people or may display anxiety and signs of loneliness in the absence of social encounters. With a strong affiliative need, a person selectively perceives situations that will offer the opportunity of gratification of this need. Furthermore, this person avoids situations in which this need cannot be gratified. Needs exert a dynamic force that influences behavior significantly.

In stressing the dynamic force of needs, Murray is placing the locus of control within personality. However, he assigns a determining role to the environment in his concept of *press*, which frequently consists of the stimuli that set off needs. Consider the case of a superstimulus: an attractive dessert that entices a person to eat more even though the person is not hungry.

The Meaning of Press

Murray (1938) uses the term *press* to stand for stimulus or situation. He believes that the difficulty with the word *stimulus* is that its meaning is too general and argues that we, therefore, need a term to personalize stimuli. Not everyone is affected by the same stimulus. Murray uses the term *press*, then, to stand for the stimulus for a particular person. *A press does something to or for a person.* A pretty blonde is a highly positive affiliative press for a certain young man. Being in her presence sets off several basic needs. Her presence exerts pressure upon him. The notion of press (the same spelling is also used for the plural) is that the environment may force the person into certain postures or predicaments.

Consider the first day of classes: the professor announces that there will be several unannounced quizzes, certainly a press for most students. Then she mentions the lengthy term paper. Here is another press that surely affects the average student. There is a source of tension that was not anticipated. The situation "presses" the students in a certain direction. The press does something to them; it makes them respond.

To arrive at significant press for yourself, consider what objects and people do, or can do, to or for you. A friend is critical, flattering, suspecting, admiring, envious, condescending. A parent may be dominating, restricting, punitive, loving, generous, frustrating. A toothache is painful, annoying, troublesome.

Frequently, a need is activated by a press and gives rise to certain activities that quiet the need and reduce the tension. It should be noted that needs may instigate behavior directly without any apparent press. But needs may confer significance upon certain press more than others.

Just as needs tell us about the determining tendencies within the individual, so press provide us with knowledge of the environment for a particular person. Specifically, we may discover which aspects of the environment are perceived as threatening, dangerous, favorable, helpful, and the like. A knowledge of needs would be insufficient without a knowledge of the significant environmental factors. Murray uses many of the same terms that he uses to designate needs also to name press: for example, affiliation, aggression, nurturance, dominance, but he prefixes press with "p" and needs with "n."

ALPHA AND BETA PRESS

Murray (1938) distinguishes between alpha press and beta press. Alpha press is what the object actually is whereas beta press is the perception or interpretation of it. Obviously, we would have to know the beta press if we desired to secure a picture of the manner in which the environment affects a particular individual. Discrepancies and distortions between alpha and beta press may lead to delusional thinking and serious behavioral disturbances. A storm may be perceived quite differently by two people. One may seriously misinterpret the potential dangers whereas the other may underrate the hazards. The manner in which a person views or interprets his or her environment is secured through knowledge of the person's interpretation of press, the beta press. Behavior is far better understood and potentially predicted from a knowledge of both needs and significant beta press (Murray, 1938).

Need-Integrate, Thema, and Dyad

All the elements associated with a need become tied together; Murray (1938) calls this a *need-integrate*. A need-integrate may be understood as a complete unit of behavior with all the elements tightly bound together as a result of repeated occurrence. The need-integrate includes the triggering stimulus (which he calls press), the deficit state (which is the need), associated images and emotions, and, finally, the particular goal or incentive that satisfies the need. As a shorthand description, Murray speaks of *themas* rather than need-integrates.

Murray focuses directly on the interaction between need and press and identifies these interactions as *themas*. A thema is the conjunction of a press and a need (Murray, 1938). Certain objects, persons, or events (press) are highly significant for a person. Cer-

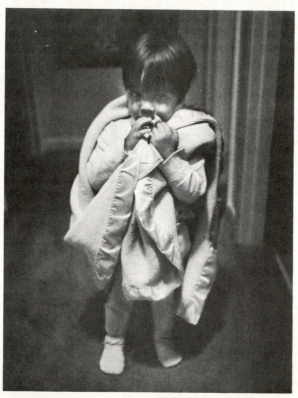

© William Strode 1980/Woodfin Camp & Associates

Forms of escape as a means of dealing with stress may be recurring themas.

tain needs are dominant and pervasive. Themas refer to units of behavior, produced by a need, directed toward a particular object, person, or event. A press such as friendliness (pAffiliation) may instigate nAffiliation in a particular person. For this person, friendly encounters activate friendly behaviors because the person has an intense need for affiliation. The friendliness thema would apply to specific press, that is, friendly people. A friendly salesperson, however, might elicit nAggression or nRejection. The thema refers to the conjunction of specific press with specific needs.

When a thema is the major determinant in personality, affecting all significant aspects of behavior, it is termed by Murray "unity thema."

> A *unity thema* is a compound of interrelated-collaborating or conflicting-dominant needs that are linked to press to which the individual was exposed on one or more particular occasions, gratifying or traumatic in early childhood. The thema may stand for a primary infantile experience or a subsequent reaction formation to that experience. But whatever its nature and genesis, it repeats itself in many forms during later life [1938, pp. 604–605].[3]

Thus we see that the unity thema for each person is the key to understanding significant features of behavior. An example is the power complex in which the person is driven to gain superiority over others. Any all-consuming passion in a person's life may be a unity thema (see *Scripts People Live By*, Claude Steiner, 1974, and *Beyond Games and Scripts*, Eric Berne, 1976).

Themas, as we have noted, are the conjunction of needs and objects. Needs involve an object, for example, loving someone or something, fearing someone or something, and so on. Consider themas such as submitting to authority, defending against an aggressor, caring for helpless creatures. Themas may be very specific, for example, a woman feeling motherly toward her sick husband or a grandfather feeling playful toward his granddaughter. Themas may also be highly general, for instance, acquiescing to any request made by a friend. Murray intended themas to be the units of behavior that psychologists use to describe, explain, predict, and influence behavior. Refer to Table 4–1 for themas based on Murray's psychogenic needs. The left-hand column is a list of these needs. Themas are named by need terms such as nurturing thema, achievement thema, and affiliative thema.

Murray introduces the term *dyad* to stand for the *relationship between the person and the environment*. The personality is complex, but the environment is also complex. Our needs impel us to take certain courses of action in order to gratify them. Our physical, social, and cultural environments also continually make demands on us. We have noted that Murray uses the term *press* to designate environmental influences and stresses needs as the dynamic influences within the personality. There are two basic classes of dyadic relationships: those involving *reactions* to the environment and those that involve *actions* upon the environment. Such reactions and actions may become characteristic of an individual; thus, they may be termed themas. Frequently, the two types of dyads are linked, as when a person reacts to a situation with intense emotion and then acts to change the situation. Murray's formulation of the two types of dyads is the same as Skinner's view of respondents and operants and Bandura's idea of mutual determinism. These views emphasize the continual interaction between the individual and the environment.

[3]H. A. Murray, *Explorations in Personality*.

TABLE 4-1 TYPICAL THEMAS

Need	Themas
Abasement	To submit passively to a motherlike person.
	To accept blame readily from a superior.
	To confess wrongdoing to anyone who will listen.
Achievement	To strive to earn a large income.
	To attain honors and awards through outstanding achievements.
	To rival and surpass associates.
Affiliation	To have a close friend.
	To please many people.
	To work closely with another or on a team.
Aggression	To overcome the opposition of another who is perceived as a threat.
	To cause another to submit: to control, to obligate others.
	To demonstrate superiority over others by hurting them.
Autonomy	To resist any form of restraint or coercion from parents.
	To quit deliberately activities which are required by authorities.
	To express needs relating to desired objects freely and impulsively.
	To seek exemptions from rules.
Counteraction	To strive anew in the face of failure.
	To overcome humiliation by taking strong positive action.
	To seek constantly to overcome weaknesses in oneself.
	To seek obstacles and difficulties to surmount.
Defendance	To defend the self against any criticism from anyone.
	To conceal quickly or justify a misdeed or humiliation in relationships with one perceived as an inferior.
	To be vindictive toward anyone who interferes with strivings.
Deference	To admire and support an older sibling, parent, friend.
	To praise, honor, or eulogize a boss, teacher, hero.
	To yield eagerly to the influence of a friend, partner, parent.
	To imitate the example of a model such as one's boss.
Dominance	To control one's environment by making things suit one's plan.
	To influence or direct the behavior of friends, classmates, parents.
	To take charge of situations: leader, boss, director, persuader.
	To persuade, to restrain, to direct, to control others.
Exhibition	To make an impression on members of the opposite sex.
	To fascinate, shock, entertain, intrigue people perceived as significant.
	To draw attention to oneself through appearance and behavior.
Harmavoidance	To avoid taking risks by a conservative approach to life.
	To take precautionary measures in any threatening situation.
	To worry excessively about the uncertainties of life.

Note: While themas involve needs and are in fact named by need terms, they also include press.

TABLE 4-1 (Continued)

Need	Themas
Infavoidance	To maintain a high level of pride in relationships with others.
	To avoid failure in undertakings.
	To be especially sensitive to belittlement, scorn, and indifference of others.
Nurturance	To be attracted to babies, small animals, and helpless creatures.
	To rally for the underdog.
	To enjoy matchmaking, directing young people, giving support.
	To sympathize with, console, comfort one who is affilicted.
Order	To organize and plan a trip or program.
	To produce a balance or orderly arrangement.
	To work out a system in the midst of confusion.
Play	To enjoy pleasure-making through sports.
	To enjoy laughing and making jokes in company with others.
Rejection	To respond to some people with an air of superiority.
	To deliberately snub or exclude certain people.
Sentience	To need activities and people that promote sensual pleasures.
	To seek unusual experiences as a means of changing moods.
Sex	To be attracted by many sexual partners.
	To be preoccupied with erotic concerns.
	To be attracted by an older man or woman.
Succorance	To respond dependently to a motherlike person.
	To cling to any authority figure who demonstrates concern.
	To seek to be counseled, advised, consoled by a sympathetic friend.
Understanding	To ask questions of a knowledgeable person.
	To speculate about unknowns.
	To attempt to identify the causes of things and events.

General Principles Concerning Needs

NEED EXPRESSIONS, VALUES, VECTORS

To say that people have a strong achievement need does not really tell us much about them because the need points only to their general orientation. Unless we understand their specific goals, knowing that they have a need for achievement is of little value. The goals are the concrete ways in which the need is expressed or satisfied. The goals are the press, and, if a pattern of behavior is repeated, it becomes a thema. The goal gives the need substance, a tangible form. A person usually would not describe himself or herself as having a strong need for achievement; there would have to be some specific goal or goals. The person might want to earn more money than any of his or her friends or possess the best-looking home or attain recognition through athletic accomplishment. In addition to goals associated with a need, there are specific means for attaining goals. Not every means of achieving is acceptable.

In the early formulation of his theory, Murray (1938) stressed the role of needs as determinants of behavior, but later he emphasized the "end states" of needs, which he terms *values* (Murray, 1951). Many needs may produce the same end state; that is, a particular value such as property, wealth, or fame may be the object of a number of needs. In like manner, Murray (1951) also classifies the diverse means of attaining values under a number of general headings, which he terms *vectors*. Murray borrows the term *vector* from physics, where it refers to the direction of a given force. In psychology a vector may be taken as the direction of behavior toward a goal. A behavior vector may comprise many acts, all of which have some specific direction or movement in common. Examples are locomotion, construction, acquisition, manipulation, and other similar general classes of activities.

Means, like goals, are highly specific. A person may want wealth desperately, but be unable to steal to get it. Another may seek recognition but will not step on another to attain it. Of course, some individuals allow themselves a wider range of means in accomplishing their goals. But even criminals have certain means that are unacceptable to them: their code of ethics may preclude stealing from a friend.

Murray takes the position that the human personality is dynamic. A structure, although described as psychic, exists, grows, changes, and functions. It is *reactive* to circumstances in the environment, but it is also *proactive* through spontaneous inner activity (Murray, 1954). An active need impels us to take action whether or not an appropriate press is present. A ringing telephone may cause a person to do something to stop the annoying sound, but the same individual may produce sound on a piano as a result of an inner urge. Of specific relevance to the operation of personality are the goal-directed efforts that arise within the personality. The main driving forces are internal.

The happenings in a person's life are brought about by the individual. He or she makes things happen, and even the things that happen to the person are interpreted within a framework of his or her needs. One man sees a plot of land as an unproductive empty field. Another becomes excited at the prospect of buying this piece of land and building a home for his family. The same situation has strikingly different significance to the two men, and the cause of the difference is within the personality of each: one does not need a home because he is not married, whereas the other has a strong need for it. It is a highly positive press for one, but not for the other. Alter the need structure of a person, and you alter his or her whole personality and its relation to the person's environment. Murray describes the role of needs in the following passage:

> A need is a construct (a convenient fiction or hypothetical concept) which stands for a force . . . in the brain region, a force which organizes perception, apperception, intellection, conation, and action in such a way as to transform in a certain direction an existing, unsatisfying situation. A need is sometimes provoked directly by internal processes of a certain kind . . . but, more frequently (when in a state of readiness) by the occurrence of one of a few commonly effective press (environmental). . . . Thus, it manifests itself by leading the organism to search for or to avoid encountering or, when encountered, to attend and respond to certain kinds of press. . . . Each need is characteristically accompanied by a particular feeling or emotion and tends to use certain modes . . . to further its trend. It may be weak or intense, momentary or enduring. But usually it persists and gives rise to a

certain course of overt behavior (or fantasy), which . . . changes the initiating circumstance in such a way as to bring about an end situation which stills (appeases or satisfies) the organism. [1938, p. 175].[4]

OTHER PRINCIPLES

Before considering in detail the subjective and behavioral manifestations of the psychogenic needs proposed by Murray, we will discuss several additional principles relating to the dynamics of needs. These ideas will enable the reader to appreciate the scope of Murray's need matrix in describing, explaining, and predicting behavior. They are not ordered in any logical form or priority system.

1. Behavior is not best understood as a collection of habits, instigated by press alone, but rather as the means that are used by needs to accomplish certain ends. Habits are the means by which needs are satisfied.

2. An indication of abnormality is lack of flexibility in behavior — following rigid patterns as in obsessive/compulsive behavior or as in the behavior of some elderly persons, and functioning predominantly on a concrete level, as in cases of severely brain-damaged persons or of the narrowed behavior of someone who is said to have a "one-track mind."

3. A need is a force that causes activity. It may be experienced as a tension, but the basis of the tension may not be known, and the appropriate goal also may not be known, as when a person feels depressed but does not know why. In most cases, however, both the need and the goal are in awareness: the person knows why he or she is disturbed and what he or she wants (Murray, 1938).

4. The two major classes of needs are the *viscerogenic*, which relate to bodily functioning, and the *psychogenic*, which are qualities of the personality. The two classes are interdependent. Culture has the greatest influence on the psychogenic needs (Murray, 1954).

5. Viscerogenic needs have a definite zone of the body that serves as the source of tension; the psychogenic needs are experienced without any particular localization: there is no bodily organ involved in feeling lonely. A "heartache" really takes place in the brain.

6. Viscerogenic needs are rhythmical and cyclical: the needs come and go periodically as a result of the requirements of the living organism. Psychogenic needs are more dependent upon press or circumstances and do not occur in a set cycle. They also come and go, but the rhythm is not regular. Generally, viscerogenic needs are more directly related to survival than are the psychogenic needs; thus, they are more potent than psychogenic needs. Under certain conditions, however, psychogenic needs may take priority over viscerogenic needs, for example, a person who has a strong nAffiliation that impels him or her to stay late at a party rather than to get a full-night's sleep.

7. The ease with which needs are satisfied is inversely proportional to their importance in personality. As Murray (1954) points out, air is the most urgent need of all,

[4]H. A. Murray, *Explorations in Personality*.

and yet as a need it plays an insignificant part in personality development and functioning. On the other hand, the need for sexual outlet, although not absolutely required for existence, is highly significant in personality growth and development.

8. Needs may fuse and operate as virtually one motivational unit. Behavior is usually the outcome of a fusion of needs (Murray, 1938). Work is satisfying because it involves being autonomous, achieving, affiliating with others, feeling dominant, and possibly many other needs. A man may fall in love with a woman because she satisfies a variety of needs. In her relationship with him she may assume such roles as a concerned mother, a working associate, a little sister needing care, even a rival to compete with. Of course, a woman also may fall in love with a man as a result of the satisfaction of a variety of needs. The more needs involved, the greater are the ties formed. The more compatible the needs of two people (and in general, similarities make for compatibility more than do differences unless the needs of each are too extreme), the greater is the attachment.

9. A need may be subsidiary to another need, as when an individual desires to befriend someone who has influence in the community (Murray, 1938). He or she needs the friendship and may strive arduously to secure it. In this example, the need for friendship is subsidiary to the need to be superior or the need for recognition.

10. The satisfaction of a need is accompanied by positive affect (feeling or emotion). Dissatisfaction accompanies need deprivation or need frustration. Activity, such as vigorous exercise or a brisk walk, in itself gives pleasure as well as a sense of achievement. Certainly, the attainment of a goal is pleasurable, particularly when it is highly valued. All need states are held to be accompanied by tension, and removal of the tension, at least in the case of negative tension, is experienced as pleasure.

The best way to appreciate the value of the need approach is to learn the meanings of the terms that designate the various needs. What follows is a lengthy presentation of the key psychogenic needs that Murray used in understanding the behavior of fifty subjects. It should be understood that these needs are expressed in unique ways by each person and vary in degree of dominance. Each need is accompanied by characteristic emotions, is expressed by habitual behaviors, and is directed toward specific ends. A further point in comprehending the needs is that several of them are extremes of a continuum, such as dominance and deference, nurturance and succorance, defendants and counteraction. But this following material can be made more manageable by learning the meanings of the terms.

Examples from Murray's List of Needs

Everyone is familiar with the viscerogenic needs. Although they are absolutely essential to the maintenance of life, they usually have little to do with the development and functioning of personality unless there is severe deprivation or excess; then the consequences are disastrous or even fatal.

A number of Murray's psychogenic needs will be discussed in order to demonstrate the power of this approach. The psychogenic needs are not usually a factor in survival but are essential for personality growth and functioning. The various behavioral manifestations or expressions of these needs will be given with actual examples of real situations. The material for this section is drawn largely from "Variables in Personality," Chapter 3 of Murray's *Explorations in Personality* (1938).

n DOMINANCE[5]

The need to dominate others is manifested in a wide variety of forms. Subjectively, it may be experienced as a desire to control others, to lead, to persuade, to take charge of situations, to set a pattern or standard that others should follow. Usually, the leader deliberately strives to dominate. He takes on responsibilities in order to be observed by those who can help him attain a position of authority. The common notion that leadership ability expresses itself naturally and that the leader will emerge because of his superior endowment, is false (Carter and Nixon, 1949). The person who attains leadership has a strong need to be in a dominative role and organizes all his or her abilities to reach that goal.

Those who are dominant often manifest their dominance in their behavior and freely report an unusual sense of self-confidence. They feel capable in relation to others. They do not shrink from those in authority or from those who hold highly respected positions. They indicate that they feel adequate to deal with most situations that confront them. Seldom do they experience feelings of inferiority, particularly in relation to other people. A not-so-obvious expression of the need to dominate, however, is the person who wishes to impose his or her desires or convictions on others. Such a person may lack the quality of reciprocity, that is, may fail to see the world from the standpoint of others. This often results in overevaluation of himself or herself.

n DEFERENCE

The need for deference is manifested in interpersonal relationships, such as ready compliance with the request of another out of high admiration. In general, it refers to willing acceptance of a subordinate position in relation to others (Lang and Lazovik, 1962). An individual who has a strong need for deference wants to work for, or be associated with, one whom he or she can admire and respect. A man is fortunate if he has a secretary who has an active need for deference because her work in serving him fulfills a need. She derives great pleasure from his accomplishments and successes and gains satisfaction from her work in promoting him.

The concept of the role model illustrates the operation of the deference need. The role model is an exemplar, one who is considered an ideal human, at least with respect to some attributes. Children often display a deferent attitude toward older children or adults. They are acutely aware of their insufficiencies and lack of perfection in comparison with older people. A child who is struggling with some problem is struck with

---

[5]The terms *n Dominance*, *n Deference*, and so forth, are Murray's way of referring to the various needs. *n* Deference, for example, may be read as "need for deference," "need to defer," and so on, for all the needs listed here.

a sense of awe by the older child or adult who solves the same problem with apparent ease. Such a child may form a completely false image of the one who seems to do what he or she cannot do. Simply being near this great person satisfies something in him or her. Deferent people actually derive satisfaction from the superiorities of others. They eagerly offer respect, admiration, and praise. They are happy to help the admired person satisfy the need to dominate. They may undertake a campaign to elect their idol to office or to promote him for an award. They take great pride if the person receives the honor, especially if they were instrumental in bringing this about. Whereas an envious person derives great pleasure from the defeat or injury of a superior rival, the deferent person delights in and actually desires the superiority of another. His or her need is fulfilled only in others' superiority.

Probably the purest form of the need for deference is devout religious surrender. Religious people offer prayers of supplication, praise, and adoration to a divine being. They believe that they are given special graces by being spiritually close to a personal God. They subordinate themselves and become a part of the divine through their acts of deference. To love, serve, and obey are ideals that are espoused by the devout of almost all religions.

n AUTONOMY

The need for autonomy is manifested in the following ways: by resisting authority (anyone who has authority over the person is automatically seen as a threat), by resistance to being coerced (the person cannot go along with something that others have suggested), by being independent, by being irresponsible or free of rules and regulations, by fighting against restrictions and constraints, by defying convention and ruling oneself in order to remain unattached and unobligated to others. You might describe a person with a strong need for autonomy as negativistic, independent, irresponsible, nonconformist, radical, willful, or stubborn.

We all at times experience a sense of confinement and an overburden of regulations and restrictions. In conjunction with such feelings are the motives to be free and independent to do whatever we please. In a sense, a vacation is a means of accomplishing these things. We arrange for certain activities that are more in keeping with what we like to do than with what we have to do (which is the normal state of things). The vacation activities satisfy many needs, among which the need for autonomy is of paramount importance to the individual.

The strength of the autonomy need may be appreciated through the many ways in which people seek to gratify it. Some young people are lured by the total freedom and rejection of counterculture movements. They throw over the mores of their class and choose freedom and independence as their primary values. Money, status, fame—the goals traditionally sought by the young—are considered the deadening values of the "establishment" and are replaced by the goal of the greatest autonomy possible.

We could argue that the need for autonomy is a natural reaction against the cramping demands of society: the long confinement in school, the confusion over a career and acceptable life-style, the conflicting demands of opposing values, and many other societal "ills." Some young people may not like what they see and what they are forced to do and rebel against the system. The rebellion may range from a felt need (which is not acted upon) to escape the responsibilities that are placed upon them to an open attack on the institutions of the society.

The need for autonomy sometimes fuses with the need for achievement, with great resultant benefits for mankind. Scientists and men of genius who risk censure and rejection to pursue an idea that goes against the current are examples of the happy combination of the autonomy and achievement needs. Freud, who was rejected by the medical profession, continued to develop his radical ideas about the unconscious at the cost of professional security. In the end he became more famous than those who derided him, and many believe he made significant contributions to the study of psychology. The history of science and philosophy is replete with stories of human beings who gave up comfort, security, and even prestige to satisfy their need for autonomy.

In the lives of ordinary people, the need for autonomy takes over behavior. Everyone must face the independence-dependence conflict. As people grow up, more and more is expected of them. Choices, judgment, decisions are constantly confronting the individual. In the final analysis, people cannot turn to others for solutions. Others may give advice, but usually the final decision is left to the person faced with the task. In such instances, the person is caught in a conflict between the need for autonomy and the fear of the consequences that autonomy may produce. Many shrink away from this situation or develop symptoms of personality disorder. Even the strongest among us are often disturbed by the conflict. But in the end, the harsh call of necessity and the great urge for freedom and independence win out for most people, and they enjoy the benefits of autonomous living by taking control over and responsibility for their lives. The achievement of autonomy is a highly valued personal attainment, but Murray frequently refers to the need for autonomy in a negative sense. His treatment of the other needs should also be understood in this same light. He deals with need exaggerations.

n AGGRESSION

The need for aggression is manifested objectively in behavior and subjectively in the need to resist force, to fight and take revenge, to win over another forcibly, to attack and injure animals or humans, to oppose and deny the rights of a rival. The emotional aspects of the need for aggression include anger, irritation, annoyance, hatred, and yearning for revenge. A person with a strong need for aggression may be described as hateful, malicious, irritable, negativistic, ruthless, cruel, destructive, vindictive, critical, accusatory, abusive, domineering, harsh, and despotic.

One of the most perplexing aspects of human behavior is the amount of aggressiveness that exists. People's inhumanity to other people has for centuries puzzled the greatest minds. War and violence have played a conspicuous part in human history. At any one time there are a dozen or more trouble spots in the world with actual shooting wars that take a high toll of lives and leave many more to suffer permanent disabilities. No one can possibly estimate the extent of violence, murder, personal injury, and crime involving the injury of fellow humans. In all the major cities of the United States the streets have become battlegrounds. You risk your life traveling alone after dark in many sections of the cities.

The daily newspapers are filled with tales of woe. A man is robbed and beaten mercilessly so that he is disabled for life. If you inquire into the motivation behind such behavior, you often find an element that goes beyond the desire to steal. If the victim does not resist, as most do not, there is no justification for violence. The violence, the unprovoked attack, must serve a strong motive. The assailant demonstrates by his or her behavior that he or she has a need to see another human hurt. Often the need to injure actually seems to predominate as when an individual is attacked by a gang and brutalized while his possessions remain untouched. The helpless victim wonders why this happened to him, as have many great minds.

Freud (1926) became more and more convinced that the need for aggression is present in everyone to a greater or lesser degree. So pervasive is it that if it is not turned outward on other people or things, then it is turned inward upon the self, with many unpleasant consequences. Most people find acceptable outlets for their aggressive needs through their work or in forms of recreation. The point is that the need to hurt is strong in some people and must be satisfied just as must the needs to achieve, to affiliate, to express our abilities, and so on. The acceptance of aggression as a need brings with it serious consequences, particularly if we assume that everyone has this need. The control of aggression and the expression of it are among the greatest problems of humans.

A popular football player, Jack Tatum of the Houston Oilers, revealed in his book *They Call Me Assassin* (1979) that he tackled players with the intent to injure them. Although a large public outcry was stirred by this book, Tatum continued to be a very popular player. There is a special fascination in sports that involve violence of the participants: boxing, football, wrestling, hunting, and hockey. Even though there has been a consistent outcry against violent sports such as boxing and football, occasionally there is an outburst of interest among the public. Boxing has lost favor for a variety of reasons, but the vast interest that can arise spontaneously in a heavyweight title fight is difficult to account for. One might understand interest that was built up through many matches, but when interest is sparked by a single bout, there is the suspicion that some basic need for aggression is being satisfied in the spectators. It is estimated that recent world heavyweight title bouts have attracted worldwide television audiences in excess of 300 million. There are few other events that have attracted such interest, particularly interest requiring a high payment. It seems to be a matter of aggression's waiting to be unleashed. If the fighters were engaged in a spelling bee, surely the audience would have been diminished considerably because spelling bees ordinarily do not involve injuries to the contestants. The need for aggression, even if it is so diluted as to be satisfied merely through being a spectator of aggressive acts, must surely be a powerful need, and its prevalence is widespread.

Not everyone exhibits this need to the same degree, however. Anthropologists (for example, Gorer, 1966) point out that certain cultures are characterized by a great deal of aggression among their members whereas others foster more benign traits. Women, in general, have been, until now, less openly aggressive than men (Oetzel, 1966), but this is probably due to cultural influences (see Lips and Colwill, *The Psychology of Sex Differences*, 1978, and Rorbaugh, *Women: Psychology's Puzzle*, 1979).

n NURTURANCE

A nurturant person is one who enjoys and strongly desires to do things involving the care of others. Some of the forms of expressing the need for nurturance are giving assis-

Photo credit: © 1982 Catherine Ursillo/Photo Researchers, Inc.

Selfless caring for others is one of the noblest human needs.

tance to one who is helpless, guiding and assisting the weak, the hurt, the young, the lonely, the infirm. Other forms of expression include protecting, nursing, caring for, feeding, sympathizing with, and feeling pity, compassion, and tenderness—traits that have been traditionally associated with femininity. This might be interpreted as sexist; however, the qualities of behavior that stem from the nurturance need are among the most noble of human attributes. The qualities of nurturance in a person represent humanity at its best. Many men do, in fact, behave in nurturant ways in relation to loved ones. In custody cases it has been customary for the judge to award the care of the children to the mother under the tacit assumption that nurturance is a feminine quality. But recently the trend is beginning to change. Judges consider which parent has the best potential for caring for the children and increasingly are awarding custody to the father.

What might go under the heading of nurturance is highly varied (see Bowlby, *Attachment*, 1969; Kaplan, *Oneness and Separateness*, 1978). A mother may have a nurturant attitude toward her baby. Although she receives little in return for her many sacrifices, she may devote most of her time and energy to caring for her child, especially if the child has an illness. If her nurturant need is strong, she does not regret or begrudge her sacrifice, even if it costs her many sleepless nights. On the contrary, she is at her best in this role. Being "motherly," at least in relation to her baby, satisfies a deep longing in her (Sears, Maccoby, and Levin, 1957). Strangely, she may feel and behave in a maternalistic way toward her baby but not feel the same impulse with respect to her older children (Fromm, 1947), a factor that may cause her to neglect them for the sake of the baby. Many persons have indicated a strong resentment of a younger brother or sister that dates back to the birth of the newcomer. All the mother's attention was directed to the baby, and the older child lost his or her position of dominance. Adler made a major point of this notion in his concept of family position and its effect on development (see Forer, *The Birth Order Factor*, 1977).

This example suggests that the nurturance need can be quite specific. Some women may feel protective and motherly toward teenagers, but not toward infants. Other women actually feel a maternal impulse for a grown man and may behave toward him as if he were a young child. There are men, of course, who seem to need this type of relationship; they may be described as having a need for succorance — a need to be taken care of, to be comforted and soothed, and to depend on someone. The marriage of a woman who has the need to nurture and a man who needs to receive succorance may be a good match. Each is satisfying the other's basic need: one complements the other; she wants what he provides and vice versa. Problems may arise when one of the partners expects or demands what the other is not motivated to give. A wife may want to lean on her husband for support and assistance in solving her personal problems, but he may not be willing or able to help her. In such instances a great deal of friction may be created.

To illustrate the varied expressions of the need for nurturance, we might consider some not-so-obvious outlets. Consider the individual who loves to grow and care for plants: there is nothing so helpless and so totally at the mercy of external forces for survival as a plant. Plants can do nothing to secure their sustenance and alter their circumstances. From the standpoint of the nurturance need, no other thing can be as compliant and dependent. Even a child can resist his or her mother's efforts at mothering. As a matter of fact, as children grow (and this also applies to animals), they become more and more independent of the caring person. But plants cannot even secure water for themselves.

Pets are often objects of the nurturance need. To feel sympathetic and protective toward infant creatures is universal among humans, and absence of this feeling is considered by some psychologists to be indicative of faulty development (Maslow, 1968d). However, the fascination pets have for humans is certainly a mystery. Perhaps a pet satisfies a number of needs: to dominate, to nurture, to feel superiority over something. Consider the relation of a dog to the one who cares for it. The dog gives itself completely to its master, irrespective of the master's status, appearance, and even style of life. Many a rejected soul has found some sense of identity and worth through a pet dog. An unfortunate young woman who suffered from facial deformities, poor vision, and an unattractive frail appearance, loved by no one, secured a guide dog to assist her in her work as a music teacher. Her personality underwent a remarkable change. Her dog was her constant companion. His response to her and the care that she gave him provided her with a whole new orientation to life. She behaved like a person who had met an exciting new friend. Everything about her improved — her work, her relationships with others, even her health. Although many needs were undoubtedly satisfied, there is no question that her need for nurturance was greatly affected by her caring for the dog, which served her as a guide and companion.

n ACHIEVEMENT

The need to achieve may fuse with virtually all other needs. One individual may strive to achieve in order to gain power over others; another may seek success to prove that he or she is not inferior; another may be driven to achieve because he or she feels insecure; still another could be the fusion of the need to achieve with the need for self-improvement; and there are many, many other such fusions. According to Murray (1938), the basic elements in achievement are to do something well and do it quickly.

Some specific ways to express the achievement need are to master difficult situations; to control, manipulate, and organize physical objects; to overcome obstacles; to attain high standards; to rival and surpass competitors; to exercise your talents and faculties; and, in general, to do things well (French, 1955). People in whom the achievement need is strong are described as ambitious, climbers, good scrappers.

© Erika Stone 1982

Our complex nature demands achievement.

The need for achievement has many people in its grip. So strong is it in some that the "what" of the achievement is not as important as the fact that some type of achievement has been attained. In such instances there is probably a fusion between achievement and dominance. Most often, however, the need for achievement is directed toward specific goals. Most persons do not want to achieve in all areas of their lives, but usually have specific directions that are significant to them. For one person, the need to achieve takes the form of earning a large income; for another, it is to hold an admired place; for another, it is overcoming obstacles that others could not conquer. You may observe from these examples that achievement is almost always subsidiary to other goals but there are examples of achievement for its own sake, as you shall see.

Achievement is usually associated with culturally desirable goals such as financial security, status, power, and so on. The one who achieves has advantages over others. A variety of basic needs may thus be served by the achievement need.

Probably the purest forms of the achievement need are found in the inventor, the explorer, and the researcher, who strive to solve practical problems or to unlock nature's mysteries. Often such persons actually forego the use of their talents in certain directions that might guarantee them easy success in order to follow their interests, at the risk of total failure in the end. Many undoubtedly do fail in their pursuit of achievement in their own chosen way. Thus, whereas the need for achievement is frequently socially oriented, it is not always so. In such instances, it might best be considered an expression of self-actualization (see Maslow, 1970). The ego ideal, which may be considered in this context to be the image of the perfected self, is sometimes the basis of the need for achievement. *To be the perfected self involves the attainment of particular goals and the renunciation of other goals.* In the individual in whom the ego ideal is dominant, the achievement motive takes its purest form: the saintly man who gives up his own comforts in order to attain his cherished goals. Tradition holds that the greatest persons are usually those who give up personal gains for the sake of ideals. If there is merit in this observation, we have an example of a strong fusion between the need for achievement and the need for autonomy. The statement "no one can demand from me as much as I demand from myself" exemplifies the essential operation of the achievement need.

n ABASEMENT

The individual who has a need for abasement may passively accept criticism, blame, or punishment; he or she submits without a struggle to the demands of others, gives up easily and surrenders and becomes resigned to fate, may readily admit mistakes and failings and take defeat as a matter of course, may seek out those to whom he or she can confess his or her sins, wallows in self-criticism, and seeks and even enjoys pain, punishment, and hurt from others. The element of *self-depreciation* is always present in the person who has a need for abasement; the deferent person, in contrast, submits because he or she gains strength and importance through the superiority of another. Some of the emotions that go along with the need for abasement are guilt, shame, depression, helplessness, and despair. A self-abasing person is described as meek, humble, servile, submissive, spineless.

A college coed who thought herself extremely unattractive and unacceptable to men because she was somewhat overweight took an abasive attitude in her relations with others. When she spoke, she could hardly be heard because she spoke softly and swallowed her words. If someone wronged her, she would not stand up for herself. She met a male student who showed some interest in her, but her sense of inferiority led her to introduce him to her best girl friend. When she was asked about this rather strange behavior, she said that she really did not have much of a chance with him, and her friend was so much more attractive.

The element of self-effacement, or self-hate, is always a part of the picture in one who has a need for abasement although its intensity may vary greatly. The following example illustrates the strength of self-aggression, and we might argue the presence of a masochistic trend. A young air force officer at a service club began to become disorderly and abusive after gulping down several drinks hurriedly. He walked up to the biggest man in the place and began to taunt him. The man did not want to fight and ignored him, but the officer continued his harassment. Finally, the officer pushed the larger man, who then began to fight with him and caused severe injury. The officer had deliberately picked the fight; he did not even know the other man. He had a history of being destructive—committing needless violence as a means of venting his hostile feelings. He would also periodically impose many punitive restrictions upon himself, such as fasting or giving up drinking. On the evening of the fight, he was on a date with his girl friend at her apartment. They had engaged in some love play when he hinted that he wanted intercourse. She pushed him away, and he reacted by slapping her. Then he left angrily and went to the service club where he picked the fight. One obvious interpretation is that he was looking for punishment for having done something that was abhorrent to him.

n SEX

The need for sex, like the other needs, has many forms of expression. All forms of expression, however, have a sensual quality. For example, the need for sex is active when one enjoys looking at, touching, listening to, and being near a person of the opposite sex. (Some find members of the same sex more attractive than those of the other sex.) The need for sex varies in intensity from a constant preoccupation to an occasional sense of tension. The forms of expression and arousal are much more varied than most people imagine. An extensive treatment of the sex need is not possible here, but it might be mentioned that, as Freud held, this need constitutes one of the major problem sources for people in Western cultures. The problem, of course, is one of gratification.

We may look at the need for sex as an example of the subordination of one need to another. A man may have a strong aggressive need; he delights in hurting others, in making them suffer. The sexual need may be brought into service as a means of expressing his aggressive tendencies. Obviously, this type of situation is highly abnormal. Again, the need to care for someone may be the dominant need in a relationship, and sexual activity may be a means of satisfying that need. A woman or a man may be very nurturant in relation to her or his spouse. The sexual need is active in their relationship, but the need to nurture may be more potent. This emphasis on nurturance may cause difficulties when the first child is born if one of the spouses finds much satisfaction in caring for the baby and begins to ignore the other. Many men complain that their wives change in relation to them with the birth of the first child. In such instances, an apparently good marital relationship is based on a strong need to nurture more than on the affiliative and sexual needs.

n SENTIENCE

The need for sentience may be described as deriving pleasure from sensory and motor experiences and as feeling tensions when such experiences are not possible. All the sensory modalities are sources of much tensions and pleasures — visual, tactual, gustatory, olfactory, and so on (see Montagu, *Touching*, 1971; Montagu and Matson, *The Human Connection*, 1979). A number of recent studies have indicated the presence of the need for a certain amount of sensory stimulation in everyone and maintain that deprivation of sensory inputs, even for short periods, can cause profound psychological and behavioral impairments (see Bowlby, 1973; 1980).

Many forms of psychotherapy have the aim of increasing sensory awareness. Gestalt therapy, for example, consists in part of techniques that are designed to sharpen the client's awareness of his or her inner experiences — to make ideas and feelings *gestalten*, that is, definitely configurated and clearly perceived. In other words, the client is encouraged to become aware as much as possible of his or her inner and outer life. All this is done to aid the client to know him or herself and also to live more richly and fully. Other sensory awareness therapies are currently coming into vogue: *Focusing, Rolfing, Awareness Through Movement, Tai Chi* (see Rolf, 1977; Feldenkrais, 1977; and Huang, 1973).

Some individuals, such as those who truly enjoy art or music or vivid poetry, have an unusual need for sensory stimulation. The person who enjoys a good physical workout probably also has a need for sentience. Certainly there is an invigorating feeling produced by exercise. There is a heightening of activity, with accompanying feelings and sensations, and then the recovery and relaxation phase, with other pleasant sensations and feelings. Not everyone is willing to go to the trouble of finding an adequate facility for exercising, and the whole thought of physical activity is repugnant to many. They do not have a need for this type of sentience.

The recent popularity of drugs and the increasing use of alcohol (see Blum et al., 1969) certainly point out the pervasiveness of the need for sentience. Of all the reasons why people drink or take drugs, the alteration of consciousness (expansion, contraction, and all the many other paranormal states) is certainly one of the most compelling (see release from *Research Triangle News*, March 20, 1981). A common expression among drug users is "taking a bad trip," which of course denotes an unpleasant experience.

There are many hazards with the use of chemical agents for the purpose of mood-alteration. Be it euphoria or a feeling of calm or tranquillity, a person using a mood-altering chemical is being profoundly rewarded through the autonomic nervous system. Mood-altering chemicals, however, have the power to be severely harmful and/or addictive. For most people, then, especially those who are addiction-prone, chemicals are not the answer to the fulfillment of n Sentience (see *The Dynamics of Addiction* by George A. Mann, M.D., no date).

Those who love the rustic beauty of the out-of-doors, who love to walk in the woods and look at the objects of nature, surely have a strong need for sentience. All the senses are stimulated in such natural settings. Our most animalistic nature finds outlets in the primitive natural environment. But not everyone has this need, it appears, because some folks want little to do with outdoor life. For such people the allurements of the urban night life are far more compelling.

n EXHIBITION

One who has a strong need for exhibition may manifest it in a great variety of behaviors. Some of the commonest are these: to make an impression; to be seen and heard; to excite, amaze, fascinate, intrigue, entertain, and shock; to try to create a reaction in others. People with this need want to be observed by others. They experience tension when not noticed or when ignored. Many people deliberately dress in a manner that draws attention. Many engage in behavior that attracts the curiosity of others. Politicians display their wares to their audiences: they want to be seen and heard; they want to exhibit their competence by making promises and displaying their verbal talents. They have a need for public and individual attention from others. A man may undertake to write an autobiography for a variety of reasons: because he thinks that others want to know about his life or maybe because he thinks that he has lived an unusual life. There are numerous reasons, but certainly the need for exhibition cannot be ruled out as a strong contributing force in many instances.

A certain degree of exhibitionism may be found in everyone under specific circumstances. The absence of this need, as in the person who has a strong need for seclusiveness, is probably abnormal. Some people have talents that make possible the satisfaction of exhibition tendencies. Others, finding repeated failure in their attempts to satisfy this need, may deliberately inhibit attempts at satisfaction and instead express an opposite need, such as seclusiveness, or take a hostile attitude toward other people. In one sense, aggressiveness toward others satisfies exhibition tendencies through the effects produced. Again, it can be seen that the desire to make an impression on others is one of the most powerful needs of humans (Jones, 1964), and it has many acceptable as well as unacceptable forms of expression.

n PLAY

The need for play may take the form of pleasure-seeking as an end in itself. It may be described as activity for its own sake — activity pleasure. Among children it occupies a large portion of the waking hours and appears to be a means of testing sensory and motor functions (Piaget, 1962). The play behavior of children is probably a fusion of several needs: sentience, dominance, achievement, understanding, and play. The small child explores the objects in his or her world by playing with them. He or she pushes and pulls, puts things together, builds and disassembles structures, and even breaks things, all for the sake of pleasure. Many adults play a great deal: bowling, golf, baseball, and so on. Often there is the element of winning or losing, of competition with yourself or opponents. But in much play activity, such as hiking, rowing, sunbathing, and swimming, there is neither competition nor achievement.

n AFFILIATION

In general, the affiliative need means to seek companions, to work closely with others in a team effort, to be liked by those who are liked, to relate in an intimate manner to certain people, to be attractive to some people. The need varies markedly with different individuals, from those who crave the friendship of everyone they meet to those who are self-sufficient and make no effort to form friendships (McKeachie et al., 1966; Kaplan, 1978). Friendships are based on a variety of factors: you may simply like anyone who likes you; another searches out people who are inferior or dependent; another tries to befriend only those who are quite similar to him or her; still others strive to befriend dominant people. Kinget (1975) points out that

> The social-emotional gratification derived from casual good fellowship with a wide variety of people may be commonplace, but, like a loaf of bread, it is the mainstay of many affective diets [p. 104].

The history of the affiliation need in each person is quite significant in personality development. At three, your need for affiliation is quite different from your need at twenty. At all ages, one of the major benefits of friendships is a sense of not being or feeling alone with your problems. Your age mates usually have the same problems to deal with, and you find support and actual solutions through contacts (see also Montagu and Matson, *The Human Connection*, 1979).

n REJECTION

When you turn away from someone considered inferior or separate yourself from certain groups or classes or consider yourself especially elite and superior, with a "better-than-thou" attitude, the need for rejection is determining your behavior. Such persons are often quite discriminating about the people they can like or accept. The qualities of humanness are not enough for them. Certain standards are demanded, and those who do not meet them are excluded as inferior or undesirable. The thinking and conversations of such people are permeated with an atmosphere of downgrading. A person who has a strong need to reject others is intolerant: he or she is not willing to respect the right of the other to hold and value a different point of view. His or her general opinion is that most people are not worth listening to or bothering with. Consider this sentiment: "Few men are raised in our estimates by being very closely examined."

n SUCCORANCE

In general, succorance means to have your needs taken care of by someone else. Other behaviors that come under the heading of the need for succorance are to be loved, advised, protected, nursed, guided, consoled, forgiven, supported, encouraged, and sympathized or empathized with. We may picture, as an extreme instance of the need for succorance, a person who is helpless, pleading, suppliant, begging forgiveness, crying for help. The element of dependence is frequently associated with a succorant tendency. The individual cannot stand on his or her own feet; he or she feels inadequate to deal with a situation and turns to others for help. But dependence is not always characteristic of one who thrives on being helped or cared for. A highly capable, self-sufficient woman may relate to the man she loves in a succorant manner: she may subordinate her ambitions for the sake of his. She desires to make him "feel masculine." She expresses appreciation and gratitude for the protection and care he wants to give her. He may have a need to nurture, and she has a need to receive the nurturance — a need for succorance. Actually, in real-life situations the roles vary: sometimes she cares for him, as when he is ill. Both of these needs are important aspects of human relationships. Giving love in a generous manner and receiving it with proper appreciation bind people together.

n HARMAVOIDANCE, n BLAMAVOIDANCE, n INFAVOIDANCE, n DEFENDANCE, AND n COUNTERACTION

Several needs relate to the fear of injury from other people and things and also to the disapproval of one's own conscience. Harmavoidance deals with avoidance of injuries of all types; infavoidance refers to avoidance of failure. Defendance is an active tendency to protect yourself against threats to status, and counteraction refers to a renewal of effort as the result of failure.

Those who have a strong need for harmavoidance are sensitive to any physical and psychological threat to their integrity. They wish to avoid pain, physical injury, and death. Strong precautionary measures are taken, such as a strict special diet, avoiding certain foods because they are "poisonous," maintaining a strict regime of exercise, visiting a doctor frequently, reading and worrying about fatal diseases. Such a person may be described as timid, frightened, worrisome, hypochondriacal, sensitive, cautious, wary, prudent. A person dominated by this attitude has many fears: he or she thinks often of death with great horror; fears animals such as snakes, dogs, cats; worries about becoming ill and losing status; fears taking any risks that could involve injury. Some people believe that they need a great deal of rest and sleep to avoid becoming exhausted. Phobias are common: fear of dying in a fire, fear of hell, fear of being alone at night, and so on.

A need for blamavoidance appears to be related to living with other people who have the power to judge your conduct. It involves avoidance of disapproval, censure, and punishment from others. This need to avoid certain behaviors exerts strong inhibitions and controls over activities that are detrimental to group living. When the controlling force is within the person, in the form of superego, the avoidant behavior is motivated by guilt. Specific forms of this need include avoiding blame, rejection, or loss of affection, and controlling selfish strivings, replacing them with socially directed behavior. Such expressions as "what would people say if they really knew me" exemplify the operation of this need. Some people cannot tolerate the idea that anyone disapproves of them. They wish to make a favorable impression on everyone, irrespective of position or closeness. Some even go so far as to value the opinions of others more than their own.

Infavoidance involves avoiding humiliation, embarrassing situations, and belittlement from others; quitting situations that are threatening; rejecting something new from fear of failing; feeling inferior; lacking self-confidence; feeling unworthy. Such a person may be described as sensitive, shy, nervous, passive. A person who has a strong need to avoid failure is sensitive to any kind of failure. Failing in unessential matters is reacted to in the same way as are more significant shortcomings. Because failure of any sort is dreaded, there is a constant inhibition of action. If you do not seek much, you cannot be deprived or hurt (Birney, Burdick, and Teevan, 1969; Good and Good, 1975).

You have a need for defendance when you display by your behavior an attitude of self-protection against criticism, blame, or any attack. This need is also operating in concealment, in self-justification, and in attempts to cover over a failure or to support your course of action. A defendant individual may easily misinterpret the actions of others, finding insult where none was intended. Such people are quick to make excuses, cover up areas of weakness, and maintain a status of reserve. Sometimes even lying is used as a means of concealment and covering up. The individual may be so ready to assume a defensive screen that he or she does not make any effort to change the things he or she is defensive about, with the consequence that the defensive strategy becomes a fixed part of the personality. When n defendance is prominent in a person, there are probably unconscious protective mechanisms that are at work, causing the hypersensitivities and distortions of perception. The blamavoidant person wants the good opinion of others so strongly that he or she is willing to make changes in himself or herself; the defendant person does not do much changing.

People who have a strong need for counteraction find renewed motivation in the status of failure. They say, in effect: "I have been knocked down, but I won't stay down." Such persons typically strive to overcome weaknesses, to seek out obstacles to overcome. Pride and self-respect are highly significant to them. Counteraction is often manifested in a strong negative reaction to receiving aid: the person would rather do without than be helped or dependent on another. Such terms as resolute, determined, dauntless, adventurous, and prideful describe one who is dominated by this need. As a striking example of its power, you may think of the suffering hero, beset on all sides by limitations and difficulties, but nevertheless, through sheer willpower and self-sacrifice, gaining the victory for himself or herself. Being a quitter is extremely distasteful to this type of person.

n ORDER

A need for order is manifested in behavior directed toward organizing the immediate environment. Some people have a compulsion to put things in order, to clean up, to arrange furniture and clothing neatly, to organize and systematize books and other possessions. The orderly individual experiences tension when his or her home or room is in a condition of disarray. He or she must "get the mess straightened out." Everything has a place and should be kept there. A need for orderliness is not easily learned by an adult, a factor that also appears to apply to most of the other needs. Many wives complain that their husbands are careless about their things, and despite persistent nagging the tendency to be slovenly does not change. An extreme tendency toward orderliness is a symptom of a malfunctioning personality. A man or woman who is constantly cleaning and dusting because of an inordinate fear of dirt is an example. The behavior has a compulsive quality about it, and the home is kept too well to be livable and comfortable.

n UNDERSTANDING

Many philosophers and psychologists have puzzled over the question of the status of cognition in relation to motivation. Some have regarded cognition as the servant or tool of motivation. One has a need and uses cognitive functioning as a means of securing satisfaction. Some, however — Murray included — have taken the position that cognition meets the requirements of a need. One may seek knowledge for its own sake. Cognitive processes may be pressed into the service of needs, but they may also function as needs themselves and have motivational force such as the curiosity drive that impels the gossip to search out information. (For further information see Richard M. Restak, 1979).

The need for cognition may take some of the following forms: to analyze experience, to abstract, to discriminate among concepts, to define relations, to synthesize

NASA/Photo Researchers, Inc.

Cognition has its own motivation.

ideas, and to arrive at generalizations. One who has this need experiences tension related to intellectual pursuits and thoroughly enjoys discovering new relationships; if the person is a scientist, he or she may delight in seeing his or her hypotheses verified by the data. Some actual behavioral manifestations of the need for understanding are, according to Murray, the tendency to ask questions, interest in theory, the inclination to analyze events and draw generalizations, a zest for discussion and argumentation, a high premium on logic and reason, self-correction and criticism, the habit of stating opinion precisely, insistent attempts to make thought correspond to fact, and deep interest in abstract formulations such as science, mathematics, and philosophy. To pursue these activities, without any other intended end, exemplifies the operation of the need for cognition and understanding.

Psychological Tests Based on Murray's Formulations

The Edwards Personal Preference Schedule is an assessment instrument that presents a profile of the subject's standing with respect to fifteen of Murray's needs. The profile is presented in Table 4–2, together with some sample items from the test. The test consists of pairs of statements that are supposed to be equivalent in desirability or undesirability. The person taking the test is required to choose one of the alternatives, thereby expressing a particular need:

> Each of the 15 personality variables in the EPPS is paired twice with each of the other variables. If, in each of the comparisons, the subject has chosen the statement for a given variable as being more characteristic of himself than the statements for the other variables, his score on this particular variable would be 28. This is the maximum score that can be obtained for any given personality variable. In order to obtain a score of 0 for any given variable, the subject would always have to regard the statements for this variable, in the 28 comparisons in which it appears, as being less characteristic of himself than the statements for the other variables [see Edwards, 1959].

Another important test that was inspired by Murray's ideas is the Thematic Apperception Test (Murray, 1943; see also Buros, 1972; Anastasi, 1976; for review). The test contains nineteen black and white drawings of a vague nature and one blank card. The person is to look at each card and make up a story suggested by the picture. The purpose of this procedure is to stimulate literary creativity and thereby evoke fantasies that reveal covert and unconscious complexes. The test is based upon the well-recognized fact that when a person interprets an ambiguous social situation, he or she is apt to expose his or her own personality more than the phenomenon to which he or she is attending (Murray, 1938).

The stories suggested by the pictures of the thematic apperception test are analyzed in terms of needs, press, and the conjunction of these in the form of themas. The clinician looks for consistencies, conflicts, and repetition of themas. The stories are also analyzed in terms of the characteristics, roles, and outcomes of the hero, who is assumed to be the person taking the test. You look for the presence of various components in the stories just as you might analyze a blood sample.

TABLE 4-2 EDWARDS PERSONAL PREFERENCE SCHEDULE

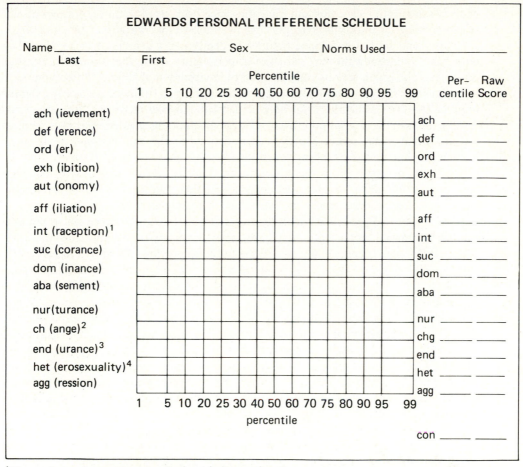

EDWARDS PERSONAL PREFERENCE SCHEDULE

Name _____ Sex _____ Norms Used _____
Last   First

[1]The need to analyze one's own and others' feelings and motives.
[2]The need to experience novelty and change in daily routines.
[3]The need to persevere at a task until completion.
[4]The need for relationships with opposite sex.

ITEMS FROM THE EDWARDS PERSONAL PREFERENCE SCHEDULE

Alternatives		Items
A	B	A: I like to talk about myself to others. B: I like to work toward some goal that I have set for myself.
A	B	A: I feel depressed when I fail at something. B: I feel nervous when giving a talk before a group.

CRITICAL EVALUATION

Murray's descriptive concepts and categories have been employed in a number of popular psychological tests. His concepts have been used as working tools by clinical psychologists, and he has developed theories to depict many aspects of personality. Not only has he suggested the key variables in personality study that should be assessed, but he has also given serious consideration to environmental factors. Those who wish to obtain a sense of the complexity and diversity of human behavior need only examine some of Murray's categories. You may be dazzled and bewildered by the variety and combinations of these descriptive categories: needs, emotions, modes, outcomes, impinging press, and many more. Murray's formulations of the motivational processes in humans are his most outstanding contribution.

On the negative side is the criticism that Murray really only describes behavior and does not provide any explanatory concepts. Furthermore, there are overlapping concepts and categories: abasement and deference, nurturance. It is difficult to obtain an integrated view of a personality with Murray's system. He *does* appreciate this problem and has introduced molar terms such as dyad, thema, unity thema, and need-integrate. Although Murray is continually modifying his concepts, his system still has an unfinished quality about it. Thus, though his ideas have been fruitful in stimulating some significant research, particularly concerning the achievement and affiliation needs (Atkinson, 1958; McClelland, 1971), they have not been generally accepted by psychologists. His language is considered unscientific and poetic by many hard-core empiricists. Like other personality theorists, Murray is more concerned with the significance of the problems than with elegance of definition and precision of measurement. He speculates freely about all aspects of personality; thus, he opens himself to criticism. Yet despite their shortcomings, his formulations have served as an inspiration for many and will continue to do so for some time. His ideas are transitional in that he maintains affiliation with the psychodynamic tradition, but he broadens the conception of human beings to include a greater role for the ego, as well as the influence of the social and cultural environment. The modifications of psychoanalytic theory which Murray introduced are given much more prominence by the three theorists to be discussed under the ego-social model in the next section, but significantly Murray anticipated many of the same ideas.

GUIDES TO RESEARCH

Theoretical constructs and postulates are difficult enough to test, but when they are taken from a personological formulation that stresses the uniqueness of each person, the empirically minded psychologists are not enticed. Murray's theoretical formulations have not directly generated much research to support his theory. The *idiographic* approach (the intensive study of the individual case) advocated by Murray has not been popular with psychologists (Maddi, 1963). Psychologists are more attracted by the *nomothetic* approach, which involves the study of the determinants of a segment of behavior of a group of people. The expected outcome of such studies is general principles of behavior. An example is that one responds more quickly to sound signals than to light signals. The hope is that when we have hundreds of such behavioral principles, we can use them to understand a particular individual. Murray would disagree and argue that we need concepts and methods to characterize and study the individual case. He has thus proposed many categories for describing the unique blend of ingredients that constitute the complex individual. Murray has a vast number of categories for each component of behavior — press, needs, emotions, outcomes, vectors, values, goals, and so on.

We can easily verify many of Murray's categories by our own personal introspections and observations of others. We can identify significant press in our own lives and relate them to our own needs. For example, we can personally validate the many subcategories of each of the components that Murray details, but we are not given constructs and postulates that explain or predict behavior; therefore, it is difficult to test Murray's formulations empirically.

Perhaps it is unfair to judge Murray's formulations from a point of view and purpose that Murray did not intend. He intended to provide conceptual categories that could be used to study and characterize the individual case. His many and varied categories and subcategories can be profitably applied to a large number of humans. His popular Thematic Apperception Test is an example of a concrete means of learning the psychological determinants of a person's behavior. It has been primarily used with pathological cases although in principle it could be just as applicable to normal people. The pictures on the cards are used to stimulate imaginative productions that reveal the dynamic forces in personality. It will be recalled that we look for significant press, dominant needs, recurrent themes, conflicts, purposes, and outcomes. The stories that are elicited by the pictures should reveal the psychological dynamics because the pictures are ambiguous. Murray terms the test "apperceptive" because the person's interpretation of the pictures is influenced by *existing sets and dispositions*. A number of systems of scoring the TAT have been developed, but none has been universally accepted. Murray offers some guidelines, but many clinicians have developed their own

system of interpretation. It would be desirable if more precision and validation in scoring responses were achieved with the TAT.

Murray recommends that the clinician look for themes that are repeated in the various stories. Again, the point is to study the content of the stories to learn about the characteristics of the person. We should look for major needs, conflicts, strategies of defense, repeated plots, and types of outcomes. It is assumed that the character of the story is the person himself and that the story reveals his or her inner and outer worlds. Common themes are revealed by similar plots in several stories. Murray advises the examiner to keep in mind questions such as the following: Is the subject active or passive in relation to his or her environment? Does the hero succeed in overcoming the major obstacle, or is he (or she) defeated in his (or her) attempts? What part do others play in the hero's struggles? What major needs are revealed by the story, and what are the significant press? Do the same themes appear in a number of stories?

The rationale and scoring procedures of the TAT represent a clear expression of Murray's interest in studying the dynamics of the individual. His basic constructs of needs, press, and thema have contributed to ego psychology in a profound way, which accounts for the continuing use of the TAT in both research and clinical practice (see Loevinger, 1976). Murray is much more interested in the study of the person rather than labeling personality types and identifying general principles of behavior. Murray's plea for dealing with the total person in natural surroundings is beginning to be heeded by current experimentalists and clinicians who have broadened the meaning of the laboratory to include actual real-life settings such as the home, the workshop, the playground, and similar unstructured settings (see Epstein, 1979).

The TAT and the Edwards Personal Preference Schedule are measurement instruments that evaluate strength of needs. They are diagnostic tools derived from Murray's formulations. Apparently, the most researched aspect of Murray's formulations is the achievement need. The studies of the achievement need are examples of the potential for research of the need approach.

Such research is an example of what could be done with other aspects of Murray's ideas.

An example of the type of research that stems from interest in the need for achievement was performed by Winterbottom (1953). He studied the relationship of childhood training in independence and the development and strength of the need for achievement. A group of boys was given a test to measure need for achievement. The mothers of both high scorers and low scorers were interviewed regarding the age at which their child was expected to be independent in a variety of tasks. Twenty specific behaviors were identified by the interviewers, such as going to bed by themselves, entertaining themselves, staying in the house alone, making their own friends, doing well in school without help, and later earning their own spending money and choosing their own clothes. All the mothers reported that they had made these demands by the time their child was ten years of age. The key result of this research is that the children who were high in achievement motivation were encouraged and pressured to perform the tasks at younger ages whereas the children with low achievement motivation tended to be overprotected.

Achievement motivation has been related to other significant variables. For example, Crockett (1962) studied the relationship of achievement motivation and differential occupational mobility. French and Thomas (1958) studied the relationship of achievement motivation to problem-solving effectiveness. Lowell (1952) studied the effect of need for achievement motivation on learning and speed of performance.

Several prominent researchers have exhaustively studied achievement motivation as it affects a variety of psychological processes and behaviors, for example, McClelland (1961, 1965, 1971); Atkinson and Feather (1966); Atkinson (1958); Atkinson and Raynor (1978); and Jackson et al (1976). Jackson found that achievement motivation is quite complex. In his research he found as many as six varieties of achievement motivation.

The great majority of studies on achievement motivation has been conducted with men.

Matina Horner (1968; 1973) has begun a movement to redress this one-sided bias. In one study she presented this brief description of a successful first-year medical student: "At the end of first-term finals, John finds himself at the top of his medical school class." For female students she used the same statement but with the name Anne. The male students were to spontaneously write their reactions about John; and the female students, about Anne. The responses of the men indicated the typical reaction and expectations for success, whereas females reacted with stories that depicted themes of fear of success. Two-thirds of the female stories described Anne as being unmarriageable, unattractive, likely to fail in the future, and in general as unfeminine. Subsequently, a considerable amount of research reflecting sex differences in achievement motivation has been carried out (see Shaver, 1976). Many people are sensitive to role expectations associated with gender and thereby consider certain behaviors and achievements inappropriate. A person fears success, then, when he or she is faced with what Tresemer calls the "gender-role-incongruent success condition," which refers to concerns associated with inappropriate work roles (see Tresemer, 1975; 1976).

Evidence is mounting that profound changes in achievement motivation, in relation to gender-specific roles, have been taking place in the last decade. Yankelovich (1981) has attempted to discern the direction of these changes and to propose solutions to the problems caused for both sexes.

The studies just noted have made a valuable contribution to our knowledge of motivation, but they are segmental approaches rather than holistic. Murray advocates a more global approach that would take into account the interactions among the many components of personality. He reports an excellent example of this type of study in his 1938 book, *Exploration in Personality*. Murray and his associates conducted an extensive study of fifty-one Harvard students in the late 1930s that exemplifies the use of idiographic approaches in personality study. Investigators from different disciplines participated in the research, which lasted for several months. Many of Murray's key ideas were drawn from the results of this extensive study. The study may be taken as a model of the idiographic approach. Each participant was subjected to rigorous observation and testing. Some of the tests and procedures were conferences, autobiographies, family relations and childhood memories, sexual development, present dilemmas, conversations, predictions and sentiments test, questionnaires, abilities test, aesthetic apperception test, and many others. There is evidence that this type of study, though difficult to conduct, is the most fruitful avenue to personality study and will become the standard for research investigations in this field.

GUIDES TO LIVING

PRACTICAL APPLICATION

Murray suggests that to use the need theory approach we should know all the needs quite well and be capable of identifying the active needs in a particular situation. Just as a physician keeps in the forefront of his or her mind symptoms of various diseases and can quickly link them with the cause, so also the individual using need theory should be aware of all the needs and their many behavioral and subjective manifestations and expressions. The same suggestion may be applied in the identification of significant press and recurring themas. These are the structural and dynamic constructs that Murray proposes as the conceptual tools for describing, explaining, predicting, and changing personality and behavior. Murray includes questionnaires for each of the needs in his *Explorations in Personality* (1938). In going over the questionnaire related to the need harmavoidance, a student exclaimed to the author: "I never realized what a coward I am." He had long recognized that he feared a lot of things, but he did not realize how extensive his fears were and how much of his behavior was in the service of them. The questionnaire brought this point home to him quite vividly, and he was determined to act upon this new insight into his behavior.

One may read over the description of the needs with the view of discovering those most characteristic of himself. The next step may be a consideration of all the ways in which the needs are expressed in behavior. Include an evaluation of the effects you are seeking to accomplish; there should be a close relation between the needs and the effects. What happens when the needs are satisfied, and what happens when they are frustrated? Is there an unnecessary amount of frustration because the goals are beyond your capabilities, or are the needs too intense? This type of examination should enable you to discover areas of difficulty to work on. One can alter goals if they are unrealistic or at least accept substitutes. The emotions associated with needs can be controlled. Even needs themselves can be moderated. It would appear that most of Murray's list of psychogenic needs are the result of learning and are continually affected by certain press; thus, principles of learning and behavior modification can be applied in changing such needs, associated personality variables, and behaviors. A person who is extremely anxious about making friends may by that fact limit his or her opportunities. Controlling the anxiety should improve the person's social relationships. While awareness of a problem does not automatically solve it, ignorance is certainly a much less likely condition for solution.

NEGATIVE AND POSITIVE NEED TENSION

In connection with need gratification, Murray subscribes to both tension reduction as a motivating force and generation of positive tensions (Murray and Kluckhohn, 1953). Some needs are associated with unpleasant tension, and we desire to rid ourselves of the tension. Examples are the viscerogenic needs. But some needs produce positive tension, and their gratification is also pleasurable. Consider such needs as curiosity, appetite for certain foods, the desire to do something competently.

One more point about need gratification should be noted: Murray believes that we strive not for happiness directly, but rather to attain certain goals or values. Happiness is a byproduct of success in meeting our goals. A tensionless state provides pleasure of a sort, but the gratification of appetitive needs provides far greater pleasure. We should strive to gratify such needs more than the deficiency ones. According to Murray:

> It is important to note that it is not a tensionless state, as Freud supposed, which is generally most satisfying to a healthy organism, but the process of reducing tension, and, other factors being equal, the degree of satisfaction is roughly proportional to the amount of tension that is reduced per unit of time. . . . A tensionless state is sometimes the ideal of those who suffer from chronic anxiety or resentment or a frustrated sex drive; but, as a rule, the absence of positive need-tension—

no appetite, no curiosity, no desire for fellowship, no zest—is very distressing. This calls our attention to the fact that the formula, tension-reduction of tension, takes account of only one side of the metabolic cycle. It covers metabolism, but not anabolism (which is the synthetic growth process by which tissues and potential energies are not only restored, but during youth, actually increased). The principle of homeostasis represents conservation but not construction. These considerations lead us to submit tentatively a more inclusive formula: generation of tension-reduction of tension. This formula represents a temporal pattern of states instead of an end state, a way of life rather than a goal; but it applies only to the positive need systems. The conservative systems that are directed toward withdrawals, avoidances, defenses, and preventions, are adequately covered by the reduction-of-tension formula [Murray and Kluckhohn, 1953, pp. 36–37].

As noted previously, Murray has in recent years placed greater emphasis upon the ends of needs, that is, the goals of needs. Goals exert influence over behavior by creating positive tension in many instances.

TYPICAL DYADS

As one technique for understanding yourself and others, Murray suggests that you begin with certain press and observe reactions to them at different times and under varying conditions. Consider your reaction to failure, making a lower mark on a test than you expected. Do you respond defensively by making an attempt at a justification? Do you seek a cause outside of yourself, such as blaming the test? Does the failure produce a depression, or are you motivated to change the situation? Reactions to specific press tend to become habitual. A person may always blame himself or herself for failure or may habitually blame other people or things or may try to find a rational explanation and ascribe the cause to impersonal forces, and so on (Rosen-

zweig, 1943). Consider other situations such as reactions to the good fortune of a friend: are you pleased or envious? You can learn about your typical reactions from an examination of typical situations and responses to them. As we have noted, Murray called these *dyadic relationships*. It will be recalled that a dyadic relationship may involve either a reaction to the environment or an action upon the environment. "I know a person well when I am able to specify quite definitely his or her reactions to specific situations, or press. I know Mary well when I can say something reagrding her typical situation-response patterns: Mary loves a surprise party; Mary dislikes a snob; Mary cannot tolerate being second best, and so forth." You can discover such dyadic relationships only by repeatedly observing the individual in a great variety of situations. The dyadic relationships that are characteristic of an individual should be understood as themas — both typical reaction and action patterns.

THE EGO HAS MANY FACTIONS

Another of Murray's ideas, which should assist in self-understanding, is his view of the complexity of the ego. Murray does not view the ego as a unitary agent as did Freud and many others. The ego is multidimensional; there are many aspects to it because there are divergent needs in the same person. It is more like a congress than a single agent. There are many factions, some of which are in diametric opposition. In a congress there are the liberals, the conservatives, the middle of the roaders, the radicals. The individual person may be conceived of in this manner. In making a decision, the conservative self says: "Don't be hasty to make a change; things are going quite well as they are." The liberal self says: "Let's do something exciting; who wants to just exist comfortably?" The conciliating self says: "Let's compromise; maybe we can take a longer vacation instead of moving away altogether."

Needs have much to do with the various aspects of the ego. Some needs are relatively unimportant in the activities of the ego. Whether you prefer sugar or cream or neither in your coffee does not cut across much of the personality. It plays no part in most decisions. Some needs are so dominant and pervasive, however, that they must be considered in virtually all personality functioning. They are constants in a person's "personal equation." Just as in the congress certain factions carry more votes than others, so also in the ego certain needs dominate others and determine the direction of judgments and decisions. You can become acquainted with these various aspects of the ego through observation. Self-improvement may be thought of, in part, as changing the influence of certain needs and the press and themas associated with them, as well as strengthening others in their place. You may conclude, from the contents of this chapter, that the need-theory approach to personality study is powerful indeed and provides a highly useful frame of reference for conceptualizing personality data.

SUMMARY

1. Murray is identified with motivational psychology. He introduced the term *personology*, which refers to the study of the total individual, including the impact of the environment, the structures and operations within the personality, and the history of the individual. Each person is viewed as being highly complex and unique and is more profitably understood by idiographic than by nomothetic methods. Idiographic refers to the study of the uniformities and determinants in the single individual. Nomothetic refers to the discovery of principles that pertain to human beings. The one is holistic; the other concentrates on specific behaviors.

2. Murray proposed that behavior is seldom predictable from knowledge of stimuli alone. It was necessary to infer intervening personality variables, and he formulated a large number of categories to designate the great diversity of inner determinants. As a result, he has been named a taxonomist, a classifier. Murray viewed the personality as a real structure with active forces — needs, abilities, competencies, and directional tendencies.

3. One of the best proofs for the existence of needs is the degree of readiness of the organism to respond to the same stimulus at different times. There are three states of a need: the inactive state, the readiness state, and the active state. A person does not experience some needs until there is an encounter with a satisfier associated with them.

4. Press is Murray's term for the impact of external stimuli. Press is a personalized stimulus, the influence that a particular event has on a person. A press does something to or for a person. Press may be viewed as being environmental factors that serve as positive or negative incentives. Needs may instigate behavior spontaneously, but frequently press activate needs, as when goals stimulate behavior. Just as needs tell us about the determining tendencies within the individual, press provide information about the significant forces of the environment for a particular person. Press are given the same names as needs, for example, pAffiliation versus nAffiliation.

5. Murray distinguishes between alpha press (what a thing actually is) and beta press (a person's perception and interpretation of a thing). Behavior is best understood and predicted from knowledge of both needs and beta press.

6. Value may be distinguished from vector. Just as a number of goals may be classified under a value, so also a number of means of attaining the goals (modes of behavior) may be classified as a vector. Needs initiate and guide behavior toward goals. Behaviors that have some essential feature in common, such as acquisition, are designated as vectors. A behavior vector comprises many acts. Many needs may lead to the same end state, a particular value, such as being popular.

7. Murray introduces molar constructs to characterize the natural units of behavior. A need-integrate refers to a complete unit of behavior including all the components tightly woven together. The essential components of a need-integrate are needs and press that interact; these are termed themas. A unity thema influences large segments of the personality and consists of a number of basic needs that activate instrumental behaviors directed toward specific goals. A unity thema is a master motivational unit and influences large segments of a person's behavior. An all-consuming passion may be a unity thema. Examples of themas are loving someone, fearing something, hating someone, submitting to authority, reacting aggressively to an aggressor.

A thema may be highly specific and personal: a grandfather reacting to and acting playfully toward his granddaughter. Themas are the units of behavior that Murray believes psychologists should identify.

8. The organism may react to the environment, but it also acts upon the environment; thus, there are both reactive needs and proactive needs. Reactive needs tend to be conservative in that they direct behavior toward tension reduction. Proactive needs tend to be expansive in that they initiate activity and promote growth. Much of human behavior is goal-directed and has the purpose of altering the environment to satisfy needs. Behavior is best understood as the means of accomplishing certain ends rather than as being a collection of S-R units or a collection of habits. Behavior is used by needs to accomplish ends.

9. Viscerogenic needs are associated with organic functioning and the maintenance of the body. Psychogenic needs have some relation to viscerogenic needs but are greatly influenced by learning and cultural factors. They are functions of the personality and have no specific bodily locus. Psychogenic needs are more important for personality growth and functioning than are viscerogenic needs. Needs may combine in the form of a need fusion, or they may conflict, or one need may be subsidiary to another. Some needs generate positive tension whereas others produce negative tension; the removal of negative tension is pleasurable. The control and expression of powerful needs, such as sex and aggression, are problems for most people.

10. Two major tests have been inspired by Murray's formulations: the Edwards Personal Preference Schedule and the Thematic Apperception Test. The former is based on fifteen of Murray's psychogenic needs and provides a profile of an individual's standings. The TAT attempts to measure covert needs, complexes, and conflicts. The stories are examined in terms of press, needs, and themas. Dyads refer to the relationships between person and the environment. Dyadic relationships that are characteristic of a person should be understood as themas. In a dyad, the significant factor may be a reaction to the situation that precedes behavior, or it may be an action that produces or changes a situation. Themas are inferred from repeated occurrences in the stories of conflicts, plots, endings, roles, and other common elements. The term *apperception* refers to significant past sets, complexes, and conflicts that influence present behavior, which are activated by the test pictures.

11. Murray viewed the ego as multidimensional rather than as a unitary agent. Needs are responsible for the various aspects of the ego. The ego is like a congress with many factions.

12. The idiographic approach advocated by Murray has not been popular with researchers who tend to follow the nomothetic approach. He sought to establish a sufficient number of conceptual categories that could be used to study and characterize the individual case. The TAT is also an idiographic approach in that the stories reveal personal material.

13. Murray's formulations have not received a great deal of interest. The achievement need and, to a lesser extent, the affiliative need have received some experimental attention. Murray himself, with several collaborators, conducted a model idiographic study that could be a pattern for other similar studies. Murray has pleaded that psychologists study the total person in natural settings rather than segmentalize behavior and study it under the highly controlled conditions of the laboratory.

GLOSSARY

Molar units: Unit of analysis that attempts to characterize coacting and interacting elements; global explanation.

> **Dyad:** Unit of analysis that includes interactions between individual and the environment; the relation of behavior to situations.

> **Thema:** Interaction between press and need that leads to a behavioral episode embodied in such phrases as submitting to authority, failing in the face of stress, overcoming obstacles.

> **Unity thema:** A master thema, a pattern of related needs and press, established early in life, which encompasses a large segment of behavior; similar to style of life; the major passion a person has.

> **Need-integrate:** A complete unit of behavior, with all the elements tightly bound together as a result of repeated occurrence; includes press, need, associated images and emotions, instrumental behaviors, and the particular goal that satisfies the need. Themas are abbreviated versions of need-integrates.

Needs: A state of deficit or excess stimulation that initiates and directs behavior to a goal that will satisfy the need; an organizing force of behavior.

> **Covert need:** Need that is not permitted direct expression, but that may lead to fantasy gratification.

> **Need fusion:** Several needs are gratified by the same behavior or goal, for example, making money by daring feats.

> **Need subsidiation:** One need may be subordinated to another, for example, need to be friendly to boss in order to satisfy the need for achievement through receiving a promotion.

> **Proactive need:** A need that initiates action toward a press; excess stimulation that may generate instrumental behavior; behavior aroused spontaneously from internal stimulation.

> **Reactive need:** Need resulting from initiating press, for example, anger as a reaction to aggressive behavior of another.

> **Psychogenic need:** Synonymous with psychological needs, not traceable to known organic processes; Murray specifies twenty-eight of them.

> **Viscerogenic need:** Need associated with biological deficits or excesses.

Personology: The scientific study of the total person; the name given by Murray to his formulations of human nature; also the study of the individual case.

Press: Aspects of the environment that influence personality and behavior in a positive or negative way; differs from the term *stimulus* in that it is personal to the individual, produces actions or movement.

Alpha press: The actual environmental object.

Beta press: Personal perception or interpretation of the press; discrepancies between alpha and beta press can cause serious disturbances in behavior.

Tests for needs: Standardized tests based on Murray's need construct. *TAT* (Thematic Apperception Test): A projective test, developed by Murray and Morgan, which consists of pictures to stimulate imaginative productions that reveal the dynamic forces (needs and press) that are significant for a person. The stories reveal basic themas in the person's life.

Edwards Personal Preference Schedule: A test that measures fifteen personality dimensions based on Murray's needs.

SUGGESTED READINGS

Murray, H. A., et al. *Explorations in Personality*. New York, Oxford, 1938.

Murray and associates report the results of a study they did at Harvard; the study exemplifies the use of idiographic approaches in personality study. Many of Murray's key ideas were drawn from the results of this extensive study, the most exhaustive treatment of Murray's formulations.

————. *Thematic Apperception Test Manual*. Cambridge, Mass.: Harvard University Press, 1943.

Instruction manual for the TAT, which outlines the testing procedures for this twenty-item projective test.

————, and D. W. Mackinnon. Assessment of OSS Personnel. *Journal of Consulting Psychology*, 10: 76–80, 1946.

An article outlining a test constructed for the United States Office of Strategic Services in World War II. Designed to measure stress; its object was to evaluate candidates for military intelligence.

————. *Components of an Evolving Personological System*. In D. L. Sills (ed.), *International Encyclopedia of the Social Sciences* (Vol 12). New York: Macmillan and Free Press, 1968.

Included in this article is Murray's description of his concept of three general eras of development, in which human energy is gradually built up and directed to significant external objects, thereby increasing the person's potential to deal with the conditions of life.

————, and C. Kluckhohn. Outline of a Conception of Personality. In Kluckhohn, C., Murray, H. A., and Schneider, S. M., (eds.), *Personality in Nature, Society, and Culture*, 2d ed. New York: Knopf, 1953.

A brief overview of Murray's theory.

EGO-SOCIAL MODEL

We have pointed out that the theories have resemblances; thus, there is some basis for classifying them, but it should also be noted that theories can be put into several categories. Both Jung and Murray, whom we have categorized as psychodynamic theorists, could also fit into the humanistic category. It should be kept in mind, therefore, that our categories are somewhat arbitrary. The major purpose is to bring out the distinctive features that several theories have in common.

The ego-social theories, which we will next consider, tend to place stress on the role of sociocultural factors in the development of personality and especially in the growth of the ego. Whereas Freud, Jung, and Murray were especially concerned with psychoorganismic determinants such as sexual and aggressive drives, complexes and archetypes, and the dynamic force of viscerogenic and psychogenic needs, the ego-social theories focus on the pervasive influence of sociocultural forces.

Freud and Jung reacted to the prevailing view of human nature that stressed the rational and conscious aspects of human functioning. They did not see humans as being characterized by rationality. As we have noted, Freud and Jung—and to a lesser extent Murray—were impressed with the nonrational forces, the motivational and emotional aspects. They felt that people behave out of loves and hates, jealousies and rivalries, envies and resentments, and other passionate interests and sentiments. Reasoned behavior and logic are not the ruling force, as the medieval scholars believed. Freud and Jung also reacted against the view that people are fully conscious and capable of making free choices. They demonstrated that the sources of human behavior were largely unconscious complexes, repressions, and archetypes. Murray is a transitional theorist in this regard because he does give greater weight to the ego than did Freud. Jung also introduced the idea of the urge for self-realization, but felt that most people do not attain selfhood but rather operate primarily on the level of primitive urges and conflicts. Although Freud and Jung were quite convincing in demonstrating the nonrational forces in human nature, their view of man was one-sided. The theorists we are now considering attempted to restore the balance by taking account of the *proper role of the ego* in the growth and operations of personality. They also have assigned greater weight to the *sociocultural factors* in shaping personality. The great learning capacity of humans makes the cultural environment extremely important. Cultural influences can be as powerful as basic biological drives and, in fact, can alter the manner in which they are expressed and gratified. During WWII, many young Japanese soldiers were willing to commit suicide by dive-bombing their planes into American warships as an expression of allegiance to their emperor. It was not uncommon for a Japanese man to commit suicide because he had brought shame to the family. Such acts are foreign to our Western mentality and seem to violate the all-powerful survival principle. These are cultural phenomena that are difficult to explain in Freudian and Jungian terms. Freud viewed the ego as being merely the servant of basic unconscious urges. Even rationality was used to serve basic drives as exemplified by rationalization and the other defense mechanisms. Freud and Jung viewed the driving forces as coming from within the personality rather than from environmental stimuli or situations. Our ego-social theorists reacted to this overemphasis on psychodynamics and the nonrational in humans.

Freud's views held such a prominent position that most of the theorists in this text can be understood in terms of supporting or reacting against one or other aspect of his theory. Erik Erikson accepted many of Freud's views on the development of personality, but he felt that Freud did not go far enough because he concentrated on the early years. The ego needed to be given more influence in personality development as well as the social and cultural determinants. Erikson proposed the view that personality development consisted primarily of the growth of the ego as the person confronts the major tasks of life. These tasks are the result of both personal and social changes; thus, Erikson speaks of the psychosocial stages of development. The problems of the ego change with the various periods of a person's life; thus, unlike Freud's view that personality is formed early in life, Erikson held that personality and primarily the ego undergo a variety of crises throughout the span of life. Success or failure by the ego in dealing with the major tasks of life has profound effects on the strengths of the ego and a person's entire orientation to life.

Alfred Adler also stressed the role of the ego in the formation of the style of life. He maintained that we are capable of self-direction and of gaining some control of our own destinies. He held that humans can only function fully in social settings, such as family, community, and team efforts. Social interest keeps us from becoming neurotic. Social concerns make communal living possible and reduce the harmful consequences of egoism and individualism. Adler believed that social sentiments stem from our inherent characteristics and are not the product of sublimation, as Freud held.

Karen Horney also stressed the role of the ego or self. She viewed abnormality as being primarily the loss of contact with the real self and the formation of an idealized version of the self. Her objective was to restore the dynamic real self as the directing force in the alienated person's life. For

Horney, some of the major problems of life were conflicts involving other people. She viewed social needs and environmental circumstances as critical in personality formation and functioning. We are born into a preformed culture to which we must conform. We all are affected by the contradictory demands of our culture and must somehow find individual expression within the cultural sanctions. Horney held that our major problems and conflicts are not created by our own nature, but rather by the conflicting demands of our culture.

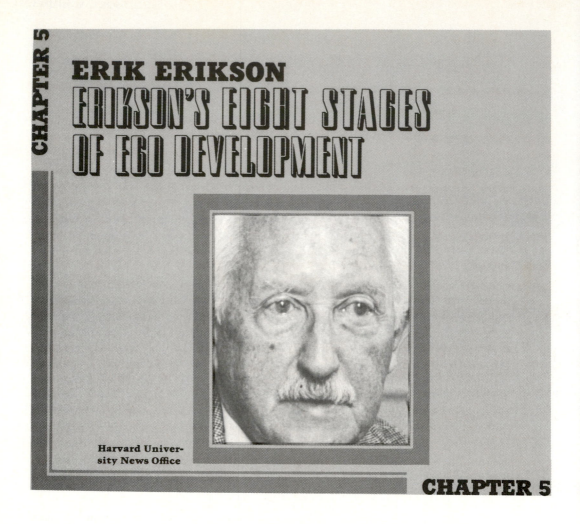

ERIK ERIKSON
ERIKSON'S EIGHT STAGES OF EGO DEVELOPMENT

Harvard University News Office

BIOGRAPHY AND HISTORICAL PERSPECTIVE

Erik Homburger Erikson was born on June 15, 1902, in Frankfort, Germany, of Danish parentage. His father abandoned his mother before his birth, and she subsequently married a pediatrician. Young Erikson was a gifted artist and resisted his stepfather's pressures to follow in his footsteps. After finishing high school, he left home, searching for his own identity, and aimlessly traveled across Europe. A schoolmate, Peter Blos, who is now a famous New York psychoanalyst, invited him to come to a training school for lay psychoanalysts in Vienna. Erikson took his friend's advice and studied under Anna Freud and August Eichorn, becoming one of the first psychoanalysts to deal with child psychiatry even though he did not have a medical degree. Sigmund Freud felt that psychoanalysts did not have to be medically trained but could specialize in the theory and practice of psychoanalysis as lay analysts.

While in Vienna, Erikson studied at a Montessori school, where special emphasis was directed toward fostering healthy growth in children. Subsequently, Erikson's formulation of a theory of child development was greatly influenced by his experiences in this school and his psychoanalytic training. He attempted to establish a psychoanalytic practice in Denmark, which was unsuccessful. He then came to the United States and established a practice in Boston. Henry A. Murray gave him his first part-time teaching position in this country at the Harvard Psychological Clinic. He also took an appointment on the staff of the Harvard Medical School, although he had only a high school education. He was called the "Ph.D. in nothing" by a fellow analyst. He was the exception; and, of course, he turned out to be the most outstanding psychoanalyst of them all.

Erikson's novel views on childhood developed through research on infantile neurosis at the Yale School of Medicine, where he held the position of research assistant in psychoanalysis from 1936 to 1939. Then, from 1939 to 1951, he was a research associate at the Institute of Child Welfare, and later he became professor of psychology at the University of California, Berkeley. During the years 1951 through 1960, he was a senior consultant at the Austen-Riggs Center and professor at the University of Pittsburgh School of Medicine. Since 1960 he has been professor of human development and lecturer on psychiatry at Harvard University. He has been retired for several years but continues to write important works in his field.

BASIC CONSTRUCTS AND POSTULATES

Psychosocial Determinants

It soon becomes apparent that Erikson's theory of personality takes in a broader area than does Freud's. Erikson encompasses aspects of personality development that he feels Freud hardly covered at all or did not stress sufficiently (Erikson, 1963). In formulating his own theory of development, he does not deny the validity of Freud's psychosexual stages. Rather he builds on them through his emphasis on the social determinants of personality growth.

Erikson's thinking is strongly influenced by the main concepts and assumptions of the psychoanalytic school. He has been innovative in his own right, however, and has introduced many new ideas, such as the pervasive role of social determinants in personality development and emphasis on the developing strengths of the ego. Because. of this, he has earned for himself the title of "ego psychologist."

Erikson holds that major conflicts in early life are caused only in part by the frustration of the sex instincts; many conflicts result from the clash between the child's nonsexual needs and desires and the expectations and limitations of his or her culture (Erikson, 1963). Because there is throughout life a total interaction between a person and his or her environment, personality growth and change cannot be restricted to the first twenty years. Erikson thus divides the life cycle into eight stages: five to cover the years up to approximately age twenty and three more to include the rest of life. Each of the stages is distinct and unique, with particular problems and needs, as well as new cultural expectations and limitations. As the ego increases in importance in the personality, a person gains increasing control of his or her circumstances and himself or herself. *Each stage presents the individual with a major task to be achieved*, such as the development of a sense of basic trust in the environment and in the self, a sense of autonomy, or a sense of industry (Erikson, 1963).

The Epigenetic Principle

Erikson holds that the eight stages of the life cycle are the result of the *epigenetic principle*. This principle states that the course of development is genetically programmed and that maturational unfolding follows a definite patterned sequence. The individual's relationships to the environment are determined by biological changes. The biological and environmental requirements must be meshed. The inner and outer requirements must fit, to some degree at least, for an individual to develop and function normally in a particular culture. Any given behavior can be understood in terms of biological, psychological, and social adjustments. While stressing the role of the ego, Erikson also accepts the role of the id through biological unfolding and the role of the superego through the influence of the sociocultural environment. Needs must be satisfied in a sociocultural setting. The genetic design directs the developing individual, but development occurs in a preexisting cultural setting, which also has a dynamic structure. Freud stressed the dynamic unfolding of instincts, but Erikson adds the dynamic operation of culture. Development does not occur in a vacuum, but rather in a cultural setting that exerts powerful demands.

Every organism, including humans, has a genetically determined nature that is manifested in growth in an orderly fashion. The course of development is remarkably similar among members of a given species and can be predicted quite confidently for a particular individual. But although growth occurs within the organism, only certain environmental conditions can make it possible, for every organism requires some form of nutrition and, in the case of humans, a great deal of sociocultural support.

What might be called schedule of development, which specifies the sequence of changes, is quite similar from child to child, although the particular time of a particular activity may vary considerably with each child. In other words, each child goes through the same steps in growth, but the time at which these steps occur varies. Many a young mother consults books on developmental norms to see whether her child is doing what the average child in his or her age group is doing. These averages are based upon actual observation of large representative samples of children at specific ages.

Virtually every aspect of personality development and functioning is the joint product of individual endowments and cultural influences. Although growth is ostensibly an organismic process, human psychobiological development is impossible without the geographical and sociocultural conditions within which growth takes place. Humans have a long childhood, and, for civilized people, the growing-up period is protracted. Many experiences, both painful and pleasureable, can alter psychobiological development during this period (Erikson, 1963).

Each culture prescribes standards that the authorities in the culture impose on its members; parents are the earliest authorities, or cultural representatives, for the child.

Because cultures differ widely on what is acceptable and unacceptable behavior, each culture produces frustrations and conflicts, thereby engendering specific personality traits in its members. Erikson (1968) believes that particular personality types and traits, such as individualism and competitiveness, may be associated with various cultures.

Cultural Changes

Cultural and physical-geographical conditions have such a pervasive influence upon the course of development that the total orientation of a people — what is worthwhile, ethical, and moral — is established by such external conditions. The powerful role of culture is manifested when there is a sudden alteration in cultural patterns, as in the case of many American Indian tribes who were brought under the influence of American education, institutions, and norms. Often the people who are the victims of such transformations are divested of cultural supports — particularly the young, who are caught between the demands, values, and practices of two divergent systems. The beliefs and practices of the primitive societies are quite opposite to the prescriptions of the imposed culture, and many new problems are created by the clash of the old and the new.

Erikson (1950, p. 14) spent some time living among the Sioux Indians, where he had the opportunity to observe the consequences of forcing them to follow American cultural practices. He discusses what happened to the Sioux Indians in South Dakota when the government took up the task of "civilizing" them.

The radical shift in cultures created many problems for the Sioux. Imagine having to give up age-old traditions and beliefs such as festivals and national and religious days of celebration. The holidays that replaced them had little meaning and, in fact, as with black Americans, actually served as reminders of racial and political prejudice and conflict. How could Washington's birthday be significant to a people who were crushed by the government whose founder was being honored?

The children particularly felt the adverse effects of the conflict between the two cultures. At home they were exposed to Sioux ideals and practices; at school they were expected to adopt American middle-class standards of conduct. Erikson (1968) reports that the teachers complained that the children were apathetic, lacking in initiative, and reeked of farm odors. The children had difficulties assimilating both cultures and adjusted to neither very successfully. Erikson believed that the sense of identity of these children, so essential to healthy development, was being seriously impaired. The young Sioux did not derive cultural supports from either source.

The discrepancy in values between the Sioux culture and the American middle-class is apparent in the following incident: A group of Sioux youngsters were taught how to play football. The teachers presented the rules repeatedly and demonstrated the game. But a strange thing occurred: No one was keeping score. The teachers were puzzled, and some made critical remarks about the impossibility of "civilizing these people." One teacher asked one of the brighter players why they were not keeping score, adding the query: "Doesn't your team want to win?" The young man pondered a bit and then quizzically retorted that everyone knew and liked everyone else, and if one team won, the other team would be unhappy. He paused for a moment, then politely added: "Why can't we just play the game; why do we have to keep score?"

Photo credits: *upper* The Bettman Archive; *lower left* Monkmeyer Press Photo Service; *lower right* NASA/Photo Researchers, Inc.

Technological advances are part of our culture and influence society.

It may be tempting to assume that the Sioux values are more natural to humans and that our values tend to be artificial. Sioux culture fitted the conditions of the environment and level of civilization that prevailed at the time of confrontation with white civilization. It was as much the product of circumstances and traditions as ours. The typical Sioux could not function well in a middle-class American setting just as the typical American would not find Sioux culture suitable for his or her aims and aspirations.

Earlier in their history the Sioux were nomads. They depended on the buffalo for survival and followed its migrations. A necessary condition of nomadic living was communal generosity. Because reserves of food were limited, an individual's very survival was contingent upon the goodwill of others. The successful hunter was expected to share his bounty. When the Sioux were forced to live on government reservations, many of the old traditions remained. Communal living and noncompetitiveness stayed key values. While the white American child is brought up with capitalistic ideals — ambitiousness, competitiveness, economic independence — the Sioux child grows up in a culture where communal values are stressed over individualism.

The ideals of the Sioux culture do not harmonize well with those of a capitalistic society. For the Sioux, competition means a victor and a loser, and to be the loser means to be put in an inferior role. The middle-class American child learns to follow rules that guide his or her competitiveness, but winning is all-important. The loser must be a "good loser," which means that he or she must accept his or her own deficiencies gracefully, at least publicly. In a society where survival depends upon sharing and the generosity of those who are able or lucky, the idea of asserting individual supremacy is not only repugnant but actually dangerous to the survival of the group. Another point here is that child-rearing practices and goals reflect the nature of living conditions, and these practices and goals pressure the child to be a contributing member of the society.

We can look to our own life situations for other examples of the influence of cultural and environmental forces. Growing up involves a continuing series of adjustments, for the world outside the home is certainly quite different from immediate family circumstances. Everyone has to learn how to get along with other children, with adults, and with authority figures. The school environment places further adjustive demands upon us. As we move up the grades, there are increasing requirements: for independence, for initiative, for industry, for self-definition. In a sense, the new requirements compete with the old habits, and, like the Indians, we may have difficulty accepting the new and shedding the old. In the early stages of a new environment, we may long for our earlier circumstances because they are familiar and we have learned to deal with them. The ability to accomodate oneself to changing circumstances is a mark of maturity, Erikson believes (1968).

The Eight Stages of Life

As we discuss Erikson's eight stages of life, keep in mind that each stage, if successfully encountered and lived through, adds something to the ego. Erikson (1964) refers to these ego attainments as *ego strengths*. He is one of a few leading psychologists who have made a place in their system for what were traditionally termed virtues—such as hope, will, courage, purpose, fidelity. For Erikson these ego strengths are not sublimations but actual attainments of the ego. As the child grows, there are changes in potentialities and abilities, but there is also increased vulnerability to injury. Learning to do more for himself or herself, the child increases his or her susceptibility to frustrations and conflicts. And although the successful attainment of a particular achievement—for instance, a sense of trust—prepares a child to live more effectively, he or she may easily "backslide" or regress. However, if a crisis is not resolved successfully at the appropriate stage of development, later experiences can provide a second chance: a trustworthy teacher, for example, can undo the psychological damage done by cruel or inattentive parents. But it should be noted that an achievement mastered at the appropriate stage may prepare the growing child to take on the tasks of the next stage; thus, it will have an even greater likelihood of becoming a continuing influence on the child's personality as the subsequent tasks are mastered.

GENERAL CHARACTERISTICS OF THE EIGHT STAGES

To Erikson, the same problems recur throughout life. He distinguishes between the *immature* phase, the *critical* phase, and the *resolution* phase of these universal problems (1968). For example, a child is confronted with the problem of self-identity (who he or she really is); so also is the adolescent, the young adult, the middle-aged person, and the elderly individual. The identity problem is not as acute for the child as for the adolescent or young adult when it reaches its *critical* phase. The problem is in its *immature* phase for the child; but if adequately dealt with during its critical phase, it is in the *resolution* phase for the later stages. On the other hand, the problem of autonomy (asserting independence) is in the critical phase at the age of two. During adolescence, the search for identity reaches the *critical* phase because, at this time, a variety of biological, psychological, and social conditions such as sexual maturity, parental and other expectations, and approaching adult status strongly bring out the need for self-definition, the so-called identity crisis. *By crisis, Erikson does not mean overwhelming stress, but rather a turning point or changed perspective in the life of the individual, when a new problem must be confronted and mastered.*

The *resolution* of those conflicts and problems associated with each period of life helps to make normal development possible. Failure to attain specific ego strengths when it is crucial to do so results in a carry-over of problems and necessarily impedes efforts to solve the new problems of the following stages. The young adult who fails to establish a firm sense of identity during adolescence cannot form an intimate association with others when this task becomes critical in the next stage of development. Thus he or she may experience difficulties in marriage, in work, and in recreational activities because he or she cannot relate with others in a satisfying way. The eight psychosocial tasks associated with Erikson's stages of life are quite general, and each influences the whole orientation to life.

Major problems are conflicts.   During each stage of life, according to Erikson (1963), an individual is confronted with a major problem *that is really a basic conflict;*

it remains a recurrent problem throughout life although it may take different forms at various periods. For instance, the lifelong dependence upon the external environment and the necessity of trusting our ability to deal with it create a conflict between a sense of trust and mistrust.

No one can ever establish a perfectly secure life situation. The sense of trust or mistrust thus determines the manner in which we face life. Erikson delineates eight major developmental crises that occur in different stages throughout the life cycle (1963). We will discuss these in detail later. To get a first impression of them, however, consider some of the basic decisions we must make: How much independence should we have? How hard and how long should we work for what we want? How much of ourselves should we give to others?

Ritualization and ritualism. The various stages of development, according to Erikson, require the harmonious interplay of unfolding maturational requirements and existing social and cultural conditions. In spite of wide geographical and sociocultural differences, Erikson (1977) holds that the human species is capable of surviving in a variety of environments. The newborn child has the task of becoming what Erikson terms *speciated;* that is, the child must become enculturated. Each individual must acquire the customs, beliefs, values, and acceptable patterns of behavior sanctioned by a particular society. The standards and practices of a culture are communicated to the young by *ritualizations*, which are *recurring patterns of behavior characteristic of a particular society*. Erikson points out the role of ritualization in the following passage:

> It is only a seeming paradox that newly born Man, who could, in principle and probably within some genetic limits, fit into any number of pseudo-species [other categories of humans] and their habitats, must for that very reason be coaxed and induced to become "speciated" during a prolonged childhood by some form of family: he must be *familiarized by ritualization* with a particular version of human existence . . . from the outset that ritualization is an aspect of everyday life which is more clearly seen in a different culture or class or even family than our own, where, in fact, ritualization is more often than not experienced simply as the only proper way to do things; and the question is only why does not everybody do it our way. I share, I am sure, with all anthropologists (professional and amateur) the wonder with which one encounters in the field old people who will tenderly describe what once was appropriate in their culture, displaying a sense of moral and aesthetic rightness in details unquestionably sanctioned by the universe. [1977, pp. 79–80][1]

For Erikson, ritualization refers to daily routines that make life meaningful in a particular society. We relate to each other with particular ways of greeting and departing, for example, kissing, hugging, handclasping. We address certain people with titles and experience a sense of respect for their status. The person is given guides of conduct that set boundaries to permissible behavior. At a dance, you are permitted to make contact with a stranger whereas this behavior is not tolerated in other settings. You may shake hands with a friend and greet your friend's wife with a brief hug under certain conditions.

[1]Quotation is reprinted from *Toys and Reasons, Stages in the Ritualization of Experience*, by Erik H. Erikson, by permission of W. W. Norton & Company, Inc. Copyright © 1977 by W. W. Norton & Company, Inc. Published in Great Britain and the Commonwealth by Marion Boyars Ltd., London.

Erikson uses the term *ritualism* to refer to an *inappropriate ritualization*. We need certain authority figures as models and sources of inspiration, but if we idealize and idolize them, we experience needless inferiority or debilitating apathy. There are right and wrong ways of doing things, but we may be caught up in the formality of situations rather than the purpose that we are trying to achieve. Ritualism may be taken as false ritualizations. They are the causes of social and psychological pathology. Ritualisms lead to excess and artificiality.

Erikson (1977) specifies ritualizations and ritualisms for each of the psychosocial stages. Again, it should be kept in mind that ritualizations are *culturally approved patterns* of behaviors that enable a person to become an acceptable member of the culture. Ritualisms are *abnormalities;* they are *exaggerations of ritualizations.* Abnormalities may also take the form of deficiencies. A distrusting person may relate to people through the ritualism of idolism, which is an exaggerated ritualization of normal social interaction. On the other hand, many distrusting people avoid human contacts altogether because they are suspicious of others.

STAGE ONE, INFANCY: TRUST VERSUS MISTRUST (HOPE)

During the first year of postnatal life, the infant faces his or her first major challenge, the outcome of which has a profound effect on all later developments, Erikson believes (1963). The infant is torn between trusting and mistrusting the things and people in his or her environment. A sense of trust develops if the infant's needs are met without too much frustration. A trustful environment also determines development of trust in one's self; self-confidence. A sense of trust is manifested in faith in the environment and optimism about the future. A sense of mistrust is revealed through suspiciousness, inwardness, and fearful and anxious concern with security. The child who has achieved a basic sense of trust views his or her surroundings as predictable and consistent.

During early life, the nature of the infant requires that he or she receive appropriate satisfaction of basic needs — especially the need for mothering — because the infant can do little to meet them. The infant's orientation is incorporative: he or she relates to the environment by receiving. There is no other time, except under certain conditions of illness and aging, when helplessness is so complete. A child's needs must be satisfied not only at the proper time but in the proper amount. Failure in either respect may result in a variety of disturbances. We can experience this feeling of infantile helplessness during highly traumatic moments, such as following the sudden loss of a loved one.

A child must also become regulated to the mother's schedule, or there will be conflict between them. How can a mother help to create a sense of trust in her child? Erikson offers the following suggestions:

> Mothers create a sense of trust in their children by the kind of administration which in its quality combines sensitive care of the baby's individual needs and a firm sense of personal trustworthiness within the trusted framework of their community's life style. This forms the very basis in the child for a component of the sense of identity which will later

combine a sense of being "all right," of being oneself, and of becoming what other people trust one will become. Parents must not only have certain ways of guiding by prohibition and permission, they must also be able to represent to the child a deep, almost somatic conviction that there is a meaning in what they are doing. In this sense, a traditional system of child care can be said to be a factor making for trust, even where items of that tradition taken singly, may seem arbitrarily or unnecessarily cruel, or lenient. [Erikson, 1968, p. 103][2]

Erikson believes that if the relationship between mother and child is mutually satisfying, the child apparently receives a sense of "inner goodness" through a harmonious interaction with the mother, which does not have to be continually reaffirmed (1968). Children lacking a sense of trust display signs of insecurity if their mothers leave even for a short while. It seems essential that the child experience security in need gratification through warm and consistent care from those who minister to him or her. The mother whose care for her child harmonizes with the child's needs engenders in him or her a sense of being *acceptable*, of being *good* and *lovable*, and these are the essential ingredients of the sense of basic trust. People who have a sense of basic trust feel at one with themselves and with others; they feel "good and all right" and acceptable to those around them. They can be themselves and like to be themselves. If their sense of trust is unusually well developed, they acquire the virtue of abiding *hope*, an optimistic outlook on life.

The sense of basic trust is never attained permanently and, in fact, even early in life, undergoes a severe test as we will see in the next crisis that confronts the growing child in the stage of autonomy. The helpless infant orients to the environment, at first almost exclusively by incorporating and receiving. But the infant soon learns to assert himself or herself by resisting, accepting, or rejecting what is offered to him or her. As the infant's needs increase and knowledge and abilities grow, his or her relationship with the surroundings takes a more active turn; instead of having an exclusively incorporate and receptive orientation, the infant begins to participate actively by using increased knowledge and skills in exploring, manipulating, and grasping the things he or she needs or wants. Taking or actively getting rather than receiving and accepting become the child's major modes of orientation to the environment before he or she is two years old. By asserting himself or herself, the child comes into conflict with the people in the world who have power over him or her. His or her sense of trust may be shaken, because at this stage the mother may begin to lose her "motherly" feelings toward the child as Fromm has pointed out (1947).

Numinous versus idolism   Erikson names the earliest ritualization the *numinous* ritualization. It occurs as a result of the repeated interactions of mother and infant. The mother acts and reacts in the presence of her baby in routine ways as she goes about caring for the child's needs. The child in turn acts and reacts in relation to the mother. There is mutual recognition and affirmation: the child needs the mother, and

---

[2]Quotation is reprinted from *Identity: Youth and Crisis*, by Erik H. Erikson, by permission of W. W. Norton & Company, Inc. Copyright © 1968 by W. W. Norton & Company, Inc. Published in Great Britain and the Commonwealth by Faber and Faber Publishers, London.

the mother needs the child. Ideally, each affirms the identity of the other in the relationship. Erikson points out that:

> There is much to suggest that man is born with the need for such regular and mutual affirmation and certification: we know at any rate that its absence can harm an infant radically, by diminishing or extinguishing his search for impressions which will verify his senses. . . . Of all psychological disturbances which we have learned to connect ontogenetically [within the life span of the individual] with early stages of life, the deepest and most devastating are those in which the light of mutual recognition and hope is early forfeited in autistic and psychotic withdrawal. [1977, pp. 88–89][3]

The formation of a sense of trust in the environment and the acquisition of the attribute of hope are fostered by social relationships in which there is mutual respect and support. In such a relationship the other person is revered. What Erikson seems to be saying is that we need people (including numinous religious figures) that inspire devotion in us. A distortion of the numinous ritualization is what Erikson terms the *ritualism of idolism*. Idolism is an exaggeration of reverence and respect. Paradoxically, it may result in overestimation of self (narcissism) on the one hand or idealization of others on the other hand.

The trusting person is capable of the numinous ritualization, by which Erikson means *social responsiveness*. The term *numinous* refers to profound emotional experiences. The sociable person experiences social feeling and sentiments in the presence of others. Social skills and customs are valued and practiced in order to please others. The exaggerated expression is the ritualism of idolism: excessive admiration and idealization of others. We should note that a distrusting person may simply lack social feelings and skills. For each of the stages, Erikson specifies a ritualism that is to be understood as an exaggeration of a ritualization, and hence it is an abnormality. However, failure in developing the appropriate ego strength may be expressed in many forms of abnormality.

STAGE TWO, EARLY CHILDHOOD: AUTONOMY VERSUS SHAME AND DOUBT (WILL)

With the development of perceptual and muscular skills, the child gains increasing autonomy of action. Two modes of dealing with his or her surroundings, although previously existing in primitive form, become dominant ways of coping: holding on to things and letting them go. These are expressions of the developing will. This necessary step in growth may put the child in conflict with the significant people in his or her life. It marks clear assertion of the ego and often the child's demands are directly opposed by others. Furthermore, because of the immaturity of the child's psychological faculties, he or she lacks discretion in the use of these modalities and may resist the demands of parents by obstinate tenacity; in toilet training, he or she may refuse to cooperate with the mother's wishes: indeed, the child may generalize this approach to

---

[3]Quotation is reprinted from *Toys and Reasons, Stages in the Ritualization of Experience*, by Erik H. Erikson, by permission of W. W. Norton & Company, Inc. Copyright © 1977 by W. W. Norton & Company, Inc. Published in Great Britain and the Commonwealth by Marion Boyars Ltd., London.

all of his or her dealings with others. A child may also "let go" in hostile and aggressive ways, creating friction and conflict, and immaturity may make him or her extremely vulnerable to feelings of shame and doubt. Shame here means feeling of being unacceptable to others whereas doubt means fear of self-assertiveness.

Because the child has not yet learned to avoid certain situations, such as the mother's bad moods, he or she easily becomes the victim of her displaced aggression. The child may make the same mistakes over and over through ignorance, and the parents may interpret this as defiance. Struggling to meet the demands of the environment and encountering frequent failures, frustrations, and rebuffs, a child may develop a sense of self-doubt. One result may be the development of obsessional and compulsive trends: doubting his or her own abilities, the child limits participation in life to fixed and rigid routines and may do only what is safe and what fits within the limits set by the significant people in his or her life. At the other extreme, a child may develop aggressive and hostile tendencies and react negatively to all external and internal controls. The need to overcome self-doubt may be so strong as to engender a rebellious and self-assertive orientation that overrides the effects of parental rewards, so that parental approval is not valued as highly as the reward that accrues from self-assertiveness. The child may actually develop a hatred of his or her parents and generalize it to any authority figure and to restriction of any kind: rules, standards, laws. Self-esteem is bolstered not by conformity to cultural expectations but by negativism. Overconformity with blocking of impulses and the total lack of respect for regulation and control are two of the extreme disturbances caused by a sense of self-doubt; there are many others as well.

In addition to a sense of self-doubt, a child may develop a sense of shame that persists throughout life. Shame results when the ego is exposed and defenseless in the face of unfavorable or unflattering scrutiny. It is an undesirable form of self-consciousness, an injury to self-esteem, produced by the censorship and disapproval of others; thus, it is caused by outside evaluations rather than by self-evaluations, which may stem from conscience and be experienced as guilt and which occur in the next stage of development. Before conscience develops sufficiently, guilt is not possible, but shame may be felt quite early. It should be noted that the child's uncontrollable impulses may be the basis for the development of a lifelong sense of doubt and shame, and subsequently guilt.

A child is small and inferior in relation to those who have power over him or her; he or she thus has a tendency to undervalue the self and, at the same time, to overvalue those who have this authority. If parents, teachers, and older children downgrade and belittle a child's accomplishments, he or she may feel worthless, dirty, and evil and begin to believe that what he or she does or produces is of no value. Here we can see the foundations of a profound sense of self-doubt, shame, and inferiority. Many parents encourage such feelings because they are impatient with their child's level of accomplishment; they either continually berate the child for doing things badly or are forever pushing him or her into things that are beyond the child's capabilities. Sometimes the child may react in a opposite way and flout all authority or callously disregard the interests and rights of others. Which reaction occurs depends upon the nature of the child and on the methods that are used to shame him or her.

As conscience begins to take shape (the foundation of the next stage), it exerts control over behavior. It exercises this control through self-rewards and self-punishments expressed as pride and self-hate. The form of guilt that is the result of a poorly developed conscience also promotes self-doubt. Conscience provides a source of inner controls and a model for desirable conduct. Before conscience develops, external regulations and controls dominate. If you obey these inner and outer sources of control, you can avoid a great deal of doubt, shame, and guilt. Why don't some individuals use their consciences in this manner? The reason is that the urge for autonomy competes with the voice of conscience. We can see the effects of this conflict between conscience and autonomy in unhealthy traits such as willfulness and rigidity in decision making or in healthy traits such as cooperativeness and conformity to expectations. These traits (which make a great difference between a satisfying life-style and one that leads to dissatisfaction, unhappiness, and a feeling of being trapped) thus have their origins during the stage when autonomy is a crisis. It should be noted that these traits are healthy or unhealthy expressions of will.

Before conscience is developed, the culture usually provides an all-important code of laws to regulate the child's conduct and to assist him or her in attaining a limited measure of autonomy while avoiding doubt and shame. Other subtle guidelines—tradition, customs, mores, folkways, taboos—help the child to know what he or she should or should not do to be acceptable as a member of the culture. Justice on the institutitional level and fairness on the individual level ensure the protection of rights and guarantee a certain degree of equality of autonomy for all. The individual, if development is normal, gradually acquires a knowledge of his or her rights and limitations and even of his or her privileges, if he or she happens to have advantages over others. The individual also learns obligations. Just as the parents' own sense of trust is communicated to their child and affects the development of the child's sense of trust, so their degree of autonomy affects the conditions for the development of his autonomy. Parents who value conservative conformity can hardly expect development of individualism in their child. A fearful, anxious mother may have such an influence over her child that these traits will become enduring features of the child's orientation to life.

In brief, some very basic attitudes are formed during the second stage of development, when the need for autonomy creates a crisis. The formation of these attitudes depends upon how successfully the crisis is resolved and on how well the ego fares. If a person develops a sense of autonomy to an unusual degree, he or she will demonstrate the virtues of *courage, self-control*, and *will power* (Erikson, 1965). Favorable or unfavorable outcomes in autonomy are best understood according to Erikson in terms of healthy or unhealthy expressions of will.

Judicious versus legalism.   Autonomy is served by exercise of will. But assertion of will can get you into trouble unless you know the limitations and boundaries within which autonomous behavior can occur. You must learn to discriminate right from wrong, the acceptable from the unacceptable. The freedom of self-expression requires sensitivity to the approval and disapproval of others. Erikson refers to the ritualization of this period as the *judicious*. He says:

> The ontological source of this second kind of ritualization is the second stage of life, characterized as it is by rapid advances in psychosocial *autonomy*. As the ability to crawl and

eventually to stand serves increased self-reliance, it also soon leads to play with the boundaries of the permissible. If, to the first stage, namely, infancy, I have ascribed the rudiments of *hope*, I consider *will* to be the basic strength founded in the second stage, that is, early childhood. The new acquisitions in cognitive as well as in muscular and locomotor capacities and the increased readiness for interplay with others fosters, under favorable conditions, a great pleasure in exerting one's will and in being found both capable of and justified in using it. This, then, is the ontogenetic origin of that great human preoccupation with "free will" which will look for and find its test in the ritualization in daily life of making judgments as to what constitutes arenas for self-assertion. [1977, pp. 92–93][4]

We need to learn to judge ourselves from the standpoint of those who judge us, so that we are not unacceptable to others, particularly those who have power over us. Eventually, the superego will aid us in this most difficult task. We are confronted with the choice of doubting ourselves or those who judge us. Neither course in extreme form is desirable. The child needs to have fairly clear indications of right and wrong if self-doubt and a sense of shame are to be minimized. The ritualization that serves the exercise of will is termed by Erikson the judicious ritualization. It refers to laws, rules, regulations, honored practices, and formality in everyday life. An abnormal form of ritualization is the *ritualism* that Erikson terms *legalism*, being preoccupied with the letter, rather than the spirit, of the law. An example of legalism is the English teacher who is more concerned with grammar than with the quality of content. Erikson warns that compliance with the law or regulations may result from fear rather than personal assent to the worth of such controls. Ritualizations prevent the harmful consequences of ritualism.

The term *judicious ritualization* is Erikson's way of summarizing *codes of acceptable conduct*. The child who enjoys a sense of autonomy knows the rules and roles that are appropriate. A child with a sense of doubt or shame may follow exaggerated expressions of rules, the ritualism of legalism. Of course, the defect in autonomy may result in other forms of abnormalities, such as lack of risk-taking or failure to participate in social interactions.

STAGE THREE, PLAY AGE: INITIATIVE VERSUS GUILT (PURPOSE)

During the ages from about three to five, the need for autonomy takes a more vigorous form; it becomes more coordinated, efficient, spontaneous, and goal-directed. In this period, the major accomplishment of the ego, according to Erikson (1963), is a sense of initiative, and failure in this task is experienced as guilt. If self-doubt and shame are the result of failure in acquiring a sense of autonomy, a profound and enduring sense of guilt and unworthiness is the result of failure in acquiring a sense of initiative. The capacities and abilities that were maturing during the stage of autonomy continue to mature; but the efforts at autonomy now take on greater activity and direction: under-

---

[4]Quotation is reprinted from *Toys and Reasons, Stages in the Ritualization of Experience*, by Erik H. Erikson, by permission of W. W. Norton & Company, Inc. Copyright © 1977 by W. W. Norton & Company, Inc. Published in Great Britain and the Commonwealth by Marion Boyars Ltd., London.

taking, attacking, planning. The child can do essential things effortlessly — walking, running, and picking things up — which previously he or she struggled to do; thus, energy can be used more efficiently. In fact the child's energy level is greater, and he or she can work and play at things for longer periods of time. Because the child can do so many more things, failure at a task can easily be forgotten as he or she quickly turns to something else. (Erikson, 1956)

Here is what Erikson thinks about the stage of initiative while offering some pertinent observations regarding all the stages of development:

> There is in every child at every stage a new miracle of vigorous unfolding, which constitutes a new hope and a new responsibility for all. Such is the sense of the pervading quality of initiative. The criteria for all these senses and qualities are the same: a crisis, more or less beset with fumbling and fear, is resolved, in that the child suddenly seems to "grow together" both in his person and in his body. He appears "more himself," more loving, relaxed and brighter in his judgement, more activated and activating. He is in free possession of a surplus of energy which permits him to forget failures quickly and to approach what seems desirable (even if it also seems uncertain and even dangerous) with undiminished and more accurate direction. [1963, p 255][5]

Following the Freudian notion of infantile sexuality, Erikson (1963) holds that the attempt at developing a sense of initiative takes on a sexual aspect, although rudimentary in character at first. The boy becomes romantically interested in his mother and actively engages in primitive courting. More broadly, the boy derives pleasure from male aggressiveness and feats of conquest. He is curious, active, and intrusive. A girl becomes romantically interested in her father. Her sexual initiative turns to modes of "catching," aggressive forms of snatching, or making herself attractive and endearing. Erikson describes the sexual aspect of the striving for initiative as follows:

> This then is the stage of the "castration complex," the intensified fear of finding the (now energetically erotized) genitals harmed as a punishment for the fantasies attached to their excitement. Infantile sexuality and incest taboo, castration complex and superego, all unite here to bring about that specifically human crisis during which the child must turn from an exclusive, pregenital attachment to his parents to the new process of becoming a parent, a carrier of tradition. [1963, p. 256][6]

In the preceding passage, the influence of Freudian concepts and principles on Erikson's formulations is quite apparent; again it should be clear that Erikson does not modify Freud's ideas as much as he extends them. In accepting such controversial concepts as the Oedipus and castration complexes, the incest motive, and the superego, he opens himself to the same criticisms that we have applied to Freud. Nevertheless, Erikson moderates Freud's ideas to an extent, bringing them more in line with conventional principles of child development by giving a strong place during this period to both the ego and social influences.

[5,6]Quotation is reprinted from *Childhood and Society*, 2nd Edition, by Erik H. Erikson, by permission of W. W. Norton & Company, Inc. Copyright 1950, 1963 by W. W. Norton & Company, Inc. Published in Great Britain and the Commonwealth by the Hogarth Press Ltd., London.

The efforts at initiative, like the strivings for autonomy, often bring the child into collison with powerful people who can make him or her feel guilty for intruding and asserting himself or herself. The child competes for and desires things that adults regard as their prerogatives — to take the mother's attention from the father, in the case of the boy; to be favored by the father, in the case of the girl; to be included in adult conversations and concerns and to be given the privileges of adult status, in the case of both. If the parents are too harsh with the child and put him or her down for interference in their activities, the child will develop a sense of guilt.

The sense of initiative is greatly influenced by the development of the *superego*. The superego consists of two components: *conscience* (internal regulations, rules, and taboos), and the *ego ideal* (internalized images and models of acceptable and laudable conduct). It is the part of the superego that supervises and watches over the active ego. It is the moral agent of personality, reflecting the values and norms, as well as the taboos, of the culture. These are communicated in a variety of ways to the child: by parents, by other children, by institutions, by model persons and heroes of society. The superego has the power to produce guilt in the ego if it does not follow the dictates of the conscience or live up to the prescriptions of the ego ideal. The guilt is felt as unworthiness, dissatisfaction with self, and often depression. With the development of the superego, then, the ego begins to receive inner censorship in addition to external censorship, which began with the stage of autonomy. The inner restrictions may become so severe that the person limits his or her potential gratifications to a remarkable degree. In such instances the person may be described as inhibited and may in fact require extensive therapy to lessen the tyranny of the superego.

In the early stages of the formulation of the superego, some children are all too willing to restrict and punish themselves. Pathological trends may thus develop: chronic self-depreciation, compulsive overconformity, deep and lasting resentment resulting from failure to meet standards the way others do. When the superego persists in an infantile form, it hampers the free expression of the ego; hence the development of a sense of initiative is blocked, and the fullest potentials of the ego are never realized. The ego must eventually lessen the tyranny and power of the superego by becoming strong and taking over the personality.

Erikson (1963) points out that although the superego can be a serious hindrance to personality development and functioning, with the appropriate training and experience it can become an important personal asset. If development is normal, the child is quite eager to identify with the important people in his or her life: parents, teachers, heroes, and other models of the culture. The child is ready at this stage for the beginnings of cooperative ventures and for rudimentary productive work. Such activities can strengthen his or her capabilities for meeting the requirements of the next stage, when new problems will be confronted. If the child's development is normal during this stage, Erikson holds that the ego gains another important strength — the virtue of purpose or directionality.

Authenticity versus impersonation. Erikson points out that children use play behavior to deal with the psychosocial crisis of the play age, namely, initiative versus guilt. Play enables the child to relive or to correct or simply to recreate past experiences as a means of clarification of what constitutes authentic roles. The play behavior offers opportunities, not available through actual behavior, of trying a variety of roles and behaviors that are approved and also suitable to the child's individuality. Exploration of guilt-producing behavior is also possible through play behavior. In solitary or cooperative play, the child assumes a variety of roles that represent both the accepted and disapproved roles of society. In the child's dramatizations, rewards and punishments sanctioned by society are imposed.

Erikson (1977) refers to the ritualization of the play age as authenticity, which refers to the dramatizations of culturally accepted roles as a means of resolving the conflict between initiative and guilt. The formation of the ego ideal occurs during this period. The child internalizes standards of conduct and roles that are sanctioned and also rejects those that are disapproved. Initiative is given concrete lines of permissibility and restriction.

The ritualism that may result is impersonation, or the assumption of fake roles and poses. Individuals may glorify themselves by pretending to have attributes that they do not possess. Other forms of pathology that may result from faulty resolution of the crises of initiative are repression of thought and inhibition of activity. The person dares not think or imagine certain lines of behavior or take certain actions. The other extreme is also possible; the person may identify with unacceptable roles and act out his or her impulses without guilt.

Children with a well-developed sense of initiative can be themselves and act authentically through acceptable cultural rules for sex, age, status, and setting. The exaggerated expression is impersonation: attempting to impress others with artificial roles. We have noted that other forms of abnormalities can also result from an improperly formed superego.

STAGE FOUR, SCHOOL AGE: INDUSTRY VERSUS INFERIORITY (COMPETENCE)

With a basic sense of trust, an adequate sense of autonomy, and an appropriate amount of initiative, the child enters the stage of developing industry. The fantasies and magical ideas of childhood must give way to the task of preparing for acceptable roles in society. The child becomes acquainted with the "tool" world at home and at school. Play continues, but productive work and real achievements are expected. *Skills and knowledge are to be acquired:* whether they are taught in a formal school setting or in a field situation depends on the culture, but every culture provides some arrangement for the training of children. Here we are reminded of one of Mischel's cognitive variables, the ability to generate appropriate knowledge and skills (Chapter 13).

The child of this age might be described as *an apprentice in the art of learning the tasks of adulthood.* The training period is usually quite lengthy in civilized societies because so much is expected of the individual. There are many possible ways of living in a highly diversified technological society, and the best educational preparation has not yet been devised; Erikson criticizes the current education system for being an independent culture, not really in tune with the requirements of living after schooling. Many others have argued the same point. Schooling seems more to deaden and stultify creativity than to enliven it; it forces everyone into a mold, which is not suitable for modern living in a complex society.

Although learning before the age of six concentrates primarily upon such basic skills as talking, walking, dressing, and eating, the grammar school years widen these skills to include productive work, independent social living, and the beginnings of personal responsibility. The child learns to win rewards and praise by making and doing things that are more than facsimiles of real achievements. Erikson (1968) holds that if all goes well during the period between six and twelve, the child will begin to develop two important virtues: *method* and *competence*. Usually children are eager to be like adults, and if they are not stifled in their efforts, they will willingly meet the demands placed upon them. But if these demands are contrary to their natural tendencies (as they often are in formal education, when, for instance, children are expected to sit attentively for long periods of time), they will rebel and resist what Maslow called "the breaking of his psychological bones." (Maslow, 1968c) What happens during this period if things go wrong? Erikson tells us:

> The child's danger, at this stage, lies in the sense of inadequacy and inferiority. If he despairs of his tools and skills or of his status among his tool partners, he may be discouraged from identification with them and with a section of the tool world. To lose the hope of such "industrial" association may pull him back to the more isolated, less tool-conscious familial rivalry of the Oedipal time. The child despairs of his equipment in the tool world and in anatomy and considers himself doomed to mediocrity or inadequacy. It is at this point that wider society becomes significant in its ways of admitting the child to an understanding of meaningful roles in the technology and economy. Many a child's development is disrupted when family life has failed to prepare him for school life, or when school life fails to sustain the promises of earlier stages. [1963, p. 260][7]

> And again: but there is another, more fundamental danger, namely, man's restriction of himself and constriction of his horizons to include only his work to which, so the book says, he has been sentenced after his expulsion from paradise. If he accepts work as his only obligation, and "what works" as his only criterion of worthwhileness, he may become the conformist and thoughtless slave of his technology and of those who are in a position to exploit it. [1963, p. 261][8]

Formality versus formalism. The ritualization of formality occurs during school age. The growing child learns appropriate skills, methodical performance, and standards of perfection. Play is transformed into work. As contrasted with the judicious ritualization, which refers to morally and socially right conduct, the ritualization of formality refers to *appropriate ways* of doing something. Problem-solving skills and strategies promote a sense of industry and competence.

Formality may be expressed in the *ritualism* of *formalism*-perfectionism, empty ceremonialism. The student whose only concern in college is grades would exemplify the ritualism of formalism. In referring to the name of this ritualism, Erikson says:

[7,8]Quotation is reprinted from *Childhood and Society*, 2nd Edition, by Erik H. Erikson, by permission of W. W. Norton & Company, Inc. Copyright 1950, 1963 by W. W. Norton & Company, Inc. Published in Great Britain and the Commonwealth by the Hogarth Press Ltd., London.

". . . whatever the name, it must express the fact that human striving for method and logic can also lead to that self-enslavement which makes of each man what Marx called a 'craft idiot,' that is, one who for the sake of a proficiency will forget and deny the human context within which it has a significance and maybe dangerous function." (1977, p. 106) One may be so captivated by making money that it becomes an end in itself rather than a means. One may be so preoccupied with proficiency that outcomes are ignored, for example, more and better nuclear weapons.

A person who has achieved a sense of industry uses the ritualism of formality, which may be interpreted as *effective ways of doing things*. The person who feels inferior may resort to the ritualism of formalism: the pretense of being competent. Again, as with the other ego failures, there are other forms of abnormalities. The person who feels inferior may avoid competition and active efforts to overcome limitations.

STAGE FIVE, ADOLESCENCE: IDENTITY VERSUS ROLE CONFUSION (FIDELITY)

The "search for identity" is a commonly used expression that has become associated with Erikson's work. Erikson (1968) holds that the search for identity, although an ever-present concern throughout life, reaches a crisis point during adolescence when many significant changes in the total person, but especially in the self, take place. Identity refers to *an integration of roles*. In the highly specialized technological society of Western cultures, the adolescent period is quite long because the preparations for independent adult status are greater than in simpler societies. The result is that the young person is caught in an identity problem: still a child in some respects, yet with adult needs, still dependent yet expected to behave independently, sexually mature yet unable to satisfy sexual needs, the adolescent does not know who he or she really is. In Western societies adolescence is a period of storm and turmoil. The adult world has difficulty defining the adolescent's roles, and so does the adolescent.

Many young persons resort to the formation of their own subculture, which is often quite different from, and even antagonistic to, the prevailing culture. This subculture may satisfy to some degree the adolescent's need for identity, but it does not deal with other needs that may be met only by taking on an approved role in the cultural mainstream. A political activist who believes in the equality of all people, whether they work or not, may run into difficulty meeting the requirements of life in our society if he or she does not engage in some kind of gainful employment. Every society sets up certain prototypes of work for both sexes, and those who deviate too much from these will encounter disapproval, censure, and even imprisonment.

It will be recalled that for Erikson ego identity is inner continuity or inner sameness; it may be taken simply as a *core ego role* that is acceptable to the individual and to the circle of people who are important to the individual. The nature of the social circle varies considerably throughout life but attains an extremely sensitive level during adolescence. Like every other aspect of personality, the search for identity follows a developmental course, with adolescence as the high point, but with another peak late

Jean-Claude Lejeune/EKM Nepenthe

Freedom expressed by conformity.

in life as we face the termination of our existence. The failure to attain a sense of identity Erikson (1963) terms *role confusion*.

The sense of identity may be considered from a measurement point of view: it may occupy a point on a continuum from extreme role confusion at one end to a firm sense of identity at the other. In actuality, a fixed point does not describe accurately the fluid state of so complex a phenomenon as ego functioning; a better picture is a range of identity feelings that vary with both internal and external conditions.

A brief look at the history of the search for identity may help to highlight the place that this aspect of ego development holds in the growth of the child. The earliest attempts at establishing a sense of identity are based on achievement: the child is praised and rewarded for doing certain things such as drinking from a cup, riding a bicycle alone, or doing homework without assistance. The earliest achievements thus relate to personal management and play activities. With respect to the latter, Erikson (1968) makes the interesting point that in civilized societies such achievements have no bearing on adult work except in a highly superficial way. Though during the stage of industry the child does learn to do many things that adults do—reading, writing, and ciphering—these accomplishments are still in the realm of training and contribute nothing to the well-being of the home. The formation of the child's sense of identity may be adversely affected; he or she may experience feelings of inferiority because he or she cannot help realizing that play activities are just play and that being an adult is a far more desirable status. In primitive cultures, on the other hand, the play activity of the child is integrated with the work of survival. The little boy learns to fish for fun, but his catch is eaten by the members of the family. He does not have complicated toys to play with, so tools associated with work activities are used for play.

During the adolescent years, the matter of achievement becomes highly critical, and often young people feel that they are not much good at anything. They are judged by their achievement, and they judge themselves by them. There are many areas of achievement and the standards are quite high. As a matter of fact, idealism colors much of what young people strive for, and often their achievements fall far short of their expectations, and there is disappointment and disillusionment. They may blame society, but usually they have a haunting notion that they themselves are ultimately to blame. Thus achievement must enable them to find a place within their social group; they must learn how to dress and act in the definitive way that the group approves. Often the standards, although strictly maintained, are not clearly specified, and for some they are not readily discernible. These young people go through a particularly trying ordeal, experiencing rejection and censorship but remaining in the dark as to the reasons.

Erikson (1968) points out that the formation of a sense of identity in a complex industrialized society confronts the young person with other peculiar problems. Young people are bewildered; their knowledge of what is available is vague, and their opportunities for trying out different life-styles are limited. Not really knowing what direction to take, they must venture along a particular path with many uncertainties and unknowns clouding their journey. There are inequities in class membership, unequal opportunities, different values, and various deviations from the mainstream culture. For example, a child growing up in a family where the only source of income is a welfare check, and in which the father has never held a steady job, surely has poor models after which to pattern his or her own sense of identity. From the foregoing discussion, it should be clear that the formation of a sense of identity is a highly complex process taking place over a long period, and frequently the individual is a victim of circumstances that he or she cannot control but that engender role diffusion and confusion.

Erikson points out that identity is related to making long-term commitments:

Adolescence is the last stage of childhood. The adolescent process, however, is conclusively complete only when the individual has subordinated his childhood identifications to a new kind of identification, achieved in absorbing sociability and in competitive apprenticeship with and among his age mates. These new identifications are no longer characterized by the playfulness of childhood and the experimental zest for youth; with dire urgency they force the young individual to choices and decisions which will, with increasing immediacy, lead to commitments "for life." The task to be performed here by the young person and by his society is formidable. It necessitates, in different individuals and in different societies, great variations in duration, intensity, and ritualization of adolescence. Societies offer, as individuals require, more or less sanctioned intermediary periods between childhood and adulthood, often charcterized by a combination of prolonged immaturity and provoked precocity. [1968, p. 155][9]

This intermediary period of prolonged immaturity Erikson terms *psychosocial moratorium.* Erikson has used the term *psychosocial moratorium* to designate some very puzzling behaviors in late adolescence and young adulthood. It refers to a temporary break from the demands of the psychological course of development. In its purest form, the moratorium is an *abrupt change* in the direction of behavior. For instance, a high school student who has indicated to every one that he plans to attend college may decide at the last minute that he does not want to go. Instead, he may join the Peace Corps, take a job, or simply do nothing for a while. This apparently irresponsible attitude is easily misinterpreted by parents and teachers as laziness, defiance, or an out-and-out personality disorder. But Erikson has a different view; he believes it is a normal response to the stresses and strains of growing up. The psychosocial moratorium offers an unusual opportunity for close scrutiny of a person's values. When young people resume their previous activities, they often have a better chance of achieving their goals.

For the many who cannot literally "drop out," there are more subtle reactions. A young person in college may begin drinking regularly, or turn to drugs, or join an extremist group and devote all his or her time to its affairs. The young person may lose the incentive to do assignments, perhaps even failing a semester, or his or her grades may drop sharply, or he or she may simply experience boredom and fatigue a good bit of the time.

If the process of attaining a sense of identity is successful, individuals have the conviction that they had to become the way they are, that there is no other possible way for them to be; further, they must feel that society sees them this way. Such a conviction implies that they feel integrated, at one with themselves, and comfortable in relation to their physical and social surroundings (Erikson, 1968). This total sense of identity is an ideal that no one attains completely or achieves once and for always. Most people feel accepted and self-accepting in some aspects of their lives, and partially or totally rejected in others. Furthermore, personality integration is always a matter of degree; we all experience divergent trends within ourselves, dissociated aspects of personality that behave like separate personalities and elements that seem totally foreign. With respect to the course of development of a sense of identity, Erikson says:

> From a genetic point of view, then, the process of identity formation emerges as an evolving configuration — a configuration which is gradually established by successive ego syntheses and resyntheses throughout childhood. It is a configuration gradually integrating constitutional givens, idiosyncratic libidinal needs, favored capacities, significant identifications, effective defenses, successful sublimations, and consistent roles.

[9]Quotation is reprinted from *Identity: Youth and Crisis*, by Erik H. Erikson, by permission of W. W. Norton & Company, Inc. Copyright © 1968 by W. W. Norton & Company, Inc. Published in Great Britain and the Commonwealth by Faber and Faber Publishers, London.

We all exper divergent trends w/in ourselves, dissociated aspects of personality that behave like separate personalities + elements that seem to- tally foreign

The final assembly of all the converging identity elements at the end of childhood (and the abandonment of the divergent ones), appears to be a formidable task . . . . [1968, p. 163][10]

In his attempts to attain a sense of identity, the youth experiences both *role confusion* and *role diffusion*, particularly toward the end of adolescence when earlier conflicts are intensified and the urgency of taking on a stable role is greatest. The adolescent "plays" with different roles, in the hope of finding one that "fits" (Erikson, 1956). The defenses of the ego during this time are quite fluid, and such role experimentation may give the impression that a serious disturbance exists in the personality, despite the fact that frequently the only means the young person has of dealing with inner and outer stresses is the trial and error use of coping and adapting mechanisms. At this time the sense of role diffusion, or lack of identity, is the greatest; when a sense of identity is achieved, it is experienced as a pleasant emotional state, as Erikson points out: "An optimal sense of identity . . . is experienced. . . as a sense of psychosocial well-being. Its most obvious concomitants are a feeling of being at home in one's body, a sense of 'knowing where one is going,' and an inner assuredness of anticipated recognition from those who count." [1968, p. 165]

Ideology versus totalism.   During adolescence many physical, psychological, and social changes occur that begin to define the adult status. A variety of roles must be integrated as the individual seeks a continuing sense of identity. The stresses of this period may lead to a number of abnormal strategies, such as regression to childhood coping techniques as a means of avoiding the stress of change, or dropping out of the mainstream (the psychosocial moratorium) in order to find oneself, or fanatic commitment to a system or cult.

The individual in late adolescence is looking for answers to some of life's basic questions in order to make a commitment to cultural values and accepted standards of conduct. The best resolution of the conflicting ideologies that confront adolescents is induction into the culture as contributing adults who occupy accepted statuses and follow approved roles. Erikson terms the ritualization of this period *ideology*, which refers to identification with the rituals and the standards of the culture. The ritualism of this stage is *totalism*. Erikson says: "The ritualistic element reserved for youth I have called *totalism*, that is, exclusive preoccupation with what seems unquestionably ideal within a tight system of ideas," (1977, p. 110) The person commits himself or herself to a system that offers an ideal way of life — a religion, a system of economics, a political system.

Certain rites and ceremonies mark the change from adolescence to adulthood, such as graduation from high school, obtaining a driver's license, attaining the voting age, being able to purchase hard liquor. A recent advertisement suggested that the attainment of adulthood be marked by the first purchase a person makes with a credit card. These various ceremonies confer rights, obligations, and privileges and also initiate the young person into the mainstream of the culture.

---

[10]Quotation is reprinted from *Identity: Youth and Crisis*, by Erik H. Erikson, by permission of W. W. Norton & Company, Inc. Copyright © 1968 by W. W. Norton & Company, Inc. Published in Great Britain and the Commonwealth by Faber and Faber Publishers, London.

A person who has achieved a sense of identity makes a commitment to an accepted ideology, a system of beliefs and values that are approved by his or her culture. Life is regulated by such beliefs and standards. A person suffering from role confusion lacks such a commitment. There are many forms of abnormality that may occur. The ritualism of totalism stresses the fanatic pursuit of ideals and absolute answers to the major problems of life.

We have given more attention to the sense of identity than to any of the other psychosocial stages because this period is so crucial in the development of personality. Failure to attain a healthy sense of identity has greater adverse effects on subsequent personality growth and functioning than do the other psychosocial achievements. Erikson ascribes two highly important human virtues, devotion and fidelity, to the attainment of a healthy sense of identity. Without a firm sense of identity, a person cannot be loyal to anything or anyone. Erikson himself has much more to say about identity than any of the other achievements; in fact, he has devoted an entire book, *Identity: Youth and Crisis* (1968), to this topic.

STAGE SIX, YOUNG ADULTHOOD: INTIMACY VERSUS ISOLATION (LOVE)

Social interactions are significant all through life, but during young adulthood they reach a crisis point. Most people have a profound longing to relate intimately to a member of the opposite sex, and marriage is the usual means by which this need is gratified. It will be recalled that if the basic requirement or task of a particular stage is successfully accomplished, it becomes a major source of activity and pleasure in the next stage. The adolescent who struggles with problems of identity approaches social relationships fearfully, with more displeasure than pleasure; but if he or she settles identity problems, social interactions also improve. As a young adult he or she meets the challenges of social interactions with competence, genuinely enjoying social relationships, the intimate as well as the casual ones.

Intimacy in human relationships presupposes other important achievements, and thus many are incapable of realizing it. One cannot form an intimate relationship without a basic trust in another. Then, too, an intimate relationship is built upon the secure autonomy of the parties; a person who stands on his or her own two feet can give more than the dependent, helpless individual who wants only to receive. A well-developed sense of initiative enables the partners to do productive things for each other. A sense of industry enables each partner to show love in a tangible way by competently doing things for the mate. A sense of identity provides the partner with a stable ego role, a healthy capacity for fidelity, and a well-defined set of values and priorities.

Erikson accepts Freud's idea that one of the marks of maturity (or what Freud called genitality) is the ability to love. To love truly requires qualities such as compassion, sympathy, empathy, identification, reciprocity, and mutuality. Compassion is the feeling of tenderness toward another and the desire to help. Sympathy means unity or harmony with another. Empathy is a feeling of sharing an experience. Identification is becoming as one with the other. Reciprocity means to accept the point of view of another as being as valid as one's own. Mutuality means wanting what the other desires to give and giving what the other desires to receive. These are the social aspects of personality without which intimacy cannot occur.

Consider marriage as an example of an intimate relationship; if a marriage is to be successful, each partner must feel toward the other the emotions previously noted. There must be mutuality and reciprocity; each must want what the other has to give and, in turn, be able to give what the other wants or needs. Each gives up some of his or her own desires for the sake of the desires of the other. Compassion, sympathy, empathy, and identification serve to smooth over the rough spots and the natural differences between man and woman, as well as adding richness to the relationship. These social feelings and emotions are quite apparent in the sex act, which is but one facet of the intimacy associated with marriage. Erikson summarizes the joint participation of the partners in the sex act as follows:

> Genitality consists of the capacity to develop orgastic potency which is more than the discharge of sex products in the same sense of Kinsey's "outlets." It combines the ripening of intimate sexual mutuality with full genital sensitivity and with a capacity for discharge of tension from the whole body. This is a rather concrete way of saying something about a process which we really do not yet quite understand. But the experience of the climactic mutuality of orgasm clearly provides a supreme example of the mutual regulation of complicated patterns and in some way appeases the hostilities and potential rages caused by the daily evidence of the oppositeness of male and female, of fact and fancy, of love and hate, of work and play. Such experience makes sexuality less obsessive, and sadistic control of the partner superfluous.

> Before such genital maturity is reached, much of sexual life is of the self-seeking, identity-hungry kind; each partner is really trying only to reach himself. Or it remains only a kind of genital combat in which each tries to defeat the other. [1968, p. 137][11]

By the term *genitality*, Erikson, like Freud, means more than a biological tension, as is evident from his description of it; it involves the total person and a complex interaction between the two partners; it brings the couple together in a way that nothing else can. Erikson (1968) believes that aspects of masculinity are offensive to women, and some aspects of femininity are offensive to men. Sharing genital pleasure is one means of dealing with the oppositeness in the partners; each needs the other for his or her needs to be satisfied.

Failure to establish satisfying intimate relationships often leaves people with a deep sense of isolation and estrangement. Although people may be able to carry on with their work and maintain some semblance of intimacy in superficial relationships, they may experience a profound feeling of emptiness and loneliness. Most human beings seem to have a strong need for love and an equally strong need to love. If these needs are not met, there is a haunting sense of incompleteness. Other reactions to failure in the need for intimacy include stereotyped social roles, such as always being sarcastic, always being the clown, or chronically submitting to the will of others.

---

[11]Quotation is reprinted from *Identity: Youth and Crisis*, by Erik H. Erikson, by permission of W. W. Norton & Company, Inc. Copyright © 1968 by W. W. Norton & Company, Inc. Published in Great Britain and the Commonwealth by Faber and Faber Publishers, London.

In stressing the role of intimacy during young adulthood, Erikson does not say much about the other major task of this period, namely, preparing for and working competently in a vocation. Everyone has the obligation to find some place in life, and this usually means some kind of acceptable work role. Perhaps Erikson believes that the need for intimacy overshadows the need for a vocation at this stage, particularly since work becomes the dominant concern for the next stage, that of generativity versus stagnation. Erikson (1968) ascribes two important virtues to the person who has successfully dealt with the problem of intimacy: *affiliation* (forming friendships), and *love* (profound concern for another).

Affiliative versus elitism.   The ritualization of early adulthood is the affiliative ritualization. It refers to the rituals associated with the mutual affirmation of identities of people who care for each other. In a man-woman relationship, the affiliative ritualization fosters *complementarity of identities*. The ceremony of marriage and the subsequent honeymoon celebrate formally the union of the two parties. There are certain ceremonial practices such as the exchange of rings, the pledge of fidelity, and other symbolic practices that mark the event with dignity and solemnity. Erikson holds that all the previous ritualizations contribute to the later ones: the marriage ceremony creates a numinous spell; it has judicious elements in that certain rights are bestowed and sanctioned; it is a dramatic occurrence with specific ceremonial practices; there is a formal aspect of the event that must be followed in great detail; the mutual pledges help to define each partner's identity as husband or wife.

The exaggeration of the affiliative ritualization is termed by Erikson *the ritualism of elitism*, which refers to a sense of superiority of one's kind or group affiliations. Erikson points out:

> Its ritualistic side is a kind of shared narcissism in the form of an elitism of exclusive groups. It must be obvious that exactly that demonstrative display of shared tastes and predilections, of enthusiastic opinions and scathing judgments that so often pervade the conversations and actions of young adults bound in love or work, in friendship, or in ideology completes the human form of those instinctive bonds which are confirmed in the greeting ceremonials by which, say, birds signify that they are *made* for each other-and for an engagement in breeding. [1977, p. 110][12]

Status symbols, snobbery, and exclusive club affiliations exemplify the ritualism of elitism.

A sense of intimacy requires the abilities and feelings that are appropriate for forming human attachments, affiliations with others. A sense of isolation is characterized by deficiencies in affiliative skills and feelings. The ritualism of elitism is but one form of abnormality resulting from failure to acquire a sense of intimacy. Elitism refers to snobbish affiliation; formation of "in" groups; a sense of superior group status.

---

[12]Quotation is reprinted from *Toys and Reasons, Stages in the Ritualization of Experience*, by Erik H. Erikson, by permission of W. W. Norton & Company, Inc. Copyright © 1977 by W. W. Norton & Company, Inc. Published in Great Britain and the Commonwealth by Marion Boyars Ltd., London.

STAGE SEVEN, MIDDLE ADULTHOOD: GENERATIVITY VERSUS STAGNATION (CARE)

Freud held that along with the ability to love, the ability to work effectively is a mark of maturity. Erikson (1963) seems to agree with both requirements, love and work, and he delineated a stage of life that he terms *generativity* to describe the requirement of sustained, productive work and caring. The period is the middle years from about twenty-five to sixty. There may be some disagreement about the upper limit of this period because life expectancy is increasing. Furthermore, as Levinson (1978) points out, it is doubtful that this large and important period of life can be understood as a single stage. It is usually the period of greatest productivity in life; people establish themselves in a vocation, bring up a family, and secure a favorable reputation in the community. In a group of elderly people who were asked to select the period of life that afforded them the greatest happiness, this was the period selected most often. It is the time when the individual reaches full physical, psychological, and social maturity. Vigorous functioning requires the achievements of earlier periods. People have most to give during these years, a fact quite apparent in the rearing of a family, which demands the utmost in generosity.

The care of a child demands an unqualified giving of oneself. Although some parents may use their children to satisfy abnormal needs, the majority of parents do not have children for selfish reasons. Erikson makes the point that parents need children quite as much as children need parents. There are marriages in which children are not desired, and many men and women seem to do quite well without either spouse or children. The fact remains, however, that, under the right conditions, having children adds a dimension to life for which there can be no substitute. There is indescribable joy in being a part of the growth of a child from infancy through adulthood. Seeing the child undergoing the same stages of development as the parent adds a richness and meaning to life that cannot be had in any other way. What can substitute for the joy a father experiences when his son takes his first job? What a sense of pride a mother derives from taking her own baby to the doctor for the first time or from enrolling the child in nursery school or witnessing the child's graduation from college, marriage, and first-born child! There are many instances in a child's life that provide the parents with the deepest pleasures, but both parents need a high degree of maturity if such joys and pleasures are to be realized. There are sorrows, frustrations, and disappointments, and many parents make a terrible mess of parenthood. A clinical psychologist remarked that most parents he has dealt with disliked or hated their children. Allowing for the fact that this clinician dealt only with abnormal people in his professional work, the fact remains that among all kinds of people there is a great deal of disharmony in the parent-child relationship.

Failure to attain generativity (taking this in the broadest sense as productivity and creativity in all spheres of life), Erikson designates *stagnation*. A sense of stagnation is a personal impoverishment. The victim may feel that life is drab and empty, that he or she is merely marking time and getting older without fulfilling his or her expectations. People who stagnate do not effectively use what they have; they do not make their life interesting or zestful. They may become apathetic and complain of chronic fatigue, or there may be a chronic grumbling and resentment. Many homemakers complain that their lives are quite dull and dreary, that they are confined and trapped with children all day long, and that they have to do menial tasks. Many men complain that their jobs, which may have been exciting for the first two or three years, are dull and monotonous and that life is a perpetual merry-go-round, with nothing very interesting to do. These are instances of the failure to use personal abilities to make life an ever-creative flow of experience.

Even the most routine work can be done in a way to bring pleasure if you use your ingenuity. To be able to work productively and creatively requires the attainment of all the achievements of the previous stages, and it is no wonder that many people fail in the matter of generativity; they fail because they are not fully prepared to deal with their life situation during this period. It appears that the problem of the meaning of existence is one of the major concerns of our day, when existence itself is so precarious. Generative persons find meaning in utilizing their knowledge and skills for their own sake; usually they enjoy their work and do it well. Erikson (1968) attributes two very important virtues to the person who has attained generativity: *production* (working creatively and productively) and *care* (working for the benefit of others).

Generational versus authoritism   The adult is a communicator of rituals to the new generation. Erikson terms the ritualization of mature adulthood *generational*. The adult assumes a variety of roles that involve ritualizations such as teacher, paternalistic guide, problem solver, provider, and protector. The culture prescribes certain roles and practices that are appropriate to the status of parent. A particular parent is aided in his or her roles by these ritualizations that enable the culture to be passed on to the next generation. Many of the earlier ritualizations play a part such as the numinous (the parental authority), the judicious (the purveyor of truth and proper conduct), the model of authenticity, the carrier of appropriate skills and traditions, the source of ideologies, the example of intimacy, the generational and productive person, and the fount of wisdom. The ritualism of this period is termed *authoritism* by Erikson and refers to a self-convinced and spurious assumption of authority. We are reminded of the parent who assumes the role of dictator, using knowledge and power to dominate the young.

Authoritism is the ritualism of the middle years, an exaggerated form of generational ritualization, referring to rigid authoritarian parental roles. The person who experiences a sense of stagnation during the middle years may suffer from a host of other abnormalities, which were noted in the discussion of stagnation. The generational ritualization is Erikson's term for the culturally accepted modes of parenting that transmit the best of a culture to the next generation.

STAGE EIGHT, LATE ADULTHOOD: EGO INTEGRITY VERSUS DESPAIR (WISDOM)

The eighth and last stage of life in Erikson's schema spans the years from sixty to death. Ego integrity, which is the major task of this period, implies a full unification of personality, with the ego as the major determining force. Although Erikson has not really

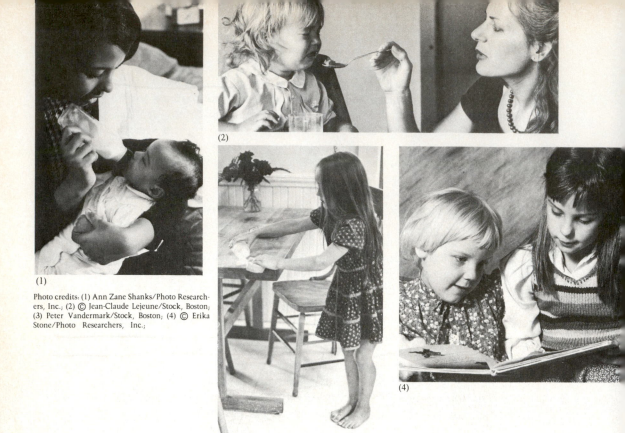

Photo credits: (1) Ann Zane Shanks/Photo Researchers, Inc.; (2) © Jean-Claude Lejeune/Stock, Boston;
(3) Peter Vandermark/Stock, Boston; (4) © Erika
Stone/Photo Researchers, Inc.;

Each stage of life confronts the ego with a major task.

detailed this stage, it would seem to resemble Jung's idea (1964b) of the individuation process, the full attainment of selfhood.

> Lacking a clear definition, I shall point to a few constituents of this state of mind. It is the ego's accrued assurance of its proclivity for order and meaning. It is a postnarcissistic love of the human ego — not of the self — as an experience which conveys some world order and spiritual sense, no matter how dearly paid for. It is the acceptance of one's one and only life cycle as something that had to be and that, by necessity, permitted no substitutions: it thus means a new, a different love of one's parents. [1963, p. 168][13]

The prospect of the termination of life results in a great deal of torment for many people. The aging person experiences difficulties ranging from physical aches and pains to apathy and loss of interest in things and people to feelings of uselessness, isolation, and despair — the term that Erikson uses to sum up all these problems. Erikson does not believe that the last period of life need be bleak and terrifying for everybody; it is not for those who have successfully accomplished the tasks of the preceding stages. For

[13]Quotation is reprinted from *Childhood and Society*, 2nd Edition, by Erik H. Erikson, by permission of W. W. Norton & Company, Inc. Copyright 1950, 1963 by W. W. Norton & Company, Inc. Published in Great Britain and the Commonwealth by the Hogarth Press Ltd., London.

(5) Mimi Forsyth/Monkmeyer Press Photo Service; (6) © Baron Wolman 1978/Woodfin Camp Associates; (7) © Erika Stone; (8) Frank Siteman/Stock, Boston

example, we need trust that we have lived a good life and trust also that death will not be a terrifying experience; in fact, for those who believe in an afterlife, death will be the threshold of a new kind of existence. Autonomy is needed to face the problems of this period with self-reliance. Initiative and industry are necessary to change circumstances that can be changed. The sense of identity is the most vital asset because the ego is valued as the most important facet in our personality. Having attained rich friendships and having worked productively and successfully, a person feels no regrets or lingering desires for the things of youth. Thus, in a sense, each achievement prepares one for the final task of life: the ability to face the prospect of death without despair and with the feeling that one's life has been complete, lived the way it had to be.

Many elderly people report that they are not terrified at the thought of their own death. Having lived their lives fully, they do not long for perpetual existence on earth. It is as if each period were lived fully at the time, and no needs remained to haunt them. The feeling can be compared to consuming the various courses of a large meal: after you have eaten soup, you lose taste for soup and want something else. If you have had a satisfactory childhood, a successful career, a good marriage, and a family that is grown and independent, the pleasures of life have been experienced, and there is not much more that a person could ask for.

It would be Pollyanna thinking to suppose that the greatest mystery of life could be faced without fear. Every new venture, no matter how well prepared you are, is approached with fear and hesitation. Consider the first day at school, the first day at work, the wedding day, the day the first child comes home, and many many more. Each major undertaking in life challenges the ego strength, and death probably presents the greatest of all challenges. However, each stage also provides the ego with greater strength and readies it for the challenges of the next stage. Having profited from the experiences of living, the elderly person faces the last period of life with wisdom, which is the virtue that Erikson attributes to this stage. Those who find death totally incomprehensible and terrifying have failed in the previous accomplishments of living.

Integral versus sapientism.   Erikson refers to the ritualization of old age as the *integral*, by which he seems to mean the unification of life's objectives. The person who has lived successfully through the cycle of life within a particular society and has met its requirements is in a position to affirm the value of his or her life. The elderly are the personification of traditional wisdom for a particular culture. The ritualism of old age is *sapientism*, which is the unwise pretense of being wise. Erikson says:

> We can see now what rituals must accomplish: by combining and renewing the ritualizations of childhood and affirming generative sanction, they help to consolidate adult life once its commitments and investments have led to the creation of new persons and to the production of new things and ideas. And, of course, by tying life cycle and institutions into a meaningful whole, they create a sense of immortality not only for the leaders and the elite but also for every participant. And there can be little doubt that the ritualization of everyday life permits, and even demands, that adults forget death as the inscrutable background of all life, and give priority to the absolute reality of world views shared with others of the same geography, history, and technology. By means of ritual, in fact, death becomes the meaningful boundary of such reality. [1977, pp. 112–113][14]

We might think of integral ritualization as embodying true wisdom and wholesome self-respect. People who have attained a sense of the value of life appreciate life's limitations. Sapientism is expressed in authoritarian forms—as knowing more than anyone else; as having the only answers; as being absolutely right. Again, this is one form of abnormality associated with failure in achieving the ego strength of integrity.

To appreciate the meaning and value of ritualizations, think of what types of behavior are appropriate and praiseworthy in our culture for an old man or an old woman. We might think of such behavior as telling stories, playing with grandchildren, engaging in certain types of hobbies and the like. For each of the stages there are appropriate ritualizations but also ritualisms that are inappropriate behaviors.

A summary of Erikson's eight stages of development is provided in Table 5–1.

---

[14]Quotation is reprinted from *Toys and Reasons, Stages in the Ritualization of Experience*, by Erik H. Erikson, by permission of W. W. Norton & Company, Inc. Copyright © 1977 by W. W. Norton & Company, Inc. Published in Great Britain and the Commonwealth by Marion Boyars Ltd., London.

TABLE 5-1 SUMMARY OF ERIKSON'S EIGHT STAGES

Stage	Ego Crisis	Virtues	Significant Task	Ritualiza-tion	Ritualism
1. Infancy	Trust vs. Mistrust	Hope	Mutual affirmation of mother and child	Numinous	Idolism
2. Early Childhood	Autonomy vs. Shame and Doubt	Courage, Self-control, and Willpower	Differentiation between right and wrong	Judicious	Legalism
3. Play Age	Initiative vs. Guilt	Purpose	Role experimentation	Authenticity	Impersonation
4. School Age	Industry vs. Inferiority	Competence and Method	Skill learning	Formality	Formalism
5. Adolescence	Identity vs. Role Confusion	Fidelity and Devotion	Establishing philosophy of life	Idiology	Totalism
6. Young Adulthood	Intimacy vs. Isolation	Love and Affiliation	Mutually satisfying social relationships	Affiliative	Elitism
7. Middle Adulthood	Generativity vs. Stagnation	Care and Production	Perpetuating the culture	Generational	Authoritism
8. Late Adulthood	Ego Integrity vs. Despair	Wisdom	Acceptance of completion of life	Integral	Sapientism

VIEWS ON IDEAL PERSONALITY AND LIVING

Despite Erikson's stress on ego identity, during each stage of our lives we virtually become a different person. We can see this in ourselves by looking back over our lives. You might consider the difference between what you were at ten years of age and what you are now. Almost every aspect of your life has changed—physical size, responsibilities, roles, and a host of new frustrations. Life continues to change, and not many years from now you will be going through another stage that will have its own set of inner and outer requirements. Erikson points out desirable and undesirable outcomes for each of the eight stages of life in terms of his psychosocial theory of development.

One way to look at the ego attainments that Erikson delineates for each stage is as a model of ideal attributes that can foster healthy personality growth and functioning. Knowing these, we can strive to promote these ego strengths in ourselves. The ego strengths increase one's potential for living effectively. They are great assets to the one who possesses them.

Trust

A sense of trust is not only essential for the helpless infant but for all of us. We are often faced with unknowns, partial evidence, and conflicting information. A sense of trust enables us to make decisions under such adverse conditions. We need to have confidence or trust in ourselves, trust in our environment, and even trust in the form of optimism for the future. Without trust, we experience fear, which is a crippling emotion that inhibits behavior. Hope refers to positive expectations in the absence of supporting evidence. We are constantly called upon to make decisions about important matters, the outcome of which entails uncertainty and risk. Erikson also includes in the sense of trust the powerful benefit of respect and reverence for people. Life is greatly enriched by our social relationships, including our relationship with supernatural persons. Our sense of trust must encompass belief in people.

Autonomy

Despite philosophical controversy regarding human will and free will, our everyday experience testifies to the important and pervasive role of will in our lives. Our ability to make choices and decisions and to abide by them plays an important role in practically everything we do. Consider the value in your life of self-control, self-discipline, self-assertiveness, and willpower. The ability to say yes or no to our impulses, to the pressures of the environment, and to our future prospects is an important dimension of effective living. We must all be courageous in the face of distractions, frustrations, and our own inner resistances and with the daily problems that plague us. Persistence and perseverance are desirable qualities that stem from courage. In order to exercise will judiciously, we need to have sound judgment regarding right and wrong conduct. Sensitivity to social, cultural, legal, and personal standards and practices certainly contributes to effective living.

Initiative

Satisfying needs and wants in an orderly manner is another important dimension of healthy living. Having purpose in living gives meaning to life. A sense of initiative is aided by our short- and long-term goals and fosters a vigorous approach to living. Erikson includes as a feature of initiative the identification with authentic roles. Feeling comfortable with culturally accepted roles that are suited to our abilities, dispositions, and needs is surely a valuable asset in living.

Industry

A sense of industry that is supported by competence in necessary areas of performance is another important ego achievement. Successful living in any society depends upon possession of valued skills. We are accorded status, and value ourselves, by the skills that we possess. Success experiences depend upon our competencies. Knowing and practicing the formalities of our culture fosters success experiences. Whether we are victims or controllers of our circumstances depends to a large degree on our competencies.

Identity

Achieving a sense of identity helps to resolve many important conflicts in our lives. Being capable of finding continuity in the various roles we assume gives our lives a certain stability and unity. Our identity defines our place in the social structure. Identifying with acceptable roles helps to confirm our sense of worth. A woman who is valued by her children is helped in establishing her identity as a mother. If she is loved and respected by her husband, her identity as a wife is affirmed and defined. If her parents think that she is an excellent daughter, mother, and wife, her identity is further supported and defined. If in her profession as a teacher she is valued by her students, principal, and fellow teachers, another aspect of her identity is strengthened. This very fortunate woman has a great deal of cultural support for the various components of her sense of identity. In addition to this cultural support, she herself would have to feel comfortable in these various roles for her sense of identity to be well-established.

Two important aspects of identity are *ideological commitment* and fidelity. By ideological commitment, Erikson means having values and priorities that are functional in a particular society. By the virtue of fidelity, Erikson means being able to make commitments and promises and to abide by them. These are essential attributes for effective living.

Intimacy

A sense of intimacy is one of the most distinctively human achievements. Its benefits are many. Its essential ingredient, the capacity to love, greatly enriches life. A sense of intimacy is made up of some of our most noble emotions and sentiments — compassion, sympathy, empathy, mutuality, tender concern for another. Life is greatly supported by our many affiliations with other people. Being able to participate in social relationships with a wide diversity of people is a valuable asset.

Generativity

The attributes of productivity, generativity, and generationality require the use of abilities in performing useful work. The society provides a large variety of acceptable work roles, although they vary in degree of status. To be capable of working productively is a major strength of the ego that contributes significantly to the quality of life. Productive work is not only confined to paid employment but also to the duties of family and community life. The virtue of care makes the family an important vehicle for the transmission of the culture. Care contributes a valuable quality to parental roles. Erikson holds that the generational person is motivated to pass on what was given to him or her by the preceding generation, a necessary attribute for the perpetuation of the culture.

Integrity

Personality is strengthened through wisdom and unification in the last stage of life. Erikson seems to ascribe greater personal control in the later stages than in the earlier ones. The model that Erikson builds contains the ingredients for healthy development and functioning, but it does not specify the means by which these ideals are to be attained. We will offer some suggestions for attaining these desirable attributes in the Guides to Living section.

CRITICAL EVALUATION

Erikson's ideas on personality development have been favorably received by some child psychologists because his concepts are amenable to testing (for example, Mehrabian, 1968). For instance, he specifies both normal and abnormal ego development for each stage of personality growth. He details specific ego strengths that can be translated into measurement procedures. He makes his concepts quite explicit: there is no question, for example, that trust is the first major task of the ego, that autonomy is the second major task, that initiative is the third, and so on.

Erikson's theory has also been favorably received because it covers stages beyond adolescence and allows for social determinants. But the later stages are not clearly delineated and are barely more than named. Thus the theory is incomplete. Furthermore, since Erikson's early stages closely parallel the four stages proposed by Freud, they are subject to some of the criticisms that have been applied to such Freudian concepts as the Oedipus complex and the formation of the superego.

GUIDES TO RESEARCH

HEURISTIC VALUE OF ERIKSON'S THEORY

Erikson has been highly influential in the general field of developmental psychology. He himself has been a pioneer child analyst and has made significant contributions to this field. He has also promoted ego psychology in his emphasis on the growth of the ego. His developmental approach is popular with child psychologists and child educators because children's ego development can be judged with respect to the degree to which they have attained the ego strengths associated with each of the psychosocial stages that Erikson specifies. Erikson has also been responsible for the increased interest in the developmental stages that occur during adulthood (see Levinson, 1978; Sheehy, 1976). Another area of study that owes a debt to Erikson is the study of the effects of particular cultures on personality development and, as an extension of this topic, the comparison of cultures. He assigned the sociocultural forces a much greater role than have the psychoanalysts who stressed the instinctual drives. Finally, Erikson has made significant contributions in a new field known as psychohistorical analysis, which has inspired others to pursue this approach in studying important historical figures. Psychohistory is a method of investigation that relates sociocultural events to the study of the lives of historical figures. Erikson analyzed the lives of Luther (1962), Gandhi (1969), and Hitler (1968). Erikson's views, therefore, have had important heuristic value in that they have moved others to pursue new lines of investigation.

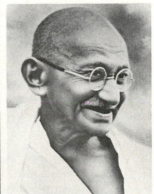

The shapers of events can be studied psychohistorically.

Photo credits: *upper left* The Bettman Archive; *upper right* Information Service of India/Photo Researchers, Inc.; *lower* The Bettman Archive

EMPIRICAL SUPPORT OF ERIKSON'S THEORY

Despite Erikson's influential position, his views have not inspired very much empirical research. One reason is that his description of some of his key constructs are more literary than scientific. They are not easily reduced to operational definitions; therefore, they remain vague generalizations. However, he has specified the attributes of the various psychosocial stages clearly enough that investigators could test their validity, and we will discuss some of this work although much more research needs to be done for the stages to be accepted as Erikson describes them. Some investigators have used Erikson's ideas to account for their research findings, but this post hoc approach (after-the-fact explanation) gives only weak support to the theory.

A developmental approach such as Erikson's is inherently difficult to study because a great deal of an investigator's and subjects' time is required. Frequently, the sample size diminishes with time. We will give a sample of some of the research that was specifically designed to test Erikson's ideas.

Erikson has strongly maintained that the development of a new ego strength in a particular developmental stage depends upon the degree to which ego strengths have been attained in previous stages. Waterman, Buebel, and Waterman (1970) sought to test this hypothesis by relating degree of ego identity with the ego attainments of the four earlier stages. Specifically, they correlated a measure of ego identity with measures of trust, autonomy, initiative, and industry. In the first phase of the study, ninety-two male college freshmen were interviewed extensively to obtain a measure of strength of ego identity. They used Rotter's test of locus of control for the measure of autonomy because it measures the degree of personal control over circumstances that a person believes he or she possesses. To assess the sense of trust, they used another test devised by Rotter that measures the degree to which a person trusts others. They found a significant correlation between ego identity and autonomy, but not with the measure of trust. From the results of this phase, it would appear that people with a firm sense of ego identity also have a strong belief in their ability to control the circumstances of their lives whereas people who experience role confusion believe that they are victims of external forces over which they have little control.

In the second phase of the study, eighty-seven male college students were given a series of self-report scales that were designed to measure the degree of resolution of the ego crises of Erikson's first five stages. The tests that were used were constructed from Erikson's ideas directly; thus, their reliability and validity are open to question. The investigators were interested in the correlations of the ego identity measure with the measures of trust, autonomy, initiative, and industry. They predicted positive correlations, and the results confirmed their predictions. The results may be interpreted according to Erikson's view that the degree of successful attainment of ego identity, the fifth ego strength, correlates with degree of successful attainments of a sense of trust, autonomy, initiative, and industry.

Peck and Havighurst (1960) conducted one of the rare developmental studies that followed a group of children beginning at age ten and continuing through age seventeen. One important finding was that the development of traits during this period was consistent in that the children tended to maintain the same rank order throughout the period. Despite changes in the strengths of traits for all the children, the relative ranks remained the same throughout study.

An important issue that this study dealt with was the part that the parents played in the development of certain traits in their children. Three years prior to the study of the children, the investigators studied the behavior of the parents toward their children. It turned out that certain qualities of the behavior of the parents were meaningfully related to the development of specific traits in their children. Ego strength and moral stability, for example, were associated with a trusting atmosphere in the home and with consistency of discipline. Superego strength, having inner controls and values, was also related to consistency of parents in their dealings with the children. The trait of friendliness was associated with two factors, the consistency factor again and a democratic family atmosphere that provided the children opportunities to make choices. On the other hand, severe discipline, lack of trust, and authoritarian control on the part of the parents engendered traits of hostility and guilt in the children. These findings support the existence of Erikson's first two stages in that the children displayed the ego qualities proposed by Erikson for trust versus mistrust and for autonomy versus shame and doubt. Healthy development seemed to be associated with parental warmth and a trusting family climate along with freedom to make personal choices.

Ciaccio (1971) tested 120 boys, five, eight, and eleven years old, for the development of traits predicted by Erikson's theory. The results supported the postulate of ego strength progression with increasing age. There was differentiation among the three age groups with respect to the ego traits of autonomy, initiative, and industry. The important idea that ego conflicts are resolved as the child progresses to the next ego crisis was called into question because all the age groups showed most conflict for the stage-two crisis, autonomy vs. shame and doubt, suggesting that this may be the focal crisis of the first five ego stages. Perhaps the problems associated with the expression of will—self-management, self-control, assertiveness, and self-doubt—are more difficult and urgent for the growing child and adolescent than the other aspects of development noted by Erikson.

Waterman and Waterman (1972) found college freshmen undergoing an identity crisis to be significantly overrepresented among students changing their majors or withdrawing from school. Problems with ego identity began earlier than the freshman year, but the demands on the young person during that period increase markedly, thereby putting the ego to a test.

Constantinople (1969), using her self-concept measure, based on Erikson's theory, found significant differences between freshmen and senior scores on industry, inferiority, and identity for both sexes, in the direction Erikson specifies.

Waterman, Kohutis, and Polone (1977) studied techniques that could help relieve the identity crisis. They compared the keeping of a diary with the writing of expressive poetry. People have long used the writing of a diary as a means of gaining insights about themselves and living. These investigators asked a group of students to keep a diary throughout the course of the study. Ego strength was measured several times to ascertain the changes that occurred. Likewise, many people have used the writing of poetry as a means of gaining self-knowledge. The investigators compared these two approaches with respect to improvement in resolving the problems of identity and found that the writing of expressive poetry was more effective than keeping a diary.

Marcia (1966) devised a test based on Erikson's concepts to measure strength of ego identity. This instrument has been used in several studies as the measure of strength of ego identity and has been tested for reliability and validity. Thus, it affirms the value of Erikson's views on the identity crisis.

We would have to conclude that, although Erikson's ideas have received acceptance in several fields, they have not generated a great deal of research that might be used as evidence to support the validity of the theory.

GUIDES TO LIVING

We will consider some psychological principles that may help you to strengthen your ego along the lines suggested by Erikson. Repeated application of the principles is the only way to benefit from them. You are encouraged to invent or find other principles.

Note: We will consider only five of Erikson's eight developmental conflicts because these are most directly relevant to the readers of this text. It should also be noted that the principles given to promote Erikson's ego accomplishments are not necessarily his principles.

A SENSE OF HOPE

Erikson ascribes one of the most important virtues of the ego to the favorable outcome of the earliest crisis of the ego, gaining a sense of hope. In this earliest period, the environment plays a predominant role in that the child is almost completely dependent on the goodwill of those who have responsibility for him or her. A trusting environment induces a sense of trust and hope. What can we do to make up for deficiencies in our sense of hope for life's potentialities?

Consider the following suggestions:

1. Optimism and pessimism are our own interpretative sets, based only in part on actual experience. Sets are learned and thus can be altered.

2. Optimism depends greatly on beliefs about important people and institutions in our lives. We can cultivate respect for the traditions, institutions, and significant heroes of our country. Our way of life greatly depends upon the toil of those who preceded us.

3. We should attempt to form friendships that are mutually affirming. Generally speaking, we need and like people who share our point of view and think and like as we do. In a relationship we may assume many roles—judge, teacher, superior, adversary. Another alternative is to be an affirming companion.

A SENSE OF COURAGE, SELF-CONTROL, AND WILLPOWER

Like the sense of trust, the achievement of a basic sense of autonomy is critical early in life, and there may be a long history of self-doubt and self-depreciation. This problem of the ego involves matters of compliance and resistance to authority. The ability to cooperate and compete is directly related to feelings of autonomy.

We cannot attain a sense of autonomy simply by asserting a desire for independence. Autonomy is based upon achievements. The status of being independent of the control of parents, teachers, and other authorities may be quite appealing to a young person, but merely asserting that we are grown-up does not in itself justify the rights of independent status. Rights are always associated with obligations. To be truly autonomous, we should be able to "pay our own way." All living involves instrumental acts. We must be willing and able to work for what we seek.

Here are some suggestions that may assist the reader to achieve a sense of autonomy: (1)

Cultivate the habit of self-respect. Your own opinion about yourself should be given the greatest weight in the choice of a course of action. (2) Be willing to make resolutions continually even if you break some of them. A resolution can motivate behavior in a particular direction. (3) Fear of making mistakes is normal, but mistakes should be dreaded only when you do not profit from them. (4) Be willing to work for what you get, and do not be misled by the good fortune of others to wallow in self-pity or to excuse yourself from effort. (5) Consider a sense of autonomy one of your major goals in life, and, like other important values, give it a high priority. (6) Intellectual judgments and decision making relating to personal matters must be your own responsibility. (7) Develop an increasing immunity against others' threats to your self-esteem. (8) There should be a gradually increasing independence of emotional ties to others, such as childish dependence on parents.

A SENSE OF PURPOSE

Self-interest requires that action be taken to meet our needs and wants. A sense of purpose gives life direction and meaning.

A sense of purpose might be promoted by following some of the suggestions for achieving autonomy, for purposeful existence is really a directed form of autonomy. Guilt is ultimately the product of our own conscience, and conscience can be brought under the control of the ego. Consider the following suggestions to promote a sense of purpose: First, examine your conscience periodically to determine if it is developing properly. Many people carry the child's conscience into adulthood. As we have noted, conscience can be either a terrible hindrance or a helpful guide to living. Proper development is not easy to specify, but conscience should become more conscious, more under control of the ego, and more flexible with age. The conscience should provide values and goals that serve as guides to behavior, giving life purpose and direction. Secondly, convince yourself that no one has a greater claim to life than you. A popular song expresses this sentiment well: "You are a child of the universe; you have a right to be here." Thirdly, be spontaneous, even though it may offend some people. A spontaneous person is expressing his or her real self, and that is the best self to be. Fourthly, learn to translate desires into instrumental behavior and to get started with the things you want and have to do. Take pride in the things that you have accomplished.

A SENSE OF COMPETENCE AND METHOD

Every society demands that its members learn certain competencies. Every adult is expected to perform some kind of work. Certain skills are valued and win for the possessor acclaim as well as material wealth. Those who possess the prized skills in abundance are accorded high status and are encouraged to regard themselves as worthy and superior to others who do not have great skills or who have not achieved the valued goals. The unskilled may be treated as inferior, and they are taught to regard themselves in an unfavorable light.

Here are some suggestions for promoting a sense of competence and method: First, consider a skill as a valuable possession, and strive to acquire it. It is an important asset in the world of changing fortunes. Secondly, recognize that one of the richest sources of pleasure for a human being is the perfecting of skills. A performer may work to the day he or she dies to improve skills though even a first-rate musician, artist, or scientist seldom attains complete perfection. Thirdly, remember that not everyone can be a great pianist, artist, philosopher, or scientist, but everyone can perfect skills, even if they are modest ones. Fourthly, realize that good work on any job level is usually highly regarded. You can always count on winning favor by good work. A habit of doing a job well and promptly is a valuable asset. Fifthly, do not forget that a social skill is just as much a skill as an art or craft, and it can be learned. Social skills may make the difference between a happy and successful life, and one that is empty and stressful.

Erikson holds that rationality is the greatest human tool; thus, the best way to deal with most problems is to reason out a solution and follow through with a plan of action. Once a plan is worked out, the total project should be broken up into small steps. Work inhibition is more readily overcome through small, easy steps than through large and difficult ones. Work toward the completion of a project can be promoted by a series of subgoals, each of which has a deadline. The best way to begin a term paper is to set a deadline for the selection and delineation of a topic. The next step is to take note cards, and this task also should have a deadline. The outline, the first draft, and the final draft should be scheduled with deadlines. We should keep these four words in mind when dealing with problems: project, plan, schedule, and goal.

The old adage to "take one day at a time" is relevant to promoting a sense of method. We should cultivate the habit of dealing with problems as they arise, letting tomorrow take care of itself. We should also learn to cooperate with the inevitables; if there is a job to be done, begin with the idea that it will get done; then do something about it even if it is only the most elementary step.

PROMOTING A SENSE OF IDENTITY

The dissatisfaction and role confusion of adolescence (or of later stages) can be replaced by a sense of identity if five principles are kept in mind. First, you can best acquire a sense of identity by anticipating a period of confusion about and reexamination of accepted values (psychosocial moratorium) and then becoming intensely involved with something. A vocation, a career, a marriage, an affiliation with an organization can serve to establish an acceptable ego role.

Secondly, the young person should select models, interpreters of the culture, with great care. Quite often young people select other young people as models, who may be just as confused as they are. One way to tell a good possible model is to notice your own reactions to the person. Some people are therapeutic and produce positive emotions in those who interact with them; others produce unfavorable reactions such as depression, gloom, and bitterness (Jourard, 1963).

Thirdly, though the values of others can certainly be taken over and learned from, ultimately they must be incorporated into the self

and made a matter of personal conviction. Values need to be reflected upon, to be made the object of one's highest critical and decision-making powers. They must become a part of the personality structure through the exercise of the ego's rational processes, not through automatic conditioning and unconscious mechanisms. An essential ingredient of the sense of identity is the formation of an adult conscience, as contrasted with the authoritarian conscience of a child (Allport, 1961; Erikson, 1968).

Fourthly, use your intellectual abilities to become increasingly aware of yourself. You should be able to describe your conception of yourself. An adult can usually describe himself or herself more completely and accurately than a child, but many people never achieve self-knowledge (Schachtel, 1962).

Fifthly, fatigue, boredom, inability to work, and uncertainty about goals are products of identity confusion. Warring elements within the personality create a dissipation of energy. As you establish a sense of identity, you begin to function more efficiently.

SUMMARY

1. Erikson builds on Freud's psychosexual stages, but with an emphasis on the social determinants of personality growth. He proposes the view that personality development consists primarily of the growth of the ego as the person confronts the major tasks of life.

2. Many conflicts result from the clash between the child's needs and desires and the expectations and limitations that the culture imposes. Any given behavior can be understood in terms of biological, psychological, and social adjustments.

3. Erikson does not view the ego as the helpless servant of basic drives or as the puppet of an all-powerful environment or as the victim of a tyrannical superego, but rather as an active agency within personality that coordinates the needs of the organism with the demands of the environment. The ego acquires strengths if it

grows normally throughout the eight stages of life.

4. Erikson divides the life cycle into eight stages, with each stage confronting the individual with a major developmental task. The major tasks are conflicts; successful resolution strengthens ego; failure weakens it. Each stage confronts the ego with a crisis, which is a turning point. Failure to resolve problems results in a carry-over to the next stage. The eight stages are: (a) basic trust versus mistrust, (b) autonomy versus shame and doubt, (c) initiative versus guilt, (d) industry versus inferiority, (e) identity versus role diffusion, (f) intimacy versus isolation, (g) generativity versus stagnation, and (h) ego-integrity versus despair.

5. To Erikson the same problems recur throughout life but in different forms. He distinguishes between the immature phase, the critical phase, and the resolution phase of these universal problems. Resolution endows the ego with a strength such as trust, autonomy, initiative, industry, identity, intimacy, generativity, and integrity. Erikson even allows for the highest human attributes, which he terms virtues, and maintains that these occur if the ego is unusually successful at each stage. The virtues in order of development are hope; courage, self-control, and willpower; purpose; competence and method; fidelity and devotion; love and affiliation; care and production; and wisdom. These may be viewed as the ideal endowments for humans. The ego strengths and virtues increase one's potential for living effectively and are great assets to one who possesses them.

6. The standards and practices of a culture are communicated to the young by ritualizations, which are recurring patterns of behavior characteristic of a particular society. Guidelines for conduct are learned through ritualizations. Erikson refers to false ritualizations as ritualism. Ritualisms are inappropriate uses of rituals that have the effect of limiting a person's actions and producing rigidity in the personality. Each stage is characterized by an appropriate ritualization and a ritualism that is an exaggerated form of abnormality. Ego failure at any stage can take

many forms of abnormality. The ritualizations and ritualisms, in order of stages, are numinous versus idolism; judicious versus legalism, authenticity versus impersonation, formality versus formalism, ideology versus totalism, affiliative versus elitism, generational versus authoritism, and integral versus sapientism. Ritualizations promote ego strength and enable the person to fit into the patterns of the culture.

7. Erikson's theory has much heuristic value, for example, research on children's ego development, developmental stages, the effects of particular cultures on personality development, and the comparison of cultures. The new field of psychohistory, a method of investigation relating sociocultural events to the study of the lives of historical figures, has also been pioneered by Erikson.

8. Erikson's views have not inspired very much empirical research because some of his constructs are presented more in a literary style than in a scientifically meaningful form. They are not easily reduced to operational definitions. A developmental approach such as Erikson's is inherently difficult to study because a great deal of an investigator's and the subjects' time is required.

GLOSSARY

Crisis: A challenge to the ego that requires a change of perspective.

Identity crisis: Occurs during adolescence in which the major task confronting the ego is the discovery of culturally acceptable core roles.

Identity confusion: Problems associated with search for core ego roles; alienation or cultural estrangement may result.

Psychosocial moratorium: Product of identity crisis characterized by abrupt change of direction. A period of value confusion.

Three phases of crisis: (1) Immature phase — mild forms of the crisis; occurs prior to the critical phase; (2) critical phase — con-

flict or problem facing ego is most intense; and (3) resolution phase — major conflict is resolved and ego gains strength, but conflict recurs in later stages in different forms.

Cultural practices: Human conventions characteristic of a social group embodied in the form of customs, traditions, folkways, taboos, and ceremonies.

Ritualizations versus ritualisms: Ritualizations are recurring patterns of behavior characteristic of a particular society. Daily routines that make life meaningful in a particular society, ritualizations at best are guides to conduct that set boundaries to permissible behavior. Ritualisms are inappropriate ritualizations, false and exaggerated ritualizations that are the causes of social and psychological pathology; ritualisms lead to excess and artificiality.

Numinous versus idolism: Numinous is the ritualization of early childhood that involves social responsiveness; profound emotional experiences engendered by or impelling one to social interactions. Idolism is exaggerated idealization of others; inappropriate admiration.

Judicious versus legalism: Judicious is the ritualization of middle childhood that embodies codes of acceptable conduct; appropriate codes of the culture. Legalism is exaggerated expression of rules; literal interpretations that may result in ridiculous outcomes.

Authenticity versus impersonation: Authenticity is the ritualization of late childhood and refers to culturally accepted roles for sex, age, status, and setting. Impersonation is an exaggerated expression of roles or adopting roles to impress others.

Formality versus formalism: Formality is the ritualization of the school years and refers to effective ways of doing things accepted by the culture. Formalism is the pretence of being competent.

Ideology versus totalism: Ideology is the ritualization of late adolescence that embodies commitment to a system of beliefs and values approved by a person's culture. Totalism is the fanatical pursuit of ideals; involvement with a cult that promises absolute answers to the problems of life.

Affiliative versus elitism: Affiliative is the ritualization of early adulthood and refers to feelings and patterns of behavior that are appropriate for forming human attachments. Elitism refers to snobbish affiliation; formation of "in" groups; a sense of superior group status.

Generational versus authoritism: Generational is the ritualization of middle adulthood that refers to culturally accepted modes of parenting, which transmit the best of a culture to the next generation; also culturally defined productive skills and worthwhile tasks. Authoritism is the ritualism of

the middle years involving rigid authoritarian roles.

Integral versus sapientism: Integral is the ritualization of old age that embodies expressions of wisdom and self-respect. Sapientism is the unwise pretence of being wise.

Ego strengths: Attainments of the ego that increase adaptive and coping potentials.

Virtue: An unusually well-developed ego strength that is the result of positive resolution of a developmental stage, for example, hope, courage (self-control and willpower), purpose, competence and method, fidelity and devotion, love and affiliation, care and production, and wisdom.

Psychosocial stages: Eight stages characterizing the human life cycle, each of which represents a particular crisis or developmental problem to be solved. Each stage is named in terms of the psychosocial conflict it represents.

1. Basic trust versus mistrust: Trust is a sense of being acceptable to one's self and confident of need-gratification by others, which, if developed fully, leads to the virtue of hope. Mistrust is lack of confidence in self and trust of others; suspiciousness; paranoid tendencies.

2. Autonomy versus shame and doubt: Autonomy refers to healthy expression of ego assertiveness or willpower, if properly developed. Shame refers to feeling unacceptable to others. Doubt refers to defects in self-assertiveness.

3. Initiative versus guilt: Initiative refers to an inner-directed sense of what is right and wrong for one's self; experimentation with different roles; adopting culturally accepted roles aided by the superego. Guilt: feeling unworthy or unacceptable to one's self; sense of being evil.

4. Industry versus inferiority: Industry is the development of skills and the acquisition of knowledge; a sense of competence. Inferiority is a sense of personal deficiency in meeting cultural requirements and in competition with others.

5. Identity versus role confusion: Identity is the sense of being and being perceived as one and the same person; having core ego roles that are accepted by others and define the self. Role confusion is the state of not having clearly defined core ego roles.

6. Intimacy versus isolation: Intimacy is the capacity to form enduring close human relationships; sense of loving and being loved. Isolation is the sense of being unlovable and unacceptable to others.

7. Generativity versus stagnation: Generativity is the sustaining of productive work and caring when an individual reaches full physical, psychological, and social maturity. Generativity nurtures and perpetuates the culture for the next generation; the embodiment and transmission of the culture; a sense of productiveness. Stagnation is the sense of the meaninglessness of life; finding life routine and boring.

8. Ego integrity versus despair: Integrity refers to a sense of wholeness and completeness; respect for self characterized by wisdom, which is defined by the particular culture. Despair is a sense of the futility of life; fear of death.

Epigenetic principle: Maturational unfolding; the emergence through growth of various parts and functions genetically determined, supported, or hindered by environmental factors.

Psychohistory: Analysis of historical personages according to Erikson's developmental theory of personality. Erikson wrote psychohistories of Gandhi, Luther, Hitler, William James, George Bernard Shaw, among others.

Psychosocial: The interaction of social and cultural factors with an organism that is maturing psychologically and physically.

Social feelings: Feelings for or evoked by other people.

    Sympathy: Unity or harmony with another.

    Empathy: Resonating emotionally with another; feeling as the other does; knowing what another feels.

    Identification: More intense form of empathy; taking on the characteristics of another; feeling of being as one with another.

    Reciprocity: Experiencing from the viewpoint of another.

    Mutuality: Giving what the other wants, and wanting what the other gives.

SUGGESTED READINGS

Erikson, Erik H. *Childhood and Society.* New York: Norton, 1950; 2d Ed. 1963.

    Erikson's first book — a classic. He introduces the eight stages of life, along with his concept that the "identity crisis" of the young has become a national concern.

————. *Young Man Luther: A Study in Psychoanalysis and History.* New York: Norton, 1962.

    A psychohistorical analysis of a noteworthy religious figure.

————. *Insight and Responsibility.* New York: Norton 1964.

    A collection of Erikson's essays.

————. *The Challenge of Youth.* Garden City, N.Y.: Doubleday-Anchor, 1965.

    Erikson discusses fidelity and diversity in youth.

————. *Identity: Youth and Crisis.* New York: Norton, 1968.

    In this book Erikson again takes up the eight stages of life, applying many of his concepts to ethnic and social groups.

————. *Toys and Reasons.* New York: Norton, 1977.

    In this little book Erikson presents his discussion of ritualizations and ritualisms.

ALFRED ADLER
ADLER'S INDIVIDUAL PSYCHOLOGY

CHAPTER 6

The Bettmann Archive

CHAPTER 6

BIOGRAPHY AND HISTORICAL PERSPECTIVE

We are by our very nature both selfish and social. We are more motivated by our social impulses than by our sexual drives. We are also conscious, not mainly unconscious. We are able to create our own destinies. We need not be the victims of primitive drives and an uncontrollable environment. We are self-conscious and capable of improving ourselves and the world around us. Our main concerns in life are a vocation, communal living, and love. We are by nature unified and consistent in what we do and not inherently torn by oppositions and conflicts as Freud and Jung maintain. These statements reflect some of the basic concepts of the great Viennese physician, Alfred Adler. They

TABLE 6-1 KEY CONTRASTS BETWEEN FREUD AND ADLER

Freud	Adler
Philosophical pessimism.	Philosophical optimism.
The individual divided against himself.	Essential indivisibility of the individual.
Predominantly antecedent determinants: the past	Predominantly future outcomes determine behavior: goals, ends.
The ego is oppressed by the superego and threatened by civilization.	The individual tends to act aggressively toward the community.
Defenses of the ego. Impulsive needdriven behavior may occur when the defenses are not strong enough.	Styles of life characterized by aggression of the individual against other people. "Barricades" when active aggression has failed.
The infant has a feeling of omnipotence (hallucinatory wish fulfillment).	The child has a feeling of inferiority (relation of midget to giant).
Basic importance of libido (psychic energy), its fixations and regressions.	Symbolism of humans sexual behavior in relation to his struggles for superiority. Using sex in power plays.
Emphasis on relationship to father and mother, and on Oedipus complex.	Emphasis on relationship to siblings and situations in the sibling set.
Neurosis is an inescapable effect of civilization and almost inherent in the human condition.	Neurosis is a trick of the individual to escape fulfilling his or her duties to the community.

Adapted from *The Discovery of the Unconscious: The History and Evolution of Dynamic Psychiatry* by Henri F. Ellenberger. ©1970 by Henri F. Ellenberger. By permission of Basic Books, Inc., Publishers, New York.

constitute a radical departure from Freudian psychoanalysis and, in fact, became the ground on which the two great psychiatrists separated (see Table 6–1).

Adler was born in Vienna in 1870 and lived there until 1935, when, as a result of a threat from the Nazi regime, he moved to the United States. In 1895 he received a medical degree from the same university at which Freud had earlier studied medicine. Although he trained to be an eye specialist, he became a practicing psychiatrist. He learned of Freud and joined his movement. Freud was much impressed by Adler and appointed him the first president of the Vienna Psychoanalytic Society. It soon became apparent that Adler's views were more than an elaboration of the psychoanalytic approach; thus he was invited to state his position before the group in 1911. Subsequently, he was voted out of the association, but about one third of the members left with him. He formed a school of psychiatry of his own, which he named Individual Psychology. Adler was very concerned with the mental health of children and was instrumental in calling attention to child training. He established a child guidance clinic in Vienna and also instituted experimental classes for young children. He died suddenly in 1937 while on a lecture tour of Scotland.

BASIC CONSTRUCTS AND POSTULATES

The Nature of Human Inferiority

Many great students of human nature have recognized human frailty and the profound sense of inferiority that seems to be so characteristic of people, but none has developed this theme as extensively as Adler (1927). Adler believed that humans, unlike many other animals, are not equipped to survive as solitary beings. They do not have claws and sharp teeth to secure food and to defend themselves. Their senses are not as well attuned to the primitive state of existence; thus they would be an easy prey to predators. In order to survive, humans had to band together into clans for mutual protection.

Consider the matter of temperature tolerance as an instance of human frailty. In the course of a year the temperature may vary as much as 100 degrees, but most people find a range of ten degrees comfortable. Some have difficulty adjusting to changes of three or four degrees. Thus in order to survive, people have had to exercise their ingenuity. They have had to build shelters with heating systems to protect against the cold. In the high temperatures of summer they have found relief through air conditioning. They have invented elevators and escalators to ease their burdens. They have invented refrigerators to preserve food and hundreds of gadgets and appliances to overcome one inferiority or another.

Adler, in brief, saw life as an uphill struggle from birth onward, with many skills to learn and many obstacles to overcome. In the course of the struggle, the individual often experiences insecurity because of an inability to adapt to or cope with the situation. People expend much effort in bringing about security, and, for the sake of preserving it, they also seek a measure of reserve. This striving for security and "security plus" may lead to a one-sided development. The highly fearful individual saves for a rainy day but also may accumulate wealth in order to exert control over others. Wealth becomes synonymous with power.

According to Adler, each person must ultimately fashion his or her own life within the context of an environment that is frequently quite demanding and must do this with the limited abilities he or she possesses. Adler points out that:

> Every individual represents both a unity of personality and the individual fashioning of that unity. The individual is thus both the picture and the artist. He is the artist of his own personality, but as an artist he is neither an infallible worker nor a person with a complete understanding of mind and body; he is rather a weak, extremely fallible, and imperfect human being. [Adler, 1956, p. 177]

Recognizing the powerful human struggle for survival, Adler early in his career viewed people as possessing an innate aggressive drive. (Adler in Ansbacher and Ansbacher, 1956) Later he attempted to concretize this aggressive drive by proposing that it is a striving for power or superiority over others. (Adler, 1930) To be strong and masterful and gain superiority is everyone's goal. Even women desire to be masculine because certain privileges relating to courting, marriage, and vocation are associated with masculinity. (Adler, 1929) Adler could have predicted the movement of women's fashions toward more masculine apparel.

Freud = inferior through penis envy + a weakly formed superego
Adler = inferior only in male-given status not inherently **217**
ALFRED ADLER

COMBATING THE INFERIOR STATUS OF WOMEN

Adler wrote repeatedly of the inferior status of women. He wrote long before the current women's liberation movement, but many of his ideas are identical with those currently being proposed (for example, Friedan, 1963). He deplored the inferior status of women and blamed the aggressive superiority of men for the roles in which women were cast. He felt that men forced inferior roles upon women so that they themselves could have advantages. Of the three major tasks of life — occupation, community, and love — women have traditionally been expected to partake of only the last.

There is no biological inferiority justifying the inferior status of women, Adler believed. Whereas Freud stressed women's inferior status through his concept of penis envy and a weakly formed superego, Adler rejected the notion that women are inherently inferior to men. He saw a complementary relationship between the two sexes (different but equal), with quite narrow definitions of difference.

Many women have rejected their own feminine identity, as Freud stated, and actively compete with men. (Adler, 1927) The solution, Adler believed, is to give women much greater freedom of choice and opportunity to express themselves. In other words, the role prescriptions should be far more flexible than they were in Adler's day and greater even than they are today.

Here is a sample of Adler's views regarding the role of women:

> All our institutions, our traditional attitudes, our laws, our morals, our customs, give evidence of the fact that they are determined and maintained by privileged males for the glory of male domination. . . . Nobody can bear a position of inferiority without anger and disgust. . . . That women must be submissive is . . . (a) superstitition. . . . [Adler, 1927; cited in Ewen, 1980, p. 138]

Development of Normal and Abnormal Strivings for Superiority

Adler held that the prolonged state of human inferiority exerts a profound effect upon the whole motivational system of the species. The child, like the adult, is always striving to improve his or her status. Everything significant that the child seeks is governed by a desire to overcome a profound sense of inadequacy. No matter what a person accomplishes or acquires, there is always more. Adler (1930) believed that life is not motivated by forces making for homeostasis or equilibrium, nor is it motivated by survival tendencies, nor is it driven by the lure of pleasure and the avoidance of pain. He believed that the main force behind everything people do, beyond the drive level of functioning, is the push to move from an inferior to a superior state, from minus to plus, from beneath to above. The healthy person is always seeking to improve his or her lot in life. Adler portrays this ceaseless striving for superiority in the following manner:

> The impetus from minus to plus never ends. The urge from below to above never ceases. Whatever premises all our philosophers and psychologists dream of — self-preservation,

pleasure principle, equalization—all these are but vague representations, attempts to express the great upward drive. [1930, p. 398]

The urge for superiority takes many forms: insatiable craving to rule others in the power-driven psychopaths, tyrannical wailing in the hypochondriacs who control everyone around them, energetic striving in the parents who want to bring up their family to be contributing members of society. In thousands and thousands of ways, humans seek to improve their lives.

Children have a vast number of things to learn. Before mastering something, they are inferior with respect to that particular thing. When they extend their sphere of activity outside the home in play with other children, a whole new source of situations that cause inferiority is opened up. Certain standards of performance are expected, and the child who fails is dealt with harshly. As children grow older, they are brought more and more into the culture. Competition is everywhere. Games are played to win. Team against team, boy against boy, and girl against girl—all create a climate of contention, of striving from an inferior status to that of a superior or victorious one. In a recent book, *Great Expectations*, Jones (1981) discusses the increased competition that the "baby boom" generation occurring after World War II is now experiencing in the limited job market.

In school, children also encounter the signs and symbols of power. The teacher is an authority who has great influence over them. Grades and awards are given for superior performance. These awards are usually based on meeting certain requirements regardless of how this is accomplished. In an atmosphere of continual evaluation and testing, great praise and honor are accorded those who meet the high standards of the test. Adler (1927) points out that even the great religions have a place after death for those who are morally superior and another place for those who are morally inferior.

In his later years, Adler came to the conclusion that for those who are developing and functioning normally the *striving for superiority* is a search for *self-perfection* (Ansbacher and Ansbacher, 1964). This concept is similar to the notion of self-actualization proposed by Maslow and by Carl Rogers—the quality of being a fully functioning person or at least of moving in the direction of actualizing our potentialities. The person who has attained a high degree of superiority in the sense of perfecting the self can be considered individualized, mature, fully functioning, or self-actualized. Striving for superiority is a general human motive which is expressed in unique ways by each individual: being excused from rules, being cared for, gaining control of others, or being exempt from work are abnormal forms of the striving for superiority. Perfecting yourself within the framework of a highly developed sense of social feeling is the healthiest expression of this striving for superiority, Adler (1939) believed. Social motives are just as much a part of human nature as the urge to be superior. To become active, however, they must be fostered and supported in the child by a tolerant and affectionate family climate. Being the recipient of the social feelings of another is one way that social feelings are stimulated. Without such encouragement, the harsher forms of superiority striving—aggressiveness and the desire for power over others—will predominate. These tendencies, characterized by selfish motives and lack of a sense of social feeling, are signs of abnormality.

UNREALISTIC EXPECTATIONS

One type of striving for absolute perfection is steadfast commitment to unrealistic goals. Such striving, which is an abnormal expression of the struggle for superiority, may be harmful to personality growth and functioning if the expectations remain unfulfilled. A child may grow up with great hopes for success in school, only to experience a succession of failures. Young persons are easily trapped into looking everywhere for perfection. The young man wishes to find a perfect wife, not one who gets angry or is moody from time to time. Even mature people search for a car without a dent in it. Because it is so important to them, they want it to be perfect. We expect the significant events of life to be without the slightest flaw. But most aspects of living are ordinarily far from perfect; thus those who cannot make compromises or accept less than absolute perfection will suffer disillusionment and disappointment. The person who desires absolute perfection is really saying, by his or her behavior, that he or she is a superior being.

Probably the greatest source of unhappiness is failure to fulfill expectations. An unfulfilled expectation may have an additional element: a sense of personal responsiblity for not being able to remedy it. Many expectations are by their very nature unfulfillable and thus inevitably lead to disillusionment.

The striving for perfection permeates all significant spheres of life. Most people, for example, have unrealistic expectations regarding vocation. A number of difficulties may arise: aspirations may be based on job status rather than on real abilities or interest. Medicine is selected by many young people because it offers so many apparent benefits. The person who expects his or her work to be challenging, exciting, worthwhile, and contributing to the betterment of humanity is bound to be disillusioned. Not that your work cannot satisfy basic needs (indeed, many find work their major interest in life), but to expect from it total fulfillment or satisfaction of needs that should be met by other activities can lead only to self-pity or other abnormal reactions. The striving for perfection is not a new phenomenon of our generation. It is just receiving more attention. Intensified competition fosters the striving for perfection — the belief that life can not only be better than it is, but perfect.

INFERIORITY, COMPENSATION, AND OVERCOMPENSATION

Adler used the term *compensation* for the strategy whereby people make up for an inferiority. Compensation helps to establish and preserve self-esteem. In the strict Adlerian sense, it means to make up for a weakness. (Adler, 1931) In a broader sense, it means to cover up or hide a weakness.

Compensation in the sense of making up for a weakness can promote healthy functioning when a person directs energy away from a weakness that cannot be changed to behavior that can be improved. If the effort is extreme, it may be termed unhealthy compensation — for example, when a frustrated football player becomes a cheerleader and devotes most of his time to that activity. Thus, we may distinguish between healthy and unhealthy forms of compensation and healthy and unhealthy overcompensation. A common unhealthy form of compensation is substitute gratification; one need is gratified for another, which is thwarted. An example of this is eating sweets to relieve frustration. You may compensate for weakness by working diligently to overcome it—for example, when a stutterer works to conquer his or her speech difficulty and actually becomes an excellent speaker. This form of compensation, which is a manifestation of the striving for superiority, is known as healthy overcompensation. It promotes healthy adaptation to life by the overcoming of a severe handicap.

Adler uses the term *overcompensation* in a healthy sense to refer to the overcoming of a weakness. Many great men and women have had to face life with serious handicaps, but they turned their weakness into strength. Helen Keller, who was both deaf and blind, became an outstanding author and lecturer. Adler pointed out that in such instances the inferiority was a powerful motivator that spurred the person to achieve prominence. Adler himself was a sickly child of short stature, who suffered throughout his life from an eye defect. Sociologists, on the other hand, have found a much higher than average incidence of abnormalities and physical impairments in prison populations; thus, the direction of compensation or overcompensation may be favorable or unfavorable. That is, there are both healthy and unhealthy forms of compensation and overcompensation, as we have noted.

Other forms of compensation and overcompensation aim more to prove superiority over others than to perfect our lives. The person who masks a profound sense of inadequacy by a blustering manner or by monopolizing conversation is exhibiting an unhealthy form of overcompensation by a pretense of strength where there is weakness.

The reason that some unhealthy forms of overcompensation are abnormal striving for superiority is that the person cannot accept a weakness in himself or herself, but tries desperately to convert it into a strength. The weakness is focused on extensively and sometimes appears to be a strong point in the person's life. The key to understanding abnormal overcompensation as a form of abnormal striving for superiority, however, is to recognize that the person rejects the self as is. The person cannot accept himself or herself with the supposed weakness. Ordinarily, the inferiority is an unalterable one, such as physique, limited talent in music, or poor sensory acuity. The behavior that constitutes the overcompensation is exaggerated, for instance, the unattractive girl who overdresses.

Fictional Finalism: The Role of Fictional Goals

quarterback story, "I wanted to be sure that Mama loved me"

As we have seen, striving for superiority is a general motivation that takes concrete form as a striving toward a particular goal. Adler (1930) greatly emphasized the role of future goals in determining present behavior. Many aspects of present behavior can be understood only in terms of a guiding goal. Rather than looking to the past as a cause of behavior, as Freud did, Adler stressed future strivings as embodied in a person's present goals: "The main problem of psychology is not to comprehend the causal factors as in physiology, but the direction-giving, pulling forces and goals which guide all other psychological movements." (1931, p. 216) With the knowledge of the guiding goal, all the elements of a behavioral unit are perceived as forming a coherent structure. This view has much in common with the Gestalt principle that the whole dominates the sum of its parts. Like the "whole" concept of Gestalt psychology, the guiding idea gives the parts a specific formal unity (Dreikurs, 1963). Frequently, a behavioral act begins with the projection of a goal, which is then followed by the specific behaviors to attain it. The behaviors would not make sense to an observer who did not possess knowledge of the goal.

Adler follows the view of teleology, which holds that one's intention or goal directs behavior. The purpose that one has guides the choice of behavior that will achieve that purpose. Thus, knowledge of a person's goals is the key to the source of motivation.

Some form of striving is characteristic of all living things, but in people striving toward goals may be a conscious process, as when a young man wishes to marry a particular girl and works to win her affection. However, goal striving need not be conscious. A school boy may behave badly in class without really knowing what his purpose is. The astute teacher may understand the purpose perfectly well: the child may be wanting and striving to get attention directed toward him. Not being capable of or willing to earn it in the usual manner, he resorts to unruly behavior. The fact that the child is unaware (unconscious) of his goal does not alter the fact that his behavior is being subordinated to a goal. Taken in this sense, so-called unconscious motivation loses some of its mystery. Unconscious motivation is simply motivation that a person does not recognize. (Adler, 1927)

Adler would counsel one who wishes to understand the behavior of another to look for the goal that the person wishes to achieve, or in some cases the goal that the person wishes to avoid. In therapy he would ask his patient: "Supposing that you did not have this ailment, what would you do?" The reply would usually reveal the particular thing the patient was avoiding: the hypochondriac, for example, would desire to work. (Ellenberger, 1970) If a psychologist is fortunate enough to hit upon the dominant goal early in his or her investigation, he or she will find that the patient's life history, as well as comtemporary style of life, is the logical outcome of this goal.

Some of the major goals around which lives may be organized are these: dominating others, leaning on others, withdrawing from the world, seeking wealth, craving fame, or desiring to be the most beautiful person in the world. Ultimately, there are as many guiding goals as there are people.

THE NATURE OF FICTIONAL GOALS

Adler derived one of his major ideas from the philosopher Hans Vaihinger, author of *The Philosophy of "As If"* (1925). Vaihinger pointed out that many of our most powerful beliefs and expectations are fictions (as if's), which we act upon as though they were facts. For example, Vaihinger stated that many people believe that there is a God, that heaven and hell exist, that certain people are their friends, and that certain values are worth striving for. In his emphasis on goals as the major source of motivation, Adler came to realize that our goals are usually fictional in nature. People behave as if something is true, even though they do not know whether it in fact is really true. Fictions can be harmful, as when a paranoid person believes that others are trying to hurt him or her. Even when the evidence may not warrant such a belief, a fictional belief can be quite real to the person who harbors it. Some beliefs, even if they are fictions, are valuable because they promote positive behavior. The old lady in a nursing home believes that her children love her, but are too busy to visit her. She is better off with this fictional belief than knowing the truth—that they do not think enough of her to take the time to see her.

Some fictions cannot be tested—for example, honesty is the best policy; some fictions can be tested, but should not be—for example, parents love their children; some should definitely be tested—for example, business people are honest. The first and second types of fictions can be judged in terms of whether or not they are useful or harmful. The third type of fictional belief should be converted into a testable hypothesis which is either true or false. A belief that business people are always honest can lead to painful consequences. When outcomes can be dangerous, fictions should be tested.

Another example of a fiction that serves as powerful motivation for many Americans is the view that, with much hard work and a little good luck, you can accomplish almost anything. Many people believe that work is the solution to all desires. If you want something seriously enough, you can get it by working hard. Yet there are many who work hard and never achieve their dreams. A graduate student who received poor marks complained that he worked hard throughout the semester. He had done a good deal of reading in his field. He could not understand why he was not doing well. He was reading in his field, but the trouble was that he was not reading his assignments. He wanted to read those things which interested him, not what was required to pass examinations.

Marc & Evelyne Bernheim 1980/Woodfin Camp & Associates

Some fictions are useful because they enable us to avoid painful realities.

He was behaving as if all "reading is a sacred thing to do" and that any kind of reading is productive. This fiction has been fostered by well-meaning teachers. A physicist who devoted all his reading time to psychology would not be true to his professional obligation.

Fictions may take the form of ideals. An ideal by its very nature is never completely attainable. Teachers may desire to be excellent in their profession. To be excellent has no final limits. They can always learn more in their subject area. Certainly, they can spend more time than they do with students. They might be able to increase their preparation time or at least to increase their efficiency. The ideal can hardly be defined, let alone attained. Nevertheless, the striving to attain their ideal greatly influences their behavior.

Some would hold that a belief in God is a guiding fiction that has proved valuable for people in general and for countless individuals. They hold that whether God really exists is not as important as that the belief is real. The effects produced by belief in a fictional God are identical with those produced by belief in a real God. Society as well as the individual profits from the belief. As we have pointed out, though much fictional thinking is useful for the person and may promote adaptive and coping behavior, some fictions are dangerous and harmful. The person who believes that power over others is a desirable thing may bend all his or her efforts to acquire this status. Such behavior is guided by a false ideal, but it impels the person toward the end of dominating those around him or her.

An example of a fiction that could be tested but probably should not be is that your physician cares about you in a personal way. Many people believe this; however, they do not expect to test this conviction by attempting to socialize with their doctor. It is as if they unconsciously know that such a relationship could not occur. Believing that the doctor really cares is a sufficient incentive to hold people to a difficult diet, or to help them take distasteful medicine regularly. One woman who had an overweight problem would tell her friends that her doctor got angry with her when she got beyond a certain point, and before seeing him for her yearly checkup she would diet stringently. Again it should be noted that whether or not her physician was really concerned about her condition does not change the matter. Even if he were not really concerned, the fact that she believed he was kept her from losing control of a potentially dangerous situation. Her behavior was being controlled by a fictional goal, namely, to please her concerned physician. We should keep in mind that all perceptions, beliefs, and expectations we form are personal constructions. They involve personal interpretations.

GOAL OF LIFE

Adler spoke repeatedly of the "goal of life," as if a person has only one goal—a concept that may be confusing. Obviously people have many, many everyday desires that set them to work toward goals. They want to get married, buy a house, follow a career. Yet in each person there is usually one outstanding goal, conscious or not, that plays a dominant role in that person's life. It may be something like being a reasonable and likable sport, possessing more wealth than one's friends, being more attractive than anyone else, making an impression on everyone, being a good conversationalist. Sometimes the guiding goal is a secret ambition that is cherished and guarded from being discovered by others. The guiding goal is frequently unconscious, although it is expressed in the person's behavior and is quite obvious to the astute observer. Adler maintained that the neurotic individual usually harbors a secret ambition of being unique and extraordinary among people. He or she may act as if the secret ambition is being fulfilled. The point is that the concrete goals of life stem from a feeling of inferiority and can best be comprehended as expressions of the one ultimate goal of striving for superiority, which takes unique form in each individual. (Adler, 1927) They must also be interpreted through a knowledge of the person's *style of life.*

The Style of Life

Adler (1929) used the expression "style of life" to designate the unique configuration of characteristics identifying a person. Each style of life is unique, though the psychology of personality has not yet advanced to a point that permits adequate characterization of the unique individual. We cannot yet, so to speak, put a person on paper. While insisting on the uniqueness and complexity of styles of life, Adler in his description of them usually used general trait names, such as the power-driven individual, the optimist, the pessimist, or the seclusive orientation. He did, however, elaborate some traits that characterize a recognizable style of life. For example, he described the optimistic style of life by characteristics such as courage, openness, social feeling, and so on. We can recognize a style of life much more easily than we can describe it.

The style of life is integrated, with all the components working together. (Adler, 1931) Every major component has an effect on all the others. If a person is intelligent, a large portion of his or her behavior is influenced by this fact. In most things this person does, although some behaviors are more affected by it than others, intelligence plays a major role. A person who is egocentric often perceives, remembers, thinks, feels, and acts with a selfish attitude. Whether such a person is driving or playing cards or participating in a conversation, his or her egocentricity plays a part. Some components are more influential, more easily aroused, more central than others. In characterizing the style of life we can usually point to a single directional tendency that is the most central determinant. This, it will be recalled, is a guiding fiction.

EARLY ESTABLISHMENT OF THE STYLE OF LIFE

Like Freud, Adler (1931) held that the style of life is formed early, usually during the first five years. He pointed out that one can observe marked differences in infants right from birth. Some children are restless and easily agitated. They may have difficulty sleeping and eating. Others seem more attuned to the demands of living and demonstrate little disturbance in meeting their survival requirements (Thomas, Chess, and Birch, 1970).

The style of life becomes more complex, more unique, and more fixed with development. It includes elements that maintain and preserve it. As it is formed, all psychological processes are organized into habitual modes of perceiving, thinking, feeling, and behaving. An optimist remembers, reasons, judges, feels, and acts quite differently from a pessimist. If two individuals with different life styles experienced the same event and subsequently described what took place, the accounts would be radically different. There would be omissions and additions by both individuals that could be traced to the particular style of life. If an interpretation of the events were given, the disparity between the accounts would be still greater.

Adler gives us a colorful anecdote that highlights early differences in the operation of the style of life:

> Perhaps I can illustrate this by an anecdote of three children who were taken to the zoo for the first time. As they stood before the lion's cage, one of them shrank behind his mother's skirts and said, "I want to go home." The second child stood where he was, very pale and trembling, and said, "I'm not a bit frightened." The third glared at the lion fiercely and asked his mother, "Shall I spit at it?" The three children really felt inferior, but each expressed his feelings in his own way, consonant with his style of life. [1931, p. 50]

One major determinant of life-style is the family environment in which the child grows. The earliest experiences are quite significant because everything is so new and unexpected. Consider such events as the first spanking, waking up cold and alone in the middle of the night, the first fall from the crib, mother and dad having a quarrel.

Adler insisted that one's philosophy of life, which is a major component of the style of life, is actually being formed during the early years of life. Through the creative power of the self, the person forms his or her style of life. Heredity provides certain abilities and tendencies, and the environment confronts the individual with a variety of experiences, but the creative power of the self selectively evolves a unique style of life. Early experiences with strongly felt inferiorities greatly determine the nature of the style of life.

Adler (1931) gave special weight to the position of the child in relation to brothers and sisters, *birth order*. Being the youngest boy with three older sisters must contribute something significant to the formation of a style of life, he would argue. Each of the many possible family configurations would exert a similarly enduring effect on its members. Other early influences are the temperament of the parents, their financial circumstances, and companions. Early attitudes, emotional responses, and expectations persist a lifetime.

Weak children, who often have to endure the hardship of being picked on constantly, may never get over the resultant feelings of profound inferiority in their relationships with others. They may develop forms of compensation that become characteristic. Their secret ambition may be to humiliate others in order to prove their superiority. Their perceptions of events, their memories, their judgments, their emotions—all are shaped by the family atmosphere and early environment into which they are born.

Many great students of human beings have accepted the notion that infancy and childhood are the formative years, a period when basic habits are shaped. Children's learning is drive-related. They learn basic social skills and reactions and a host of other "tool" skills. Their learning might be described as the "art of living" learning. But

Adler went beyond saying that the first five years are important formative years. He held that the form of personality is *established* during the first five years (Adler, 1954). In other words, the basic structure is laid down, and whatever modifications later occur are elaborations and extensions of the basic style of life.

Although imprinting had not yet been discovered in Adler's day, the principles that have since been laid down (Hess, 1964) would tend to support the notion that certain time periods and appropriate experiences combine to produce learning that is quite resistant to change. Birds that mimic can be trained to utter sounds or vocalizations during a relatively brief critical period. Learning is rapid during this period but does not occur before and after it. Extending this concept to childhood, early pleasureable and painful experiences (and probably attitudes, prejudices, and general orientation to life) are especially well learned and preclude being replaced by other experiences. It is certainly true, at least, that children have difficulty dealing with experiences and situations that were lacking in their early history. A child who has not been respected may not know how to respond to the regard of others and may thereby frustrate their expressions of regard. Hurtful experiences foster faulty learning, which interferes with later corrective learning.

STYLES OF LIFE AND STRIVING FOR SUPERIORITY

As Adler often pointed out, some individuals react to their inferiority by developing a faulty style of living, whereas others distinguish themselves by superior achievements. Pampered children may find that they can rule their parents by making their demands conspicuously felt. Neglected children gain their superiority by withdrawing and becoming self-sufficient although they grow up lacking social feeling, a handicap that hinders them in everything they do. Petted children win a place of superiority through weakness. Sickly children gain their significance from the care that is given them. Yet Adler found that in the lives of many great men and women there existed a physical or psychological inferiority that was especially difficult to bear.

Psychological inferiorities are just as powerful determinants of behavior as the more obvious physical inferiorities. A child who is adequately endowed physically and mentally may acquire a terrible sense of inferiority as a result of adverse comparison with an older brother who is favored by the parents. Such a child develops the secret goal of someday defeating and humiliating the brother and earning his or her parents' esteem, and this attitude may generalize to all people: this child needs to have everyone's highest regards. Those who care for the child can greatly influence whether the style of life becomes constructive or destructive.

Table 6–2 is a summary of the major Adlerian concepts. It depicts the differences between normal and neurotic strivings for superiority.

VIEWS ON ABNORMALITY

Adler related abnormality of personality development and functioning to the various aspects of his model of humans: profound sense of inferiority, faulty compensations and overcompensations, abnormal strivings for superiority, mistaken life-style, useless

TABLE 6-2 ADLER'S BASIC MOTIVATIONAL PRINCIPLES

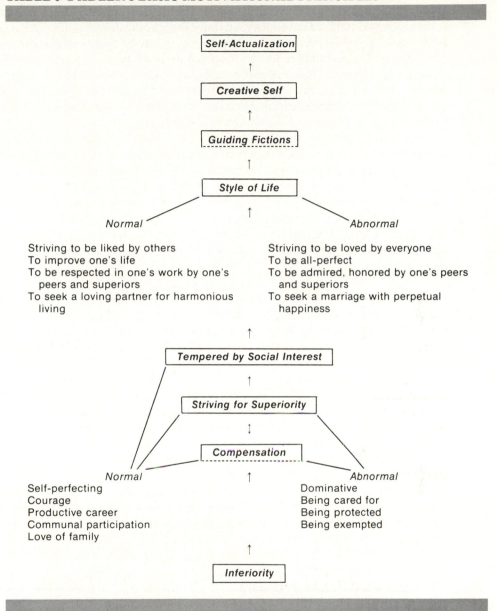

fictions, self-preoccupations, inadequate social interest, and low activity level. Everyone experiences inferiority in striving to improve himself or herself and his or her circumstances. The beginner and novice sense their inferiority in comparison with the master or expert, whether it be as a homemaker, an artisan, a physician, or a garage mechanic. The striving to improve constitutes a healthy superiority striving in such instances.

Both the sense of inferiority and the striving to overcome it, when normal, promote constructive behaviors. Personality disorders result from a profound sense of inferiority and exaggerated forms of superiority strivings. People may develop unhealthy compensations and overcompensations. Their guiding goal may be highly unrealistic and selfish. The guiding goal may reflect an irrational drive for power, success, perfection, or other idealistic goals. Their fictional beliefs may lead to behavior that is highly inappropriate to their life requirements. The inferiority feelings may be so disruptive that the people are driven to establish some type of superiority over others. The resulting behavior may be highly maladaptive and self-defeating.

Adler (1917) traces the development of abnormalities such as neuroses to the childhood period. In a child who is constitutionally predisposed to illness or nervousness, abnormality develops when conditions are "overburdening" (stressful) such as organ inferiority, neglect by the parents, or even pampering. Certainly, we would have to include, as an overburdening condition, the many forms of abuse that parents inflict upon their children. The child under conditions of stress creates what Adler terms a *mistaken life-style*. The child is severely handicapped in meeting the major problems of living. His or her orientations to reality are seriously distorted; thus he or she makes many mistakes.

Many strategies that are part of the disordered style of living are termed symptoms by psychiatrists and psychologists. Although the symptoms are painful, they are less painful than facing the real or contrived inferiorities. The more the individual experiences inferiority, the greater is the effort to compensate and the more urgent is the striving for superiority. Failure is inevitable when such developments occur. Life becomes a desperate struggle to fulfill self-imposed expectations that are impossible of attainment.

Adler frequently stressed that the striving for superiority was a desperate attempt to overcome a sense of inferiority. But it should be borne in mind that being in a superior status brings many benefits. The sickly child enjoys a privileged position in the family. Being the life of the party or the admired leader or the most talented member of a crowd satisfies many basic needs, and often these positions are sought for their own sake. We are always seeking to establish the extent of our capabilities and our personal effectiveness. Abnormality occurs when the individual strives in vain to establish his or her superiority rather than accept his or her position. The desperate striving for superiority may be due to the unwillingness to be simply an average member of a group.

Abnormal Strivings for Superiority

Why does a person become a pathological liar? The pathological liar may lie about the most trivial things. Some people love to deceive their listeners by making up lies. They gain a sense of superiority over those who cannot refute their deceptions. The kleptomaniac (one who steals for apparent pleasure rather than from a desire for the object) is also demonstrating a striving for superiority, Adler believed. Such a person is "pulling something off" — is "getting something for nothing."

There are those who constantly seek to gain an advantage over others through exemptions or privileges. Again, the superiority striving is evident: "If there are rules, they apply to the masses but not to me. If there is an obligation, it applies to ordinary people but not to me." By their behavior cynical people say that nothing is good enough for them; thus nothing is worthwhile. The criminal is looking for an easy way of getting what others must work for. The cultural dropout puts himself or herself above the ordinary requirements of day-to-day living. Many forms of striving for superiority are maladaptive and, in the long run, produce more difficulties for the individual. In his therapeutic work, Adler was vigilant in identifying these abnormal forms of the striving for superiority. He found that many of his patients were trying to get away with doing less than their share of work. *Neurotics*, for Adler (1929), were cowards who used their illness as a means of exempting themselves from the responsibilities that others had to take.

Safeguarding Tendencies and Barricades

In order to create a sense of adequacy, people may use what Adler called *safeguarding tendencies*. These are protective devices, similar to Freud's defense mechanisms. For example, a common way of dealing with difficult situations is by getting sick. The child may learn early in life that he or she can be excused from unpleasant tasks by illness or by the pretense of illness. This may become a habitual pattern of behavior: The person becomes sickly and frail although there may not be anything really wrong. We are all tempted to find a way out of facing the many problems of growing up and living, but somehow we muster the courage to face them. Sickly persons gain a measure of superiority because they are not judged by the same standards that are applied to everyone else.

They enjoy not only the benefits of exemption from work but even a degree of superiority over those who grant them such privileges. In addition, illness can be used as a means of *excusing ourselves* from participation in any competition. Just as others may apply less stringent standards for a person who is ill, so individuals may evaluate themselves in this way. They may continue to harbor great visions of the accomplishments they will someday achieve when their illness passes. A persistent illness preserves their self-esteem by keeping them out of battle and at the same time obviating the possibility of a test of their abilities. With these conditions in mind, it should not be surprising to find that many people are in a chronic state of illness. Usually, this takes the form of vague aches and pains, digestive difficulties, or headaches. No treatment seems to bring about a cure, for, unconsciously, the individual does not want to be cured. According to Adler (1927), such an illness is a means of attaining a position of superiority: should this person succeed despite the supposed sickliness, he or she is all the more worthy of glory because, as it were, he or she "accomplishes with one hand what others do with two." Adler termed the use of illness to control others the *weapons of weakness*.

Safeguarding tendencies are security measures or strategies for dealing with feelings of inferiority. (Adler in Ansbacher and Ansbacher, 1956) Everyone is constantly assailed by demands and pressures. These external requirements and personal needs lead to insecurity that is accompanied by anxiety, fear, anger, doubt, and other unpleasant affective states. Efforts are expended to deal with the internal or external demands when they occur, and even to anticipate them before they occur. If we are overwhelmed by the demands placed upon us, our adaptive and coping mechanisms may break down, and we may resort to protective strategies. Safeguarding strategies (in contrast to coping and adaptive procedures) may include distorted or selective perception, prejudicial thinking, memory impairment, obstinacy, compulsiveness, general nervousness, depression, and, in short, those behaviors and emotions which are considered symptoms of personality disorders. Certainly no one is free from safeguarding tendencies and barricades; everyone uses protective devices at times. But the normal individual uses them less often and in less exaggerated forms.

Adler refers to safeguarding tendencies in the following passage:

> All neurotic symptoms have as their object the task of safeguarding the patient's self-esteem and thereby also the life-line [life-style] into which he has grown. To prove his ability to cope with life the patient needs arrangements and neurotic symptoms as an expedient. He needs them as an oversized safeguarding component against the dangers which, in his feeling of inferiority, he expects and incessantly seeks to avoid in working out his plans for the future. [Adler, 1913, p. 263][1]

Adler used the term *barricades* to describe various withdrawal techniques such as shyness, weakness, tiredness, and sensitivity of all sorts. Such devices may preserve the sense of self-esteem by keeping the individual out of the mainstream of life. If the person claims to have a great talent, it is never really put to the test. The undiscovered composer, artist, or writer may nourish a fantasy of greatness for years. Zimbardo (1977) introduces the notion of "the prison of shyness," which exemplifies clearly Adler's construct of barricades. Safeguarding tendencies and barricades provide an excuse for failure.

Adler's Typology

Adler developed a schema for typing people that may be helpful in understanding in simple terms the nature of abnormalities. He views *degree of activity* and *degree of social interest* as significant factors in living. We must be active in order to deal with the three major problems of living: vocation, community, and family; we must also be capable of relating to other people because they are so intimately involved with success or failure in these aspects of our lives. Keeping these two dimensions in mind, let us consider the possibilities.

[1]"Individual-Psychological Treatment of Neurosis," cited in Ansbacher-Ansbacher, *The Individual Psychology of Alfred Adler*.

© Sepp Seitz 1979, 1980/Woodfin Camp & Associates

One's style of life often becomes more conspicuous with age.

HIGH ACTIVITY, LOW SOCIAL INTEREST: THE RULING TYPE

People of the ruling type are energetic and aggressive in pursuing their own ends. They get what they want because they are willing to work hard and take the required steps, but because they lack social interest, they work strictly for selfish goals, even at the expense of others. They may exploit or manipulate others.

LOW ACTIVITY, HIGH SOCIAL INTEREST: THE GETTING TYPE

The getting type is oriented toward people and, in fact, is liked or loved by others. He or she uses charm and personal power over others to establish a parasitic relationship, in which he or she receives rather than gives. Such a person's activity level is not sufficient to meet his or her problems and the demands placed upon him or her; thus he turns to others for care.

LOW ACTIVITY: LOW SOCIAL INTEREST: THE AVOIDING TYPE

People of the avoiding type lack both activity and social interest. They seek exemptions and avoidance of responsibility. They may limit their participation in life in order to avoid failure, disappointment, and other painful experiences. They make a mess out of their lives because they neither do much to work out their problems nor relate well to people with whom they must deal.

HIGH ACTIVITY, HIGH SOCIAL INTEREST: THE NORMAL PERSON

Normal people energetically confront their problems and the requirements of living. They keep in touch with reality and profit from their mistakes and keep their goals in line with their achievements. They are successful in part because they relate to and work well with other people who are important in all aspects of their lives. Socially oriented people work amicably and cooperatively with others. They achieve personal goals in the context of various social groups: their work setting, family, and community.

Neurosis: A Cowardly Orientation to Life

A neurotic may be characterized as being low in activity, low in social interest, low in self-regard, high in superiority striving, high in grandiose fictional goals, and high in self-preoccupation. Neurotics expect much from life, but do little to achieve their aims. Their inferiority feelings drive them to set highly unrealistic goals. They resort to what Adler calls "cheap tricks" to cover up their weaknesses and lack of real achievement. They seek easy solutions: making it big in the lottery, becoming famous, finding an alluring marital partner who will make life interesting and exciting, being popular and outstanding in some way.

Many aspects of neurosis have been stressed: superficiality of self, childishness, overdeveloped conscience, and repression. But Adler's is perhaps the most descriptive. For Adler, the neurotic is a coward, one who avoids facing the requirements of living. The neurotic avoids work and any form of frustration at all cost. At the same time he or she is convinced that his or her sufferings and hardships are much greater than anyone else's; thus a neurotic easily sets himself or herself apart as being something rather special and extraordinary. He or she has more difficulty with the major tasks of life because the cowardly orientation prevents him or her from dealing with problems.

Russell Abraham 1976/Stock, Boston

The neurotic avoids any form of frustration at all costs.

He or she is always looking for exemptions, for an easy way out, yet craves great success and respect.

In the following passage Adler describes some of the attributes of the neurotic life-style:

> Neurosis is the natural, logical development of an individual who is comparatively inactive, filled with a personal egocentric striving for superiority and is, therefore, retarded in the development of his social interests. [1917, p. 24][2]

An essential aspect of neurosis is the preoccupation with self. The neurotic is a highly selfish person for whom other people are one of the major problems in life. The neurotic is so preoccupied with his or her own problems that he or she does not consider other people. In a sense, the neurotic is like a grown-up child. The social sentiments are not highly developed. Just as the coward is very much concerned about his or her own life, so the neurotic is not sensitive to the needs and feelings of others, often hurting people without realizing that he or she is doing so. Such a person is frequently puzzled by the reactions received from others because he or she cannot understand why they are angry, hurt, or slighted. The neurotic does not understand because of being so wrapped up in himself or herself as not even to perceive his or her own selfish behavior. Adler was insistent that people should learn to be courageous and be willing to tolerate pain and sorrow. Children who are pampered and overprotected are not really prepared for life.

VIEWS ON IDEAL PERSONALITY AND LIVING

We can learn about ideal personality and living by looking at what a personality therapist does with his or her clients or patients. Adler sought to develop a warm and friendly relationship with his patients for the purpose of gaining respect and confidence. His approach was probably the first reality therapy. He encouraged a realistic orientation to life's problems by gently but firmly helping his patients face their unrealistic notions of things and people instead of blaming their illness on early painful experiences. The past was probed not to uncover the unconscious but to identify the neurotic style of life. He believed that earliest memories and experiences might reveal this style of living. He urged his patient to begin living on the useful side of life; above all, he worked to encourage the social tendencies in the patient. In most cases, the primary difficulty was lack of real social feeling.

Adler became convinced that although humans are selfish by nature, social tendencies are also a part of their nature. We need other people to satisfy many of our most basic needs and desires—love, sex, companionship, working partner or team, friends and acquaintances, models. The social aspect is apparently weaker than the more selfish drives; thus, social interests should be supported by the important people in the life of the growing child. Adler felt that he could awaken social interest in his

---

[2]*The Neurotic Constitution.*

Copyright Ray Ellis '76/Photo Researchers, Inc.

Most of our needs are satisfied in special settings; thus social feelings and social skills help us.

patients through his own warm personal contacts. The genuine human encounter would be such an enjoyable experience that it would prompt the patient to seek such experiences outside of therapy. The mature person does many things as a result of social interests and concerns. Even when he or she is working for his or her own ends, it is usually in a social setting and in cooperation with others—family, work setting, members of the community. Adler believed that people should work to improve and perfect themselves and to overcome inferiority feelings in social settings. The highest attributes of a person stem from well-developed social feelings. These feelings temper the power drive and make a person responsive to the needs of others.

Children, according to Adler (1939), are not antisocial by nature. They have innate dispositions to respond with social feeling and interest, but they are also highly egocentric. Life in a community is social in almost every respect. Children cannot avoid relationships with others. Success in satisfying individual needs is contingent upon success in dealing with social relationships. A warm, tolerant, supportive home atmosphere fosters the development of social feeling and social skills. Normal people want and value social relationships. They recognize that social interest is a criterion of social-emotional maturity. They accept the requirements of the culture and become contributing members. Abnormal people direct their motivation to egocentric goals and reject the culture. They are aliens in an enemy country.

Regarding social feelings, Adler says:

> It is always the want of social feelings, whatever be the name one gives it—living in fellowship, co-operation, humanity, or even the ideal-ego—which causes an insufficient preparation for all the problems of life. [1964, p. 110][3]

Table 6-3 presents a number of attributes that one of Adler's disciples discovered in the socially mature individual.

The Creative Power of the Self

Consideration of Adler's views on ideal personality and living requires an understanding of Adler's concept of the creative power of the self. It is similar to the traditional idea of ego as a free agent. The creative self plays an important role in the formation of the style of life; it is the basis for change in personality. There would be no point in personality therapy unless there is a potential for change, and the creative self is the agent that is at work in effective therapy. We can change our own circumstances and reactions by making things happen the way we want them to be. Adler strongly believed that we are not the helpless victims of our unconscious mind or of our past or present circumstances. Above all, we can even surmount our own selfishness and allow the social side of our nature greater opportunity for expression. He felt the style of life can be altered although with difficulty. We can learn self-control, how to arrange priorities and satisfy our needs, how to work toward goals, and how to express our values in our everyday behavior. We can learn to push ourselves by doing one thing more or by taking the first step even if it is a small one. The creative self exercises much control

TABLE 6-3 THE SOCIALLY MATURE INDIVIDUAL

Respects the rights of others	Is courageous
Is tolerant of others	Has a true sense of his own worth
Is interested in others	Has a feeling of belonging
Cooperates with others	Has socially acceptable goals
Encourages others	Puts forth genuine effort

Meets the needs of the situation
Is willing to share rather than say
"How much can I get?"
Thinks of "we" rather than just "I"

From Don Dinkmeyer, "The 'C' group: Integrating Knowledge and Experience to Change Behavior, An Adlerian Approach to Consultation, *Journal of Counseling Psychology*, 3:63–71, 1971. Copyright 1971 by the American Psychological Association. Adapted by permission of the author.

[3]*Social Interest: A Challenge to Mankind.*

Paul Schmick/Monkmeyer Press Photo Service

Courage is a necessary ingredient for successful living.

over how we perceive things. Many of our problems are a matter of false interpretations of reality, which lead us to exaggerate the difficulty of a situation. We may also use the creative self to establish a plan with clearly defined objectives and the proper means of attaining them. The creative self can bring unity and integration within personality. Adler strongly believed that the forces of a creative self should be harnessed as individuals give up their useless fictions and courageously direct their efforts instead to the areas of life in which they can function effectively.

It might be interesting to compare the attributes of ideal personality and living proposed by Adler and Maslow, who delineated characteristics of the self-actualized person. Table 6-4 presents this comparison. Although the terminology differs, the attributes presented by both theorists are strikingly similar.

CRITICAL EVALUATION

Students usually find Adler's theory easy to comprehend and relevant to the understanding of others and themselves. The theory contains several commonsense notions

TABLE 6-4 IDEAL PERSONALITY: ADLER AND MASLOW

Objects of Concern	Adler's Well-Adjusted Person (Striving with Social Interest)	Maslow's Self-actualized Person (Growth Motivation)
Self	Feelings of worth and value, courage and optimism	Acceptance of self, others, nature
Opinions of others	Independence of others' opinion	Independence, autonomy, detachment
Problems Outside Self	Overcoming common instead of private inferiority feelings	Focusing on problems outside oneself
Fellow Man	Being a fellow, friend	Enriching interpersonal relationships and friendships
Human	Equal, cooperative footing with fellows	Democratic, not authoritarian character structure
Mankind	Love of humankind	Identification with humankind
Realities of Life	At home in life, acquiescing in common advantages and drawbacks	Comfortable relations with reality, more efficient perception of it
Universe	Harmony with the universe, cosmic feelings	Oceanic feeling, mystic experience
Ethics	Religious and ethical feelings	Clarity in ethical norms and dealings, religious in a social-behavioral way
Esthetics	Better aesthetic judgment	Freshness of appreciation of beauty
	Improved mind, spontaneous social effort	Creativity, spontaneity in inner life, thoughts, impulses

Note: The comparisons between Adler's and Maslow's ideals for humans are strikingly similar, yet each theorist arrived at these attributes independently, a fact that enhances their credibility. Adapted from Guy Manaster, *Journal of Individual Psychology*, 24:131–149, 1968.

that fit everyone's experiences. Commonsense appeal, however, is not a valid criterion of the soundness of a theory. But Adler's theory is used widely as a guide to therapy as is attested by the existence of Adlerian institutes in every major metropolitan area of the Western world. There are many counselors and therapists who follow the concepts and methods of Individual Psychology, the school that Adler founded. There are also a number of therapies that seem to reflect Adler's ideas, such as Ellis's rational emotive therapy, Glasser's reality therapy, and the many varieties of cognitive therapies that are currently in vogue.

Adler's theory suffers from overgeneralizing of its components. The universal striving to overcome inferiority is so generalized by Adler that it encompasses the whole of human motivation. Adler does not adequately account for the wide range of variation of individual expressions of the striving for superiority. Destructive and constructive strivings for superiority are equated with healthy and unhealthy growth. Is the feeling of inferiority a factor that differentiates the criminal from the productive individual? Degree of social interest is also a factor in the direction of the striving for superiority, but there are productive people who are just as egocentric as the criminal. Adding the dimension of activity helps to account for variation in striving, but it does not completely solve the problem of the difference between healthy and unhealthy strivings for superiority. Reducing abnormality to combinations of the two dimensions of degree of activity and degree of social interest may be appealing as a typology, but it greatly oversimplifies the causes of psychopathology.

The view that many forms of psychological and behavioral disturbances are simply "cheap tricks" to gain exemptions and an easier life is greatly overgeneralized by Adler. The symptoms of psychopathology frequently create a host of problems that are more disturbing than the responsibilities the person is trying to avoid. Escaping into invalidism may hardly be less painful than facing reality. Yet, of course, Adler's idea that people get sick in order to avoid facing unpleasant tasks is certainly valid, but it is overused by Adler. We might use this idea as a hypothesis in surveying the potential causes of pathology in any particular case.

A major criticism of Adler's theory, as with Freud's, is its emphasis on the early years as permanently forming the style of life. The major argument opposing his views on this matter is that there are too many external and internal changes after early childhood to make this position tenable. Even if we define the style of life in terms of general traits and dispositions (such as optimism-pessimism, ambitiousness-carefreeness, and so on), the evidence for early establishment of the style of life is weak.

Allport (1961) deals with the problem of the prediction of personality traits from early to later years and cites the following study:

> Shirley wrote personality sketches of nineteen children during the first two years of their life. Fifteen years later, Neilon was able to locate sixteen of these children, tested them again, and without any reference to the original sketches, wrote new descriptions of their personalities. The question arose, Can outside judges match the originals with the later sketches? In other words, is a young person identifiably the same at the ages of two and seventeen? The judges had far greater than chance success, especially with girls. They were able to match nearly all of the girls' sketches at seventeen with those at two, but in one case there was complete failure. [1961, pp. 80–81]

Comparing his view with those who hold that personality is fixed early in life, Allport says: "My own view is less fatalistic. Directions may change drastically in later childhood, in adolescence or in adulthood. But that the child, to some extent, is father of the man we cannot completely deny." [1961, p. 81]

Taking up the same issue, Thomas and Chess point out that there are both amazing consistencies in development over a wide age spectrum but also that there are remarkable inconsistencies. One child impressed her nursery school teacher as being unusually competent, self-confident, and responsible and left the same impression with an interviewer at age twenty-one. Another girl, who as a child and teenager was friendly, cooperative, and openly communicative with her family, changed remarkably, so that by early adulthood she became self-centered, impulsive, secretive, and unreliable. "In a similar vein, Vaillant (1977) has documented in his vivid vignettes both the continuities and the wide range of changes in personality from the college years through the decades of middle age in the men of the Harvard Grant Study." (Thomas and Chess, 1980, p. 231)

Adler speaks repeatedly of the uniqueness of an individual's style of life, but his descriptions are usually stated in single terms or phrases. He suggests that one need only identify the individual's guiding goal of life and the means of pursuing it. We are also counseled to look for specific areas of actual inferiority or "felt inferiority" and the forms of compensations the person uses.

The concept of the creative self and its role in shaping the style of life is also quite vague. Adler argues that heredity provides abilities, and the environment, experiences, but the creative power of the self is the primary agent in molding the style of life. What Adler seems to say is that the creative self is influenced by heredity and environment but can selectively resist these forces and form a style of life as it chooses. But what determines the directions it follows if not heredity and environment? We are confronted here with the old problem of free will as an autonomous agent that exerts causal control. The problem is further complicated by Adler's insistence that the style of life is formed in the first five or six years of life. Even the advocates of free choice are more likely to attribute the operation of this process to the years beyond infancy and early childhood. As we work out a value system, a process that occurs in adolescence and beyond, the potential for free choice increases. Furthermore, if the creative self is the major determinant of the style of life and if the creative self continues to operate throughout a person's life (and, in fact, is the basis for change in personality), then why is the style of life not a continually evolving process? Significant early experiences such as organ inferiority and birth order are definitely potent factors in shaping the style of life, yet Adler assigns the major role to the creative self.

Despite the shortcomings in Adler's formulations just noted, his constructs and postulates have a wide-ranging explanatory scope. His ideas on overcoming inferiority, compensation, striving for superiority, guiding fictions, social interest, and style of life can be applied to many personality and behavioral phenomena. These ideas do, in fact, highlight many major problems of life. As we noted earlier, his theory is a working tool for numerous therapists and counselors. It can be, and is being, used to describe, explain, predict, and modify behavior. Adler has called attention to certain aspects of human nature that were being neglected by the psychoanalysts—people's social nature, the important roles of consciousness and self-consciousness, and the ability to construct a better world.

GUIDES TO RESEARCH

HEURISTIC APPLICATIONS OF ADLER'S THEORY

What can we say of Adler's theory with respect to generating new ideas for research? Whereas Adler's theory has been remarkably influential in inspiring the thinking of several prominent psychologists and psychiatrists, it has not been highly productive of research. The problem seems to be that the constructs and postulates of the theory are so general that they cannot easily be translated into testable hypotheses. How can we go about demonstrating that everyone is driven to compensate for inferiority by striving to be superior in some respect or that everyone lives by fictions? These propositions are more in the nature of general assumptions than postulates that can be suggestive of empirical hypotheses. Adler's idea regarding style of life being formed early as a function of family climate has apparently intrigued many researchers. It will be recalled that Adler placed much stress on order of birth as a major determinant of the style of life. A great number of studies have been inspired by this proposal, some of which we will review later. Adler's idea about social interest as being crucial in the life of the healthy personality has received some attention as well, but much more could be done with this topic. Its significance warrants serious consideration by researchers (see Worthen and O'Connell, 1969; Greever et al., 1973). In his theorizing, Adler stressed goal setting as a major determinant of behavior. Significant research dealing with children's goal setting behavior is receiving experimental attention (see Chatterjee and Eriksen, 1962; Mischel and Liebert, 1966).

Adler's disciples use the theory primarily to account for abnormalities in personality and behavior. In other words, they explain various forms of psychopathology in terms of the constructs and postulates of Adler's theory. Application of therapeutic procedures suggested by Adler are also discussed in the typical journal article. *The Journal of Individual Psychology* is the official organ for disciples of Adler, although articles are published in other journals such as the *Journal of Humanistic Psychology*. Many of the articles are reports of cases analyzed and treated with Adlerian concepts and procedures. Certainly one of the most important functions of a working personality theory is using it as a guide to therapy.

Typically, a theory is used to explain problem areas and then as a tool in therapeutic intervention. As we have noted, explanation is one of the major benefits of a theory. The theory should propose the causes of specific problems. For example, we might work out a program of treatment for a juvenile delinquent based on Adler's notion that criminal behavior among youth is a destructive form of the striving for superiority. The superiority striving would be rechanneled to constructive activities that will secure desirable benefits. In this instance, Adler's views would serve as the basis for rehabilitation rather than punishment. Adler interpreted the causes of criminal behavior as faulty character development that can be altered through appropriate treatment. Other articles written by Adlerians deal with the application of Adler's ideas to broader issues of community and society, but, again, such efforts in applying Adler's ideas are more in the nature of explanations than of predictions. Some experts would argue that a theory is best tested by the predictions that it can generate. Others might argue that using a theory to suggest solutions to problems is the ultimate test of a theory. Some people are satisfied if a theory can help us understand the causes of our problems because we then have directions in attempting to find solutions. The substance of what we are saying here is that theories serve many purposes, including the elucidation of global problems as well as individual ones.

Another interesting application of Adler's ideas is the analysis of lives of well-known personalities. Freud also used his own theoretical views in this manner, and Erikson formalized analysis of historical figures in his development of psychohistorical methods. With this interesting reconstructive approach the sequence of a particular set of events can be accounted for by the theory. Furthermore, the theory's predictions can be verified through the case analysis, but the great weakness of such explanation and prediction is that the constructs and postulates of personality theories such as Adler's are so general that they can be applied to a broad spectrum of events, especially in after-the-fact explanations and predictions. The reader will recall that both Erikson and Freud applied their constructs and postulates in psychohistorical analysis of important figures. An interesting possible variation of this technique is to use several theories in dealing with the same data.

EXPERIMENTAL SUPPORT OF ADLER'S THEORY

A significant problem area suggested by Adler's theorizing is the relation of type of parenting (or family atmosphere) and the style of life developed by the child. Birth order plays a significant part in this relationship because both parents and the family climate change markedly as more children are born. There is little doubt that the reactions and actions of parents to the first child are quite different from what they are to the second child. Then, too, the second child has to contend not only with parents but also with the older brother or sister. The picture becomes more complex as the structure of the family does.

An important aspect of one's style of life is the matter of *internal* versus *external locus of control*. Rotter's well-known dimension can be applied to style of life with respect to its origin in the family atmosphere. Internal locus of control means that the individual believes that his or her personal effort enables him or her to gain control, at least in some degree, over external circumstances and himself or herself. Those who possess a high degree of internal locus of control generally act to bring about change in their lives. External locus of control means that a person believes that the sources of influence in his or her life are outside the person and are not under his or her control. This person may accept conditions as they are and expend little effort trying to change external circumstances or himself (or herself). An individual's standing on this dimension certainly makes a great difference in total functioning and greatly influences that person's style of life. It would be highly desirable to know the type of family climate that fosters the formation of internal locus of control.

Lefcourt (1976) found that parental warmth, support, and encouragement were essential for the development of a sense of internal locus of control. Many psychological studies have stressed these roles as desirable for parents because they allow children to develop according to their own potentialities without crippling inhibitions and other forms of abnormality. Many of these studies have relied upon the accounts of young adults regarding family-child relationships in early life. Crandall (1973), however, has conducted longitudinal studies and obtained such data as (1) home observation of maternal behavior during the subject's first ten years, (2) interviews with subjects during early adolescence, and (3) assessment of locus of control of young adults. She found that independence training was critical in promoting a sense of internal locus of control. The child had to be permitted, encouraged, and even forced to act independently. Crandall observed that the child needed to learn the relationship between actions and outcomes without having the parents intervene in behalf of the child. Warmth and support were necessary but, without independence training, were not sufficient to promote internal locus of control.

Lefcourt (1980) sums up the relation of style of parenting and internal or external locus of control as follows:

> From Crandall's research and that which preceded it, it is possible to surmise that the ideal home atmosphere for producing children that will grow up with an internal locus of control is one that changes with the child's needs; warm and nurturant when the child is helpless, but increasingly challenging and encouraging of independent pursuits as the child becomes of age to test his developing powers. Accelerating demands for competence as the child's abilities mature may be a necessary ingredient that supplements the security created by the initially supportive, dependency-gratifying home. [In Staub, 1980, pp. 222–223]

To return to birth order, a great deal of research has been inspired by Adler's idea that birth order influences the type of life-style that is developed. The flood of research is by no means totally the result of Adler's ideas, but Adler did make some specific proposals that have been tested. This notion has been termed *positional psychology*.

An example of the type of specific proposals Adler has made is that the personalities of the oldest, middle, and youngest children in a family were different because the family climate changes. Not only is the relation with the parents altered as the family grows, but the interactions among the children becomes a major factor, perhaps of greater developmental importance than the influence of the parents. The oldest child of a family may be forever favored by the parents, particularly in Western societies, a factor that can make for a sense of responsibility and stability. On the other hand, older children may suffer from the insecurity of being dethroned by the new child. Adler (1931) believed that many drunkards, neurotics, and perverts are only children or firstborn. Schachter (1959) has tested several of Adler's contentions regarding birth order and found some support for them. His research started the trend of studying birth order effects. Vockell et al. (1973) lists 272 studies on birth order conducted between 1967 and 1972. Perhaps a greater number have been carried out since then.

Schachter (1959) found that under stress firstborn and only-born college women were likely to seek the company of others twice as often as later-born college women, who more frequently preferred to face stress alone. The study consisted of assembling a group of college women who were to be participants in an experiment that involved receiving an electric shock. An elaborate description of the procedure was given along with a sample shock. The subjects were then given a choice of being alone or going into a room with other women while they waited for the experiment to begin. The results were analyzed according to birth order as noted earlier. The firstborn and only children chose significantly more often to be in the company of others.

Schachter reported in 1963 an extensive investigation of eminence in which eldest children are more likely to become famous than later-born children. He also found, as have others, that the typical college population consists of from 50 to 65 percent of firstborn people, proportions that are much greater than the distribution in the general population. (Schachter, 1963; Danskin, 1966; and Altus, 1966) Schachter (1963) also found that firstborns had higher grade averages, a finding that supports Adler's notion that firstborn children (as contrasted with later-borns) become more ambitious adults. There are many other studies that might be discussed regarding birth order and personality factors, but the sample we have given should suffice to show how a theory can be translated into empirical research. Adler has been quite explicit in proposing causes of behavior, but researchers have not conducted tests of these propositions. One major stumbling block is that Adler's followers are therapists and not researchers. This is the case with most of the personality theorists discussed in this text. As therapists resort more to empirical demonstration of therapeutic outcomes, a trend that is gaining momentum, we may see more of Adler's ideas tested experimentally in the laboratory or empirically in the consulting room.

GUIDES TO LIVING

HIDDEN STRIVINGS FOR SUPERIORITY

Consider the many forms that strivings for superiority can take, both in yourself and others. Each person seems to have one goal that he or she is trying to live out. It may be something like being quicker and smarter than anyone else or like being a great lover. Although we may be unaware of the existence of a particular goal, our behavior makes the inference of the goal necessary. We need only observe our behavior in a variety of situations in order to become aware of our guiding goal. We have many specific goals, but they are an expression of one overriding central goal.

Adler was fond of tracing behavior to the striving for superiority. There are many explanations for depression, but Adler in his characteristic fashion reduced it to thwarted feelings of superiority. When we feel depressed, the reason could be that we feel we deserve more than we are getting. Our depressed state stems from an unrecognized feeling of self-importance.

It takes courage to face up to the problems of living. It is more comfortable to watch a television mystery than to study your lessons. It is easier to engage in recreation than to work. It is simpler to let someone else solve your problems than to do it yourself. But only by assuming your responsibilities courageously can you live independently.

Many of our feelings and emotions stem from a sense of superiority. Consider such emotions as impatience and intolerance; envy and resentment; feeling slighted, offended, and rejected; being avaricious or arrogant; and many other similarly negative emotions.

SUGGESTIONS FOR EXAMINING GOALS

1. Inferiority feelings may arise from repeated comparisons either with others or with mythical standards.

2. To have the most or the best may be far more than is necessary for a satisfying life.

3. Guiding fictions play an important part in producing a sense of inferiority. When your goals are grandiose and fantastic, however, they serve only to hinder personality growth and functioning. Guiding fictions should foster healthy growth and functioning. Fictions should be constantly examined, and when they hinder adjustment and growth, they should be altered.

4. You can deliberately create fictions that foster healthy functioning. For instance, an optimistic attitude toward the future sustains present acitvities better than does a pessimistic view. The fortunes of the future are not known; thus, an optimistic approach is just as much a fiction as a pessimistic one. But the optimistic view is a better fiction than the other, so why not adopt it? You can arrive at other similar fictions in the same manner.

5. Adler has offered us an interesting way of identifying our major guiding goal in life. He termed the method "tracing the lifeline." Unlike Freud, who sought to uncover early repressed memories, Adler sought out early known memories. He believed that one could learn many highly personal matters through such earliest memories. He compared the earliest memories to our attitudes and postures in current dreams; thus, the "lifeline" consists of two poles, the significant events of the past and the manifestations of the guiding goal in the present. This method can reveal the deepest source of motivation for an individual. Often this motivation turns out to be selfish, grandiose, and impossible to attain.

6. Adler frequently found that his patients were operating on the useless side of life, and he encouraged them to change to a more useful way of living. His advice to his patients could be taken by everyone. So much of what we do is uselessly destructive, self-defeating, antisocial. We should look instead in the direction of growth, expanded outreach, courageous confrontation, social and family experiences, and the fulfillment of our native talents. In advocating usefulness and personal growth, Adler offered his own view of the ideal personality.

7. Adler also advised us to look for a person's compensations. The particular means of striving for superiority or the specific compensations the person seeks reveal the nature of his or her felt inferiority. The belligerent individual may feel inferior about adequacy as a male or female. The person who is always pleasant may be compensating for strong antisocial tendencies. The compulsive person may be compensating for a tendency to be chaotic and disorganized. In any case, compensations reveal inferiorities.

USE AND MISUSE OF FICTIONS

For most people day-to-day activity is most meaningfully comprehended in the framework of a guiding fiction of perpetual life, but even this fiction may take an unrealistic form. An example of the exaggeration of the fictional goal of living forever is the case of the person who is reckless and does not exercise adequate caution in driving, caring for his or her health requirements, or saving for a rainy day. Although the person cannot verbalize his or her attitude, the behavior manifests the operation of this fiction. In this case also, if there occurs an event that intensifies the person's feeling of vulnerability, the operation of the fiction will decrease so drastically that he or she will experience a profound death anxiety. It may be seen from this example that fictions, although having no counterpart in reality, may vary in degree of usefulness; thus, everyone's life is directed by fictional goals, but some are harmful and hinder adjustment whereas others serve it.

The person who suffers from a personality disorder formulates fictions that are not useful. In fact because they are so vague, unrealistic, and impossible of attainment, they provide faulty objectives and lead to chronic inferiority and discontent.

A person need not be conscious of his or her guiding fiction for it to be active. Adler believed that most people think that they are pursuing one end whereas the real end is quite different. We are usually aware of some of our goals, but we may not be aware of our overriding goal, which, in Adler's view, is a guiding fiction. We can study our goals as a means of identifying this guiding fiction. A woman may state that she likes to be friendly with everyone, but in fact her behavior may indicate that she is seductive of men and jealous of other women. Obviously, individuals are aware of some of their goals, but they may not be aware of their overriding goal, the one that is the pivotal point of their lives and that subordinates all the others. Degree of awareness of goals is an indication of degree of normalcy.

To sum up, human experiences are brought together in the form of fictions. Fictions are cognitive representations of events. They may be thought of as cognitive constructs, frames of reference that the person uses to depict the events of the world in a personal way. Unable to have an exact picture of things as they really are, we always structure our own ideas of them. These ideas are usually centered around a single major goal, or guiding fiction, which becomes the principal focus of our activity. A single guiding fiction may have both healthy and unhealthy manifestations (see Table 6-5). Obviously, if the interpretations are completely false, behavior that is based on them will be highly maladaptive. For most people, fictional representations are constantly in a state of flux to meet the requirements of reality.

TABLE 6-5 USEFUL AND HARMFUL FICTIONS

Normal Person	Neurotic Person
Alters fictions when they are no longer useful.	Chooses fictions on the basis of appeal rather than usefulness.
Moderates fictions when they cause repeated frustration.	Clings to fictions tenaciously even when they produce hurt and frustration.
Has at least partial awareness of the unreality of fictions.	Adopts fictions that are grandiose and idealistic.
Derives the benefits of certain fictions without putting them to the test, because he or she knows the difference between a hypothesis and a fiction.	Treats fictions as if they were hypotheses to be put to the test, but responds irrationally to the outcome.
Careful to adopt fictions that will foster living when there is absence of knowledge about the proper course of action.	Frequently is unconscious of fictions and reacts to their failure with faulty adaptive responses rather than by changing the harmful fictions.
Willingly examines the effectiveness of fictions.	Unwilling to examine fictions with respect to their utility value.

Note: A hypothesis has value only if it is tested and confirmed. Before visiting the supermarket on Sunday, I may call to see if it is open. A *fiction* is useful or not: I believe that the people who run the supermarket are honest; thus, I do not weigh and measure every item I purchase. If it is called to my attention that they are dishonest, I alter my fiction. However, some fictions (such as belief in divine providence) cannot be tested.

SUMMARY

1. Adler founded the School of Individual Psychology, which is based on such premises as these: humans are motivated more by social impulses than sexual drives; humans are distinguished by being conscious and not unconscious; humans are self-aware and capable of profiting from mistakes and changing themselves, as well as the world around them; personality has unity and direction; conflict results from faulty life conditions and is not inherent in humans. Rather than sex and aggression being the major problems of life, the main concerns are vocation, community living, and love.

2. A major motivational force for humans, both collectively and individually, is the sense of inferiority. We strive to establish security and security plus in the form of superiority. Compensation means to hide or substitute and is an unhealthy consequence of inferiority feelings. Adler blamed men for the inferior roles in which women were cast and held to a complementary relationship between men and women: different but equal. To be masterful and dominant and to be free to fulfill individual potentials are common aspirations of both sexes, but women's roles have been highly limited.

3. Many behavior disorders may be understood as abnormal forms of striving for superiority. Children are especially vulnerable to feelings of inferiority because they are continually tested and evaluated. Rewards and awards are given for superiority whereas punishment and criticism are given for inferior performance. Such external conditions greatly influence self-esteem, and eventually, we evaluate our own performance by the same standards and inflict the same consequences to self.

4. In a healthy child, inferiority feelings are experienced in mild degrees and serve as motivation for self-perfecting: the actualizing of the child's potentialities and the attaining of standards and skills.

If self-perfecting is to occur in a healthy rather than an unhealthy form, it requires highly developed social interests and feelings. Most of our activities take place in social contexts; thus, self-centeredness is an unhealthy approach in meeting our needs. Adler believed that the tendencies to be self-centered and also to have social feelings are inborn, but whereas self-centeredness is based on powerful drives, social sentiments are weak and require a loving home atmosphere to emerge. Expecting perfection is a common reaction to a profound sense of inferiority and is an indication of abnormality. One of the greatest sources of unhappiness is the inability to fulfill expectations, our own or those set by others.

5. Adler places much emphasis on compensation as a reaction to inferiority. Compensation refers to making up for or covering over a weakness. Overcompensation, in an abnormal sense, refers to the futile attempt to excel in one's weakest area and involves denial of an aspect of the individual that cannot be changed. Overcompensation, in a healthy sense, involves turning a weakness into a strength.

6. Adler stressed the role of guiding goals in determining our present behavior. Each person has an overriding guiding goal of being superior in some respect. Many behaviors are traceable to this goal. The guiding goal may be conscious but more often is unconscious. It determines which subgoals will be pursued and which will be avoided.

7. Adler also held that many of our guiding goals are fictions. We believe and act as if certain things are true even when we have no evidence. We may harbor harmful fictions such as believing that everyone is better than we are.

Some fictions cannot be tested, but they can be judged in terms of whether or not they are useful for us. Some fictions can be tested, but should not be, because their testing could lead to needless hurt. Some fictions should be tested because they can lead to dangerous consequences. Fictions may take the form of ideals and personal constructs that represent our own interpretations and constructions. Their worth should be judged by their usefulness. Harmful fictions, even if they are ideals, should be discarded. The neurotic tends to hold to such fictions.

8. Each person develops a style of life that becomes fixed during the early years. It refers to the unique configuration of characteristics that constitute our personal identity. The style of life has at its center a guiding fiction, a goal of superiority, which gives it coherence and direction. The style of life guides the interpretive processes, as well as the types of behavior that are characteristic of the person. A philosophy of life is evolved early. Significant early experiences—or the absence of them—are essential. Adler assigns much weight to the child's innate constitution, early traumas, parental treatment, the general home climate, and especially birth order. Siblings can influence children more than parents. Organic or psychological handicaps, abuse, and other overburdening conditions could lead to a faulty style of life. Adler identified children who were likely to develop faulty life-styles: the pampered child, the neglected child, the abused child, the sickly child, the handicapped child.

9. Adler related abnormality of personality development and functioning to the various constructs of his theory of personality: profound sense of inferiority, faulty compensations and overcompensations, abnormal strivings for superiority, mistaken life-style, useless fictions, self-preoccupation, inadequate social interest, and low activity level. The child constructs a mistaken life-style as a result of being constitutionally nervous and being exposed to overburdening conditions. The child may resort to what Adler terms cheap tricks to gain superiority and avoid dealing with the realities of life. Safeguarding mechanisms and barricades may be developed to bolster self-esteem and to avoid facing painful realities. Safeguarding techniques are security measures for dealing with inferiority. Adler developed a typology based on two dimensions: degree of activity and degree of social interest. The three abnormal types are the ruling type, the getting type, the avoiding type. Adler refers to many disorders as neurosis. He views the neurotic as having a cowardly style of life with abnormal self-preoccupation and marked lack of social sentiments.

10. Adler probed the past of his patients in order to identify the origins and true nature of the unhealthy life-style. He sought to provide a corrective by pointing out the manner in which the person was living ineffectively and what the person should do in order to live more usefully. In his therapeutic contacts, he stressed a warm and accepting climate as a means of promoting the potential social interest that is so deficient in unhealthy personalities.

11. Adler maintained that courage is the mark of a healthy personality. The healthy person is active in dealing with life's demands and is motivated by well-developed social interest and feelings. The major problems of living — vocation, community, and family — are confronted squarely and with regard for the rights and requirements of others.

12. The highest human attributes stem from well-developed social interest and feelings. Most individual needs depend upon social relationships for their satisfaction. The creative self plays an important role in the formation of the style of life and is the basis for change. Adler felt that a person's style of life could be altered although it required heroic efforts at times. The creative self exerts influence over our perceptual and other cognitive functions, the guiding fictions we maintain, and the types of behavior that are possible for us.

13. Adler's views have attracted followers who practice his brand of therapy, but they have not inspired much research. Some work has been done with family climate, particularly the influence of birth order on style of life.

GLOSSARY

Birth order (positional psychology): One's position in the family. A major determinant of the style of life; reflects Adler's concern with changing family constellation.

Coping strategies: Habitual methods of dealing with problems; an important feature of the style of life.

> **Compensation:** Make up for a weakness; attempting to cover up an inferiority, real or imagined; the opposite of a realistic approach to a problem.

> **Substitute compensation:** Making up for a weakness by displaying your abilities in a different area; a pretense of superiority.

> **Overcompensation:** A form of denial of an inherent weakness by attempting to excel in that particular aspect. Some writers refer to overcompensation in a healthy sense, as turning a weakness into a strength.

Creative self: The agent ego. Adler viewed the creative self as the organizing and controlling conscious force that fashions personality; it is influenced by hereditary dispositions and environmental experiences, but it is the molder of the style of life. It is the source of change.

Early recollections: Using the earliest memories as a means of discerning the nature of the style of life.

> **Tracing the lifeline:** Relating the occurrences in current dreams with early experiences to highlight major directions in the style of life.

Mistaken style of life: A faulty orientation to life established early as a result of overburdening conditions.

> **Overburdening condition:** Unusual stress situation; organ inferiority or psychological inadequacies; parental and sibling abuse; these conditions produce a profound sense of inferiority and lead to a mistaken life-style.

> **Neurosis:** Adler emcompasses a number of

psychological disorders under this category; a cowardly orientation to life in which a person uses cheap tricks to gain superiority.

Safeguarding tendencies: Protective strategies that preserve self-esteem.

Barricades: Avoiding mechanisms, shielding self from injury through escape mechanisms; a sickly orientation to life.

Sense of inferiority: A major motivational force in human life inherent to humans as a species and individually.

Inferiority feelings: Felt inferiority; feeling of ineptitude and inadequacy; a natural condition of infancy in childhood (relation of midget to giants); serves as motivation for improving one's lot.

Inferiority complex: A profound sense of inferiority, leading to exaggerated forms of compensation and superiority strivings; an integral component of a person's style of life.

Organ inferiority: Sense of inferiority due to a physical weakness or disorder, more generally feeling inadequate as a result of real or imagined deficits.

Social interest and feelings: An inborn potential to experience emotions and motives that involve other people; a social sense that requires a loving and caring environment to flourish. It promotes three major tasks of life — vocation, communal living, and family — and is the mark of a healthy personality for Adler.

Striving for superiority: The great dynamic force of life; the will to live and improve. Abnormal expressions stem from exaggerated feelings of inferiority; tempered by social interest, it is the basis of communal and family living.

Style of life: The unique configuration of characteristics that constitute your personal identity; your orientation to life made up of enduring, coping, and adapting characteristics that produce consistency across situations.

Avoiding type: Abnormal type characterized by withdrawal from facing reality; low activity level and low social interest.

Getting type: Abnormal type characterized by demanding or expecting things from others; high social interest but low activity level.

Ruling type: An abnormal style of life that is characterized by high activity level but low social interest; the person exploits others.

Normal type (socially useful type): The healthy personality that actively strives to meet needs within social context; high activity level and well-developed social interest and feelings.

Striving toward goals (a teleological view): Present behavior is governed by goals or future striving; an alternative to causality.

Fictional finalism: The view that many of our guiding goals are fictions that we accept without confirmation. They are "as if's" that may be evaluated in terms of their usefulness rather than truth.

Fiction: Personal constructs, assumptions, and goals; some are not testable; some are harmful; some should be tested; and some that could be tested should not be.

SUGGESTED READINGS

Adler, Alfred. *Practice and Theory of Individual Psychology*. New York: Harcourt Brace Jovanovich, 1927.

Adler presents a rather complete statement of his theory of personality in this book. He introduces such principles as "striving for superiority," "style of life," "creative self," "Fictional finalism," and "social interest."

———— *Science of Living*. New York: Clinton, 1929.

This is a highly readable account of Adler's basic principles, designed for the lay person and intended as a book on mental health.

———— *The Education of Children*. Chicago: Henry Regnery, 1930.

In this book Adler seeks to apply the principles of mental health to the school setting. He is guided by the view that formal education should include knowledge of and practice in the art of living. He also introduces his pioneer ideas on group counseling and family therapy.

——— *The Problem Child.* New York: Putnam's, 1963.

Adler presents clinical cases which comprise faulty life styles. He describes and explains these life styles in the light of his theory of personality.

Ansbacher, H. L., and Rowena R. Ansbacher. *The Individual Psychology of Alfred Adler.* New York: Basic Books, 1956.

Two devoted disciples of Adler have collaborated to bring together a series of excerpts from his original writings. Adler's theoretical thinking is represented in an evolutionary perspective.

KAREN HORNEY
THE REAL VERSUS
THE IDEAL SELF

Karen Horney
Psychoanalytic
Institute and
Center

BIOGRAPHY AND HISTORICAL PERSPECTIVE

Karen Horney (pronounced horn-eye) was born near Hamburg, Germany, in 1885. The child of a sea captain father, she distinguished herself as a pioneer in the field of psychiatry and was instrumental in eradicating the image that medicine was strictly a man's profession. Her father resisted Karen's attempts to enter the field of medicine, an interest that began as early as the age of twelve. She came from an unorthodox family made up of an older brother, and stepbrother, and two step-sisters from her father's two previous marriages. Her freethinking mother, however, reacted against her father's chauvinism and probably served as a model for the young Karen's pioneer spirit (Rubins, 1978). She received her medical training at the University of Berlin. For fourteen years she was associated with the Berlin Psychoanalytic Institute—from 1918 to 1932.

She came to the United States in 1932 and became associate director of the Chicago Psychoanalytic Institute. Her first major work, *The Neurotic Personality of Our Time*, was published in 1937. The most complete statements of Horney's theory can be found in *Our Inner Conflicts* (1945) and *Neurosis and Human Growth* (1950). Her last book, *Feminine Psychology* (1967), was published posthumously; it is a collection of essays written early in her career regarding the differences between male and female sexuality and illustrates her major differences with Freud on this issue. Horney also wrote *New Ways in Psychoanalysis* (1939) to illustrate further her differences with Freud's view on human nature.

Early in her career Horney was analyzed by Karl Abraham and Hanns Sachs, both of whom were closely associated with Freud. As her own views developed, however, Horney found that she could not remain an orthodox Freudian. She moved from Chicago to New York in 1934 to teach at the New York Psychoanalytic Institute and also to set up a private practice. By 1941 it became clear to her and to the members of the institute that their concepts were in serious disagreement and that she could not teach and practice psychoanalysis within the orthodox framework. Subsequently, she helped found the Association for the Advancement of Psychoanalysis to promote her own ideas. She headed this school until her death in 1952.

Horney gradually became convinced that psychoanalysis was one-sided in its stress on the genetic and instinctive determinants of behavior. (Horney, 1939) When she came to America, during the Great Depression, she came face to face with the powerful role of environmental forces—economic, social, and educational. In dealing with the problems of her patients, she found Adler's ideas and Fromm's stress on social forces more helpful than Freudian theory. Rather than being tormented by sexual fixations, a man might be struggling with problems associated with career, marriage, and setting feasible goals for himself. Furthermore, Horney believed that women were not by nature inferior to men but were being treated as if they were. She disagreed with Freud about feminine penis envy, the desire for masculine roles. She demonstrated by her own example that a woman could fulfill herself both in a profession and as a homemaker. She pursued an active career and brought up three daughters. Horney (1937) did not accept the notion that conflict is inevitable; rather, she believed that it is acquired through the faulty training and expectations imposed upon the child. Her basic ideas regarding the formation of neurotic trends are these:

1. The child is subjected to a stressful environment that produces *basic anxiety*, the feeling of isolation and helplessness in a hostile world.
2. A strategy is developed to cope with the stress.
3. Because the strategy reduces anxiety, it becomes highly significant for the individual. It actually becomes a need.
4. The strategy (or need) may be elevated to the status of a general orientation to life. It becomes *compulsive* and is *indiscriminately used*.

Some of the adverse home conditions that foster the development of maladaptive strategies are overdomination by parents, indifference, erratic treatment, lack of respect for the child's individual needs, lack of real guidance, disparaging attitude, too much admiration (or the absence of it), lack of encouragement and warmth from parents, too

Home atmosphere fosters maladaptive coping strategies.

Erika Stone/Photo Researchers, Inc.

much (or too little) responsibility, overprotection, isolation from other children, injustice, discrimination, unkept promises, hostile atmosphere, quarrelsome parents, and so forth. (Horney, 1945)

Under such conditions the child becomes insecure and works out a strategy to alleviate his or her feelings of insecurity. One child finds that she can reduce her insecurity by compliance with her parents' requests, even though she must sacrifice her own wishes. Another finds that he can get what he wants by becoming hostile and aggressive, but that he must suppress his more tender emotions in the process. Still another discovers that aloofness and detachment work in her family setting, but that she has to hold back her own desire for self-assertion and love. In each orientation, something is lost while anxiety-reduction is accomplished. The particular strategy becomes habitual and generalized as a total approach to life.

It is important to remember that Horney considered neurosis a matter of degree. Both healthy and unhealthy forces exist in all persons:

> Neurosis, it must be said, is always a matter of degree—and when I speak of "a neurotic" I invariably mean "a person to the extent that he is neurotic." For him awareness of feelings and desires is at a low ebb. Often the only feelings experienced consciously and clearly are reactions of fear and anger to blows dealt to vulnerable spots. And even these may be repressed. (Horney, 1945, p. 28)[1]

Horney (1942) identified ten neurotic needs and then later derived from them three orientations toward social relationships (Horney, 1945): *moving toward people, moving against people, and moving away from people*. These major orientations have normal and abnormal expressions. In her last formal statement of the theory, Horney expanded the social orientations to encompass a wider scope, the total orientation to life. She named these general orientations: (1) *self-effacing solution* (compliance and striving for

[1]*Our Inner Conflicts.*

love), (2) *expansive solution* (striving for mastery), and (3) *resignation* (striving for freedom).

Horney listed ten neurotic needs in her 1942 book. These are need for affection and approval, a dominant partner in life, power, exploitation of others, prestige, personal admiration, ambition in personal achievement, narrowly confined limits of life, self-sufficiency and independence, perfection, and unassailability. Everyone may possess these needs, but in the neurotic person one or more are quite strong and generalized. (Horney, 1937) The needs develop as a consequence of the child's efforts to find solutions for disturbed social relationships. However, the solutions are irrational.

Although Horney focused almost exclusively on the neurotic aspects of personality, both her work as a therapist and her definition of neurosis as a matter of degree obviously demonstrate that she was interested in bringing about health and normalcy. Her conception of normalcy, following the medical model, was more a matter of eliminating symptoms than of promoting health and growth. A number of personality psychologists (for example, Allport, 1961; Maslow, 1970) would oppose this approach and argue for a distinction between not being sick and being healthy. Yet despite Horney's influence by the physician's bias—to treat the sick rather than to promote optimal growth and functioning—her theory offers us many useful insights and guides to healthy living.

Horney was more impressed with social pressures as sources of neurotic problems rather than difficulties with instincts and drive gratifications. Life in a capitalistic system seems to hold out many benefits, but it also creates many stresses. One is tempted by "the good things"—status, power, wealth, and fame—with the expressed hope that everyone may have them, whereas in reality the competition is fierce and the attainment of great success is possible for relatively few. From the earliest period of life, the child is tantalized with a glamorous world of make-believe; television, newspapers, and magazines—indeed all the media, including parents, of course—portray the "beautiful people" who live the glamorous lives. One of the basic points Horney (1937) made regarding the relation of culture to personality growth is that the culture imposes the stresses that hamper growth and at the same time provides false solutions that are appealing and simple to follow. Such solutions are a mirage that can lead only to a chronically disordered personality. They take the form of an abandonment of the *real self* for the sake of pursuing an *idealized version of the self*. Many striking changes in personality development result from the rejection of the potentialities of the real self and the vain attempt to actualize the idealized or glamorous self. This is the theme that will be taken from Horney's work.

BASIC CONSTRUCTS AND POSTULATES

Real Self Versus Idealized Image of Self

In describing ourselves, we draw upon our concept of self, which may or may not be an accurate representation of our real self. We may also have a more or less vague notion of what we would like to be, our idealized version of self. For the normal person this distinction is maintained. In the case of neurosis, the idealized version of self is adopted as the real self, which, in Horney's view, creates inner strain and conflict. We all confront the tasks of setting goals for ourselves and working out our aspirations toward a better life. We form an idealized self-image, which is the self we would like to be. We might think of this self-image as the conception of the perfected or ideal self. Yet there is always the danger of confusion between our notions of our real self and of the self we would like to become. If in fact we adopt the idealized image of self as the real self, the basis for neurosis is established, in Horney's (1950) view. The distinction between the real self and the ideal self is blurred, and the person begins to distort reality.

Horney believed that there are many factors that promote a faulty conception of self. We need an accurate self-image as a guide to conduct, but our capacities and abilities are difficult to assess: it is quite natural to overestimate or even underestimate them.

Horney also believed that we should constantly examine our ideal image of self and compare it with our actual achievements and performances. There should always be a fairly clear awareness of the difference between the real self and the aspired or ideal self. Ultimately, we should attempt to actualize our real self in order to perfect it. We should continually strive to insure a *close correspondence* between what we really are and our conception or image of self. Adequate functioning of the self presupposes a favorable environment, and especially the early environment. During this period of time the self lacks the resources and strength to administer the organism. This vital function is the major task of the parents; they make the decisions for the child. Gradually the self emerges as a source of control and growth, and inner controls are substituted for the outer forces.

Horney believed that children have their own individual nature, which must be given full freedom to develop. The deceptively simple key to liberating the forces of the self is self-knowledge (Horney, 1950). The individual, no matter how favorable his or her environment, will possess both constructive and destructive tendencies. The destructive tendencies may be dealt with by a punitive environment, by severe inner dictates of a harsh conscience, or by suitable learning. Horney favored the *outgrowing of the undesirable tendencies* as a result of learning, particularly learning about the self. To work at one's self is a requirement of liberating and cultivating the forces of the self.

For the self to unfold to its fullest, children must be given opportunity in accordance with their inner potential. This requires warmth, encouragement, being a part of the family, respect of their rights, and even a certain amount of friction with those about them. (Horney, 1950) When parents do not provide the appropriate atmosphere and ingredients to promote growth, the following development ensues: children experience insecurity or anxiety; they work out strategies to defend against the anxiety: these usually relieve only some tension temporarily and at the expense of the attainment of full growth. Basic anxiety is painful and threatening. It is difficult to describe. Horney (1937) defined it as the *feeling of being isolated and helpless in a world that is potentially hostile.* Feeling utterly helpless and alone in a life situation that you cannot master is certainly a terrifying state.

CLARIFICATION OF THE NOTION OF THE IDEAL SELF

The reader may find some confusion in the distinction between the real and ideal selves as Horney used these concepts. At times she spoke as if there were *two selves.* For instance, she used the analogy of a civil war raging within the personality—a war between the real self and the ideal self. It may help to clear up the confusion to make a more detailed distinction between the real self and the self-image. We are capable of reflecting upon our psychological and physical processes. We may know something and know that we know. Just as we may form perceptions of objects in our world, so we may also form a perception of ourselves. The perception of self (we may call it a self-image) stands for the self. It is not the self, but a representation of it, just as a perception of an object is not the same as the object. The representation or image of self may or may not correspond quite well with the existing self. Thus "what I am" may or may not correspond with "what I think I am." A peculiar situation exists with respect to the causes of actual behavior when the self-image and the real self do not correspond.

One major source of motivation—if not the most important—centers about the self-image. If a man pictures himself as a great athlete, he will entertain fantasies of his great feats and subsequent acclaim. Many psychological activities will be organized around this self-image. Ultimately, he will act upon the image; he will try out for the football team, or whatever. The self-image sets expectations, aspirations, or demands upon the real self.

People who follow the dictates of their image of self and who firmly believe that their representation of self is their real self create problems for their real self. The false concept of self may initiate behavior, but the quality of that behavior depends upon the attributes of the real self. Actions stemming from a faulty representation of self

An idealized version of self is the basis of loss of contact with the real self.

Vinnie Fish © 1976/Photo Researchers, Inc.

serve only to block even further a person's awareness of what is real; the person is less able to perceive the discrepancy as more is invested in the faulty self-image. *The conflict between the ideal and the real self, which Horney took as the basis of neurosis, derives from a faulty representation of self that is acted upon.*

MULTIPLE CONCEPTIONS OF SELF

Horney followed the simplest distinction with her notions of the real self and the self-image. The actual picture is much more complex, as Jourard (1963) has pointed out. A person may have images of potential selves. Thus, as we have noted, in addition to the image of self, there may be an image or conception of the perfected real self. You might say: "I know what I want to be; I also know what I ought to be; and I know what my parents want me to be." You may also have an image or conception of what might be termed "the despised self." Horney did in fact bring out these various selves, or self-images, but she did not name them explicitly. Her major concern was with the discrepancies between the real or actual self and the idea of self that the person possesses.

Moving Toward, Against, or Away from People

Depending on the nature of the child—his or her learning experience, temperament, and abilities—and depending upon the nature of the parents, the child may react by acquiring a fixed behavior pattern. For instance, the child may find (1) that compliance with the parents (doing what they ask and demand) is the only way to keep anxiety away; (2) that aggressiveness and resistance to the wishes of the parents, if pursued long enough, will also get the desired results; or (3) that escape—keeping away physically—is the best strategy. These three trends can be summarized as moving toward, moving against, and moving away from people.

Compliant individuals acquire needs, sensitivities, inhibitions, and even values that center about winning affection and acceptance by others. They desire to be saintly, good, perfect, true friends. Aggressive people seek to win the good things of life by being powerful and masterful, to be in control of things and themselves, to be a tower of strength and composure. People who solve their problems by aloofness aim at detachment and inviolability. They desire total self-sufficiency. *Any one of these three directions can become the focal organizing principle which pervades the total personality of the neurotic.* (Horney, 1945) *Any one of the three directions is a major limitation to growth.* Each of the three directions blocks the satisfaction of vital needs and thereby creates inner conflicts. Compliant people who are undeviatingly amiable have a need to assert themselves. People who must always dominate must suppress their social tendencies. The aloof, shy person avoids some problems, but he or she denies both vital requirements, self-assertiveness, and social needs.

The three trends that Horney maintained become fixed styles of life are glorified by literature, drama, parents, and in general by the carriers of the culture. Consider individuals whose major orientation is moving toward people: their idealized type is the saintly, selfless, noncombatant person who gets along with everyone and is loved and admired by all who know him or her. Such a person is a real lover of humankind, a true humanitarian. This ideal is exemplified by the suffering hero who, despite great adversity and misunderstanding by others, emerges victorious in the end. His or her glory is all the greater because he or she is humble and courageous.

For people who move against people in their effort to secure safety for themselves, the ideal image is also readily available. The conquering hero who is strong and masterful and willingly obeyed is an appealing model for the young child. Everything desirable — power, fame, wealth, and adulation — accrues to the strong, powerful individual. Many people admire the manipulator, as a shrewd conquering hero.

The person who by temperament and circumstance takes a direction away from people has an idealized image too. Some of the most highly respected humans are the philosophers, the great theologians, the dedicated scientists — the great benefactors of humankind with enviable status — who live above the mundane and commonplace. Horney stated that the person who moves away from people "feels himself akin to a rare oriental rug, unique in its pattern and combination of colors, forever unalterable. . . . He takes extraordinary pride in having kept free of the leveling influences of environment and is determined to keep on doing so." (1945, p. 18)

The Alienation from Self

The process of alienation that Horney described as the *central inner conflict* is, in its extreme form, the total abandonment of the real self for the sake of the ideal self. People who reject their real self have lost touch with their greatest source of strength (May, 1953). Everyone confronts this conflict. In striving to improve the real self, an image of the perfected self is formed and used as a guide. The image may be unrealistic, or the person may believe that he or she is closer to being perfected than he or she really is. These matters are difficult to assess, and you can easily make mistakes.

Gradually the person *becomes his or her ideal self.* Being much more appealing than the real self, the idealized self is easily identified as real. To the frustrated child, the discovery of the ideal self is a momentous event because it opens up a variety of possibilities that previously did not exist. Then too, it offers the prospect of solving all the child's problems. The feelings of inadequacy, alienation from others, inner discord — feelings the child continues to experience — can be easily rationalized, for what the child really has become, in his or her own view, is a wonderful, glorious person with extraordinary powers and endowments whom no one has discovered yet! Being one's ideal self becomes a tantalizing prospect and is sought after tenaciously. Frustrated people are driven; they are not the drivers. So strong is identification with the ideal self that people cling to it at all cost. The biggest price they pay is neglect of the real potentialities they have. They chase after the talents and abilities they do not have. The great qualities we attribute to ourselves, even though they are unreal, flow naturally from the alienation of the real self and the identification with the ideal self. It should be noted that by *alienation* Horney did not mean cultural estrangement or rejection by others, which is a current meaning of the term, but rather the much more devastating process of the *loss of the real self. Horney pointed out that the ideal self is the logical outcome of conditions during early development, and when it occurs, it is the beginning of a new line of development.*

In brief, the ideal self becomes more real for the person than the real self. As there is always a natural thrust outward, toward self-expression, the person's life is changed radically in the direction of expressing the glamorous self. The real assets are overlooked, and eventually even demeaned, for the sake of the ideal qualities. *The search for glory is Horney's way of designating the abandonment of the real self to pursue the actualizing of the ideal self.* (Horney, 1950)

Harmful Consequences of Identifying with the Idealized Self

THE SEARCH FOR GLORY

The "search for glory" is regularly accompanied by three needs that take unique form in each individual: (1) the need for perfection, (2) neurotic ambition, and (3) the need for a vindictive triumph. These needs may vary in form of expression throughout life, but as long as the individual pursues the idealized self, they will continue to influence the direction of behavior.

1. The need for perfection.   The need for perfection is a logical implication of the desire for glory. The search for perfection is a common quest of youth, but in the course of development, the normal person learns to accept compromises and less than perfection—the good with the bad. When a person believes that he or she is the idealized version of self, imperfection is intolerable. The person *must* be perfect. As Horney says: "The neurotic is the Faust who is not satisfied with knowing a great deal, but has to know everything." (1950, p. 35)

The nature of the perfection will be determined by the direction toward which individuals have organized their personality: toward, against, or away from people. If they move toward people they must be not only morally good but saintly and without flaw. If they move against people, they must be not only capable but most extraordinary: supermen or superwomen. If they move away from people, they must be not only independent but absolutely self-sufficient. Whatever the direction, there *must* be perfection and nothing less.

2. Neurotic ambition.   Neurotic ambition also takes individual form on the basis of one of the three directions. The main component is excelling, or supremacy over others. This indiscriminate and insatiable urge to excel is part of the fabric of American culture. The child is early taught to be a good competitor. As one popular expression has it, "To win isn't everything, but to lose is nothing." The goals sought are grandiose and fantastic. They may be totally unrealistic and not at all in tune with the individual's potentialities. But the fact that they are lofty and highly desirable endows their pursuit with a sense of significance and urgency.

3. The need for vindictive triumph.   This need manifests itself consciously as a desire to surpass and humiliate others. Despite the noble ideals, neurotics experience a great deal of misery. They do not really accomplish their goals, and thus the solution they adopt dooms them to continuous failure. They do not abandon the search for glory, however, as they *have rejected their real self*. Instead they become bitter and resentful of those who have power over them. They blame such people for their problems and frustrations: the reason they lost their job was that the boss hated them; the teacher failed them because he or she did not like the truly bright students; someday those who have hurt these people will appreciate their true worth—and will pay for what they have done.

NEUROTIC NEEDS AND VICIOUS CIRCLES

Neurotic needs lead to a condition that may be described as a vicious circle (Horney, 1937). The neurotic need creates conditions that intensify the need. To begin with, the need is unrealistic in that it cannot be satisfied, at least to the extent the person desires. *Because the need cannot be gratified completely, fear is always associated with its arousal. Fear becomes a regular component of all the neurotic's major needs. This fear, in turn, increases the intensity of the need and the urgency to gratify it.* The greater need instigates more intense fear, and greater effort is expended to gratify it; hence the vicious circle.

If people seek glory by means of domination—by being always the winner, the leader, the feared and respected one—they have a strong fear that these needs will be frustrated. As they inevitably fail (because the need to dominate admits of no exception), the fear associated with their desire to dominate is increased. Even if they succeed to a remarkable degree, their success is never enough, and the fear continues. Rather than decreasing the desire, they actually increase it and may go to extremes to ward off the fear. Thus a condition of insatiability may occur; they never get enough power or control or respect from underlings. Because fear is associated with their needs, there is a compulsive quality about them: they are trapped. Neurotics are locked into a certain course by their needs, and the only real solution to their trapped existence is to return to their real self.

IMAGINATION AND THE SEARCH FOR GLORY

Normal people may have whimsical moments—daydreams—when they temporarily flee from harsh reality to an inner world of make-believe, but they are fully aware of this excursion into the unreal. They do not make decisions, plan, or take action on the basis of sheer daydreams; they do not live by them (Singer, 1966). Whereas the normal person keeps in touch with reality, the neurotic distorts it, sometimes quite seriously. Horney pointed out that the imagination of neurotics often soars into unlimited possibilities. For example, they believe that posing puzzling questions about life is sufficient to prove that they have great depth of personality and are different from the masses. Imagination goes to work to serve the ideal self, and this is largely done unconsciously. There begins to be an air of artificiality about the person. His or her relationships with others are superficial and as the alienation process progresses, his or her conception of self becomes ever more distorted. Even his or her feelings, which are often displayed dramatically, are hollow and not genuine. Paradoxically, such a person agonizes and worries about things that he or she cannot change and overlooks those things that he or she should. (Temerlin, 1965)

The glorious image of self drastically changes the approach to life.

The Museum of Modern Art/Film Stills Archive

As the attributes of the ideal self are grandiose and fantastic, the neurotic must have recourse to imagination to bring about the many distortions that support them. It is noteworthy that the ideal self emerges as a result of neurotic needs to relieve basic anxiety. Once it takes shape, the process of distortion must intensify. The glorious image of self *drastically changes the approach to life.* The neurotic who has lost the appreciation of reality renounces the ordinary means of obtaining gratification of his or her needs. Such a person wants to be on the mountain without climbing it; work may become abhorrent to the neurotic, for his or her goals are so far beyond anything he or she can accomplish that other techniques must be substituted.

THE DEVIL'S PACT

Horney presented a vivid analogy, which she called "The Devil's Pact," to describe the process of alienation from the real to the ideal self. The basis of the pact is the *desire for greatness* and the equally strong desire for an *easy way out.* The despicable real self is renounced for the glorious ideal self. All one has to do is to give up the claim to the real self. This the neurotic does quite readily, for the real self is despised because it is so grossly inferior to the ideal self. The price to be paid is eventual hell for the total self, but there are moments of grandeur and the immediate expectation of relief from an unbearable life situation. The person sells his or her soul, the real self, for fabricated glory, the ideal self. (Horney, 1950) Horney says:

> I now saw gradually that the neurotic's idealized image did not merely constitute a false belief in his value and significance; it was rather like the creation of a Frankenstein monster which in time usurped his best energies. It eventually usurped his drive to grow, to realize his given potentialities. And this meant that he was no longer interested in realistically tackling or outgrowing his difficulties, and in fulfilling his potentials, but was bent

© Bettye Lane/Photo Researchers, Inc.

Alienation occurs when the real self is renounced.

on actualizing his idealized self. It entails not only the compulsive drive for worldly glory through success, power, and triumph but also the tyrannical inner system by which he tries to mold himself into a godlike being; it entails neurotic claims and the development of neurotic pride. [1950, pp. 367–369].[2]

Like the Frankenstein monster, the idealized self is a creation of the individual that becomes unmanageable and takes over the person's life.

Attempts to Sustain the Idealized Self-image

Horney delineated four methods by which the neurotic, assisted by his or her imagination, seeks to maintain a godlike or glorious image of self: (1) *neurotic pride*, (2) *neurotic claims*, (3) *tyrannical shoulds*, and (4) *auxiliary protective strategies*.

1. NEUROTIC PRIDE VERSUS REAL PRIDE

Real pride. Pride stems from an evaluation of self and takes the form of self-regard or self-love. The person who overvalues himself or herself suffers from false pride, which Horney considered neurotic pride. Neurotic pride consists of converting weak-

[2]*Neurosis and Human Growth*, by Karen Horney, M.D. Copyright 1950 by W.W. Norton & Company, Inc. Copyright renewed 1978. Used by permission of W.W. Norton & Company, Inc

nesses into virtues. Through a process of distorted imagination and faulty reasoning, the true attributes of self, which are unacceptable to the person, are transformed into highly prized virtues. When this occurs, the person experiences a false sense of self-esteem, but self-condemnation ultimately follows. This undercutting of the self may range from misguided humility to a deep sense of personal inferiority.

A genuine pride requires a basic foundation in fact. A student, for instance, may be justly proud of his or her marks if he or she earns them honestly and has worked hard for them. Genuine pride, because it is grounded in fact, is not usually demonstrated in pompous displays. The person enjoys a deep sense of accomplishment and may experience a momentary elevation of self-esteem.

Neurotic pride: Needs become virtues. To bolster the ideal self, people may transform neurotic needs into virtues by means of distortion, rationalization, displacement, and compartmentalization. An appreciation of this process is vital if we are to understand the operation of neurotic pride. Not all neurotic needs are converted to virtues, only those that suit the dominant character structure. If an individual's primary reaction in human relations is one of compliance and submission, a giving in rather than an asserting of self, this compliant tendency will be transformed. As compliance is considered a sign of weakness in our culture, it cannot fit the idealized self-image. It thus becomes a sensitivity to the needs of others, a genuinely human desire to promote harmony. Conversely, the individual who is uncontrollably self-seeking and uses any method at his or her disposal to dominate over others may transform this basically selfish motivation by calling it competitive spirit, being a "good scrapper." Such a person further justifies his or her unscrupulous behavior by reasoning that the loser has learned a lesson. Again, people who pursue their activities in solitude, unable either to relate well to others or to deal with them by open competition, may glorify their conduct by holding that they are rejecting being slaves to common cultural practices. They find their fulfillment in self-sufficiency. They do not need "big happenings" to make them content.

Thus, under the influence of his or her dominant orientation to life, each person's particular weakness is easily touched up and converted from a flaw that he or she cannot accept into a highly prized virtue. Obviously, such hypocrisy and sham ultimately hinder the development and functioning of the personality. No real change in behavior occurs with the transformation of weaknesses into strengths, neurotic needs into virtues. If anything, the person is less equipped to deal with his or her problems as he or she has converted weaknesses into presumed strengths by means of self-deception. Until the real self gains ascendance, the real potentials for growth will be overlooked.

Because neurotic pride is an exaggerated form of self-valuation, it sensitizes the one who possesses it to threat and injury to a remarkable degree. A slight irritation may provoke a strong and prolonged fear or rage reaction. The reasoning is something like this: "I am a very special person—how could you do this to me? It would be bad enough to do it to others, but to do it to me is absolutely despicable." The fear of injury is also reflected in the neurotically proud individual's rejection of situations that might provoke shame or humiliation, such as competing in sports, asking for a date, or giving a talk before a group. The pride system demands that such situations be *avoided*, not overcome. This may involve a general emotional suppression that inhibits the most alive portion of the personality. A rigid caution against spontaneous expression of thoughts and feelings may be adopted as a method of dealing with social relationships.

Often the very quality of which the neurotic is most proud is the one that needs the greatest change. He or she may flaunt a refusal to be pushed around but would do much better if he or she were not so driven to win every battle that the fear of losing deadens his or her personality.

The demands of the ideal self, with accompanying neurotic pride, convert existing needs into neurotic claims and imperfections of the self into impossible shoulds. We will now turn our attention to these claims and shoulds.

2. NEUROTIC CLAIMS

Neurotic claims—neurotic needs transformed by the imagination—involve the *groundless assertion of a right or title*. They are quite different from genuine needs in that an element of personal due is added. The neurotic says in effect: "I am an extraordinary person, and therefore deserve the best."

Cultural practices often support the formation of neurotic claims. On Christmas, birthdays, and other holidays, children are showered with gifts and much attention. The statement "Christmas is really for children" exemplifies this practice. (A child who came from a large family with many unmarried members asked her mother, upon receiving a large number of gifts, "Why does everyone love me so much?") During infancy the child's main strategy, although obviously not consciously formulated, is to obtain gratification of his or her requirements on the claim of being helpless but very lovable. This is normal childhood behavior, but if allowed to continue too long, it becomes the foundation of the alienation process. Our culture sanctions loving care for children, but if this care is not supplemented by independence training, development will be abnormal. The child reared under conditions of pampering and indulgence readily claims all sorts of things solely on the basis of being a "glorious person." The tendency to idealize the self comes rather naturally, and thus this tendency should be restrained rather than encouraged by the parents. Usually restraint is achieved by requiring more and more from the child. Children must eventually earn what they get, develop their real abilities, and adjust to and master their environment.

An unfulfilled need that has been *converted* to a claim produces much more intense frustration than the same need not so transformed. The claim is a demand that the neurotic person believes is due him or her. Frustration is an unpleasant psychic state for all, but the people who have transformed their needs to claims consider it a direct affront and a cause for righteous indignation. Normal people with a need for affection know that they must work to gratify it. The neurotic with a claim for affection expects to receive affection without earning it.

The relation of claims to moving toward, against, or away from people. Like most aspects of their search for perfection, the neurotics' claims are organized around their major direction in life. If they move toward people (the self-effacing, compliant orientation) as a means of getting what they need, their claim will take the form of expecting unqualified love. They must be constantly reassured of the love of the other. An example is the wife who expects her husband to call her several times a day from work. She may be obsessed with jealousy and nag him incessantly for supposed infidelity. The irony of such a situation is that the person who is claiming the devotion of his or her partner usually does not do anything to deserve the love. The love is demanded by the assumed qualities bestowed by the ideal self. (Horney, 1950)

People with the expansive orientation who manipulate other people for their own ends (moving against people) claim that something should be theirs simply because it is available. Why should they not have the good things of life, since they know others who possess them and are obviously inferior? The fact that those who possess the good things had to work hard and sacrifice a great deal is conveniently glossed over. They claim respect and allegiance from others on the basis of their assumed qualities of leadership and competence. (Horney, 1950)

Detached people with the resigned orientation (moving away from people) do not seem to make claims. They want to be left alone. But they do make at least one claim: not to be held responsible for ordinary obligations. This requirement may not appear to be a claim at all, but it is. These people may object that as they criticize no one and make no demands of anyone, they should not be criticized. If they are reproved for not doing what is expected of them at home, they may feel unjustly persecuted (Horney, 1950). This example clearly illustrates the subtlety of neurotic claims. As the claim is not based on real attributes, its fulfillment may be presumed. *The implicit desire for an easy solution underlies all neurotic claims.*

How to deal with claims.   As we have noted, Horney held that the basis for claims is the identification of the self as the idealized self-image. The best preventive measure is not to allow the real self to make the transformation. We should strive continually for self-knowledge and exploration. As it is easy to convert a need to a claim, we should frequently examine our basic needs and expectations. Needs and expectations are revealed by wants and desires, a scrutiny of which may identify possible underlying claims. Horney (1942) held that the self is highly complex: it is analogous to a large city that one could explore for years before finding all the major and minor points of interest. Learning about one's claims is like learning about the city's governing agencies.

Even the most balanced person will discover some claims behind his or her behavior. Expectations may be set too high, given present accomplishments. An examination of the means necessary to reach desired goals, as well as the feasibility of the goals themselves, will guard against insidious conversion of needs to claims. We must also develop effective ways of dealing with the frustration that inevitably accompanies goal pursuit. Incidentally situations that are especially frustrating may reveal hidden underlying claims.

3. THE TYRANNY OF THE "SHOULDS"

One characteristic of the search for glory, it will be recalled, is the need for personal perfection. Personal perfection, which helps to sustain a godlike image of self, is brought about through a system of inner dictates or expectations which Horney designated "the tyranny of the 'shoulds.'" Like claims, shoulds are intended to suit the individual to the level required by his or her ideal self (Table 7–1). The difference is that whereas claims are unrealistic demands of people and things outside the person, shoulds are unrealistic expectations of oneself.

Horney's concept of the shoulds applies to everyone to a greater or lesser degree. The task of dealing with personal expectations is universal. "How much should I demand of myself? When am I falling short of or exceeding my potentialities? How generous, or moral, or considerate, or hardworking, or humble should I be?" These are constant concerns of the healthiest of people. We should frequently examine our shoulds and attempt to bring them into line with our real self.

Shoulds versus realistic self-demands. The realistic expectations that normal people impose upon themselves—those that take account of real assets and liabilities and prevailing circumstances—are the product of the real self. Shoulds, on the other hand, are grandiose and unattainable expectations that result from the influence of the idealized self. The justification for shoulds is obviously erroneous. Because a

TABLE 7-1 METHODS OF MAINTAINING THE IDEAL SELF

Claims	Shoulds
Feels entitled never to be criticized, doubted, or questioned	Should be the epitome of honesty, generosity, justice, dignity, courageousness, unselfishness
Feels entitled to blind obedience	
Feels entitled to fool everyone	Should be the perfect lover, spouse, teacher
Feels entitled to immunity and exception	Should overcome difficulties easily
Expects to be loved by all he or she meets	Should overcome bad moods simply by willing
Claims to impress all	Should be able to endure everything
Claims to be honored by all	Should be able to like everyone
Claims to be close to others	Should be able to love his or her parents, country
Claims to live in peace; deplores combat	
All needs must be fulfilled	Should be spontaneous
Feels self-sufficient (does not want to be bothered by others)	Should know and understand everything
	Should never be tired or ill
Disdainful of others' rights	Should be able to work endlessly and productively
Requires admiration	
Claims to be openly aggressive and ambitious	Should be all things to all people
Claims to be allowed to maintain his distance	Should be above pleasure
Claims not to have any problems	Should control his or her feelings
Claims to be better than everyone else and recognized for it	Should never feel hurt
	Should always be serene and unruffled
Claims to be exempt from illness	Nothing should matter to him or her
Claims to be pleased by others all the time	

Note: Not all the "claims" and "shoulds" noted in the table will be found in any one neurotic person; rather both claims and shoulds follow the individual's major personal orientation: self-effacing, expansive, or resigned. Claims may be contradictory and create serious inner conflicts, for example, expecting to be both loved and feared. Shoulds, too, may be contradictory and produce inner conflicts, for example, being composed and dynamic at the same time.

person has attained superiority in one field, for example, he or she expects to be superior in all. Another individual assumes that work should be easy for him or her, for if he or she wills something, it should come to pass. Obviously, the shoulds place the individual in great jeopardy and vulnerability. The uncompromising quality of a system of shoulds insures failure. One of the most devastating consequences of a system of shoulds is self-hate because fulfillment is impossible.

To summarize briefly: becoming the idealized self causes a hatred and contempt for the real self. This point is necessary for an understanding of Horney's conception of neurosis. The idealized self, endowed with false pride and supported by claims and shoulds, has as one of its objectives the obliteration of the hated and despicable real self. The seemingly contradictory observation that neurotics often display both inordinate pride and vicious self-contempt makes sense in Horney's system. The *pride* stems from the ideal self; and the *contempt*, from the inadequacy of the real self.

The idealization of the self causes the person to experience inordinate self-love. To support the false image of self, the person attributes to himself or herself extraordinary qualities, the possession of which would be highly laudable and the basis for respect. But the attributes are fake and sham; they simply do not exist; the person has deluded himself or herself into believing that he or she is an extraordinary person. At times, the person senses his or her pretense and sham existence, and the great pride changes to vicious self-hatred and self-condemnation. Furthermore, the person's everyday behavior is the product of his or her real self and not of the idealized image of self. Repeated failures reveal a different picture from what the individual imagines himself or herself to be, a picture that is not very flattering. Mechanisms of self-deception and reality distortion are typically used to alter the unpleasant truths about self, but the distortion and denial do not alter the facts forever. Occasionally, the person experiences painful realities about himself or herself that contradict the idealized self-image, and the result is self-hatred and merciless self-accusations. In the long run, the negative features predominate, and the person may undergo a catastrophic breakdown psychologically and physically.

Horney summarizes some of the preceding ideas in the following passage:

> Roughly speaking, a person builds up an idealized image of himself because he cannot tolerate himself as he actually is. The image apparently counteracts this calamity; but having placed himself on a pedestal, he can tolerate his real self still less and starts to rage against it; to despise himself and to chafe under the yoke of his own unattainable demands upon himself. A person reacts to this inner dictatorship just as a person might react to a comparable political dictatorship: he may identify himself with it . . . he may stand on tiptoe to try to measure up to its demands; or he may rebel against the coercion and refuse to recognize the imposed obligations . . . . All these consequences combine to build a mighty barrier against development. The person cannot learn from his mistakes because he does not see them. [Horney, 1945, pp. 112–113][3]

4. AUXILIARY PROTECTIVE STRATEGIES

The auxiliary protective strategies can best be considered in outline form (Table 7–2).

[3]*Our Inner Conflicts.*

Mechanism	Description
Blind spots	Ignoring the conflict Being oblivious to the true situation Being "stupid" in certain areas of one's life Example: a husband who will not consider his inefficiency as a possible cause of family money problems
Compartmentalization	Segregating contradictory roles Behaving inconsistently without conscious awareness Solving conflicts by freely expressing both alternatives at different times Example: a person who regularly attends church on Sundays but is unscrupulous in his or her business dealings
Rationalization	Self-deceiving by reasoning Minimizing or remodeling conflicting factors so that conflict is diminished Example: a person who calls his or her efforts to take advantage of others "a matter of good business"
Excessive self-control	Undue exertion of restraints over certain emotions and thoughts, which are in conflict with opposite tendencies Resistance against distractions and healthy motives Example: one who holds under control certain emotions or motives such as enthusiasm, sex, rage, tenderness
Arbitrary rightness	Eliminating doubt from within and influence from without Regarding doubt and indecision as the worst evil Settling conflicts once and for all by declaring arbitrarily and dogmatically that one is invariably right Example: the politician who interprets all issues from the standpoint of the party line
Elusiveness	Avoiding being pinned down to any statement Choosing to remain undecided rather than resolve a conflict in favor of the wrong decision Considering all ramifications, consequences, and alternatives, then postponing a decision Example: the lawyer who refuses to give a definite opinion on the outcome of a case, but details all the possibilities instead
Cynicism	Denying and deriding moral values Not forming any values because there are none that are worthwhile Finding most things and people uninteresting Being overly discreet in tastes Example: the tired old man who wants to be left alone because there is nothing much left for him in life

CRITICAL EVALUATION

Horney was one of the first psychiatrists to call attention to cultural factors as major determinants of personality growth and functioning. Like Freud, she perceived the significance of the home environment, but she took a wider view and included the cultural forces — economic, social, political, educational, and the like. She saw that cultural practices could foster the development of abnormal trends. Whereas Freud attempted to identify common factors that were universal in people, such as life and death instincts and their alterations, Horney focused upon the specific conditions of the culture and even subculture.

Horney was a master at deriving implications from a key concept. She would rival any medieval scholar in her deductive skills. In reading her work, we are easily drawn away from the original assumptions and postulates and are caught up in the many ramifications and elaborations that she derived from them. Furthermore, it is difficult to separate empirical observation from inference because her only support is testimony from her own clinical experiences. Although her hypotheses have a commonsense appeal, they must be tested empirically if they are to gain the status of behavioral principles. Although she has a number of practicing disciples, it does not appear that her views are inspiring the necessary research support.

Nevertheless, the reader can certainly profit from the richness and depth of Horney's insights into the deepest human motivations. It should be possible to apply her ideas in promoting mental health. She devoted her entire career to this problem although, like other clinicians, she had more experience with the abnormal than with the normal. She was quite optimistic about the natural potential for growth and healthy functioning both in people in general and in each individual: "My own belief is that man has the capacity as well as the desire to develop his potentialities and become a decent human being, and that these deteriorate if his relationship to others and hence to himself is, and continues to be, disturbed. I believe that man can change and go on changing as long as he lives. And this belief has grown with deeper understanding." (1950, p. 22) To Horney, our best hope, both collectively and individually, for realizing potentials lies in positive support of our own constructive forces by the social environment.

GUIDES TO RESEARCH

HEURISTIC VALUE OF HORNEY'S THEORY

The training school that Horney founded, the Association for the Advancement of Psychoanalysis, continues to attract students; thus, her views about psychiatry and human personality are being perpetuated. Horney has influenced the thinking of several prominent personality theorists. Eric Fromm and Harry Stack Sullivan, who were affiliated at one time with her school of psychiatry, have espoused and elaborated on her stress on the cultural determinants in personality. She was among Freud's earliest disciples to turn away from Freud's heavy emphasis on biological determinism.

Another area in which Horney's views have been influential is in feminine psychology. Some of her earliest papers were written as reactions to Freud's male-dominated psychology. A collection of her articles dealing with the problems of women, sex differences, and a number of other pertinent issues relevant to her differences with Freud are gathered together and published in a volume entitled *Feminine Psychology* (1967). See also *The Adolescent Diaries of Karen Horney* (1980) for the origins of some of her ideas about women. She argued against the prevailing view of feminine inferiority and eventually proposed a psychology of persons as an overriding concern for psychology and psychiatry. She certainly appreciated the special problems of each sex; thus, in a real sense, it is valid to speak of masculine and feminine psychology, but the remarkable similarities of the two sexes as members of the human species are best encompassed in a person psychology.

Horney's writings contain many ideas that reflect the humanistic and existential point of view, although she has not often been claimed by the adherents of these movements. For example, she came to disagree with Freud's ideas about normal and abnormal processes in personality and behavior. Freud held that abnormal processes were exaggerations of the normal; thus, one could see the normal personality more vividly through studying the abnormal. Horney began to see a significant difference between a sick and a healthy orientation. She spoke of constructive and destructive forms of growth, using a physical analogy. Her ideas influenced personality theorists such as Maslow and Rogers, who subsequently propounded a health and growth psychology—the idea that being a psychologically and physically healthy person involves a great deal more than *not* being sick. As a matter of fact, Rogers' theory of the self has marked similarities with Horney's views. His notion of incongruence is virtually identical with Horney's construct of the alienation of the self.

Horney's theory of personality takes into account both biological and psychosocial determinants. Humans are born into a physical and sociocultural environment, which greatly shapes the genetic potentials. Horney felt strongly that many differences between men and women are culturally determined rather than biologically set. Humans have a species nature and an individual nature, but there are also powerful social and cultural forces that shape personality. (See Juanita Williams, 1977, pp. 64–65, for further elaboration of this point.) The behavior of both sexes varies considerably from society to society, and no particular society exists that is ideally suited to bring out the best potentials of human beings.

Views on Sex Differences

Horney attempted to right some of the wrongs and injustices that she believed were perpetuated by Freud and others, who viewed women as inferior to men. She did not deny the rather obvious and important differences between the sexes, which some recent feminists seem to do. She saw differences, but these were not to be construed on a dimension of superiority. It might be instructive to examine some of her views on sex differences. For example, women have a different role in sexual intercourse in that a woman is receptive whereas the man must be active to perform adequately. The female partner, of course, can be active in participating in mutual stimulation and enjoyment. Women, even frigid women, can engage in intercourse, but an impotent man cannot. Another important difference between the sexes is that women bear the children, a fact that has many physical and psychological implications for both sexes. For example, some psychoanalysts have made this difference the basis of male envy, the so-called birth envy, which is supposed to cause strife between men and women. Typically, men are larger and stronger than women, factors that create dread in some women and sadistic tendencies in some men. There are certainly major differences between men and women that are not culturally determined.

In her book on feminine psychology, Hor-

womb envy

ney attacks many of the current misconceptions about the differences between the sexes. Freud's ideas are frequent targets. For example, she attacks his notion of penis envy on the part of the woman, as we have noted. She does not believe that women are born with the desire to have masculine attributes. However, many women protest against their inferior status in society and their lack of opportunity for fulfillment, desires that have nothing to do with wanting to be masculine. Penis envy is a pathological development, not a normal aspiration. When it occurs, it is the product of circumstances.

the 2 primary drives in women
1) Sex
2) mother-hood

When Horney began to analyze men, after her long experience with women, she was impressed with the mutual distrust of the sexes. She discovered that men envied women for pregnancy, childbirth, and motherhood, and also for their breasts and the act of suckling. Horney came to believe that men's attitudes and behavior toward women hinder the natural unfolding of feminine potentials and the opportunity for uniqueness in development and functioning. One of her most challenging ideas is that women have a sexual drive independent of the maternal drive. This view is one of the cornerstones of modern feminism. The desire for a child in a woman is a primary drive, as is the sexual drive.

In attempting to arrive at real differences between the sexes, Horney suggested that researchers measure observable behaviors in both sexes, for example, rather than assume that masochism is natural to the female personality. She said:

> Reviewing then, the observable masochistic attitudes, regardless of their deeper motivation, I suggest that the anthropologist seek data concerning questions like these: under what social or cultural conditions do we find more frequently in women than in men:
>
> **1.** the manifesting of inhibitions in the direct expression of demands and aggressions;
>
> **2.** a regarding of oneself as weak, helpless, or inferior and implicitly or explicitly demanding considerations and advantages on this basis;

> **3.** a becoming emotionally dependent on the other sex;
>
> **4.** a showing of tendencies to be self-sacrificing, to be submissive, to feel used or to be exploited, to put responsibilities on the other sex.

These formulation, said Horney, . . . are direct generalizations of the psychoanalytic experience with masochistic women. (1967, p. 229)[4]

An example of the kind of research that has been influenced by the questions Horney asked is that of Eleanor Maccoby, who has done a great amount of work in the area of sex roles and sex differences. (Maccoby, 1966; Maccoby and Jacklin, 1974) For instance, Maccoby and Jacklin found three areas in which sex differences exist when they reviewed the literature on cognitive and intellectual ability. These were verbal ability, mathematical ability, and spatial ability. Girls excel in verbal ability; boys do better in mathematical and spatial ability. There is evidence today that such differences may be the result of sex-linked cerebral dominance. (Kagan, 1971; 1972) As we can see, there is not much research directly attributable to Horney's theory, but she spurred others to pursue lines of investigation that she suggested. A number of important studies have dealt with the actual differences between sensory, perceptual, cognitive, and motor functions of boys and girls that are not caused by cultural factors.

It is difficult to assess Horney's influence in these studies, but she did pose the questions that later investigators are currently attempting to answer in respect to biological versus cultural determinism.

In the introduction to Horney's book *Feminine Psychology*, Harold Kelman writes a fitting tribute to her approach to the study of human nature. "After confronting Freud's male-oriented psychology with her own so-called female psychology, she prepared the way for a philosophy, psychology, and psychoanalysis of whole people living and interacting with their changing environments." (Kelman in Horney, 1967)

---

[4]*Neuroses and Human Growth*, by Karen Horney, M.D. Copyright 1967 by W.W. Norton & Company, Inc. Used by permission of W.W. Norton & Company, Inc.

GUIDES TO LIVING

In 1942, Horney wrote a book entitled *Self Analysis.* It was an attempt to provide the layperson with insights from psychoanalysis that could be applied by everyone. She discussed free association, dream analysis, resistance, and transference. Though the book is not a guide to mental health, it contains many valuable suggestions for improving one's life. We will consider some of these ideas.

ONE PROBLEM AT A TIME

Horney suggested that one should begin his or her self-analysis by identifying one problem area that is unmistakable. Undesirable traits or trends that are doubtful should not be taken up in the early stages of self-analysis. These problems will emerge as the analysis proceeds, if they are truly problems.

RATIONAL AND INTUITIVE APPROACH

Horney maintained that an approach that is both rational and intuitive should be applied. One basic step in a self-analysis is to discover all aspects of a problem area. In looking at actual behavior, consider the various ways in which the problem is manifested. To achieve this objective, you can rely on Horney's views of neurotic trends. Is the major difficulty social relationships? Is it a matter of inflexibility in seeking to be loved or to dominate or to withdraw from others? Is the particular trend so compulsive that it rules the personality?

To Horney, one of the problem areas with which everyone must deal is the search for glory:

> For his well-functioning, man needs both the vision of possibilities, the perspective of infinitude *and* the realization of limitations, of necessities, of the concrete. If a man's thinking *and* feeling are primarily focused upon the infinite and the vision of possibilities, he loses his sense for the concrete, for the here and now. He loses his capacity for living in the moment. He is no longer capable of submitting to the necessities in himself, "to what may be called one's limit." He loses sight of what is actually necessary for achieving something. . . . If, on the other hand, a man does not see beyond the narrow horizon of the concrete, the necessary, the finite, he becomes "narrow-minded and mean-spirited." It is not, then, a question of either-or, but of *both*, if there is to be growth. The recognition of limitations, laws, and necessities serves as a check against being carried away into the infinite, and against the mere "floundering in possibilities" [1950, p. 35].[5]

In addition to the manifestations of the undesirable trait, Horney suggested that we should look for interrelation of the trait with other characteristics. For instance, a trait of helplessness may be linked with a more general orientation of dependency. The dependency, in turn, may be associated with a profound fear of self-assertiveness. We should ask the question: How is the particular personality trait or trend embedded in the total structure of the personality?

We must also inquire about the scope of a trait—its centrality in the personality structure. Is the trait or trend a troublesome quirk that is occasionally set off, or is it a way of life?

Insight into the nature of a neurotic trend is often promoted by an understanding of the

---

[5] *Neurosis and Human Growth*, by Karen Horney, M.D. Copyright 1950 by W.W. Norton & Company, Inc. Copyright renewed 1978. Used by permission of W.W. Norton & Company, Inc.

origins of the trend. Such analysis requires that you probe into your past. The probing should be done leisurely and without producing too much anxiety. If you begin to experience resentment or hostility or undue self-pity, it should be dropped until another time. One more point is salient here: Horney advised us to follow thoroughly one problem area rather than attempt a complete coverage of personality difficulties. As we gain insight into one problem area, other problems will emerge. But more importantly, personality functioning will begin to improve, and other problem areas will become easier to analyze.

DISCOVERY OF CLAIMS AND SHOULDS

Horney made a significant contribution to our knowledge of the psychodynamics of abnormal personality formations through her brilliant insights into the nature of neurotic claims and shoulds. We have already discussed the nature of both of these, but here we are concerned with the means of detecting them. Whether neurotic or not, everyone harbors some neurotic claims and shoulds, and their existence hampers the full development and functioning of personality. Table 7–3 contrasts normal and neurotic growth and summarizes the changes that take place in personality with the development of a neurosis.

It will be recalled that neurotic claims are unrealistic or unwarranted expectations or demands of people and things outside the person whereas shoulds are unrealistic demands or expectations of oneself. A claim is an undeserved or unearned title that the person believes he or she has whereas a should is a perfectionist demand that is applied to oneself. By their very nature claims and shoulds cannot be satisfied; thus one who possesses them will experience needless suffering—anxiety, resentment, disappointment, and anguish (in the case of unfulfilled claims)—and needless torture—self-accusation, self-contempt, self-hatred, negativism, and resistance against doing anything for oneself (in the case of shoulds).

Horney pointed out that shoulds are not simply ideals or high moral standards, the attributes of the perfected self, but rather are glamorous and grandiose expectations. If anything, they are immoral because they are based on an

TABLE 7-3 NORMAL VERSUS NEUROTIC GROWTH

Normal Growth Includes	Neurotic Growth Includes	Neurotic Solutions
Actualizing self	Unrealistic claims	Compliance
Growth	Host of "shoulds"	Mastery
Self-realization	Neurotic striving for perfection	Detachment
Maturity	Unrealistic ambitions	Blind spots
Fulfillment	Triumph over others	Compartments
Spontaneity	Pride, self-hate, contempt, self-accusations	Rationalization
		Excessive self-control
		Arbitrary rightness
		Elusiveness
		Cynicism
		End Results
		Alienation from real self
		Striving to actualize ideal self

inflated sense of self. Consider some of the following points:

1. We approach a task with the attitude that we should be able to do it easily. When we fail, we begin to find excuses for ourselves. Our approach to life is counterfeit.

2. We may expect to be consistently serene and calm, even in situations in which other emotions are appropriate. This attitude may produce a blunting of emotional responses, and in fact we may begin to lose touch with our emotions, so that we do not feel them when they occur.

3. Frequently there are contradictory shoulds, and the ensuing conflict may be extremely intense. "I should be all-loving, but also dynamic and aggressive." In such instances there may be sudden shifts of mood.

4. People often deal with the problems of aging or attractiveness or the other inevitables in life by converting them into shoulds. "It is unfair and totally unjust for this to be happening to me." "I hate the thought of growing old, so I simply won't allow it to happen; thus I am not getting old." Such thinking can become highly irrational and lead to reckless behavior to support the should.

5. Shoulds may result from erroneous inferences. Because a person happens to be intelligent, he or she assumes that he should be able to write or play the piano or do almost anything—and furthermore, do these things easily and without too much work.

6. If a particular should is especially powerful, the entire personality is made over. Real feelings, emotions, and desires are not experienced but are replaced with fictitious ones that suit the character of the should. One who is dominated by the inner dictate that he or she should love everyone is incapable of genuine love because he or she has killed off this potential in himself or herself. Instead, he or she experiences a pseudo, sham, or illusory love. His or her unreal love neither benefits nor convinces others; rather it becomes progressively unreal and shallow. If we had to select one word to characterize Horney's view of a neurotic, it would be "a phony." The examination of such inner dictates to discover their grandiose and fantastic nature is absolutely essential to mental health. Horney said of the shoulds:

> We are less aware of the harm done our feelings by these pervasive shoulds than of other damage inflicted by them. Yet it is actually the heaviest price we pay for trying to mold ourselves into perfection. Feelings are the most alive part of ourselves; if they are put under a dictatorial regime, a profound uncertainty is created in our essential being, which must affect adversely our relations to everything inside and outside ourselves. We can hardly overrate the intensity of the impact of the inner dictates. The more the drive to actualize his idealized self prevails in a person, the more the shoulds become the sole motor force moving him, driving him, whipping him into action. [1950, p. 84].[6]

There is a striking similarity between Horney's notion of counteracting one's shoulds and challenging hidden assumptions proposed by Albert Ellis (1975) and also with the current emphasis in cognitive behavior modification on cognitive restructuring. (Meichenbaum, 1978)

Shoulds are interrelated with each person's style of life. As these trends in the personality can only block the use of real abilities and the satisfaction of genuine needs, we should vigilantly question the bases of our assumptions, expectations, and demands, with respect to both ourselves and others. As we rid ourselves of neurotic trends, the potentialities of our real self begin to emerge.

TACKLING PROBLEM AREAS

The study of the self need not be an intensively critical self-scrutiny. There are degrees of self-exploration, and not everyone should attempt to plumb the depth and breadth of his

---

[6]*Neurosis and Human Growth*, by Karen Horney, M.D. Copyright 1950 by W.W. Norton & Company, Inc. Copyright renewed 1978. Used by permission of W.W. Norton & Company, Inc.

Photo credits: *upper* © Erika Stone/Photo Researchers, Inc.; *lower left* © Hella Hammid/Rapho, Photo Researchers, Inc.; *lower right* © Hazel Hankin/Stock, Bosto

The normal person uses the three orientations flexibly.

Neurotics repress the tendencies to move in the other orientations.

or her inner life. But we certainly can tackle problem areas that are obvious. Taking Horney's analogy of the self as a large city, we might ask: What are the most important landmarks (traits or tendencies) in my self? Consider a typical problem: "People do not like me." Horney might

suggest posing the following questions to ourselves: Is it true that no one likes you? Do you think that you are more likable at some times than others? In your own opinion are you not likable? What particular behaviors do you think are most unattractive about you? What is the simplest first step you can take to change a particularly undesirable behavior? Can you work out a simple program to change this behavior? Answers to such questions can set positive tendencies toward growth and mastery to work for everyone, Horney believed. We all have both destructive and constructive tendencies. The constructive ones must be supported and fostered if they are to operate spontaneously. Again we see in Horney's thinking anticipation of later trends, as for example, the method of self-instruction as a means of changing behavior (Mahoney, 1974).

Horney believed that humans can reduce or even eliminate inner conflicts, though the process may be painful:

To experience conflicts knowingly, though it may be distressing, can be an invaluable asset. The more we face our own conflicts and seek out our own solutions, the more inner freedom and strength we will gain. When conflicts center about the primary issues of life, it is all the more difficult to face them and resolve them. But provided we are sufficiently alive, there is no reason why in principle we should not be able to do so. Education could do much to help us to live with greater awareness of ourselves and to develop our own convictions. A realization of the significance of the factors involved in choice would give us ideals to strive for, and in that a direction for our lives [1950, p. 27].[7]

SUGGESTIONS FOR HEALTHY LIVING

Horney believed that the normal person is one who can integrate the three orientations to life—moving toward, against, and away from people:

From the point of view of the normal person there is no reason why the three attitudes [orientations to life] should be mutually exclusive. One should be capable of giving in to others, of fighting, and of keeping to oneself. The three can complement each other and make for a harmonious whole. If one predominates, it merely indicates an overdevelopment along one line. [1945, pp. 45–46][8]

Her description of the work involved in self-improvement and integration parallels Maslow's concept of self-actualization and Rogers' picture of the fully functioning person. Consider the following brief recipe for healthy living that Horney outlines:

Putting the work to be done in positive terms, it concerns all that is involved in self-realization. With regard to himself it means striving

toward a clearer and deeper experiencing of his feelings, wishes, and beliefs; toward a greater ability to tap his resources and to use them for constructive ends; toward a clearer perception of his direction in life, with the assumption of responsibility for himself and his decisions. With regard to others it means his striving toward relating himself to others with genuine feelings; toward respecting them as individuals in their own right and with their own peculiarities; toward developing a spirit of mutuality (instead of using them as a means to an end). With regard to work it means that the work itself will become more important to him than the satisfaction of his pride or vanity and that he will aim at realizing and developing his special gifts and at becoming more productive. (1950, p. 364)[9]

Horney held that neurosis does not develop if the child is given the opportunity to grow and to actualize his or her inner nature. Neurosis is a thwarting of the constructive inner

---

[7] *Neurosis and Human Growth*, by Karen Horney, M.D. Copyright 1950 by W.W. Norton & Company, Inc. Copyright renewed 1978. Used by permission of W.W. Norton & Comnpany, Inc.
[8] *Our Inner Conflicts.*
[9] See footnote 7.

forces that are basic to human nature. Conflict is not inherent but is created. Horney makes the excellent point that we may become victims of our culture by overidentifying with its values and practices. We may take the cultural prescriptions and allurements too seriously.

> ... the person who is likely to become neurotic is one who has experienced the culturally determined difficulties in an accentuated form, mostly through the medium of childhood experiences, and who has consequently been unable to solve them, or has solved them only at great cost to his personality. We might call him a stepchild of our culture. [1937, p. 290][10]

Horney's concept of the basic discrepancy

between the real and ideal selves is succinctly summarized in a passage that she cited from the poet Christian Morgenstern on the power of self-hate when the ideal self is dominant:

> I shall succumb, destroyed by myself
> I who am two, what I could be and what I am
> And in the end one will annihilate the other,
> The would-be is like a prancing steed
> (*I am* is fettered to his tail)
> Is like a wheel to which *I am* is bound
> Is like a fury whose fingers twine
> Into his victims hair, is like a vampire
> That sits upon his heart and sucks and sucks

[1950, pp 113–114][11]

SUMMARY

1. Horney rejected Freud's notions of the genetic and instinctive determinants of behavior and also Freud's division of the psyche into warring systems. She became convinced that personality illness was caused by powerful environmental demands—economic, social, and educational—which created problems of adjustment rather than intrinsic inner conflicts. A pattern of unfavorable circumstances in the home produces in the child a condition that Horney termed basic anxiety, a feeling of being isolated and helpless in a potentially hostile environment. Such insecurity is the basis for the formation of a neurotic style of life, and healthy patterns of growth are blocked as deviant ones predominate.

2. Horney delineated three social orientations—moving toward people, moving against people, and moving away from people—as abnormal strategies for dealing with anxiety. The social orientations eventually become generalized as total orientations to life. When adopted, an orientation creates inner conflicts because competing tendencies must be suppressed. A person may conpulsively adopt either

(a) the self-effacing solution (striving for love), (b) the expansive solution (striving for mastery), or (c) the detached solution (striving for freedom).

3. Horney viewed society and culture as providing the stresses that caused personality problems, and at the same time offered simple and appealing solutions. One of the major solutions was to provide ideal models for people to follow. These ideals inspired the dissatisfied individual to pursue the process of alienation, the abandonment of the real self for the sake of an idealized version of self. Creating basic anxiety in the child induces dissatisfaction with self, and the easy solution is to identify with an ideal version of self. Instead of actualizing the potentialities of the real self, the alienated person attempts to actualize the potentialities of the ideal self, a situation that creates serious disturbances in personality growth and functioning.

4. The false self-image is a motivating force in the personality, but the behavior that actually occurs stems from the attributes of the real self. Serious personality disturbance may occur because there is inconsistency between

---

[10]*The Neurotic Personality of Our Time.*

[11]"Entwicklungschmerzen" ("Growing Pains"), trans. Caroline Newton from a collection of poems, *Auf Vielen Wegen*. (Munich: R. Piper and Company, 1921).

expectations and actual behavior. In order to preserve the idealized self, a person finds defensive distortion necessary. The defensive strategies will tend to fit one of the major orientations to life, which then becomes highly compulsive, creating severe inner conflicts because vital needs must be suppressed. As the culture provides ideal models for each of the three basic orientations, the one best suited to the individual is readily adopted by one who suffers profound dissatisfaction with self.

5.　Horney terms the central inner conflict the struggle between the real self and the ideal self. When a person abandons the real self, the greatest source of strength, alienation occurs. For the insecure and self-dissatisfied child, becoming the idealized self is a tantalizing prospect because it apparently solves many problems. The person is captivated by a search for glory and projects an image of self as extraordinary. The search for glory involves the need for perfection, the need for neurotic ambition, and the need for a vindictive triumph. Strong needs are associated with fear, which further intensifies the needs, creating a vicious circle. The needs become insatiable, and the strategy to gratify them, ever more compulsive. The desire for greatness and the equally strong desire for an easy way out lead to the devil's pact, the renunciation of the real self for the sake of a glorified self.

6.　The idealized self is supported by four strategies: (a) neurotic pride, (b) neurotic claims, (c) tyrannical shoulds, and (d) auxiliary protective mechanisms. Neurotic pride is false pride because it consists of converting weaknesses into virtues. Alternating with inordinate self-love, which stems from the glorified self, is self-hatred because the true attributes are manifested in the person's behavior when the defenses break down. Neurotic pride sensitizes a person to a remarkable degree to insults or threats; thus, the person may limit participation in any activity that might expose the sham existence.

7.　Neurotic claims are unwarranted expectations of others or the external world. They are groundless assertions of title, based on the grandiose nature of the ideal self. Needs may

be transformed into claims, such as the need for affection to the claim of affection. The particular claims stem from a person's dominant orientation to life, centering about expectations of either love, mastery, or detachment. Unusual sensitivities and low frustration tolerance may reveal the presence of claims.

8.　Personal perfection, a quality of the ideal self, requires a system of inner dictates that suit the individual to the demands of the ideal self. These are tyrannical shoulds that are directed to making over the self. They also lead to self-accusations and self-hatred as the individual inevitably encounters the truth about the real self.

9.　Auxiliary protective mechanisms also support the idealized version of self. They are (a) blind spots, (b) compartmentalizations, (c) rationalizations, (d) excessive self-control, (e) arbitrary rightness, (f) elusiveness, and (g) cynicism.

10.　With the formation of neurotic pride, claims, shoulds, and the auxiliary protective mechanisms, all supporting the false image of self, Horney's picture of the neurotic is of one who lives a sham existence, a pretender and a phony. Horney maintains that the three basic orientations are effective coping strategies if they are used properly, which is the case with the normal person. They should complement each other rather than being compulsively followed. Horney pointed out that a person may become a victim of his or her culture by overidentifying with its values, a factor that promotes the alienation process.

11.　Horney wrote a series of articles on feminine psychology, later compiled as a book, in which she argued against the inferior role of women that Freud promoted. While recognizing the differences between the sexes, she proposed a psychology of persons as an overriding concern for psychology and psychiatry. In general, her views have not inspired much scientific research, although some current scientific interest is being directed to sex differences that are independent of cultural effects, but how much Horney's views are responsible for this development is difficult to assess.

GLOSSARY

Alienation process: Horney's term for the loss of contact with the real self and the formation of an idealized version of self; an unhealthy process of denial of the potentials of the real self due to feelings of self-dissatisfaction caused by environmental circumstances.

Ideal self: A distorted conception of self that reduces basic anxiety and inner conflicts; a false solution for the problem of self-dissatisfaction.

Glory: A search for glory, characteristic of the alienation process in which a person attempts to impress others as being extraordinary; involves the needs for perfection, neurotic ambition, and vindictive triumph over others.

Neurotic pride: A false sense of self-esteem based on the attributes of the idealized self, involving converting weaknesses into virtues.

Claims: Faulty expectations of others and the world that are logical outcomes of identification with the idealized self, experienced as rights or entitlements.

Neurotic needs: Need converted to claim becomes compulsive, insatiable and indiscriminate, for example, driven to be loved all the time and by everyone.

Shoulds: Faulty expectations of self to suit the requirements of the idealized self; harsh inner dictates for perfectionistic standards. The basis for self-contempt and self accusations.

Auxiliary protective mechanisms: Defensive strategies that maintain the idealized version of self.

Central inner conflict. The conflict resulting from the requirements of the idealized self and the attributes of the real self; especially acute when defensive distortion breaks down and one senses the truth about himself or herself.

Devil's pact: The renunciation of the real self and acceptance of the idealized version of self as the real self. The notion that one sells his or her self for temporary glory.

Anxiety: Dread; diffuse fear, fear of the unknown.

Basic anxiety: For Horney the feeling of being helpless and alone in a potentially hostile world. Results from parental mismanagement; the prototype of later anxiety situations.

Security: For Horney a major motive of life that wards off anxiety.

Neurotic trends: Also called neurotic needs. Ten powerful needs that result from basic anxiety become the basis for the three neurotic orientations to life.

Self: The governing core of personality. The true attributes of the self.

Self-image: The concept one has of self.

Idealized self-image: The concept of the perfected self.

Ideal self: Faulty conception of self; accepted as the real self.

Self realization: The process of fulfilling the potentials of the real self, as contrasted with neurosis, which involves the vain attempt to fulfill the attributes of the ideal self.

Self-contempt: Intense hatred for the self caused by the tyranny of the shoulds for failing to meet the demands of the ideal self.

Tyranny of the shoulds: The impossible demands placed by the individual on himself or herself when the ideal self is substituted for the real self.

Social orientations: Three possible types of social relationships; the source of inner conflicts when one of them becomes a dominant orientation; developed early in life as security measures to reduce basic anxiety.

Moving toward people: Gaining acceptance through compliance with the wishes and expectations of others; being liked and likeable; requires suppression of self-assertive needs.

Moving against people: Exploiting power over others to satisfy needs; places high premium on mastery and domination in social relationships; requires the suppression of healthy needs for affiliation and love.

Moving away from people: Gaining security through avoidance of problems associated with social relationships; requires suppression of social needs and the need to compete with others.

Total orientation to life: A general orientation to life stemming from one of the three social orientations; it becomes a way of life that is followed, irrespective of its utility.

    Compliance: A self-effacing orientation in which one gains acceptance and security through conformity and subordination to the desires of others.

Mastery: An expansive orientation in which aggressive control over others is compulsively sought; being dominant and masterful are ideals.

Detachment: A resigned orientation in which self-sufficiency is the ideal goal; requires suppression of healthy social needs and self-assertive behavior.

SUGGESTED READINGS

Horney, Karen. *The Neurotic Personality of Our Time.* New York: Norton, 1937.

    Horney presents her sociopsychological view of neurosis, which holds that cultural influences, rather than the thwarting of sexual instincts, set the climate for neurosis. She stresses the striving towards security and away from anxiety.

————*New Ways in Psychoanalysis.* New York: Norton, 1939.

    In this book Horney brings out clearly her differences with the traditional Freudian views. She attempts to correct the one-sided stress on instinctual determinants by her analysis of the cultural determinants.

————*Self Analysis.* New York: Norton, 1942.

    The book is an attempt to convey to the layperson some of the methods and concepts of psychoanalysis. Horney suggests that everyone could apply them with some benefit. The book deals with self-exploration and understanding.

————*Our Inner Conflicts.* New York: Norton, 1945.

    In this book Horney presents her three social orientations; moving toward, away from, and against people. She discusses the role of conflict extensively. She details the differences between normal and neurotic social relationships.

————*Neurosis and Human Growth.* New York: Norton, 1950.

    Horney rounds out her theory of neurosis by introducing the concept of the idealized self. She stresses the alienation from the real self through the pursuit of the idealized self. She coordinates the three social orientations with more generalized orientations to life: the self-effacing, the expansive, and the resigned. She views the neurotic as one who abandons his or her real potentialities and attempts to actualize his or her idealized version of self.

HUMANISTIC-EXISTENTIAL MODEL

The humanistic and existential psychologists have attempted to formulate theories of human nature that are based on *distinctively human attributes and problems of existence* caused by the condition of being human. They have rejected the typical models used by psychologists that depict humans in mechanistic or biological terms. Gordon W. Allport, Carl R. Rogers, Abraham Maslow, and Erich Fromm, the representatives of the humanistic-existential movement we will consider next, have rejected the machine model of humans, the animal model, the pathological model, and the model of the child as being inappropriate characterizations of fulfilled human nature. The machine model conceptualizes human nature as a complicated computer. The animal model views people as being simply more complex animals, being governed by drive-reduction motivation and pain avoidance. The pathological model stresses the nonrational and unconscious aspects of personality. The model of the child views the human adult as being simply a more complex child. These models neglect the radical changes that occur from childhood to adulthood in motivation, in cognition, in the growth of the self, and in the development of abilities. According to the humanistic-existential psychologists, an adequate theory of personality must take account of these attributes and the meaning they have for living as a human. Furthermore, humans have created, and are greatly affected by, a social-cultural environment, as we have seen in the theorizing of the ego-social theorists. Our humanistic psychologists are sympathetic to the pervasive role of social and cultural forces in shaping human behavior, but they would caution against overemphasis on such determinants of behavior.

If you wanted to build a theory of personality that adequately depicted our human nature, you would have the challenging and difficult task of determining what components to include in your theory and how much weight to give to each of them. Would you stress biological drives and selfish concerns? How much weight would you give to negative emotions such as hatred, envy, jealousy, and fear? Would you distinguish between people's animal nature and higher nature? What would full development and ideal functioning be, and what environmental conditions would be required to promote these ideals? What place would you give to inborn tendencies, and how much weight would you assign to learning potentials? Learning is such a key process in humans that its nature should be clearly delineated. Would you stress the automatic habit learning of conditioning or the more cognitive and personal aspects of human learning?

Humanistic and existential psychologists claim that they include components in their theories that encompass much more of human nature than other theories. Maslow, for example, studied the "highest reaches" of human potentials in his study of self-actualizers. Rogers dealt with college students who were experiencing life adjustment problems and currently works with a great variety of normal adult problems in his group work. Allport and Fromm have also focused on normal people who are striving to be better than they are. The psychodynamic and ego-social theories were geared toward the abnormal although Erikson did have some views on the formation of human virtues. The adherents of the humanistic and existential theories maintain that they incorporate into their theories the psychodynamic and ego-social determinants, but that they also include constructs and postulates that enlarge the scope of their theorizing to encompass normal and ideal personalities.

An interesting development in the thinking of some current cognitive behavior theorists, who, of course, identify themselves with the behavioristic and not the humanistic position, is the inclusion of humanistic and existential ideas (such as self-regulatory systems, intentions, and plans) that were so vehemently rejected by the radical behaviorists. This provides support to the contention of the humanistic-existential theorists that their views are more comprehensive than those of the psychodynamic, ego-social, and strict behavioristic theorists.

Humanistic and existential psychologists have included in their theories the notion of the self as a free agent. They hold that we can control our own destinies, if conditions are not too restrictive. They also view humans as having the ability for self-examination and self-induced change. We can rationally interpret, criticize, monitor, and evaluate our own behavior. We can evaluate both present and past behaviors and make plans for the future. We can also anticipate the long-term consequences of present behavior. Many people do not actually function on these levels, but the fact that they can, under the right conditions, provides a great challenge for behavior scientists and our community leaders.

Take away any of the ingredients that the humanistic and existential theorists propose, they insist, and the result is something less than a human being, or, certainly, less than a fully functioning human. They portray humans as having a much greater potential for living effectively than do the other theorists. Their view of abnormality is also quite broad because it encompasses everything less than the ideal. Deficiencies in human attributes are the causes of behavior disorders.

There are a variety of existential schools, several of which view human existence in pessimistic terms. The theorists we will be considering (Fromm is our best example) tend to follow the position that certain problems of existence result from the attributes of being human. In other words, because we are made the way we are, we must face certain problems and tasks. Our wonderful abilities create problems for us. We can anticipate the future, but that causes anxiety about aging, illness, and death. We have the capacity to make commitments, but often we must do so with only partial information. We can imagine perfection, and yet we must face imperfection everywhere. As conscious and self-conscious, future-oriented, creative, reasoning persons, we must cope with certain problems created by these very qualities.

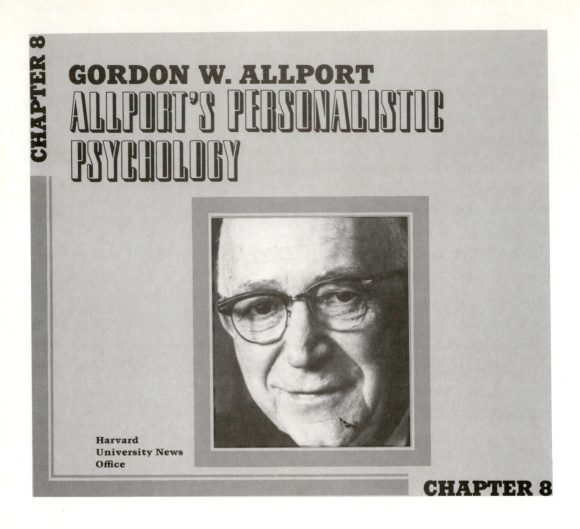

GORDON W. ALLPORT
ALLPORT'S PERSONALISTIC PSYCHOLOGY

Harvard
University News
Office

CHAPTER 8

BIOGRAPHY AND HISTORICAL PERSPECTIVE

From the beginning of his professional career, Gordon Allport was daring enough to follow his own line of thinking in psychology. While other psychologists were studying people with methods and concepts used for the study of animal behavior, Allport held strictly to the view that humans alone are the proper object of psychology. For this reason he has been termed a humanistic psychologist, although the term is not used in a complimentary sense by some of his detractors. In his book *The Person in Psychology* (1968), Allport clearly identifies himself as a humanistic psychologist and accepts intellectual kinship with Rogers, Maslow, and Fromm, the other humanistic psychologists who will be discussed in this section.

Allport was equally insistent on a strict differentiation between normal and abnormal, between mechanical and living systems, and between child and adult. He held that the concepts and principles that explain child behavior, the behavior of animals, and the operations of a machine cannot be applied to the mature adult personality. Allport likewise objected to a strong emphasis on the all-powerful role of the unconscious in the life of the normal person. He held that normal people know pretty well what they are doing and what they want to do.

He advocated the intensive study of the unique individual. For Allport (1961), *the psychology of personality is the science of the individual case.* While the main thrust in psychology was to discover principles of behavior common to all people, or at least to a definable group of people, he held that each person is highly unique and can be understood only through discovery of the principles of his or her own behavior. Allport did, of course, accept general behavior principles as a valuable aid, but the individual was to be the object of direct study, so that the psychologist might discover how these principles applied to him or her.

Allport was born in 1897 in Indiana but grew up in Cleveland, Ohio. He did his undergraduate work at Harvard, not in psychology but in philosophy and economics, receiving his B.A. in 1919. He then went to Roberts College in Istanbul to teach sociology and English. He returned to Harvard to complete a Ph.D. in psychology in 1922. During the next two years he studied in several famous European universities and during that time visited Sigmund Freud. Though he later taught at several American colleges, he was at Harvard from 1930 until his death in 1967.

Allport was primarily a college teacher, but his activities were wide and varied. He wrote about a dozen books, many research papers, reviews, introductions for the works of others, and monographs on specialized topics. His style of writing is a delight to read: he wrote clearly, concisely, and, above all, with the intent to communicate. A beginning student of personality would do well to begin his or her study with Allport.

BASIC CONSTRUCTS AND POSTULATES

Personality psychologists, because of their interest in the integrated functioning of the single individual and their belief that all aspects of personality are interactive in development, have in general concentrated on global approaches rather than on specific dimensions. One of the most challenging of the global approaches is the study of the evolution of the self. Gordon Allport has done more with this topic than any other personality theorist, but he also considers the changes that take place in other specific dimensions of personality: learning, cognition, motivation. We will begin by considering his views on the various ways in which the self is experienced, describing some characteristics of each life period associated with the self-experiences. Throughout this chapter the reader should bear in mind Allport's insistence that his constructs and postulates be individualized; thus, for example, a discussion of the development of the proprium and the requirements for maturity are to be understood within the context of each individual's life. Then we will take up his other key concepts with the same view in mind.

The Problem of the Self

The concept of the self has created many difficulties for the psychologist who wishes to follow the concepts and methods of science in a study of humans. (Wylie, 1968) Why the self should be such a problem, so much so in fact that many psychologists have even denied its existence, is an extremely puzzling phenomenon to Allport. The subjective experiences of self cannot be doubted: they are existential facts. Allport holds that to question their existence is absurd; to inquire into their genesis, their development, and their various roles in personality can promote fruitful scientific knowledge. To deny the existence of the self because of the difficulties encountered in its study is contrary to the spirit of inquiry, which has led to so much progress in the various departments of science. But why should the notion of self as a determining factor in personality present so many difficulties? The problem is that once the self had developed, it becomes a source of spontaneous activity and control that appears to mediate between antecedent conditions and behavior. In other words, the major problem is that the self seems to be a primary cause of behavior, different from other causes. Whatever the problems are, Allport believes that we should acknowledge the self as the central core of personality and make it the object of rigorous experimental study.

Several people, similar in learning ability, may be exposed to the same conditions and demonstrate a striking difference in actual absorption of knowledge. What is learned is affected greatly by the degree of relevance of the material to the self. One may read over a poem a hundred times, but, without the intent to learn, the poem will not be memorized. As we shall see, intentions constitute significant aspects of the self. Mere exposure or even many repetitions do not produce mechanical learning. Learning is influenced by attention, concentration, motivation, perceived value, factors that are related to the self.

Hugh J. Stern Studio/Monkmeyer Press Photo Service

Ego involvement greatly influences motivation.

Passive Attending, Task Involvement, Self-Involvement

In analyzing the role of activity in learning, Allport (1961) notes that attention, which is partly determined by self, is a necessary condition for learning. Passive attending is not as effective in promoting learning as what Allport calls task involvement-active participation in the learning of the task. Learning is facilitated by such active participation: if you reconstruct or rehearse material, you will learn with greater understanding and retention. A more complete participation in the learning process—such as deliberate memorizing, taking notes, rephrasing the ideas in your own language—enhances the learning significantly. Thus although task involvement is much more conducive to learning than is passive involvement, the task itself requires completion; self-involvement is still more effective, because personal motivation is active.

Self-involved participation may be considered participation based on interest. Interests bring into play the deepest levels of motivation. A student may be self-involved in learning a foreign language because he or she is corresponding with a pen pal who knows the language. Another student may devote the same amount of time to studying, but with only superficial self involvement: because this student is learning just to pass the course, he or she has little sense of purpose and does not learn well. In self-involved learning, the outcome of the learning meets an important need, and the learning is instrumental in attaining the goal. Participating without self-involvement does not call into play motives of the self. Thus, the method of learning, though important in facilitating learning, does not tell the whole story: more crucial is the type of involvement. Many high school students are accused of being remarkably lazy or unmotivated, yet the problem is rather that they are motivated in different ways from those expected by their parents and teachers. They may not be self-involved by the subjects or methods taught in school, but let them find a job where they can become self-involved, and the motivation factor will soon be evident. Many apparent high school failures later turn into vocational successes. (McClelland, 1973)

When the self comes into play, then the total relation between the individual and his or her activities is different: more intense, more significant, and more consequential. If the self exerts such influence on personality, it cannot be ignored simply because its study presents some problems. Better knowledge of the self may help to solve some of these problems. The self is highly complex when it is fully developed; tracing this development should foster understanding.

Allport delineates at least seven different self-experiences, each maturing at a different period during the first twenty years of life. These are (1) bodily self, (2) self-identity, (3) self-extension, (4) self-image, (5) self-esteem, (6) self as rational coper, and (7) propriate strivings. Yet he cautions that the self should not be equated with the whole of personality; in fact, the self is not even as broad as consciousness.

Self-Experiences

It should be understood that when Allport uses the term *self*, he refers to experiences of the self (the self as known and felt), not the self as agent knower. As a matter of fact, he has invented a new term to stand for self-experiences, the proprium, which he distinguishes from the self, traditionally considered the active agent in personality (Allport, 1961). He wishes to avoid the homunculus notion of the self which assigns it the role of puppeteer, the agent that presides and decides.

Before his or her self begins to develop, however, the child must pass through the sensorimotor stage, which covers approximately the first eighteen months of life. During this period, experiences "happen" to the child. No mediational process intervenes between sensory inputs and response outputs. The child's behavior is controlled by impulses on the one hand and external stimuli on the other. He or she is stimulus-bound, unable to interpose an evaluational process between an impulse or an attractive stimulus and reaction to them. The self does not yet play a part in the child's behavior.

1. THE BODILY SELF

Recurring organic sensations (which the infant perceives as belonging to himself or herself when the memory has developed to a certain level), as well as frustrating encounters with objects, eventually lead to the formation of a sense of "me" as distinct from other things: this is the bodily self. (Allport, 1961) It is not the total self because

© Elizabeth Crews/Stock, Boston

A sense of "me" is the earliest self-experience.

it is constituted only of sensations of the body. Under normal circumstances the bodily self is not experienced, but under certain conditions such as illness or injury it stands out. Some experiments on the effects of reduced sensory stimulation, which even produces psychoticlike states, indicate the vital role that the continuing flow of bodily sensations plays in normal functioning. The bodily self becomes salient during the growth period, when the child is quite alert to the changes in his or her own body. The child may feel inferior because he or she is smaller or weaker or larger than others.

When sexual concerns become acute, they are accompanied by an increased attention to appearance, and this of course includes the bodily self. Many young people view themselves as puny, clumsy, fat, ugly, or the like.

2. SELF-IDENTITY

Different from the bodily self is the sense of self-identity, the awareness of continuity of personal identity (Allport, 1961). It is the awareness of the self as the core of personality. In other words, self-identity involves the sense of self that is ordinarily described as the "I," the ego. Despite the many changes that take place from infancy to old age, there is a perception of continuity. When you awaken in the morning, you are immediately aware of your identity as the same person who went to bed. These observations may seem rather obvious, but the attainment of the sense of identity, as Erikson has so ably portrayed, is a difficult matter indeed. Identity is acquired gradually with many hazards, and some never have a firm sense of it.

Assigning a name to a child establishes a point of reference. Furthermore, holding the child responsible for what he or she does—rewarding and punishing certain behaviors—fosters the experience of being an active agent. The child soon learns that his or her parents and siblings and everyone else for that matter have names and that they too are accountable for their conduct.

3. SELF-ESTEEM

As the sense of identity begins to take shape, a new self-experience becomes apparent during the second or third year of life: self-esteem (Allport, 1961). It is manifested in the efforts of the child to become acquainted with his or her surroundings, and it may be equated with pride. When a child struggles valiantly to get something off the table and fails repeatedly, he or she may express the disappointment in crying; but success, when it comes is a great event, and the child may exclaim with glee. He or she tells everyone of this feat and is willing to demonstrate it again and again.

Allport holds that negativism in the child is one of the earliest manifestations of self-esteem. As children assert themselves effectively, they develop a positive self-valuation. Children make a great discovery when they learn to say no; they find a means of asserting their ego. Rewards and punishments may fail to modify this behavior because this need for ego assertion now outweighs the consideration of consequences. Thus, although a child is consistently praised and rewarded for certain behaviors and criticized and punished for others, he or she may persist in following his or her own line of activity, irrespective of what parents or teachers do. This point is quite significant in child rearing and has too often been overlooked.

James R. Holland/Stock, Boston

Self-esteem is behind many achievements.

4. SELF-EXTENSION

Between the ages of four and six, two other dimensions of self-experience are prominent: self-extension and self-image. (Allport, 1961) Self-extension is what a person values. For healthy people, it embraces a wide range of objects and people, and its scope generally increases with age. One of the earliest manifestations of self-extension is ownership; a child may learn early by hard experience what is his or hers and what belongs to the parents. If there are several children in the family, the child must also learn that he or she cannot have all the toys because some belong to a brother or sister. With age the child's interests broaden to include a football team, a church, the welfare of his or her city and country. In fact, we can learn a great deal about a person from a knowledge of the person's extended self: as Allport points out, "A person is what he loves." (Allport, 1961, p. 122) A person has a sense of self-extension when there is a sense of ownership, things which belong to or are important to the self.

5. SELF-IMAGE

The self-image refers to the image of the total personality, including the bodily self and the sense of identity. Roughly, it may be taken as one's self-conception. In this respect it differs from self-identity, which refers to the self or ego exclusively. Yet, like self-identity, self-image is to a great extent the product of the roles in which the child is cast. If a child happens to be small and weak, he or she may be treated like an invalid. Gradually this will form a self-image that corresponds to the role expectations of significant others: he or she will begin to think of himself or herself as physically inadequate and helpless. Sometimes the formation of an unfavorable self-image is unavoidable, if a child with a physical impairment perceives differences between himself or herself and schoolmates. Other children may, of course, treat him or her with scorn and rejection, and the fact that he or she cannot compete on the same level will also affect this child's self-image.

Like other aspects of the self, the self-image is a slowly evolving process. At first it is vague and ill-defined, having no elements of what one wants to be or should be — no notion of a perfected self. But as conscience becomes a salient feature of personality and as the child begins to acquire the capacity to project into the future, the self-image broadens to include not only an approximate image of the real self, but also images of potential selves. There may be a failure in development of these aspects of self. A person may have only vague notions of what he or she is, wants to be, or should be, and as a result, his or her orientation to life may lack direction. The person's growth will be limited, for you cannot change unless you have some ideal self-image as a goal. As we shall see when we discuss the "must" versus "ought" conscience, failure in development of the self-image can result in a protraction of the childhood conscience into adulthood.

6. THE SELF AS RATIONAL COPER

Between the ages of six and twelve, children become aware of their growing intellectual powers. They begin to know and sense that they can solve problems and that some children are better at it than they are. While in school, of course, their efforts at certain intellectual tasks are either rewarded or punished, and this factor helps to highlight their growing awareness of the ego as an active problem-solving agency. During this period the child is fond of word games, puzzles, codes, and riddles. In relationships outside the home with other children of his or her age, there is a continual testing of skills, including intellectual ones.

Two trends that often compete with each other are active during this period: the child needs to test and assert his or her ego but also needs the support that comes from conformity. It is a moralistic and legalistic period in which rules acquire sacred power over the child (Allport, 1961). It should be noted that self-identity is an awareness of the self as an object experienced whereas a sense of self as rational coper is the experience of self as an active agent. The awareness of self as a rational coper is a significant self-experience that can contribute, depending on the circumstances, either to the enrichment of self or to its impoverishment.

7. PROPRIATE STRIVING

As we follow development from age twelve on, we of course encounter the second greatest period of change, adolescence. During this period a new dimension of self-experience emerges, the projection of goals and long-term objectives. Allport (1961) calls this aspect of the self *propriate striving* — a term he uses to indicate that all aspects of self are involved in the process of striving for goals — bodily self, self-identity, self-extension, self-image, and self as rational coper. As the individual attains adult status, he or she must take over more and more of his or her own affairs. A person is held responsible for choosing a vocation, for selecting a marital partner, and, in general, for working out a life plan. In order to do these things, a person must consider the future and try to work out goals on the basis of current potentialities, interest, and available facilities. Table 8–1 illustrates the evolving sense of self.

MUST VERSUS OUGHT CONSCIENCE

A significant aspect of propriate functioning is the growth and operation of conscience. Conscience may be thought of as an internal indicator of right and wrong conduct that becomes active when behavior violates accepted standards or values. The values and standards may be imposed by others and enforced by punishment or rewards, or they may arise from the developed self. The conscience that is formed on the basis of an

Sensory/motor 0–18 mths

Self-Experience	Age	Identifying Characteristics
1. Bodily self	From eighteen months	Sense of "bodily" me Configuration of bodily sensations Normally not experienced
2. Self-identity	From eighteen months	Awareness of continuity: inner sameness Self as core of personality The "I": ego
3. Self-esteem	From two to three years	Equated with pride: self-love Capable of self-evaluation Basic influence in life style Manifested by negativism, egoism
4. Self-extension	From four to six years	Sense of ownership: possession Expands with age Equation of "me" and "mine"

5. Self-image	From six to twelve years	Early Form:
		    Conception of total person
		    Conception of one's self
		Mature Form:
		    Potential selves: What one wants to be
		                What one should be

6. Rational coper	From six to twelve years	Sense of self as a doer and problem solver Sense of competence Submission to external rules and regulations
7. Propriate striving	From twelve years	Projection of stable goals and long-term objectives Beginnings of "ought" conscience Formulation of personal values

external code is termed by Allport the "must" conscience whereas the conscience that results from the fully developed proprium is the "ought" conscience. The growing child is at first controlled largely by external authorities who have the power to punish and reward behavior. These authorities determine the standards that the child must meet. Children's fear of rejection and punishment makes them obey. As they begin to take over their own lives, that is, as the proprium develops and propriate strivings come to the fore, they begin to set their own standards. They formulate what Allport terms a "preferred style of life," which greatly influences their goals and plans. Conscience is then a matter of success or failure in fulfilling the goals. Children do many things because they fulfill ambitions and self-image, and also avoid doing certain things because they distract from their objectives. When they slip, they feel guilty. There are still "musts" in addition to "oughts," but now they become matters of rational consideration: "I must go to class rather than sleep if I want to become a lawyer or a doctor," for example. The anticipated consequences, rather than fear, determine behavior: the gas tank must be filled, or the consequences are uncomfortable.

Whether people remain on the level of the "must" conscience, dominated and controlled by fear, or attain the level of the "ought" conscience, motivated by long-term objectives and the preferred style of life, depends upon the nature of their self-development, which, in turn, depends upon many conditions. There is not an automatic change from the "must" to the "ought" conscience, and many people remain stuck with the "must" conscience of childhood, never enjoying the benefits that the "ought" conscience confers. (Kohlberg, 1969) If the "ought" conscience is functioning well, it warns us as a friend before it punishes us as a judge.

To sum up: Allport views the self as a complex aspect of personality, gradually evolving and exerting a greater and greater influence over behavior. If it has developed normally in the adult, it is the major internal or subjective source of behavior. Usually, it is not experienced unless there is something wrong. A single behavioral act, however, may involve all the various self-experiences. During special circumstances, such as mental stress or physical suffering, the self is experienced quite acutely. Allport highlights this point by an example:

> Although the seven aspects of the proprium do seem to evolve at successive stages of life, I do not mean to imply that they function separately. In our daily experience several, or even all aspects coexist. Suppose you are facing a difficult and critical examination. No doubt you are aware of your high pulse rate and of the butterflies in your stomach (bodily self); also the significance of the exam in terms of your past and future (self-identity); of your prideful involvement (self-esteem); of what success or failure may mean to your family (self-extension); of your hopes and aspirations (self-image); of your role as the solver of problems on the examination (rational agent); and of the relevance of the whole situation to your long range goals (propriate striving). The propriate functions are the foundations of consistency within personality—they make for stable attitudes, intentions, and evaluations. [Allport, 1961, p. 137][1]

[1]From *Pattern and Growth in Personality*, by Gordon W. Allport. Copyright 1937, ©1961 by Holt, Rinehart and Winston, Inc. Renewal ©1965 by Gordon W. Allport. Reprinted by permission of Holt, Rinehart and Winston, CBS College Publishing.

Allport's Views on Development of Personality

Allport accepts such conventional developmental concepts and principles as heredity, physique, temperament, and intelligence. He considers these the underpinnings of personality. Once they attain their mature status, they remain personality constants throughout life. He also accepts maturation as a continuing factor: as a result of growth activity, many changes occur which are not dependent, except in a supportive way, on environmental forces. We will now consider some of Allport's more unique developmental principles: principles of learning, intentions, functional autonomy, and personal dispositions.

COGNITIVE AND PERSONAL LEARNING VERSUS CONDITIONING

Allport delineates three types of learning: conditioning, cognitive learning, and personal learning. Conditioning involves the automatic linking of responses to stimuli or behaviors to consequences. It applies to humans to a much less degree than cognitive and personal learning. Cognitive learning involves the knowing operations. It includes information processing, understanding causes and relationships, and the formation of cognitive structures. The ability to use cognitive processes begins early in personality development and grows rapidly with age. Personal learning is the learning that stems from propriate functions and involves a deliberate focusing of attention. When we say that learning matters for the person, it is personal learning, for example, learning to ride a bicycle, play the piano, or bowl. Even when learning is relatively automatic as in conditioning, the cognitive operations may play a part, as when we turn attention away from a painful scene.

Early in life, cognitive and perceptual sets (predispositions to perceive or respond in a certain way) are formed and begin to play a significant role in the child's views of the world. By the time adulthood is attained, the perceptual and cognitive sets have become important determining tendencies that intervene between the environment and personal reactions to it. A child may develop early in life a pessimistic outlook and interpret everything in the light of this general set. If we arrange situations to promote the learning of principles of mental health through conditioning, we might find that the child still responds primarily on the basis of this pessimistic set. A mother's promise of a tantalizing reward may fail to promote learning in her child because the child has a cognitive set of expecting the mother not to follow through. Thus the learning that is predicted by the reinforcement theorist does not occur because the cognitive set may so alter the nature of the reinforcement that it is no longer operating for the individual.

Insight is another cognitive process that plays an increasing role in the development of the child. Cognitive insight is the formation of a conceptual representation of an event. The growing child attempts to cognize or make some meaning of the events about him or her. Allport cites the case of a little girl of three who was found by her mother turning on the gas cock of the kitchen stove. The mother mildly slapped the child's hand as she said, "No, you mustn't do that." According to the principles of conditioning, the sight of the stove should thereafter be a sufficient *condition* to cause the child to avoid it. If a neutral stimulus occurs at the same time as a painful stimulus, the neutral stimulus acquires some of the properties of the painful stimulus. Thus, the pain in this instance should be transferred to the neutral stimulus, the sight of the stove, which originally attracted the little girl. The next day, however, the mother again observed the child playing with the gas cock. When she approached her daughter, the girl put out her hand to be slapped. Apparently, she had put together a sequence of events; she was cognitively structuring incoming information rather than simply responding in a mechanical manner as specified by principles of conditioning. Instead of being a passive recipient of circumstances, she was actively organizing the impressions she received. Generally, this activity increases with age. We continuously cognize our world within a subjective frame of reference.

Three basic orientations characterize the individual's progress from childhood to adulthood, Allport believes (1955). At first, children are almost totally dependent on their environment; then, gradually, as their psychological abilities mature and a great deal of learning takes place, they grow in autonomy and independence. Finally, having reached adulthood, they take responsibility for their own lives. These changes are characterized by an increase in cognitive activities, such as insight.

INTENTIONS VERSUS DRIVES

Some of Allport's major ideas are brought out by his use of the term *intention* to signify motivation that is usually conscious, contemporary, blended with cognition, and future-oriented. For Allport, intention is roughly synonymous with interest. "Intention is a much-neglected form of motivation, but one of central importance for the understanding of personality. It enables us to overcome the opposing of motive and thought. Like all motives, intention refers to what the individual is trying to do. There are, to be sure, immediate and short-run intentions (getting a glass of water, brushing off a fly, satisfying any drive); but the term has particular value in pointing to the long-range dispositions in personality." (Allport, 1961, p. 223)

Allport holds that knowledge of a person's intentions provides insights that other aspects of his or her personality do not. We may know a person's aptitudes, but without knowing his or her intentions, we have no way of knowing which of those aptitudes the person is going to develop. Because no one employs and perfects all his or her potentialities (some are preferred over others), we cannot know which are propriate and which are not, simply by knowing aptitudes. Thus, some psychologists, such as Henry Murray (1938), have attempted to approach personality through need motivation; if we know basic needs, we can comprehend and predict behavior. Others, rejecting the future orientation of intention theory in favor of a theory that stresses the influence of the past upon the present, have tried to reduce all motivation, both in the child and in the adult, to basic physiological drives.

Yet needs, like abilities, are often subordinated to intentions. A student may have a strong need to marry, but if he or she also has the intention of finishing college, the intention will override the need. We might argue that intention is equivalent to need, but Allport disagrees because he believes that intention includes cognitive as well as conative striving elements. He also finds the drive theory one-sided, with too much emphasis on tension reduction. In humans, when a physiological drive is satisfied, interests begin to dominate the scene. After a day's work people eat and relax a while, but then they begin to look for something to do. Consider curiosity and the desire to play: they do not satiate. We can see this even in the play behavior of children: if they lose interest in one toy, they do not stop playing; they find some other toy. Drive psychology and emphasis on basic needs stress the tendencies to conserve, to adapt, to deal with tensions; but they ignore spontaneous activity, growth, and expanded outreach, so characteristic of normal behavior in both child and adult. The sick or immature person may be driven by his or her drives—caught up in excessive eating, drinking, sexual activity—but the normal, mature person puts these in their place and does much more. Drive motivation accounts for the essentials in humans but not for the more typical human activities. An individual who gradually grows toward an acceptance of marriage and family responsibilities could hardly be satisfying a basic, physiological drive or any motive remotely associated with drives.

FUNCTIONAL AUTONOMY

Allport says: "Functional autonomy regards adult motives as varied, and as self-sustaining, contemporary systems, growing out of antecedent systems, but functionally independent of them" (Allport, 1961, p. 227). The principle of functional autonomy holds that an activity is motivational in its own right: it does not stem from another motive except itself. A musician makes music because he or she enjoys doing so: the musician may take a reduction in salary to take a job where he or she can play his or her instrument. The musician may work for money through necessity, but the principal motive is to make music because this is the activity that he or she finds self-sustaining and motivational in its own right. An investment broker may continue to invest, even when he or she has enough to retire.

Functional autonomy may be contrasted with sublimation. A sublimated behavior can be traced to an unacceptable motive and represents a disguised outlet for that motive. A sadistic child who enjoys torturing insects may find a sublimated outlet through dissecting animals during, say, premedical training. A dedication to the vocation of surgeon could also be explained as a sublimation of sadistic needs. Allport does not deny the mechanism of sublimation, but he argues against the view that all adult motives and behaviors are sublimations. The dedicated surgeon may be fulfilling a self-image that includes the core role of healer and obtains satisfaction by exercising skills and applying knowledge. He or she is not playing out childish needs but rather has worked out a style of life that is being expressed in part by work as a surgeon. In other words, his or her motivation is functionally autonomous, that is, independent of the past.

The principle of functional autonomy also holds that an activity that is in the service of a motive can itself become motivational. What begins as an activity performed out of necessity may come to fit into the propriate sphere and may hence become a strong autonomous motive. A man may work hard for money, and when he has more than enough to retire, he may continue working for other motives such as prestige, feeling useful, or companionship or because he hates to stay at home. In order to be autonomous, the motive to work must not be reducible to any other motive. He works because he enjoys his work. Actually, any particular behavior is the outcome of a blend of many motives, some of which may be autonomous in varying degrees. Of course, some early motives may also continue to be active in the total pattern operating at any given time.

Suppose we ask the man in the preceding example, "Why do you continue working when you have enough money to retire comfortably?" and he replies, "Because I like to work." Allport would argue that this motive for working is functionally autonomous or self-sustaining. But as a psychologist he would also wish to carry his analysis beyond the man's superficial explanation by asking: "Why do you like to do it? How did you come to like to do it?" He believes we should attempt to relate the motive to the rest of personality, to the history of the person, and to the proprium, which is the explanatory principle for autonomous motives. Major functionally autonomous motives, such as intentions, may be explained in terms of one's style of life, which is made up of self-image, propriate strivings, self-extensions, adult conscience, temperament, and so on. It should be noted that the style of life may be either a continual reliving of the past, or it may have the mature adult status. Within the developed personality, including the developed proprium, lies the explanation of the major functionally autonomous motives.

It will be recalled that with the development of the proprium the motivational picture changes. Though the process occurs gradually, the change in motivation is quite marked. Allport offers a colorful analogy to bring out this point. A ship mired in the mud may be gradually lifted by the tide until it is afloat. The change that is occurring is imperceptible, but the outcome is completely different from both the original state and each of the intermediate stages. In like manner, the proprium gradually evolves as the child grows: it plays a major role in his or her adaptation to the environment. If its development is normal, it comes to have an autonomous existence and manner of functioning and becomes a major controlling force in the personality. Many behaviors serve only the proprium. We can trace the development of functionally autonomous motives by retracing the growth of the proprium and the changes in the individual's circumstances, but the important point is that functionally autonomous motives are independent of past motives. Allport offers some ideas to clarify the nature of functional autonomy.

Utilizing the energy level.   Allport (1961) suggests that drive-related activity does not, in fact, exhaust the available supply of energy for most people and that free-floating energy must be utilized in some kind of motivated behavior. When drives are efficiently satisfied, more energy is available for functionally autonomous motives. Propriate functions put this energy to work if development has been normal. Seeking to develop competence in knowledge and skills does not serve just drives but rather helps to fulfill an evolving self-image.

Abilities often turn to interests.   The exercise of abilities may attain motivational significance and serve as the basis for the acquisition of abiding interests or long-term intentions. We have here one possible explanation for the principle of functional autonomy: a developed ability has its own motivation. Interests, nevertheless, are often formed around a particular ability or talent. A person who has musical talent is likely to develop an interest in making music, partly because the skill comes easily for him or her. Such a person delights in using his or her skill and perfecting it without any other apparent reason than the pleasure it provides. There may also be an element of challenge, as the individual attempts to perfect his or her musical skill. The use of one's talents may be a ruling passion around which the total life-style is organized (see Crutchfield, 1973). Scientists may devote their entire lives to their work, and even their leisure time may be filled with activities related to their dominant interest. Not everyone has abilities or talents that become the source of such compelling passions, but everyone has some abilities that can and do become the focal point of interests. We tend to enjoy doing what we can do well.

Self-image and life-style are organizing factors. The evolving self-image, which is another significant component of the proprium, points out the main directions of development and is functionally autonomous in adulthood.

Allport succinctly summarizes several key aspects of functional autonomy in the following passage.

> The principle of functional autonomy holds (1) that ... motives are contemporary, that whatever drives must drive now; that the "go" of a motive is not bound functionally to its historical origins or to early goals, but to present goals only; (2) that the character of motives alters so radically from infancy to maturity that we may speak of adult motives as supplanting the motives of infancy; (3) that the maturity of personality is measured by the degree of functional autonomy its motives have achieved; even though in every personality there are archaisms (infantilisms, regressions, reflex responses), still the cultivated and socialized individual shows maturity to the extent he has overcome early forms of motivation; (4) that the differentiating course of learning (reflecting ever more diversified environmental influence), acting upon divergent temperaments and abilities, creates individualized motives. The dynamic structure of every personality is unique, although similarities due to species, culture, stages of development, climate, may produce certain resemblances. [1940, p. 545][2]

Traits: Basic Units in Personality

COMMON TRAITS VERSUS PERSONAL DISPOSITIONS

A great many traits on which a large number of people can be compared have been identified, such as level of aspiration, degree of neuroticism, and introversion-extroversion. For instance, we might measure by means of a standardized test how well a particular person compares with other people on these and similar traits, and assign the person a percentile score that reveals the standing of his or her performance in relation to a large number of other people who have taken the same test. Such standings can be

---

[2]"Motivation in Personality: A reply to Mr. Bertocci," *Psychological Review*.

quite useful to a counselor: a personality trait profile might be used to advise a student not to pursue medicine because his or her trait pattern is quite unlike that of the typical physician.

Yet traits as they exist in the individual are quite complex because they involve a great variety of different behaviors and are triggered by a wide range of different stimuli. Neither the range of behaviors that are expressive of individual traits nor the range of stimuli that set off the core disposition is revealed by the trait name or the percentile standing of a person on a particular trait dimension. In other words, knowing a person's percentile score on a common trait dimension is only a crude beginning in the task of understanding the nature of the trait as it exists in the individual. Then, too, each trait interacts with all other traits within the same individual and is altered by that fact. For example, suppose that Mary falls at the eightieth percentile on a test of dominance; we might conclude that Mary is quite dominant compared with other people her age. Suppose that Jean also scores at the eightieth percentile on the same test; we might be tempted to interpret her score as being identical with Mary's and to view her as the same in dominance standing. But such an interpretation is erroneous because Mary's dominance may not be expressed in the same way as Jean's or may not be elicited by the same situations. Mary's qualities of dominance, like Jean's, interact with everything else in her personality. Dominance is not expressed in the same way by an introvert as by an extrovert, by the highly intelligent person as by the mentally retarded, by the self-lover as by the self-hater. A number of trait scores on a test profile cannot faithfully represent the unique configuration of qualities making up the individual personality. Allport (1961) believes that this "patterned individuality" can be better approached through individual traits, which in his later formulation he terms personal dispositions.

left © Frostie 1981/Woodfin Camp & Associates; *right* Jean-Claude Lejeune/Stock, Boston

Traits determine our perceptions and behaviors.

Much of what has been said of common traits applies also to personal dispositions because, after all, common traits are approximations of individual traits. Two people may be the same height, but they have quite different natures. Allport defines a personal disposition as "a generalized neural-psychic structure peculiar to the individual with the capacity to render many stimuli functionally equivalent and to initiate consistent or equivalent forms of adaptive or stylistic behavior." (1961, p. 373)

By "equivalent forms of behavior" Allport means the various ways of expressing the core tendency. Suppose that a certain girl is considered "motherly" by her friends. They would have identified this personal disposition by specific behaviors, because a trait is inferred from the repetition of behaviors having the same meaning. We could verify the existence of the disposition by observing her under a variety of circumstances, looking for these behavior congruences. She loves to feed and care for small animals; she brings home any stray dog or cat she finds; she enjoys sending get-well cards; she likes to host parties; she loves to prepare meals for her family. If we knew her better we could specify even more behaviors associated with her core disposition of mothering, and we could give more specific details of the way she responds. Allport's own example of a man who has a phobia against communism (Figure 8–1) further demonstrates the operation of equivalent forms of behavior.

A personal disposition may be so powerful that it appears to become active spontaneously, but Allport disavows this idea; he believes that there is always a triggering stimulus. The stimulus may be difficult to identify, or because the core tendency is so powerful and pervasive, it may be triggered by minimal stimuli or by almost any stimulus. A person who is driven to talkativeness may respond in a great many situations with an outpouring of verbal utterances. It seems that anything will set him or her off. Many neurotic symptoms fit this picture; the person manifests the symptom in a wide range of situations.

A personal disposition, then, has the capacity to render stimuli functionally equivalent. This means that many stimuli or situations are capable of setting off the

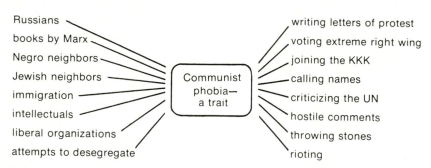

Russians
books by Marx
Negro neighbors
Jewish neighbors
immigration
intellectuals
liberal organizations
attempts to desegregate

Communist phobia—a trait

writing letters of protest
voting extreme right wing
joining the KKK
calling names
criticizing the UN
hostile comments
throwing stones
rioting

FIGURE 8-1
Generality of a trait. The range of a trait is determined by the equivalence of stimuli that arouse it and by the equivalence of responses that it provokes.

disposition to a greater or lesser degree. The disposition remains in a latent condition until an appropriate situation activates it. Just as we inquired into the range of responses that express a disposition, so also may we inquire about the range of stimuli that are functionally equivalent, that have the same meaning for the individual. A person who has an aggressive disposition may display various aggressive responses in a variety of situations as when an underdog is being beaten or whenever the person must deal with an authority figure or in any competitive situation or with any stranger. Only an exhaustive knowledge of the person will bring out the many situations that activate this aggressive tendency. Thus we can see from Allport's view of an individual trait that a great deal of information must be obtained if we are to recognize the trait as it exists in the individual. A single adjective or noun label is the bare beginning; there must be information about the various responses that express the disposition as well as about the range of situations in which the disposition becomes active. Then too, a particular trait always occurs with other traits, and the picture becomes quite involved, as Allport sees it.

Personal dispositions versus habits.   Allport (1961) has held to the view that the personal disposition is the basic structural unit of personality. The popular stimulus-response approach is that the habit, defined as a measurable response to a measurable stimulus, is the irreducible unit; traits are categories invented for the purpose of classifying habits and have no real existence of their own. The S-R psychologist would argue that many habits may have similarities, but they are nevertheless distinct. Little Mary learns to wash her hands and face as soon as she gets up in the morning, and gradually this becomes a habit. Then she learns to comb and brush her hair, another distinct habit. She learns to change her clothes, a third habit that bears some similarity to the other two. Allport believes that although, during the process of learning, each habit is at first distinct and separate, as the self-image and the life-style begin to take shape, the habits are gradually subsumed under a personal disposition of cleanliness. As Mary grows up, still other habits will be integrated into this core disposition of cleanliness: she will inspect her clothes for cleanliness and keep her room and things neatly. New habits will enter the sphere of existing dispositions, and her personality will acquire more and more stability and unity with age. Hence traits are more truly descriptive of Mary than single habits.

Now there may be some inconsistencies: Mary may have the disposition toward personal cleanliness, but her room may be constantly in disarray. Allport (1966) holds that there is never total consistency, even in the best of lives. Such inconsistencies should be studied, because they reveal a good deal about a person's course of development. Why does Mary, who is so meticulous about her person, neglect her room? One explanation of inconsistencies is that there are opposing dispositions in the same personality.

Consider another example of the priority of traits over habits. A certain man has the disposition of being polite, which is expressed, among other ways, in being a good listener. In conversation, instead of worrying about putting in his piece, he listens carefully and asks many questions. But he finds that questioning causes displeasure to one particular friend, so when he is with this friend, he contributes his own ideas more actively. For the sake of the disposition to please others, he alters his habit of listening and asking questions. Not only is concentration on the habit level inefficient; it may also mislead the observer to perceive inconsistencies in behavior where there are none. The man in question was being polite although his behavior is quite different when it is altered for the friend. A trait involves at least two habits, but there are usually many more than two, and new habits are formed within the existing framework of dispositions.

SECONDARY, CENTRAL, AND CARDINAL TRAITS

Secondary traits are relatively specific personality units with a limited range of effective stimuli and responses. They are on the periphery of personality and are quite independent of other traits. Examples are the preference for chocolate to vanilla ice cream, beef to chicken, sandwiches to full meals, and so on. Aversions are typically secondary traits as well. There are hundreds of such relatively isolated traits. They can be easily altered because they are not propriate. Furthermore, to know such traits does not tell us very much about a person. Knowing that John prefers tea to coffee does not tell us much about the major forces in John's life.

Central traits are broad personality units that influence large segments of behavior and are set off by a wide range of stimuli. Knowing fully a central trait tells a great deal because much behavior is covered. In other words, knowing some things about a person (central traits) tells us considerably more about other aspects of personality than knowing certain other things (secondary traits). Some examples of central traits are generosity, neatness, thriftiness, promptness, and industriousness. If one of these becomes dominant in personality, it becomes a cardinal trait. A central trait such as politeness influences much of a person's behavior and thereby constitutes a significant component of the person's identity.

The *cardinal trait*, in the strict sense for Allport, applies to only a few people because it must exert such a pervasive influence in personality as to affect all major areas of behavior; for example, chauvinistic, Machiavellian, and Dionysian are trait terms named after notable people who exemplified them. The cardinal trait is the one around which a great deal of behavior is organized. The individual may be identified by it. Often we use a single trait name to describe a person, and this may be taken as his or her cardinal trait.

SOME CAUTIONS ABOUT TRAITS

To summarize: a trait never occurs alone; many determinants are always simultaneously active. The effects of a trait can often be detected by consistencies in behavior. We can usually identify important goals and purposes that reveal a trait. Repeated observations are necessary in order to observe the consistency produced by a trait. A particular trait may be blocked or inhibited by an opposite trait, but we can usually discover the conditions under which each is dominant.

Another difficulty with traits is that we must rely upon observable behavior to make inferences, and our observations may be incorrect. For example, it may appear that a man is friendly because he likes us whereas his real motive is to get us to like him so that he can use us for some purpose. Here we are dealing with a false inference; self-seeking rather than friendliness is the true trait.

Still another difficulty is that we may think we know a core disposition when, in fact, we have identified only a surface expression of the trait. For instance, we may think that a friend is thrifty when he or she is actually suffering from a trait of compulsive hoarding. Thriftiness is only one manifestation of the hoarding trait. The difference in this case is between a phenotypic trait, which is a behavioral manifestation of a trait, and a genotypic trait, which is the core disposition itself.

VIEWS ON ABNORMALITY

Allport was not a practicing therapist, and his theory of personality does not have a lot to say about the great variety of possible abnormalities. He does deal with abnormal behavior in general terms. He is in accord with some of Freud's notions of the stunting of personality as a result of unpleasant circumstances in childhood. He does not adhere to the psychosexual stages that Freud delineates, but he does stress the supportive role that parents should assume in rearing children. Stunting of personality may occur through parental deficiencies such as child abuse and neglect, inconsistencies in setting and maintaining standards, and failure to serve as proper role models.

Allport also provides a place in his theorizing for two other major causes of abnormality, environmental stress and poor genes. One may inherit body structures and nervous system mechanisms that make living in our complex world highly frustrating. The individual who is physically handicapped or mentally and emotionally deficient will have great difficulties coping with environmental and personal demands. On the other hand, one who must cope with conditions of excessive stress also may suffer psychological and physical stunting or malfunctioning. An overload of stress hampers the adjustive and coping resources of a person.

Propriate Versus Opportunistic Functioning

Allport contrasts opportunistic functioning with propriate functioning. The fully developed proprium involves such attributes as an evolving self-image, propriate strivings, self-esteem, and rational coping. The individual has a value orientation to life with specific short- and long-term goals to serve as guides. Abilities are used to accomplish the goals, which are determined by the person's intentions. Unity of personality is maintained by the vigorous operation of the proprium. The "ought" conscience has a directing and unifying influence in its role as an indicator of proper and improper behavior. The "ought" conscience is an important motivating force of the proprium. It directs conduct toward fulfillment of propriate strivings and the self-image.

Opportunistic living for Allport means preoccupation with drive satisfaction and momentary pleasures. The sick or stunted personality is compulsively concerned with drive satisfaction and pleasure-seeking. The healthy person is occupied with bringing about a desired future by working toward goals whereas the opportunistic person is tied to present requirements or reliving past problems. Opportunistic living stems from the power of immediate stimuli or compelling drives. Without the developed proprium, a person may suffer from a deficiency of inner controls. If he or she functions under the domination of the "must" conscience, personality growth and functioning are greatly restricted. By taking into account the many ways in which the self may fail to develop, we can gain a notion of the many possible ways one might be abnormal.

Comparison of Neurotic and Normal Orientations

Allport is rather specific about the differences between the neurotic and the normal orientation to life. He tends to follow the view that the difference is not just in degree but rather in kind: We either face reality or try to deny it. But we could argue the point that there are degrees of denial and specific circumstances that may set one person to deny at one time more than another.

Allport's view that the normal and neurotic are discontinuous seems to go counter to our everyday experience. We observe in others and sense in ourselves marked changes in behavior that range at times from a rational and realistic orientation to a host of abnormal behaviors that encompass the whole spectrum of psychopathology. It also seems rather obvious that people vary in degree of mental health just as they vary in degree of physical health, yet Allport holds tenaciously to the discontinuity of normal and neurotic.

Allport maintains that the underlying processes for the normal and neurotic are quite different. A person who is typically reality-oriented may have a bad day, during which his or her behavior is maladaptive and resembles the everyday behavior of the neurotic. But when this person recovers his or her equilibrium, he or she functions adequately again. The disturbance may be the result of external or internal stress. Allport argues that there are different degrees of normality and different forms of neuroses, but normal and neurotic are discontinuous because the underlying processes are essentially different. His view clarifies some issues dividing normal and neurotic personalities, but it does not appear to account for the wide variations and fluctuations within both categories of behavior. The borderline cases would be difficult to explain with Allport's view.

Allport provides us with seven dimensions in which normals and neurotics differ:

1. The neurotic attempts to avoid quickly anything that produces pain or tension whereas the normal person generally confronts the requirements of his or her life circumstances and works aggressively to satisfy his or her needs. Reality can be a problem for everyone but is especially difficult for the neurotic. (Horney, 1950)

2. Neurotics habitually try to deny their difficulties, but they usually fail because their problems continue to plague them, often with greater force. The normal person can effectively dispose of certain matters and not think about them. The normal person has a fairly good idea about the problems he or she can or cannot solve whereas the neurotic is indiscriminate in this regard.

3. The neurotic is characterized by many splits in personality in that the various segments are not properly integrated under propriate control. Goals and values may conflict, and opposite trends and traits compete. Normal people are characterized by integration and unity. The various components of their personalities work harmoniously. They do not fight themselves in getting things done.

4. Neurotics not only try to deceive others about their true nature, but they are also actually self-deceiving. With respect to motivation, they exhibit lack of insight. Normal people pretty well know their motivations and goals and are aware of their limitations and possibilities. These qualities are brought together under the term *insight*.

5. Neurotics are characterized by a stunting in personality growth. Their emotions may have a primitive quality, and their motives may be childish. A child may display infantile qualities; an adolescent, childish tendencies; and an adult, remain fixated at the adolescent stage. The normal person thinks, feels, and acts in accordance with his or her age expectancy.

6. Neurotics find their impulses troublesome. They find themselves doing things they do not understand. Normal people can restrain impulsive expression and tolerate frustration while they work out a course of action. They are typically aware of what they want and what is missing. When what they want is not available to them, they can accept substitutes or nothing at all if that is the only alternative.

7. The neurotic's perspectives are restricted and tied to the immediate situation. He or she may focus all his or her attention on the one bad experience of the day and forget all the good things that happened. The normal person has a more abstract point of view and can remove himself or herself from the situation and survey and evaluate it in a more realistic perspective. In most situations the normal person can take charge of his or her own thoughts, feelings, and reactions.

VIEWS ON IDEAL PERSONALITY AND LIVING

The ideal personality state for Allport is *maturity*. The mature person has evolved an orientation to life that entails several achievements in the major aspects of living. We might use the analogy of a mature plant or tree to illuminate what is meant by a mature human. The tree is mature if it is fully developed—if it has fulfilled all its potentials as a particular species of tree. The mature person is fully grown and uses his or her abilities well.

You should bear in mind that the attributes of maturity that Allport holds as the ideal for humans presuppose the developmental changes in the aspects of personality we have discussed. The mature personality is characterized by a well-developed core self (proprium), which includes an "ought" conscience and a system of intentions. The knowing functions operate vigorously and are functional for the person. The person has worked out a value orientation to life, so that there is an order of priorities.

Allport is very clear in stressing the generality of his ideal model. Each person must apply the attributes in an individual manner. Furthermore, the ideal life is not a static state that is achieved once and for all. Each period of life brings new changes both within the personality and in external circumstances. A mature orientation requires constant adjustment and flexibility. We will begin our discussion with several general considerations of maturity and then deal with the specific criteria that Allport has delineated.

General Characteristics of Maturity

A CONTINUING PROCESS

Maturity is not a state that one reaches and then maintains. It should be thought of as an ongoing process. Accomplishments do not leave a person satisfied for long. The opposite of this forward thrust is stagnation or backward orientation or preoccupation with security or, in pathological cases, an inordinate focusing on drives.

Figure 8-2 presents Allport's criteria of maturity. (Allport, 1961, Chapter 12) These are compared with the goals of psychotherapy proposed by a group of psychiatrists.

Goals of Psychotherapy
1. To remove unwanted symptoms
2. To adjust the person to the society in which he or she lives
3. To enhance the experience of well-being
4. To encourage mental health, which includes the following characteristics:
   a. Cheerfulness
   b. Optimistic serenity
   c. Ability to enjoy work
   d. Ability to enjoy play
   e. Capacity to love
   f. Ability to achieve goals
   g. No extreme show of emotion
   h. Self-insight
   i. Social responsibility
   j. Appropriate reaction to situations

Allport's Criteria of Maturity
1. Extension of self
2. Warm relating of self to others
3. Emotional security
4. Realistic perceptions
5. Skills and assignments
6. Self-objectification
7. Unifying philosophy of life

FIGURE 8-2
Allport's Criteria of Maturity

Note: The conditions for happiness as seen by the psychotherapists are insufficient to the state of maturity as specified by Allport.

NO ONE BEST WAY TO LIVE

Each person is unique in personality structure, and there are ultimately as many ways to live properly as there are individual humans. Allport, more than any other personality theorist, focuses upon this uniqueness.

Carl Rogers, whose views we will consider next, makes some pertinent observations about various life-styles:

> The good life has had very different meanings for different groups and in different ages. For some it has meant a life given over to meditation—the holy man on the mountaintop. In sharp contrast, to others it has meant a life of achievement—gaining wealth, status, knowledge, or power.
>
> For many it has meant strict adherence to a creed, a set of rules or principles—whether found in the Bible, the Koran, or emanating from a religious leader. For still others it has meant selfless dedication to a cause outside of themselves—Christian missionary work, Communism, or Hitler's German youth. For some it has been the indulgence of every pleasurable appetite; to paraphrase from the Bible: "Eat, drink and be merry, for tomorrow we die".[3]

GOAL-SEEKING MORE SIGNIFICANT THAN DRIVE SATISFACTION

The mark of maturity for Allport (1961) is setting and striving to fulfill goals. The most basic quality of people is not their drives but their goals, not the past but the future, not so much their limitations but their possibilities. Goals and values configurate a life and give it stability and direction.

MATURITY MORE THAN THE ABSENCE OF ILLNESS

A sound personality is characterized by a zest for living, a forward thrust, always having "irons in the fire." Warding off ill health and relieving tensions are necessary, but only as a base for attaining maturity. For Allport (1961) maturity is more than being normal or not being sick.

MATURITY INVOLVES NOT MERELY LACK OF TENSION BUT ALSO CREATING TENSION

The mature person actually creates tensions. Although the tensions resulting from conflicts, frustrations, and pressures of day-to-day living are unpleasant and impel us to remove them as quickly as possible, certain types of tensions are not only pleasurable but have a tonic effect on everyday living. Thus, one manifestation of a mature personality is tension-seeking, which takes the form of short- and long-term goals. When one goal is reached, a new one is projected to replace it, utilizing the available energy.

[3]From Carl R. Rogers, "The Good Life: What Is It? How Is It Being Achieved?" *America and the Future of Man*. Courses by Newspaper, University Extension, University of California, San Diego, Copyright 1973, by the Regents of the University of California.

MATURITY REQUIRES THE ESTABLISHMENT OF A FIRM SENSE OF IDENTITY

Each person is born into a culture that forces upon him or her many impositions and restrictions, shaping him or her according to the cultural molds. Each individual has his or her own inner nature, which must assert itself within the cultural setting. This inner nature, which on a psychological level may be thought of as the self, is something that develops, grows, and changes from birth onwards.

A WELL-FORMED SELF-IMAGE THAT IS BEING FULFILLED

The self-image refers to the picture we have of ourselves, which should be fairly accurate, but it also includes a picture, more or less clearly defined, of what we would like to become.

Criteria of Maturity

It is important to remember that, despite its general characteristics, maturity to Allport is not a general factor but a series of continuing attainments. The normal adult is highly complex, with many facets of involvement. All through life we must interact with others in varying degrees of intimacy; we must fix upon a stable self-identity. Goals must be worked out, both long-term and short-term, and appropriate means to attain these goals must be learned. Methods must be developed for dealing with frustration, failure, disappointments, losses, and the many adversities that beset even the most gifted. Thus, for Allport, maturity involves a multidimensional series of continuing attainments, all of which necessitate continual attention and flexibility.

SELF-EXTENSION

As the self grows and develops, it reaches out to more and more things. At first, the major focus of concentration is the organism itself. Then the surroundings of the home life are perceived and brought into relation with the self. As the child grows older, if development is normal, the self extends beyond the home to playmates, school, sports, and clubs. Still later, self-involvement includes members of the opposite sex, church, country, career, and a host of other attachments. These attachments and involvements, though changing from period to period throughout life, are absolutely essential to the pursuit of maturity.

The whole point of the requirement of self-extension is that there is vastly more to life than simply surviving and satisfying drives. Self enters into drive satisfaction, particularly when a drive is deprived for some length of time, but such a condition does not promote the attainment of maturity. A person whose energies are entirely devoted to just "getting on" cannot fulfill his or her other potentialities, and life for such a person must necessarily be routine and drab.

WARM RELATING OF SELF TO OTHERS

Allport holds that the social adjustment of the mature personality is characterized by two types of warmth: the capacities for *intimacy* and for *compassion*. Warm human experiences of a social nature, as in a successful marriage or in a strong friendship, add zest to life and are tonic to personality growth and functioning. Intimacy is a form of self-extension that deeply binds one person with another. Human attachments are as potent a motivational force as any motive can be.

To see another person as a mirror image of oneself, a fellow human who despite differences shares a basic human nature, is probably the foundation of empathy and also the root source of intimacy. It may be objected by some that an intimate relationship is frosting on the cake, not really necessary for effective living. Some people, such as the self-sufficient husband who relates to his wife only to the extent of providing for her support, seem not to require any but superficial relationships. However, in this case at least, the psychological well-being of the person may be questioned. One can survive without intimate human relationships, but maturity is not mere existence; rather it entails an ideal type of existence. An intimate relationship provides the participating parties with profound experiences that have no substitute. (Dahms, 1972)

Compassion stems from an appreciation of the human condition of all people. If we understand our own limitations, weaknesses, sufferings, and the many inevitables and unknowns in life and if we are able to perceive those of others in the same light, we possess compassion. Despite wide differences in life situations, natural gifts, and liabilities, all people have much in common. No one is the complete master of his or her destiny; no one is without adversity and suffering; all must face an unknown future. No one really understands completely the riddles of life. Our most penetrating questions have never been answered to our complete satisfaction. The mature person, seeing and appreciating these conditions of human life, experiences a sense of oneness with all humans. Even if the great religions had not placed high value on brotherly love, the mature personality would become aware of this aspect of his or her relations with other humans. The noblest qualities of humans are based on this emotion. Its expression ranges from the selfless generosity of a parent toward his or her children to a host of charitable and altruistic acts that often return nothing except the feeling that one has helped a fellow mortal.

EMOTIONAL SECURITY

A number of qualities, particularly self-acceptance, are covered under this heading. Acknowledging inherent imperfections but always striving to better themselves with a genuine self-regard, mature persons appreciate the fact that no one is all that he or she would like to be. Our culture often presents us with the beguiling image of the perfect man or woman. Mature people come to recognize, sooner or later, the fictional and unrealistic character of such ideal roles and bend their efforts toward fulfilling their individual potential. The difference between what they are and what they wish to become is not as large as for the unhappy, anxiety-ridden, self-hating neurotic.

Another aspect of emotional security is accepting emotions as a normal part of the self. In this regard the culture may be a hindrance; men are expected to hold back on emotional expression whereas women are given much more freedom of outlet. Most people have a great deal of difficulty harmonizing their natural emotional reactions with cultural models. Mature people accept their emotions as a part of themselves, neither allowing the emotions to rule their lives nor rejecting them as alien to human nature. They not only learn to live with their emotions but also use them for constructive purposes as when a man who is angry with his employer turns the energy into more vigorous efforts in his work. One of the most significant aspects of emotional control is not allowing the emotions to take charge to the point of interference with others. Infantile and neurotic individuals easily play out their emotions. They wear their hearts on their sleeves, so to speak. When they are in a bad mood, everyone knows it and is affected by it. In contrast, mature people in the same state may not even be noticeably different in demeanor though some become quieter in mood (Wessman and Ricke, 1966). Living entails taking risks, being rejected, falling short—a host of frustrating events. Somehow the mature person lives with these frustrations and learns to carry on. (Hutt, 1947) He learns to "cooperate rather than continually fight with the inevitables of life."

REALISTIC PERCEPTION

One of the most basic requirements of maturity is keeping in touch with reality, seeing things as they are. Often events and situations are complex and difficult to perceive correctly on this account alone. Add to this powerful needs and ego defenses, and distortion becomes commonplace. (Bruner and Goodman, 1947) Into every situation a person brings a whole history of experiences that may interfere with a correct perception of reality. The mature person cooperates with reality and does not try to bend it to meet his or her needs and purposes. The not-so-sound individual creates events through perceptual distortion to suit his or her expectations and desires. Behind perceptions are sets; healthy people's sets assist them in obtaining a correct representation of their surroundings while neurotics' sets lead them to see things that are not there. They react to a world that does not exist.

PRODUCTIVE SKILLS

Allport believes that mature people possess skills and competencies in one or more areas of their lives. Without basic skills, a person cannot establish the kind of security that is necessary for the building of a mature approach to living. An outstanding psychologist, R. W. White (1959), holds that competence is a major motive of life. We all strive to master our circumstances. Children learn to care for themselves by mastering simple skills. Later, they extend their competence to school work and little chores around the home. Still later, they train for some kind of work. Cutting across all these forms of competence-seeking are the social skills that they must acquire. Successful living is highly contingent upon an individual's competencies.

WORTHWHILE ASSIGNMENTS

The person who has skills usually experiences the need to express them by doing some task. The concepts of task absorption and ego-relevant activity are applicable in this context. The psychological as well as the physical machinery needs activity. If the activity is not guided and channeled appropriately, there may be degeneration and even self-destruction. Freud recognized the power of self-destructive tendencies and even postulated the existence of death instincts that can work havoc on the individual. Allport, though not accepting the death instincts, recognizes the devastating effects of idleness. We need to lose ourselves in a task. Some existentialists (for example, Boss, 1963) have expressed this point in the notion that we should seek rather than avoid responsibilities. Having a duty to perform gives most people meaning in life. A father who takes seriously his duties of supporting his family, bringing up his children properly, and doing these tasks as well as he can experiences unity and integration of personality, and his life will have meaning for him.

BEING OBJECTIVE ABOUT SELF

Closely allied with realistic perception is a quality that Allport designates *self-objectification;* by this he means knowledge of oneself. Self-awareness is a concern that begins early and continues throughout life. There are wide individual differences in the degree of attainment. The mature person possesses it to a high degree; the immature person is as much baffled by this aspect of his or her life as by other major aspects. Immature people are a mystery to themselves. Their behavior frequently does not make sense, or they do things that in retrospect seem completely ludicrous and irrational. Knowing ourselves involves three qualities: knowing what we can do, knowing what we cannot do, and knowing what we ought to do. People may aspire to goals that are far beyond their possibility of attainment, or, of course, they may set their aspirations lower than they should be. In both instances, frustration is inevitable. Learning about our limitations is as essential an ingredient of self-knowledge as is learning about our possibilities.

UNIFYING PHILOSOPHY OF LIFE

Allport (1960) holds that one of the key attributes of maturity is having a philosophy of life, a frame of reference that gives meaning to life. One who derives meaning from the activities of everyday life might be described as having directedness — by which Allport means living with purpose or meaning. In more tangible terms, directedness means having values that set our priorities and having goals that achieve them.

Contrast the person who has no clearly defined goals and who lives only by momentary desires with the person who has a strongly held religion that gives meaning to his or her life. Many different facets of life may be made meaningful by the pursuit of a guiding goal, as in the case of a person who strives vigorously for vocational success in order to support a family adequately. However, we should not think of a guiding purpose in glamorous terms. Some people find the ordinary things of everyday life full of meaning and value. A hardworking house painter may strive to please his favorite customer. The high point of his job is the compliment he receives when the job is well done.

Many successful people report that interest in, and satisfaction with, their work for its own sake is what gives their lives direction. (Allport, 1961) Work for many people is the major source of meaning, but, as we have pointed out, we can find meaning in family, community, recreation, politics, and social relationships. It would seem that participation in the major aspects of living would enrich our lives.

We can expect young people to have some trouble with their long-term goals because they go through a period of uncertainty and confusion. Allport (1955) holds that maturity does not usually occur before the thirties, when one begins to settle on important goals and a unifying philosophy of life.

Conclusions

The criteria of maturity are not possessed by all people. Many conditions are unfavorable and hinder personality growth and functioning. Everyone is caught in a conflict between cultural expectations and personal requirements. Some are blocked from the very beginning of life from ever attaining fulfillment. Just as a plant requires an intact seed and favorable elements in the environment for the attainment of full growth, so also does a human being depend upon heredity and nourishing surroundings to an even greater degree. However, many more can live mature lives if educators (including parents) and behavior scientists utilize the knowledge about personality growth that is now available. Of course, this power to improve life will also increase with new discoveries in the science of human behavior.

If we accept Allport's standards for maturity, it should be evident that having the qualities he describes should provide many satisfactions and joys, yet Allport held that happiness and maturity are not the same. (1968) Happiness is probably an unattainable goal if it is taken as mental tranquility, euphoria, or being "turned-on." Many people's lives are filled with hardship and sorrow: happiness could hardly describe the lives of such people. But maturity, taken in the sense of a certain orientation to life, is certainly much more of an attainable goal. We may be victims of circumstances over which we have no control, but we can surely control our reactions to them by the way we perceive and respond to them. Happiness is perhaps found only in heaven, but Allport believes we can hope to approach life in a mature way.

CRITICAL EVALUATION

Allport has been highly influential in the field of personality, and, in fact, has voiced the problems that are major concerns in the field. As we noted earlier, he has persistently criticized the stress in American psychology and psychiatry on the irrational and unconscious determinants of behavior. Principles and methods appropriate to the study of psychologically sick people have been applied to the normal individual, creating a distorted model of normal personality. As was noted earlier, Allport (1953) holds that the information obtained through the popular projective tests (Rorschach Ink-Blot Test and Thematic Apperception Test) is not substantially different from what we can get simply by asking the person to tell about himself or herself. At best, the projective tests are not necessary to understand the normal person; at worst, they give a distorted picture by overemphasizing irrational and unconscious behavior patterns.

Allport has criticized many other current trends in psychology, proposing what he believes are more fruitful approaches. As we have seen, he finds serious difficulties with the attitude that a number of percentile standings derived from psychological tests give an accurate picture of personality. His ideas about traits, values, and personal dispositions; his principle of functional autonomy; his distinction between the "must" and the "ought" conscience; his stress on intentions and propriate strivings in the adult; and his emphasis upon the central role of expressive behavior — have provided psychologists with ways of understanding the single individual.

Nevertheless, Allport's ideas have not garnered many disciples who continue to develop and test them. He himself admitted that he did not conduct enough research to support his theories, many of which are simply untested hypotheses. Furthermore, he has focused his theorizing primarily on the personality rather than on social and other environmental factors. He recognized the influences of environment in his treatment of the importance of culture, situation, and role expectations, but exactly how these forces interact with his conceptualization of personality is never considered. (Allport, 1960) On the basis of these and other criticisms not presented here, Allport's theory will probably continue to diminish in influence. We might infer, from the spirit of the following quotation, that Allport himself would have accepted this conclusion, for he appreciated the fact that his theory was merely a rough first approximation of an adequate model of humans:

> How shall a psychological life history be written? What processes and structures must a full-bodied account of personality include? How can one detect unifying threads in a life, if they exist? The greater part of my own professional work can be viewed as an attempt to answer such questions through piecemeal and stepwise research and writing. If my theoretical writing exceed in bulk my output of research, it is because of my conviction that significant, not trivial, questions must be posed before we lose ourselves in a frenzy of investigation. [1968, p. 377][4]

The kinds of questions with which Allport was concerned are difficult to answer, but at the same time they are most relevant to the goal of depicting adequately the single case — his cherished ideal.

GUIDES TO RESEARCH

FOCUS ON INDIVIDUALITY

Allport has conducted research that was suggested by distinctive features of his theory. In his theorizing about the normal person, Allport has stressed conscious awareness of motivation and future aspirations. He has inveighed against the use of indirect methods of assessment, such as projective tests, in the evaluation of normal people. The indirect methods are based on the view

[4]*The Person in Psychology: Selected Essays.*

that unconscious determinants play a major role in everyone's life. Allport held that unconscious factors play a greater role in the lives of psychologically disordered individuals than in normal lives. Allport's theory has dignified the intensive study of the normal individual. His theory stresses the role of goals and values in the normal person, and these can be discovered through direct methods such as interviews, self-description, and case studies. As the editor of the *Journal of Abnormal and Social Psychology*, Allport promoted the publication of single case studies.

Allport's theory contains constructs and postulates that are designed to highlight what he has termed "patterned individuality," by which he means the unique configuration of traits that are characteristic of a person. Measuring a person's values can assist in this task. He was instrumental in developing a test of values (the Allport-Vernon-Lindzey Test of Values, 1960) which assesses one's value profile. The test measures a person's relative standing on the six value orientations proposed by Spranger—theoretical, economic, political, social, aesthetic, and religious. The typical psychological test assesses dimensions by comparing one's standing in a test with the performance of a large number of peo-

ple who have taken the same test under similar conditions. Allport wanted to measure the unique configuration of values of the particular individual, not as compared with others taking the test, but as they exist within the individual.

Learning general principles of behavior is helpful as a first approximation, but Allport believed that the individual should be the prime focus of concentration. There are consistencies, congruences, and uniformities in individual behavior, and these should be brought out in psychological studies. Furthermore, Allport's theory stresses the dynamic organization of personality. Each personality is made up of a unique blend of interacting traits. He felt that one should approach individual study from the individual's frame of reference—from the "inside." To achieve this end, he introduced techniques of studying personal documents (1942) such as letters, diaries, school papers, autobiographies and personal impressions. He published a series of letters (*Letters from Jenny*, 1965) in which he analyzed the contents of more than 300 letters that a mother wrote to her son. He attempted to arrive at a characterization of the woman in terms of his views of personal dispositions.

ADAPTIVE AND STYLISTIC TRAITS

Every behavior may be viewed from two aspects, *adaptive* and *stylistic*. Adaptive behavior has a purpose: it accomplishes something; it may be termed coping. An adaptive act points toward some goal, and it may be judged as to whether or not the goal is accomplished or to what degree it is. A person may be writing a letter to a friend, eating an apple, buying a book, or simply laughing, coughing, or crying. Adaptive behavior consists of the "what" of a person's behavior whereas stylistic behavior deals with the "how," the manner in which an adaptive act is carried out. Allport described stylistic behavior as "adverbial." We can learn about a person from both aspects of behavior, but probably stylistic behavior tells us more about underlying personality dispositions.

Consider a child answering a question on a test: he or she answers either correctly or incorrectly, and we learn something about his or her knowledge. But the child's manner of answering may tell us a great deal more of significance about his or her personality. We might learn whether the answer is superficially given or deliberated and considered thoroughly. It may be vague, confused, and delivered hesitatingly or presented confidently, with clear demonstration of understanding. To the astute observer, the stylistic expression will reveal things that the person may attempt to cover up; an individual may be so occupied with the coping aspect of behavior that he or she does not pay attention to the manner of expressing it. A smiling face may be accompanied by a harsh manner of speaking.

Other expressive behaviors include posture, gait, gestures, and facial expressions. By studying stylistic behaviors, we can learn about enduring temperamental traits, ingrained early habits, and strongly held attitudes.

Allport conducted research on expressive behaviors. He believed that expressive behaviors were outward manifestations of stylistic dispositions. A person might be slow-moving or nervous, deliberate or careless, active or passive. For instance, graphology, or the study of handwriting, is not a quack field if it is approached scientifically. Handwriting is a product of expressive behavior and thus should reveal stylistic dispositions. Allport, after extensive research in expressive behavior, came to agree with the famous Greek physiognomist, Lavater, that "one and the same spirit is manifest in all that a person does." Physiognomy is the art of determining personality traits from studying the face. Stylistic dispositions are manifested in many forms. Interest in expressive or stylistic behavior has received renewed research attention under the new name of body language.

The following differences between *coping* and *expressive* (or stylistic) behavior should be helpful in promoting knowledge both of others and of self. (1) Coping is purposive and specifically motivated; expressive behavior is not. (2) Coping is determined by the needs of the moment and by the situation; expressive movement reflects deeper personal structure. (3) Coping is formally elicited; expressive behavior is spontaneously "emitted." (4) Coping can be readily controlled (inhibited, modified, conventionalized); expressive behavior is hard to alter and often uncontrollable. (A change in our style of handwriting can be kept up for only a short time.) (5) Coping usually aims to change the environment; expressive behavior aims at nothing though it may incidentally have effects (as when our manner of answering questions during an interview creates a good impression and lands us the job). (6) Typically, coping is conscious even though it may employ automatic skills; expressive behavior generally lies below the threshold of our awareness. (Allport, 1961, p. 463)[5]

GUIDES TO LIVING

We will now consider Allport's requirements for maturity from the standpoint of fostering them in ourselves. Unfortunately, like so many other personality theorists, Allport does not give us much in the way of implementation; thus, some of the suggestions will be derived from his works and some from other sources.

SELF-EXTENSION

Ideally we should participate at an ego level in all the major areas of living. Thus, we should be involved with vocation, learning, recreation, the community, religion, and home. We might begin by considering these areas of living from the standpoint of authentic participation. With respect to participation in the various spheres of life, Allport points out that it is probably too much to expect even the mature person to become passionately interested in all these spheres of activity. But unless autonomous interests have developed in some of these areas—unless our work, our study, our families, hobbies, politics, our religious quest become significantly propriate—we cannot possibly qualify as mature personalities.

[5]From *Pattern and Growth in Personality*, by Gordon W. Allport. Copyright 1937, ©1961 by Holt, Rinehart and Winston. Renewal ©1965 by Gordon W. Allport. Reprinted by permission of Holt, Rinehart and Winston, CBS College Publishing.

True participation gives direction to life. Maturity advances in proportion as lives are decentered from the clamorous immediacy of the body and ego-centeredness.

Self-love is a prominent and inescapable factor in every life, but it need not dominate. Everyone has self-love, but only self-extension is the earmark of maturity. [1961, pp. 284–285]

WARM RELATING OF SELF TO OTHERS

Here are some suggestions relative to forming warm, social relationships. First, certain behaviors hamper relationships with others. Don't be overly concerned about winning every point or argument. Remember that the desire to impress everyone is very tempting but is quite unrealistic. Avoid imitating the apparently successful social techniques of one who seems to be liked. Being a jokester, a hearty extrovert, always loving and pleasant, a powerful and masterful person may be highly appealing, but if it does not express your real self, it will not be suitable. Second, although most people respond to indications of liking or loving, there are some who are not prone to reacting to demonstrations of concern. Take a tolerant attitude toward others. Because we are all members of the human species, no matter how favorable our life situation seems to be, we are confronted with unsolvable problems and dilemmas such as fear of the future, growing older, suffering pain and disappointment, inconsistencies between what is and what should be, and the like. Third, learn social skills by watching others and by observing the consequences of

your own behavior. Be willing to adopt new approaches and to vary your roles with different people. Fourth, Allport is the champion of the idea that each person is a unique creation of nature. You should strive to perfect your style of life: discover your assets and bring them out more fully; work continually to improve your shortcomings; avoid fixed poses and artificial roles.

Allport tells us some attitudes to avoid and also some to cultivate if we would relate warmly with others.

> Both intimacy and compassion require that one not be a burden or nuisance to others, nor impede their freedom in finding their own identity. Constant complaining and criticizing, jealousy and sarcasm are toxic in social relationships. A woman of marked maturity was asked what she considered the most important role of life. She answered, "Do not poison the air that other people have to breathe." [1961, p. 285][6]

EMOTIONAL SECURITY

In the following passage Allport details some of the negative and positive qualities related to mature self-acceptance:

> Irritations and thwarting occur daily. The immature adult, like the child, meets them with tantrums of temper, or with complaining, blaming others, and self-pity. By contrast, the mature person puts up with frustration,

takes the blame on himself (by being "intropunitive") if it is appropriate to do so. He can bide his time, plan to circumvent the obstacle, or, if necessary, resign himself to the inevitable. It is definitely not true that the mature person is always calm and serene, nor is he always cheerful. His moods come and go; he may even be temperamentally pessimistic and depressed. But he has learned to live with his emotional states in such a way that they do not betray him into impulsive acts; nor interfere with the well-being of others. [1961, p. 188][7]

REALISTIC PERCEPTION, SKILLS, AND ASSIGNMENTS

Allport groups as important qualities of maturity the ability to perceive the world realistically, the development of functional skills, and working on worthwhile tasks. These qualities need not go together, but they usually do. Certainly we can neither meet our world head on nor employ our skills correctly without a realistic perception of things.

Skills are valued possessions, no matter how humble they may be. We should guard against devaluating our accomplishments and skills because they seem less spectacular than someone else's. We should cultivate the attitude "My skills are more important to me than whatever someone else can do." Improvement and not evaluation and comparison should be the goal. We might think of the confidence and poise of the skilled painter, carpenter, teacher, or surgeon performing his or her craft easily, smoothly, and seemingly without effort. Performing a skill well can be experienced as pleasurable in itself. We should view our skill and work as absolute values rather than fit them into the cultural mold. Bear in mind that what is highly paid for or valued in a particular culture is not necessarily intrinsically valuable. According to Allport's notion of self-extension, what we are and what we can do are closely identified. We have a right to feel pride in our skills, just as we need to feel positively about outselves.

Allport takes up the question of freedom of action by relating freedom of choice to the number of skills one possesses:

A person whose stores of experience and knowledge contain many "determining tendencies" is freer than a person who has only a meager store. If I have only one relevant skill, or if I know only one solution, I have only one degree of freedom. I act in the only way I can. But if I have much relevant knowledge, a broad education, and have wide experience with the kind of problem I face, then I can select, on the whole, the most appropriate solution, or create a new one. A many-channeled mind is freer than a one-track mind. [1961, p. 562][8]

We see a striking resemblance between Allport's view of increased freedom through knowledge and skill and Mischel's view on the same point, namely, the ability to generate knowledge and competencies of a situation.

Allport considers the existential problem of commitment in the following passages:

Fortunately we have the capacity to make commitments and to take risks. We can, if we wish, gamble our life on the value of some personal project, even though we cannot prove its worth, or be assured of its success. Our faith in a project may be only half sure, but that does not mean that we will have to be halfhearted. To be able to make a life wager is man's crowning ability. [1961, p. 558][9]

SELF-OBJECTIFICATION: INSIGHT

Allport asks this question:

How is the psychologist to tell whether or not an individual has insight? [Insight in the psychiatric sense means self-knowledge.]

[7,8,9]From *Pattern and Growth in Personality*, by Gordon W. Allport. Copyright 1937, ©1961 by Holt, Rinehart and Winston, Inc. Renewal ©1965 by Gordon W. Allport. Reprinted by permission of Holt, Rinehart and Winston, CBS College Publishing.

According to an adage, every man has three characters:
1. that which he has
2. that which he thinks he has
3. that which others think he has [1961, p. 291][10]

To elaborate: self-knowledge is clouded by overestimation of self. Look for pretense, false masks, and exaggeration of self-worth. Of course, one may err in the opposite direction by chronic self-devaluation and self-contempt. Many people take themselves much too seriously for their own good. Do not be afraid of the truth about yourself because there are more positives than negatives in most lives.

UNIFYING PHILOSOPHY OF LIFE

Values are more characteristic of adults than of children and of the mature than of the average or the psychologically disturbed. If you are not certain of your values, begin by looking at your interests. If you are not clear about your interests, you might look at your preferences and aversions and ultimately at your typical behavior patterns. In this way you may arrive at a pattern of values that was not previously formulated.

Allport agrees with Spranger that the religious sentiment, if it is mature, is the most comprehensive value. Here are some points to think about regarding religious belief. (1) Mature religious beliefs are not pathological or a sign of personality weakness. (2) The religious sentiment may be one's response to the problems of living, and it may be a guide for future behavior. (3) Religion can offer the most complete explanation for living. (4) Important values often have to be sacrificed or cannot be attained. A religious sentiment can make even this fact acceptable. (5) Religious sentiment offers an optimistic approach to life. If a belief cannot be disproved, then we are justified in harboring it as long as it promotes a positive approach. (6) Allegiance to any cause is a form of directedness. Surrender to religion can be the most compelling form of directedness. (7) Most religions foster social and humanistic values.

He also offers us a guide to the normal development of conscience if we bear in mind that conscience is a major component of the proprium and a major determinant of behavior:

> A mature person has a relatively clear self-image by virtue of which he can imagine what he would like to be and what he ought to do as a unique individual, and not merely as a member of his tribe, or as the child of his parents. He says to himself in effect, "I ought to do the best I can to become the sort of person I partly am, and wholly hope to be." This type of conscience is not the obedient "must" of childhood. [1961, p. 303][11]

SUMMARY

1. Allport has been called a humanistic psychologist because he stressed the necessity of formulating a theory of personality that depicted the distinctively human attributes. Allport focused on the evolution of the self by means of studying self-experiences. He maintained that significant changes also take place from childhood to adulthood in learning, cognition, and motivation.

2. When self-experiences are active, learning, motivation, and emotions are greatly affected. Involvements vary from passive attend-

---

[10,11]From *Pattern and Growth in Personality*, by Gordon W. Allport. Copyright 1937, ©1961 by Holt, Rinehart and Winston, Inc. Renewal ©1965 by Gordon W. Allport. 'Reprinted by permission of Holt, Rinehart and Winston, CBS College Publishing.

ing, through task involvement, to participation that is personally relevant. Allport uses the term *proprium* to designate self-experiences, which he distinguishes from the self as agent.

3. The sensorimotor stage during which the self has not yet developed occurs in the first eighteen months. The first self-experience that emerges is the bodily sense, which refers to the "sense of 'me-ness.'" Self-identity refers to the awareness of continuity of personal identity and core self roles. Self-esteem refers to the sense of pride or shame or is often manifested in negativism as the child attempts to prove his or her mastery over things and people. Self-extension, which emerges during four to six years of age, includes as part of the self the sense of ownership, what one values and what belongs to the person. A child begins to form a self-image also during this period that embodies conceptions of self. These are promoted by the expectations, reactions, and actions of significant others.

4. The sense of self as an active agent is termed by Allport the self as rational coper. Such experiences become evident during the ages of six to twelve. Propriate striving refers to the sense of self as striving toward goals. Another dimension of the proprium is the shift from the must conscience of childhood to the ought conscience of adulthood. The musts of the mature proprium are governed by anticipated consequences.

5. Allport assigns a much greater role in human life to cognitive and personally motivated learning than to classical and operant conditioning. Examples of cognitive learning are perceptual and cognitive sets and insight experiences (forming correct cognitive structures). Cognitive development enables the child to progress from dependence, to autonomy, to a sense of responsibility for his or her own life.

6. Drive-motivation is characterized by tension reduction. Intentions are the major motives of mature adults and are important components of the proprium. They determine which needs and abilities will be stressed and promote growth and stimulate activity. Rather than tension-reduction, intentions create tension.

7. The principle of functional autonomy holds that certain activities are motivational in their own right. They depend upon one's self-image and preferred life-style. The proprium is the source of significant intentions that embody functionally autonomous motives. Many behaviors serve only the proprium. With its development, there are marked changes in the character of motivation. Activities that serve a particular motive may acquire motivation of their own.

8. Common traits are approximations of individual traits. They are expressed as single terms and frequently measured by standardized tests, which provide percentile scales. The problem with common traits is that they are incomplete because they do not take account of interactions among traits, as well as the unique stimuli that set them off and the specific behaviors that express them. Individual traits are also termed personal dispositions. These exert a selective influence on perception and behavior. Allport argues that personal dispositions and not habits are the basic descriptive units of personality. Traits may be divided into cardinal, central, and secondary, depending upon the amount of influence they exert over behavior. Traits are identified by consistencies in behavior.

9. Allport accepts some of Freud's ideas on the stunting of personality as a result of neglect. He also agrees with the views concerning the harmful effects of stress and the handicapping disabilities of having poor genes. He distinguishes between propriate and opportunistic living. The latter stems from the power of immediate stimuli and compelling drives. Allport views a discontinuity between the normal orientation and the neurotic orientation. Seven dimensions on which normals and neurotics differ are (a) avoidance-confrontations; (b) denial — reality orientation; (c) splits in personality — unity and integration; (d) lack of insight — self-knowledge; (e) fixations — age-appropriate coping; (f) impulsivity — control; (g) restricted perception — abstract and global point of view.

10. The ideal personality for Allport is maturity. It refers to being fully functioning. The mature person has a well-developed and well-functioning proprium. General characteristics of maturity are a continuing process; no one best way to live; goal-seeking more significant than drive-satisfaction; maturity is more than the absence of illness; maturity involves creating tension, establishing a firm sense of identity. Allport's specific criteria of maturity are self-extension (participation in significant aspects of life); warm relating of self to others (capacity for intimacy and compassion); emotional security (self-acceptance and emotional control); realistic perception; productive skills; worthwhile assignments; objectivity about self; unifying philosophy of life (directedness and value-orientation).

11. In his research, Allport utilized direct methods rather than indirect methods of assessment. He stressed the study of expressive and stylistic behavior in addition to adaptive behaviors. He sought for methods that highlight an individual's patterned individuality. The Allport-Vernon test of values attempts to accomplish this objective. Allport desired to discover the unique configuration of traits that characterized a person. He introduced the study of personal documents. He also used biographies and autobiographies, case studies and interviews, and certain standardized tests to attempt to know the individual case. Allport concluded, after much study of expressive behavior, that there is much consistency in the manner in which we perform our everyday tasks. Expressive behavior has been receiving renewed research interest in the form of the study of body language. Allport's ideas have not generated much research although many of them have been incorporated into the body of accepted psychological knowledge.

12. Allport is one of the champions of humanistic and existential psychology, and he pleaded for a theory of personality that would encompass the distinctively human attributes and consider the problems associated with living as a human. He, like Maslow, Rogers, and Fromm, was interested in the highest possibilities for humans and not simply in the deficient and abnormal personality. These men held that existing models of humans are patterned after the models used by the physical and biological sciences and are inadequate to portray human nature and human existence.

GLOSSARY

Approaches to personality: Research methods appropriate to personality study.

Adaptive and stylistic behavior: An approach to personality study in which a distinction is made between a behavioral act or product and the manner in which it is performed or accomplished.

Expressive behaviors: Facial features, gestures, posture, gait, and other stylistic behaviors used to study tempermental dispositions.

Idiographic method: Focus on the consistencies, congruences, and lawfulness of the single case.

Nomothetic method: Studying groups of people to ascertain broad principles of behavior that apply to humans in general or to large segments of people.

Personal documents: An idiographic method; the study of personal expression by means of autobiographies, letters, personal journals, and diaries.

Conscience: Self-regulatory functions.

Must conscience: Early conscience felt as unexplained imperatives governed by fear of authority (like Freud's primitive superego) derived from introjected standards.

Ought conscience: Mature conscience; self-regulatory function of the proprium based on evolving self-image; preferred lifestyle and values felt as a sense of pride or self-dissatisfaction.

Adult musts: Sense of duty based on rational considerations of outcomes.

Criteria of maturity: Allport's ideal adult personality; refers to the fully developed and fully functioning person; also to a healthy orientation to life. Includes the attributes of self-extension, warm relating of self to others, emotional security and self-acceptance, realistic perception, productive skills and worthwhile assignments, objectivity about self, unifying philosophy of life (directedness and having a value orientation to life).

Functional autonomy: A motive of the proprium that serves no other motive but itself; an activity serving one need may acquire its own motivational force.

Intention: Major components of the proprium, which are a blend of cognition and striving; a natural motivational unit; similar to interest; it refers to tension-maintained rather than tension-reduced.

Levels of participation: Degrees of self or propriate involvement; greatly affects learning, motivation, emotion, and behavior.

> **Passive attending:** Low-level of participation not involving proprium.

> **Task involvement:** Absorption resulting from task requirements.

> **Ego involvement:** Participation that involves the proprium.

Proprium: The unifying core of personal identity; it refers to the modes of experiencing oneself, the felt self.

> **Bodily self:** The organic sense of self.

> **Self-identity:** The sense of continuity of personal identity.

> **Self-esteem:** Sense of pride; the emergence of self-evaluation.

> **Self-extension:** The sense of ownership; something belonging to the self.

> **Self-image:** The sense of self-concept or concepts of potential selves.

> **Objectivity about self:** Self-knowledge, insight into oneself.

Propriate striving: The sense of self as a striver after ends; the striving for short- and long-term goals.

Self as rational coper: The sense of self as a problem solver.

Trait: A neuropsychic structure that initiates and guides behaviors that accomplish a common purpose, usually set off by a range of stimuli that have some essential feature in common. Traits account for consistency in behavior.

> **Cardinal trait:** A broad disposition that enters into much of what a person does. The single outstanding quality of a person. A cardinal trait applies to only a few people, in Allport's sense. It is an essential feature of one's identity.

> **Central traits:** Core dispositions that are constants in one's personal equation. Each influences large segments of behavior. They account for the distinctiveness of each person.

> **Common traits:** Approximations of individual traits, measured by standardized tests, an indication of the strength of a disposition, but highly general, usually expressed as a percentile standing.

> **Individual trait:** A trait as it actually exists within the individual.

> **Personal disposition:** Refers to the core of an individual trait, but also is synonymous with individual trait. Allport stresses the uniqueness of personal disposition, having a specific range of functionally equivalent stimuli and leading to a range of functionally equivalent behaviors.

> **Secondary traits:** Tendencies that have a limited influence over behavior and are set off by quite specific stimulus conditions. Preferences and aversions are common examples.

SUGGESTED READINGS

Allport, Gordon W. *Personality: A Psychological Interpretation.* New York: Holt, Rinehart and Winston, 1937.

> This book established Allport as a pioneer in the field of personality theory. He outlines the major areas of the personality field, weaving in his own theory of the person.

————. *Becoming: Basic Considerations for a Psychology of Personality.* New Haven: Yale University Press, 1955.

This short book presents Allport's views on the ideal state for man. It discusses the nature and evolution of the self, the requirements for maturity, the social aspects of behavior, and the future orientation of the individual.

————. *Personality and Social Encounter.* Boston: Beacon Press, 1960.

This volume contains a selection of essays which are neither "technical nor popular." Allport contends they were written "either to amplify the theory of personality contained in my *Personality: A Psychological Interpretation* or to express my concern with topical problems in social psychology."

————. *Pattern and Growth in Personality.* New York: Holt, Rinehart and Winston, 1961.

Allport presents his last major statement of his theory in this book. He stresses the uniqueness of each individual and introduces his concept of the personal disposition, which he considers the basic unit of personality make-up. The book is highly readable and is suggested for the beginning personality student.

————. *The Person in Psychology: Selected Essays.* Boston: Beacon Press, 1968.

This book is a collection of writings emphasizing Allport's humanistic approach to psychology.

CARL R. ROGERS
ROGERS' FULLY
FUNCTIONING PERSON

CHAPTER 9

*Deny and distort will come up repeatedly
Neither are good judgment.*

BIOGRAPHY AND HISTORICAL PERSPECTIVE

In his work as a psychotherapist, Carl R. Rogers became increasingly convinced that those coming to him for help with their personal problems were actually searching for their real selves. Although he had ruled out the possibility of the self as an explanatory concept, he was forced to reexamine its place in his own life and in the lives of his clients. He made a complete turnabout, so that his name is now associated with self theory. He holds that psychological imbalance and disharmony results from a discrepancy between the conception of self and the real self and that congruity between self and self-awareness promotes healthy personality growth and functioning. Speaking of his position on the self, Rogers says:

> I began my work with the settled notion that the self was a vague, ambiguous, scientifically meaningless term, which had gone out of the psychologist's vocabulary with the departure of the introspectionists. Consequently, I was slow in recognizing that when clients were given the opportunity to express their problems and their attitudes in their own terms, without any guidance and interpretation, they tended to talk in terms of the self.... It seemed clear . . . that the self was an important element in the experience of the client, and that in some odd sense, his goal was to become his real self. [1959, pp. 200–201][1]

Carl Rogers was born in 1902 in Oak Park, Illinois. He came from a family with strong Protestant convictions. After graduating from college he attended Union Theological Seminary, but he transferred to Columbia to study clinical psychology. He received an M.A. in psychology in 1928 and a Ph.D. in 1931. For the first ten years of his professional career, Rogers worked at a child guidance clinic. During this period, he came under the influence of several outstanding neo-Freudian psychoanalysts, such as Theodore Reich and Otto Rank. In 1940, he made a radical change in his life by accepting a professorship in psychology at Ohio State University. He formulated many of his clinical insights and presented them in a book that he wrote in 1942, *Counseling and Psychotherapy*. In 1945, Rogers moved to the University of Chicago, where he headed the counseling center and taught psychology. Many important research projects came out of this experience. He developed the technique of recording counseling sessions and worked out elaborate methods for studying the responses of his clients. In his 1951 book, *Client-Centered Therapy: Its Current Practice, Implications, and Theory*, Rogers presented his ideas on counseling and also attempted to formalize a theory of personality. In 1957 he went to the University of Wisconsin, his alma mater, to hold a joint appointment as professor of psychology and psychiatry. In 1964 he accepted a position as resident fellow at the Western Behavioral Sciences Institute in La Jolla, California. He is currently a resident fellow at the Center for Studies of the Person in La Jolla, which he helped to found.

Rogers has applied his client-centered concepts and practices in a wide range of situations. For many years he was personally involved in individual counseling. (Rogers, 1951; 1977; 1980) He has also applied his concepts and methods to family life (Rogers, 1961), to education and learning (1969), and to group tension and conflict (1959). He is currently interested in encounter groups and is steadily becoming the leader in this area (Rogers, 1970).

Mowrer (1969) has divided Rogers's work into two periods, one focusing upon client-centered counseling and the other reflecting his interest in group dynamics. Mowrer has also observed a shift in Rogers's approach from tender loving care to tough loving care. The shift reflects the increasing responsibility that is required of the participant.

Rogers has long held the conviction that every person has powerful constructive forces within his or her personality that need to be allowed to operate. Growing things

---

[1]"A Theory of Therapy, Personality, and Interpersonal Relationships as Developed in the Client-Centered Framework."In S. Koch (ed.), *Psychology: A Study of Science*.

do not need to be grown but need only be given the conditions that will permit growth, for they have an inherent tendency for growth and actualization. He expresses this conviction with a vivid observation in the following passage:

> During a vacation weekend some months ago I was standing on a headland overlooking one of the rugged coves which dot the coastline of northern California. Several large rock outcroppings were at the mouth of the cove, and these received the full force of the great Pacific combers which, beating upon them, broke into mountains of spray before surging into the cliff-lined shore. As I watched the waves breaking over these large rocks in the distance, I noticed with surprise what appeared to be tiny palm trees on the rocks, no more than two or three feet high, taking the pounding of the breakers. Through my binoculars I saw that these were some type of seaweed, with a slender "trunk" topped off with a head of leaves. As one examined a specimen in the interval between the waves it seemed clear that this fragile, erect, top-heavy plant would be utterly crushed and broken by the next breaker. When the wave crunched down upon it, the trunk bent almost flat, the leaves were whipped into a straight line by the torrent of the water, yet the moment the wave had passed, here was the plant again, erect, tough, resilient. It seemed incredible that it was able to take this incessant pounding hour after hour, day after night, week after week, perhaps, for all I know, year after year, and all the time nourishing itself, extending its domain, reproducing itself; in short, maintaining and enhancing itself in this process which, in our shorthand, we call growth. Here in this palmlike seaweed was the tenacity of life, the forward thrust of life, the ability to push into an incredibly hostile environment and not only hold its own, but to adapt, develop, become itself. [1963, pp. 1–2][2]

Rogers attempts to detail the general nature of healthy growth in his theory of personality. He says his theory "pictures the end-point of personality development as being a basic congruence between the phenomenal field of experience and the conceptual structure of the self — a situation which, if acheived, would represent freedom from internal strain and anxiety, and freedom from potential strain; which would represent the maximum in realistically oriented adaptation; which would mean the establishment of an individualized value system having considerable identity with the value system of any other equally well-adjusted member of the human race." (1951, p. 532)

For Rogers, the phenomenal field of experience is the total realm of psychological experiences. It is the total psychological field, of which some parts are conscious and some parts are unconscious. The conceptual structure of self is the self-concept, which may or may not correspond with the real self. He defines the unconscious as psychological experiences that are not symbolized, or, in other words, not available to the conscious self. When all psychological experiences can be consciously experienced, the person is in a state of *congruence*. He or she then has a conception of self that corresponds to his or her real self.

Rogers broadens his conception of congruence to include harmony between experience and awareness and between awareness and communication. He says in his most recent publication:

> In place of the term "realness" I have sometimes used the word "congruence." By this I mean that when my experiencing of this moment is present in my awareness and when

[2] "Actualizing Tendency in Relation to 'Motives' and Consciousness," in M.R. Jones (ed.), *Nebraska Symposium on Motivation*.

what is present is present in my communication, then each of these three levels matches or is congruent. At such moments I am integrated or whole, I am completely in one piece. Most of the time, of course, I, like everyone else, exhibit some degree of incongruence. [1980, p. 15][3]

BASIC CONSTRUCTS AND POSTULATES

Actualization Tendency, Self-Actualization, and the Organismic Valuing Process

Living things have a genetic design that contains a growth potential. This innate growth potential is termed by Rogers the *actualizing tendency*. The actualizing tendency impels the organism to become what it is genetically designed to be. Rogers describes the operation of the actualizing tendency as follows: "The inherent tendency of the organism to develop all its capacities in ways which serve to maintain or enhance the organism." [1959, p. 196]

Our organism follows a predictable course of growth. The body resists disease and repairs itself. The medicine the physician prescribes does not cure disease, but rather enables the growth forces to heal. The environment does not create the growth potential, but it may foster or hinder it. A child may be forced to engage in patterns of behavior that are contrary to native tendencies. The child who does not take readily to a musical instrument is demonstrating that such behavior does not fulfull a growth tendency. The actualization tendency is expressed in a variety of motives that have the common purpose of maintaining and enhancing the organism. When the environment and the organism are in tune, the organism thrives and fulfills its potentialities. A stressful environment or an unhealthy organism will hamper the operation of the actualizing tendency.

The tendency for growth and unfolding is also manifested psychologically when the self begins to emerge. Rogers uses the term *self-actualization*, a subsidiary of the actualizing tendency, to refer to the *growth potential of the self*. We have motives to preserve, maintain, and enhance ourselves. The operation of self-actualization is seen in the urge to establish our identity or to preserve self-esteem. We are reminded of Maslow's growth motives as being manifestations of self-actualization. Healthy people strive to expand their lives to enrich and improve conditions for themselves. Again, the environment may either foster or hinder the operation of self-actualization. Healthy people are motivated to fulfill their potentials. They seek much more than security, safety, and sameness. A key point is that a major source of motivation is the self, in addition to the organismic drives and the conditions of the environment. The developing self is a significant component of the total organism and increasingly imposes its own motivational requirements. Meeting the requirements of the self contributes to the well-being of the person, quite as much as meeting the requirements of the organism.

Another subsidiary of the actualizing tendency is what Rogers terms the *organ-*

[3]*A Way of Being.*

ismic valuing process. (Rogers 1961; 1977; 1980) This process of valuing things depends upon affectively toned experiences that are felt as agreeable or disagreeable, pleasant or unpleasant, satisfying or dissatisfying. It feels good, and is good, for us to be hugged when we are depressed, to be cared for when we are lonely, to be helped when we are frustrated. If the organismic valuing process is functioning properly, it directs the person to make choices that promote and sustain life and well-being. We get hungry and enjoy eating certain foods. We reject foods that might be poisonous. The mechanism is not infallible: We can learn to enjoy foods that are not good for us. You can see the operation of the organismic valuing process in an animal like a cat who sniffs at food that is offered to it. The cat is slow to try new things. It explores and tests before it chooses. Its very survival depends upon making the right choices.

There is some similarity between Rogers' organismic valuing process and Freud's pleasure principle. The healthy personality does and should make choices on the basis of positive or negative feeling-tone. If a course of action feels good, it should be followed; and if it feels bad, it should be avoided. We should be able to trust our intuitions and hunches in making decisions. Rogers terms this *organismic trusting.* (Rogers, 1961, 1977) Here we are dealing with something like "a gut feeling," or "I feel it in my bones." The person senses what to do, but cannot give a complete and coherent explanation of the reasons. Rogers would argue that this person is being aided by his or her growth tendencies. Again, we must stress that although these growth tendencies have great utility for us, they are not infallible. Sometimes it is necessary to countermand a "natural impulse," or the momentary feeling. Rational evaluation is, at times, superior to the organismic valuing process. A man may have an overwhelming desire to marry, but his circumstances make that course totally irresponsible.

INTROJECTION HINDERS THE ORGANISMIC VALUING PROCESS

One of Rogers' major tenets is that the self-structure is formed by introjecting the values and standards of others although, ideally, the concept of self should reflect the requirements of the real self. Introjection means to internalize — to incorporate as an integral part of the self — ideas, standards, and values that are external. Decision making is greatly influenced by such introjections, and the choices may be totally inconsistent with the requirements of the organism. A student might choose a premedical program in college as a result of introjecting the value society places on the medical profession rather than because of having a true feeling for this work. He will probably find that he can not sustain the required effort to complete the program because he is not choosing to do what his own nature requires. The operation of the organismic valuing process is severely limited by introjections that are at odds with the actual requirements of the person. The student does not sense his own true desires. When the self-structure is so distorted that it does not mirror the requirements of the person, many forms of abnormality may result. The path to normality is to make the self-structure, the concept of self, correspond to the real self.

Rogers points this out in the following passage:

> As the individual perceives and accepts into his self-structure more of his organic experiences, he finds that he is replacing his present value system, based so largely on introjec-

What feels good or bad is often good or bad for us.

© 1978 Alice Kandell/Photo Researchers, Inc.

tions which have been distortedly symbolized, with a continuing organismic valuing process. [1951, p. 21]

In a real sense, people begin to take over their own lives and make choices that reflect their own needs and desires. They choose what is good for them rather than what someone else tells them is good for them.

Rogers (1977) elaborates this point further in the following passage:

> I have myself stressed the idea that man is wiser than his intellect, and that well-functioning persons come to trust their experiencing as an appropriate guide to their behavior . . . when a person is functioning in an integrated, unified, effective manner, she has confidence in the directions she unconsciously chooses, and trusts her experiencing, of which, even if she is fortunate, she has only partial glimpses in her awareness. [p. 246][4]

Respect for Individuality

A high regard for individuality underlies client-centered therapy. Although the individual may be judged irritable and obnoxious by common social standards, he or she must be treated with respect and accepted as a human being who has difficulties and problems that impede his or her fulfillment as a person. The individual merits positive

[4]*Carl Rogers on Personal Power.*

regard, even when, in a social sense, he or she does not deserve it. By positive regard Rogers means *unconditional acceptance* of the person. The client-centered therapist gives positive regard not because the person deserves it but because the person needs it. Every person has a genuine need for such positive regard. Sometimes this need is so distorted that the person who has been deprived of positive regard may not know how to deal with it when he or she does experience it. At first the person may look upon it as a threat, but in the warm, accepting relationship of nondirective therapy, he or she gradually comes to accept and welcome the warmth of another person. It should be noted that the warm, accepting, nonjudgmental relationship between therapist and client is as important as any therapeutic procedure, if not more so, in promoting the therapeutic effects. (Rogers, 1951; see also Rogers 1977; 1980; and Kirschenbaum, 1979)

The Dual Nature of the Self

The ability to sense our own experiences is a remarkable human quality. It is the basis of self-awareness. We can know ourselves and form a self-concept. Like other concepts, the concept of self may or may not correspond well with the actual self; that is, we may or may not know ourselves. Of course, the degree of correspondence varies considerably from person to person. Serious discrepancy between the concept of self and the actual self causes abnormal personality and behavior, according to Rogers. Sometimes a particular behavior is more the result of the self-concept than of the real self. At other times, behavior is directly caused by the real self, irrespective of the nature of the self-concept. A man who has the self-concept of being a "lady-killer" may actually be gauche and crude. His behavior is determined by his actual self although his expectations are the product of his concept of self.

If the self-concept is distorted or malformed, as it often is in those who seek therapy, the person's full potentials are severely blocked, leading to psychological or physical disorders. Consider the woman who believes that she is basically unlovable; her conception of self will certainly influence significant facets of behavior. Social contacts may be greatly restricted. The ability to demonstrate and receive affection may be seriously impaired. The person may set up defenses to block out any feelings of affection in herself. She may also misinterpret demonstrations of affection from others in order that she may continue to maintain her self-concept of being an unlovable person. Such defensive distortion and perceptual misinterpretation are highly detrimental to personality growth and functioning.

Rogers (1951) reports that in successful therapy the self-concept is modified to include the *totality of sensory and visceral experiences.* In other words, the senses are utilized and trusted fully. Material is not censored or altered to conform to the distorted self-concept. Visceral experiences are feelings and desires associated with vital psychobiological needs, and these too are experienced freely and are accepted as a part of the real self. Gradually, the concept of self comes to reflect the real experiences of the self. After successful therapy, clients report an exuberantly positive self-feeling, a genuine liking for the self that they are or have newly discovered. The person, for the moment at least, may be totally accepting of his or her "whole self" without qualification. One of Rogers' clients described this experience as a childlike delight and awe, a new and exciting discovery. The real self is a joyful thing to discover and to be.

Basic Goodness of Human Nature

Some religions assume that people are born with a nature tainted with antisocial and destructive tendencies and that the growing child must be socialized and civilized. We must tame the wild beast. The cliché "Spare the rod and spoil the child" embodies the view that strict discipline is essential in child-rearing. Freud (1927) expressed this idea when he made the id the locus of the most powerful motivation in the personality: inherently selfish, antisocial, and primitive. If the id had full reign over the personality, individual survival would be reduced to the law of the jungle. Survival and civilization are made possible by channeling the tendencies of the id into socially oriented forms of expression. The power of conscience from within and the fear of punishment from without keep the basically animalistic individual in line with the standards of social living. When people are behaving "naturally," they are at their worst; witness the old aphorism "Evil comes on by natural bent, while virtue needs encouragement."

Departing sharply from Freudian theory, Rogers (1961) believes that one of the most basic principles of human nature is that human motivations and tendencies are positive. Even our primitive impulses are not animalistic, egocentric, or antisocial. We are essentially forward-looking, sensitively humane, and "good." Rogers agrees with Maslow (1970) that our negative emotions—hatred, destructiveness, jealousy, and the like—are merely by-products of the frustration of such vital desires as security, acceptance, love, and self-fulfillment. Negative emotions are not in themselves the core of human nature.

Incongruence

For Rogers, *incongruence* refers to a discrepancy between the concept of self and the actual experiences of self. The person suffering from incongruence may be particularly prone to displaying negative emotions. As we have seen, such a person has, in Rogers' view, a distorted self-concept, a view of himself or herself that is incomplete or grossly out of tune with the rest of his or her personality. (Rogers, 1959) If the self-concept is incongruent with the *real* needs of the self, frustration results. In such cases, negative emotions and antisocial behavior are common occurrences.

All too often, children are brought up to believe that they are "bad" or "immoral." In impressing upon children that they constantly need to improve, many parents and teachers convey the notion that children are unworthy, bad, or undesirable as they are. In the process of stressing a negative self-evaluation, they frequently discourage positive feelings toward the self, treating such feelings with scorn and even punishment. Praise and recognition must come from others, never from oneself. "The meek shall inherit the earth." Humility is a virtue that the child is encouraged to adopt as a guiding principle. This leads to a one-way evaluation process: the person can be

I want to learn counseling psychology so that I can help myself and help others. That may be received ambivalently. However, I cannot belong to others until I belong to myself.

only bad, or at best neutral. Perceiving himself or herself as bad or inferior, the child interprets, filters out, and distorts sensory inputs to support this self-conception. In therapy, or under certain other conditions such as warm human relationships, he or she may gradually experience positive self-feelings, and if this aspect of the personality is incorporated into the self-concept, it will be expanded. The child will learn to like and genuinely approve of certain aspects of himself or herself and to dislike and disapprove of other aspects. In other words, the child will gain a more realistic picture of his or her personality. The conception of self will become more congruent with the real self.

INTROJECTION

As we have noted previously, a common form of self-distortion results from introjection, which is the taking over of the values, beliefs, or behaviors of another—usually one who has authority over the person—and accepting them as if they were truly one's own (Rogers, 1951). This process may lead to incongruity between one's real needs, feelings, and desires and the awareness of them. A child may introject the idea that his or her mother must always be liked or that he or she should not have any feeling of hostility toward her, or that he or she should always like her no matter what she does. The feelings the child actually experiences may be incongruent with this introjected value. In order to preserve the self-concept, the child must deny or distort these real feelings to be somehow acceptable. Sometimes the defenses break down, and the person does experience true feelings, with a resulting catastrophic reaction, such as an anxiety attack. For example, a boy who has always been taught to love his mother may experience extreme hatred for her when she punishes him unfairly.

Another common distortion of the self-concept is the introjected belief that no one can care for me, that I am unlovable. When this attitude comes about, it limits the information-gathering functions. The person may fail to see genuine affection when it occurs and may by his or her actions preclude a close, intimate human relationship. The person may have to blunt positive feelings toward others to maintain this distorted self-concept. Personality growth and functioning are then greatly limited, for _people cannot function fully when their concept of self, or self-awareness, is a poor approximation of what they really are._

CONDITIONS OF WORTH

Conditions of worth take the form of prescriptions (do's and don'ts) that must be followed in daily conduct if we are to be acceptable to or valued by others. They cause a distortion of the concept of self and contribute to the incongruence between the concept of self and real self. Children cannot eat their food in any way they please; they must learn to adhere to certain standards of etiquette. Furthermore, the requirements are variable: they do not have to follow the same strict manners with their age-mates as at a formal dinner, but conditions of worth are always present. As a matter of fact, knowledge of and adherence to conditions of worth in all the varied situations we encounter is considered an indication of good adjustment. However, according to Rogers (1972), indiscriminate conformity has detrimental effects on the operation of the self. In other words, in order to conform to conditions of worth, people may have to sacrifice their spontaneity and their personal desires, and in general fit themselves to a pattern that may not correspond to their true nature. A man is not considered truly masculine if he cries as a means of emotional expression and outlet; he must maintain composure under stress. This is a condition of worth that defines masculinity in our culture. It is a limitation on personality functioning, on individuality. Yet most men accept this standard as absolutely infallible. Thus if you were to object, you would be fighting not only against something external but against something in which you really believe, as a result of the introjection of the conduct appropriate to men. The fact that conditions of worth may not be at all attuned to the individual's true nature does not change the consequences of failure to meet them. The sensitive man will be judged (and will judge himself) as deviant, no matter how masculine he is, if he expresses his emotions through crying, whether alone or in the presence of others. The concept of self is greatly influenced by the introjected conditions of worth and may lead to *conditional positive self-regard* (self-criticism) rather than *unconditional positive self-regard* (self-acceptance).

NEED FOR POSITIVE REGARD

In addition to the rewarding and punishing power the parents and other significant people naturally possess, there is another aspect that is a part of the nature of the child that promotes the formation of conditions of worth, namely, the child's need for positive regard. (Rogers, 1959) The normal child behaves in a way that reveals a strong need for acceptance, respect, and love from those who care for him or her. Giving and withholding positive regard can have profound effects upon behavior. Early in the child's life the parents, or parent substitutes, are the "biggest" happening in the child's experience. They can play with and fondle the child and provide a warm, accepting surrounding, or they can punish, reject, mistreat, and in general make life very difficult and unpleasant. There is no time in life when we are so utterly dependent on the good will of others as in infancy. The growth of children is best promoted by positive regard because eventually they will come to regard themselves as they have been regarded by others. (Rogers, 1961; see also Rogers, 1977, for an expanded view of what is needed during early infancy and beyond. See also Leboyer, 1975.)

Imposing conditions of worth on children's behavior is tantamount to telling them: "If you want to be in my good graces, you should think, feel, and act the way I want you to." Imposing such requirements upon the child is making positive regard conditional: "You are acceptable only if you behave in certain prescribed ways." Rogers (1959) advises the parent who wishes to rear a psychologically healthy child to give unconditional positive regard—to accept and respect the child as he or she is. For example, disapproval should be registered in a manner that communicates that the child himself is not disapproved of, only his objectionable behavior. If the child takes a toy from his brother, the parent may indicate disapproval and even take the toy away from him and return it to the other child—and do this without a great deal of emotion. The child can still feel that he is respected. But if the parent uses such expressions as "You are bad; you are terrible; you are naughty and selfish," the stress changes from disapproval of a particular behavior to disapproval of the child.

One last point: parents are important people in the child's life (and this is true of other significant people as well) and what they desire can influence the child a great deal. If the parents disapprove of something, the child should be informed so that he or she can weigh this fact with the existing configuration of material; thus the child can take action on the basis of a full awareness of all his or her perceptions, motives, and possibilities, among which are the parents' wishes. The value of conditions of worth can best be appreciated if we consider the spirit or intent of the concept, namely, the imposition of a variety of preconditions for accepting another person.

VIEWS ON ABNORMALITY

Examining his numerous recorded interviews, Rogers was led to the conclusion that the people who came to him with personality problems were actually trying to find their real selves. Although the symptom picture was quite unique in each case, it could generally be traced to one or more problems of the self. The most common complaint was that life seemed artificial and unreal. Often the person felt that he or she was nothing but a hollow shell; the person made his or her life conform to what others wanted rather than what the person wanted. Instead of being a vital agent to promote his or her own needs and wants, the patient was playing out cultural roles or expectations of those who had power over him or her. Rogers found that improvements in personality functioning occurred when the client could discover and express his or her real self.

Rogers came to promote such ideals for people as expanded consciousness, emotional freedom, and the enjoyment of a rich inner life. He has encouraged his clients and students to follow their own ways rather than the directions others have forced upon them.

Faulty Self-Concept as Cause of Abnormal Behavior

There are many causes of our behavior: the ringing telephone is annoying, so we answer it; when we are hungry, we begin to think of ways of obtaining food. For Rogers, the most important cause of behavior is our self-concept. What we think of ourselves plays a part in everything we do. The person who thinks of himself or herself as loving, kind, considerate, and attractive also thinks, feels, and acts in ways that are consistent with this conception of self. Such a person expects to be treated by others with respect and acceptance. An individual who has an unfavorable conception of self may find that his or her behavior follows and agrees with this faulty conception of self and may believe that he or she is unlovable, unattractive, and uninteresting, and this person's behavior is appropriate to these conceptions of himself or herself.

Consider some other abnormalities which Rogers would ascribe to faulty self-concepts. One person may always look outside of himself for standards, so he never knows what the requirements of his true self really are. Another person usually adopts a compliant style of relating to others, so she typically blocks her own impulses and feelings. Some people are so ashamed of what they consider their true self that they play-act all the time. They become so involved in their various roles that the real self is not experienced. Another common form of abnormality is the person who has a self-concept that includes many musts and shoulds: the self is thereby distorted by a host of interjected conditions of worth. Keeping their feelings and desires constantly under control or denying them altogether, these people never feel comfortable inside because they always fall short of the artificial standards that they have accepted as their own values (see also Branden, 1971).

Rather than deal directly with these various symptoms, Rogers has found that helping the person discover the true self is the best approach. When this discovery occurs, the symptoms disappear.

Emotional Disturbance

It appears that when things go wrong in personality development and functioning, emotions and feelings are most injured. Our emotions are the part of us that suffers the most in an abnormal home or school environment. When attempts to express genuine emotions are met with punishment and frustrations, we begin to deny or repress them. If emotions repeatedly cause trouble for us, we might respond by trying to do away with them altogether. But, of course, this means cutting off vital aspects of our personality. It also means becoming an artificial person. Karen Horney (1950) terms this process *alienation*; Rogers calls it *incongruence*. The milder reactions to this loss of contact with emotions are feelings of being trapped, of being restricted, or of having to be guarded and cautious. The more serious reactions include feelings of unreality, a sense of being superficial, and a sense of not having any identity. The person may complain of feeling empty and of not participating in life.

An essential ingredient of self-exploration is sensing one's feelings and emotions, even those which are negative and most unflattering. Negative feelings toward parents may be difficult to accept as one's own, but they are better felt than covered up, because at least the person knows that he (she) has them. One can then take steps to change conditions by dealing with the problems with one's parents. Denial and distortion can make matters only worse.

Psychological Breakdown

As we have noted, the person with a false conception of self has to cut off vital experiences—both those coming from within and those coming from the external world. A protective system of defenses is formed in order to preserve the concept of self. Occasionally, the correct impressions overcome the defenses, and then the person may experience a psychological breakdown or a great deal of anxiety. Suppose a young man conceives of himself as being brave and unafraid, but in a situation which threatens his life, he panics and loses control of himself. Now he is faced with evidence that contradicts his conception of self, and he cannot deny it. He may experience a terrible sense of confusion and distress. He is now confronted with his own cowardice, and this is extremely unacceptable to him. He may respond in a number of ways. For one thing, he may simply recover from shock and further increase his defenses, so that he can preserve his false self-concept. This alternative means further distortion of personality and also the greater likelihood that he will encounter his unacceptable behavior again. On the other hand, he may perceive the need to change his self-concept.

Getting Behind the Masks

When Rogers uses the term *mask*, he is referring to artificial or unauthentic roles that are either self-imposed or imposed from without. If major aspects of personality are in conflict as a result of opposed role expectations, a firm sense of identity will not occur. The person may complain of being trapped or of not knowing who he or she is or of instability. He or she cannot take a stand on anything nor make a decision on his or her own.

For many persons, roles are difficult to perform in the prescribed way. One may not like the assigned role of father; he may have his own definition of that role. A man may desire to be married but reject the role that his wife and the culture in general expect of him (for a discussion of male and female roles, see Rogers, 1972). The manner of performing our assigned roles may vary from a complete redefinition of the role to grudging perfunctory performance of it to a wholehearted acceptance and identification with the role. In this last instance, the role may be practically identical with the real self. (Gergen, 1971)

The basic problem of the growing individual is to *discover and express his or her real self within the roles that are imposed upon him or her.* Children come into the

We wear many masks.

Arthur Tress ⓒ/Photo Researchers, Inc.

world as members of a preformed culture. They are "fitted" to the culture, not the culture to them. (See Walkenstein, *Don't Shrink to Fit*, 1977.) Their parents demand that they learn many things, among which are the roles they are expected to perform. They are rewarded and punished for their knowledge and performance of these roles. No matter how permissive the home environment, a variety of roles must be learned. Conformity to expectations is as much a part of successful living as is individuality. One-sided development is a major source of psychopathology. But people who are so immersed in their culture that they do not dare to be their real self will experience a sense of emptiness and lack of identity. On the other hand, people who reject most or all of their culture will experience alienation and estrangement, a sense of not being a participant in life. They will have nothing with which to replace their lost cultural roots. Obviously, neither extreme is a desirable way of life.

Rogers describes the changes that have taken place in one of his clients in the following passage:

> I find that many individuals have formed themselves by trying to please others, but again, when they are free, they move away from being this person. So one professional man, looking back at some of the process he has been through, writes, toward the end of therapy: "I finally felt that I simply had to begin doing what I wanted to do, not what I thought I should do, and regardless of what other people feel I should do. This is a complete reversal of my whole life. I've always felt I had to do things because they were expected of me, or more important, to make people like me. The hell with it! I think from now on I'm going to just be me — rich or poor, good or bad, rational or irrational, logical or illogical, famous or infamous. So thanks for your part in helping to rediscover Shakespeare's 'To Thine Own Self be True.'" [1961, p. 170][5]

THE POWER OF CULTURAL ROLES

Many young people conceive of themselves as possessing culturally favored attributes to a high degree. Their conception of self fits a cultural stereotype. Because such roles are or appear to be highly rewarding, developing young people cling to them with everything they have. They strongly desire to be lovers, the men-about-town, wealthy, and famous. They work diligently to structure their self to suit these goals. They block off experiences that tell them a different story about themselves. Their defenses keep such information out, unless they encounter a situation that is totally unexpected and beyond their defensive measures. Then, of course, the awful truth may come home to them in a most painful manner. Yet even this realization of the truth about the self does not usually produce personality change. The distorted self-structure and its defenses are firmly established; and habitually the disturbing experience is quickly glossed over as a bad one, and the distorted self-structure is maintained. (Coopersmith, 1967; see also Branden, 1969; Wylie, 1974, 1978.)

A person may, of course, be unrealistic in the opposite sense: the conception of self may include attributes of inferiority and of being incompetent and unlovable. This distortion of self is also quite common because there are so many ways in which one

[5]Carl R. Rogers *On Becoming a Person*. Reprinted by permission of Houghton Mifflin Company.

may feel inadequate. A culture that offers such glamorous and alluring possibilities to the young person necessarily sets the stage for failure and disappointment.

A conception of self as inferior or unlovable is also firmly structured and resistant to change. Defenses are erected to maintain this erroneous self-conception. A person who believes he or she is inferior may actually disregard or minimize contrary evidence. This may explain the depression that sometimes accompanies the achievement of a highly prized goal. Discovering emotions such as hatred for our parents when only love is acceptable is indeed a painful experience. Giving up false ideals and roles is also painful. But the result of the process is a new person or better, a new self that is more in keeping with the person who was potentially there all the while.

VIEWS ON IDEAL PERSONALITY AND LIVING

Awareness and Becoming the Real Self

One key factor in the discovery of the real self is awareness — awareness of sensory and visceral experiences. With awareness, people know what is going on in their environment and within themselves. Their experiences are not screened and transformed to suit a distorted self-concept. As Rogers says: "The person comes to be in awareness what he is in experience." He may thus become a complete and fully functioning person. (Rogers, 1961)

The remainder of this section will deal with the fully functioning person as viewed by Rogers. It may be helpful to obtain an overview of the main directions that personality growth takes. Table 9-1 depicts both negative and positive directions in this growth process.

MOVING AWAY FROM FACADES AND OUGHTS

The fully functioning person easily recognizes and definitely avoids putting on a facade or demeanor that does not fit his or her real self. (Rogers, 1961, 1980) Being an extrovert may appear to be a highly desirable personality trait, but for the fully functioning person, such a trait, if it did not fit him or her, would be a perversion of the self and thus highly distasteful. Many young persons — and older people who should know better — cling to the belief that outgoing, talkative, humorous qualities make for popularity and success in social and vocational endeavors. Under the influence of this erroneous idea, they misshape their behaviors and selves to fit the cultural model. Our culture does place a premium on appearance. We put on personality traits just as we might put on clothing for different occasions (Goffman, 1959). But even when appearance is stressed, success is ultimately based upon real, not merely apparent, qualities.

Moving away from parental or cultural expectations is, for many people, another indication of becoming a fully functioning person. As we have seen, many values and goals are simply taken over and accepted uncritically as our own even though in actuality they are incongruent with our real needs. A high school student may believe that he or she wants desperately to go to college and that if he or she does not finish college,

TABLE 9-1 NEGATIVE AND POSITIVE DIRECTIONS CHARACTERISTIC OF THE FULLY FUNCTIONING PERSON (LARGELY DERIVED FROM STATEMENTS OF CLIENTS)

Negative Directions (Moving Away From)	Positive Directions (Moving Toward)
Away from shells, facades, and fronts	Being in a continual process of change and action
Away from a self that one is not	
Away from "oughts" (being less submissive, less compliant in meeting standards set by others)	Trusting intuitions, feelings, emotions, and motives
	Being a participant in experience rather than being its boss or controlling it
Away from disliking and being ashamed of self	Letting experience carry one on, floating with a complex stream of experience, moving toward ill-defined goals
Away from doing what is expected, just for that reason alone	
Away from doing things for the sake of pleasing others at the expense of self	Moving toward goals behaviorally, not compulsively planning and choosing them
Away from "musts" and "shoulds" as motives for behavior	Following paths which feel good
	Living in the moment (existential living); letting experience carry one on
	Possessing greater openness to experience
	Being more authentic, real, genuine
	Moving closer to feelings and self (more willingness to yield to feelings and not to place a screen between feelings and self); journey to the center of self
	Accepting and appreciating the "realness" of self
	Increasing positive self-regard (a genuine liking and sympathy for self)

Rogers (1974) attempts to illuminate the role of the person-centered therapist by using the analogy of a gardener. The plants in the garden grow to their optimal potential if the gardener removes negative conditions and introduces positive conditions that foster growth. The therapist is a growth-facilitator—not a behavior shaper or a healer or an adviser or a giver of inspiration. The growth potentials of the person need to be allowed full expression.

life will be filled with hardships and disappointments. This view was common among the children of many European immigrants, who saw in education the glorious way to successful living. However, intellectually and emotionally a student may not be suited for college work. He or she may feel constrained to go and actually make it through, but all the while will feel tense and uneasy. The student may feel trapped. He or she is doing something he or she does not really believe in, and this is the cause of the distress, although the student may not recognize it. Many people complain that their lives are regulated from without rather than from within. They are slaves to certain things, such as money, prestige, or power.

Toward Self-Direction

As we have just implied, the fully functioning person takes responsibility for the main directions of his or her life. Although the move toward self-regulation and autonomy is a gradual and painful process, self-direction yields great satisfaction. To be dependent requires less of the person than to be independent. To accept ready-made standards of conduct, values, and goals requires less effort and poses less threat than to work these out for oneself. People who introject the values of their or their parents' culture subject themselves to the likelihood of incongruity between what they *believe* their real wants and needs are, and their actual wants and needs, which must be distorted in the process. Whereas breaking away from dependence is terribly painful and arriving at personally determined goals is highly frustrating at times because we must inevitably make mistakes, self-direction is ultimately the best approach to life. *We function most fully when we are fulfilling ourselves in our own way*. This can be accomplished only by self-direction. (Rogers, 1961, 1977, 1980) Rogers perceives the difficulty of this task, as he indicates in the following statement: "This is not to say that the process would be smooth or comfortable . . . to be oneself is worth a high price." (Rogers, 1980)

It should be noted that to take charge of your life by examining the appropriateness of values for yourself does not imply that the culture should be rejected. To Rogers, becoming a fully functioning person does not mean breaking away from tradition and espousing an unconventional movement. Being a fully functioning person means being autonomous, formulating or choosing one's own style of life. The culture is broad and flexible, and most people can function as individuals within it.

Process Living

By *process living*, Rogers (1961, 1980) means spontaneity, creative living, flexibility, and a dynamic and changing orientation to life. It is the opposite of adjusting by attaining a static and adequate manner of dealing with our needs and pressures, of achieving a "state" of adequate functioning. Rogers says of process persons that "They are keenly aware that the one certainty of life is change—that they are always in process, always changing. They welcome this risk-taking way of being and are eager to face change." [Rogers, 1980, p. 48]

People who are characterized by process living accept inner and outer experiences as they are, without imposing requirements and standards. Such people flow with their experiences. They do not rule out certain things or set boundaries regarding what needs and sensory elements will be recognized. In other words, their self is not fixed and static. Rogers sees the ideal state as a fluid, changeable, unstructured, moment-by-moment existence.

Rogers is quite clear about what the good life is *not*. It is not a fixed state, a glorious state of virtue, contentment, nirvana, or happiness. Furthermore, process living is not attaining homeostasis or tension reduction or equilibrium. Rogers even rejects the notion that those who are fully functioning are "actualized," a term used by several outstanding personologists to describe ideal human living. The good life is not a destination but a process or direction in which people are participating fully according to their true natures. An essential feature of this process is inner freedom, continuing flexibility to select the direction of living.

Openness to Experience

To live fully requires that we fully know what is really going on within and outside ourselves. Openness to experience is the opposite of defensiveness. All organic experiences and sensory inputs are freely relayed through the nervous system. People can sense their deepest emotions even if they are quite negative, but at the same time they do not rule out positive ones. All of their emotions are permitted to pass into the self-structure. In fact, the openness quality rules out false masks, leaving the self-structure mobile and fluid. Such people do not feel comfortable being someone other than themselves. They are at their worst when they are play-acting. They do not cling to culturally determined expectations and allurements. Their judgments, choices, and decisions are natural outcomes of their own evaluation of experience, both internal and external. They are willing to live with their experiences as these are rather than impose an artificial order upon them.

LISTENING TO ONESELF

An integral aspect of openness to experience is "listening to oneself." (Rogers, 1972) This is recognized in Eastern cultures, which place much stress on becoming acquainted with one's deepest nature. In Western cultures, however, the focus is outside the person, and there seems to be a taboo against introspection. The child is admonished to keep busy, to always be doing or looking or listening or playing with something. This external orientation and avoidance of inner experiences produce a one-sided development that in the long run is harmful because it blocks out a major source of knowledge. Individuals faced with a decision find that they cannot make it because they really do not know themselves and hence do not know what they want. Obviously they cannot predict the future, and certain critical decisions that may change our course in life cause hesitation and doubt. Yet in many instances the difficulty lies with the lack of self-awareness.

For such people, awareness of self is vague, with conflicting elements, and the self that is experienced may seem unreal. According to Rogers' view of the nature of the self, it may well *be* unreal. The self is not what the organism is. Listening to oneself is one way in which everyone can discover his or her real self. (Moustakas, 1972; see Gendlin, 1978, for his description of the technique of self-focusing; also Masters and Houston, 1978.)

Existential Living

Rogers (1961, 1977, 1980) believes that people should let their experiences tell them what they mean rather than force a meaning upon them. We are living existentially if we can react flexibly to the total complex of internal and external experiences without imposing general constructs on our perceptions of events. The self should emerge from the complex of momentary experience rather than determine it. Rogers cannot mean that there are no psychological structures or preformed ideas affecting the pattern of stimulation that is perceived, because obviously we bring into every situation the complex of attitudes, experiences, and dispositions that are an integral part of our personality. But the person who lives existentially continually evaluates the constructs that affect his or her style of life, allowing them to change under the influx of experience.

Trusting One's Organism — — — — intuition

Using his own experiences, Rogers attempts to convey what he means by trusting one's organism:

> One of the basic things which I was a long time in realizing, and which I am still learning, is that when an activity feels as though it is valuable or worth doing, it is worth doing. Put another way, I have learned that my total organismic sensing of a stiuation is more trustworthy than my intellect. All of my professional life I have been going in directions which others thought were foolish, and about which I have had many doubts myself. But I have never regretted moving in directions which "felt right," even though I have often felt lonely or foolish at the time. [1961, p. 22][6]

In this passage, Rogers is referring to the operation of the organismic valuing process, which, it will be recalled, is revealed through positive or negative feeling states. It functions optimally when a person is in a state of congruence. It cannot be trusted as a guide to living when a person is in a state of incongruence.

Rogers does not mean that we should act rashly, and on the whim of the moment change our whole course of life. His meaning appears to be more in the nature of acting spontaneously, freshly, and freely, without too many constraints. His reasoning goes something like this: The person who is open to all his or her experiences can consider all the components because at least they are all available. Obviously if part of the evidence is missing, behavior that is based on the existing evidence may be undesirable for the person. In a particular situation, such as leaving home for a promising job, all the elements are inspected and evaluated. We may dislike leaving our parents and friends. We may fear starting a new life in a strange environment. At the same time, we see the value of the opportunity and some exciting challenges to our creative talents. We may also appreciate that the decision does not have to be binding for life. All these elements are brought together; a judgment or several judgments emerge, and finally we fix upon a decision. The decision, when it arrives, may feel like an intuition, but it is not. It is more like a conclusion based on premises that are not totally in awareness. If we are open to experience, we can feel confident that our choices are rational at the time we make them, even though they may lead to behavior which must be reevaluated later.

[6]Carl R. Rogers *On Becoming a Person*. Reprinted by permission of Houghton Mifflin Company.

You can trust your organismic valuing process when you are congruent

Many people are fearful of expressing themselves freely because they fail to trust their spontaneous actions or reactions. They are careful to censor what they say and do, and usually they are quite uncomfortable and tense (Laing, 1967). Rogers has observed that persons who have profited most from therapy are able to trust their emotions and behave on what appears to the observer to be the impulse of the moment. But we do not arrive at this point only through therapy. Learning about ourselves and testing the insights that have been gained can lead to a trust in our organism. Our emotions can be acted upon with favorable results. When the person is fully functioning, he or she begins to see that his or her total organism is often wiser than awareness alone. The person can come to rely upon "intuition" and both positive and negative feelings for certain matters. (For more on the development of self-trust, see Rogers, 1977, 1980.)

A Sense of Freedom

Fully functioning people experience a feeling of freedom, a sense of self-determination (Rogers, 1961). They can choose to move in a direction of growth or stagnation, to be themselves or a facade, to open themselves to their experiences or shut them out. On the other hand, people who hold to strict cultural standards or the expectations of others feel that their behavior is determined by forces over which they have no control. (Rotter, 1971, 1980) A man, for example, complained that he was like an automaton. He had gone through the same daily routines so frequently and mechanically that he began to accept the idea that there was no other way for him. He expressed his sense of being trapped by comparing himself to a wind-up toy that is programmed for a certain sequence of movements and executes them exactly according to the program.

One young woman complained that her life was so permeated with "shoulds" and "oughts" that she felt she had no real desires of her own. Her decisions were virtually foregone conclusions. She had to earn good grades, take a college prep course in high school, and attend college with a major in teaching. All this and much more was determined for her by her parents. She began by questioning her religious beliefs, which she felt did more to block her growth and functioning than to promote them. She seemed to have an excessive amount of guilt and complained of feeling that she was basically an evil person. Her environmental circumstances and internal controls engendered a style of life that did not permit freedom of choice. It should be noted that by the time people reach an age at which they can begin to make choices for themselves, they may have already internalized (introjected) the standards of conduct that were forced upon them with the consequence that they cannot violate these standards without experiencing a profound sense of guilt. They tie themselves up and block their own channels of expression.

There are two points regarding the subjective sense of freedom that may cause the reader some confusion: (1) the relation of conscience to freedom: Does the fully functioning person have a conscience? And (2) freedom versus determinism: Is not human nature subject to the laws of causality?

not automatons
not permeated w/ "shoulds" & "oughts"

FREEDOM AND CONSCIENCE

The question of conscience is somewhat complex. The fully functioning person does not have a conscience in the Freudian sense of an unconscious set of principles that have a censorship function. Yet such persons can certainly be described as people who have principles. There may appear to be a paradox or contradiction here. The fully functioning person has values, moral standards, and a host of other determining sets. But for the most part these guiding tendencies and sets are conscious. People are aware of having them, or can bring them to awareness if pressed to do so. They do not operate (as they do in the rigid, compulsive, guarded individual) as a mysterious inner force, a split off superego that oversees the doings of the ego. The guiding principles and values of the fully functioning person are his or her own; although they may have come from parents or friends, they are now an integral part of the real self. People *may* work diligently at a task not because they are driven to do so by an inner compulsion to succeed, but because they consciously desire a particular end. They know what they want and take steps to secure it.

In addition to the factor of awareness of sets, there is also the factor of flexibility. The fully functioning person's constructs, values, and so forth are not compulsively held or immutable. Such people are open to experiences and can modify their sets accordingly. They have a "set to change their sets." A young man may value making money, but if he finds that this goal is not satisfying his genuine desires, he changes his valued objective. Rather than allowing his sets to order experience, he governs his sets by his experience. His constructs are fluid and easily adjusted; thus he can accommodate himself to a changing world or to change in himself. Aging, for example, does not become a dreaded specter because he changes his constructs to suit the changes in his total organism. (Rogers, 1980) He has *guiding sets*, and these are consciously apprehended and easily modifiable.

FREEDOM VERSUS DETERMINISM

If there is a significant movement on the part of the client undergoing psychotherapy, the result is a greater sense of freedom. Such people feel more control over their lives, but whether they have increased what might be termed their actual freedom is difficult to answer and involves philosophical questions beyond the scope of this book. Some observations may aid you in thinking through the issue. In a sense, you are freer because more potentialities are open to you. However, fully functioning people are also subject to the laws of causality. Their behavior, including their sense of subjective freedom, is determined by antecedent conditions. But the point that Rogers seems to make is that such people are giving expression to much more of their real organismic self when they are fully functioning and thereby satisfying their needs effectively. What they choose is what they really need; what they consciously want mirrors what they need.

One of the attributes of functioning fully is a sense of self-determination because a person utilizes potentials efficiently. An engine that is out of tune and one that is in tune are both "determined" to function the way they do, but the one that is functioning properly maintains a certain heat level and power efficiency, whereas the malfunctioning one overheats and is highly inefficient. Aside from the philosophical difficulties involved, the fact remains that the fully functioning person *feels* a high degree of inner freedom, and this attribute is greatly valued. Freedom from constraints, whether internally or externally imposed, is an essential condition of being one's real self. In common with other humanistic psychologists Rogers (1969, 1977, 1980), now goes beyond his earlier view that the fully functioning person feels free, believing that in a real sense he *is* more free. Rogers believes that one of the defining attributes of human nature is freedom; namely, autonomous functioning, and this ability is optimum in the fully functioning person.

Table 9–2 summarizes the traits of Rogers' fully functioning person and of the incongruent person.

Creativity and Spontaneity *Summary of the ff*

When people are open to their internal and external experiences, when they do not fear being themselves and give up facades, when their constructs are flexible and can change with experience, these people are both spontaneous and creative (Rogers, 1961).

TABLE 9-2 TRAITS OF THE FULLY FUNCTIONING AND INCONGRUENT SELVES

The Fully Functioning Self	The Incongruent Self
Self-aware	Out of touch with the self
Creative	Lacks firm sense of identity
Spontaneous	Introjects
Open to experience	Frustrated impulses
Self-accepting	Negative emotions
Self-determining	Distorted self-structure
Free from constraints	Antisocial behavior
Lives in his or her "now"	Puts forth masks
Allows full outlet of potentials	Unrealistic appraisal of potentials
Trusts his or her organism	
Possesses firm sense of identity	
Avoids facades	
Has sense of free choice	
Moves from introjection	
Moves toward self-direction	
Willing to be process	
Lives existentially	

Note: Represented here are the extremes of a continuum with fully functioning at one extreme and incongruity at the other as considered by Rogers.

They can conform to the requirements of the setting when this suits their needs, but they can resist the pressures placed upon them if these compel them in directions that are opposed to their self-picture.

Creativity requires a freedom from constraints. People who must do things in a certain way or who must meet certain standards, limit their freedom and consequently hamper their creative forces. Rather than seeking to make their lives predictable, safe, orderly, and tensionless, they are fully functioning people, confident in their ability to meet life head on, relish new experiences, challenges, immediacy, stimulation, and excitement. They do not have to maintain a fixed style of living compulsively; thus they are mobile psychologically, a quality that makes for creativity. (Bloomberg, 1971; see also Rollo May, 1975; Barbara Brown, 1980, for two humanists' views of creativity and the powers of the human person.)

The Greater Richness of Life

Rogers believes that the human being is truly a rational animal. When humans are functioning properly, their behavior is not fearsome, not antisocial, not self-destructive. Most people are not rational to the degree that they could be. Rogers says:

> When man's unique capacity of awareness is thus functioning freely and fully, we find that we have, not an animal whom we must fear, not a beast who must be controlled, but an organism able to achieve, through the remarkable integrative capacity of its central nervous system, balanced, realistic, self-enhancing . . . behavior as a resultant of all these elements of awareness. To put it another way, when man is less than fully man — when he denies to awareness various aspects of his experience — then indeed we have all too often reason to fear him and his behavior, as the present world situation testifies. But when he is most fully man, when he is his complete organism, when awareness of experience, that peculiarly human attribute, is most fully operating, then he is to be trusted, then his behavior is constructive. [1961, p. 105][7]

Many people are driven by the quest for unattainable goals, or they hold rigid standards of conduct that cramp and imprison them. The good life should involve a wide range of experiences. It is possible to live sensitively, with a greater variety, richness, and depth of experience than most people enjoy. We can be "a trustworthy instrument for encountering life." Rogers believes that the *good life itself* is described not by terms such as happy, blissful, content, enjoyable (although a *person* who is functioning fully can be characterized by these terms), but rather by terms such as enriching, exciting, rewarding, challenging, meaningful. The good life is not for the timid because it involves the courage to be, to stretch and grow in one's potentialities. It means having to tolerate uncertainty, ambiguity, and even pain, but it also means freedom to be ourselves, to live in the moment and enjoy rich experiences freely.

Rogers specifies some of the steps in healthy development and effective therapy in the following statement:

> The path of development toward psychological maturity, the path of therapy, is the undoing of the estrangement in man's functioning, the dissolving of conditions of worth, the

---

[7]Carl R. Rogers *On Becoming a Person*. Reprinted by permission of Houghton Mifflin Company.

Increasing the capacity to enjoy enriches life.

Peter Menzel/Stock, Boston.

achievement of a self which is congruent with experience, and the restoration of a unified organismic valuing process as the regulator of behavior. [1959, pp. 226–227; see also Rogers, 1980]

CRITICAL EVALUATION

Rogers' views have been extremely influential in the field of psychology. During the 1950s and early 1960s he held the position that Skinner occupies today, and he continues to be influential. His client-centered approach to counseling has spread outside of psychology to diverse fields, such as nursing, business, industry, and the ministry. It has become fashionable to respect the rights of the client, whether he or she be the patient in a nurse-patient relationship, the employee in a management-labor dispute, or the child in a parent-child relationship. (Ginott, 1965) Even employee evaluations are often presented to the employee by a supervisor so that both may discuss the evaluation. Currently, Rogers is involved with group dynamics and the human potential movement, but his concepts are essentially the same as they were when he was primarily a client-centered counselor, a factor that attests to the flexibility of his formulations.

Rogers has made a significant contribution to the scientific study of counseling and psychotherapy through his analysis of therapist and client responses. By recording therapy sessions, he has opened this field to scientific investigation. (Rogers and Dymond, 1954) His views about the therapeutic relationship have spurred researchers to investigate the qualities and activities of the therapists — genuineness, empathy, and unconditional positive regard. Of special concern to Rogers was the development and influence of the self. Nevertheless, his view of a benign, unfolding self that requires simply to be accepted has been criticized as naively optimistic. He offers few direct suggestions either for self-improvement or for promoting personality change in others. Although he spends a great deal of time discussing the benefits that result when a person attains a state of congruence, he really does not tell us how to get that way except in rather abstract and general terms. To be a fully functioning person may require the learning of specific attitudes and skills of daily living, something that is overlooked by Rogers in his preoccupation with openness to experience and self-exploration. All the self-exploring in the world will not give the person a course to follow; no amount of self-acceptance will bring into being the kinds of skills required to satisfy needs. The behavior modification movement is a reaction against the kind of thinking that Rogers's theory represents. Despite the shortcomings in Rogers' theory of human nature, he is an able spokesman of the phenomenological point of view. Viewing the personality from the "inside," the subjective perspective, has certainly become a legitimate method of studying people.

GUIDES TO RESEARCH

HEURISTIC VALUE OF ROGERS' THEORY

Rogers' ideas and methods of therapy have been highly influential. He is one of the pioneers in the humanistic approach to psychology. He has garnered many disciples who not only practice his brand of psychotherapy, but many of them also conduct research suggested by Rogers' theory. He has also influenced significantly the phenomenological approach and helped to make self-psychology a respectable endeavor in contemporary psychology. Rogers has also made significant contributions to group therapies in his work with encounter groups, T-groups, sensitivity training, and other group approaches to therapy. He has demonstrated that group therapy can be effective with diverse problems and a wide variety of people, ranging from the newly divorced to business executives undergoing a midlife crisis. He is widely recognized as a leader in the encounter-group approach to therapy and

has written several books and articles describing his methods and experiences.

His person-centered therapy continues to attract many adherents. His concepts and methods are followed by counselors and therapists in many fields in the helping professions — nursing, social work, school counseling, and marriage counseling — and in industry. In his writings he has advocated a profound respect for the individual person, whether it be the child in relation to parents, the student in relation to teachers, the patient in relation to doctors and nurses, or the employee in relation to management. Rogers has stressed openness and honesty in communication and evaluations and has urged respect for the rights of the individual in any relationship in which one person possesses power over another. Current practices in many fields reflect Rogers' respect for the individual. For example, major changes have taken place in the procedures for arrest and interrogation in recent years that protect the accused from possible intimidation and coercion by law enforcement authorities.

It is difficult to determine the extent to which Rogers' ideas have contributed to such developments. Rogers' writings are widely read, and his ideas about the dignity of the individual have been broadly disseminated, but whether Rogers is reflecting the spirit of the times or has been an agent in shaping ideas is difficult to assess. Another development in the past thirty or forty years to which Rogers has at least provided impetus is a benevolent child-centeredness in our society. As a matter of fact, his name has been associated with permissiveness in child-rearing, a view that Rogers would probably not ascribe to himself. He has long inveighed against traditional roles of parents as disciplinarians, as owners of their children, and as judges and prescribers. He has instead recommended that parents serve as growth facilitators, models of excellence, and guidance counselors for their children. Again, these views have taken hold among the middle classes, but whether Rogers is the shaper of this movement cannot be readily determined. We can see from the foregoing that Rogers' ideas fit well the ethos of the times; thus he has been highly influential in American psychology and in many other fields as well.

EMPIRICAL RESEARCH SUGGESTED BY ROGERS' THEORY

The earliest tests regarding Rogers' hypotheses were carried out by Rogers himself and his followers (Rogers and Dymond, 1954). They were concerned with the effectiveness of nondirective therapy—now referred to as a person-centered therapy. Rogers was a pioneer in using recordings for analysis of therapists and client behaviors. Many of the early studies involved establishing categories for evaluating statements of the clients and also the therapists. Changes could be determined by noting the frequency of certain statements and the changes in them that occurred during the course of therapy (Raimy, 1948). Measures of therapeutic success were based on ratings made by the therapist, the clients, and independent judges. Some of the later studies employed standardized tests such as the MMPI (the Minnesota Multiphasic Personality Inventory), the California Test of Maturity, and the like. Rogers is fond of citing client statements to support his ideas. This is an informal method of testing the validity of his ideas and therapeutic methods, but more formal techniques have been subsequently used by Rogers and his followers. It will be recalled that Rogers stressed the role of genuineness, unconditional positive regard, and empathy on the part of the therapist as necessary for effective therapy. These qualities were assessed by having trained judges evaluate recorded excerpts of actual therapy sessions. Truax and Mitchell (1971) reviewed the early studies dealing with these attributes and concluded that a substantial number of studies do support the idea that the presence of these attributes in therapy is associated with varying degrees of success, and their absence produces deterioration. The findings seem to apply to a wide variety of clients and also to group as well as individual therapy. A further point should be noted: Truax and Mitchell found that Rogers' idea that all three qualities are necessary for effective therapy to occur was not quite what the studies demonstrated. It turned out that one quality, such as genuineness, might correlate with the measure of therapeutic success, but the other two did not. In a different study, another quality, or perhaps two, correlated with therapeutic success, but not the third. The studies used different measures of therapeutic success; thus it is possible that the variations were due to this factor.

Mitchell et al. (1977) reviewed a number of later studies that cover a greater variety of therapeutic approaches, not Rogers' alone, and found that about half the studies supported Rogers' triad of qualities and half did not. Again, it should be stressed that other forms of therapy were used in some of the cases.

Rappaport and Chinsky (1972) point to what they consider a flaw in many of the studies attempting to assess the behavior of the therapist. The raters usually work with written excerpts of the recorded sessions, and these are frequently inadequate to evaluate the interaction between the therapist and client. Brief samples of therapist behavior taken out of context do not reveal the qualities that Rogers suggested. Furthermore, many of the studies have used ratings of trained judges rather than the ratings of clients. Rogers is quite explicit about his views of the client-therapist relationship; he holds that improvement depends upon the *clients' perception* of the qualities of the therapist. Therapy may be effective even if the therapist does not possess the three attributes. The essential condition is that the client perceives the therapist as possessing them. In most of the studies, no effort was made to test the consistency between raters' judgments and the clients'.

Rogers (1967) conducted an interesting study with schizophrenics undergoing client-centered therapy in which he obtained ratings of the qualities of the therapists from (1) the clients, (2) from college students who were given transcripts of the therapy sessions, and (3) from the therapists themselves. He found that the clients improved if they rated the therapist as being genuine, and those that rated them low on genuineness did not improve. Whereas the clients and the student judges agreed in their ratings of the therapists, the therapists' ratings of themselves were just the opposite of those of the clients and the students. For example, a therapist who rated himself as genuine was not rated as genuine by the clients and the students. Bearing in mind that this was a single study, Rogers cautioned therapists to attempt to discover the clients' perception of them and not rely solely on their own self-evaluations as an indicator of therapeutic effectiveness. Rogers' phenomenological theory places the stress on the clients' perception. The crucial test is the correlation between the clients' perception of the therapist and therapeutic outcome.

Gurman (1977) reviewed twenty-two studies in which the clients' perceptions of the therapists were obtained. Twenty-one of the studies reported positive correlations between client perceptions and therapeutic outcome. The qualities of the therapist were those suggested by Rogers: positive regard, empathy, and genuineness. In the same report, Gurman reviewed ten studies that dealt with group therapy approaches. The group members rated the qualities of the group leaders, and measures of therapeutic outcome were taken, but therapeutic outcome did not correlate with group members' ratings. Group leaders do not occupy the same status or play the same roles as do individual therapists. Parloff et al. (1978) found methodological flaws in the studies reported by Gurman and questions whether the outcomes of the studies really support Rogers' view, but the results were strong enough to warrant at least moderate acceptance of Rogers' view about the correlation of clients' perceptions of the therapist and the success of therapy.

Q-Sort Studies

A large number of studies designed to test the effectiveness of client-centered therapy have used the Q-sort technique to assess changes that occur during and after therapy in the client's perception of self. (See Seeman and Raskin, 1953; Wylie, 1974, 1978, for comprehensive summaries.) The Q-sort technique was developed by Stephenson (1953) and involves sorting through a deck of cards that contain descriptive statements or trait names that are descriptive of self. The client places the cards in piles that range from most descriptive of self to least descriptive. There are many variations, depending upon the number of cards and the number of categories, but typically the client is required to follow the normal curve. Cards that are most or least descriptive of self constitute the smallest piles whereas statements that fit in between the extremes make up the larger piles. We might think of the descriptive statements as varying on a dimension of self-description, ranging from most applicable to self to least applicable to self.

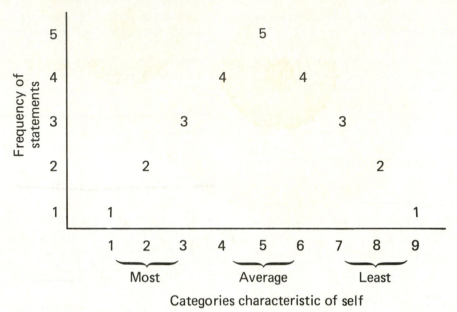

FIGURE 9-1
Sample Q-Sort Distribution

Rogers postulates that effective therapy should lead to increase in positive self-perception. Raimy (1948), using Q-sort techniques, confirmed Rogers' prediction concerning the changes in positive self-ratings with therapy (see Figure 9-1).

Rogers places much emphasis on congruence between actual self-perception (the manner in which the person describes himself or herself) and the ideal self (what the person would like to be). When these perceptions of self are quite consistent, the person enjoys a state of congruence, a condition that characterizes the fully functioning person. The cards may be sorted first for self-perception, the self sort, then for the ideal self, the ideal sort. If there is a discrepancy between the two sortings, the same card might be in different categories. For example, the statement "I let people push me around" might be given a placement of 1 in the self-sort and placement of 5 in the ideal-sort. In other words, the person perceives himself or herself to be easily manipulated by people, but would rather have that attribute be less characteristic of himself or her-

self. A correlation may be obtained by using the two sets of categories: each card thus has two numbers. Negative correlations indicate degrees of discrepancy or incongruence whereas positive correlations indicate degrees of congruence.

Using the procedure just described, Butler and Haigh (1954) found in the initial tests of a group seeking therapy a marked discrepancy between self-perception and ideal-perception, with correlations in the negative or zero range. After the completion of client-centered therapy, most of the correlations moved in a positive direction with the average correlation being .34. The movement varied with each individual, but the general trend was toward greater congruence of self-sort and ideal-sort. The control subjects who were not seeking therapy showed correlations of perceived and ideal self that averaged about .58, which indicated that there was considerably more congruence in them than in the case of those seeking therapy. The narrowing of the discrepancy as a function of therapy may be due (1) to an increase in self-esteem, as Rogers predicts; (2) to a decrease in ideal goals toward the direction of more realistic expectations; or (3) both changes may take place. Rudikoff (1954) found that ideal sorts do tend to become more like self-sorts in successful therapy. Ideals are brought more in line with perceived attributes.

Several important studies have tended to support Rogers' notion that degree of congruence between perceived and ideal self is associated with general effectiveness in living (Brophy, 1959). Turner and Vanderlippe (1958) obtained a variety of measures of general effectiveness and degree of satisfaction with life for 175 college students for whom they also secured measures of the discrepancy between the perceived self and the ideal self. Subjects who might be described as being congruent, that is, as having small discrepancies between self and ideal self, were found to be active, ascendant, sociable, stable emotionally, and thoughtful in their social relationships. These investigators also found that the congruent subjects participated in extracurricular activities, had a higher scholastic average, received higher sociometric ratings, and scored higher on certain measures of adjustment when compared with subjects who had a wide discrepancy between self and ideal descriptions.

Rosenberg (1962) related degree of self and ideal discrepancy with scores on the eighteen scales of the California Personality Inventory, a test that assesses a variety of significant dimensions of effective living. He found that the greater the self and ideal discrepancy, the lower the scores on fifteen of the scales. Rosenberg concluded that people who experience a marked discrepancy between perceived and ideal self are deficient in traits, interests, and skills that are necessary for successful living. In a similar vein, Mahoney and Hartnett (1973) found that degree of self-actualization correlated with degree of congruence as measured by the discrepancy between perceived and ideal self. This finding is predictable because many of the same attributes that characterize the self-actualizing person also apply to the congruent person as Rogers views him or her.

Q-sort studies have provided a means of measuring self-feelings and self-perceptions. The technique provides access to subjective experiences that can be measured. However, there are some problems with the Q-sort procedure, particularly in respect to the forcing of self-descriptions into set numbers. The nature of the Q-sort technique forces the person to assign self-descriptive statements into a set format; thus one may be required to assign high categories to statements that are not characteristic or be forced to give lower ratings to characteristics that *are* applicable to self.

Other Rogerian Hypotheses

Another of Rogers' ideas that has been the basis of research is that self-acceptance correlates with acceptance of others. Suinn (1961) studying high school boys found that self-acceptance was associated with acceptance of their fathers and also their teachers. Medinnus and Curtis (1963) found that mothers who were more accepting of themselves were also more accepting of their children, and vice versa. It will be recalled that self-acceptance is a major attribute of the fully functioning person. Several investigators (Seeman, 1949; Stock, 1949) have not found this relationship. Further research led other investigators (Gordon and Cartwright, 1954; Stock, 1949; and Sheerer, 1949) to conclude that self-attitudes do, in fact, correlate with attitudes toward others; thus one who has favorable attitudes about self also sees others in a favorable light, and vice versa.

Coan (1972) constructed a test to measure Rogers' notion of openness to experience. He constructed his items from statements taken directly from Rogers' description of the components of this attribute. He administered the preliminary test to 382 college students and subjected the data to a factor analysis. He obtained sixteen factors. He then obtained correlations between the sixteen factors and scores on standardized personality tests and found positive correlations of many of the factors and the personality measures. After eliminating some of the items that did not correlate very highly with the personality tests and constructing some new items, he readministered the tests to another large sample of college students. The correlation of the factors with the personality tests improved. Coan then reduced the original sixteen factors to seven more general factors, and the final test, which he purports measures openness to experience, consists of eighty-three items with seven scoring scales. The following dimensions are covered in the test: (1) aesthetic sensitivity, (2) openness to hypothetical ideas, (3) constructive utilization of fantasy, (4) openness to unconventional views of reality, (5) indulgence in fantasies, (6) unusual perceptions and associations, and (7) deliberate and systematic thought.

Rogers' ideas have inspired many researchers to put them to empirical test. He himself has conducted many empirical studies and claims that his theory is the outgrowth of his experiences and research rather than a speculative formulation. He has demonstrated that subjective experiences and states can be translated into measurable behavior.

GUIDES TO LIVING

LISTENING, REFLECTION, CLARIFICATION, AND POSITIVE REGARD

We can look to Rogers' ideas and practices in his client-centered therapy for some guidance in improving social relationships.

Being a Good Listener

Rogers found that his clients wanted very much simply to talk about their problems to someone who would listen. The emphasis is on the word *listen*, not criticize, judge, advise, or console. A client would often report that he felt much better after an hour or so, during which time Rogers had offered no directives or advice, but had listened attentively in a warm, permissive manner. Rogers (1951) points out that the major hindrance to being a good listener is the compulsion to assert or express ourselves. We do not really listen to the other because we are so busy preparing our next utterance. Most people respond positively to a sympathetic listener. What Rogers advises for counselors applies to anyone in a social relationship:

> . . . it is the counselor's aim to perceive as sensitively and accurately as possible all of the perceptual field as it is being experienced by the client . . .; and having thus perceived this internal frame of reference of the other as completely as possible, to indicate to the

client the extent to which he is seeing through the client's eyes. [1951, p. 34][8]

Reflection

Rogers found another procedure extremely valuable in conveying to his clients that he had a positive regard for them. He termed this technique "reflection." (Rogers, 1942) It involves acknowledgment of the other person's thoughts and feelings through verbal repetition of them, through calling attention to them, and through talking about them.

Clarification

By listening attentively and utilizing the technique of reflection, you can enable the other person to experience a clarification of his or her ideas and feelings. The specific ideas that you select to reflect can also promote the process of clarification. The important factor of insight, which is so potent in bringing about personality change, is fostered through clarification. Difficulties in a personal relationship may be reduced if a person uses the techniques of listening, reflection, and clarification judiciously. Hearing

[8]*Client-Centered Therapy.*

a faulty attitude or thought expressed by someone else sometimes makes it appear more vividly irrational or unrealistic.

Positive Regard

Positive regard from another, however it is expressed, is usually welcomed by anyone, particularly one who is having psychological problems. We can use our power of giving unconditional positive regard to help another discover self, as well as promote warm social relationships. Rogers speaks of unconditional positive regard that (as we noted earlier) is accepting the other as he or she is, without setting conditions, although psychologists such as Skinner (1953) would argue that giving unconditional positive regard for neurotic behaviors constitutes a reinforcement of the very behaviors that are causing the individual difficulties. Rogers has long held that accepting others as they are aids significantly in effecting change (see also Rogers, 1980, pp. 137–163).

Rogers presents an introspective account of his own reactions and efforts to apply the insights he has gained in his counseling and therapeutic work. Again his ideas are applicable to one's own efforts at improving mental health:

1. In my relationships with persons, I have found that it does not help in the long run to act as though I am something that I am not.

2. I find that I am more effective when I can listen acceptantly to myself, and can be myself.

3. I have found it of enormous value when I can permit myself to understand another person.

4. I have found it enriching to open channels whereby others can communicate their feelings, the private perceptual world to me.

5. I have found it highly rewarding when I can accept another person.

6. The more I am open to the realities in me and in the other person the less do I find myself wishing to rush in to fix things.

7. I can trust my experience.

8. Evaluation by others in not a guide for me.

9. Experience is for me the highest authority.

10. I enjoy the discovering of order in experience.

11. The facts are friendly.

12. What is most personal is most general.

13. It has been my experience that persons have a basically positive direction.

14. Life at its best is a slowly changing process, in which nothing is fixed. [1961, pp. 16–27][9]

SELF-AWARENESS

The views of Carl Rogers are quite compatible with the views of the phenomenologists. A phenomenologist is one who accepts psychological states as important determinants of behavior. As with Rogers, understanding the real self is of utmost importance. This means understanding our values, goals, and those things that give meaning to our lives. It should be noted that we do not become self-aware merely by pondering events of the day. Self-awareness is acquired most fully through observation of the self in action, particularly in social relationships, for it is then that the self is called forth actually to be what it has become.

The following five steps apply specifically to inappropriate reactions, but they may be applied to any problem areas in which one wishes to improve one's awareness.

Step 1. Recognize an inappropriate reaction. For example, a student might wonder why he becomes very angry with a certain instructor

[9]Carl R. Rogers *On Becoming a Person*. Reprinted by permission of Houghton Mifflin Company.

over seemingly minor matters when this does not occur with other teachers. In cases of inappropriate responses (for example, anger), the emotion felt is often a cover for some genuine emotion that a person fears to experience.

Step 2. Feel the apparent emotion. Allow yourself to experience the anger within you. Do not be satisfied with pushing feelings aside.

Step 3. Ask yourself what else you felt at the time. In the case of an inappropriate response or emotion, there is usually some subtle feeling that occurs just prior to the experienced emotion. For example, the angry student may recall a stab of fear felt just before the onset of anger.

Step 4. Of what does this remind you? Recall as many situations as possible in which you responded similarly. What other authority figures, for instance, have elicited inappropriate anger from you? What did you feel toward them besides anger?

Step 5. Look for a pattern. Try to discover what hidden emotion was being covered with what apparent one. Once you are aware of such a replacement, you may intelligently deal with the situations that precipitate such inappropriate responses. Once you recognize a pattern, you are predictable to yourself and can look forward to an opportunity to face this problem again and handle it another way. [Schiffman, 1971, p. 18]

Another technique that may prove helpful in developing self-awareness is the Q-Sort Test. The Q-Sort technique consists of a series of cards that have descriptive statements or trait names that can be used to describe the self. Begin by making a list of ways of perceiving the self, such as responsible, lazy, kind, generous, cruel, and the like. Then sort these statements into several piles, running from the least to most like the way you perceive yourself. Follow this by again sorting the same topics into piles indicating how you would most like to be seen. In this manner, you may obtain a somewhat objective measure of the discrepancy between your self and your

self-ideal: how you perceive yourself and how you would like to be perceived. To support your findings, you might ask a friend or relative to sort the same statements, ranging from most to least characteristic of you. You can thus detect any discrepancy between your self-perception and the image that you project to others.

Rogers considers self-awareness to be a notable accomplishment that has many benefits as he points out in the following passage:

> With greater self-awareness, a more informed choice is possible, a choice more free from introjects, a *conscious* choice . . . such a person is more potentially aware, not only of the stimuli from outside, but of ideas and dreams, and of the ongoing flow of feelings, emotions, and physiological reactions that he or she senses from within . . . such a person is free to live a feeling subjectively, as well as be aware of it . . . The crucial point is there are no barriers, no inhibitions, which prevent the full experiencing of whatever is organismically present. This person is moving in the direction of wholeness, integration, a unified life. [Rogers, 1980, pp. 127–128][10]

Rogers would counsel people who wish to become more self-aware and function more fully to examine the constructs underlying their behavior so that they can become aware of why they are doing what they are doing. Knowing the constructs is only the first step, however, and in itself cannot lead to personality change. You must be willing to discard or change your constructs. You should adopt the attitude that nothing is so sacred that it cannot be scrutinized critically and that no behavior, aside from the inevitables in life, is beyond your ability to change. Living is a dynamic process; both the individual and his or her circumstances change. A fixed style of life can only produce rigidity and a disordered personality.

One caution regarding self-exploration is in order here, however. Like so many other good things, self-study can become self-preoccupation; introspection may degenerate into morbid self-absorption, which many experts hold to be the

---

[10] *A Way of Being.*

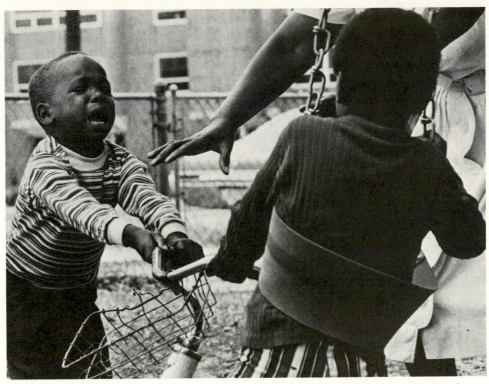

© 1976 Chester Higgins, Jr./Rapho, Photo Researchers, Inc.

Experiencing and expressing anger not only feels good, but is good.

most outstanding characteristic of a disordered personality. A neurotic, for instance, is overly concerned with himself or herself and is acutely aware of his or her own needs, emotions, and problems.

SELF-ACCEPTANCE, NOT SELF-EVALUATION

Just as Rogers stresses the value of accepting rather than evaluating others, so he insists that an acceptant attitude toward yourself is favorable to healthy personality growth and functioning. The popular view is that if you are to make steady improvements, you should be continually dissatisfied with yourself. An implication of this view is that self-acceptance engenders complacency and stagnation. But Rogers believes that self-acceptance is a condition for bringing about change in personality. The self-accepting person need not fear what he or she discovers about himself or herself and can be open to inner experiences without being overwhelmed by them. Accepting what he or she is essentially, he or she can face up to the things he or she dislikes about himself or herself. Not to be underestimated is the subjective feeling of tranquillity and inner harmony, which is in sharp contrast to the turmoil, anxious striving, and agitation characteristic of the person who strives furiously to be something greater than what he or she is. A further advantage of a basically self-accepting attitude is that it actually promotes acceptance of the individual by others.

THE HAZARDS OF EMOTIONAL EXPRESSION

Rogers has stressed openness and expressiveness in human relationships. He maintains that we should acknowledge our feelings and emotions rather than bury them. If we feel angry with a friend, this should be communicated, not as a criticism but as a statement of an impression or feeling that the friend has been unfair or unreasonable or whatever may be the case. Unacknowledged feelings are potentially dangerous. They may disrupt a friendship in subtle ways if they are not perceived and confronted. On the other hand, relating to others on an emotional level can be quite risky. In many instances, it might be better to inhibit feelings and assume instead a neutral posture.

Acute sensitivity to our feelings and emotions may endow them with a reality that they do not have: that is, emotions may be experienced more intensely by focusing on them. This condition may result in frequent fluctuations and mood changes. The person who experiences such changes makes a poor social partner and frequently a very poor working associate as well. Allport (1961) holds that the emotionally mature person does not "poison the air that others breathe" by expressing his or her bad moods freely. (See also Burns, 1980.)

On this issue we are, of course, dealing with a matter of degree. Total emotional inhibition and control are dangerous and unhealthy. But unrestrained and indiscriminate expression and overpreoccupation with emotions are also unhealthy. With some people we may be more open that with others; under certain conditions we may be more expressive than under others. It would be extremely unwise to be emotionally expressive in all situations and with all people.

Furthermore, as Jourard (1963) points out, being our "true" selves in relationships with others may produce highly inappropriate behavior. He believes that roles can serve as guides to aid us in emotional expression. We should take our various roles seriously and live them out fully. The roles that sons and daughters assume in relation to their parents are quite different from an intimate relationship with a member of the other sex. Many problems arise from inadequate role awareness and participation. Jourard holds that we are more ourselves with certain people and in certain situations than in others. Being oneself in every role would appear to be an impossibility, according to Jourard's view. The reader might ponder the difference between playing out roles well (Jourard) and being one's real self. (Rogers) Despite our dire warnings against extremes of morbid introspection and free emotional expression, Rogers' views on self-awareness, openness to experience, self-acceptance, and freedom can convert a dully normal life into an exciting adventure. They can enable us to become *fully functioning* rather than simply normal individuals.

SUMMARY

1. Rogers is associated with the phenomenological approach, which refers to the study of subjective experiences as the major determinants of behavior. The self-concept is the key internal source of behavior, according to this view. Psychological imbalance and many personality and behavior disorders result from incongruence between the concept of self and the actual self. Full congruence results from correspondence of the real self, the concept of self, and the communication of one's experiences to others.

2. Rogers holds that living organisms have an innate actualizing tendency that is expressed through a number of specific motives that have the common purpose of maintaining and enhancing the organism. In humans, when the self develops, it also has a tendency toward fulfillment of its potentials, the self-actualizing tendency. The organismic valuing process is a growth tendency by which experiences and courses of action are evaluated positively or negatively by their affective tone. The operation of the organismic valuing process may be hampered by conditions of worth, which refer to internalized standards of others that are made a part of one's own self-structure. The self-concept may become so incongruent with the actual attributes of the self that it does not reflect the person's nature, a situation that is highly detrimental to growth and healthy functioning. When the concept of self corresponds with the real attributes of self, a person then chooses what is best for self rather than what others prescribe.

3. A child is totally dependent on others for care. It has a need for positive regard, which is acceptance by others. The care and acceptance may be given unconditionally: unconditional positive regard, or it may be associated with conditions of worth, which refer to conditions that must be met to receive positive regard. The child introjects the conditions of worth in order to receive positive regard from others and itself. The process involves a distortion of the concept of self and interference with the organismic valuing process. This is the basis of incongruence between the concept of self and the real self. The distorted concept of self may set expectations that the real self cannot achieve. Distortion of external and internal information takes place in order to preserve the false self-concept.

4. In his client-centered therapy, Rogers stresses (a) unconditional positive regard (acceptance without setting conditions), (b) a relationship that promotes genuineness (authenticity on the part of the therapist), and (c) empathic listening (paying attention to the client cognitively and emotionally). A warm, accepting, nonjudgmental relationship is an essential ingredient in the therapy, which allows the client to explore the concept of self and the actual self. Both positive and negative emotions are experienced, and, typically, we come away with more positive feelings about self. The person becomes more in touch with internal as well as external impressions. New dimensions of the self are incorporated into the self-concept, so that it matches more nearly the true self.

5. Authority figures frequently criticize and punish to force or encourage prescribed behavior, but they may succeed in producing negative self-feelings and a distorted conception of self. Introjections limit the self-concept and block potentials. Establishing congruence by forming a correct self-image releases one's potentials. Disapproval of behavior should be clearly differentiated from disapproval of the person.

6. For Rogers the self is the most important source of behavior; thus, distortions of the self-concept cause abnormal behavior. Abnormality may take the form of feeling artificial, of feeling unreal, of not knowing oneself, of being like an empty shell. Other abnormalities related to the self include feeling inferior, unlovable, and evil; being artificial and phony; putting on a false front; meeting the standards of others to be acceptable; and adhering to musts and shoulds prescribed by others. Instead of dealing with such abnormalities directly, Rogers found that helping the person discover and be his or her true self was the most effective remedy. Rogers promoted such ideas as expanded consciousness, emotional freedom, and the enjoyment of a rich inner life.

7. Rogers believed that the most serious disturbance he found in his clients was disorders of emotion. The person suffering from incongruence loses contact with his or her true feelings and emotions. A protective system of defenses is formed to preserve the distorted concept of self. Occasionally, the defenses are not sufficient, with the consequence that the true feelings are experienced. The person then either intensifies the defenses or suffers a psychological breakdown. The most desirable alternative is to change the distorted self-concept so that the person becomes aware of the real self and then can take steps to make necessary changes.

8. The therapist is a growth facilitator who removes conditions that hamper growth and fosters those that support growth. The whole point of therapy is to help the person discover and express the real self.

9. Being a fully functioning person is Rogers' ideal. Helping a person to get behind the mask is one way to accomplish this state. We need not reject roles on the one hand nor reject self on the other. The fully functioning person has some of the following attributes: an internal locus of evaluation, being autonomous in formulating one's own style of life, and being capable of process living. Another characteristic is existential living, by which Rogers means accentuating the present and letting experiences reveal their meaning rather than imposing meaning on them. We should also make use of the organismic valuing process for making judgments. When a person is fully functioning, he or she is giving expression to much more of what his or her potentials are. Both the sense of freedom and actual freedom are increased. Greater spontaneity and creativity are also attributes of the fully functioning person. According to Rogers, the good life may be described by such attributes as enriching, challenging, rewarding, meaningful, and exciting.

10. Rogers made a significant contribu-

tion to the study of the processes that take place in successful and unsuccessful therapy by introducing recordings of therapy sessions. Responses of both the therapist and the clients were categorized and evaluated. Perceived genuineness, empathy, and unconditional regard have been found to be necessary for effective therapy. Although Rogers has had a major role in influencing the phenomenological approach and self-psychology, he has been criticized for being naive about the unfolding of a benign self. Much research has been generated by his views and therapeutic procedures.

GLOSSARY

Client-centered therapy: Rogers' approach to therapy, which attempts to promote growth by means of a relationship characterized by empathy, genuineness and unconditional positive regard.

    Reflection: An active form of listening in which thoughts and feelings of another are acknowledged.

Growth potential: Maturational unfolding of the genetic blueprint; inborn tendencies to fulfill species and individual nature.

    Actualizing tendency: Innate organismic growth tendency; the life force that underlies the growth and maintenance of the organism.

    Self-actualizing tendency: A subsidiary of the actualizing tendency that is inherent to the self; the innate tendency within the self that enhances and promotes its growth and expression.

    Organismic valuing process: The innate capacity to choose a course of action by means of negative or positive affective quality; a subsidiary of the actualizing tendency; it is hampered by conditions of worth.

Phenomenological view: The position that holds that the major causes of behavior are subjective.

    Phenomenal field: The contemporary subjective field.

Regard: Concern, acceptance, interest and approval.

    Conditional positive regard: Demonstration of interest and acceptance based on meeting conditions of worth; common in relationships, such as parent and child and teacher and student; fosters incongruence.

    Unconditional positive regard: Unqualified acceptance of another; concern for another without imposing conditions of worth; one of the three attributes of a successful therapist.

    Conditions of worth: The requirements that are imposed for receiving positive regard; promotes interjected values; hampers the operation of the organismic valuing process.

    Introjection: Internalizing values and standards of others and making them part of your self-concept, the major cause of incongruence.

Self: A major source of behavior; felt as the subject and object of action; the phenomenal self.

    Self-concept: The conscious experience of self; views, concepts or images of self.

    Ideal self: The aspired self; views, concepts or images of the self the person would like to be.

    Real self: The self as it is; the true characteristics of the self.

Incongruence: A discrepancy between one's views of self and the real self; the major form of abnormality for Rogers.

Congruence: Correspondence between the concept of self and the real self; a state in which growth potentials are functioning optimally.

Symbolized and unsymbolized experience: Symbolized refers to experiences that are named or that are cognitively represented by means of concepts or images; unsymbolized refers to unconscious material (similar to Freud's meaning of the unconscious).

Anxiety: A state of tension caused by experiences that the person senses to be inconsistent with the self-concept.

Defense: A process of counteracting threats to the concept of self, which involves distortion or denial of experience.

Openness to experience: The quality of the fully functioning person in which experiences are permitted access to the self without distortion.

SUGGESTED READINGS

Rogers, Carl R. *Counseling and Psychotherapy*. Boston: Houghton Mifflin, 1942.

In this book, Rogers introduces his nondirective therapy, contrasting this with other approaches to therapy. Ultimately his concern for the client led him to change the name to client-centered therapy.

——— *Client-Centered Therapy*. Boston: Houghton Mifflin, 1951.

Here Rogers deals with the nature of the therapeutic process and with related counseling problems. Procedures by which clients may be assisted in achieving new and more effective personality adjustments are discussed.

——— *On Becoming a Person*. Boston: Houghton Mifflin, 1961.

Rogers has gathered many of his manuscripts into this book, which represents his major areas of interest. The book is organized to portray a developing theme from the highly personal to topics of larger social significance.

——— *Freedom to Learn*. Columbus, Ohio: Merrill, 1969.

Rogers explores ways to make the classroom learning experience more meaningful to the student. Emphasis is placed upon the educator's role in creating the appropriate atmosphere for learning. Such an atmosphere has its roots in the client-centered approach to therapy.

——— *A Way of Being*. Boston: Houghton Mifflin, 1980.

The person-centered approach is described here as both an approach to therapy and to life. Rogers' latest thinking includes his views on growing older and on the ways our culture copes with change. This is the most all-encompassing view, to date, of Rogers' work.

CHAPTER 10

ABRAHAM MASLOW
MASLOW'S HEALTH AND GROWTH PSYCHOLOGY

CHAPTER 10

BIOGRAPHY AND HISTORICAL PERSPECTIVE

Araham Maslow was born in New York in 1908. He received his B.A., M.A., and Ph.D. from the University of Wisconsin, ending his formal education in 1934. After teaching at Wisconsin, Columbia, and Brooklyn College, he went to Brandeis University, where he became chairman of the Department of Psychology. Maslow received many awards and honors, including election to the presidency of the American Psychological Association in 1967. He died in 1970 at the age of sixty-two. Well-liked by his students and colleagues, he had a profound trust in the human capacity to work out a better world both for humanity as a whole and for each individual. He risked professional censure to pursue his convictions and was one of the pioneers of, and major contributors to, the

360

so-called *third force* in psychology. The *third force* represents a *humanistic approach* to personality science, in contrast to the other two systems, behaviorism and psychoanalysis.

Like Murray and Freud, Maslow places much stress on motivation, but he is especially concerned with the higher needs and motives (those that are distinctively human); thus we are including his views under the humanistic-existential model rather than the psychodynamic model.

In his educational and professional career, Maslow was exposed to the major currents in psychology. However, he came to the conclusion that the humanistic view of people was the most fruitful. His early training in psychology was in the structuralist tradition, which regarded the proper object of psychology to be a chemistry of conscious experiences. It sought to discover the elementary components of subjective experience. Maslow began to realize that this approach to psychology did not deal with the significant issues of human nature. He then turned to the strict behavioristic concepts and methods, which stressed the stimulus-response unit of behavior. But he soon found the behavioristic concentration on drive-related behavior inadequate to deal with the full range and complexity of human experience and behavior. He discovered that behaviorism was not adequate even in explaining the behavior of the higher animals.

Working with Harlow at the University of Wisconsin, Maslow saw firsthand the weaknesses of the drive-reduction hypothesis. He was impressed with the complexity of behavior of the primates they were studying. Chimpanzees would work for long periods solving a puzzle just out of curiosity and not for any form of drive-reduction. A monkey would learn a complicated instrumental behavior with the only reward being to look out into another room. Harlow was finding that baby monkeys reared in isolation without their natural mothers demonstrated an affectional need—a need for contact comfort with a motherlike object. Maslow's views on growth motivation as a natural aspect of healthy organisms were further shaped by his observations of pigs: The healthy pigs, as contrasted with weak or sickly ones, were interested in exploring their environments and demonstrated motivation of a different order from the physiological drives. (Harlow, 1953)

Maslow was also knowledgeable regarding psychoanalytic thinking and coauthored a text in abnormal psychology, relying heavily on psychodynamic theory. But, as with structuralism and behaviorism, he also found problems with Freudian psychology. He did not like the emphasis on the irrational, the animalistic, and the pathological in humans. He felt that Freud built his views of the normal person on the basis of people who were stunted in their growth and who were desperately struggling with life. Freud viewed humans as hampered by repressions and torn apart by conflict and discord—dominated by a primitive unconscious that kept the individual in a continual state of insecurity and turmoil. Maslow sought for a view of human nature that encompassed not only the animal in people but also the qualities that are distinctively human. He wished to learn what humans were like when they were at their best.

As a humanistic psychologist, Maslow (1955) questioned the traditional assumption that pain avoidance and tension reduction are the major sources of motivation for humans. He proposed instead that personality scientists examine human strivings for growth, for happiness, and for satisfaction. He viewed human motivation as made up

Peter Simon/Stock, Boston

Healthy animals display growth motivation in rudimentary form.

of different levels, his construct of the need hierarchy that varies in degree of potency. He distinguished between *deficit needs* and *growth needs* or *metaneeds*. Deficit needs include physiological needs, safety needs, love and belonging needs, and esteem needs. The growth needs are encompassed by the general term self-actualization. Maslow held that the higher needs (growth needs) are as much a part of the human makeup as the more rudimentary needs. By concentrating only on the lower needs, some personality psychologists have taken the one-sided view that people are selfish, evil, antisocial, and animalistic by nature. Maslow believed that there are degrees of humanness, with functioning on the higher need levels representing the high end of the humanness dimension.

BASIC CONSTRUCTS AND POSTULATES

Basic Issues in Human Motivation

In discussing human motivation in general, Maslow (1970) distinguished between a *need* and a *motive*, or *desire*. A need is a lack of something, a deficit state. By a motive he usually meant a conscious desire, a felt impulse or urge for a specific thing. You may have a hunger need and a motive or desire for a hamburger. The purpose of making this distinction is to point out the difference between basic ends and the specific means that are experienced. The individual may need food (an end) in a physiological sense, but experience hunger (a means) for a specific food. There are many more motives than there are needs. Two people may have the same need, for instance, for respect; one may attempt to achieve it by being an elder of his church, whereas the other may aspire to be the best salesperson in her company. As we shall see, motives may be distorted expressions of needs.

Need Suppression and Distortion

Maslow suggested that both the deficit (lower) needs and the growth (higher) needs are subject to distortion. Distortion of lower needs is strikingly evident in individuals suffering from psychophysiological disorders. A person may eat not to satisfy hunger but to relieve tension. Thus the basic hunger drive may be used as a channel or outlet for other motives, such as the desire for love, that have nothing to do with the need for food. This misuse of drives is harmful to the total economy of the organism, Maslow believed. (1970)

If the physiological drives can be severely distorted by faulty learning or misuse, the higher needs are much more readily disturbed and misdirected by harmful experience. The so-called virtues and noblest strivings of people—excellence, affectionate response, altruism, the creation of beauty, the discovery of truth, and the like—are not as powerful and fully structured as the typical physiological drives of hunger, thirst, sex, pain avoidance, and rest. Hence, they can be so modified and overridden by learning that they fail to function at all. In other words, people may learn to like things that are contrary to their best interests or to behave in a manner opposed to their growth needs. They may learn to be cold, unresponsive, and unaffectionate toward others even though they have within their nature the need to express and to receive affection.

The maintenance of the higher needs demands a great deal of support from cultural influences. Current institutions and prevailing views of human nature actually promote practices that suppress the highest needs of people, Maslow believed. If a child cries as a result of being hurt, his or her parents eagerly rush to help him or her, but if the child expresses his or her inner feelings of well-being in a free and natural man-

Elizabeth Hamlin/Stock, Boston

Need gratification fosters creativity.

ner, he or she may be rebuked or punished for behaving "childishly." The guiding assumption here is that the child needs to be controlled. A further implication of this assumption is that when the child is behaving naturally, he or she is behaving badly.

Many great thinkers have commented on the lack of socially oriented qualities in humans and on the prevalence, in fact, of the opposite qualities (hostility, selfishness, tendency to hurt others, jealousy, and envy). The prevailing Judeo-Christian view is that the individual is naturally selfish and even destructive of others, and socially oriented needs must be taught; they are not natural, but learned. Maslow held an opposing view, namely, that the tender emotions and socially oriented needs are native to people, but they are weak and not as complete in their structure as the basic drives. They need support, and one way to support them is to satisfy the basic needs and drives completely. If a person is not concerned about the requirements for existence, he or she can allow his or her more human impulses to surface. (Maslow, 1970)

The Survival Value of Needs

Humans do not inherit complete units of behavior (instincts) but only impulses or tensions in the presence of certain stimuli. The person must *learn* to find appropriate satisfiers and the means of securing them. The consequences of failing to satisfy certain (but not all) requirements are quite obvious: the person who does not obtain the proper nutrition suffers from some form of physical illness and may die. However, *some essential needs may go unheeded, and the consequences of not satisfying them may not be so obvious.*

Instinctive Versus Instinctoid Behavior

Maslow (1970) made a valuable distinction between a *total instinct* and an *instinctoid tendency*, or *instinct remnant*, which should aid in understanding the difference between lower needs and higher needs. A total instinct involves all the elements of a behavioral act: perception of relevant stimuli, appropriate coping behavior, and selection of goals so that behavior terminates when they are attained. For instance, a sparrow does not have to learn how to build a nest, nor must it learn to discriminate among suitable and useless objects for its goal. In fact, it does not even learn the goal for which its activity is so well coordinated. All these elements, plus whatever emotions are experienced — if any — are biological, genetic "givens." Instinctive behavior is behavior not acquired through learning.

People present a difficult problem from the standpoint of instinctive behavior. There are no full-blown instincts in humans. There are inborn reflexes and still more complex forms of behavior such as physiological drives. Even drives require for their satisfaction the learning of appropriate incentives and instrumental behaviors for obtaining these incentives. The child surely does not instinctively know what is good or harmful but must learn these things as a result of encounters with a variety of objects in the environment or must be told or shown. Figure 10–1 depicts the difference between a complete instinct and the instinctoid nature of the higher needs of humans.

Because of the apparent absence of inborn total instincts in humans, some psychologists have assumed that human behavior and experiences are entirely due to learning. Maslow, however, believed that although people may not have a complete instinct in their makeup, they do have instinct remnants, or instinctoid tendencies. A woman does not have a maternal instinct as do the lower animals in the sense that all the elements that are involved in bearing and caring for children are present without any learning, but she may certainly possess a strong impulse to tend and care for children. The point is that in the complex setting of civilized living this impulse or instinct remnant is not in itself sufficient to guide child-rearing behavior, but requires the sup-

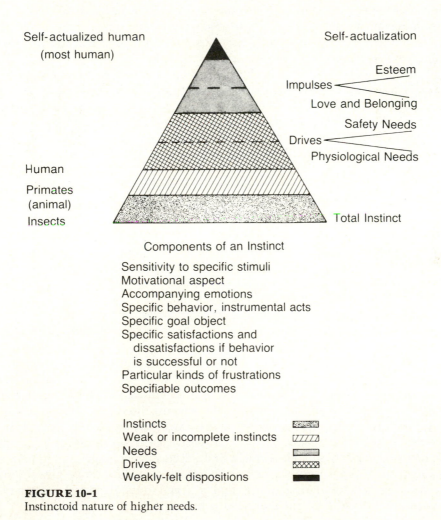

FIGURE 10–1
Instinctoid nature of higher needs.

port of correctly learned skills and attitudes and the formulation of a philosophy of child-rearing. (Caudill and Weinstein, 1969) Contrary to popular opinion, child-rearing is not a natural endowment of woman. If all such qualities were simply a matter of doing what comes naturally, there would be no personality disorders.

Humans should learn to follow their instinctoid remnants more honestly and freely. This is Maslow's essential resolution of the conflict between instinctive and learned behavior: all the agents of the culture should support the instinctoid tendencies.

Motivation Versus Metamotivation

Generally, Maslow (1971) meant by motivation desires associated with deficit states and by metamotivation desires associated with tendencies to seek certain growth ends, such as truth, goodness, beauty, and order. Metamotives do not involve reduction of tension; rather, they may increase tension when they are satisfied.

It has always been known that, but never well understood why, some people are apparently motivated by unselfish desires, such as being altruistic, helping others, striving for goodness, seeking truth — even if doing so means self-sacrifice. These metamotives have been variously described as spiritual, moral, transpersonal, the eternal verities. Maslow, after discovering that self-actualizing people experience them, named them metamotives because they go beyond ordinary motives, which are based on deficit states. (Maslow, 1971)

Motives are directed toward values that are end states. Maslow distinguished between *D-values*, which are the ends of deficit needs and motives, and *B-values*, which are the ends of metaneeds and motives. The attainment of D-values leads to tension reduction and the cessation of behavior. The attainment of B-values increases tension (positive growth-promoting tension) and stimulates further behavior. Freudians and many others have, of course, perceived such metamotives in people, but they have attempted to translate them or reduce them to more basic, selfish desires. B-values, for Maslow, promote one's being or existence as a human.

In his work with self-actualizing people, Maslow found that every one, without exception, seemed to have a mission or calling, something outside of himself or herself to live for. This was always the person's vocation or work — work not just for its own sake but because it fulfilled metaneeds (growth requirements). The work was a means of satisfying the person's metaneeds: the scientist, for instance, sought truth through research activities. His or her quest for truth was an ultimate value for him or her. It could not be reduced to any other motive; the scientist loved discovery, not for fame or power or wealth, but simply because he or she loved this pursuit. Other people might find order as a dominant value; they might derive great satisfaction from seeing a machine work properly. Still others might find the creation of beauty an ultimate end; they might work beyond normal retirement age because they derive pleasure from work. A mother's unselfish care for her child is an end in itself and cannot be reduced to a more basic, selfish need: she is expressing her very nature.

Hierarchy of Needs

Maslow introduces the important concept of hierarchy of needs. A hierarchy refers to an organizational structure with different degrees of potency. When one level of needs is sufficiently gratified, the next higher level becomes the focus of attention. The needs for growth are at the top of the hierarchy. The lower needs are deficits whereas the highest needs involve growth requirements. This distinction may be understood by keeping in mind the difference between the *need for* something versus the *need to do* something.

As we have seen, Maslow held that the lower needs are more potent and take priority over the higher ones. A hungry man does not concern himself with impressing his friends with his daring and skills, but rather with securing enough to eat. A man whose life is threatened by a murderer does not experience a threat to his sense of pride, but seeks to escape by whatever means are at his disposal. When lower needs are taken care of, then the next higher needs make their appearance in awareness, and the person is motivated to deal with their gratification. Only when all of the lower needs are at least partially gratified can the person begin to experience the self-actualizing needs. The lower needs are themselves arranged in a hierarchy; in order of potency and priority, they are the physiological needs, the safety needs, the belonging and love needs, and the esteem needs.

PHYSIOLOGICAL NEEDS

The most potent needs of all, and yet the least significant for the self-actualizing person, are the physiological needs (Maslow, 1970). When these needs are deprived for a relatively long period, all other needs recede or fail to appear. (Keys et al., 1950) Occasionally, one hears of instances that seem to contradict this view: a religious man who starves himself to death or a young woman who burns herself to death in moral protest. These are instances of higher needs that appear to function more powerfully than basic survival needs.

Maslow could have pointed out that some instances of "self-sacrifice" result from serious psychological disturbance. But it also appears to be a characteristic of the highest human needs that once a person has attained that unusual level of functioning, the consequences are so satisfying that lower needs are subordinated to higher ones, at least under temporary conditions. It would appear that prolonged deprivation of basic needs would eventually destroy the higher needs. This is not totally resolved, however.

SAFETY NEEDS

If the physiological needs do not constitute a serious problem for the person, then the safety needs become dominant forces in his or her personality. These include a variety of needs, all related to preserving the status quo—conserving and maintaining order and security. Examples of safety needs are the need for security, the need for stability, the need for order, the need for protection, and the need for dependency. Safety needs may be revealed by fears: fear of the unknown, of chaos, of ambiguity, and of confusion. The person may fear loss of control over his or her circumstances, becoming vulnerable and weak, or being unable to meet the new demands of life. Many people strongly desire structure, lawfulness, and direction from someone else. (Adorno et al., 1950)

Although many adults complain that they want to be more independent in their work to do things their own way, when they are actually given this freedom, they find it hard to accept. A large firm adopted the policy of giving new junior executives as much freedom as possible. The newly hired executives were told what their jobs were and to whom they were accountable and then were left pretty much on their own. There was no supervision or checking of minute-to-minute activities. It soon became apparent that something was wrong, because many of the employees were resigning within a period of three to six months. Their reason for quitting was not financial but a lack of structure — not having limits or standards by which to judge the adequacy of their work. Of course, the ones who left did not give these reasons, but rather found something wrong with the company practices. Some commonly given reasons were these: "They don't really take much interest in what you do around here"; or "You get the feeling that you are never doing enough"; or "No one gives any real help in this company; you are given enough rope to hang yourself."

There is a tendency to overvalue the safety needs if these are not adequately met. Most people seem unable to get beyond the safety level of functioning. (Maslow, 1970) They are security bound. This is reflected in the concern with building up large savings, overbuying of insurance, preferring a job with many fringe benefits. Uncertainty is not to be tolerated. Make the future as knowable as possible. The psychologically disturbed person may be so terrified of the unknown that he or she constructs rigid routines and standards for himself or herself and obsessively follows certain beliefs and compulsively carries them out. This is an extreme attempt to obtain a sense of security. Whereas the normal person may prefer familiar events and circumstances, he or she does not need the crutch of total control over his or her world.

LOVE AND BELONGING NEEDS

Maslow (1970) included under the category of love and belonging needs a variety of socially oriented needs such as desiring an intimate relationship with another person, being an accepted member of an organized group, needing a familiar environment such as family, living in a familiar neighborhood, and participating in group action in working for a common end with others. These needs depend for their occurrence upon a certain degree of satisfaction of the physiological and safety needs.

The crowded living conditions of contemporary life seem to block the expression of love and belonging needs. Although people live close together in apartments and houses, they do not interact. Except in small rural communities, there is an unwritten taboo against getting too close to the neighbors. People hardly know the name of the people next door, let alone socialize with them. Many people reveal that they feel alone and isolated, lonely though there are people all around them. (Riesman, 1952)

The love needs are particularly evident during adolescence and young adulthood. (Friedenberg, 1959) They vary from strong desires to have a "buddy" relationship with a member of the same sex to being an accepted member of a closely knit gang to the intimate, all-consuming passions of a romantic relationship with a member of the opposite sex. The concern with these needs is embodied in the lyrics of popular songs. A great percentage of these songs express in one way or another the powerful hold that love needs have and the hurt and fear produced by their frustration.

ESTEEM NEEDS

Just as we have needs associated with our organic makeup, so also we have needs associated with our psychological makeup. Esteem needs are examples of needs that derive from the self. The esteem needs (Maslow, 1970) may be subdivided into two classes: (1) those relating to self-esteem, self-respect, self-regard, and self-valuation; and (2) those relating to respect from others: reputation, status, social success, fame, glory, and the like.

   The concern with self-esteem, particularly regarding our own evaluation of ourselves, usually occurs in individuals who may be described as "comfortably situated." They are quite secure in the satisfaction of the lower needs. A carpenter who has established a sound reputation and does not have to worry about getting work may become quite discriminating about what type of work he or she accepts. The carpenter may accept only those jobs that can challenge his or her skills rather than taking on routine work merely for the sake of earning money. The quality of his or her work is a matter of some concern to the carpenter; thus, it fulfills a need for self-respect, a need to feel good about himself or herself. The satisfaction of this need has an internal locus. The carpenter's reasoning, although not explicitly expressed, may be as follows: "I am a competent judge of good carpentry, and this is certainly good work; of course, it is my work." Feelings of achievement, of competence, of meeting high standards of excellence in performance are not the concerns of the struggling beginner but the "extra touches" of the comfortable artisan. (Gelfand, 1962)

   Prior to attaining a level of prideful involvement in our activities, we seek the respect and assurance of others that we are worthwhile. Coopersmith (1967) has noted that failure to gratify the need for respect, reputation, or adulation from others can produce widespread personality disturbance. The most frequent form of disturbance is a sense of inferiority, of being different from others, of being a misfit. The person experiences a sense either of guilt or of shame.

SELF-ACTUALIZATION NEEDS

The self-actualizing needs are most difficult to describe because they are so highly unique and vary from individual to individual. In general, self-actualization means fulfilling our individual nature in all its aspects, being what we can be. (Maslow, 1970) The person who is talented in music must make music and experiences tension if he or she does not. The carpenter who is retired itches to take up his or her tools and put them to use again. The man who enjoys nature wishes to spend much of his time in the wild. The motherly person is at her best when caring for someone, giving a party, ministering to someone who is sick. Not only is the type of activity the person desires to perform important as a means of meeting the end of self-actualization, so also is the manner of performing the activity. Artists have their own identifiable style and their particular manner of working, also identifiable by those who know them.

An essential aspect of self-actualization is freedom — freedom from cultural and self-imposed restraints. Self-actualizing people want to be, and must be, free. (Grossack, Armstrong, and Lussieu, 1966) They want to be free to be themselves. Generally, self-actualizing people are not revolutionaries, radicals, anarchists, or against their culture; they do not adopt any extreme movement, nor do they overidentify with their culture. They perform their cultural requirements out of a sense of duty, but when such practices seriously interfere with self-actualization, they easily and freely react against them. In the section on Views on Ideal Personality and Living we will elaborate on the topic of self-actualization in greater detail.

Self-actualization is possible if the more basic needs are met to the degree that they neither distract nor consume all available energies. When people are comfortable with their lower basic needs, they can more adequately experience and act upon their higher needs. Accepting this frame of reference, we can see that in order for a person to become self-actualizing, many preconditions must be satisfied.

Table 10–1 presents Maslow's need hierarchy.

TRANSCENDENCE NEEDS

We have noted that Maslow was interested in the highest potentials of humans and identified the most distinctively human needs. For many years he held that self-actualization needs were most expressive of our individual nature and promoted growth for the individual and ultimately for humanity. His argument was that as we attain our highest potentials, even though they are related to self-fulfillment, we make a contribution to the community, to a career, to family, and other significant aspects of living. He came to see that self-actualization is not the ultimate level of motivation. There is in some people a *need for transcendence*, which refers to a *sense of community*, the need to contribute to humanity. An example is the medical doctor who perceives that research is needed in a particular field and, for the sake of filling a communal need, gives up a promising office practice. A person may join the peace corps or some other service organization to meet a need of society rather than pursue a career that might be more personally rewarding. Maslow did not elaborate much on this need for transcendence, however.

The Needs to Know and Understand

Although Maslow did not assign the so-called cognitive needs a specific place in the need hierarchy, he definitely affirmed their status in man and even in animals. (Maslow, 1970) The desires to know and understand are real motives that arise from basic needs. The normal human being cannot be passive about his or her world and does not take things for granted but wants to know the causes. From the research scientist to the "nosy" neighbor, we can see the powerful operation of the need to know. We do

TABLE 10-1 MASLOW'S NEED HIERARCHY

6. *Transcendence Needs*
Needs associated with sense of community
Need to contribute to mankind
Needs associated with a sense of obligation to others based on one's gifts (noblesse oblige)

   5. *Self-Actualization Needs*
   Need to fulfill one's personal capacities
   Need to develop one's potential
   Need to do what one is best suited to do
   Need to grow and expand metaneeds: disover truth
                                  create beauty
                                  produce order
                                  promote justice

      4. *Esteem Needs*
      Need for respect
      Need for confidence based on good opinions of others
      Need for admiration
      Need for self-confidence
      Need for self-worth
      Need for self-acceptance

         3. *Love and Belonging Needs*
         Need for friends
         Need for companions
         Need for a family
         Need for identification with a group
         Need for intimacy with a member of the opposite sex

            2. *Safety Needs*
            Need for security
            Need for protection
            Need for freedom from danger
            Need for order
            Need for predictable future

               1. *Physiological Needs*
               Need for relief from thirst, hunger
               Need for sleep
               Need for sex
               Need for relief from pain, pshysiological imbalances

Note: The "actualization needs" imply activity whereas the lower needs imply the fulfillment of a deficit ("need to" versus "need for"). In his later writings Maslow has attempted to be more specific about the qualities of self-actualization. He found self-actualizing people (1) capable of satisfying lower needs comfortably, (2) lacking obvious personality and behavioral symptoms, (3) capable of using abilities efficiently, and (4) possessing a value orientation to life.

not have to learn to know, according to Maslow, because cognition has its own needs and motives.

Satisfaction of the cognitive needs leads to the same consequences as satisfaction of the more usual needs, and likewise frustration of these needs is followed by disturbances in personality growth and functioning. Some disorders that occur as a result of cognitive frustration are a lowered zest for living, uninvolvement, and lack of curiosity. The marvelous and miraculous events pass by unnoticed. Like a child who has everything, the person may simply take what he or she has for granted and not value anything very much. Another common manifestation of cognitive distortion is the centering of concern inward, within the self. The self-centered person is not only denied a source of great pleasure from satisfying cognitive needs but also suffers harmful consequences as a result of lack of a concern with a vital aspect of his or her life.

The Aesthetic Needs

Although little is known about the operation of the aesthetic needs (Maslow, 1970), their part in human life is quite significant, especially in the lives of specific individuals. Some people find disorder, chaos, and ugliness quite intolerable. They crave the opposites of these qualities. The aesthetic needs include the needs for order, symmetry, and closure (the desire to fill in gaps in situations that are poorly structured), the need to relieve the tension produced by an uncompleted task, and the need to structure events (classify and systematize knowledge). Whereas beautiful surroundings, good music, and charming people can be exhilirating, ugly surroundings, unpleasant circumstances, and nasty people can cause illness.

VIEWS ON ABNORMALITY

Maslow presents a capsule summary of his views on human nature and the manner in which growth may be frustrated in the following statements:

> Now let me try to present briefly and at first dogmatically the essence of this newly developing conception of the psychiatrically healthy man. First of all and most important of all is the strong belief that man has an essential nature of his own, some skeleton of psychological structure that may be treated and discussed analogously with his physical structure, that he has needs, capacities and tendencies that are genetically based, some of which are characteristic of the whole human species, cutting across all cultural lines, and some of which are unique to the individual. These needs are on their face good or neutral rather than evil. Second, there is involved the conception that full, healthy, and normal and desirable development consists in actualizing this nature, in fulfilling these potentialities, and in developing into maturity along the lines that this hidden, covert, dimly seen essential nature dictates, growing from within rather than being shaped from without. Third, it is now seen clearly that psychopathology in general results from the denial or the frustration or the twisting of man's essential nature. By this conception what is good? Anything that conduces to this desirable development in the direction of actualization of the inner nature of man. What is bad or abnormal? Anything that disturbs or frustrates or twists the course of self-actualization. What is psychotherapy, or for that matter any therapy of any kind?

Any means of any kind that helps to restore the person to the path of self-actualization and of development along the lines that his inner nature dictates. [1954, pp. 340–341]

This inner nature is not strong and overpowering and unmistakable like the instincts of animals. It is weak and delicate and subtle and easily overcome by habit, cultural pressure, and wrong attitudes toward it. Even though weak, it rarely disappears in the normal person—perhaps not even in the sick person. Even though denied, it persists underground forever pressing for actualization. [1968c, p. 4][1]

Deprivation of Physiological Needs

Our physiological needs are, of course, essential to life, and long-continued frustration may produce serious and irreparable illness. Protracted hunger, thirst, and deprivation of other physiological needs can create strong tensions and can totally occupy the foreground of attention. Although we are often unclear about our higher needs, we are usually quite aware of the tensions of the lower needs. As powerful as they are, they are nevertheless capable of being distorted. We may eat for pleasure rather than for sustenance. We may drink to produce a pleasant state of mind rather than for quenching thirst. The satisfaction of physiological needs may be equated with happiness; thus, many people become unduly preoccupied with them. But overeating is harmful to health, and excessive drinking of alcoholic beverages can produce serious physical and personality problems. Free sex, too, is not without its problems—unwanted pregnancies, venereal diseases, and perhaps a guilty conscience. Being tied to basic drive satisfaction is hardly the model life for Maslow, who so strongly believed that the higher needs are far more important for happiness than are the lower needs. Maslow, however, did not pit higher against lower needs. He argued that we should put the lower needs in their place and move up to the higher needs.

Deprivation of Safety Needs

The question of security is particularly relevant for children. Not having a great deal of control over his or her surroundings, the child is frequently the victim of fear-producing situations. Maslow believed that children should be brought up in an environment that is somewhat protective and structured. They should be shielded from hurtful experiences until they have learned sufficient skills to cope with stress. The feelings of insecurity in childhood can be carried over into adulthood. Imposing a structured environment helps to promote security and healthy growth. Children seem to prefer being given direction because, after all, they cannot provide it for themselves. Permissiveness may place too much of a burden upon a child. If given too much freedom, he or she does not know what to do with it and may use it to get into terrifying situations. Freedom and self-control should be given only in amounts that the child can bear. A warm, accepting, yet structured atmosphere is the best climate for child-rearing.

---

[1]*Toward a Psychology of Being*, 2d ed; by Abraham Maslow. Copyright 1968. Reprinted by permission of Brooks/Cole Publishing Company.

Deprivation of Love Needs

The strength of the love needs is so great that, for many, thwarting of these needs is the major source of psychological disturbance. The nature of the disturbance depends upon the period of life when the need is frustrated. The elderly person may feel alone and cut off from the world. He or she may have lost most of his sources of human contact through death or the moving away of friends and family. This need for human contact is expressed in the increasing tendency among elderly people to form their own groups, golden-age organizations and the like.

At the other extreme, the infant who does not receive human love in a direct physical manner suffers from developmental retardation that is manifested in a variety of forms: physical, psychological, and social. (Bowlby, 1952) Although infants may have the best physical care, they will not develop properly unless they are also given *tender loving care* by a motherly person. Whether the physical care is a matter of satisfying the infant's safety needs (children are particularly troubled by safety needs) or whether the desire for human contact is a rudimentary expression of the love and belonging needs is not altogether clear. Probably both needs are involved. Unlike the adult, who needs both to give love and to receive it, the child seems to want more to be loved than to love.

One of the differences among humans that has preoccupied philosophers and psychologists is the wide range in the development of the peculiarly human qualities of empathy, sympathy, identification, guilt, shame, embarrassment, and similar states which seem to involve the operation of conscience and the self. (for example, Hoffman, 1970) There are people who demonstrate by their behavior that they do not experience such emotional and motivational states. They range from the bizarre psychopathic rapist and murderer to the unscrupulous businessperson, professional shyster, or politician who cheats clients through legal loopholes. What causes one person to be thoughtful, considerate, and nonaggressive and another to be just the opposite? Are some people by nature antisocial, and do they still bear the imprint of their animalistic origins, as many great philosophers and psychologists have held? Maslow believed that the answer might be a simple deprivation of appropriate human love during the time when it is essential for the healthy development and growth of a child—during the first eighteen months of life. Harlow and Griffin (1965) have demonstrated that even monkeys need mothering or "contact comfort" and that when they are deprived of this, they develop abnormally. Furthermore, the longer the deprivation and the earlier it occurs, the more enduring and damaging are its effects. Common sense tells us that babies also need mothering and that, when deprived of it, they develop badly.

An absence of love during the earliest months may permanently hamper the need and expression of love in the growing child. When they reach adulthood, such people may be blocked from fulfilling their fullest potentialities as human beings; they continue to bear the marks of their early childhood neglect. Not having received love, they can neither respond to it nor express it themselves. The result may be a severe distortion in development of conscience, culminating in lack of social and ethical values; the total behavior is adversely affected.

The person who does not have affectionate relationships with others will not die or suffer from malnutrition. The consequences of this lack of satisfaction of a basic human need are much more subtle and not easily detected. One may experience unexplainable restlessness, general tension, and free-floating anxiety as a reaction to lack of love. Though survival is possible without such need gratification, the fullness of development and functioning may be severly hampered.

Deprivation of Esteem Needs

Low self-esteem means lack of self-worth — positive self-feelings. In the fierce competition of our society, we are often left to wonder about our status. Frustration and failures of basic needs make us feel inadequate and worthless. The complaint that "I am not really good at anything" is quite common. A profound sense of inferiority is found at the root of many personality disorders. Children are often made to feel small and insignificant in comparison with adults but many adults never outgrow these feelings. They see almost everyone as being superior. Some forms of depression can be traced to a sense of low-esteem. A person who carries a lot of shame and guilt feelings is also the victim of low self-esteem. How many people really feel loved enough by the ones they care about?

Deprivation of Growth Needs

As we have noted, Maslow was especially concerned about the types of illness that resulted from frustration of the higher needs. These disorders are widespread in modern civilizations because of the rapidity of life, the loss of rootedness, and the lack of enduring social contacts among people. Many of the disorders that the existentialists have identified are, in Maslow's need schema, the product of higher need frustration. Many people, for example, complain of lack of meaning in life. Nothing seems to make sense. Others find that they are not really interested in anything and that nothing really counts or matters for them. Many complain of marking time, of routine living, of emptiness. Some people simply say that they are bored. Even with the easy availability of many luxuries, life has become quite drab and empty for many. Maslow believed that such conditions are caused by overpreoccupation with material possessions, with gratification of appetites, with status seeking, and with the other lower needs. Nothing is wrong with having the lower needs taken care of. In fact, these are essential for getting to the higher levels, the most subtle of needs. Gratification of all needs — dynamic, cognitive, or aesthetic — is essential for the good life.

Deprivation of Needs as Pathology

In Table 10–2, the standard personality abnormalities are categorized and interpreted as frustrations of deficit needs. However, Maslow held that what some psychologists consider normal behavior may also be forms of personality disorders. He termed these

TABLE 10-2 PERSONALITY DISORDERS AND HEALTH ACCORDING TO DEFICIT AND GROWTH NEEDS

Deficit Needs		Growth Needs	
Pathology	*Normalcy*	*Metapathology*	*Actualization*
Psychosis:	Well-adjusted	Bored	Creative
Schizophrenia	Social	Unauthentic	Spontaneous
Paranoid reactions	Emotionally stable	Shallow	"Selfish"*
Manic-depressive	Realistic self-concept	Alienated	Insatiably curious
Involutional reactions	Positive self-image	Meaningless	Realization of potentials
Personality Disorders:	Respectful of others	Limited horizons	Functioning on level of B-values
Paranoid	Content	Living uncreatively	Peak experiences
Cyclothymic			Brotherly attitude
Schizoid			Dedication to a vocation
Explosive			
Obsessive-compulsive			
Antisocial			
Inadequate			
Passive-agressive			
Neurosis:			
Anxiety			
Hysteria			
Phobia			
Obsessive-compulsive			
Depression			
Neurasthenia			
Depersonalization			
Hypochondriasis			

Note. These descriptions are not intended as an exhaustive list of pathologies, but rather as an illustration of the role of deficit and growth needs in personality disorders and health. Within the same individual, various levels of pathology may exist depending upon the types of needs that are deprived. It should also be noted that metapathologies are only found in people who are regarded as normal, but are considered abnormal by Maslow because they fall short of self-actualization.

*Self-loving or self-respecting.

disorders metapathologies because they involve the frustration of growth and meta-needs. Deprivation of a need produces some form of illness. The deprivation of the deficit needs may be directly experienced: for instance, one is usually definitely aware of intense hunger or loneliness. Deprivation of the growth or metaneeds is not as clearly felt, but the consequences may be just as evident. A person may feel uneasy and not realize that his or her unpleasant circumstances are producing the disturbance. To use an organic analogy, the absence of Vitamin C produces a serious disorder known as scurvy. The symptoms of the disorder are present, whether or not the person is aware of the cause. As a matter of fact, people do not experience a need for vitamin C directly.

Some disorders occur as a result of need deprivation, and the person experiences need tensions; however some disorders, such as the metapathologies, occur without the needs even being experienced. Yet whether or not the individual experiences the meta-needs does not change the fact that their frustration hinders growth and functioning. We will now consider metapathologies in some detail. Maslow had some interesting ideas on this subject that should open up new vistas for clinicians.

METAPATHOLOGIES

Metapathologies are illnesses resulting from frustration or deprivation of higher needs (Maslow, 1971). They have been the concern of the clergy, dramatists, novelists, poets, and biographers. Parents and teachers have had to cope with them without fully under-standing their nature and origins. One common form of metapathology is a stunting of development. The resulting disorders include the immature, the inadequate, and the infantile personality types, and other character disorders. The person may lack social feeling or may not develop a sufficient conscience to maintain control of impulses or

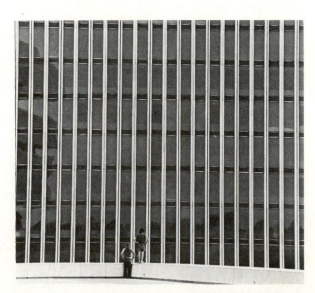

Dehumanizing conditions of modern life block higher need gratification.

Fredrick D. Bodin/Stock, Boston

may fail to develop values such as generosity, considerateness, or respect for the good opinion of others.

Maslow believed that many clinicians have ignored pertinent cognitive disturbances as well. He was referring to disturbances in curiosity. Some people view passively, without any interest, everything that goes on around them. All the mysteries about them are simply ignored or taken for granted. Even when they are exposed to new ideas or facts, they may simply be indifferent to them. There is no question that cognitive stunting or disturbance is at the root of many of the traditional illness categories. Paranoid thinking is ultimately a cognitive disorder: the person fails to interpret an event correctly either as a result of omission of details pertinent to the situation or through the addition of material that is not a part of the picture.

Other examples of metapathology are being unable to love anyone deeply, not really enjoying anything, not being able to see the value of personal accomplishment, perceiving nothing as virtuous, and behaving immorally. The existentialists have dealt with these pathologies: although they have not named them metapathologies, they have referred to existential depression, meaninglessness, alienation, directionlessness, search for meaning. Such disorders, which are manifestations of metaneed frustration and deprivation (Kierkegaard, 1954), are often not obvious either to the practitioner or to the person who suffers from them. A person may perceive that something is wrong with his or her life, but not know what. These ideas can alter the whole field of mental health when they are better understood, Maslow believed.

The Average Is Abnormal

In his study of peak experiences, Maslow came to the conclusion that healthy people are on a totally different level of motivation. He believed that most people are the victims of a host of symptoms of illness and that even some of those who set themselves up as experts in the art of living are not aware of the full extent of the human potential (1968c). Because mild pathologies are so common, they overlook human possibilities and accept as normal (or even healthy) standards that are far less desirable than the highest abilities of humans. They might say that everyone is depressed some of the time, that everyone needs an outlet for frustrations in the form of drinking, drugs, sex, or whatever. These experts on mental health gear their ideas to standards that apply to the prevailing, the average, the modal because they have not studied the most highly evolved, healthy, mature human beings. "You can be better than you are" means that you can suffer less from mental strife, not that you can live on a higher psychobiological plane. Self-actualizers are foreign to the average person; their motivations and cognitions are on a B-level, a level that most people experience only fleetingly or not at all. Maslow introduces a new term, *Being-psychology*, to embody his ideas on healthy functioning:

> I call it Being-psychology because it concerns itself with ends rather than with means, i.e., end-experiences, end-values, end-cognitions, with people as ends. Contemporary psychology has mostly studied not-having rather than having, striving rather than fulfillment,

frustration rather than gratification, seeking for joy rather than having attained joy, trying to get there rather than being there. [1968c, p 73][2]

Absence of Psychological Symptoms When They Should Be Present

The absence of psychological symptoms, when we should have them, is unhealthy. Our symptoms tell us that all is not well. Denying or suppressing symptoms frustrates the normal response of the organism to abnormal conditions. Personality problems, apparent or not, may be "loud protests against the crushing of one's psychological bones" (Maslow, 1970). Many symptoms should not be denied and are to be interpreted not as personal failings and weaknesses, but rather as the result of an unfavorable life situation: unreasonable parents, stressful school requirements, forced dependence, unnatural surroundings.

Maslow held that environmental circumstances may either promote or retard self-actualization. As he viewed current cultural practices and institutions, he found them based on a distorted model of human nature. (Maslow, 1968a)

VIEWS ON IDEAL PERSONALITY AND LIVING

Maslow looked for self-actualizing people among students, but found few that were. Students have needs and goals which cannot be met satisfactorily while still in college. As they move into better positions to meet these needs and attain their goals, they will begin to look at life differently. As basic needs are gratified, other needs will take their place. According to Maslow's need hierarchy theory, the process of self-actualization can occur only when the basic lower needs (physiological, safety, love and belonging, and esteem needs) are met, and many of these are frustrated in young persons. For instance, they are forced into a dependent role; they must postpone some of their deepest desires, and postponement means frustration.

Then there is the lack of knowledge about many things. They do not yet know clearly what to expect from themselves, from their parents, from work, from recreation. Their lives may be filled with confusion and conflict. They are lacking in certain basic learning experiences; as they expand their outreach and take over their own lives, they will learn to know more about themselves, to know about the harsher side of living, to take responsibility for their own actions. All this takes place after college days. Settling on a vocation, getting married, the birth of the first child are experiences that lie ahead. These and many other experiences will have profound effects on their total orientation to life. Maslow was led to make a distinction between healthy growth and self-actualization. A ten-year old might be growing in a healthy manner but a ten-year old could not be self-actualized.

First we will discuss some of the methods Maslow used to study the topic. Then we will take up the traits that he found characteristic of his healthy subjects. Some of

---

[2]*Toward a Psychology of Being*, 2d ed, by Abraham Maslow. Copyright 1968. Reprinted by permission of Brooks/Cole Publishing Company.

the ideas will be foreign to you and may contradict some of your expectations and beliefs, but bear in mind that Maslow was studying the highest levels of humanness, the superstars in the art of living. He himself was surprised by a number of his findings, and he concluded that the total life orientation of self-actualizers is of an order different from that of the average person. His study of the healthiest people also led him to the conclusion that many changes should be made in our most cherished institutions — education, economics, child-rearing, work patterns, pay incentives — so that they may promote rather than hinder personality growth and functioning. Even morality and ethics — what constitutes good and bad conduct — should be based on the nature of people. A knowledge of the highest human potentialities can help us to arrive at the true definition of the nature of humans as a species. We can learn from the healthiest persons what may be possible for all of us, given the optimum conditions of growth.

Characteristic Traits of Self-Actualizing People

Maslow attempted to identify healthy human growth and functioning by studying people he knew personally, contemporary public figures, and historical personalities. Starting with a "folk" definition of self-actualization, he selected his subjects from a large sample. He then reexamined his definition in the light of his clinical studies and changed it accordingly. He made further clinical tests and observations and again modified his definition. The definition had both a positive and a negative aspect: on the negative side he eliminated subjects who showed evidence of neurosis, psychosis, and psychopathic disturbance; on the positive side he looked for signs of health and for self-actualization, which were at first intuitively defined because these are what he set out to identify. "It may be loosely described as the full use and exploitation of talents, capacities, potentialities, and other factors. Such people seem to be fulfilling themselves and to be doing the best that they are capable of doing, reminding us of Nietzsche's exhortation 'Become what thou art.' They are people who have developed, or are developing to the full stature of which they are capable." (1970, p. 150) Because of his subjects' resistance, he had to study them indirectly, even surreptitiously. He included such well-known public and historical figures as Albert Einstein, Franklin Roosevelt, Albert Schweitzer, and William James.

The reader should bear in mind that Maslow derived his descriptions of self-actualizers from interviews, biographies, autobiographies, and casual observations of behavior; they were not based on standardized tests or obtained from experimental situations. Thus, they should be considered only as global impressions and first approximations to the subject. Maslow himself regarded his work as a pioneer investigation that might point out certain major directions and possible pitfalls for further study.

Maslow (1970) formulated the following list of traits characteristic of self-actualizers:

1. More efficient perception of reality and more comfortable relationship with it. The unknown is readily accepted and indeed arouses the greatest curiosity.
2. Acceptance of self, others, and nature.

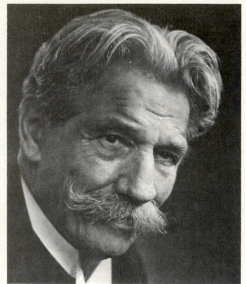

Become what thou art.

Photo credits: (Roosevelt) Acme Photo/Photo Researchers, Inc.; (Schweitzer) © Karsh, Ottawa/Woodfin Camp & Associates; (Einstein) © Karsh, Ottawa/Woodfin Camp & Associates

3. Spontaneity, simplicity, naturalness. Self-actualizers work out their own sets of values which truly influence their conduct. Their inner lives are highly individualistic.

4. Problem centering. Decisions leading to goal fulfillment are made unemotionally. Work is the expression of the most personal motive and is a source of identification to the self-actualized.

5. The quality of detachment, the need for privacy. Self-actualizers enjoy being alone and sorting out their thoughts and values.

6. Internal locus of decision making. Factors determining conduct come from within rather than from the external world. Self-actualizers are self-movers who view free will as an active process.

7. Autonomy. Self-actualizers are self-sufficient, being independent of environmental conditions.

8. Continued freshness of appreciation. Pleasures do not diminish with repetition; renewed joy from commonplace events often repeated.

9. Peak experiences. States of unusual well-being, characterized by loss of sense of time and self; being transfixed, awe-inspired, and in a state of wonderment.

10. *Gemeinschaftsgefuhl.* A sense of brotherhood. Healthy people identify with humans in general. Affection, understanding, and sympathy are given freely.

11. Interpersonal relations. Friendships are limited but strongly bound.

12. Democratic character structure. Self-actualizers accept all types of people.

13. Discrimination between means and ends, between good and evil. Self-actualizers are certain about their convictions and lack confusion, chaos, and conflicting beliefs. Means are easily interchanged while ends remain fixed.

14. Philosophical, unhostile sense of humor. Self-actualizers find humor in their own shortcomings and inconsistencies.

15. Creativeness. Self-actualizers are inventive, original, and spontaneous.

RESISTANCE TO ENCULTURATION, OR THE TRANSCENDENCE OF ANY PARTICULAR CULTURE

Are self-actualizing people well adjusted; are they likable, easy to understand? Do they fit the image of the "hail fellow well met," the hearty extrovert whom everyone loves? The answer to all these questions is "NO!" It seems that the healthiest humans are strong-willed, self-sufficient, independent of cultural norms. The stereotype of the socialized American does not fit them at all. In fact, they are considered strange, eccentric, and even antisocial by those who are incapable of appreciating them or who do not know them. There is an air of self-sufficiency about them that is offensive to some people.

Maslow (1970) believed that self-actualizers are less "flattened out," less molded, less dominated by the culture than average people. Every culture necessarily produces certain forms of pathology. Some individuals are fortunate enough to resist the harmful effects of their culture, and this seems to be the case with self-actualizers.

PERSONALITY INTEGRITY

Healthy people do not experience personality fragmentation, dissociations, splits within the personality, isolated elements functioning as separate "personalities." They do not have oppositions and conflicts within them—conflicts between basic urges and conscience, between self-seeking and ideals, between childlike impulses and adult behavior. Here is the way Maslow described the failure in personality integration:

> The normal adjustment of the average, common sense, well-adjusted man implies a continued successful rejection of much of the depths of human nature, both conative and cognitive. To adjust well to the world of reality means a splitting of the person. It means that the person turns his back on much in himself because it is dangerous. But it is now clear that by so doing, he loses a great deal too, for these depths are also the source of all his joys, his ability to play, to love, to laugh, and most important for us, to be creative. By protecting himself against the hell within himself, he also cuts himself off from the heaven within, flat, tight, frozen, controlled, cautious, who can't laugh or play or love, or be silly or trusting or childish. His imagination, his intuition, his softness, his emotionality tend to be strangulated or distorted. [1968c, p. 142][3]

TRANSCENDENCE OF DICHOTOMIES

Probably the one most outstanding quality of self-actualizing people is their transcendence or overcoming of dichotomies (Maslow, 1968b). In this context the term *dichotomy* indicates split or "oppositeness," the extremes of a dimension, such as work and play, being adult and being childlike, masculinity and femininity, being selfish and altruistic, self-seeking and generous, rational and emotional. The "transcendence of dichotomies" means that opposite qualities are integrated and expressed by the same behavior, not either/or, but both. Most people are at either one end or the other of these dimensions; they distinguish between what is work and what is recreation, between acting childishly and acting adultlike, between being rational and being irrational. The alternatives appear worlds apart. Precisely to the degree that oppositions and conflicting elements exist within the personality do we, according to Maslow, suspect and in fact find pathology. Integrated functioning is a sign of health. Consider the carpenter who enjoys working with wood: he does good work as a matter of pride; he is acting selfishly to the limit because he loves his work, but his work also provides pleasure and joy for others. By being as good a carpenter as he can, he is benefiting both himself and others, thus transcending the dichotomy between selfishness and altruism. For him, the difference between working and playing is not sharp because his work provides him a form of recreation. He thus also transcends the dichotomy between work and play.

Many traditional views of the good life have sharply separated the so-called "animalistic" or lower nature of humans from their higher nature. Interestingly, Maslow in effect did the same thing with his need hierarchy, but by *complementation* rather than *opposition*. He did not oppose "spirit" with "flesh," the higher with the lower. This is an important point in his theory of motivation: the higher needs build on, complement, and in fact transform the lower needs.

---

[3]*Toward a Psychology of Being*, 2d ed, by Abraham Maslow. Copyright 1968. Reprinted by permission of Brooks/Cole Publishing Company

In contrast to Freud, Maslow held that primitive primary processes can give breadth to living and engender creativity, spontaneity, and free expression. (Wild, 1965) He believed that suppression or denial of the so-called primitive forces diminishes the personality. Part of the personality is killed off if the superego is dominant, if the ego holds complete control, or if the id is untempered. The person who behaves rationally — and at the same time spontaneously and creatively — is living more effectively than the person suffering from a one-sided development. Conscience, impulse, and reasoning each play a part in promoting health. The balanced person allows all aspects of personality to be expressed, as Jung held. Maslow agreed with Jung (1964b), although he arrived at the same conclusion from a different perspective.

Some Basic Questions About Self-Actualizers

Maslow himself admitted that his findings fall far short of empirically derived principles. They are to be taken as tentative, as hypotheses to be tested. He pointed out in an article that the pioneer does not have the foundation of solid knowledge to conduct rigorous experimentation; he is ahead of the known; he is reaching out beyond the frontier of knowledge. (Maslow, 1969) At the present level of knowledge about self-actualizing people, it is impossible to determine how much is Maslow's own projections and constructions and how much represents "real" people. The answer probably lies somewhere between these extremes. One point in Maslow's favor is that his formulations do agree in part with those of others: with Rogers' on the fully functioning person and with those of theorists who have taken up the study of ideal human existence. At the present time, Maslow's hypotheses appear more thorough than the others, but ultimately the traits he has proposed must be subjected to empirical test — although the task is a formidable one — and then we will know how accurate he was.

With respect to the question of individual differences in traits, Maslow attempted to identify traits that were common to all his healthy subjects and also to identify traits found in some, but not all, of his subjects. By doing so, he recognized the uniqueness and variability of the people he studied, but he did not deal adequately with the topic. Furthermore, in many ways the traits are not irreducible; they presuppose one another. For example, he believed that we cannot have the attribute of freshness of appreciation without creativeness. Individuality still remains a problem because the traits Maslow abstracted are general attributes and, therefore, approximations to individuality. (Allport, 1961)

Subjectively, the healthy subjects do experience guilt, anxiety, sadness, self-criticism, internal strife, and conflict; but these psychic states are caused by nonneurotic conditions. We might list such things as discrepancies between what is and what should be, injustices, inequalities, lack of certain perfection in the self, struggling to work out a philosophy of life. It should be kept in mind that even healthy subjects live in a far from perfect environment; thus, some of their imperfections are undoubtedly the consequences of environmental conditions. As Horney (1937) pointed out, the culture may be "sick."

B-Values: Expressions of Metaneeds

Maslow discovered what he termed B-values in his study of "peak experiences." Peak experiences are states of being or experiencing that may be described as the highest human experiences. They are states of mind that are not means to anything else but are complete in themselves. They cannot be appreciated by anyone who has not experienced them, anymore than you can taste chocolate by description. Maslow found that his self-actualizing people reported having such experiences rather frequently. He at first thought that they were a defining characteristic of such people, but later (1968c) he found that even people falling far short of self-actualization have them, though much less frequently. He also found a few self-actualizers who did not have them. Such experiences may be described as "turning on," "being inspired," "being awed." They evoke wonderment, amazement, awe, joy, inspiration, fascination, exaltation, and captivation.

Need gratification is accompanied by emotion and pleasure. The type of pleasure or emotion that occurs varies with the level of need gratification. At the level of B-values there may be a lack of emotion or pleasure and instead a state of quiescence or tranquillity. Usually, however, there are distinct emotions and pleasures that do occur on the B-level of gratification. It should be remembered that we are dealing here with the highest reaches of human experiences and consciousness, and these have not been studied, although they have been reported by mystics, the religious, and even common folk for hundreds of years. The conditions leading to such experiences are not known. Maslow was the first experimentalist who attempted to illumine them. In the following passage he has given us a graphic description of the different emotions associated with his hierarchy of needs. It provides a neat summary of his theory of motivation:

> At the lowest basic need level we can certainly talk of being driven and of desperately craving, striving, or needing, when, e.g., cut off from oxygen or experiencing great pain. As we go on up the hierarchy of basic needs, words like desiring, wishing, or preferring, choosing, wanting, become more appropriate. But at the highest levels, i.e., of metamotivation, all these words become subjectively inadequate, and such words as yearning for, devoted to, aspiring to, loving, adoring, admiring, worshipping, being drawn to or fascinated by, describe the metamotivated feelings more accurately. [1968d, p. 61][4]

Table 10–3 summarizes the relation between personality functioning and the conditions of need gratification and deprivation. Note the differences in emotional states as one goes up the hierarchy.

Enumeration of B-Values

Maslow attempted specifically to identify the B-values by listing fourteen of them (Table 10–4). In considering these B-values, bear in mind that although they are presented in highly abstract form, in actual life situations they are quite concrete and

[4]"A Theory of Metamotivation: The Biological Rooting of the Value-Life." *Psychology Today*.

TABLE 10-3 NEED HIERARCHY AND LEVELS OF PERSONALITY FUNCTIONING

Need Hierarchy	Condition of Deficiency	Fulfillment	Illustration
1. Physiological	Hunger, thirst Sexual frustration Tension Fatigue Illness Lack of proper shelter	Relaxation Release from tension Experiences of pleasure from senses Physical well-being Comfort	Feeling satisfied after a good meal
2. Safety	Insecurity Yearning Sense of loss Fear Obsession Compulsion	Security Comfort Balance Poise Calm Tranquility	Being secure in a full-time job
3. Love	Self-consciousness Feeling of being unwanted Feeling of worthlessness Emptiness Loneliness Isolation Incompleteness	Free expression of emotions Sense of wholeness Sense of warmth Renewed sense of life and strength Sense of growing together	Experiencing total acceptance in a love relationship
4. Esteem	Feeling of incompetence Negativism Feeling of inferiority	Confidence Sense of mastery Positive self-regard Self-respect Self-extension	Receiving an award for an outstanding performance on some project
5. Self-Actualization	Alienation Metapathologies Absence of meaning in life Boredom Routine living Limited activities	Healthy curiosity Peak experiences B-values Realization of potentials Work which is pleasurable and embodies values Creative living	Experiencing a profound insight

TABLE 10-4 MASLOW'S LIST OF B-VALUES

Value	Characteristics
1. Wholeness	Unity, integration, tendency to oneness, interconnectedness, simplicity, organization, structure, dichotomy transcendence, order
2. Perfection	Necessity, just-rightness, just-so-ness, inevitability, suitability, justice, completeness, oughtness
3. Completion	Ending, finality, justice, "it's finished," fulfillment, destiny, fate
4. Justice	Fairness, orderliness, lawfulness, oughtness
5. Aliveness	Process, non-deadness, spontaneity, self-regulation, full functioning
6. Richness	Differentiation, complexity, intricacy
7. Simplicity	Honesty, nakedness, essentiality, abstract, skeletal structure
8. Beauty	Rightness, form, aliveness, simplicity, richness, wholeness, perfection, completion, uniqueness, honesty
9. Goodness	Rightness, desirability, oughtness, justice, benevolence, honesty
10. Uniqueness	Idiosyncrasy, individuality, noncomparability, novelty
11. Effortlessness	Ease; lack of strain, striving, or difficulty; grace, perfect functioning
12. Playfulness	Fun, joy, amusement, gaiety, humor, exuberance, effortlessness
13. Truth, honesty, reality	Nakedness, simplicity, richness, oughtness, pure and unadulterated beauty, completeness, essentiality
14. Self-sufficiency	Autonomy, independence, not-needing-other-than-itself-in-order-to-be-itself, self-determining, environment transcendence, separateness, living by its own laws

From *Toward a Psychology of Being* by Abraham Maslow. Copyright 1968. Reprinted by permission of Brooks/Cole Publishing Company.

specifiable. For instance, the person who derives joy or pleasure from the "wholeness" value may be the business executive who delights in the integrated functioning of all the departments he or she supervises. Every unit does its part to manufacture the product. You might also think of each member of a baseball team contributing effectively. Fortunate is the manager who has such a team; he is satisfied not just because he is winning games but also because of his own role in bringing about the orderly functioning of the team members.

Maslow's list of B-values may be viewed from the standpoint of positive need tensions and from the standpoint of B-value incentives. A person may actually experience tension from the need to produce order or create beauty or bring about integration or organize things into an articulate structure. In such instances, the need tensions are felt as positive emotions, such as anticipation, delight, yearning, and zestful risk-taking. The values are also incentives that satisfy the metaneeds. When attained, the incentives produce certain pleasures and emotional states. There are delights and pleasures associated with the contemplation or creation of beauty, order, perfection, wholeness, unity, balance, and so on. The metaneeds can be powerful "movers"; their gratification can occupy most of a person's waking behavior provided that his or her deficit needs are comfortably gratified.

We might ask how a person feels when he or she is functioning on the B-level. How does this person impress others? The subjects studied report that they feel at the peak of their powers, are able to operate smoothly, effectively, effortlessly. They report feeling more intelligent, more perceptive, wittier, stronger, more graceful than at other times; they do not waste effort fighting and restraining themselves; inhibitions are dropped. They feel themselves fully responsible, creative, in total control. They appear to others more effective, decisive, strong, single-minded, able to overcome opposition, self-assured. To the observer they look more trustworthy, reliable, dependable. They seem to be people with a mission that will be accomplished. (Maslow, 1968c)

Rating Scale for Self-Actualizers

Psychologists have long used rating scales and checklists to assess personality. The items vary with the intention or purpose of the test, but they typically include significant areas of life: work habits, promptness, social qualities, motivation level, assessment of abilities and capacities, and so-called character traits such as honesty, trustworthiness, reliability, and egocentricity. Consider Maslow's traits of a superior human being with an eye to a rating scale: spontaneity, expressiveness, innocence, guilelessness, naivete, candidness, ingenuousness, childlikeness, artlessness, unguardedness, defenselessness, naturalness, simplicity, responsiveness, unhesitant manner, plainness, sincerity, unaffectedness, immediateness, primitiveness (in an open sense), uncontrolledness, freely flowing outwardness, automatic behavior, impulsiveness, instinctiveness, unrestrainedness, unself-consciousness, thoughtlessness (in the sense of lack of censuring), unawareness. (Maslow, 1968c) In order to construct a rating scale to measure these qualities, we would have to define the foregoing terms operationally. If we allow for the vagueness and overlapping of meanings of the various terms, the difference between these dimensions and those typically used is quite striking. Such descriptive categories may be the personality rating scales of the future, when we know more about the highest human potentials.

CRITICAL EVALUATION

Beyond emphasizing the necessity of gratifying needs, Maslow did not specify the particulars for dealing with them. Allport (1961) and Maddi (1965) have pointed out that there are numerous instances of high human achievement among those who have had anything but easy gratification of needs. Maslow might have responded that gratification is not the only, but rather the *best*, way to deal with needs. Yet the experimental application of his need hierarchy has yielded conflicting results: in some work settings, providing conditions that seem to gratify higher needs produced evident improvement in performance and employee morale (Marrow et al., 1967); however, in other settings there was no improvement. (Hall and Nongaim, 1968) Table 10–5 presents a potential application of Maslow's need hierarchy to occupation.

The most obvious objection to Maslow's ideas on self-actualization is that the traits and characteristics he discovered are his own constructions rather than actual qualities of living people. Maslow did admit that the traits that have emerged from his

TABLE 10-5 MASLOW'S NEED HIERARCHY RELATED TO OCCUPATION

In our society there is no single situation which is potentially so capable of giving some satisfactions at all levels of basic needs as is the occupation.—Ann Roe, *The Psychology of Occupations*, 1956, p. 31.

Needs	Work-Related Fulfillments
6. Transcendence needs	Helping fellow employees, working beyond call of duty to promote department participation in outside activities sponsored by company
5. Self-actualization needs	Creative behavior Use of talents, pursuit of interests Productiveness
4. Esteem needs	Representing adulthood, independence, and freedom Sense of accomplishment, responsibility, and prestige Being valued by work associates
3. Love and belonging needs	Working with a congenial group Being needed and welcomed by peers and superiors
2. Safety needs	Shelter: renting an apartment, buying a house Fringe benefits: pension, savings Clothing Personal property: furniture, car
1. Physiological needs	Earning money to secure the essentials for living: food, water

Adapted from Ann Roe *The Psychology of Occupations*. Reprinted by permission of John Wiley & Sons, Inc.

investigation are his clinical impressions. In his favor is the observation that his characteristics of self-actualizing people resemble those proposed by other mental health experts.

There is an optimistic tone in Maslow's formulations, and we may be beguiled by his confidence in human prospects into thinking that self-actualization is merely a matter of self-reflection and exploration once we know the traits of self-actualizers. We might be tempted to conclude that all we have to do is make the traits of the self-actualizers a part of our own personality. Students are often quite interested in the traits of geniuses because they think or hope that they can foster the same traits in themselves. This is wishful thinking. There is value in knowing the qualities of genius and healthy personality, but knowledge alone is insufficient to engender such qualities in one's self.

Maslow recommended that in keeping with people's true nature there should be radical changes in all the major social and cultural institutions. Child-rearing practices should promote growth; education should foster creativity and spontaneity in the child; religion should stimulate our innate positive tendencies and responses; work should permit gratification of the highest needs, for self-esteem and the pursuit of meaningful personal goals. The good things in life should be available to all. But how can parents be made need-gratifying rather than punitive? How can unpleasant jobs be made fulfilling? How can all of us learn high levels of skills so that we can comfortably satisfy our needs? Perhaps the objective should indeed be to create conditions that would allow more people to attain the fullness of their potentialities. But Maslow's approach is more descriptive than functional: he told us what should be the case, but he did not reveal the methods of attaining his ideals.

Maslow has been a significant figure in the humanistic psychology movement. His theorizing and experimental work have directed attention to the highest potentials of which humans are capable. The human potentials movement, which deals with human fulfillment, growth possibilities, human enrichment, has derived nourishment from Maslow's thinking. Curing the sick is no longer the only function of the personality and behavior therapist. There are professionals who deal directly with such humanistic concerns as increasing our capacity for emotional experiencing, fulfilling our potentials in a variety of aspects of living, and accentuating the positive side of life. It is beginning to be professionally acceptable in many fields such as medicine, psychology, psychiatry, and social work to have practitioners who are concerned in promoting health rather than alleviating illness. It may well turn out that Maslow's ideas on B-values, metamotivation, peak experiences, and self-actualization will receive experimental and clinical support from these disciplines.

Maslow's theory has also been fruitful in spurring the researchers to try out his ideas in various settings such as the school, the workshop, even in the pastoral consulting room. Not all of the studies have been supportive of Maslow's theory, but the findings of such studies have increased our knowledge of the important topic of motivation, and Maslow's theory deserves credit for that. In the end, perhaps Maslow's theory will prove to be outmoded, but it is serving a useful purpose in stimulating research and controversy. These are the methods by which answers are found.

GUIDES TO RESEARCH

STUDIES RELATING TO NEED HIERARCHY

The core of Maslow's theory is the degree of priority that various need levels may occupy. Maslow specified an orderly arrangement of needs: physiological, safety, love, esteem, and self-actualization—which follow the fulfill-ment-progression model. The needs initiate, sustain, and direct behavior toward the specific gratifiers. In the case of the deficit needs, the theory predicts that the most potent concerns arise from the level of needs just above those which are being met fairly comfortably. The need hierarchy construct could be tested in a variety of settings—school, home, industry, recreation.

The implications of the need hierarchy concept have received the most research attention in industry. Most of the studies have been cross-sectional in that they have compared various job categories with Maslow's need levels. An example is a study by Porter (1961) in which differences in the importance of various need levels were related to bottom- and middle-management positions. Porter concluded that the management position was certainly a factor in determining the extent of satisfaction of need levels. The lower-level jobs provided gratification only of the lower-level needs whereas the higher-management jobs provided gratification for both lower- and higher-level needs. The higher-management positions paid better (security and esteem needs); provided greater freedom of decision making (belonging, esteem, self-actualization needs); and permitted the utilization of potentials through more freedom of individual action (self-actualization needs).

Steers and Spencer (1977) studied the relationship between performance and satisfaction in people who have a high need for achievement (high-need achievers) and people with a low need for achievement (low-need achievers). High performance and satisfaction go together for those who have a strong need for achievement but not for those with a low need. Those low-need achievers who performed well did not particularly derive satisfaction from their work.

Steers and Spencer interpret their finding to mean that good performance is rewarding in itself to the high-need achievers whatever other rewards may be received. Making a job more challenging by providing opportunities for greater participation would be more stimulating for those with a high need to achieve, but wasted for those with a low need to achieve. Steers and Spencer caution, however, that the need-achievement effect may be overridden by the powerful effects of rewards and the pressures of production.

Surveying the research literature on Maslow's need hierarchy, Landy and Trumbo conclude:

> While a good deal of cross-sectional research has been done on Maslow's model, only recently have longitudinal studies been undertaken. There is an important difference between the two approaches. If Maslow's proposition is to have any value in the explanation of work motivation, it must be supported by data that describe the progress of individuals through the need hierarchy. For example, the theory must be supported with data that show that when an individual's love needs are satisfied his esteem needs become more important. [1980, p. 338]

In the cross-sectional approach, different job levels are compared with respect to motivational concerns and satisfactions. Such a study would attempt to answer such questions as these: For example, do day laborers satisfy the same needs as corporation executives? What need levels are expressed in their respective fears and anxieties? On the other hand, the longitudinal approach traces the changes in motivation as one progresses in job categories.

Hall and Nongaim (1968) found that the intensity of a need, rather than diminishing with increased satisfaction (as Maslow's theory would predict), actually increased. As workers moved to higher-level jobs, the higher-need levels were manifested, but the lower-level needs also increased in intensity. This finding may be interpreted thus: The more a need is satisfied, the more important it becomes; making more money increased the desire to make money. These data support the reinforcement theory of Skinner more than Maslow's views on need progression. Satisfying a need stimulates it. Maslow did argue for increased intensity of the self-actualizing needs with gratification, but this is not supposed to happen for the deficit needs that are satiated with gratification.

Mathes (1981) studied the order of potency of Maslow's need hierarchy. Maslow argued that each need level had to be gratified to a certain degree before a person experiences concerns related to the next level of needs. Subjects were to fill out a questionnaire that involved a series of forced-choice comparisons in which a higher-need satisfier was paired with a lower-need satisfier. The question that the subjects had to keep in mind was which satisfier they would rather do without. By this procedure preference for the various need levels could be measured. Subjects stated that they were most willing to do without esteem satisfiers—followed by security,

self-actualization, belongingness—and they were least willing to forego physiological satisfaction. The results, according to the author, suggest that a revision of Maslow's hierarchy should contain only three levels—physiological, belongingness, and esteem needs. Safety needs form a part of the physiological level, and esteem needs fit into the self-actualization level.

Wahba and Bridwell (1976) reviewed both cross-sectional and longitudinal studies and found little support for the need hierarchy arrangements and the implications that can be derived from the theory. They found no support for the longitudinal studies and only weak support from the cross-sectional work. They find many problems with the concept of needs, the measurement of needs, and the ordering that Maslow proposes. They pose some interesting questions that challenge the soundness and utility of the need hierarchy theory: " ... why should needs be structured in a fixed hierarchy? Does this hierarchy vary for different people? What happens to the hierarchy over time? How can we have a fixed hierarchy when behavior is multidetermined?" (p. 235)

STUDIES RELATING TO SELF-ACTUALIZATION

A test has been developed to assess the major traits that Maslow specified as characteristic of self-actualizers. Shostrum (1963) names the test, the Personal Orientation Inventory (POI). It is a self-report questionnaire that consists of 150 items, each having two-alternative choices. The test is designed to measure the values and behaviors of a self-actualized person and provide scores that indicate degrees of self-actualization. The taker of the test is required to select one of a pair of alternatives that most applies to him or her. There are problems with this type of test because it forces a choice that may not apply at all for the person. Forced choices do not permit a person to express individuality. In many instances, the items do not specify degrees of an attribute. Sometimes both alternatives may characterize a person at different times and under different conditions. Take the choices "I prefer to save

good things for future use" and "I prefer to use good things now." In specific instances, both alternatives would apply to a person's life. Take the statements "I worry about the future" and "I do not worry about the future." The same point holds. These statements are too categorical to bring out individual differences in the two orientations.

Another difficulty with the test is that you might present a flattering picture of yourself by selecting items that depict yourself as creative, spontaneous, and flexible. In other words, the test is definitely open to falsification. People familiar with the goals and ideals of the humanistic psychology movement would have little difficulty in portraying themselves as being highly self-actualized. Keeping these shortcomings in mind, the test should be considered a crude measure of self-actualization as envisioned by Maslow. Shostrom (1981) has developed another test, the Actualization Assessment Battery, which corrects some of the deficiencies of the earlier test.

Ryckman (1978) reviews some of the studies that have attempted to assess the validity of the POI test:

> In terms of validity, a number of studies show that the POI measures can be used to distinguish between groups in society that we would ordinarily consider to differ in their actualization levels. For example, two studies have shown that groups of psychiatric patients scored lower (were less self-actualized) on virtually all the POI scales than groups of people judged by experienced clinical psychologists to be self-actualized (Fox, Knapp, and Michael, 1968). Another study has shown that all scales of the POI discriminated among groups of alcoholic wives, non-alcoholic wives, and clinically judged self-

actualizers in the expected way. A group of normal subjects also scored higher on many of the POI scales than the alcoholic wives. (Zaccaria and Weir, 1967) In general, these studies and others indicate that the POI is a valid discriminator between normal and abnormal groups.

> A number of studies have indicated that the POI can be utilized effectively to measure changes in self-actualization following encounter group experiences. In one investigation, for example, there were changes in the POI scores on most of the subscales as well as on the two major scales in the direction of greater self-actualization following counseling that emphasized expression of feelings and the need to be sensitive to the desires of others, as compared to a variety of control groups who received no counseling. [Pearson, 1966; cited in Ryckman pp. 323 and 325]

GUIDES TO LIVING

BECOMING ACQUAINTED WITH THE HIGHER NEEDS

As so many others have done from a different frame of reference, Maslow advised that we should become acquainted with our real self and, in fact, with our entire organism. We should endeavor to identify the subtle impulses that may be contrary to cultural values, but that nevertheless are a vital part of our individual behavior. These impulses should be expressed in behavior even if this requires going counter to the culture. In the long run, the benefits will be

greater than those from blindly following the cultural ideals. Being a mother may be more satisfying, if the proper attitude is taken, than being a working wife. According to Maslow (1955), following prevailing practices and values may bring about certain apparently favorable results—wealth, power, prestige—but at the cost of fulfillment of a person's individual nature. Again, we can learn to like what is not good for us.

NEED-DEPRIVATION VERSUS NEED-GRATIFICATION

Maslow proposed an interesting notion concerning the motivating power of need-deprivation and need-gratification. Certainly people are motivated to do something about a deprived need; thus, deprivation of a need is commonly used to instigate motivation. Parents may deprive their

child of freedom, love, or respect in order to motivate the child to do better in his or her school work, for instance. But consider the value of gratification as a better means of inducing motivation (see also Skinner, 1953, on the effects of positive reinforcement). Gratification of basic needs renders them inactive, and hence the higher needs take their place. These higher needs are not satiated but rather stimulated by gratification. Reaching out for others and giving love freely have no limit. The more we give, the more we seem to have to give, and the greater is our motivation to give it. Maslow seems to be saying that the best thing to do with our needs is to gratify them. Skinner holds that lower-need gratifiers can be powerful controllers of behavior, but Maslow would argue that higher-need gratifiers are still more potent. One thing is clear: gratifying all of the need levels increases one's potential pleasures.

DEALING WITH FEELINGS OF INSECURITY

Courage is a helpful attitude in dealing with feelings of insecurity. No one can take full control of his or her life and eliminate threats and fears, dangers and hurts, but we can take the attitude of faith in ourselves and meet most situations head-on. Such an attitude equips the individual to function in spite of the unknowns. Security obviously depends upon external circumstances, but not completely so, because there can never be full control of these events. A sense of safety is to a great degree a matter of attitude.

WORK AS NEED-GRATIFICATION

Table 10–5 presents the relationship between needs and potential work-related fulfillments based on Maslow's need hierarchy.

LOWER-NEED GRATIFICATION IS LIMITING

Some people mistakenly believe that the degree of fulfillment we attain is directly related to the extent of basic lower-need gratification. Indulging the appetites for food and drink to great excess will not lead to fulfillment. To attempt to find contentment by compulsive satisfaction of physiological needs is to neglect significant aspects of our nature. Moderation in lower-need gratification is not simply a moralistic practice; it is dictated by the requirements of successful living.

THE HIGHER NEEDS ARE WEAK

A person cannot avoid his or her physiological lower needs for long, but can overlook, postpone, or even deny the higher needs all his or her life. Closely related to this lack of urgency is the difficulty of recognizing the higher needs. Many people have trouble mapping out a desirable lifestyle for themselves. They can more easily identify what is wrong in their lives — what they dislike — than specify what they really want and like — what constitutes an ideal existence for them. The key to successful living, according to Maslow, is to recognize our most personal higher needs and take steps to satisfy them even if only in a small way at first. One of our priorities should be to spend some time each day doing what we want to do.

FOCUS ON HIGHER NEEDS

Although any food will do to eliminate hunger, the love of a loved one cannot be replaced. Furthermore, the amount of food or water or sexual gratification is limited, but the capacity to give love, to know, or to appreciate and value something is virtually unlimited. The higher needs, affording such a varied scope of gratification, should always provide motivation enough to make life interesting and exciting.

The pleasure of an excellent meal, especially when you are hungry, is great, but it may be described as relief or comfort, pleasure, relaxation, and the like. Usually, of course, the pleasurable experience is short-lived, and you again begin to experience hunger pangs. Satisfaction of higher needs leads to feelings of self-respect, self-love, self-satisfaction. Certain pleasurable experiences (the term is not to be interpreted as "sensual") are not possible without higher-need gratification. What Maslow (1962) called "peak experience" is one such pleasure: the feeling of great joy at the birth of a child or the marriage of a daughter or graduation from school. We can promote such experiences by placing ourselves in certain situations. Receiving an honor for your work produces a sense of pride that has no substitute. You may value such possessions for a lifetime. Consider such emotional states as wonderment, awe, adulation, bliss, reverence, and exaltation. The gratification of the higher needs does not weaken with time. As a matter of fact, once an individual has experienced gratification of his or her higher needs, he or she cannot find substitutes for them through gratification of his or her lower needs. Maslow advises us to value our achievements continually and to count our blessings as a means of experiencing positive emotions. The value of accomplishments should not diminish with time.

LIVING FOR THE PRESENT VERSUS LIVING FOR THE FUTURE

A striking example of the transcending of dichotomies (harmonizing what appear to be opposing attitudes toward life) is the philosophical principle espoused by the Shakers. The Shakers were an austere religious sect whose adherents took a vow of celibacy. They were a communal group whose Christian beliefs were organized around two principles that seem to contradict each other: "Live this day as if it were your last, and live this day as if you were going to live a thousand years." The first part of the proposition advises us to live as fully as possible each day because we do not know how long our lives will be. Living for the day has many implications, such as being concerned with immediate ends rather than overpreoccupied with means, not worrying excessively about the unknown future, and not being overly ambitious, so that failure to accomplish objectives is not a tragedy. But the second part tells us to view our lives from the opposite frame of reference: to expect a long life. We are advised to plan, to look optimistically to a better tomorrow, to have hopes and dreams, and not to be caught up in momentary setbacks and tensions. Actually, these are not really opposite guides to living; they both imply living as fully as possible. One may have many long-term goals and objectives but at the same time live fully in the present. Working toward goals can be need-gratifying. Having plans and goals makes the present more invigorating. We could continue with these apparent paradoxes, but the point is that what appear to be opposite and irreconcilable approaches to living can, in practice and given the appropriate level of maturity, be integrated within a person's style of life. The mature person accomplishes both objectives at the same time by the same behavior.

D-LIVING VERSUS B-LIVING

Maslow has given us some insight into his view of the highest human potentialities by contrasting the D-life with the B-life. He has also advised us how to live on the B-plane:

> I have found it most useful for myself to differentiate between the realm of being (B-realm) and the realm of deficiencies (D-realm), that is, between the eternal and the "practical." Simply as a matter of the strategy and tactics of living well and fully and of choosing one's life instead of having it determined for us, this is a help. It is so easy to forget ultimates in the rush and hurry of daily life, especially for young people. So often we are merely responders, so to speak, simply reacting to stimuli, to rewards and punishments, to emergencies, to pains and fears, to demands of other people, to superficialities. It takes a specific, conscious, ad hoc effort, at least at first, to turn one's attention to intrinsic things and values, e.g., perhaps seeking actual physical aloneness, perhaps exposing oneself to great music, to good people, to natural beauty, etc. Only after practice do these strategies become easy and automatic so that one can be living in the B-realm even without wishing or trying, i.e., the "unitive life," the "metalife," the "life of being," etc. [1968c, p. 61]⁵

BEING AS SELFISH AS POSSIBLE

Maslow repeatedly reminded his students of the cardinal principle of his brand of growth psychology: being as selfish as possible. He meant that we should respect ourselves enough to want to be our most developed self. Furthermore, if we are engaging in an activity that meets our needs, we will perform the work better and benefit both ourselves and others. For example, if a professor uses his lectures to clarify his thinking on a research project, the students will profit from his knowledge and enthusiasm, and he may learn something from their questions. The point is that we should take our lives seriously enough to live as fully as possible.

GROWTH-PROMOTING ACTIVITIES

Growth is promoted through using one's powers. We may gain many delights from exploring, manipulating, experiencing, being involved, being interested, exercising choice, knowing, liking, loving — without filling any deficits or hungers. Frequently we are so occupied with satisfaction of our deficit needs (physiological, safety, love, and esteem) that we overlook many easily available gratifications. It may be useful to consider the many ways of deriving pleasure from growth-promoting activities without paying a heavy price. Some of these are so obvious as to appear trivial: reading a good book, enjoying the beauties of nature, cultivating a genuine appreciation for other people, making good use of all the senses both for pleasure and utility, enjoying one's feelings and emotions, appreciating cognitive experiences such as insights, integrating ideas, and logical order. Perhaps the old saying "The best things in life are free" may acquire new meaning in the light of Maslow's growth concepts.

⁵*Toward a Psychology of Being*, by Abraham Maslow. Copyright 1968. Reprinted by permission of Brooks/Cole Publishing Company.

USING NEED TENSIONS AS GUIDES

If you study your own behavior, you can usually identify some of the needs that are active. A lower need is active because there is insufficient gratification. A higher or growth need may be active because its gratification results in a positive emotional experience. The lower or deficit needs are experienced as unpleasant tensions. By using this difference in feeling tone, you can identify and emphasize behaviors associated with the higher needs. For example, if it "feels good" to write poetry, you should enjoy this activity, regardless of lack of remuneration or recognition. Growth experiences are self-validating: they are ends in themselves, and the emotions that accompany them are enjoyable.

MORE HUMAN, LESS AMERICAN

Maslow suggested the challenging idea that in order to become more human, we might have to become less American. He meant that the more we identify with basic human experiences, the less we are German, Italian, Mexican, or any other nationality or cultural type. We ought not to espouse our culture at the expense of fulfilling our individual natures. Being one of the herd is not conducive to self-actualization, according to Maslow.

FEAR OF POTENTIAL GREATNESS

Maslow believed that many people fear their own potential greatness. Everyone is, according to Maslow, both worm and God. We may fear our potential because it places upon us a heavy burden to act in ways counter to the expectations of the culture and of significant people in our lives. We may easily emphasize security, the good opinion of others, and material success over self-fulfillment. It should be noted that Maslow equated the highest levels of need gratification with self-actualization, not with physical health or material well-being or social effectiveness though all of these to a degree are preconditions for attaining self-actualization. Maslow would exhort us to "dare to be great."

PERSONAL GROWTH

Maslow suggested that although we may not be able to rid ourselves of severe neurotic conditions or make our lives perfect, there are always some things about ourselves that we can improve. He gave us an additional guideline in his observation that during peak experiences we can often perceive and understand things about ourselves and the world with a high degree of clarity. We may actively question and probe during these experiences and thereby open ourselves to new insights. Small growth steps are possible in every life; we must be willing to endure the fear of change resulting from the pull of the safety needs when growth-promoting change is attempted.

GROWTH COGNITION

Cognition can be an expression of one's natural growth tendencies in the same way that a healthy apple tree bears fruit. A new discovery, a sudden insight, a novel way of viewing an old problem—all promote an expanded outreach. Maslow (1968a) compared such illuminating cognitive experiences to an increase in sensory acuity: seeing things more keenly, hearing things more acutely, feeling things more intensely. We can, of course, utilize our cognitive talents in a wide variety of growth-promoting ways and experience some of the greatest joys of living.

SUMMARY

1. Maslow was a pioneer and an advocate of the humanistic approach, termed the third force in psychology. His work with animals and later with humans led him to a distinction between deficit and growth motivation. Healthy animals displayed motives that might be described as growth motivation rather than only drive-reduction, which characterizes deficit motivation. In humans, deficit motivation is related to organic requirements. With the emergence of the self, self-actualization tendencies become evident.

2. Maslow distinguished between need and motive: a need is a deficit state, which is not experienced, whereas a motive is a conscious desire or impulse for a specific thing. There are many more motives than there are needs.

3. All needs are subject to distortion. The higher and subtler needs are much more easily distorted and misdirected by inappropriate experiences. Higher needs are instinctoid in that they are like partial instincts, lacking the other components of a total instinct. Maslow believed that current cultural influences and institutions do more to suppress the higher needs than to support them.

4. Satisfying the lower needs is a condition for experiencing the higher needs. The needs exist in a hierarchy of levels governed by the principle of prepotence.

5. Need deprivation is the basis for pathology for Maslow. The pathology resulting from deprivation of the deficit needs fit the categories of neuroses, psychoses, and personality disorders. Pathology resulting from the deprivation of growth needs is termed metapathology. Many metapathologies are accepted as normal problems of living, but Maslow terms them abnormalities because they constitute impairments of self-actualization.

6. A total instinct is unlearned behavior universal to a species, which involves all the elements of a behavioral act. Higher needs may be characterized as instinctoid tendencies or instinct remnants, which under the right conditions are felt as impulses and are gratified through learning. The basic needs are associated with more complex patterns of behavior known as drives.

7. In addition to Maslow's distinction between needs and motives are the distinctions between metaneeds and metamotives and between D-values and B-values. Metaneeds are growth needs and have corresponding metamotives. Needs are deficit states whose gratification reduces tension and that are related to D-values (deficit-values). Metaneeds are related to B-values (being-values). Metamotivation is defined as tendencies to seek growth ends. Metamotives may increase tension and stimulate behavior when they are gratified whereas deficit motives are reduced through gratification. Maslow believed that metaneeds and metamotives are essential to human nature, but that they are often frustrated because deficit needs and motives have not been satisfied adequately. Metapathologies may be considered a stunting of development. Examples of metapathologies include chronic boredom,

sense of alienation, lack of involvement or direction, routine living, cognitive disturbances, existential depression, and immoral behavior.

8. The lower or deficit needs are (in order of potency) physiological needs, safety, love and belonging, and esteem. The physiological needs are the most potent because they are necessary for survival. Safety needs involve the preservation and maintenance of the organism and become dominant when physiological needs do not present a serious problem. With physiological and safety needs adequately gratified, the person experiences love and belonging needs, which include socially oriented needs, such as being a member of a group or family or a partner in an intimate relationship. The highest form of love is B-love, which is valuing the being of another. D-love is based upon a deficit need, not upon the qualities of the loved person. Esteem needs are related to self-valuation and to respect from others. Esteem needs are usually externally based before they become internally based. Self-actualization needs refer to growth requirements. Self-actualization is highly personal. Maslow specifies a number of key traits of self-actualization that must be understood as they are expressed in the life of a particular individual. Self-actualization is possible if the lower needs are met without consuming or distracting all available energies. Maslow introduced a level of needs beyond self-actualization needs, which he termed the transcendence needs that are based on concern for others.

9. Cognitive needs include the need to know the world, to analyze, to theorize, and to build systems. Frustration of cognitive needs can lead to forms of pathology such as paranoia. The need to know has its own motivating force. Aesthetic needs, which include the need for symmetry, order, and closure, play a significant role in human personality.

10. Abnormality, for Maslow, is the result of the frustration of people's essential nature. Maslow relates all types of abnormality to the various forms of need deprivation. Anything less than full growth and functioning is abnormal for Maslow. Maslow considers average behavior as abnormal in that it is not motivated

by metaneeds. Maslow has named healthy or self-actualizing functioning as "Being-psychology." For Maslow, the B-values are the highest human ends. The B-values are related to metaneeds as incentives. B-values include such ends as wholeness, perfection, truth, and justice. Maslow defined self-actualization generally as the full use and exploitation of talents, capacities, and potentialities; according to Maslow, the self-actualizing person perceives reality efficiently; is curious about the unknown and readily accepts it; accepts self, others, and nature; is spontaneous, simple, and natural; has a highly developed individualistic inner life; is problem-centered; views work as a source of identification and fulfillment; values privacy; is motivated from within rather than from the external world; is autonomous and self-sufficient; gains pleasure from everyday experiences; enjoys the same experiences repeatedly; has peak experiences that may involve loss of sense of time; identifies with universal humanness; has few but strong friendships; has a democratic character structure (accepting all types of people); discriminates between ends and means (ends are strongly held, and means are easily interchanged); has a philosophical sense of humor; is creative, inventive, and spontaneous. The most outstanding quality of self-actualizing persons, according to Maslow, is their ability to transcend dichotomies, harmonizing oppositions, such as work and play, rationality and emotionality. Self-actualizing people are motivated by B-values such as wholeness, perfection, completion, justice, aliveness, richness, simplicity, beauty, goodness, uniqueness, effortlessness, playfulness, truth, and self-sufficiency. Maslow believed that environmental conditions have an important effect on our potential for self-actualization. He advised getting to know both the self and the culture in order to know how to best become what we are.

11. Maslow is identified with the human potentials movement, which stresses a health and growth psychology. Rather than restricting treatment to obvious forms of pathology, therapy is expanded to include promoting health and fulfillment.

GLOSSARY

Health and growth psychology: An approach to psychology, espoused by Maslow, which focuses on the highest potentials of humans; views health as being qualitatively different from the absence of illness.

Human potentials movement: A movement that studies the highest possibilites that humans can attain and the means of attaining them; stress on growth potentials of humans.

Humanistic psychology: An approach to psychology that emphasizes the distinctively human attributes; deals with fulfilled human nature; stresses the attributes of the self, freedom, and creativity; the third force in psychology; contrasted with psychoanalysis and behaviorism.

Needs: Requirements of an organism.

Deficit need: A deficiency or lack of a necessary ingredient; a need for something; gratification appeases the need and reduces tension.

Metaneed: Synonym for growth need; a need to do something; the gratification of metaneeds stimulates activity and often promotes growth.

Need hierarchy: The arrangement of needs in order of priority; the lower needs are prepotent in that they take priority over the higher needs. Gratification of lower needs is a condition for sensing the next level of needs.

Self-actualization needs: Needs associated with the self that promote the full development and functioning of the self.

Need versus motive: Need is a requirement, an end that is not consciously felt; motive is the specific desire associated with a need; the same need may give rise to several motives.

Transcendence need: A need beyond self-actualization that impels a person to stress and seek communal ends; for example, a person chooses a course of action because it is needed to promote the welfare of the community.

Aesthetic needs: Needs associated with appreciation of beauty, art, orderly arrangement, and balance.

Cognitive needs: Knowing operations have a dynamic force of their own independent of their instrumentality for other needs.

Pathology: The general term for illness or sickness or dysfunction.

Need deprivation: The major source of pathology for Maslow.

Metapathology: Pathologies resulting from frustration of growth or metaneeds; examples include certain existential illnesses, such as existential depression, a sense of futility, routine living.

Peak experience: A profound emotional experience analogous to Jung's meaning of numinous experiences and Erikson's notion of the numinous ritualization; being transfixed, awe-inspired, in a state of wonderment.

Transcendence of dichotomies: A quality of self-actualizers in which opposite behaviors are harmonized or expressed by the same person; overcoming oppositions in one's nature.

Values: Ends, the objects of needs and motives; need and motive gratifiers.

D-values: The incentive for deficit needs; for example, food for a hungry organism; safety for a frightened man; love for a lonely person.

B-values: The end states of the metaneeds and metamotives; the growth objectives associated with the higher needs. The attainment of B-values stimulates rather than satiates behavior.

D-cognition: Knowledge that is motivated by a deficit need.

B-cognition: The need to know for its own sake.

D-love: Emotional attachment to another based on a deficit need such as sex or the love and belonging needs.

B-love: Emotional attachment to another based on the qualities of that person; valuing the being of another.

SUGGESTED READINGS

Maslow, Abraham. *Religions, Values and Peak Experiences*. New York: Viking, 1964.

In this brief work, Maslow proposes that the religious experience be considered scientifically. He believes a better understanding of the need for spiritual expression, as manifested in peak or religious experiences, can be obtained through science.

———— *Toward a Psychology of Being*, 2d ed. New York: D. Van Nostrand, 1968.

As a pioneer in psychology's movement away from the negativistic view of man, Maslow presents his theories of B-values, peak experiences, and self-actualization.

———— *Motivation and Personality*, 2d ed. New New York: Harper & Row, 1970.

This is the best known of Maslow's books. It presents his theory of personality, with special attention to the need hierarchy and self-actualization.

———— *The Farther Reaches of Human Nature*. New York: Viking, 1971.

This book integrates Maslow's views on creativity, biology, cognition, synergy, and the need hierarchy with the role of science in the study of human nature.

ERICH FROMM
FROMM'S HUMANISTIC PSYCHOANALYSIS

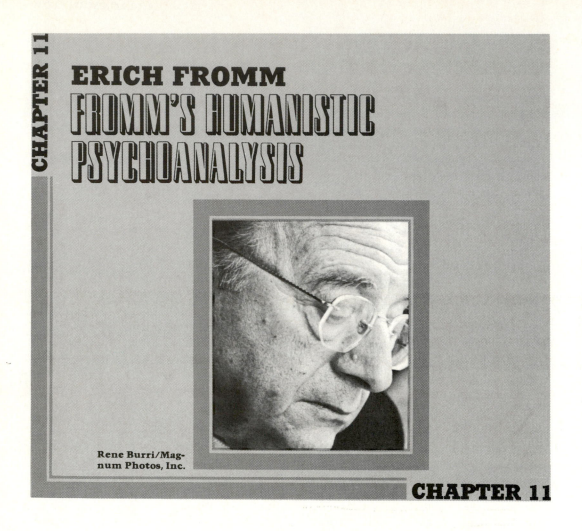

Rene Burri/Mag-
num Photos, Inc.

BIOGRAPHY AND HISTORICAL PERSPECTIVE

A rich fund of suggestions for ideal living can be found in the writings of the philosophers, particularly in the field of ethics. The content of ethics might be considered as
ideal guides to living, which have some similarity to principles of mental health. One
significant difference is in the degree of perfection in living: mental health principles
are concerned with promoting healthier optimal behavior whereas the principles of
ethics usually stretch human strivings to the ultimate of perfection, to the best that
humans can attain. In some ethical systems, even mental health and well-being are
sacrificed for the sake of ideal human functioning. Proper human conduct may be
defined by the state or the majority of the people or by a formalized moral code.

Because of this lack of concern for the well-being of the individual, many scientific psychologists refuse to accept ethics as a source of the ideals of human conduct. Then too, ethicians are more concerned with ends than with means: they prescribe the ideals of the good life but do not deal with the ways of attaining them. For example, you might argue for the absolute indissolubility of marriage on the basis of the so-called natural law or on the grounds of the benefit to society as a whole, but disregard difficulties in individual cases that might justify divorce. One of the major problems in ethics is the application of universal laws, or principles based on human nature in general, to the specific individual (Brandt, 1959). Thus most psychologists and psychiatrists have turned away from philosophical speculation as a means of learning about human behavior — both as it is and as it should be. Erich Fromm, a well-known psychoanalyst and author, is an exception: he holds that ethics can teach us much of value about the ideal life, if it is brought into line with scientific findings. For him ideal human existence is healthy existence: the two are one and the same. He believes that what is objectively right must also be good for people. This proposition represents an attitude toward the good life that deserves a hearing.

Fromm's books are likely to be quite popular on a college campus because his ideas are pertinent to several subject areas in the typical college curriculum: sociology, philosophy, psychology, and psychoanalysis. His *The Art of Loving* is required reading in many courses. Fromm was a noted lecturer, professor, and psychotherapist. He was born in 1900 in Frankfort, Germany, and received his education in several of Europe's outstanding universities: Frankfort, Munich, and Heidelberg (where he received his Ph.D. in psychology). In 1922 he undertook instruction in psychoanalysis as a lay analyst at the Berlin Institute of Psychoanalysis. He came to the United States during the Great Depression and pursued an active career in writing, lecturing, and teaching. He spent his later years teaching at the University of Mexico and served as director of the Mexican Psychoanalytic Institute. He died in Switzerland in 1980.

The influence of Karl Marx on the formulation of Fromm's philosophical orientation cannot be overlooked. He mentioned Marx along with Buddha, Jesus, and Master Eckhart as espousing the philosophy of *being* rather than *having*, saying: "Marx taught that luxury is as much a vice as poverty and that our goal should be to *be* much, not to *have* much. ("I refer here to the real Marx, the radical humanist, not to the vulgar forgery presented by Soviet Communism."). (Fromm, *To Have or to Be?*, 1976, p. 15)

BASIC CONSTRUCTS AND POSTULATES

Fromm is considered a humanistic psychoanalyst because he deals extensively with the issue of what it means to be human. He has attempted to identify the attributes that are distinctively human. If we can specify what attributes constitute humanness, then we can go on to the question of what is meant by fulfilled human nature. Fromm theorizes about optimal personality, growth, and functioning. If we know what the defining attributes of human nature are, we can then attempt to perfect ourselves according to this model. Our human nature creates for us specific problems that Fromm terms "the human situation." If we were made differently, our existence would be different. Fromm begins his specification of the attributes of human nature by identifying five basic distinctively human needs. The quality of our life greatly depends on the manner of gratifying these needs. They are so basic to our nature, Fromm holds, that if we do not deal with them adequately, we may either die or go insane (1955). These are certainly dire consequences for needs that are not ordinarily considered survival needs. In Fromm's view, we must pay attention to these five needs, which in today's world seem more threatened than ever before. In reading Fromm, we should keep this question in mind: What does it mean to be fully human? We will begin with a discussion of the five distinctively human needs.

Fromm's Five Human Needs

Fromm disagrees with Freud about the role of sex in human life. It is not sexual frustration that is our biggest problem, but rather the simple fact that we are human beings. According to Fromm, the very qualities that make us human — the ability to know and reason about the things of the world; the ability to reflect upon our own thoughts, feelings, and activities; the ability to project into the future; the ability to perceive contradictions, injustices, and discrepancies, and so on — present us with difficulties and challenges. To be human means to have a specific makeup with specific needs and specific problems to solve. We are unlike any other creature in the world. We are aliens because we are not linked to nature by instincts. We depend upon a cultural heritage — our traditions, customs, values — but these are rapidly changing; thus many of us are in a state of confusion. We must depend on our abilities to reason correctly, to develop skills, and to love productively as the best means of dealing with the problems associated with being human. If we do not meet our specifically human needs adequately, we suffer serious psychological and physical impairment. These needs are, according to Fromm (1955), relatedness, transcendence, rootedness, sense of identity, and a frame of reference. Each person must deal with these needs. They are the basic psychological requirements for living effectively.

1. Relatedness.   The feeling of loneliness and isolation is common to all humans, according to Fromm. The only means of overcoming this feeling is some type of relatedness to others. But not every form of relatedness will promote happiness. Submission and dominance are forms of relatedness, but these are harmful to us. We should use our ability to love productively in dealing with others. There are several forms of productive love: maternal love, paternal love, erotic love, brotherly love, and love of self. Productive love is the only way to overcome the feeling of aloneness and isolation common to all people.

2. Transcendence.   The need for transcendence refers to the need to gain control of one's life, to have choices, and to determine one's destiny. Relating to the world in a passive manner is contrary to human nature. Although there are wide differences among people, everyone has the capacity for knowledge and skills. When these capacities are not used, or are used incorrectly, personality development and functioning are

If all the essential ingredients are present, it is one of us.

The Museum of Modern Art/Film Stills Archive

impaired. Because people are not guided by their instincts, they must solve their problems by means of their own resources, including the culture in which they live. Each individual person must create his or her own world.

3. Rootedness. The desire for rootedness may be interpreted as a need for meaningful ties with our immediate surroundings and past. We might think of Maslow's belonging and acceptance needs. We should be a part of our community, of our job, of our school. People need traditions, customs, and rituals that stand for things or beliefs that are greater than the individual and help us to feel that we are a part of our community. In a rapidly changing world, the need for rootedness becomes strongly felt (Lifton, 1970).

4. Sense of identity. Fromm agrees with Erikson on the need for identity. We may also think of Maslow's esteem needs in this respect. We all have a need to identify our place in the world and to have suitable roles by which we perceive ourselves and are perceived by others.

5. Frame of reference. Each person has the need to make sense of his or her life and to understand his or her world. Fromm holds that even an incorrect picture of the world is better than none at all. To be in a state of chaos and confusion is highly frustrating to most people.

We should note that Fromm often speaks of people in general rather than of the individual person. It is easy to misinterpret his ideas as being highly abstract, but bear in mind that what applies to others also applies in some form to you. For Fromm, every person has a profound feeling of aloneness and isolation. Every person has contradictory elements within himself or herself. Every person in one degree or another has to deal with certain problems of existence. Whenever the term "man" is encountered in Fromm's writing, it might be more effective to substitute the term "I."

Values as Guides

Many psychologists have rejected value judgments on the ground that they cannot be tested. For example, some people believe that being charitable is a better way of living than being selfish or that being free is more desirable than being a slave or that self-directed behavior enhances mental health more than being ruled by an authoritarian force. To apply the empirical test of validity to value judgments appears impossible to many behavior scientists; certainly the test is fraught with difficulties. Ultimately there is the question of just what is desirable: What is an adequate measure of healthy functioning? Yet, despite these objections, Fromm (1960) maintains that value judgments are the basis of our actions and that these actions in turn have much to do with our mental health. He argues that certain values promote effective living and others impede it. He thus opposes ethical relativism. Most of our basic expectations and significant choices are rooted in values. (Simon, 1974; Harmin et al., 1973) Whether we choose to marry or to remain single is a value judgment; so also is our choice to engage in gainful employment because this way of earning a livelihood is valued over others. The values may thus be our own, or they may be forced upon us.

Numerous psychologists argue that values are a matter of personal preference. For them there are many ways to live and many different values that justify these diverse modes of living. Fromm holds to norms and value judgments that apply to all because they are based on the very nature of humans — a nature that despite the uniqueness of each individual is the common inheritance of all. The person who suffers from neurosis has failed to meet certain requirements of his or her own nature. Fromm would say that the failure is a moral one even though the fault may not be totally one's own. In many instances the neurosis is the outcome of the inability to resolve conflicts of values. (See Simon, et al., 1972, for a discussion of the issue of value clarification.)

Some Ethical Problems

Ethics is an applied branch of philosophy, which means that it is concerned with actual behavior. It is functional in that it offers guides to living. The principles of ethics deal with decisions having a direct bearing on conduct. For the reader who has not studied ethics formally, it may be instructive to examine some questions of an ethical nature.

Consider abortion. Should a woman have the right to determine whether a fetus is to be aborted? Does the unborn child have rights even though he or she cannot take up his or her own case? What about the welfare mother who is already overburdened with children or the unwed pregnant teenager or the rape victim? What place should the state have? Certainly the laws governing abortion have traditionally been quite strict. If abortion is allowed, how far on in the pregnancy should it be permitted before it is considered illegal? Should it be a matter of personal preference, scarcely different from choosing one's clothing or type of food or recreation? Does it violate the best interests of humanity, both as a whole and as individuals? Or is it really in the child's best interest to permit him or her to be born hopelessly retarded or deformed or into a family that will not care for him or her? These questions have puzzled the greatest minds. Is there anything in the nature of people that can tell us the answers? Fromm holds that human reason can find solutions. Just as humans have made sound judgments about physical nature that have resulted in marvelous achievements, so they ought to be able to make sound judgments about their own best conduct. There are right and wrong ways to build an automobile, to construct a home, to perform surgery, to grow old. Reason is our only hope. Knowledge of human nature is the foundation of valid ethical judgments. (Fromm, 1947)

Consider another ethical issue. A young woman with a widowed father may be tormented by a conflict between his expectation of her and the concerns both of herself and of her husband-to-be. Her father exerts pressure to keep her home, and she has a profound sense of obligation to him. At the same time, she wants to marry and have a family of her own. Is there a solution to this dilemma? The young woman may have difficulty weighing one value against another, but there is an order of priority here. She may believe that her obligation must take precedence over her "selfish" desires for marriage, but her own rights are really more important and outweigh her duty to her father, according to Fromm. To affirm the priority of her rights is not to imply that her obligations to her father are nonexistent. His expectations of her are unjust, but there is some middle ground. She can still be a vital part of his life, while living her own. The solutions to such problems are not arbitrary, nor are they simply a matter of cultural practice. There are definite rights and wrongs that transcend cultural beliefs.

These are but two examples of the literally hundreds of ethical issues. Every aspect of life involves value judgments, and we cannot really treat the good life psychologically without considering values and their bases. Proposing a humanistic ethics, Fromm believes that the norms for ethical conduct have their source within human nature itself. In his view, ethical conduct is equivalent to health. The mature, integrated, and happy person is virtuous. Vice, on the other hand, is self-mutilation. The productive orientation to life is ethical; nonproductive orientations are unethical.

Authoritarian Versus Humanistic Ethics

We may question the source of the guiding principles: who determines the "oughts" for us? We may also inquire about the justification or validity of the source. In authoritarian ethics some authority imposes the laws or rules (Fromm, 1947). It may be the government, parents, teachers, religion, or even the culture. There must be compliance without questioning the validity of the norms. Fear of the authority's power keeps the followers in line. It should be pointed out that authoritarian ethics may harmonize with humanistic ethics if the authority imposes controls and rules that promote human living, but frequently this is not the case. The norms may be injurious to the ones who must follow them.

The rights of those subject to authority are minimized. Rewards and punishments are determined by the authority, with no participation by the subject. In the slave-master relationship, slaves have rights that are given them by the master and no rights from their own nature. Although most people are not slaves, authoritarian controls are a part of everyone's life. The parents are the authorities for the infant and young child.

Codes of conduct are prescribed and enforced by authorities.

They make all the rules and set the conditions for rewards and punishments, often exercising their power despotically. In the early grades, the teacher also has great power, imposing conditions for success and failure that greatly affect the child's development. Like parents, many teachers do not give adequate consideration to the rights of children and young adults. They expect them to perform all requirements and tasks uniformly and neglect to acknowledge individual differences in talent, motivation, home circumstances, and the like. The failure of the system to bend to the individual often produces the learning casualty in school (Holt, 1964). Frequently the social deviant is the victim of circumstances that do not harmonize with the requirements of the individual's nature.

In contrast to authoritarian ethics, humanistic ethics is based on the requirements of human nature. (Fromm, 1947) What is right and wrong is at the same time good or bad for us. Fromm believes that life should be lived fully. Failure to attain fullness is a capital sin in humanistic ethics. Irresponsible living that squanders talents and fails to actualize potentialities constitutes vice.

The Human Situation

According to Fromm (1947), every individual faces distinct problems by virtue of the fact that he or she is human. Although each person is unique as a living being, the tasks and difficulties that he or she must confront are frequently similar to those of others. All the circumstances of two people's lives may be different, but the nature of certain problems is the same. Fromm terms the state of humans *the human situation*.

Fromm attaches considerable importance to the condition of being human. He holds that we are a freak of nature, an anomaly in the world by comparison with other animals. Our very nature confronts us with conflicts that can never be totally resolved. We must work out some expedient way of living with the human situation. Fromm describes these peculiarly human conditions as existential and historical dichotomies.

EXISTENTIAL AND HISTORICAL DICHOTOMIES

Existential dichotomies. To say that we are confronted with existential dichotomies means that we must face unsettling and unavoidable discrepancies, double-horned dilemmas (Fromm, 1947). For example, you did not choose to be born, but suicide is highly disapproved socially and repugnant psychologically. You have many potentialities that you know can never be fulfilled. You must live with the fact that injustices that you cannot right will plague you. You must also live as fully and completely as possible with the recognition, acute at times, that death is inevitable. As you go about satisfying your needs, you know that you can never reach a state of complete harmony and tranquillity. Whenever a certain level is reached, there is renewed striving for improvement. With the greatest brain evolved, the human being is nevertheless the eternal wanderer. There are always new things to be known, gaps in knowledge to be filled. Although we can appreciate the role of happiness in our lives, we know that we cannot attain it as a permanent condition. We strive for perfect relatedness with others, and we are doomed to failure in our attempts. The human being is the only creature who can be bored, who can be discontented, who can project a better life but cannot always achieve it. It is our lot to find harmony within ourselves and between ourselves and nature through the use of reason. We do not discover harmony; we must create it. *We must make our own world because the world we find is not suited to us.* (Fromm, 1947) The existential dichotomies present each person with insoluble contradictions, unlike the historical dichotomies, which are contradictions that might not have taken place.

Historical dichotomies. The historical fact that wealth is unevenly distributed is a matter that could have been otherwise. That certain people were and are treated as inferior is another incomprehensible aspect of human life. Reason dictates that this does not have to happen. The use of valuable knowledge and resources for war and for defense against war is another historical enigma. These are dichotomies that could be resolved through reason. Some people have a vested interest in explaining such problems as inequities in wealth as a natural outcome of the inferior status of certain groups. An authoritarian leader may have the power to convince the masses that inequities are a fact of life, but the consequences remain to plague society. Many problems that appear to be existential dichotomies are really historical dichotomies instead.

Our only answer is to face our problems and realize that we must find solutions. For the unsolvable problems, the answer is to try to develop all one's potentialities and live productively. Fromm's unproductive orientations are unsuccessful means of dealing with the human situation. Productive love and productive work are the best remedies to the human condition. Table 11-1 lists some of the most outstanding existential and historical dichotomies. In his writings Fromm enumerates others.

Fromm (1955) believes that the human situation creates a need for passionate involvement in something. For some the devotion and involvement are centered about a supernatural being. In Western culture there is a passionate pursuit of wealth, power, and prestige. One must be involved in something to a high degree, and both the type of attachment and the nature of the object that is sought have much to do with the quality of living. Neurosis may be considered an irrational religion, an immature passionate pursuit that is an attempt to find meaning. One person may strive to be loved by everyone. Another may believe that he or she can be happy only if he or she is successful in sports. Another looks for romantic love as the answer and falls in love indiscriminately. One cannot just live; there must be meaning to life. By "meaning" Fromm refers to involvements, attachments, and interests.

Conscience

Conscience is a regulating agency within personality, an attribute of self-awareness that enables a person to observe, reflect on, and evaluate his or her own conduct. The judgments of conscience may stem from internalized prescriptions that have little to do with a person's major aims or needs. They may also represent self-evaluations based on the person's own ideals and values. These in turn may be the products of the real self,

TABLE 11-1 EXISTENTIAL AND HISTORICAL DICHOTOMIES

Existential Dichotomies

1. Life-Death: people desire immortality yet possess knowledge of their imminent death.
2. Each person is the bearer of vast human potentials, yet his or her life span does not permit their realization.
3. Each one is alone in his or her unique identity, and owing to this uniqueness he or she remains dissimilar to others. Yet no one can remain alone, unrelated to others: that is, I want to be an individual, but I must conform in order to be related to others.
4. We desire security and predictability, but conditions of life make for insecurity and unpredictability.
5. We desire to know truth yet are confronted with partial truths, misrepresentations, and limitations of knowledge.
6. We desire health and freedom from accidents but are subject to both ill health and accidents.
7. We desire to control things but are subject to many factors over which we have no control.
8. We must make binding decisions but with uncertainty of outcome and only partial evidence.
9. We strive for freedom but cannot cope with it once it is attained.
10. We strive for perfection and improvement, yet mistakes are inevitable and often irreparable.

Historical Dichotomies

1. Abundant technical means for material satisfaction exist, yet there also exists the incapacity to use them exclusively for peace and the welfare of humanity.
2. We desire long-lasting peace yet have a history of war.
3. Discrimination exists among people despite purported equality.
4. Wealth is unequally distributed in the face of poverty.
5. The benefits of science and technology are available to relatively few.

playing a part in meeting the needs of the person and the demands of the environment. Whether conscience consists of internalized authority (what Fromm [1947] calls the *authoritarian conscience*) or of self-imposed prescriptions, based on requirements of the real self (what he calls *humanistic conscience*), has much to do with productiveness. The authoritarian conscience hinders growth and functioning: it leads to conformity, lack of spontaneity, and suppression of the real self. Humanistic conscience promotes growth, freedom, spontaneity, and the fulfillment of the self's potentialities. Both types of conscience will be discussed in some detail because everyone has within himself or herself a measure of each.

HUMANISTIC VERSUS AUTHORITARIAN CONSCIENCE

Humanistic conscience, according to Fromm, consists of the formation within the personality of values and aims that exert a directive and restraining influence on conduct,but are based on the individual's nature and not on the precepts of external authority. The primary capacities involved in the development of humanistic conscience are the powers to reason and to love (Hoffman, 1970). The conscience is the *voice of the real self*. It points to the goals that can help us to become our real selves. It tells us what is morally good for us (moral in this sense means what is healthy and productive). It embodies not only our major aims in life but also the acceptable means by which these may be achieved.

Whereas the authoritarian conscience issues orders that are supported through fear (I must do this or that because I am afraid of the law or my parents or my teachers), the humanistic conscience rules through precepts based on obligations to oneself. You might say: I owe it to myself to study diligently in school, to make good grades in order to prepare for a career. I owe it to myself to keep physically and psychologically fit, to rest adequately, to make my life as enjoyable as possible. You might use the expression "I owe it to myself" as a means of identifying the demands of your own humanistic conscience, which, Fromm believes, is the spokesperson for the real self. If the humanistic conscience is a dominant force, it keeps people to their objectives. Because they have worked out these objectives themselves, the objectives exert considerable strength against competing desires, such as the desire not to work or the desire for recreation or even the crippling effects of self-doubt.

Conformity to humanistic conscience is congruent with fulfillment of the real self. The voice of conscience is in a sense a commentary upon success or failure in fulfilling oneself. A machine that is functioning properly has identifiable characteristics: it makes a certain sound; there may be a particular output, and so forth. When it is out of order, it also produces definite indications. Similarly, conscience can indicate success or failure in living productively. The "bad conscience," experienced as guilt, depression, or fear, is a sign that a person is not living productively whereas the "good conscience," experienced as a sense of well-being, of inner and outer harmony, is a sign of productive living. The humanistic conscience can be a good guide for judging success or failure in the art of living, and *only the humanistic conscience* can serve this function. The authoritarian conscience is active or inactive only in relation to whether you obey or disobey the precepts of an authority. A general sense of well-being or of guilt may not be trusted in this case. In fact, a person may be comfortable in his or her state of conformity to the authority but actually be living unproductively. Psychologically the person may have a sense of tranquillity while suffering physically from some dysfunction. Usually both body and mind are affected. But the point is that the authoritarian conscience cannot be trusted as an indicator of good living. (Fromm, 1947)

Table 11-2 summarizes Fromm's views on the humanistic and authoritarian consciences. It should be noted that aspects of both forms of conscience may be operating in the individual simultaneously.

If humanistic conscience is the voice of the real self, pointing the way to successful living, then why does it so often go unheard? Fromm believes there are a number of reasons: first of all, many people are so controlled by an authoritarian conscience that they distrust their own thoughts and desires. In fact, they identify the dictates of the authorities as their own, as when a man believes that successful living requires the attainment of wealth and fame. Another reason is that our culture emphasizes an outer orientation; it promotes the idea that one should always be busy doing something— reading, working, socializing. Fromm says:

> In order to listen to the voice of our conscience we must be able to listen to ourselves, and this is exactly what most people in our culture have difficulties in doing. We listen to every voice and to everybody but not to ourselves. We are constantly exposed to the noise of

TABLE 11-2 HUMANISTIC VERSUS AUTHORITARIAN CONSCIENCE

Humanistic Conscience

1. Is independent of external sanctions and rewards.
2. Is listening to the true self.
3. Consists of a response of the total personality, being both cognitive and affective in character and involving the productive use of abilities.
4. Is a reaction of the self to the self.
5. Summons one to live fully and productively, and to realize one's potentials.
6. Is the "Voice of our loving care for ourselves" (Fromm, 1947, p. 159).
7. Is an expression of self-interest and integrity.
8. Possesses the goal of productiveness.
9. Is the spokesperson of the real self.
10. Is active as pride and a sense of well-being or self-dissatisfaction and tension.

Authoritarian Conscience

1. Consists of prescriptions of authorities which are internalized.
2. Is "good" or unfelt when there is adherence to the prescriptions of authority and/or to internalized rules; is "bad" when guilt is experienced as a result of displeasing the authority: i.e., "If I obey, my conscience is quiet or good, and if I disobey, my conscience is felt or bad."
3. Involves a sense of inner security as a result of a symbiotic union with a figure who is perceived as more powerful. (Obedience means benefits from the authority.)
4. Depends upon love and approval from authority; thus pride and self-satisfaction are experienced when there is total compliance.
5. Is a submission of the self, as a result of fear, to the will of others who are regarded as morally superior.
6. Fromm says of the authoritarian conscience: "Paradoxically, the authoritarian guilty conscience is the result of feelings of strength, independence, productiveness, and pride, while the authoritarian good conscience springs from the feelings of obedience, dependence, powerlessness, and sinfulness." (1947, p. 150)*
7. May involve self-destructive strivings which are perceived as virtuous.
8. Results in the formation of a pseudo-self which is an embodiment of the expectations of others.

*Guilty conscience associated with healthy self-assertion versus good conscience associated with unhealthy compliance.

opinions and ideas hammering at us from everywhere; motion pictures, newspapers, radio, idle chatter. If we had planned intentionally to prevent outselves from ever listening to ourselves, we could have done no better. [1947, p. 161][1]

Closely related, Fromm believes, is our phobia of being alone. Any kind of company is preferable to none at all: being with ourselves is undesirable because we are

[1]From *Man for Himself* by Erich Fromm. Copyright 1947, ©1975 by Erich Fromm. Reprinted by permission of Holt, Rinehart and Winston, Publishers.

afraid of what we may discover. The positive aspects of conscience are not experienced strongly. More often, we encounter conscience in its negative aspects, as feelings of guilt, anxiety, depression, and lack of meaning. "The paradoxical — and tragic — situation of man is that his conscience is weakest when he needs it most." (Fromm, 1947, p. 160)[2]

According to Fromm, three inordinate fears stand out as consequences of ignoring the real conscience: fear of (1) death, (2) growing old, and (3) disapproval of others. Not having fully experienced the present and past, we fear the future, especially old age. Not having lived fully, we find death totally unjust and incomprehensible. Not being satisfied with ourselves, we continually look for approval from others. Everyone, of course, has some difficulty with these three fears, but for some persons they become insurmountable and constantly plaguing concerns that interfere with living.

CONSCIENCE AS A GUIDE TO PRODUCTIVE LIVING

Fromm (1947) holds that conscience can foster or hinder productive living. It hinders when it blocks and suppresses the expression of the real self. The authoritarian conscience, for instance, often requires conformity to norms of conduct that may actually produce illness, as when a soldier is commanded to kill innocent victims of war. When the conscience is an expression of the real self (the humanistic conscience), complying with its dictates should be conducive to joy and happiness, if environmental conditions are favorable.

Consider the same behavior from the standpoint of the humanistic and the authoritarian conscience. Masturbation may cause guilt feelings in one with a strong authoritarian conscience, because he or she is violating a precept of an external authority that proclaims that such behavior is wrong. A person with a humanistic conscience may also feel guilty for practicing masturbation, but the guilt stems from a personal conviction that one ought to be satisfying his or her sexual needs in a more fulfilling manner. Soon a person's guilt indicates that he or she is not living as productively as possible; this is what Fromm holds is the essence of the humanistic conscience.

Fromm makes another important point about the authoritarian and humanistic consciences that might easily be missed. He does not hold that all external codes are arbitrary and contrary to man's nature. The great religions of the world and the systems of the moral philosophers foster ethical principles that harmonize with the human condition. Most of the precepts of the Old and New Testaments, for instance, can be the foundation of a humanistic conscience; the commandment against stealing should be taught to every child. The golden rule, promoted by the major religions of the world, is an excellent tenet for the humanistic conscience, because it promotes individual and social well-being. As we acquire the ability to understand the reasons for our precepts, traditional beliefs should be reexamined to determine whether they are arbitrary and merely ritualistic or important guides to living. We could make a case for the authoritarian conscience's being gradually replaced by the humanistic as the individual more and more takes charge of his or her own life. We have stressed the negative aspect of

---

[2]It is felt more strongly in matters of avoidance than in matters of approach.

conscience, the consequences of not paying attention to it. How do we know when conscience is functioning properly, or what constitutes signs of good conscience? Fromm believes that we can be guided by certain emotional states, both positive and negative. He has some interesting modifications of the hedonistic notion.

A Sense of Well-Being

HAPPINESS: A TOTAL ORGANISMIC RESPONSE

In Fromm's view happiness is not merely a subjective state but a total organismic response, manifested in increased vitality, physical well-being, and utilization of potentialities. Unhappiness, whether conscious or unconscious, also affects the organism, producing such conditions as chronic lethargy, low energy output, headaches, backaches, and a host of psychosomatic disorders. Fromm believes that a person may consider himself or herself happy but have bodily symptoms that suggest that his or her happiness is an illusion or a form of pleasure that is not happiness. Fromm says:

> Happiness and unhappiness are so much a state of our total personality that bodily reactions are frequently more expressive of them than our conscious feeling. The drawn face of a person, listlessness, tiredness, or physical symptoms like headaches—are frequent expressions of unhappiness, just as physical feelings of "well-being" can be "symptoms" of happiness. Indeed, our body is less capable of being deceived about the state of happiness than our mind. [1947, p. 181][3]

A sadistic boss may not only fail to recognize his enjoyment of the suffering of those whom he controls, but may also rationalize his behavior and turn it into a virtue. He may believe he is helping his employees to work at their best so that they will receive promotions. He rationalizes that he wants to help them, but sometimes this means hurting them temporarily. He wants his department to be the best in the company. He is deriving pleasure from his sadistic activities, but he is not aware of it. Because sadism is an unsatisfactory mode of living, he will experience deleterious consequences—if not psychologically (because he has effectively rationalized his behavior), then in some bodily dysfunction such as chronic fatigue. Here we have a person who feels pleasure but whose total organismic response reveals that he is unhappy.

Another form of pleasure-craving stems from irrational psychological needs. Usually having their source in fear, insecurity, or loneliness, they include possessiveness, envy, and jealousy and the cravings for power, domination, or submission to authority. Often they result in lack of productiveness, or inability to work or love spontaneously. Unlike physiological needs, which follow a rhythmical sequence of arousal and satiation, irrational psychological needs are often intensified but rarely satiated. How much does it take to satisfy the miser, to please the distrusting mate, to quiet the fame seeker, to quell the passions of one who seeks revenge? Even when they are satisfied, such needs produce only irrational pleasure, not true happiness.

[3]From *Man for Himself*, by Erich Fromm. Copyright 1947, ©1975 by Erich Fromm. Reprinted by permission of Holt, Rinehart and Winston, Publishers.

In the following passage, Fromm affirms the frequently overlooked principle that violation of psychological laws can be just as injurious as violation of physical laws:

> While a person may succeed in ignoring or rationalizing destructive impulses, he — his organism as it were — cannot help reacting and being affected by acts that contradict the very principle by which his life and all life are sustained. We find that the destructive person is unhappy even if he has succeeded in attaining the aims of his destructiveness, which undermines his own existence. Conversely, no healthy person can keep from admiring, and being affected by, manifestations of decency, love, and courage; for these are the forces on which his own life rests. [1947, p. 225][4]

Everyone seeks joy and happiness, but these are scarcely found in the lives of most people. According to Fromm, "man's happiness consists of 'having fun.'. . . The world is one great object for our appetite, a big apple, a big bottle, a big breast; we are the sucklers, the eternally expectant ones, the hopeful ones — and the eternally disappointed ones" (1956, p. 87). Certain values are sought after as the means for attaining happiness, but these are often the wrong values, or the means are confused with ends. Making money is a necessary requirement for survival in Western civilization; money buys the necessities and luxuries of life. But valuing money for its own sake or judging our worth by our earning power is a confusion of means with ends. Fromm points out that a person works hard to make money, and then, instead of using it to promote happiness, invests it to make more money.

For many people, what money can buy is the definition of happiness. Fromm describes the haven of this personality type as

> a vision which would look like the biggest department store in the world, showing new things and gadgets, and himself having plenty of money with which to buy them. He would wander around open-mouthed in this heaven of gadgets and commodities, provided only that there were ever more and new things to buy, and perhaps his neighbors were just a little less privileged than he. [1955, p. 135][5]

PSYCHOLOGICAL SCARCITY AND ABUNDANCE

Fromm (1947) makes an interesting distinction between psychological scarcity and psychological abundance. This distinction is similar to Maslow's distinction between deficit and growth motivation. Scarcity refers to a deficiency or lack. Physiological needs fit this model; so also do neurotic cravings. In each case the pleasure is derived from relief of tension. But although the tensions resulting from physiological needs provide motivation for the maintenance of life, the tensions resulting from neurotic needs are rooted in nonproductive traits such as insecurity, anxiety, and fear, and may lead to detrimental emotions such as hatred, envy, and possessiveness. "Abundance pleasure," which Fromm equates with joy and happiness, derives from the productive use of capabilities — activities that go beyond the level of necessity and tension relief. To live abundantly is to use our abilities in a creative and constructive manner to achieve what we

---

[4]From *Man for Himself*, by Erich Fromm. Copyright 1947, ©1975 by Erich Fromm. Reprinted by permission of Holt, Rinehart and Winston, Publishers.
[5]*The Sane Society*.

want to do rather than what we must do. There are many pursuits that have no practical significance in the maintenance of life yet add zest and sparkle to living; literature and the arts are examples. The greatest achievements of people are products of abundance rather than of scarcity motivation.

Sex is a tension state, which can provide genuine pleasure when there is relief of tension, but Fromm believes that there is a great deal more to sex than tension, a mistake that Freud made. Aside from the manner of preparation, the manner of performing the sexual act, and the mechanics of satisfying this need, there are other factors such as feelings which the partners have for each other, moral considerations, and a host of others.

Abundance pleasure, in contrast to tension relief, requires active efforts. A father may derive great joy from having his son in medical school: what tensions are at the root of this pleasure? A distinction between joy and happiness is relevant: joy is the pleasure of single situations whereas happiness is an enduring state punctuated by moments of joy. It should be noted that, according to Fromm, joy and happiness are not goals in themselves but rather byproducts of the productive use of abilities.

HAPPINESS AND CONSCIENCE

According to Fromm (1947), productive living is associated with joy and happiness. The humanistic conscience, if it holds a dominant role in a person's life, will react positively or negatively depending on whether or not behavior is productive. Fromm does not elucidate the specific relationships between conscience and happiness or unhappiness, but it would seem that the operation of conscience plays an important role in both. Furthermore, the subjective state of happiness, as we noted previously, is not necessarily a valid indicator of true happiness; there must be a total organismic response. When the humanistic conscience prevails, the subjective states of pleasure and displeasure may be trusted.

Suppose we take the example of a mother who derives great joy and pride from buying her son his first two-wheel bicycle. Why should this act produce joy, according to Fromm's views? First of all, it is a productive activity, involving productive work and productive love. The mother buys the bicycle with money she has earned, not stolen. Second, she is giving to another human: brotherly love, Fromm's term for love of other humans. Third, her love has no strings attached: she expects nothing in return. Fourth, her activity is motivated not by a painful tension but by the desire to make another happy, a condition that stresses abundance rather than scarcity. Consider other possible reasons for engaging in the same activity. A mother buys a bicycle because she wants her son to win a race and bring honor to her as the mother. Or she really hates her son and gets him things as a reaction-formation against her unmotherly feelings. Or her son may nag her incessantly, so that she complies in order to find relief. There are many other possible reasons. We can see from the preceding illustrations that there is a considerable difference between motives stemming from a productive orientation and motives of nonproductive orientations. Fromm considers the productive orientation morally good and the nonproductive orientations morally bad. Let us now examine these orientations in more detail.

The Productive and Nonproductive Orientations

To comprehend better the meaning of Fromm's productive and nonproductive orientations, we should consider some terms that he uses in a rather unique way. Fromm views personality as being composed of behavior traits, character traits, and character types. By behavior traits he means traits that may be identified by an observer and that are overt manifestations of character traits. Character traits make up the core of personality and are the source of a number of behavior traits. Economy is a behavior trait that may be due to lack of funds (external cause), or it may express the character trait of stinginess (internal cause). What appears to be ethically undesirable when judged strictly as a behavior trait (such as stealing) may be an expression of a character trait (such as a desire for conformity) and thus not a deliberate misdemeanor. For example, a child may steal in order to fit in with the gang. The character traits rather than the specific behaviors must be judged. A character type is a constellation, a patterned organization of traits—what others have termed personality type. A person's character becomes fixed and represents habitual ways of thinking, feeling, and acting. Character types may be productive or nonproductive. The way a person perceives, thinks, feels, and acts is determined by the nature of his or her character type rather than by rational evaluation of situations. According to Fromm (1947), distinct character types, each consisting of a syndrome of traits, are identifiable.

NONPRODUCTIVE ORIENTATIONS

In Fromm's view, each of the nonproductive orientations is a faulty character type. Fromm terms the healthy character type the productive orientation. Although each person is unique, there are many factors that are similar for everyone in a culture. We have mentioned the existential dichotomies with which we all must deal as a result of our humanness. In childhood we are helpless and dependent on others for the satisfaction of needs. Each of us must gradually take over his or her own life and learn to accomplish the tasks that are associated with specific life periods as Erikson (1963) points out. Things can go wrong all along the way. Quite often the difficulties begin early, with the parent-child relationship. If the development of certain basic functions is arrested, these frustrated processes remain as a source of problems for the individual. A person's whole character may be centered about a particular mode of activity. Each of the *nonproductive orientations* represents a *failure in one of the basic tasks of life.*

The receptive orientation   In order to grow properly, each person must learn to receive from others and to give in return, to take things, and to save a part of what he or she has. We must learn to follow authority, to guide others, to be alone, to assert our claims and rights. In the receptive orientation, the dependence on others has not been outgrown. (Fromm and Maccoby, 1970) The lesson that we must earn what we want has not been learned. The individual's relatedness to others is one-sided: he or she is more comfortable receiving than giving or taking.

The exploitative orientation. The exploitative orientation stems from another basic early activity: the explorative and acquisitive activities of the child. A child soon learns that having to wait to be given what he or she needs can produce considerable frustration, and that taking things can be a much more effective means of getting one's way. Eventually, the child also learns that there are many regulations to be followed and that one must acquire rights to things rather than simply appropriate them. Failure to learn this lesson may result in a character structure whose dominant trait is to exploit others. The source of gratification is outside the individual; things are acquired simply by taking, irrespective of others' rights. Frequently the exploitative person harbors a harsh view of life: the only good he or she sees in others is their use value for him or her. Life is viewed as a constant struggle in which a person must dominate others before they gain the upper hand. The qualities of sympathy and empathy have not developed. Fromm refers to this orientation, in its extreme form, as cannibalistic, because others are used (devoured) to further oneself.

The hoarding orientation The hoarding orientation involves preserving and saving. There is suspicion of what is new. Frequently there is compulsive ordering of the events in a person's life. Spontaneity and creativity are likely to be absent; rigidity and adherence to routine are characteristic. There is often a negative tone in the behavior of these persons toward others, but, unlike the exploitative type, they react not with aggressiveness and hostility, but rather with obstinacy and distrust. Fromm describes the hoarders as individuals to whom "the act of creation is a miracle of which they hear but in which they do not believe. Their highest values are order and security; their motto: 'There is nothing new under the sun.'" (Fromm, 1947, p. 67)

The marketing orientation Although the receptive, exploitative, and hoarding orientations are elaborations of Freud's pregenital character types, the marketing orientation belongs to Fromm alone. Unlike the three orientations just discussed, the marketing orientation is not based on fixation or faulty development but rather springs from overidentification with the socioeconomic precepts of capitalistic society. The major theme of this orientation is a person's value as a commodity—as a worker, as a love object, as a person in general. One is not only the product but also the seller and must fit the demand of the marketplace with respect to his or her career, in his or her search for a marital partner, indeed in practically all spheres of living. What the person really is must be subverted to the expectations set by others. (Maddi, 1972) Standards of value are defined by external authorities. The person may conceal his or her real qualities to meet the demands of the marketplace and comes to judge personal worth in terms of the ability to meet these outside standards. The person thus becomes a victim instead of a master of his or her circumstances. There is always a sense of insecurity and inferiority because status, being outside the person's control, is constantly threatened.

Fromm holds that in a capitalistic society a person's sense of self-identity is also impaired. Identity is related to the individual's abilities and to what he or she does with them. Fromm points out, "Both his powers and what they create become estranged,

TABLE 11-3 POSITIVE AND NEGATIVE ASPECTS OF NONPRODUCTIVE ORIENTATIONS

Positive Aspects	Negative Aspects
Receptive Orientation	
Accepting	Passive, without initiative
Responsive	Opinionless, characterless
Devoted	Submissive
Modest	Without pride
Charming	Parasitical
Adaptable	Unprincipled
Socially adjusted	Servile, without self-confidence
Idealistic	Unrealistic
Sensitive	Cowardly
Polite	Spineless
Optimistic	Wishful thinking
Trusting	Guillible
Tender	Sentimental
Exploitative Orientation	
Active	Exploitative
Able to take initiative	Aggressive
Able to make claims	Egocentric
Proud	Conceited
Impulsive	Rash
Self-confident	Arrogant
Captivating	Seducing
Hoarding Orientation	
Practical	Unimaginative
Economical	Stingy
Careful	Suspicious
Reserved	Cold
Patient	Lethargic
Cautious	Anxious
Steadfast, tenacious	Stubborn
Imperturbable	Indolent
Composed under stress	Inert
Orderly	Pedantic
Methodical	Obsessional
Loyal	Possessive
Marketing Orientation	
Social	Unable to be alone
Experimenting	Aimless
Undogmatic	Relativistic
Efficient	Overactive
Curious	Tactless
Intelligent	Intellectualistic
Adaptable	Undiscriminating
Tolerant	Indifferent

TABLE 11-3 (*Continued*)

Positive Aspects	Negative Aspects
Witty	Silly
Generous	Wasteful
Purposeful	Opportunistic
Able to change	Inconsistent
Youthful	Childish
Forward looking	Without a future or a past
Openminded	Without principle and values

Adapted from Fromm, 1947.

something different from himself, something for others to judge and use; thus his feeling of identity becomes as shaky as his self-esteem; it is constituted by the sum total of roles one can play: 'I am as you desire me.'" (Fromm, 1947, p. 73) There may be no market for our abilities, not because they are useless or without value in themselves, but because they are not in demand at the time. Social relationships are also colored by the demands of the market.

Blending of orientations.   Fromm (1947) introduces the idea that character orientations may be blended: no person is totally unproductive or exclusively centered in a single orientation. As a matter of fact, even the nonproductive orientations are styles of living that consist of traits that range from extreme nonproductiveness to productiveness. All the unproductive orientations can be moved toward the positive end of the continuum if the constructive trends in the personality are sufficiently strong. The stubbornness characteristic of the hoarding orientation, for example, can be shaded into tenacity and persistence in achieving goals; the deadening passivity of the receptive orientation can become adaptability. The positive and negative qualities of each orientation, as Fromm listed them, are given in Table 11–3.

Read Table 11–3 with the view that traits listed under Positive Aspects make up a productive orientation. Each of these traits contributes significantly to adapting and coping skills. Under the heading Negative Aspects are listed highly unproductive traits. In a real sense each orientation — receptive, exploitative, hoarding, and marketing — has a productive and nonproductive mode. A concise view of Fromm's model of the productive orientation may be had by noting all the traits under Positive Aspects. The orientations may also be described as (1) accepting, (2) taking, (3) preserving, (4) exchanging, and (5) producing. These terms may be used as healthy expressions of Fromm's nonproductive orientations to life.

Fromm pictures the productive orientation as a properly balanced blending of all the desirable traits of the nonproductive orientations. Each trait adds something useful to the personality although no one ever acquires all of the positive traits, and no one has just the proper balance.

THE PRODUCTIVE ORIENTATION

As we have noted, Fromm's orientations have a productive and nonproductive mode. The traits of the productive mode of each orientation contribute vital ingredients to the formation of personality. For example, there are desirable forms of receptivity — agreeableness, cooperativeness, sociability. There are also desirable forms of exploitation (self-assertiveness) — standing up for one's rights, actively working for what one needs and wants, not allowing other people to interfere with one's rights. The hoarding orientation also contributes vital qualities to the personality, such as protecting our interests, conserving and saving our resources, preparing for the future. In our society, the marketing orientation is necessary in its desirable forms such as selling ourselves, making ourselves attractive and youthful-appearing, cultivating appealing social traits. Like Freud, Fromm views the fully developed personality as being complex and composed of many traits acquired in successive stages of development.

The productive orientation is a mode of relatedness to the world in which we develop and utilize our potentialities as fully as possible. (Fromm, 1947) Two basic modes of dealing with the world are knowing and loving. Through knowledge we become aware of people and things; through love we experience relatedness.

There are parallels between some of Fromm's characteristics of productiveness and Allport's characteristics of maturity; for example, ego involvement in the activity (Allport) and concern and respect for objects (Fromm); warm relating of self to others (Allport) and brotherly love (Fromm). The basic idea of productiveness is activity, not compulsive work that is directed toward making something tangible, but rather activity that fosters the development of all a person's potentialities. Fromm quotes a passage from Ibsen's *Peer Gynt* that brings out the essence of frustrated productiveness. Laziness is an enemy of productiveness, but so also is compulsive work. Unlived aspects of our lives will haunt us in the form of regrets and resentments.

> The Threadballs (on the ground)
> > We are thought
> > > You should have thought us;
> > Little feet, to life
> > > You should have brought us;
> > We should have risen
> > > With glorious sound;
> > But here like threadballs
> > > We are earth-bound.
>
> Withered Leaves
> > We are a watchword;
> > > You should have used us;
> > Life, by your sloth,
> > > Has been refused us.
> > By worms we're eaten
> > > All up and down;
> > No fruit will have us
> > > For spreading crown.

A Sighing in the Air
    We are songs;
        You should have sung us;
    In the depths of your heart
        Despair has wrung us.
    We lay and waited;
        You called us not.
    May your throat and voice
        With poison rot!

Dewdrops
    We are tears
        Which were never shed.
    The cutting ice
        Which all hearts dread
            We could have melted;
    But now its dart
        Is frozen into
            A stubborn heart.
    The wound is closed;
        Our power is lost.

Broken Straws
    We are deeds
        You have left undone;
    Strangled by doubt,
        Spoiled ere begun.
    At the Judgment Day
        We shall be there
    To tell our tale;
        How will you fare?[6]

It might be interesting to relate the productive orientation to the humanistic and authoritarian consciences. The individual who has a strong authoritarian conscience may enjoy a sense of pride because he or she has not violated the laws of the community, the precepts of the religion, the rules of the household, the regulations of the setting. However, because the individual has been so busy avoiding certain behaviors, he or she has not really done anything positive and has used abilities and talents to protect against the power of the authorities in life, but at the cost of limiting the use of abilities and potentialities. In contrast, the person in whom the humanistic conscience is dominant not only avoids certain behaviors but also engages wholeheartedly in self-expression. His or her conscience operates most fully when the person is functioning productively — actively meeting goals and using abilities. He or she is attempting to "get to heaven" by positive achievements rather than by backing away from

[6]*Eleven Plays of Henrik Ibsen.* (New York: Modern Library, Act 5, Scene 6. Quoted in *Man for Himself* by Erich Fromm. Copyright 1947, ©1975 by Erich Fromm. Reprinted by permission of Holt, Rinehart and Winston, Inc.

hell. There is surely more joy and happiness in using our abilities to produce things than in simply avoiding punishment and censure. Often the best way to avoid doing something wrong appears to be to do nothing, but thereby you gain nothing. For the humanistic conscience, sins of omission are just as serious as, if not more so than, sins of commission. What you can do, you ought to do.

Love of Death Versus Love of Life

To sharpen his views on the difference between the productive and nonproductive orientations, Fromm, in his later writings, has introduced a distinction between the *necrophilous* and the *biophilous* orientations to life (1964 and 1973). The necrophilous person is a *lover of destruction, decay,* and *death.* This person hates life and derives pleasure from destroying it. Our modern technological and impersonal age fosters the necrophilous character because it stresses economic values rather than personal values. The industrial revolution began the process of mechanizing humans, using people as machines. The process of dehumanization has progressed as technology has increased in sophistication. The alienated human, the product of industrialization, has deteriorated into the hater of life, the necrophile. Fromm holds, in common with many other growth-oriented theorists, that when growth forces are blocked, destructive processes take over. Much human work is being taken over by machines, and humans are being conceptualized and treated as if they were machines. In a rather strange way, dehumanization is fostered by development of artificial limbs and synthetic, mechanical organs. We are witnessing the development of sophisticated robots that perform the work of humans. Work that once gave meaning to life is being denied to many people. We are living in the era of worship of machines, preoccupation with gadgets, and ever-increasing efficiency of production. This environment does not permit the gratification of the five basic human needs that Fromm holds to be essential to healthy living.

In our society, we are seeing widespread human killing. Among the poor and disadvantaged, who are most victimized by the byproducts of dehumanizing mechanization, the rate of killing is astoundingly high. Furthermore, we are much more accepting of this malignant destructiveness in certain segments of our youth. Little is being done to reverse the conditions that foster this senseless human destructiveness.

In recent years we have seen riots by alienated youths that have destroyed their own neighborhoods. The results of these riots have hurt not only innocent people but those who perpetrated the violence and destructiveness. Fromm could point to the necrophilous tendency in this self-destructive activity. Merchants and other business concerns that were the victims of riots have moved elsewhere; thus, the people in the riot areas have to travel great distances for their supplies and services.

Another area in which destructiveness is becoming a major problem is the schools. For many years the educational system produced learning failures who simply dropped out of school and found whatever work was available to them. But the picture is changing: the thwarted young people are attacking teachers and setting schools on fire. The dehumanization process appears to be increasing in the schools, with the consequence that malignant necrophilic destructiveness is also increasing.

We have been speaking in generalities. Of course, individual people and family climates vary in the balance between life-orientation and death-orientation. Generally speaking, our society tends to foster the necrophilic orientation, but individual circumstances may support or resist the tendency. Fromm (1973) believes that a cold, disinterested mother who is a victim of necrophilia will engender this orientation in her children. They fail to develop the warm attachment to her that is characteristic of normal development and fail to develop social sentiments and a respect for human life.

In contrast, the biophilous orientation affirms human life. A person with a biophilous orientation seeks to expand his or her outreach and fulfill his or her potentials. Human values are given high priority. Even death is viewed as the reason to live life more fully rather than as the factor that negates the value of life. The necrophilic person says: "Death makes life meaningless." The biophilic person says: "Death makes living all the more urgent."

HAVING ORIENTATION VERSUS BEING ORIENTATION

Fromm (1976) distinguishes between a *having* mode of living and a *being* mode of living. The being mode is characterized by participation in, and experiencing of, life-promoting activities. It exemplifies the biophilic orientation, in which life is affirmed and increased. We are reminded of Rogers' fully functioning person, Jung's individuated personality, Maslow's self-actualizing person, Allport's requirements for maturity. For Fromm, the "being" mode of living is an essential attribute of the productive orientation.

The "having" mode of living stresses possessions. Happiness is equated with having many things and abundant consumption. We are reminded of Fromm's marketing orientation, which fits the American dream of wealth, beauty, and popularity. A person's self-worth depends upon his or her bank account, property holdings, and other symbols of wealth and possessions. The motto of the "having" mode is "I am worth more if I have more of what others value." Obviously, we need certain things for survival, and, in fact, Fromm has pointed out that the productive life depends on abundance. If all our energies were required simply to survive, we could not develop and utilize our most distinctively human potentials. Having many things beyond the requirements for survival does not in direct proportion increase our enjoyment of life. Fromm has repeatedly pointed to the insanity that our "having" society creates as we struggle to have more and more material things and to surpass our neighbors. Technological society has made life better in some respects, but the byproducts of unemployment, inflation, restlessness, alienation, insecurity, and a host of other problems created by humans challenge the true value of these developments for humanity. We see again Fromm's insistence on the great influence of society in setting the problems for us. We are not born with a "having" orientation, but acquire this distorted form of adaptation and coping as a result of socioeconomic forces.

Fromm was so impressed by the difference between the having and the being modes of living that he viewed this difference as the major problem of existence as he points out in the following passage:

> What I saw has led me to conclude that this distinction, together with that between love of life and love of the dead, represents the most crucial problem of existence; that empirical

It is better to be than to have.

Photo credits: *upper* Peter Menzel/Stock, Boston; *lower* Mimi Forsyth/Monkmeyer Press Photo Service

anthropological and psychoanalytic data tend to demonstrate that having and being are two fundamental modes of experience, the respective strengths of which determine the differences between the characters of individuals and various types of social character." [Fromm, 1976, p. 16][7]

[7] *To Have or to Be?*

The Role of Love in Human Life

If you were asked to reveal the most basic and most personal striving you have, it would probably be the desire to be part of an intimate love relationship. Fromm holds that union with others, particularly erotic love between man and woman, is one of the strongest human motives. You can hardly attend a movie, a play or an opera, or become acquainted with a person without encountering the theme of unrequited love. The craving for love is the major theme of the vast majority of popular songs. Why is love so significant in human life? Fromm holds that the craving for love, whether normal productive love or the many distortions of it, is one of our basic strivings because it points to the answer to the human situation: it is the only way that we can truly solve our condition of separation and aloneness. "In the experience of love lies the only answer to being human, lies sanity." (Fromm, 1947, p. 33) In a recent lecture, Fromm stated that love is potentially the greatest power on earth.

It will be recalled that, by virtue of being human, we experience a loss of harmony and oneness with nature. We are separated, strangers in our world. We heavily depend upon our cultural supports for our stability — traditions, customs, values, practices — but these have been changing rapidly in recent years; thus, our anchors have been lost and our sense of alienation has increased.

Our sense of separation and isolation is the basic cause of our anxiety. To overcome this painful state, many means are used. Alcohol and drugs dull the realization of alienation and estrangement. In the intoxicated state, a person cuts off the outside world and thus temporarily feels euphoria because he or she has blocked out the problem of isolation. The internal state of awareness is the person's only world. But the relief is temporary, and the only way to cope again with the problem is to use more intoxicants. Some drugs, such as mood elevators, enhance participation and union with the outside world by increasing sensory acuity and energy expenditure, but this again is a transitory and artificial means of solving a basic human problem. The only real and lasting solution is productive love (Fromm, 1955). (See also *Love and Addiction*, by Stanton Peele and Archie Broddey, 1975, for further insight into the ways we humans seek to reduce alienation and find fulfillment through means external to ourselves).

Fromm believes that many people deal with the requirement of loving in the wrong way. They seek to be loved rather than to love. They view love as an intensely emotional experience, as an involvement with a highly appealing person that simply happens when the appropriate partner is encountered. According to Fromm, "they are starved for [love]; they watch endless numbers of films about happy and unhappy love stories, they listen to hundreds of trashy songs about love — yet hardly anyone thinks that there is anything that needs to be learned about love." (1956, p. 1) Fromm portrays some of our other mistaken notions about love: "Love and affection have assumed the same meaning as that of the formula for the baby, or the college education one should get, or the latest film one should 'take in.' You feed love, as you feed security, knowledge and everything else — and you have a happy person!" (1955, p. 200) He goes on to say that many individuals "take the intensity of the infatuation, this being 'crazy' about each other, for proof of the intensity of their love, while it may only prove the degree of their preceding loneliness." (1956, p. 4)

Loving involves much more than emotional reaction; it is an active process of the total personality that brings into play thought, feeling, and behavior. The highest forms of human love do not "just happen" in the presence of another person. Romantic love is often confused with true erotic love; the sexual component is quite prominent, but romantic love is based on sudden discovery, on physical attraction, on hormonal changes; it is only an allurement to a deeper form of love. (Harlow, 1971) Romantic love is not the highest form of love, if it is love at all. There is motherly love, brotherly love, love for oneself, love for God (Table 11-4). All types of productive love are rooted in activity of the total personality and involve caring, responsibility, respect, and knowledge of the loved one. These four elements are necessary conditions for any loving relationship to occur. The specific type of love relationship would include other ingredients. Through a deliberate striving to love, the ability to love can be developed. Loving can become an enduring trait of personality—like generosity, truthfulness, promptness—that exerts a continuing influence on human relationships. Love does not happen to a person; it must be cultivated. (Fromm, 1956)

Because being human means to feel alone and separated, there is a strong motivation to unite with others, frequently in a loving relationship. This may be seen in a great variety of behaviors. Conformity to the standards set by the culture (or by subgroups within the culture) is an expression of the need for relatedness. Despite the plea that everyone wants to be different and unique, the fact remains that the urge to conform is much more conspicuous than is individualism. (Fromm, 1941) The rebel-

TABLE 11-4 FIVE OBJECTS OR TYPES OF PRODUCTIVE LOVE

1. Brotherly love: Care for, responsibility for, respect for, and knowledge of another human being; a love between equals.
2. Motherly love: Unconditional affirmation of a child's life and needs; care and responsibility for the child's life and growth.
   a. Motherly love is an attitude that instills love for life.
   b. Motherly love is by nature a love of inequality: the mother gives and the child takes.
   c. Fatherly love is conditional: it is acquired or earned by the child's performance of duty, by his or her obedience, or by his or her fulfillment of the father's expectations.
3. Erotic love: A craving for complete fusion, for union with one other person.
   a. Erotic love is directed toward one person of the opposite sex with whom oneness and fusion are desired.
   b. Without brotherly love, erotic love is mere sexual desire and not true love.
4. Self-love (love of self): Not selfishness, not narcissism.
   a. Love for oneself is inseparably connected to love for any other being.
   b. Love of self is a prerequisite for brotherly love ("Love Thy Neighbor as Thyself").
   c. According to Fromm, love of self is a loving, affirmative, friendly attitude toward oneself.
5. Love of God: The highest value, the most desirable good to which human aspire and represent by the concept "god."

lious young person who joins a militant radical group may actually be more of a conformist than those he or she criticizes. His or her feeling of alienation and aloneness impels him or her to unite in a common cause almost to the exclusion of his or her individuality. Without knowing it, this person is striving desperately for brotherly love. If a member of such a group becomes involved in a productive love relationship with another person, the sense of relatedness and security provided by the affiliation with the radical group may be replaced by the intimate personal relationship; you may see a total change in life orientation.

LOVE AND THE NONPRODUCTIVE ORIENTATIONS

Love is such a significant function of the total personality that any personality defect will affect the ability to love. The disturbance will produce a distortion of one or more of the aspects of loving: dominating rather than giving, demanding rather than accepting, dictating rather than reciprocating, loving as satisfaction of tension rather than as expression of regard for the other. (Fromm, 1956)

Love and the marketing orientation. In the marketing orientation, people view themselves as packages to be displayed. Fromm (1947) distinguishes between the *use value* and the *exchange value* of an object. The exchange value is what the object will bring in the marketplace; the use value is its real worth. The real worth may have little to do with the actual exchange value. A man may value a woman because she fits a cultural image. In our culture that might include being physically beautiful (and standards of beauty are also defined by the culture; in some cultures the fatter the woman, the more beautiful she is thought to be). Love based on exchange value rather than real value is superficial and temporary; it is founded on qualities that are bound to change. Marketing types have a terrible dread of growing old because they then lose the value that they had as young persons. What is valued is a persona, a social mask that makes for the "good package." The relationship between two such people is thus rooted in an artificial involvement. There is even the idea that you can buy a new package if the old one loses the qualities that were a part of the original package. The marketing orientation, so common today, creates terrible stresses for the young person. He or she must keep in style, but not everyone fits the expected pattern; hence there is a great deal of self-depreciation. (Hirsch and Keniston, 1970) The desirable traits of the marketing orientation keep a loving relationship alive.

LOVE AND THE PRODUCTIVE ORIENTATION

Freud, when asked to indicate the qualities of the mature person, answered that the mature person should be able to work and to love. Certainly, neurotic people commonly suffer from an inability to do either. The love of one who suffers from a nonproductive orientation to living is one-sided, distorted, and not conducive to the mutual development of each of the parties. What then characterizes productive love, and how does it differ from other forms?

Fromm's description of productive love resembles the popular notion of intense

© 1981 Susan Rosenberg/Photo Researchers, Inc.

Love is the most powerful force on earth.

liking. Consider the attraction between a man and a woman: she may describe him as cute, sharp, exciting, smooth, groovy, and the like; he may describe her as doll-like, heavenly, sweet, lovable, or neat. In both instances we get the impression of physical attraction, but there is more; there is an infatuation with personality traits. You may be especially attracted to the smile, the voice, the laugh, the wit, and so on, of the other. The attraction is often due more to what the person is or has than to what the person does. Whatever this is called, Fromm does not consider it love. The qualities that make for physical and psychological attraction are merely preconditions that may set the stage for the formation of a love relationship. Productive love is not a mysterious quality that arises in a person when the appropriate object is present and available; there must be certain activities, namely, (1) care, (2) responsibility, (3) respect, and (4) knowledge of each other. (Fromm, 1947)

Many young people are concerned about being attractive to members of the other sex. Fromm would counsel them to work at loving. To be loved means to be loving just as to be interesting means being interested. A loving person will be attractive to others. People are lonely and quite eager to form close relationships: this is one answer to the human situation. We whose plight is to feel alone seek relatedness, but we also need to be independent. To be intimately related with someone or something, and at the same time remain an independent individual, a person must love productively. Although there are many other forms of relatedness, they fail to satisfy these seemingly contradictory needs. In a loving relation, erotic feelings may be prominent, but other components are required.

1. Care.   Care for the loved one involves activity, giving of oneself, doing something, working for another. When a person works to produce something, it becomes a part of him or her. Two people who care for each other produce something new that neither has alone. A growing thing, the relatedness between them, is created. Again, we may comprehend the idea if we keep in mind that Fromm means by love what others call intense liking.

2. Responsibility.   The notion of responsibility also implies activity. Responsibility to another does not mean domination, control, or depriving another of autonomy. It means answering to the needs of the loved one. One of the highest forms of loving is a mother's love for her child. She expects nothing in return for her care; she responds to the child's needs, desiring only his or her growth and development. The mother's love is unconditional, at least during infancy, according to Fromm. In a productive love relationship, each accepts the needs of the other as genuine rather than attempting to change them and strives to gratify those needs. The integrity and autonomy of the loved one must be guarded; otherwise, the love may deteriorate into domination.

3. Respect.   Respect implies concern for the rights of the loved one. A relationship based entirely on an idealized image of the other is bound to falter. The relationship should be based on the real attributes of the person and not on imagined qualities that are projected onto him or her. If there is a desire to remake the other person, although the one desiring the change may plead strongly that he or she really loves, the love cannot be real. Some imperfections must be tolerated; some change is always taking place. The two create a new thing, their relationship.

4. Knowledge.   Knowledge can occur on different levels. In loving, you should penetrate to the core of the other, get to the essence of his or her nature. Here knowing requires experiencing the other in his or her totality. Knowledge should be objective, not colored by desire and distortion. You must get to know the other as he or she is.

All four aspects of productive love are interrelated and required for a loving relationship to be formed. The various types of loving relationships involve additional elements, as we have noted. Self-love, care and responsibility for oneself, self-respect, and self-knowledge are also conditions of productive love.

CRITICAL EVALUATION

Fromm has been quite bold in attempting to identify specific traits of the various orientations to life. In the case of the nonproductive orientations, he presents the traits in bipolar form, so that we have both the positive and the negative traits associated with each orientation. Fromm does not really tell us how to move from the negative to the positive traits except in a highly general manner. We have attempted to concretize some of his ideas in this regard in the Guides to Living section.

Fromm's distinction between the authoritarian and humanistic consciences is a valuable one, but there are problems that he does not deal with adequately. Although the nature of the authoritarian conscience is depicted quite clearly, the humanistic conscience seems vague and even mystical. Fromm says that the humanistic conscience is the real self. But what is this real self, and how does it come about? Does it include needs, abilities, interests? And are not these subject to learning? What part does culture play? Can we really rely on joy and happiness, defined by Fromm as psychobiological well-being, as valid indicators of the humanistic conscience?

Fromm's idea of humanistic ethics as a guide to healthy living is still more a hope than an actuality. No one has yet solved the perennial problems of birth control, abortion, euthanasia, premarital sexuality, and extramarital sexuality. Are these good or bad for people? Can we really establish values that are equally good for all people because they are based on human nature?

GUIDES TO RESEARCH

HEURISTIC VALUE OF FROMM'S THEORY

Fromm's writings cover a wide range of topics in sociology, philosophy, mental hygiene, economics, and political structures. His ideas are cited by such eminent psychologists as Maslow, Horney, and Sullivan. As we have noted, his works are widely read in colleges and universities, but the degree to which his ideas have stimulated new lines of research is difficult to assess. His many suggestions for improving society have not had much impact and have not been applied. Fromm has not founded a school of psychology or attracted a large discipleship who promulgate his views; thus, we would have to conclude that Fromm's ideas have not had significant heuristic value. He has propounded a humanistic psychology, a movement that seems to be gaining momentum in the eighties. The social, economic, political, and personal problems that Fromm pointed out so frequently are becoming ever more acute.

For example, he deplored the inferior status of women and wholeheartedly supported feminine emancipation in political, economic, social, and vocational life. Fromm strongly promoted the idea that people, all people, should be given the opportunity to fulfill their potential. Like Karen Horney (1967), Fromm accused Freud of demeaning women. He succinctly summarizes Freud's view of women in the following statement: "To look at women as castrated men, with a weakly developed Super-Ego (sense of morality), vain and unreliable, all this is only a slightly rationalized version of the patriarchal prejudices of his (Freud's) times." (Fromm, 1959, p. 22) Fromm has not only acutely perceived the problems that plague us, but he has also proposed remedies that may turn out to be workable in the near future.

EMPIRICAL RESEARCH SUGGESTED BY FROMM'S THEORY

Many of Fromm's views are explicit enough to translate into testable hypotheses: for example, the various character types, the role of the five basic human needs, and the place of existential dichotomies in human life, but researchers have not turned to Fromm for their ideas. One difficulty is that Fromm writes in a literary style and tends to speak in generalities about humanity. He often deals with what might be described as "grand" social and economic issues that are not easily reduced to testable form. It is extremely difficult to duplicate under controlled conditions of experimentation various types of socioeconomic systems such as democracy, autocracy, and communism and to observe their long-range effects on character formation.

Fromm and Maccoby (1970) report an extensive study of the character types in a small Mexican village in which a team of investigators studied the adult population of about 500 people. It was an extensive investigation that involved a multidisciplinary approach covering several years. It was a broad social-psychological study, which involved psychologists, anthropologists, physicians, and statisticians, who studied the people in terms of their history, social structure, attitudes, changing traditions, and health. The people in the village were studied in depth by means of interviews, questionnaires, paper and pencil tests, direct observation, and even projective tests such as the TAT (Thematic Apperception Test) and the Rorschach Inkblot Test.

The social, political, and economic conditions that prevailed tended to create fairly distinct classes. Most of the townspeople were farmers who worked for a landowner. Their lives were simple and limited. Some people worked as fishermen and were mainly self-employed. Still others were potters who earned a meager living from the sale of their wares. Some of the farmers had small plots of land, which they worked with their families, using primitive methods of farming. They were better off than those who worked for the landowners, because they profited directly from their own effort.

Most of the people lived rather insecure lives, barely on a subsistence level. Fromm describes the general tone of the people as selfish, suspicious of one another, pessimistic, and fatalistic about the future. Many passively accepted their lot and depreciated themselves in comparison to city people. They felt helpless to change conditions and powerless to influence either nature or the industrial machine that controlled them (see Fromm and Maccoby, 1970, p. 37).

In this study we have the opportunity to observe the powerful influence of environmental conditions—physical, social, economic, and cultural—on the character types that developed. Here were people living under varying conditions in a relatively small area.

It will be recalled that Fromm specifies bipolar traits that, at one extreme, constitute nonproductive orientations and at the other end of the continuum contribute to a productive orientation; thus, one could speak of productive and nonproductive versions of the receptive orientation, the exploitative orientation, the hoarding orientation, and the marketing orientation. Several of the character types proposed by Fromm applied to the people of the village, depending upon their life circumstances. A character type may be thought of as a person's psychosocial adaptation to the conditions of life to which he or she has been exposed.

The nonproductive receptive character type was found among the poorest group, the farmers who worked for the landowners. These people had the least control of their circumstances and tended to be passive and submissive to external authority. They were the victims of powerful external control, which left them in a subservient state.

Fromm and Maccoby found that those who owned the small plots of land were better off than the serf farmers because they could influence to some degree their own destinies. If they worked hard and if the conditions were favorable, they would have surplus food that would enable them to save some money. These people fitted the hoarding productive type, which might be described as self-reliant and independent. Their circumstances permitted initiative and a certain amount of self-determination in controlling their own circumstances. There were also people who fitted the nonproductive hoarding type and could be characterized as unduly security-oriented and self-limiting in the face of greater productivity potential. They accepted less than they might have achieved because they were unwilling to take risks.

Although in the minority, productive and nonproductive forms of the exploitative character types were found among the villagers. The unproductive types were likely to engage in fighting and manipulation of others through power plays. Women who were of the nonproductive exploitative type were characterized by Fromm and Maccoby as the "most malicious gossip mongers." (1970, p. 48) The productive exploitative character types were the smallest group, a few rich men who owned the land (which the serfs worked) and the few commercial enterprises that existed in the village. They had adopted the capitalistic spirit and methods of Western societies and were the entrepreneurs. They were the people who not only possessed the bulk of the wealth in the village, but were also respected and regarded as the leaders of the community although they were hated by the serfs.

Fromm's marketing orientation did not emerge from this study, probably because the simple conditions of life in the village did not foster such traits as play-acting, exhibitionism, and popularity-seeking that are found among certain classes in our modern urban centers. One might predict that such traits would be more common as the conditions of life improved.

This study is a good example of theory-inspired research. It was supportive of Fromm's views on the formation of character types, but, more importantly, it serves as a model of significant research that is guided by a well-conceived theory. Fromm has proposed solutions to our most urgent problems, but unless they are actually tried in field situations, they will remain mere speculations.

GUIDES TO LIVING

THE PRACTICE OF LOVE

Fromm holds that love is an art that can be acquired through the aid of the following factors.

The overcoming of narcissism.
In the strict sense of the word, narcissism means excessive selfishness. It may be extended to include an egocentric interpretation of events. Objective observation is not possible when narcissism is present. The person sees everything from the standpoint of his or her own needs, attitudes, and prejudices. No one ever succeeds completely in eliminating subjective elements, but one can more closely approximate objectivity. (Elkind, 1967) Certainly, one can deliberately strive to remove the narcissistic focus. Preoccupation with oneself and distortion caused by selfish desires block the possibility of productive love. (Fromm, 1947) Everyone must deal with the narcissistic aspect of his or her personality. It is probably the most outstanding hindrance to productive love. Self-love and self-ishness for Fromm are not the same. In fact they are opposites. Loving oneself means respect for self and also respect for others because they are like self.

Faith.
We may distinguish between rational and irrational faith. Rational faith is grounded in sound observation and reasoning, whereas irrational faith is blind trust in an authority, or wish fulfillment. Fromm believes that, through practice, faith can be developed as a trait of personality. It is an essential aspect of productive love. (Fromm, 1947)

An interesting aspect of faith in a loved one is that it tends to foster that which we desire in the other. If a man trusts his wife and child, they may live up to the trust, whereas if he expects them to disappoint him, they probably will. Loved ones may live up either to faith or to the lack of it; thus, faith is more productive than its opposite. Again there must be a rational basis for faith: you would not trust a two-year-old with a large sum of money she received as a gift. Through practice one can increase his ability to have faith in himself and others. Fromm would counsel us to look for instances in ourselves of lack of faith and to try to understand the reasons for them. Consider qualities within yourself that make you distrustful or doubting. For example, if you have to choose between having faith in an unknown future and assuming a gloomy outlook (because you are dealing with unknowns anyway), it would seem much more beneficial to proceed with faith. You may question the meaning and value of going to college and become discouraged and depressed, but if you have faith that the benefits will come, the work will get done without as much pain. Here we are reminded of Adler's useful fictions.

Promoting a loving nature.

Fromm believes that we have a social, loving nature, but it can be brought out only under certain cultural conditions. No culture exists that fits humanity well. Capitalism, for example, at best stresses fairness rather than love. A business deal is good if each party gets something and maybe gives in to the same degree: one does not benefit at the expense of the other. But loving goes further than fairness: it implies care and concern for others. Society should promote a sense of brotherly love in all. People should work harmoniously with a sense of mutual concern. Caring for one another should be a widespread condition in a society. This is the only hope in the face of human loneliness and alienation. The development of greater communal spirit is Fromm's (1955) answer to the human situation.

FREEDOM *FROM* VERSUS FREEDOM *TO*

Fromm (1941) offers us an interesting insight into an important human concern through his distinction between freedom *from* and freedom *to*. This distinction refers to the negative and positive aspects of freedom. There is a significant difference between being free *from* external controls, regulations, or restrictions and being free *to* use our capabilities, abilities, and resources.

Being able to make productive use of capabilities is the most liberating type of freedom for meeting the problems associated with being human. To be free from submission to authority does not guarantee that the positive freedom will occur. Freedom to do things is an outcome of the productive orientation.

MEETING FROMM'S FIVE HUMAN NEEDS

1. Relatedness. How can we satisfy our need for relatedness? Fromm tells us to cultivate the art of loving. Loving, and hence relatedness, can be encouraged through a concentrated effort to get to know another person. A loving attitude is strengthened by caring enough for the other to do things for him or her. Love is also fostered by being sensitive to the other's needs, likes, and dislikes and adjusting our behavior to them. Finally, love is promoted by respecting the other—giving him or her positive regard, accepting the person as he or she is, respecting individuality and uniqueness. These are the attributes of true love, productive love as Fromm terms it. This type of relatedness cannot help but engender love in return from at least some others. Just as hate begets hate, so love begets love.

2. Transcendence. How can we overcome dependency, passivity, the pressures of immediate circumstances? Fromm suggests that we use all our abilities productively. He agrees with Maslow's problem orientation to life in his own notion of intelligence, by which he means the use of our abilities to solve the problems of living. This implies profiting from past mistakes, looking at all possible alternatives before making a decision, and dealing unemotionally with personal challenges. We should use our ability to reason, according to Fromm, as a means of perceiving things as they really are. We may contrast and compare, analyze and synthesize, integrate and coordinate the impressions we receive. Agreeing with Kelly (1955), Fromm holds that we should take the scientist's approach by forming tentative constructs of the events in our world and then testing these through the deductions derived from them. In brief, we can use our abilities to meet our needs if we develop these abilities as fully as possible. Like other personality theorists, Fromm places great stress on active and skilled participation in our world.

In characteristic fashion, Fromm emphasizes the role of productive love as a means of overcoming the feeling of being trapped and victimized by the environment. Thus transcendence is achieved by productive use of reason, intelligence, skills, and emotions. The whole person is involved through thought, feeling, and action.

3. Rootedness.

How can we promote a sense of belongingness? Fromm suggests involvement (similar to Allport's idea of self-extension) in something bigger than ourselves. Examples might be our church and religion, a social or civic organization, our family, a cause. We should especially appreciate the importance of customs, traditions, places that we enjoy. Cherishing friends and acquaintances can help to satisfy the need for rootedness. Establishing our own traditions and customs can also help to satisfy this need: for example, a family dinner together every Sunday. In an unfamiliar environment, such as a new job, we may gain a sense of rootedness simply by bringing some familiar objects to our place of work: a set of pipes, a plant, or a book rack. However it is accomplished, rootedness is one of our requirements for productive living.

4. Identity.

How can we develop a sense of identity? Fromm says that we gain a sense of identity through creative and productive activities. We may become identified by our skills, our accomplishments, our professions. He also points out that productive love helps to foster identity because it provides for an intimate and enjoyable union between two people and at the same time fosters a sense of individuality and uniqueness. I experience vital powers in myself when I demonstrate love for another, and the love I receive affirms my identity and sense of worthiness. It should be noted that an act of loving in itself has value for personality functioning even if it is not reciprocated.

5. Frame of reference.

How can we promote better understanding of ourselves and of the world? Fromm would agree with Frankl (1955) on the importance of meaning in human life. There are some things about which we are quite clear. Understanding and meaningfulness would be enhanced if we periodically reminded ourselves of those things that are important to us. Counting our blessings is one means of doing so. We may count our blessings in a negative way by considering all the things that could have happened but did not: "I cried because I had no shoes, until I met a man with no feet." A more positive approach is to affirm the value of the things we consider desirable, reviewing our achievements and instances of good fortune. Another way to foster understanding is to cultivate patience with ambiguities and deficiencies of knowledge. Learning about ourselves and our world is an ongoing process. The mysteries of life may never be known, but there can be a continual improvement in understanding and meaning. Again, we can look to science as a guide with the expectation that the same techniques and safeguards applied to the study of the universe can be applied to our own lives. For the mysteries that have no answers, we can experience a sense of reverence and invoke an attitude of acceptance.

SUMMARY

1. Fromm proposes a humanistic psychoanalysis that attempts to restore the distinctively human attributes to psychoanalysis. He takes up the issue of what it means to be human and goes on to consider productive and nonproductive orientations. A value-orientation is one of the most important human attributes. Fromm holds that ethics can teach us much of value about the ideal life, if it is brought into line with scientific findings. For Fromm, ideal human existence is ethical existence. Value judgments are the basis of our actions and expectations. Neurosis is the inability to resolve value conflicts. The source of norms for ethical conduct lies within our nature, if we are functioning normally. Ethics deals with ideal standards of conduct for humankind, whereas mental hygiene is concerned with promoting optimal mental health of the individual.

2. Fromm delineates five basic psychological needs, the frustration of which leads to alienation, insanity, or death. They are relatedness, rootedness, transcendence, identity, and frame of reference. The major problems of life are not sex and aggression but rather stem from the human situation, the problems associated with the attributes of being human. Fromm terms the human species the freak of the universe because we do not have instincts to guide us, but must depend on our own reasoning abilities and skills. Societies provide solutions to our problems, but existing societies themselves promote abnormalities. The major problem of life is alienation (a sense of loneliness), and the solution is found in productive work and loving relationships. security

3. We cannot attain a productive orientation without considering ethical issues and values. The mature, healthy, and integrated person is virtuous in the sense of fostering the fullness of self-development and communal living. Vice and sin are forms of self-mutilation.

4. Authoritarian ethics imposes a code of values and practices that may be contrary to human nature. Humanistic ethics are based on the requirements of our natures collectively and individually. In humanistic ethics, what is right or wrong is good or bad for us. Failure to live fully is a sin in humanistic ethics. Conscience is a regulatory agency within personality that enables us to observe, reflect on, and evaluate conduct. The judgments of conscience may stem from internalized prescriptions (the authoritarian conscience) or self-evaluation based upon one's own ideals and values (the humanistic conscience or the dictates of the real self). Humanistic conscience promotes growth, spontaneity, and the fulfillment of the self. The authoritarian conscience is like Freud's superego and represents introjected precepts of authority figures that are either admired or feared. Authoritarian conscience hampers growth and limits freedom and may lead to behavior that is contrary to our nature. Humanistic conscience rules through self-determined precepts that are based on obligations to oneself, what Allport calls "oughts" rather than the "musts" of the authoritarian conscience. Humanistic conscience is experienced as a sense of well-being or self-dissatisfaction. Humanistic conscience consists of values that stem from requirements of the person.

5. Our very nature confronts us with insoluble problems—problems of existence that Fromm terms existential dichotomies. These refer to unresolvable contradictions, such as desiring immortality but knowing that we must die. Historical dichotomies are contradictions that need not have occurred, such as poverty in the face of abundance.

6. Fromm's unproductive orientations are unsuccessful means of living. Fromm observed that we must be passionately involved with something. In Western cultures, there is a passionate pursuit of wealth, power, and status. Neurosis may be considered an irrational religion. Life must have meaning, by which Fromm means involvements, attachments, and interests.

7. Fromm argued that joy and happiness can be good guides to living, if we define them in terms of a total organismic response: a sense of well-being that includes both the psyche and the body. Unhappiness is expressed in physical symptoms. Fromm holds that our body is less capable of being deceived by unhappiness than our mind.

8. Scarcity motivation and abundance motivation have radically different outcomes. The former results in tension-relief whereas the latter results in growth. The difference is in doing what we have to do versus doing what we want to do.

9. Behavior traits are expressions of character traits, and character traits make up character types, which may be either productive

Love

or nonproductive. Each of the four major nonproductive orientations is an unhealthy character type. Each is a failure in the major tasks of life. In the receptive orientation, dependence becomes the major mode of satisfying needs; in the exploitative orientation, aggressive taking from others is exaggerated; in the hoarding orientation, conservation and security are stressed; in the marketing orientation, selling ourselves as a commodity is the means of satisfying needs. The nonproductive orientations consist of bipolar traits that range from productive qualities at one extreme to nonproductive ones at the other. The productive orientation consists of all the desirable traits of the nonproductive orientations in proper balance. It includes (a) receiving, (b) taking, (c) preserving, (d) exchanging, and (e) producing. "What one can do one ought to do" is a good characterization of the productive orientation. The productive orientation is also characterized by a biophilous mode of living, the affirmation of the worth of life. Fromm refers to a necrophilous orientation as a nonproductive mode, which refers to orientation to death and destruction, based on dehumanized living. Fromm also distinguishes between a being orientation, which emphasizes experiences, and a

having orientation, which places value on possessions. The alienated human, the product of the industrial revolution, has deteriorated into the hater of life, the necrophile. Fromm made an important distinction between freedom *from* and freedom *to*: We may be free from external restrictions and controls but not free to use abilities because we resort to escape mechanisms, rather than face the risks of failure associated with activity.

10. Loving relationships are our answer to alienation. Love involves an active process that can be cultivated; it is an art. The essence of loving relationships is care, respect, responsibility, and knowledge. Other types of love, such as brotherly love, motherly love, fatherly love, erotic love, self-love and love of God, have additional elements. Love is expressed in distorted forms in the nonproductive orientations. The most productive love is that which allows the fullest development of individuality. Fromm stressed the active nature of love rather than defining it in terms of highly emotional states.

11. Fromm's ideas have attracted wide interest and have influenced many thinkers, but they have not generated much empirical research.

GLOSSARY

Alienation: In Fromm's meaning, feelings of loneliness, of not belonging in your important settings; one of the consequences of failure to satisfy the five basic human needs.

Automaton conformity: A form of escape in which a person submits to a guiding authority or follows socially defined roles for the sake of being acceptable.

Freak of the universe: Fromm's description of humanity's peculiar state of existence; not being guided by instincts, each person must work out his or her own destiny; also refers to the problems resulting from the human situation.

Human needs: Fromm proposes five basic

psychological needs, which are distinctively human and which must be met in order to avoid the sense of alienation.

    1. Relatedness: Need to have meaningful human contacts; many loving relationships of all types.

    2. Rootedness: Need to feel that you belong or are a part of your various social settings; having a sense of tradition.

    3. Transcendence: Feeling of having control over your circumstances; of not being trapped and controlled by others; a sense of creativity; pathological transcendence involves hate and malignant aggression; gaining control by destruction and death.

4. Identity: Need to have acceptable roles by which you are known and with which you are identified.

5. Frame of reference: Need for meaning; to make sense of what you do.

The human situation: The problems associated with the attributes of being human; facing death, imperfection, aging, and unknowns.

Existential dichotomies: Contradictions that stem from human attributes; insoluble conflicts, such as wishing for immortality and knowing that you must die; wishing for perfection but having to live with imperfection.

Historical dichotomies: Inconsistencies and contradictions that have existed but could have been prevented.

Humanistic communitarian socialism: Fromm's Utopian society in which people live in small communities and have a great deal of mutual concern.

Humanistic psychoanalysis: Fromm's brand of psychoanalysis, which stresses the distinctively human attributes and needs; the highest possibilities for humans; a humanizing of psychoanalysis.

Nonproductive orientations: Faulty life-styles developed early in life that represent failures in the major tasks of living; the development of a faulty character type; the life-style is centered about an exaggeration of a basic mode of survival.

1. Receptive orientation: An exaggeration of dependency; life is organized about the mode of receiving from others; the characteristics for accomplishing this task are developed, such as being lovable, conforming, and passive.

2. Exploitative orientation: Life-orientation is centered about taking from others; traits of aggressiveness and callousness are prominent.

3. Hoarding orientation: A life-style that is characterized by restricted participation in life, including traits of miserliness, compulsive orderliness, obstinacy, and disinclination to take risks.

4. Marketing orientation: The prod-uct of a capitalistic society; people suit themselves to the demands of the marketplace; a person is a commodity that is valued according to the worth that others bestow.

5. Necrophilous orientation: Love of death and destruction; results from dehumanizing conditions of industrialization.

Norms of behavior: Sources of values and standards.

Authoritarian ethics: A code of standards imposed by an external authority; requires obedience out of fear or through admiration; may not be conducive to fulfilling one's potentials.

Humanistic ethics: A code of values based on the requirements of human nature; good is defined as what promotes life; evil is defined as what hinders life.

Authoritarian conscience: Like Freud's superego in that external prescriptions are internalized; may be the source of guilt and self-limitation.

Humanistic conscience: The loving care for ourselves; the sense of promoting our welfare; humanistic conscience is felt as a sense of well-being or self-dissatisfaction.

Productive orientation: Orientation to the world that is characterized by reasoned solutions, loving relationships, productive skills, biophilia (love of life), and a being mode of living. It consists of the positive traits of the nonproductive orientations.

Biophilia: Love of life and affirmation of human values.

Being mode versus having mode: The being mode stresses human experiences; the having mode stresses material possessions.

Loving orientation: Active concern for others; involves care, respect, responsibility, and understanding. These common elements are necessary for all forms of love, but specific types have additional components, such as motherly love, fatherly love, and erotic love.

Freedom *from* versus freedom *to*: Freedom *from* is a negative form of freedom, in which restrictions are removed, but one may not be free to act and may resort to forms of escape. Freedom *to* is a positive form of freedom, which involves taking action.

SUGGESTED READINGS

Fromm, Erich. *Escape from Freedom*. New York: Holt, Rinehart and Winston, 1941.

Considered Fromm's most important work, this book is an exploration of the causes of human submission to tyranny.

———. *Man for Himself*. New York: Holt, Rinehart and Winston, 1947.

In this work, Fromm inquires into the psychology of ethics, considering the role of morality in the world today.

———. *Psychoanalysis and Religion*. New Haven: Yale University Press, 1950.

Both priests and analysts are summoned to respond to the challenges of technocracy's spiritual wasteland.

———. *The Sane Society*. New York: Holt, Rinehart and Winston, 1955.

Both a psychoanalytic and a socioanalytic work. *The Sane Society* considers the effects of contemporary Western culture on the mental health of Western people.

———. *The Art of Loving*. New York: Harper & Row, 1956.

In this popular book, Fromm presents tangible steps for fostering the ability to love productively. Many of his major ideas are introduced briefly: the book represents a good introduction to Fromm.

———. *To Have or to Be?* New York: Harper & Row, 1976.

A summary of Fromm's lifework, this important book outlines the distinction between the having and being modes of existence, along with a number of suggestions for socioeconomic changes that Fromm believes would alter the future of humankind.

BEHAVIORISTIC MODEL

The theories we have been considering have one theme in common, namely, that personality is a something. Its structures and operating principles can be understood and manipulated. We have been introduced to active psychic agents or personality variables such as traits, needs, instincts, intentions, dispositions, id, ego, superego, and so on, and to a variety of dynamic factors such as the pleasure and reality principles, the construct of need hierarchy, the principles of self-actualizing tendency, and striving for superiority. For the most part, these constructs and postulates were derived from observations of behavior in clinical settings although Murray, Maslow, and Allport used normal populations.

Those who hold that personality comes between the environment and behavior maintain that when we know the nature of personality, we are in a much better position to relate behavior to its causes because personality variables themselves are major causes of behavior. When Freud spoke of the id, he really meant to refer to instincts and basic drives that are a fundamental feature of the personality. When Allport referred to central traits, he was saying that there is something within the core of the personality, in fact, within the nervous system, which actually influences behavior. Situations and behaviors are interpreted and directed by the nature of such traits.

Now what of the behavioristic tradition? It seemed to many that a bright new day began in psychology when early in the development of American psychology John B. Watson proposed a behaviorism, which was a daring new idea that psychology should dispense with the psyche. This view came to be called the "empty organism" approach because it considered only observable behavior in relation to environmental stimuli and not the unobservable personality agents. Watson argued that we could obtain dependable knowledge about animal and human behavior by observing what the individual does in different situations. If music is introduced into a work setting, we can easily record the changes in behavior without trying to determine what is going on within the personality of the workers. We can measure such tangible variables as production output, amount of waste, time spent at the drinking fountain, tardiness and absentee records, and a host of other behavior and output indicators. It would be quite difficult to determine whether the workers feel better or like their jobs more with music playing, but anyone can observe the changes in behavior and behavior outputs. We surely would not ask a thermometer to tell us how it feels as it registers changes in temperature. The animal psychologist does not depend upon the animals' introspections to learn about the causes of their behavior. "Why should we treat humans any differently?" Watson pointed out.

Watson was fascinated by the great potential for learning in humans. He held that the normal child comes into the world with little in the way of inborn behavior. What the child becomes is the result of the type of environment and learning experiences that are encountered. Children can be taught effective habits and useful skills. Watson actually proposed that he could take an average child and make of him or her whatever was specified: a genius or a dullard, a productive member of the community or a criminal. The learning history of the individual makes all the difference in the type of person one becomes. It was a challenging new program for psychology that held the promise of putting psychology on an equal footing with the more rigorous sciences. It also held a great deal of hope for humanity as well. It became highly fashionable to be called a behaviorist.

Currently, B. F. Skinner is making many of the same claims. Skinner argues that personality cannot be known except through inferences from behavior; thus, why bother to make guesses about internal variables when we can relate behavior to environmental events? He holds that human behavior can be engineered, not by trying to influence minds or change personalities, but by changing the environment. Skinner is particularly concerned with controlling behavior by controlling its consequences: that is, by setting up contingencies of reinforcement by which certain behaviors are rewarded. Skinner's operant procedures can be applied to ourselves if we learn the principles involved. We will discuss personal applications of these procedures after we review Skinner's contributions in Chapter 12.

Skinner is termed a "radical behaviorist" because he attempts to explain behavior without making use of *intervening personality variables,* but close examination of Skinner's ideas would lead one to question whether he really succeeds in his program of denying intervening variables. There are some other behaviorists who have been termed "moderate behaviorists" for whom *intervening variables are essential* for explaining, predicting, and controlling behavior. These personality scientists call themselves "cognitive social learning theorists." The major difference between their personality variables and those proposed by the traditional personality theorists is that they tie them more rigorously to stimulus situations and behaviors. In other words, they are much more rigorous in the manner in which they derive their variables. They usually infer them from experimental investigations and use them as explanatory constructs that account for the observed behaviors. This is good scientific procedure. The traditional personality theorists were not so careful about relating inferred personality variables to observable behavior. It is frequently difficult to specify the behaviors that a construct or postulate denotes in these traditional theories. We will consider the cognitive and social learning theorists Albert Bandura, Julian Rotter, Albert Ellis, and Walter Mischel in Chapter 13. In the critical evaluation section of that chapter, we will examine the issue of whether the cognitive and social learning theorists are really following the mission that Watson had in mind. They meet the requirements of rigor and objectivity, but not the requirement of eliminating personality variables as explanatory devices.

Many behaviorists of all varieties are associated with learning theories because learning is so fundamental to development. Furthermore, learning represents a clear case of the formation of new behaviors, whatever one's view on the role of inheritance. The behaviorists were attracted to learning phenomena because they fitted well their emphasis on objectivity. It was possible to study the conditions that promoted or hampered learning. The stimuli that precede and follow behavior are observable, as well as the learned behavior. Even the broader conceptions of learning, which encompass changes in cognitive, affective, and motivational determinants, could be subjected to rigorous investigation. Behaviorists have long been associated with the learning approach because it exemplifies their stress on objectivity, for example, S-R bonds; but learning in humans involves mediating psychological processes, which are inferred from behavior.

The fantastic progress of knowledge is evident to anyone who is in touch with our world. In just a few years, we have seen the development of totally new fields such as space exploration, open-heart surgery, the computer, drugs for the treatment of the mentally ill, and many more. Our parents could scarcely dream of these developments. The high school students of today can solve problems that were not even known as problems a few years ago. They can solve them because they have *learned* to do so. Each generation passes on the knowledge of the preceding ones in addition to its own new discoveries. The achievements of great minds who may have studied and labored a lifetime can often be communicated easily to many who are willing to learn. Euclid's principles of geometry are taught to millions of tenth graders. What we have learned to do with the physical world all around us we can learn to do with ourselves. Better ways of dealing with needs and personal problems can be discovered and communicated. We already have much more knowledge than is being used to improve human life.

The learning approach to personality study and improvement is one of the most optimistic personality theories. It holds that personality, normal or abnormal, is largely the product of learning. As we grow up, we learn a multitude of habits, skills, attitudes, emotional responses, prejudices, and complexes. Neurosis and other abnormalities may thus be thought of as learned responses. A person is not born neurotic, but acquires "bad habits," which can be accounted for by principles of learning. For J. Dollard and N. E. Miller (1950), neurosis is a deficiency blocking the full use of the higher mental processes. Their optimistic note is that if neurosis is learned, then it can be unlearned by understanding and applying principles of learning. In this context, psychotherapy consists of teaching: the neurotic is the student who wishes to replace bad habits with good ones. Psychotherapy restores the higher mental functions and frees patients of their symptoms so that they may have a clear and efficient mind.

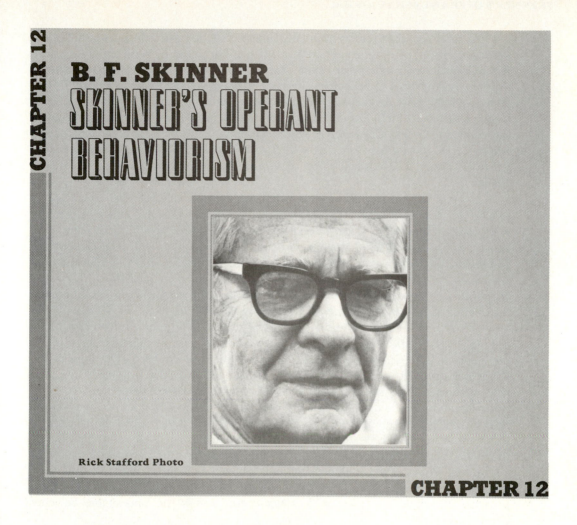

Rick Stafford Photo

CHAPTER 12

B. F. SKINNER
SKINNER'S OPERANT BEHAVIORISM

BIOGRAPHY AND HISTORICAL PERSPECTIVE

The concepts and work of B. F. Skinner are exerting a profound influence on many areas of contemporary psychology. Skinner is a radical behaviorist, and he has developed operant reinforcement procedures that he and his students have applied to many aspects of behavior control in a variety of settings. In the strictest sense, a radical behaviorist relates behavior to environmental causes and rejects personality variables as explanatory constructs. His reinforcement concepts and procedures have been used to modify behavior among institutional psychotics, in penal and correctional institutions, in business and work environments, in schools and other instructional settings, and in individual psychotherapy. (Goodall, 1972)

Skinner is probably more influential today than any other psychologist. Several journals carry only operant conditioning studies, and an entire division of the American Psychological Association, with more than a thousand members, is devoted to the experimental analysis of behavior. There are many psychologists who identify themselves as Skinnerian, and several graduate schools offer programs in behavior modification, leading to a Ph.D. For applications of operant procedures with humans, consult the following books: *Cumulative Record* (Skinner, 1972b), *Handbook of Operant Behavior* (Honig and Staddon, 1977), *Behavior Therapy, Techniques and Empirical Findings* (Rimm and Masters, 1979), *A Primer of Operant Conditioning* (Reynolds, 1968).

Skinner was born in 1904 in Susquehanna, Pennsylvania. He received a Ph.D. in psychology from Harvard in 1931. He worked in Professor Crozier's biology laboratory as an assistant until 1936, when he received his first teaching appointment at the University of Minnesota. In 1938 his first major book was published, *The Behavior of Organisms*. He remained nine years at Minnesota, and after a brief period at the University of Indiana, he went to Harvard to teach. He has remained there ever since, winning many honors and awards both in psychology and outside the field and becoming one of the outstanding figures in the behavioral sciences.

To obtain a preliminary picture of the application of Skinner's reinforcement procedures, let us contrast his approach with two others, a "loving" approach and a "punitive" approach, in dealing with the behavior of retarded children. The basis of the loving approach is that children should be influenced to behave in socially approved ways by means of suggestions supported with demonstrations of respect and concern. But workers in the field report that the love and tenderness method does not always instigate the type of behavior they desire. A negative child does not become cooperative just because he or she is treated kindly. Under the punitive approach, the children are threatened with punishment if they do not behave according to the wishes of the school authorities. This method is something like: "If you want to get along in this place, you'd better follow the rules." Yet even when punishment is actually used, in many instances the desirable behavior does not occur; nor is the undesirable behavior eliminated.

In contrast to these two approaches, Skinner uses rewards *(positive reinforcement)* to strengthen prescribed behaviors. When the prescribed behavior is rewarded by tokens that can be redeemed for a variety of goods, privileges, and exemptions, the degree of behavior control that can be achieved is amazing. The children will perform many tasks for the tokens that they simply would not do under either the loving or the punitive conditions. Using rewards to modify behavior has been applied effectively in many other settings as well (for example, Ayllon and Azrin, 1965). Skinner and his students maintain that they can control the behavior of humans as effectively as they can the behavior of animals. Put simply, the principle is that reinforcement raises the frequency with which behavior occurs: organisms do what pays off.

Another feature of Skinner's approach is his concern with the *consequences of behavior*. Although he recognizes the importance of behavior that is *elicited* by stimuli (antecedent causes), he is more concerned with operant behavior that is *emitted* and strengthened by a *reinforcer*. (Skinner, 1938) He is greatly interested in controlling the behavior of the individual organism or human. Many psychologists deal with the behavior of groups of subjects, using statistical tests of significance and thereby obliterating individual differences. Furthermore, they concentrate on predicting behavior. Skinner, in contrast, holds that it should be possible to control and engineer the behavior of every individual organism if the appropriate conditions are known and applied.

BASIC CONSTRUCTS AND POSTULATES

Most of the personality theorists we are considering view personality as a real structure that can be depicted in terms of constructs such as traits, needs, values, habits, style of life, sentiments, the self, id, ego, superego, and the like. Knowledge of these components and their interactions will assist in accomplishing the aims of a science of personality, namely, to describe, to explain, to predict, and to control the behavior of a single individual. In addition, most personologists believe that behavior must be viewed as the product of an interaction between internal personality structures and environmental factors. Knowledge of either alone is insufficient to accomplish the aims of personality science, but one difficulty with this view is that the personality variables must be inferred from behavior: they cannot be approached directly.

In the science of behavior, Skinner believes, personality variables are really only verbal labels for specific behaviors. *Dependency*, for instance, is a term that stands for certain types of behaviors in relation to certain types of people. It is not something that exists in the personality structure as a trait. The behaviors designated as dependency have something in common and substitute for one another; they may result in similar consequences; they occur in specifiable types of situations, but they do not emanate from a personality structure that can be called dependency. A knowledge of the behaviors designated as dependency, according to Skinner, is better promoted by learning the reinforcement history of the behaviors classified as dependent and the situations that elicit such behaviors than by attempting to learn about the nature of the supposed trait and its interactions with other purported traits in the personality. A practical control of "dependency" behavior can occur only when antecedents and consequences of such behavior are altered. (Skinner, 1953) Personality constructs appear to increase our knowledge of the determinants of behavior, but they are merely fictions—carry-overs from psychology's mentalistic past. (Skinner, 1971) Skinner believes that they are names for classes of behavior rather than personality variables.

Actions Determined by Consequences of Behavior

As we have suggested, a simple but most powerful guiding principle of Skinner's brand of behaviorism is that *behavior is determined and maintained by its consequences.* An animal or human can be controlled by those who possess reinforcers. Just as a rat can be trained, with the proper use of reinforcers, to press a bar, jump over a fence, run a maze, turn to the right, fight with other rats, and perform other adaptive or unadaptive behaviors, so people are much more under the control of reinforcers than they think.

Behavior is determined and maintained by its consequences.

Michael Kagan Photography/Monkmeyer Press Photo Service.

Control does not necessarily mean conscious control exerted by a person or group though, of course, it can be carefully planned and executed. It refers to the influence of environmental stimuli, both preceding and following behavior. One of Skinner's (1953) major contributions is his elaboration of the countless ways in which the human power of self-determination is under environmental control.

Everyone knows that, in order to get certain results, we have to take certain steps, that is, perform instrumental acts. Skinner terms instrumental acts "operants" because we must operate on the environment to achieve an outcome. *Instrumental acts* are the means to a goal. A behavior becomes an instrumental act or an operant if it leads to reinforcement. Furthermore, reinforced behavior tends to be repeated. (Skinner, 1963) Much of our behavior has been acquired through trial-and-error success. By success, we mean that certain behaviors have attained the status of operants; they have become means to reinforcers.

In his program for behaviorism, Watson (1914) suggested that the environment affects behavior, but he placed the emphasis on the determining power of situations and failed to distinguish between reacting to the environment and acting upon the environment. His S-R position stressed the power of the impinging stimulus and the plasticity of the person who simply reacts to the pressure of the stimulus. No doubt much behavior is molded by the events in a person's life, but reaction is not the only property of the organism. Thus Watson's S-R model is one-sided because it takes account of reaction only. Even the simplest organism behaves. In Skinner's approach to the study and control of behavior, behaving, rather than reacting, is studied. Behavior produces changes in the environment that may in turn change behavior. No doubt Watson perceived the fact that the consequences of behavior will influence the behavior that produced the consequences, but his preoccupation with the "molding" power of the environment led him to study this aspect alone. It soon became apparent that this model of behavior study was inadequate. By emphasizing behavior (for example, acting upon the environment) and the consequences of behavior (the reinforcers), Skinner comes much closer to controlling behavior. The environment selects behavior.

Respondent and Operant Behavior

Skinner has made an important distinction that should help us to understand the nature of conditioning: the difference between respondent and operant behavior. We may think of the difference between a reaction and an action or between response and behavior: The aroma of soup may cause me to get hungry, a reaction, which in turn leads to my going to the kitchen to eat. Respondent conditioning is the substitution of one stimulus for another in producing an already existing response. The same response is made to a different stimulus; thus, the learning that takes place in respondent conditioning increases the effects of the environment, that is, the number of stimuli that will elicit a response. The reader will recognize this as Pavlovian conditioning. A child may burn his or her hand with a lighted match and, as a result of the painful experience, may acquire an avoidance response to matches in general. We will discuss this type of conditioning more thoroughly, but for now the reader should bear in mind that responses are not increased through respondent conditioning; only stimuli are increased. Existing responses become linked to new stimuli. In operant conditioning, behaviors are modified. Native behaviors are organized in a great many different arrangements. Simple finger movements may be learned in many complicated patterns. In one sequence, the child drinks from a cup; in another pattern, he or she eats with a fork; in another, the child learns to dress himself or herself. The same behaviors can be used for countless instrumental acts. As we noted previously, the specific movements (the learned habit or sequence of habits) depend upon the consequences. These may be arranged by an experimenter who wishes to engender the particular habits, or the consequences may occur in an unplanned manner (natural reinforcements or punishments).

A good way to remember the difference between the two forms of behavior is that, in respondent conditioning, the stimulus *elicits* a response whereas, in operant conditioning, a behavior is *emitted*. Operant behavior occurs in the presence of occasioning stimuli that serve as cues for specific behaviors.

The concept of emitted behavior will help to clarify the meaning of operant behavior. Emitted behavior is the observed random or spontaneous behavior of an organism that cannot usually be traced to specific stimuli (Skinner, 1938). If a rat is placed in a Skinner box, it will be active; its behavior is emitted behavior because there are no stimuli that can be identified as causing its actions. When the rat in its course of activity presses a bar in the box, a pellet drops, which it eats. Something happens to the pattern of behavior as a consequence of the reinforcement, the food pellet: the emitted behavior of bar-pressing is strengthened. The rat begins to press the bar more frequently, gets more food, and presses more often. Once reinforcement begins, then, behavior starts to come under the control of the reinforcing stimulus, the food. The rat's actions become much less random. Time is now largely spent in regular and predictable bar-pressing. The differences between respondent and operant conditioning are summarized in Table 12-1, in which paradigms for both are presented. In this context, *paradigm* means "design."

TABLE 12-1 PARADIGMS FOR RESPONDENT AND OPERANT CONDITIONING

A. Respondent Conditioning:

$$\text{UCS} \text{_____} \text{UCR}$$
$$\text{CS} + \text{UCS} \text{_____} \text{UCR}$$
$$\text{CS} \text{_____} \text{CR}$$

In classical conditioning, an unconditioned stimulus (UCS), such as a tap to the knee, elicits the unconditioned response (UCR) of a knee jerk. A conditioned stimulus (CS) may then be paired with the UCS repeatedly until the CS, such as a bell, elicits a knee jerk in the absence of the UCS.

B. Operant Conditioning (Skinner Box):

$$\text{S} \text{\_\_\_\_\_}$$

B_1 Exploring
B_2 Scratching
B_3 Grooming
B_4 Defecating
B_5 Urinating
B_6 Bar-pressing: operant response

Total stimulus situation: Skinner box
Occasioning stimuli: Hunger stimuli
Discriminable stimuli: Sight of bar, walls, floor, ceiling, food dish.

In operant conditioning, the organism emits a variety of behaviors, but once the behavior desired by the experimenter is emitted, it is immediately reinforced. Such reinforcement causes an increase in frequency of this behavior. The paradigm above depicts the exploratory behavior of a rat in a Skinner box. There is a total stimulus situation within the box that includes the walls, lever, water tube, eating dish, and so on. The rat thus has many things to act upon. In this total situation, a variety of behaviors are possible, as listed above. But only when bar-pressing occurs does the rat receive any reinforcement, usually consisting of a food pellet.

RESPONDENT-OPERANT UNITS

We have spoken of respondents and operants as if they were separate processes, but typically a complete unit of behavior begins with a respondent and is followed by an operant. A stimulus or situation sets off a conditioned or unconditioned emotional respondent, which, in turn, triggers an adaptive or maladaptive operant. A friend makes a cutting remark; one reacts with anger, a respondent; then an angry physical attack ensues, a pattern of operants. We often react to situations by means of conditioned fear, anger, or pleasure, and then we act upon the environment by means of conditioned operants. A significant point to draw from the preceding analysis is that our behavior is under the control of powerful emotions. Frequently, conditioned or unconditioned stimuli elicit powerful emotional respondents, which then lead to highly maladaptive operants. Changing such units should begin with the conditioned respondents because they evoke the operants directly. Agressive behavior is the result of the evocation of anger. A person may overreact to certain stimuli and behave in antisocial and destructive ways. Treatment can certainly focus on methods of behavior channeling and extinction, but it should also deal with the extinction of emotional respondents.

Contingencies of Reinforcement

The term *contingency* may be defined as "dependence upon." To say that reinforcement is contingent upon a specific operant behavior means that it depends upon the occurrence of that behavior. An individual is not reinforced unless he or she acts appropriately. Let us consider a typical situation: John asks Mary for a date, and she accepts. He has now asked her ten times, and each time she has accepted. The operant behavior is John's invitation for a date. Mary's acceptance is the reinforcement. The schedule of reinforcement may be described as total; she has accepted every time. As we have noted, contingency implies a relationship in which there is mutual dependence; in this instance John's behavior depends upon Mary's, and Mary's behavior is influenced by John's. Obviously, Mary cannot reinforce behavior that John does not emit. But when John does emit behavior, Mary can influence future behavior by her reinforcement power.

After reinforcing John's invitations by accepting a number of dates, Mary may suddenly stop accepting. John will continue asking her for a while, but eventually the operant behavior of asking will be extinguished. However, the contingency (the relation of behavior and reinforcement) may not be all or none; Mary may choose to refuse from time to time. This type of reinforcement is known as partial or intermittent reinforcement, in this case, "playing hard to get." A clever way to remember the meaning of intermittent reinforcement is to think of a "now and again schedule." Mary wants to keep John's rate of responding high and to use her reinforcement power to best advantage. Animals can be made to work quite hard for smaller and smaller reinforcements, and there are parallels in human behavior. Work output is generally better on a piece rate than by hourly pay. Commissions can be highly motivating even if their

Stimulus leads to reaction; reaction leads to action.

occurrence is highly unpredictable; the salesperson may emit a great deal of behavior for modest reinforcements. Gambling is another example: a few wins may sustain many tries. Skinner (Skinner and Ferster, 1957) has given names to the contingencies (the specific manner in which the reinforcement is related to operant behavior), such as fixed and variable interval schedules, fixed and variable ratio schedules.

SCHEDULES OF REINFORCEMENT CONTROL BEHAVIOR

That reinforcement can influence behavior has been known for a long time, but Skinner has demonstrated the intricate ways in which reinforcements can be used. Specific schedules of reinforcement have characteristic rates of responding associated with them. In the interval schedule, the reinforcement is based on time, not on the behavior of the subject. In contrast, ratio reinforcement schedules do depend on the behavior of the subject in that the subject can increase the likelihood of reinforcement by emitting more responses. Skinner and his collaborators have demonstrated the capability of such

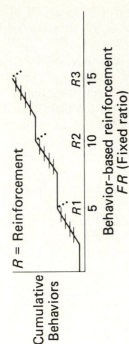

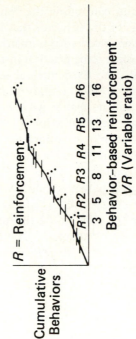

Behavior-based reinforcement
FR (Fixed ratio)

FR (Fixed Ratio): Reinforcement occurs after a fixed number of responses. FR-5, for example, means reinforcement is given after every 5th response made by the subject. FR schedules result in high and stable rates of responding with a pause immediately after each reinforcement is given. Factory piecework (workers paid after a fixed number of items are produced) is an example of an FR schedule.

Time-based reinforcement
FI (Fixed interval)

FI (Fixed Interval): Reinforcement occurs after a determined amount of time, such as every 5 minutes. Reinforcement is provided at these time-intervals despite the organism's responses or lack of responses. A cumulative record of FI responding typically reveals a scalloped graph. Pauses occur after reinforcement and responding increases as the end of an interval approaches. When one is expecting an important letter, the checking of a mail box may be on an FI schedule. The rate of checking the mailbox increases greatly just before the mailman arrives. After his arrival, behavior ceases abruptly, then increases again just before his next scheduled arrival.

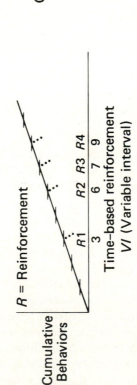

Behavior-based reinforcement
VR (Variable ratio)

VR (Variable Ratio): Reinforcement comes after varying numbers of responses. For example, reinforcement in one FR schedule may come after the 3rd then 5th then 8th responses, repeating the pattern of 3-5-8. Variable ratio schedules result in high steady rates of responding. Gambling devices such as slot machines employ the principle of variable ratio scheduling.

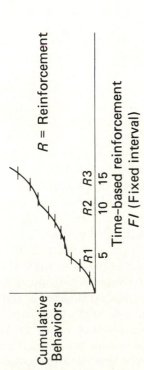

Time-based reinforcement
VI (Variable interval)

VI (Variable Interval): Reinforcement occurs after varying quantities of time. In one period, reinforcement may occur after 3-6-7-9 minutes successively. VI reinforcement results in sustained responding at a low rate.

FIGURE 12-1
Fixed interval, variable interval, fixed ratio, and variable ratio behaviors.

schedules in controlling the behavior of animals. The observer is impressed by the orderliness of the behavior that is being manipulated. Much of the same control has been demonstrated with humans.

Consider some practical instances of behavior under the various schedules of reinforcement. The fixed interval schedule, so commonly used, produces low levels of responding. A weekly salary is an example. Unless the worker gets into trouble, the salary is paid no matter what he or she does. Many supervisors complain that their workers are lazy, but Skinner would argue that the difficulty lies instead in the fixed interval schedule of reinforcement. The same may be said of fixed salary increases. In some professions there is a guaranteed yearly increase in salary according to a negotiated schedule. In such instances, merit has little to do with the salary increments. Another fixed interval schedule that may produce unfavorable consequences is the practice of giving gifts to children on certain days of the year. Ordinarily, the child does nothing to deserve the gifts. Could this practice foster the development of faulty expectations regarding the nature of the good life? One more example is the welfare program: what does it do to a person to receive doles regularly without doing anything to receive them, except not working?

Consider the difference in behavior under a fixed and a variable interval schedule in the case of regularly scheduled tests and those unannounced. Let us regard testing as an aversive stimulus and the preparation as a form of avoidance behavior. (Many students study primarily to avoid failing tests.) When the tests are regularly announced, the studying behavior increases just before the tests and drops right after. In the unannounced schedule, the behavior is steady because students must be prepared for each class lest they experience unwanted aversive consequences.

In ratio reinforcement, the behavior of the subject can influence the occurrence of the reinforcement. In a piece-rate program of paying, the worker's output can augment and speed the salary rate. Even if the piece-rate requirement is increased, the worker's behavior can still influence the reinforcements. An example of an effective ratio schedule is the merit increase if it is truly based on work output rather than on other aspects of working. Sometimes schedules may be combined as when a person receives both a fixed base salary and a commission.

Operant behavior is not only "built up" by means of reinforcers but the strength and frequency of the operant behavior also depend upon the way the reinforcer occurs, the particular schedule. Thus reinforcement both builds behavior and sustains it after it is formed. The question of the maintenance of behavior is highly crucial in many aspects of life. Behavior can be sustained with remarkably sparse reinforcement if the appropriate schedule of reinforcement is followed. (Jenkins and Stanley, 1950) In general, we begin with total reinforcement, and gradually less and less is used while more and more behavior is required of the organism for the same reinforcement. In the building of behavior, reinforcements are given at first for partial responses if they move in the direction of the correct behavior. Reinforcement is such a powerful factor in controlling behavior that it can be used to shape learning. We will look at this most important aspect of operant conditioning in a moment, but now let us return momentarily to John's asking Mary for a date. We have seen that John has to emit behavior before it can be reinforced by Mary, but what causes John to emit the appropriate behavior?

Mary can play a part by providing a *discriminable* or noticeable stimulus that may serve as an *occasioning* stimulus; in other words, she may give John a hint. But John has to be able to discriminate the meaning of the hint, or he will not emit the behavior that Mary wishes to reinforce. A word more about discriminable stimuli. A discriminable stimulus is one that stands out because it has meaning for the individual. A green traffic light informs the driver to proceed. When the discriminable stimulus is present, it is an occasioning stimulus for certain behavior.

Shaping and Chaining

Shaping is a term that is associated especially with Skinner's procedures for operant conditioning. It is sometimes called the "method of successive approximations." Shaping behavior means building behavior patterns, or operants, by means of reinforcement of partial or graded responses. Undifferentiated behavior is molded gradually in an ordered series of steps that increasingly approximate the desired behavior pattern. (Skinner and Ferster, 1957) A rat in a Skinner box will eventually learn to depress the bar that causes a pellet of food to drop into the food dish. It may be argued that the operant behavior of bar-pressing is formed by the natural contingencies of the Skinner box; the hungry animal learns the response simply because it is active and eventually depresses the bar accidentally. But it is possible to shape the bar-pressing operant with the use of the method of successive approximations.

Bar-pressing behavior is far from a simple reflex response. The animal has to orient toward the bar, move in its direction, approach it, and press the bar with enough pressure to activate the mechanism. It is only because the Skinner box precludes many competing behaviors and because it is so arranged that bar-pressing is a likely behavior, given the nature of a laboratory rat, that the operant behavior can be learned without any prompts and assists from the experimenter. Reinforcing behavior that more and more approximates the final pattern greatly speeds up the process of building up the operant. The rat is reinforced first whenever he turns in the direction of the bar, then when he advances toward it, then only when he approaches the bar, then only when he touches the bar, and finally only when he depresses it. Shaping procedures not only hasten the process of building operants, but may also be used to produce operants that would never occur under natural contingencies or conditions. Skinner has been able to get pigeons to play Ping-Pong, dance with each other, peck for hours at a time on a switch, and engage in many other unpigeonlike behaviors. He has successfully regulated the speed, the strength, and the pattern of responses.

Shaping is a common experience among people in everyday life. A father utters a word; his child attempts to imitate it; the parent reinforces the partially correct (approximate) response by saying "good"; he then repeats the correct version of the word. Some parents insist on the correct version before giving a reinforcement. Skinner (1957) suggests that they would obtain better results if they reinforced approximations of the exact word. It might be objected that reinforcing wrong responses makes those responses more likely to occur than the proper response. Many children are, in fact, reinforced for "baby talk" and carry this to adulthood, because the parents are appar-

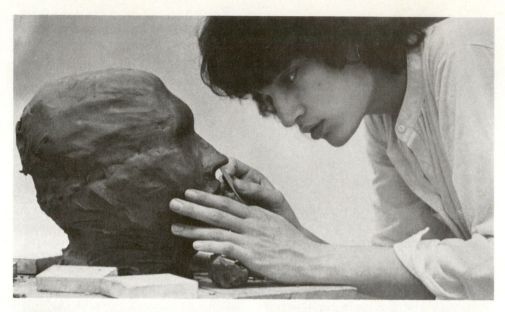

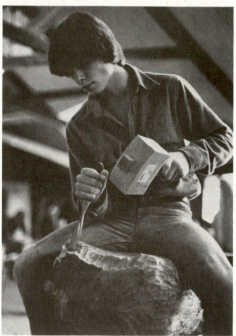

Photo credits: *upper* © Thomas E. England 1979/Photo Researchers, Inc.; *lower left* David S. Strickler/Monkmeyer Press Photo Service; *lower right* Peter Vandermark, Stock, Boston.

The final product results from systematic changes.

ently reinforced by such talk and, in turn, reinforce it in their children. But to say that reinforcing approximations is reinforcing wrong behavior misses the whole point of shaping. Reinforcement should be given only when the approximations progressively resemble the final form; thus, reinforcement is not given for approximations that have already been reinforced. Finally, only the correct word or phrase is reinforced. Instead of perpetuating "baby talk," the method of successive approximations is an excellent way of eliminating such incorrect verbal forms.

Shaping is sometimes confused with *chaining*. Chaining procedures refer to building behavior through combining in sequence a series of simple behavioral units. The total pattern of behavior may be quite complex, but it is made up of a series of simple units that have been acquired through operant conditioning.

Another point is relevant to shaping and chaining: if approximations are reinforced, they are strengthened; thus, their likelihood of recurring is increased. How can we explain the progression to the next level of approximation? The answer is that reinforcers have such a powerful effect on behavior that they stimulate general behavioral activity. Thus, the active organism is likely to make the next approximation simply because it is more active as a result of the stimulating power of the reinforcer. The methods of shaping and chaining, along with the elaboration of schedules of reinforcement, are among Skinner's most significant contributions to behavior modification procedures.

Skinner and many others have used operant procedures in education. Skinner (1968) is one of the pioneers in the field of teaching machines and programmed instruction. The learner proceeds, in a short time, through a series of graded steps, from a low level of performance or knowledge to almost complete mastery of a particular skill or subject. Many of the principles discovered in the animal laboratory are used. For example, the learners' behavior is shaped; the material is presented in small chunks. They may be given prompts to foster correct responses. Incorrect responses are undesirable because they can also be learned and will interfere with the recall of correct ones; thus, in a well-developed program these are kept to a minimum by having the learner advance one small step at a time. Learners are informed by the machine each time their answer, which is filled in, matches the one given in the program. This knowledge of being correct is the reinforcer. Complicated sequences of ideas are arranged so that the learners proceed systematically, going on to the next step only after they have mastered the one on which they have been working. The program is designed to shape the behavior of the learner, using principles of operant conditioning.

DIFFERENTIAL REINFORCEMENT

A variation on shaping is the technique of differential reinforcement (Skinner, 1953). This means selective reinforcement and extinction — reinforcing only desired behaviors and not others. Not only do certain operants acquire greater strength by this procedure, but others are weakened. Suppose that a friend whom you like very much emits both sarcastic and nonsarcastic behavior. Given the notion that you have "reinforcing power," it should be possible to shape your friend's actions. You would like to increase the occurrence of nonsarcastic behaviors and decrease the sarcastic ones. You can reinforce with approval, laughter, smiles, praise, or attention when your friend displays behavior that you prefer and remain silent, turn away, interrupt, or change the subject when the friend is acting sarcastically. You are using differential reinforcement, and if you have reinforcement power over your friend, his or her behavior will be modified. It should be noted that Skinner advises against the use of punishment to eliminate the unwanted behavior. As we shall see, punishment does not automatically eliminate undesirable conduct and may in fact provoke worse behavior. The unwanted behavior should be ignored or extinguished by other nonpunitive methods.

Application to biofeedback work.   Some recent work in the area of biofeedback conditioning has demonstrated the powerful role of differential reinforcement in promoting the control of organic processes by the individual. The traditional notions of self-control may have to undergo drastic changes. It has been possible to control physiological functions such as heart rate, digestive activities, the contraction and expansion of blood vessels, and even electrical brain activity. A typical procedure is to allow a subject to hear a signal that goes on when the heart rate drops several beats per minute. The signal informs the person that his or her heartbeat has slowed slightly. This signal may be set so that it goes on only if the rate is several beats less than the previous setting. As a rule, there is a signal that matches the heartbeat all along and a different signal that is heard when the rate of heartbeat drops. This second signal is the reinforcer. By this procedure, subjects have been able to reduce their heart rate as much as fifteen beats per minute.

Such work offers the hope that we may be able to control moods, motivation, and even temperament with our own behaviors. A device known as an alpha sensor makes an audible signal when the alpha waves in the brain are present. The device is attached to the head, and the person listens for the signal that tells him or her that the brain activity is characteristic of relaxation. The signal increases gradually in intensity and frequency as the alpha rhythm of the brain predominates. The person engages in certain relaxation exercises, the operant behaviors, which produce the alpha waves and the corresponding signal, the reinforcer. It takes some time to acquire the ability to keep the signal on, but it can be done. Subjects who have learned this technique report that they experience profound relaxation when the alpha rhythm emerges. (Nowlis and Kamiya, 1970) The feedback of the alpha sensor provides the differential reinforcement that shapes the operant behavior. Some recent studies have cast doubt on the effectiveness of biofeedback in aiding an individual to gain control of mood states. (See further application of biofeedback in the Guides to Research section.)

Reinforcement is such a basic concept for Skinner that his entire psychology may be described as "reinforcement psychology." To sum up, operant conditioning occurs only if there is a reinforcement following an emitted response. Shaping is the systematic use of reinforcers to produce a behavior by reinforcing approximations of that behavior. Chaining is the formation of complex sequences of simple operants by using reinforcers in a progressive manner. Scheduling refers to the timing, patterning, and amount of reinforcement. The basic principle of Skinner's psychology is that behavior is formed and maintained by reinforcers. We have already said some things about reinforcers and reinforcement, but the process is so universal that certain further ideas should be considered. We will look at positive and negative reinforcers, punishment and aversive procedures. If reinforcers play such a significant role in living, we ought to know what they are, how they can best be used, and what consequences occur when they are not used properly. Most of us prefer to be reinforced rather than punished, and Skinner (1971) believes that punishment to form or change behavior is used much too often. A highly significant fact about punishment is that it is an unpredictable, and often ineffective, means of controlling behavior. Some operant researchers (Lovass et al., 1965) dispute Skinner's negative views of punishment and have found punishment to be an effective controller of behavior. On the other hand, reinforcement increases the likelihood of the desired behavior. It would seem that those who have control of the behavior of others should take this difference into account. These ideas will become clearer as we discuss reinforcement. Skinner advises accentuating the positives by using reinforcement to promote such behaviors, instead of eliminating negatives by using punishment.

Positive Reinforcement, Negative Reinforcement, and Punishment

POSITIVE REINFORCEMENT

Reinforcement, whether positive or negative, is ultimately an individual matter, but because of similarities among people, we can identify typical classes of reinforcers. The broadest classification is the division of positive reinforcers into *unlearned* and *learned*. These classes are also termed *primary* and *secondary*, *unconditioned* and *conditioned*. Organismic requirements are clear cases of primary reinforcement: food, water, sexual object, rest, activity, curiosity. There are some obviously learned reinforcers such as money, awards, medals, and honors. There are also reinforcers—such as affection, approval, and attention—which Skinner (1953) calls *generalized conditioned reinforcers*, by which he means that they are learned reinforcers that can reinforce many different behaviors. Some psychologists would argue that these generalized reinforcers are primary because they stem from the needs of the self. Food is reinforcing to someone who is hungry or who has a craving for it, but praise, approval, attention, and affection can reinforce a great variety of behaviors. For instance, some people will do almost anything for attention, approval, or affection. It is significant to note that many of these generalized reinforcers are within the power of all of us to give. In other words, we have the power to pay attention to someone, to praise, to approve of his or her responses, to give affection. (Rheingold et al., 1959) As we noted earlier, the manner of giving reinforcers (when, how much, and what type) is a critical factor in behavior control and modification. One advantage of a generalized reinforcer is that it is not linked to any specific class of behaviors but can be used to reinforce many different behaviors.

As we noted, while respondent and operant conditioning are distinct processes, they frequently occur together. When behavior is successful in securing reinforcement, certain aspects of the reinforcing situation may become eliciting stimuli for emotional responses. These emotional responses may be either negative or positive. A child writes a good paper and receives praise from his or her teacher. Skinner considers praise to be a learned reinforcer, but there are those who would argue that it is a primary psychological reinforcer. Let us take this position. The praise is accompanied by a grade or a percent value. If this is repeated a number of times, the grades or percent standings acquire the status of conditioned reinforcers; they are reinforcing in their own right, at least for a time. It is argued that such conditioned reinforcers must be strengthened from time to time with primary reinforcers, or they will extinguish; the grades must be supported by teacher or parental approval if they are to control the child's behavior. But the conditioned reinforcers have remarkable reinforcing power. Our lives are controlled by them much more than we suspect (Wilson and Verplanck, 1956), and those who wish to take over their own lives must identify such conditioned reinforcers as a first step.

The author conducted an informal experiment with his two children with conditioned reinforcers. Paul, who was ten, and Laureen, who was eight, were told that they were going to receive points for certain jobs around the house. A chart would be provided for the points, but they were responsible for recording their own points. The rules were simple: certain jobs such as wiping the table and emptying the rubbish would earn specified points. They had to choose the job and submit it for evaluation. Nothing was said about the "pay off" for all this work. The first evening both children scurried about doing a variety of chores and assigning themselves the points. They continued doing jobs that they did not like to do for several days despite their waning enthusiasm for the program. About the fourth day, Paul began grumbling about the prize. Instructions were simply repeated without any mention of an ultimate reward.

About the sixth day, Laureen wondered what would happen if she won and what constituted winning in any case. Again the question was evaded and the instructions repeated. The children complained from time to time, but they continued working for the points, although at a diminished rate, for about three weeks, until finally a reinforcer, a banana split, was given to each of them.

This home experiment demonstrates the remarkable reinforcing power of something as unrewarding as points. Competition may have played a part, parental encouragement may also have contributed, but these factors were minimized as much as possible. Simply earning empty points was reinforcement enough to get the children to do things they disliked doing. We might consider how much we do for flattery, for status, for approval, to get ahead of others, to have more of certain intangibles such as better grades, awards, honors. Many conditioned reinforcers are the unpaying aspects of a culture: for instance, the tremendous amount of work that is performed for secondary reinforcements by volunteers (Skinner, 1953).

NEGATIVE REINFORCEMENT

Negative reinforcement occurs when behavior *removes* or *avoids* an unpleasant or aversive stimulus. The removal or avoidance of the unwanted stimulus reinforces the effective operant behaviors. We are referring to escape and avoidance learning which can be highly motivating. We will take up punishment separately, but for now it should be kept in mind that one form of punishment adds something unpleasant to behavior in order to weaken or eliminate it whereas negative reinforcement is designed to strengthen avoidance or escape behavior by adding something unpleasant that the behavior can remove. (Skinner, 1972) The following example will illustrate negative reinforcement in escape behavior versus negative reinforcement in avoidance behavior. Finding shelter during a rainstorm is escape behavior that is negatively reinforced. Running to the same shelter when the sky threatens rain is avoidance behavior that is negatively reinforced. In both these instances, behavior is strengthened by its outcome. Good attendance as a means of avoiding the final examination is an example of negative reinforcement: the unwanted final exam may be avoided. In this case, the behavior eliminates an unwanted aspect of a situation, and the outcome is highly desirable. Not every instance of negative reinforcement is so clear-cut, and frequently some punitive elements remain, as we shall see. Another example of negative reinforcement is the reduction of a prison term by good behavior. The prisoner's behavior does not obtain anything directly, as in the case of positive reinforcement, but it does give him or her the opportunity to secure positive reinforcement by reducing his or her sentence. Still other examples are the reduction of the number of periods in school by the earning of a certain grade average and the lowering of a fine if the offender attends safety classes.

The examples of negative reinforcement that we have presented may be viewed as variations upon positive reinforcement because when the unpleasant aspects are totally removed by the behavior, the person is free to seek other reinforcements. Yet many other cases fitting the pattern of negative reinforcement are more like punishment than reward: instances of avoiding the consequences of threats are of this type. An employee works in order to avoid the consequences that his or her boss might impose — being fired, being given an undesirable job, losing a promotion. This type of aversive control is often effective and is probably the most frequently used method of behavior control. Children avoid the punishment of their parents by conforming to their demands and expectations. Students avoid the power of the teacher by fulfilling the requirements of the course no matter how irrational and distasteful they may be. There is no question that avoiding threats is reinforcing to a degree, but it is weak in many instances and may have unpleasant by-products. (Brady, 1958) One of the problems with negative reinforcers is that their consequences are unpredictable; sometimes they are effective and sometimes not. The worker may stop working after a period of time unless threatened anew by the boss. The boss has to keep a close watch and check on the employee. The inclination not to work or to do other things competes with the work activities; it is suppressed by the power of the boss, which must take the form of a continuous threat. The employee's behavior at best avoids the boss's power, but it does not eliminate it; therefore, a punitive element remains. The good behavior really does not obtain anything for the worker as is the case with positive reinforcement. Thus, it seems to this writer that most instances of negative reinforcement are really an admixture of rewards and punishments.

CONSEQUENCES OF NEGATIVE AND POSITIVE REINFORCEMENT

Let us contrast positive and negative reinforcement. A father might get his son to study his lessons by offering him a positive reinforcer such as the use of the family car Saturday evening, or he may use a negative reinforcer by threatening an earlier curfew. In both instances the father may get results, but the consequences of positive reinforcement are much more desirable than those of negative reinforcement. (Skinner, 1971)

Threatening punishment may induce emotional responses in the son: the boy may become antagonistic toward the father; he may not come home on time in the evenings; he may talk back to his father; he may actually refuse to follow his father's wishes; he may even deliberately fail in his studies as a means of retaliating. One thing is clear: behavior that produces positive reinforcement tends to be repeated whereas behavior that simply avoids a threatened punishment will not necessarily be sustained and, in fact, other undesirable behaviors may occur. Behavior that is punished is subject to the same conditions as negative reinforcement, and the unwanted by-products may be even more serious. Because the person cannot avoid punishment, the emotional responses may be intense.

One point should be clear: in his criticism of punishment, Skinner does not advocate using positive reinforcers to prevent unwanted behavior. Rather, he advocates use of positive reinforcers to promote certain desirable behaviors and use of methods other than negative reinforcement and punishment to eliminate undesirable behavior. What do you do with undesirable behavior if you do not use negative reinforcers and punishment? There are alternative methods of behavior modification: extinction (not paying attention to the behavior), satiation (allowing the person to engage in the behavior until he tires of it), changing circumstances (for example, distracting a child or changing the subject), promoting counteracting behavior, and simply allowing forgetting to take place. (Skinner, 1953) Children are often controlled by threats of punishment; the mother follows the child about with a constant flurry of "nos" and "no-nos." Skinner advises the harassed mother to remove the objects she wishes to preserve until the child reaches the age when he or she is no longer interested in them. The child who has an intense interest in the telephone may be punished or threatened a hundred times but still continues to play with the phone when the mother is not around. Better to let the child play with the phone until he or she tires of it, until he or she is satiated with it, than to engage in aversive control. We could go on with such examples, but the point should be clear: negative reinforcers and punishment are not the only ways to prevent or block unwanted behavior and promote desirable behavior.

PUNISHMENT

Punishment occurs when behavior is followed by an unpleasant consequence or when behavior causes a desirable thing to be withdrawn. Some investigators distinguish between *positive* and *negative punishment:* positive punishment follows behavior with something undesirable; negative punishment follows the behavior with the removal of something desirable. The purpose of punishment is to stop or change undesirable behavior. A child who has wandered off from home may be punished by being confined to the house for a period of time, or the mother may display strong disapproval and direct hostility. The purpose is to protect the child, but it may not be effective. Punished behavior is not necessarily eliminated (Estes, 1944); instead, the punished one may find other ways to secure what he or she wants. The boy who is punished for wandering off has not been changed by the punishment. If he were trying to find his friend's house, he may persist in his desire to seek out his friend. Perhaps the mother should seek the cause of the child's wandering and deal directly to change it. For instance, she may instruct him to ask for help in getting to his friend's house.

Punishment, then, may stop or block behavior, but it does not necessarily change the cause of the behavior. The punishment builds up fear, but gradually the fear extinguishes if the person avoids the punishment, and eventually the behavior that was originally punished will recur. Imprisonment punishes the criminal and engenders fear, among other emotions. The fear persists at a sufficient intensity after imprisonment to block the antisocial behavior for a while, but it may diminish so that antisocial behavior again emerges. Some ex-convicts do not commit crime again; it may be that while the fear prevented them from committing crime, they became involved in other activities such as work, family, religion, and so on. The finding of these new interests should not be left to the ex-convict; it should be engineered by rehabilitation experts. (Skinner, 1971) If punishment is not the answer to crime, then what is? Skinner would argue that rehabilitation is better than punishment and that prevention, by reinforcing socially acceptable behavior, is better than treatment.

Like negative reinforcement, punishment may produce unfavorable by-products. The prisoner comes to hate society even more after imprisonment. Resentment may induce him or her to seek still more devious ways of expressing his or her hatred and bitterness. A person with a prison record is discriminated against; thus, many conditions make return to crime the only way open to him or her. The identification of a child with his or her parents may also be greatly disturbed by repeated punishment (Mischel and Grusec, 1966). The positive reinforcing power of the parents wanes in the process. The same notion may be applied to husband and wife relationships: a nagging, complaining, critical mate will induce negative emotions in the spouse, and these will counteract any positive reinforcers that are used.

Because punishment cannot be avoided, it is actually violent, aggressive behavior on the part of the punisher. Negative reinforcement is a much more humane way to treat people because persons being negatively reinforced can prevent the negative consequence of their actions. Many behavior therapists believe that punishment is only permissible when absolutely all other avenues have been explored and have failed. (Rimm and Masters, 1979)

If punishment is to be used in blocking behavior, it should be informative: it should communicate the notion that the behavior is undesirable. A parent informs a child by disapproval. The purpose is best accomplished by mild punishment, and many of the undesirable consequences are thus avoided. But Skinner, in general, prefers the use of positive reinforcers to foster behavior. Drivers should be reinforced for driving safely, not just punished when they do not. Children should be rewarded when they are behaving well and not just attended to when they misbehave. Misbehavior may become their only means of getting attention. In Tables 12-2 and 12-3 characteristics of positive and negative reinforcement, punishment, and extinction are summarized.

VIEWS ON ABNORMALITY

Skinner deals with abnormality in terms of operant reinforcement constructs and procedures. He also uses classical conditioning principles (what he terms respondent conditioning) to account for faulty emotional reactions. Rather than offering any unique

TABLE 12-2 CHARACTERISTICS OF REINFORCEMENT AND PUNISHMENT

Positive Reinforcement	Negative Reinforcement	Punishment
1. Produced by instrumental behavior	1. Consists of the removal of unwanted consequences	1. Used to weaken behaviors, but frequently ineffective
2. Increases the probability of a particular instrumental response	2. Strengthens instrumental avoidance behavior	2. Consists of following instrumental responses by an unpleasant consequence, or removing one that is desired
3. Increases the intensity of a particular instrumental response	3. Strengthens instrumental escape behavior	3. Suppresses behavior, but does not necessarily weaken it
4. Sustains instrumental responses that have been learned	4. Increases the behavior that removes it	4. May instigate other instrumental responses that accomplish the same goal (being caught stealing during the day instigates stealing at night)
5. Elicits respondent emotional behaviors that induce approach behavior (enthusiasm, zest, encouragement, joy, excitement, pleasure)	5. Resembles positive reinforcement when instrumental responses remove certain aversive consequences (shortening a prison sentence by good behavior; receiving reduced work load as reward for good work)	5. May result in conditioned emotional responses (ulcers, chronic headache, resentment, and other psychosomatic processes; anger, hatred, fear, anxiety, distrust)
	6. Resembles punishment when instrumental responses simply prevent punishment (performing a job to avoid punishment by the boss; cleaning one's room to prevent mother's nagging)	6. May result in avoidance or escape behaviors (active avoidance: learning what to do to avoid the punishment; passive avoidance: learning what not to do to avoid or escape from the punishment)
		7. If mild, may stimulate alternative behaviors

NOTE: Reinforcement strengthens, punishment weakens. Strictly speaking, punishment cannot be avoided: an angry parent who is motivated to punish his or her child will administer the punishment in spite of the child's cries, protests, and pleadings. If punishment can be avoided or escaped, then we are dealing with negative reinforcement.

insights about the possible causes of abnormality, *he translates personality and behavior disorders into the language of respondent and operant conditioning.* Basic to his views on abnormality is the idea that psychological disorders are to be understood as disordered behavior. He does not accept the distinction between personality and behavior; thus, faulty personality traits or disturbances in the formation of the self and, in general, explanations that assume the existence of psychological variables are rejected. Also rejected by Skinner is the distinction between causes and symptoms. This distinction, taken over from the medical model of pathology, refers to the notion that some-

TABLE 12-3 REINFORCEMENT, EXTINCTION, AND PUNISHMENT

Types of Outcome	Description	Effects on Behavior
Positive reinforcement	Something desirable follows behavior	Strengthens approach operants
Negative reinforcement	Something undesirable is removed or avoided	Strengthens escape and avoidance operants
Extinction	Absence of usual outcome of behavior	Weakens approach, avoidance, and escape operants
Punishment	Something undesirable follows behavior or something desirable is removed	Weakens approach, avoidance, and escape operants

The outcome of reinforcers, the strengthening of behavior, is much more predictable than the outcome of extinction or punishment, the weakening of behavior. Forms of counter conditioning appear to have a greater effect on weakening behavior than extinction and punishment procedures for both respondents and operants.

thing within the personality, the pathogenic cause, may be functioning abnormally with the symptoms being manifested in a behavior disorder.

Behavior Disorders Related to Environmental Causes

Skinner relates both normal and abnormal behavior to environmental factors. A person may have problems with social relationships as a result of lack of appropriate social skills. Perhaps the individual is an only child living in a community without children of the same age. The child lacked the opportunity to learn the types of behavior that promote social interactions and, therefore, did not enjoy the reinforcers associated with normal social relationships. Treatment should consist of designing an environment in which social behavior with children of his or her own age could be shaped with appropriate reinforcers. The program could be carried out in a nursery school setting under the supervision of a behavior modification specialist. However it is done, Skinner would deal with this behavior problem by arranging the appropriate contingencies in the environment rather than through psychotherapy, play therapy, role-playing, and similar traditional procedures.

We have noted that Skinner places much more stress on operants than on respondents. He does not deal very much with the abnormalities that result form either faulty conditioned emotional respondents or failures in acquiring appropriate conditioned emotional reactions, but he is sympathetic to the behavioral methodology used to eliminate or foster such behaviors. (Eysenck, 1965) Behavior therapists use such procedures as extinction, counterconditioning, desensitization, and a host of new techniques to eliminate phobias, compulsions, obsessions, tics, and many other abnormal behaviors. Skinner finds many of these methods congenial with his thinking, but he has not made any significant contributions in this area. His main focus is on operant reinforcement principles and methodology.

Reinterpreting Abnormal Psychic States

Skinner has redefined many typical psychological concepts in operant conditioning terms. He has attempted to rid psychology of "explanatory fictions," as he terms them. These are constructs that Skinner believes are used to explain things psychologists cannot explain. We might diagnose a personality disorder as low self-esteem and institute therapy designed to bolster self-esteem. However, such vague terms do not help us either to treat the difficulty or to prevent it. Psychological entities such as traits, needs, sentiments, and feelings only add confusion, Skinner believes. What we need is to identify the reinforcers and to do something about changing them. He contrasts his approach to the traditional one by considering some typical explanatory fictions:

> The condition of low operant strength resulting from extinction often requires treatment. Some forms of psychotherapy are systems of reinforcement designed to reinstate behavior which has been lost through extinction. The therapist may himself supply the reinforcement, or he may arrange living conditions in which behavior is likely to be reinforced. In occupational therapy, for example, the patient is encouraged to engage in simple forms of behavior which receive immediate and fairly consistent reinforcement. It is of no advantage to say that such therapy helps the patient by giving him a "sense of achievement" or improves his "morale," builds up his "interest," or removes or prevents "discouragement." Such terms as these merely add to the growing population of explanatory fictions. One who readily engages in a given activity is not showing an interest, he is showing the effect of reinforcement. We do not give a man a sense of achievement, we reinforce a particular action. To become discouraged is simply to fail to respond because reinforcement has not been forthcoming. Our problem is simply to account for probability of response in terms of a history of reinforcement and extinction. [1953, p. 72][1]

As noted earlier, in many of his writings, Skinner considers traditional abnormalities such as depression, cynicism, lack of impulse control, low self-esteem in terms of the principles of operant conditioning. Consider the case of the individual who suffers from depression. Skinner would point out that depression results from inability to produce positive reinforcers. The person who is dissatisfied with life is not securing the quality or quantity of reinforcers that are desired. The condition known as reactive depression would certainly meet Skinner's translation because it is the result of unpleasant conditions over which a person has no control. A person may be depressed because he or she has lost a lover, and no other has replaced the person. There are many instances when we are depressed because we cannot get what we seek, but some forms of depression do not have an identifiable loss or environmental cause. The person may complain of being depressed and yet not have any good reason for the depression. Here we may be dealing with biochemical conditions that can be ameliorated by appropriate drugs. However, reactive depression could be aided by teaching a person the types of skills that would obtain more desirable reinforcers.

A person complains of profound feelings of inferiority. A psychologist who stresses self as a major determinant of behavior might interpret the problem as low self-esteem caused by unrealistic parental expectations that were introjected by the child.

---

[1] *Science and Human Behavior.*

The explanation might go on to involve an overly strict ego ideal that places impossible demands on the ego. The cure, according to this interpretation, is to help the person to become more realistic about his or her aspirations and to adjust his or her expectancies to actual abilities. Skinner would translate the problem into the language of reinforcement. The person is not satisfied with the types of reinforcers that he or she can obtain currently. One solution is to design a behavior modification program that would shape new skills or improve existing ones so that better reinforcers could be obtained. Another solution might be to change directions: the person might utilize other skills that would lead to greater success in securing desirable reinforcers. The person might change majors or vocational objectives and would be directed to focus on the reinforcers that he or she could obtain rather than those he or she could not.

One more problem area should make the reinforcement approach clear. Some people have difficulty working on long-term projects. They work only for immediate reinforcers and find it difficult to sustain effort under conditions of postponed reinforcers. Skinner would point out that the cause is that the person has not been exposed to variable ratio schedules, but rather has a reinforcement history of receiving immediate gratification for work done. By establishing a program of variable ratio reinforcement, the problem could be remedied.

Only empirical tests of the outcomes of these contrasting approaches can establish which one is superior. The evidence seems to indicate that certain problems respond to the behavioral approaches and others are more successfully treated with the traditional therapies. (Patterson, 1973) But even if the behavioral approaches are effective only for specific types of abnormalities, they would still be welcomed innovations.

VIEWS ON IDEAL PERSONALITY AND LIVING

Good Person Depends on Good Environment

Skinner has not confined his thinking to the rat in the Skinner box. He has wanted to do more than design better teaching devices, for his thinking extends to a Utopian society. (Skinner, 1948) Unlike other psychologists such as Rogers, Allport, Jung, and Fromm, he has not defined an ideal human state from the standpoint of personality makeup and functioning. He has concentrated on an ideal environment.

Skinner seems to believe that human beings are largely what the environment makes of them. The astronaut in space traveling to the moon is a very different person from the dirt farmer in the Bible Belt who is barely eking out a living from the soil. The difference between them is due largely to the environments in which they live. The environment selects behaviors that are appropriate to the circumstances, but of course humans have the capacity to act upon and thereby change their environment. (Skinner, 1953) Certainly, heredity plays a determining part as the raw material that the environment molds, but the fact remains that heredity cannot operate independently. Assuredly, a man is what he is by virtue of his native potential, but the moldability of a man is so great that his environment determines what he becomes. Aristotle could not transcend the limitations of his environment. Because he lacked a vast amount of knowledge, he could not have devised a space program.

Skinner, through his behavior engineering, has induced behaviors in animals that have never occurred in the history of the species; he has used behavior technology to do so. Human superiority has been expressed in a highly complex world that is largely of our making. The world, however, is in dire trouble; science and technology have created almost as many problems as they have solved. Humans themselves remain one of the greatest.

The natural and biological sciences have faced many human ills, such as disease, the overcoming of food shortages, and, in general, the control of nature. But pollution, population explosion, poverty, war, and a host of other hardships, many of them human-made, are very much with us. Skinner believes that even with the knowledge we now possess, life could be much less aversive and, in fact, more fulfilling. In addition to improving the environment, we have the capability of improving ourselves.

Perhaps Skinner does not attempt to specify what ideal existence is on an individual level because he does not yet know all the possibilities of a technology of human behavior. His methods and concepts have been used only on specific problems such as behavior modification, behavior therapy, programmed instruction, and teaching machines. There are many other areas where traditional methods could be replaced by Skinner's. Many parents do not do a good job of bringing up children; many educational practices are highly punitive, and, for the most part, foster a distaste for learning. Economics is geared toward unwholesome competition, and industry and business still resort to aversive controls. Many people simply do not like their work. Life, in general, is much more stressful than present knowledge and technology warrant.

Skinner, speaking through Frazier, the main character of *Walden Two*, offers a program for a benevolent control of behavior through the use of positive reinforcers. By their nature, positive reinforcers promote the operant responses that are required to secure them. The one who seeks them may be controlled willingly. Many persons forego pleasures for the sake of money reinforcement that they obtain through their work. The designers of the society can use behavior technology to foster certain values and behaviors, but this poses many problems regarding what those values should be and who will determine them. Frazier says:

> Now that we know how positive reinforcement works, and why negative doesn't, we can be more deliberate, and hence more successful in our cultural design. We can achieve a sort of control, under which the controlled, though they are following a code much more scrupulously than was ever the case under the old system, nevertheless feel free. They are doing what they want to do, not what they are forced to do. That's the source of the tremendous power of positive reinforcement—there's no restraint and no revolt. By a careful cultural design, we control not the final behavior, but the inclination to behave, the motives, the desires, the wishes. The curious thing is that in that case the question of freedom never arises. [Skinner, 1948, p. 218][2]

Skinner believes that what is needed is to engineer the environment so that behavior is brought under control. Some people, for example, should not procreate, but

[2]*Walden Two.*

they do not have enough self-control to discipline themselves. The workers should be controlled by positive reinforcers administered by benevolent controllers. Many personality theorists hold that the model person is a responsible, contributing member of society who pursues his or her own interests within the limitations of the rights of others. But Skinner (1971) holds that freedom and responsibility assume the existence of an autonomous agent within the person. This view, he believes, is hopeless and even fatalistic. The environment determines behavior; change and improve the environment, and desired behavior will occur. The hope of humanity lies in the judicious control of the environment so that social, responsible, productive behavior is promoted in the members of society. It should be noted that Skinner seeks many of the same ends as the humanistic psychologists do, from whom he received the Humanist of the Year award; he advocates the use of behavior methodology, however.

Those who have reinforcement power over others can use such power to promote desirable behavior. Skinner's hope is that they will use reinforcers in the most efficient manner possible, so that there are fewer failures as parents, teachers, employers, and judges. The good person depends upon the good environment, in Skinner's view, but there are some problems defining both the good environment and the good person. We still do not know what the highest human potentials are; thus, we would have difficulties designing the environment to produce them.

One more point is crucial in understanding Skinner's view on ideal personality and living. Though he does not provide us with a model of the perfected human, he does stress the idea that we can act upon our environment and produce positive reinforcers. Furthermore, whether or not he has a right to call self-management a behavioral technique, he does make allowance for designing one's own program of self-improvement. This is a significant attribute that can be fostered in an individual.

CRITICAL EVALUATION

As we suggested in the introduction to this chapter, Skinner's methods are highly influential in contemporary psychology, and his methods are being applied in other fields as well. The greatest support for Skinner is the empirical validation that his techniques are receiving. Behavior is being modified and controlled in many settings, ranging from penal institutions to the classroom, from the athletic field to the consulting office, with white rats and graduate students, with retarded children and superior adults. Behavior engineering is a widespread phenomenon in our day, and it seems to be increasing in scope. But there are questions that are still not answered. How enduring are the changed behaviors? If we remove the reinforcers, the behavior extinguishes. If the deviant is reinforced for socially approved behavior, what will assure the continuation of the behavior when the contrived reinforcers are removed? Regarding the long-continued use of contrived reinforcers, Skinner says:

> You don't need to maintain a system of contrived reinforcers indefinitely. People get the impression that I believe that we should all get gumdrops whenever we do anything of value. There are many ways of attenuating a system of reinforcement. Certain schedules of reinforcement permit you to reduce the frequency of reinforcement steadily. But the

main thing is to let the noncontrived reinforcers take over. The students who get prizes for doing their homework eventually discover the natural reinforcers of getting work done. They discover that they are learning something, possibly in contrast with their brothers and sisters in other classrooms, but in any case something which makes them more successful. [Skinner, 1972, p. 130][3]

Consider an example of a study in the use and removal of reinforcers in a junior high school math class that challenges Skinner's view that natural reinforcers replace contrived ones. The study was divided into three phases. In the first, the students were given the usual instructions for turning or not turning in assignments. In the second phase, reinforcers were introduced for prescribed behaviors, including turning in completed assignments on time. Performance improved markedly as a result of the reinforcers. In the third phase, the reinforcers were removed, and there was a return to the instructions and sanctions of phase one. The children then demonstrated less interest in the course than they did in the first phase. The students complained that they wanted the reinforcers and did not want to work without them. The natural reinforcers did not take over, and, in fact, personal motivation seemed to have deteriorated. (Greene, 1974)

Citing a number of studies in which the results of behavior modification programs were examined, Deci concludes that:

> The evidence from the studies reported here as well as many other similar studies indicates that behavior modification falls sadly short of what it is claimed to accomplish by many of its advocates.
>
> Results of studies show that rewards, etc., do work effectively to bring behavior under their control. The problem, however, is that the "improved" behavior persists only so long as the rewards or tokens persist.
>
> What seems to happen is that the behavior comes under the control of the rewards, so when the rewards stop, the behavior stops. [Deci, 1972, p. 118]

Whether or not intrinsic interest is destroyed by the removal of extrinsic reinforcers requires further investigations that consider a greater variety of reinforcing conditions.

It is tempting for one who advocates a whole new approach to the total field, as Skinner does, to explain everything with concepts that apply adequately to only a part of the total. For example, Skinner (1953; 1971) attempts to relate concepts of operant conditioning to self-management, with the individual being both the controller and the controlled. He makes a distinction between the controlled self and the controlling self in order to demonstrate that personal management of behavior (what was traditionally called willpower) can be brought within the framework of reinforcement theory. The controlling self can act as the behavior engineer and map out a program of behavior modification and control. A person can institute a set of contingencies for himself or herself. For example, certain desirable activities (positive reinforcements) may be made contingent upon certain behaviors; thus, a person may allow himself or herself a trip to the snack bar only if he or she studies a given amount of time, or may buy a new record as a reward for studying hard for a test.

A critic from the humanistic camp might point out that it is doubtful that Skin-

---

[3]"Will Success Spoil B. F. Skinner?" (Interview transcription.) *Today*.

ner can legitimately claim this form of self-control under his notion of behavior engineering. Though it is true that we can be taught specific techniques of self-management, the application of these techniques requires an element of personal striving and decision making. Working out a program of behavior modification for ourselves involves such processes as choosing among alternatives, establishing priorities, making decisions and choices, and other functions that were traditionally associated with a self-structure. Skinner defines a self in terms of verbal behavior and social responses from others, but his definition is not very convincing. Furthermore, we may create our own methods of self-control. How can this be explained behavioristically? In addition, after we have worked out a plan with all the behaviors and reinforcements specified, we may simply not be able to carry it out. It is a common observation that all the good intentions in the world may not be sufficient to guarantee that they will be executed. Saint Paul says: "The spirit is willing, but the flesh is weak." It would seem that Skinner is outside his domain when he delves into self-management even though he attempts to relate it to past reinforcement schedules. Why one person can carry out a personally developed program of self-management and another cannot remains an unanswered question. Perhaps one can more vividly sense the consequences of his or her behavior than the other person can. Then, too, how can the various schedules of reinforcement that have been found to be so effective in controlling behavior be applied to oneself? In any case we are dealing with variables that are outside the Skinnerian system. It seems likely that a different conception of people and different techniques will be required to promote better self-management.

Further, operant reinforcement theory seems limited to explaining learned behaviors that are chiefly under the control of rewards and punishments. Skinner, despite active attempts, has not been particularly successful in accounting for cognitive behaviors such as concept formation, creativity, problem solving, and acquisition of language. He is also unable to account for learning by observation (imitation).

When we broaden the concept of reinforcement to include contrived and natural, specific and generalized, extrinsic and intrinsic, other imposed and self-imposed, the range of possible applications in human life is almost unlimited. There is no question that reinforcements play an enormous role in every aspect of living. It has always been so, but Skinner more than any other psychologist has refined the techniques of utilizing reinforcers for behavior management. Science is cumulative, and there is no reason why those who may have a different conception of humans, such as the humanistic psychologists, cannot utilize and build upon the behavior modification procedures of Skinner. A model of humans that allows for a certain degree of self-determination can incorporate Skinner's techniques and discoveries even if not his general conception of humanity. It is unlikely that Skinner's technology will ever be replaced completely.

GUIDES TO RESEARCH

HEURISTIC VALUE OF SKINNER'S VIEWS

As we have noted, Skinner's views on operant reinforcement concepts and procedures are receiving widespread interest and application. Many people in the helping professions apply

Skinner's reinforcement principles in changing or controlling behavior. These methods have been especially helpful with people having problems with impulse control, such as autistic children, the retarded and learning disabled, institutionalized psychotics, and social deviants such as juvenile delinquents and criminals. These types of personality and behavior disorders have not responded well to the typical interview procedures of the traditional psychotherapies. For many therapists, behavior modification procedures have been a welcomed therapeutic innovation.

There are many advantages in using behavior modification techniques. Their proponents claim that they are especially effective in dealing with specific behavior problems such as speech difficulties, phobias, compulsive behaviors, tantrum control in children, obesity, and a host of other trait and behavior disturbances. Because the treatment strategy is directed to a specific problem rather than to the total personality, the duration of treatment is usually much shorter than is the case in the traditional forms of therapy.

Another advantage is that the effectiveness of the procedures can be easily assessed. Changes in behavior occur rapidly if the behavior problems come under the influence of the reinforcement regime. Reinforcers are powerful controllers of behavior, especially when one can use primary or very strong secondary reinforcers.

Another advantage of behavior modification procedures is that they can be taught to personnel who do not have training in the behavioral sciences: hospital attendants, nurses, teacher's aides, and paraprofessionals in a variety of fields. Many of the traditional therapies not only required extensive training, for example, psychoanalysis, but also did not make provision for using therapeutic aids. A program of behavior modification or of behavior therapy may be designed by an expert (a behavior engineer or trained behavior therapist) who then directs the implementation of the program, utilizing the services of the type of assistants noted earlier. Training the staff in the concepts and procedures of behavior modification may be necessary prior to the initiation of the actual program.

Problem areas may be matched with specific behavior modification programs. For example, a specific program may be developed to deal with delinquent offenders living in a residential treatment facility. Specific procedures may be worked out in great detail for treating phobias. In fact, such programs are being sold commercially. (Goodall, 1972)

The operant conditioning of Skinner fosters rigor, precision, and objectivity more strictly than did Watson, the founder of behaviorism. The behavior researcher and behavior therapist keep continuous and detailed records of rates of behaviors, behavior changes, and precise measurements of stimuli. They use automated devices to measure behaviors precisely; they graph, chart, and log behaviors. (Bassett, Blanchard, and Koshland, 1977) One result of this strict record-keeping is that the behavior researchers and therapists can readily determine whether or not their program of behavior modification is working. (Skinner, 1978) Reports of behavior change by subjects in experiments or clients in therapy may be used as data, but more reliance is placed on changes that occur (or do not occur) in specific behaviors. The victim of an elevator phobia may state that he or she feels more comfortable in riding elevators than previously, but the behavior therapist depends more on observable behaviors: for example, signs of anxiety. Behavior researchers and therapists are their own best critics. (Rimm, 1976)

Some critics have pointed out that behavior modification is becoming a prestigious label that is being applied to a host of methods that are not strictly behavioristic. In one treatment program for delinquent boys a great variety of techniques that ranged from token reinforcers to rap sessions with a group leader were all labeled behavior modification techniques. Even Skinner has broadened the notion of reinforcers far beyond the simple delivery of food to a rat for bar-pressing behavior or receipt of a kernel of corn for pecking behavior of a pigeon. For humans, strong reinforcers may include praise, attention, flattery, a pleasant smile, and other similar intangibles. Skinner, who terms these "generalized conditioned reinforcers" has not used them in his research, and his description of how these are learned does not really explain their power or persistence, in the view of some critics. (Hilgard and Bower, 1975) Such reinforcers make more sense as primary reinforcers for a psychological entity that Skinner rejects, the self. When the original behavior modification procedures are so broadly expanded, it becomes impossible to assess their efficacy. When everything under the sun psychologically is termed behavior modification, the true value of the procedures is difficult to assess.

Research, correctly or incorrectly performed, dealing with behavior modification is abundant. Several journals specialize in such work, for example, *Journal of the Experimental Analysis of Behavior* and *Journal of Applied Behavior Analysis*. Many other journals also carry such research reports. There is no question that Skinner's views have been credited as the source of much research and application in behavior management, but, again, it should be noted that what is often termed behavior modification or behavioristic research is loosely defined as "anything that works."

Instructional Applications (Programmed Instructions and Teaching Machines)

Skinner is a pioneer in the development of programmed instruction and teaching machines. He advocated the use of principles of operant conditioning in working out a step-by-step teaching program that might be presented by an exposure device or in book form. Many combinations are possible: programmed instruction packages have used audio and video recordings, filmstrips, slides, regular films, along with written forms that the learner completes. Even computers have been used for programmed instruction. Such learning systems are used primarily in educational settings, but they are also being widely used in business and industrial training facilities.

The extent of the use of programmed instruction and teaching machines is difficult to determine. The early proponents of this approach predicted a major revolution in instructional procedures, but these have not "caught on" quite as extensively as these enthusiasts predicted. However, they continue to be used on a wide scale. Skinner definitely deserves credit for being a major contributor in this area.

EMPIRICAL SUPPORT FOR SKINNER'S VIEWS

Characteristics of Operant Conditioning Research

Skinner has derived his principles primarily from his research with laboratory rats and pigeons. He sought to identify the stimulus variables that could be manipulated so as to gain control of specific behaviors such as bar-pressing by the rat and picking on an electric switch by the pigeon. He has not hesitated to generalize his findings based on relatively simple responses of relatively simple animals to the highly complex and diverse behaviors of humans. The variables he investigated were also introduced in a straightforward manner. He arranged the laboratory environment, so that one variable at a time could be studied under highly controlled conditions. He obtained (1) a baseline measure of a specific behavior and then (2) introduced a variable and then (3) noted the changes that occurred in the particular behavior. The variable was then removed, and again the specific behavior was measured. If the behavior changed with the introduction of the variable and returned to baseline when it was removed, the variable would be clearly established as the cause of the behavior change. This research design has been frequently used by investigators who attempt to demonstrate the effectiveness of behavior modification, using operant conditioning procedures. The following study is a typical example.

A promising application of reinforcement procedures was carried out with institutionalized psychotics in a so-called token economy (Ayllon and Azrin, 1965, 1968), in which tokens were used as reinforcers that could be cashed in for desired items and activities. Prior to the implementation of the project, a pilot study had to be conducted to determine (1) the types of behaviors that were to be reinforced, (2) the methods of reinforcing that were most effective and feasible, and (3) the types of reinforcers to be used. Furthermore, the reinforcers would be given by several people involved with patient management; thus, there had to be some agreement and consistency in delivering the reinforcers. Forty-five long-term patients formed the population of the ward that was being studied.

The preliminary study and training period lasted eighteen months. A host of behaviors was established as desirable—personal hygiene activities, helping serve meals to other patients, performing kitchen duties, secretarial activities, and general ward duties. The patients were given tokens for performing these various tasks. The number of tokens, of course, depended on the nature of the work done. Patients could accumulate tokens to purchase the more attractive reinforcers such as new clothing, a trip into town, or a meeting with the very popular social worker. These were typical long-term hospitalized psychotic patients who exhibited a variety of symptoms of debilitation—low activity level, apathy and depression, poor cleanliness habits, and generally a low level of self-management skills. With the institution of the token economy, the conditions changed rapidly. The patients began to work for the reinforcers by performing the specified behaviors, which were selected as being representative of normal functioning. We could argue that the changed environment resembled conditions in the real world more than the typical hospital setting. In another phase of the project, the investigators studied the effects of removing the reinforcers. Extinction of the targeted behaviors occurred, and the patients again exhibited the typical psychotic behaviors.

Critics of Skinner argue that one of the difficulties of using reinforcers such as the tokens in the preceding study is that the environment is contrived and not really like conditions in the real world. We do not receive tokens for proper self-care. The proponents argue that contrived reinforcers are used to elicit behaviors that will eventually produce natural reinforcers. They would point out that extinction occurred because the experiment had not continued long enough for the change in reinforcers to occur. The token economy research was undertaken for forty-two days.

Functional Analysis of Behavior

Those who use operant conditioning for therapeutic purposes advocate that one begin with a *functional analysis* of behavior. They relate a particular behavior to environmental events—to the antecedents and to the consequences of that behavior (Skinner, 1978). Certain stimuli are the cues for a particular behavior, and other stimuli maintain the behavior. Suppose you wished to conduct a functional analysis of smoking behaviors. It would be necessary to identify the stimulus events that would occasion smoking behavior. Common smoking situations are these: smoking after eating, smoking with certain beverages, smoking during breaks, smoking during work. Analysis of the reinforcing consequences might include relating the degree of pleasure to the specific occasions for smoking. It might involve a fine-grained analysis of the various pleasurable aspects of smoking, such as the flavor, occupying one's hands, nervous tics such as tapping the cigarette, flicking the ash, and so on. A program of behavior change would require altering both the antecedents and the consequences. The occasions for smoking could be altered; and the pleasures (the reinforcers), changed. Specific procedures would have to be developed to accomplish these objectives, of course. This general procedure has been applied to a host of behavior problems.

An actual application of reinforcement procedures was used with a three-year-old child in a nursery setting to extinguish crawling and crouching behavior and to promote normal walking and standing behaviors. (Harris, et al., 1967) The child's behavior in the nursery school was continuing to regress during the first three months of attendance. The child was spending more and more of her time crawling and crouching. The teachers attempted to correct the behavior by affection and demonstrations of concern. A functional analysis revealed that the teachers were actually reinforcing the very behavior they wanted to eliminate and ignoring the instances of normal behaviors. The approach was reversed.

The child was ignored when she was crawling or crouching, and was given praise and attention when she walked and stood up. The predicted results occurred rapidly. Within a week the child was showing a marked increase in the normal behaviors and a corresponding decrease in the undesirable ones. The researchers also identified the cues that elicited the unwanted behaviors, and these were altered. Thus, undesirable behavior was lessened by changing both the antecedents and the consequences.

We cannot do justice here to a survey of the vast literature in operant conditioning. It has been used so widely that behavior modification, taken in the broadest sense of techniques to change behavior, has created a revolution in the behavioral sciences. Skinner certainly deserves some credit for this movement.

Operant Conditioning and Biofeedback

As noted previously, biofeedback refers to the use of sensitive recording devices that measure neural, chemical, and physiological processes that are not ordinarily consciously experienced or under conscious control (Miller and Banuazizi, 1968; DiCarra, 1973). These investigators used operant conditioning procedures to enable both rats and humans to gain control of bodily processes that had previously been considered not subject to conditioning. Using sensitive feedback monitors, they could observe changes in intestinal and cardiac functions. They administered reinforcers for specific changes such as increases or decreases in blood pressure and in intestinal dilation or constriction. In the case of humans, the changes in bodily functioning can be monitored by the individual subject or client through the conversion of the electrical signal into audible tones and a blinking light. For example, the sound may begin to turn on when the blood pressure drops a given percent or when the arteries of the neck constrict in the case of the migraine sufferer.

The signal informs the individual that he or she has been able to alter the particular bodily function. The signal serves as a reinforcer, in

that control is being achieved. We regulate normal voluntary functions through a similar process of feedback. We learn to control our hands effectively because we experience what we are doing with them. Biofeedback devices enable us to monitor functions that are not typically open to us although some people have learned to sense and control autonomic functions even without formal training. Some of the feats of the mystics and the Eastern fakirs are probably the products of natural or learned sensitivity to autonomic processes. Biofeedback research has demonstrated that many people can learn to gain control of bodily functions with biofeedback training. Some people, after training, can produce the changes without the feedback devices. It should be noted, however, that a number of people do not respond to the training.

There are a number of physical ailments that are apparently greatly influenced and partly caused by emotional and attitudinal factors. These have been termed psychosomatic or psychophysiologic disorders, as noted in the recent publication of the American Psychiatric Association. (See the *Diagnostic and Statistical Manual of Mental Disorders*, American Psychiatric Association, 1980, 3d ed., p. 303.) They include certain skin disorders, musculoskeletal reactions, respiratory reactions, cardiovascular reactions, gastrointestinal reactions, and genitourinary reactions. Holistic medicine is concerned with the intricate relationship of the psychological and physical realms. Many illnesses considered purely organic seem to respond to some of the newer forms of therapy, including cognitive restructuring, self-instructional procedures, and, of course, biofeedback procedures. (McReynolds, 1975; Simon, 1977) Investigations have reported success with the use of biofeedback procedures in treating such disorders as chronic backache, high blood pressure, and migraine headache. (Engle and Shapiro, 1971) Some patients have been aided in regaining the function of limbs

that were paralyzed but that did not return to normal functioning during recovery. (Johnson and Garten, 1973) Researchers are finding that some people can gain control of physiological functions even without the biofeedback training. (Benson, Beary, and Carol, 1974; Benson, Kotch, Crassweller, and Greenwood, 1977) Further applications and refinements of operant conditioning procedures may open up the possibilities of treatment of a host of other disorders. This remarkable application of operant reinforcement offers an alternative to drug therapy. It is still a new area of research, and there are some indications that the early enthusiasm of its proponents who viewed it as a panacea was somewhat extreme.

GUIDES TO LIVING

TYPES OF REINFORCERS

Reinforcers play so important and pervasive a role in operant conditioning and behavior modification programs that it might be instructive to consider some of the various classes. We have already indicated some of the major types, for

example, positive and negative reinforcers, learned and unlearned reinforcers, specific and generalized, natural and contrived, conspicuous and inconspicuous, self-administered and other-administered.

Conspicuous and Inconspicuous Reinforcers

Consider the class of conspicuous and inconspicuous reinforcers. Skinner (1953) holds that all behavior is maintained by reinforcers. Some reinforcers are conspicuous in that they are obvious to an observer and to the behaving person. A person shooting at a target for a prize is an example of the operation of a conspicuous reinforcer. Frequently, however, a person is not aware of the reinforcers that are controlling behavior. Skinner would argue that the reinforcers are present nevertheless, but they are not obvious to the person or the observer.

What makes the difference between a dedicated and nondedicated teacher? Skinner would point out that the dedicated teacher is being controlled by perhaps unplanned but powerful inconspicuous reinforcers. Making good lesson plans, working closely with students, and

spending extra time on marking papers may produce some natural reinforcers such as pride, feeling of accomplishment, and also attention from students and respect from fellow teachers. We are terming these reinforcers inconspicuous in that they are not a part of the formal program for motivating and rewarding teachers and because the teacher who is influenced by them may not be aware of their effect on his or her behavior.

Skinner argues that dedicated teaching should be operationally defined, and then appropriate reinforcers and schedules should be used to promote it. Dedicated teaching is too important to permit it to occur by chance. Existing incentives and pay schedules represent crude and inefficient use of reinforcers.

Self-Administered Reinforcers

Reinforcers may be self-administered or administered by others. Self-administered reinforcers can be just as effective as reinforcers administered by others. (Skinner, 1978) We can establish contingent reinforcers to use as rewards for specific behaviors. A contingent reinforcer is one that is used conditionally, that is, only for rewarding specified behaviors such as studying for a certain period or working on a term paper and doing work that is not intrinsically motivating. Intrinsic motivation may be defined as natural reinforcement; thus when a task does not produce natural reinforcers, we can use contingent reinforcers. In other words, we can reward ourselves for doing work even though the reward has nothing to do with the work. We can contingently use such reinforcers as relaxing in an easy chair, drinking a cup of coffee, watching television, or even giving ourselves points for a record album as a reward for doing a variety of tasks. It may seem to the reader that this procedure is a form of game-playing, but the important thing is that it is a good way of gaining control of behavior. We can get ourselves to do distasteful work by using contingent reinforcers in the manner just described.

Reinforcers can take many forms, as we have noted. If we set up a routine, we feel compelled to follow it. Following the routine is itself reinforcing. If we establish a deadline, the deadline is a goal, and attaining it is reinforcing. When we follow a plan we have made, we receive reinforcement from our own behavior. Dividing a major project into subgoals is also another way of obtaining reinforcers along the way to the completion of the task. No matter what other reinforcers we derive, just getting a job done is a form of reinforcement—relief from tension. The curious thing is that we create the tension and then find it reinforcing to remove it.

We might even use Skinner's notions of shaping and chaining in our effort to achieve self-management. We might approach a difficult writing task by preparing a rough draft as spontaneously as possible and then reworking the material one or more times until it meets the specifications of the project. We might use the chaining procedure by dividing the project into units and dealing first with those units with which we feel most comfortable.

Using Negative Reinforcers

People can use negative reinforcement to promote behavior, for example, by determining to sit at the typewriter for an hour no matter how much is accomplished. If such a procedure is followed, we must be honest enough with ourselves to stick with the plan. The reinforcement is relief from the unpleasant task. Again, the important thing is that it can be an effective way

of gaining self-control. People who exhibit high degrees of self-control have probably designed such procedures for themselves even without knowledge of principles of operant conditioning. We can learn to use such principles and invent our own unique methods of applying these principles to ourselves.

Self-Control

Skinner believes that an experimental analysis of the behavior termed self-control should assist us in understanding the sense of freedom of decision making that people experience. As long as

we hold that there is an independent, autonomous will, or self, operating outside the laws of the material universe, we can do nothing about improving or strengthening the will. (Skinner,

1971) It was assumed by some philosophers that the will is similar to a muscle, a "mental muscle" that could be strengthened through discipline and exercise. Thus, to strengthen your will, you can deny yourself things you like, force yourself to do things you dislike, and practice habits of punctuality, hard work, and clean living. According to Skinner, these methods are effective only when they lead to positive reinforcements or the avoidance of negative reinforcements. How is the self formed? The consequences of behavior change behavior. The self consists of certain learned responses resulting from the consequences of our behavior as well as from the manner in which others relate to us.

MEANS OF SELF-CONTROL

Just as variables can be manipulated to influence the behavior of others, so also can we design conditions to manipulate our own behaviors. (Goldiamond, 1965; Rosenbaum, 1980) Self-management techniques are being advocated by behavioristic psychologists such as Skinner as falling within the domain of behaviorism. Some critics object that the rationale for their inclusion is not very sound because they imply free will, which the behaviorists reject. We shall include these methods here with this caution in mind.

Skinner, along with Bandura, resolves some of the problems of the freedom-determinism issue with the notion of *reciprocal determinism*, which refers to the mutual interaction of the individual and the environment. The environment acts upon the individual, but the individual can alter the environment; this increased freedom is gained through appropriate knowledge and skills. Self-initiated activity is still not accounted for by this view, however.

People who know from past experience that they have a tendency to succumb to the flattery of a salesperson can deliberately turn a deaf ear in such situations. If they adopt the policy of thinking over, for at least a day, any major purchase, even if there is a promise of a discount for signing on the spot, they will avoid a hasty decision that they may later regret. Reputable business people generally do not coerce their potential customers by offering discounts for immediate commitment. We can see here that susceptibility to flattery and the allure of a discount are definite variables that can be brought under self-control.

People may also develop techniques to control their temper; they may, for instance, count to ten before responding while angry. As a rule you should not write a letter when you are upset; or if you write a letter, you should read it at a later time and then decide whether or not to send it. Many people have regretted the hasty words of criticism or hate or whatever they wrote in a state of anger. Unlike spoken words, the written can become a permanent record.

Some people find that they can control their tendency to spend money only by limiting the amount they take with them. One man said that he did not use charge accounts simply because it was so tempting to spend more than he could afford. Here is an example of a system of payment, a great convenience if used properly, that exerts control over the behavior of many. Skinner would point out that the aversive consequences are delayed: you do not pay until much later; thus, the positive reinforcements of the purchase are not offset by the negative consequences. The misuse of charge accounts makes sense in terms of reinforcement theory. If you understand the dynamics of their use, you can take steps to guard against their dangers.

Suppose that you have some difficulty remembering things. There are many ways of controlling behavior to facilitate remembering. You may use the "displacement method": altering something you are bound to see. For example, you may displace the cover of the coffee pot or place a cup upside down at your place at the table. The displaced thing will remind you of what you want to remember. Or you may have a certain place where you put things you want to remember the next morning.

WHY SELF-CONTROL IS NOT ALWAYS EFFECTIVE

Skinner points out that, frequently, natural aversive consequences are insufficient to control behavior; they have to be bolstered by additional reinforcers. He means that the natural consequences must be supplemented and this is where self-control techniques can play a significant role. A man who drinks excessively may experience repeated hangovers, but he continues the inordinate drinking. Skinner would argue that the natural consequences of his drinking apparently are not sufficient to change the behavior that caused it. Perhaps the reason is that there is a time lapse between the positive effects of the drinking and the aversive effects of the hangover. In any case, the natural aversive reinforcer in this instance would have to be augmented by other aversive consequences. A better attack, in Skinner's view, is to engage in behaviors that would produce desirable positive reinforcers.

Bandura (1969) points out that aversive consequences often fail to alter behavior because they occur long after the behavior. Thus they do not compete with the reinforcing consequences of the same behavior. The drinker enjoys the euphoric effects of alcohol before experiencing the aversive effects of the hangover. Bandura suggests finding a way of moving the aversive consequences so that they occur earlier in the drinking sequence. An example might be a set of written instructions that one might read before a party.

If welders do not wear goggles, they are endangering their vision, but some welders who know this still will not wear goggles. The driver who passes another car on a hill is risking his or her life and threatening the lives of others, yet many drivers still insist on passing. Many people smoke even though there is possible danger to their health. In such instances, the possible consequences apparently do not change the behavior. The welder may go for weeks without an injury; the smoker may not experience the ill effects for years; the driver may pass many times without an accident. Other aversive reinforcers must be provided: the man who does not wear his goggles will get fired; the driver who passes on a hill risks a stiff fine; the smoker is warned by highly placed medical authorities. Such additional aversive consequences are effective for many people, but there are still those for whom they are not effective. This is one of the reasons that Skinner argues against the use of aversive control and emphasizes the use of positive reinforcers to instigate desirable behavior.

Perhaps what is needed is to make the aversive consequences vividly apparent to the person or to ourselves so that we will be motivated enough to prevent those consequences from occurring. Sometimes, for instance, just writing down what we eat is enough to create an awareness of poor eating patterns and produce a change in those patterns toward health (see Komaki and Dore-Boyce, 1978). Bandura's suggestion about using aversive control is certainly relevant here.

HINTS FOR SELF-CONTROL

Here are some questions that may help you to work out methods for self-control. First, what techniques can you use to alter your mood? Dress up. Take a bath. Read a favorite poem. Go someplace. Secondly, how can you get yourself to do things you have to do but don't want to do? Establish objectives. Work out a plan. Schedule a timetable for completing each step. Third, how can you break a habit? Avoid certain situations. Practice weak forms of the habit: smoke a brand of cigarettes you don't enjoy, or touch, with gloves on, an animal you dread. You may counteract one emotion by its opposite. It should be borne in mind that when an unwanted behavior, such as overeating, is being extinguished, there is a period in which you may experience a void. This condition opens the possibility of acquiring a new unwanted behavior, such as increased smoking. Thus, you should take account of this in planning a behavior modification program for yourself and include a desirable target behavior to replace the old. Fourth, how can you overcome a symptom? You can tell yourself that the symptom is distressing but will not endanger health. If you feel fatigued when you have done nothing exhausting, you can simply endure the feeling of fatigue as a psychological reaction to an unpleasant life situation.

WHERE DOES SELF-CONTROL ORIGINATE?

Consider the question of teaching a child self-reliance. Parents and teachers control the child's behavior through their power to administer positive and aversive reinforcement. Mother makes sure that the child gets to school on time, and the teacher makes sure that he or she works when he or she gets there. Both mother and teacher issue verbal commands and support their requests and commands with threats of punishment if need be. The child eventually learns to tell time and to get off to school without being told. In a study hall, he or she works on a project that has been assigned. If we analyze the child's behavior, we can see that the environment is still the effective cause. He or she comes to depend on the clock rather than on the mother. Having been punished by parents for being late, the child uses the clock to avoid such punishment. At school he or she works on the assigned project rather than reading comic books because his or her environmental history has reinforced such behavior.

Whether or not techniques of self-control will be learned and utilized depends upon the previous history; if there have been prior reinforcements for utilizing techniques of self-control, then these will be used. Behavior that in the past has avoided aversive consequences will also tend to acquire strength. Thus, those who take control of themselves have been reinforced either positively or negatively for doing so.

Not only does Skinner attribute self-management skills to the learning history of the person, but he also holds that we can be our own behavior modifiers. According to this view, we can work out our own program of behavior modification to gain better control of our circumstances. In other words, in being our own behavior modifiers, we can correct past deficiencies. This highly controversial viewpoint is significant for our own efforts in applying operant reinforcement principles. Though rejecting the notion of free will, Skinner's idea that we can design our own program of behavior modification seems to restore the essence of freedom that is self-management, some might argue. Irrespective of the philosophical issues involved here, the point is that self-management techniques can be learned and implemented by those who wish to improve their lives.

SUMMARY

1. Skinner is a radical behaviorist because he does not accept psychological variables as determinants of behavior, but rather relates behavior to environmental stimuli. He has developed operant reinforcement constructs and methods. Skinner argues that trait terms are merely labels for classes of behaviors that would be better explained by discovering the environmental determinants.

2. A major guiding principle for Skinner is that behavior is determined by its consequences. Behavior becomes an operant if it leads to a goal.

3. Watson, the founder of American behaviorism, emphasized reactions and adaptations to the environment, an *S-R* model, whereas Skinner stresses actions upon the environment, an operant behaviorism. The outcomes of behavior may be controlled by the behavior modifier. Consequences of behavior are either reinforcers or punishers.

4. Respondent conditioning is another

versions of the Skinner box --

name for classical conditioning, which involves stimulus substitution. In operant conditioning behavior produces consequences that increase or decrease the probability of the behavior. In respondent conditioning, a response is elicited; in operant conditioning, a behavior is emitted. Operant conditioning increases the behavior repertory of the subject whereas respondent conditioning increases the stimuli to which one reacts. A complete unit of behavior includes both respondents and operants. We often react in a situation with fear, anger, or pleasure and then emit an operant that may change the situation. Much of our behavior is, therefore, under the control of powerful emotions that are set off by conditioned stimuli in our environment.

5. Contingencies of reinforcement refer to the conditions of reinforcement. Skinner uses the term *contingency* to stand for behavior and its outcome. Reinforcements can be used in intricate ways. The particular arrangements are known as schedules of reinforcements, also termed contingencies, by Skinner. There are fixed and variable interval schedules and fixed and variable ratio schedules. Interval schedules are based on time; ratio schedules are based on behavior. Specific schedules are associated with characteristic rates of behavior. Reinforcers may be used to promote learning and to sustain performance. A continuous reinforcement schedule fosters learning, whereas intermittent reinforcement schedules are used to sustain performance.

6. In respondent conditioning, an eliciting stimulus sets off the unconditioned response. In operant conditioning, an occasioning stimulus leads to the operant or emitted behavior. A discriminable stimulus is one that serves as a sign, or a cue that has meaning for the subject. Antecedent and consequent stimuli play different roles for respondent and operant conditioning.

7. Undifferentiated behavior is molded gradually in an ordered series of steps that increasingly approximate the desired behavior pattern through a process known as shaping. Through shaping, one can regulate the speed, strength, and patterning of behavior. Shaping is also termed the method of successive approximations. Chaining refers to combining behavior

units into a sequence that may be quite complex. Another form of shaping is differential reinforcement, which refers to selective reinforcement and extinction in producing a particular operant. Differential reinforcement has been used with biofeedback conditioning, in which the subject is informed of changes in physiological functions by a signal and is able to gain control of them.

8. Skinner's distinctive contributions include shaping, chaining, and the various schedules of reinforcement. Skinner is also one of the pioneers in the development of teaching machines and programmed instruction, using operant reinforcement constructs and methods.

9. Reinforcement is so basic to Skinner's methods that his approach has been termed a reinforcement psychology. Some important distinctions relevant to reinforcement are these: positive and negative, learned and unlearned, natural and contrived, specific and generalized, self-administered and other-administered, and conspicuous and inconspicuous. Positive reinforcement strengthens approach behavior, whereas negative reinforcement strengthens avoidance or escape behavior. Removing or preventing a threat is a form of negative reinforcement. Punishment is intended to weaken behavior but has been frequently demonstrated to be ineffective. It also produces unwanted respondents. Punishment is defined as undesirable consequences produced by behavior or desirable consequences removed by behavior. Extinction refers to the absence of the usual outcomes of conditioned responses and behaviors, also intended to weaken behavior. A generalized reinforcer can be used to strengthen many different behaviors. Behavior may be changed by satiation, counterconditioning, changing circumstances, and promoting counteracting behavior, and through forgetting. Although mild forms of punishment can aid in changing behavior by serving as informative cues, Skinner rejects punishment as a method of behavior change because its outcomes are unpredictable.

10. Skinner deals with abnormalities by translating personality disorders into the language of operant and respondent behavior. Skinner relates both normal and abnormal behavior to environmental determinants. He rejects such

personality variables as the self; thus, disorders that require the self as an explanatory principle are translated into behavioristic terms.

11. Skinner has not proposed an ideal state of personality and living, but rather has concentrated on the factors that determine behavior. The good person is the product of the good environment. Skinner does appreciate the active nature of operants and argues for learning appropriate operants for effective living, but he does not define what that means. He protests frequently the widespread use of aversive control and maintains that the controllers of behavior, such as parents, teachers, and law enforcement authorities, should rely more on the powerful effects of positive reinforcers in shaping desirable behavior. Human superiority has been demonstrated in a world that is largely made by humans, but humans have created many problems as well. Skinner provides constructs and methods for a self-administered program of behavior modification. Whether this type of program is really behavioristic is open to question because it implies that the self can exercise control over itself.

12. Skinner's ideas have inspired a great deal of research. Behavior modification is a widespread phenomenon in contemporary life. One advantage of using behavior modification methods and constructs in therapeutic settings is that the therapy team can be taught them in a relatively short time. A major proof of the effectiveness of operant procedures is the change in behavior that occurs when the reinforcer is introduced and the elimination of the changed behavior when the reinforcer is removed. This is also one of the weaknesses of operant procedures in that the operant behavior becomes tied to the reinforcers. Proponents of behavior modification argue that natural reinforcers will occur when the appropriate behavior is instigated by the contrived reinforcers, thus making the contrived reinforcers unnecessary. This point is a source of controversy because there is supporting evidence for both sides.

GLOSSARY

Behaviorism: Approach to psychology that stresses environmental control of observable behavior; founded by J. B. Watson; Skinner is the most popular current representative of radical behaviorism, which rejects conscious states and psychological variables as determinants of behavior. Moderate behaviorists accept intervening personality variables but operationally define them.

Contingency: The type of relationship between an operant and the reinforcer; Skinner uses the term to stand for the schedule of reinforcement. Behavior depends on contingencies.

Functional analysis of behavior: Identifying the antecedent and consequent environmental determinants of specific behavior.

Learning: A general term for acquisition of responses or behaviors.

Conditioning: A form of habit learning that involves connections or bonds. The two basic types involve bonds between stimuli and responses and between behaviors and outcomes.

Respondent: Synonym for classical conditioning; a type of conditioning in which emotional responses become attached to neutral stimuli.

Operant: A type of conditioning in which behavior produces outcomes that influence the strength and probability of that behavior.

Chaining: A complex form of conditioning in which simple conditioned units are linked in sequence.

Shaping: Using reinforcers to promote the learning of a graded series of behaviors that eventuate in the correct sequence of operants. Successive approximations of the correct behaviors are reinforced until reinforcement is given only for the correct sequence.

Discrimination: Learning the specific meaning of stimuli through the use of reinforcers and extinction.

Reinforcers: Stimuli that increase the probability of behaviors; stimuli that strengthen behavior.

Unlearned and learned (unconditioned and conditioned): Natural reinforcers as contrasted with learned reinforcers, for example, food versus awards.

Natural and contrived: Natural reinforcers are those that are the direct outcome of operants; contrived reinforcers are desirable stimuli that are used by a behavior modifier to instigate operants, for example, tokens. This distinction applies also to punishment.

Specific and generalized: Specific reinforcers relate directly to a specific need, for example, food for a hungry animal; generalized reinforcers encompass a broad spectrum of behaviors; for example, praise can serve as a reinforcer for many different behaviors.

Conspicuous and inconspicuous: Reinforcers that are perceived as reinforcers and reinforcers that operate without awareness.

Other-administered and self-administered: Reinforcers arranged and delivered by others versus reinforcers arranged and delivered by oneself.

Positive and negative: Both strengthen behavior; positive reinforcers strengthen approach behavior; negative reinforcers strengthen avoidance and escape behaviors.

Contingent and noncontingent: Reinforcers that depend on the emitting of an operant versus reinforcers given without any required behavior.

Schedules of reinforcement: The particular arrangements of delivery of reinforcers; schedules determine rate, strength, and quality of behavior.

Fixed interval: Reinforcement based on a fixed time interval; sometimes at least one correct behavior is required and sometimes not.

Variable interval: The reinforcer is given according to an average time interval, but particular instances of delivery vary.

Fixed ratio: Reinforcement based on fixed number of behaviors.

Variable ratio: The reinforcement is given for varying numbers of behaviors; usually based on an average number of behaviors.

Intermittent reinforcement: Partial schedule of reinforcement; reinforcing a fraction of the correct behaviors.

Continuous reinforcement: Reinforcement given for each correct behavior; useful during the acquisition phase.

Stimulus: In the strict sense, any impinging energy to which the organism is sensitive; used broadly as situation.

Discriminable: A stimulus that has meaning for an organism; serving as a cue or sign for response or behavior.

Occasioning: A discriminable stimulus that indicates that an operant is appropriate.

Antecedent: A stimulus that precedes a response or behavior.

Consequent: A stimulus that follows behavior and is produced by behavior.

Stimulus Substitution: Another name for classical or respondent conditioning, by which a neutral stimulus acquires some of the properties of a natural stimulus through pairing of the two stimuli.

Eliciting: Stimulus that evokes a response.

Aversive: Stimulus that is painful and which the organism wishes to terminate or avoid.

Stimulus generalization: A range of stimuli that have a common property and evoke varying degrees of the same behavior.

Types of behavior: Behavior is a general term that stands for a variety of reactions and actions.

Approach: Behavior directed toward a goal; an operant that secures reinforcement; strengthened by a positive reinforcer.

Avoidance: Behavior that prevents an unwanted stimulus; strengthened by a negative reinforcer.

Escape: Behavior that removes or terminates a painful stimulus; the successful outcome is negatively reinforcing.

Operant: Behavior that acts upon the environment and which produces a goal; synonymous with instrumental behavior; operants may be classified as approach, avoidance, or escape.

Respondent: A response or reaction to a stimulus; unlearned respondents are unconditioned responses; learned respondents are conditioned responses.

Elicited: Reaction to an antecedent stimulus; elicited behaviors are termed respondents.

Emitted: Spontaneous behavior; may occur in the presence of an occasioning stimulus; means operant behavior.

Weakening behavior: Lessening the frequency of behavior; inhibiting or blocking behavior.

Extinction: Weakening behavior by removing usual reinforcing consequences.

Punishment: Following behavior with undesirable consequence or removing desirable consequence of behavior.

Counterconditioning: Blocking a particular behavior by conditioning an opposing behavior to the same stimulus; one emotion may be substituted for another through counterconditioning.

SUGGESTED READINGS

Skinner, B. F. *The Behavior of Organisms*. New York: Appleton, 1938.

Presented here is a useful formulation of behavior in terms of the principles of conditioning. Selected experiments are used for illustrative purposes.

———. *Walden Two*. New York: Macmillan, 1948.

Skinner constructs his Utopia based upon the principles of behavior engineering.

———. *Science and Human Behavior*. New York: Macmillan, 1953.

Topics include thinking, self-control, government and law, psychotherapy, group control, education, and many others.

———. *Contingencies of Reinforcement: A Theoretical Analysis*. New York: Appleton, 1954.

Skinner restates his entire scientific position. He stresses the relevance of science in broad social problems.

———. *The Technology of Teaching*. New York: Appleton, 1968b

Here Skinner offers his views on how learning should be approached in the schools to optimize student potentials.

———. *Beyond Freedom and Dignity*. New York: Knopf, 1971.

In this book Skinner questions the traditional views of freedom and responsibility and proposes instead an environmental control of behavior. He views the answers to human problems in terms of a designed society in the hands of benevolent designers.

———. *Cumulative Record*. New York: Appleton, 1972b.

A collection of Skinner's research papers, giving detailed analysis of experiments.

———. *Notebooks*. Englewood Cliffs, N.J.: Prentice-Hall, 1981.

Skinner relates all things to operant conditioning; for Skinner, behavior is always shaped by consequences. This book is a compilation of twenty-five years of notebook keeping; it reveals Skinner's literary bent and a thoroughly human picture of Skinner the man.

A. BANDURA, J. ROTTER, A. ELLIS, AND W. MISCHEL

COGNITIVE AND SOCIAL LEARNING THEORIES

Bandura

Rotter

Ellis

Mischel

CHAPTER 13

THE MANY APPLICATIONS OF LEARNING THEORY

Do we learn responses to situations, or do we learn information that can be used to guide our responses? Do we learn by responding, or do we respond after we learn? Furthermore, can the learning of humans be understood through the principles of the animal laboratory, or is the nature of humans so different from that of the lower animals that different principles are involved? Are our abilities to cognize and interpret our world such that we cannot apply the principles of animal learning to human learning? What about the social aspects of human learning: much important learning takes place in social contexts and involves social activities. Albert Bandura (1963, 1969, 1977), without denying the value of other learning approaches, stresses the imitative and observational aspect of learning in social contexts. Julian Rotter, Albert Ellis, and Walter Mischel inferred cognitive variables that they believe others have not dealt with adequately. The learning approach has an applied side, which is termed *behavior modification* or *behavior therapy*. We will consider the applied uses of learning concepts and principles in bringing about personality change.

DISTINCTIVE FEATURES OF COGNITIVE AND SOCIAL LEARNING THEORIES

In this chapter we will discuss the cognitive and social learning theories of Albert Bandura, Julian Rotter, Albert Ellis, and Walter Mischel. These theorists refer to themselves as behaviorists, but there is some question as to whether their approaches reflect the intent of the behavioristic movement, which was to eliminate from psychology psychological or personality causes. John Watson, the founder of American behaviorism, wanted psychology to focus on observable behavior and measurable environmental causes. He rejected psychological explanations based on personality variables.

The cognitive and social learning theorists have made extensive use of intervening personality variables and especially the cognitive determinants of overt behavior. Such theories have stressed the role of learning in humans. Bandura is the most explicit in his emphasis on observational learning. Furthermore, human learning occurs primarily in social settings although, of course, we learn by direct experience and from our own cognitive processes such as reasoning and problem solving. Even habit and associationistic learning involve active cognitive processing. The cognitive operations and attainments are highly stressed in the theories of Rotter, Ellis, and Mischel. Another distinguishing feature of these theories is their empirical basis. Except for Ellis' views, which are primarily derived from his therapeutic experiences, the cognitive and social learning theories are derived from experimental work. Like the traditional personality theories, personality variables are used as explanatory devices and are inferred from behavior, but unlike the traditional personality theorists, who derived their constructs and postulates from their experiences in psychotherapy, the cognitive and social learning theorists derive their intervening variables from rigorous experimentation. Their methods of treatment and outcome-evaluation also involve rigorous measurement and control. These theories reflect the great interest in cognitive psychology that has occurred in recent years.

Biographies

ALBERT BANDURA

Albert Bandura was born in Alberta, Canada, in 1925, and came to the United States in 1949. He received his bachelor's degree from the University of British Columbia and his M.A. and Ph.D. from the University of Iowa in 1952. His views on social learning and modeling were first presented in 1963 in a book with R. Walters, entitled *Social Learning and Personality Development*. In his 1969 book, *Principles of Behavior Modification*, Bandura presents the therapeutic applications of modeling procedures. He wrote a book on aggression with that title that was published in 1973. His latest presentation of his constructs and research appeared in his most recent book, *Social Learning Theory* (1977). His teaching career has been at Stanford University since 1953 in the Department of Psychology. He served as the president of the American Psychological Association in 1974.

JULIAN ROTTER

Julian Rotter grew up in Brooklyn, New York, and graduated from Brooklyn College in 1937. After that he did graduate work at the universities of Iowa and Indiana, receiving the Ph.D. in clinical psychology in 1941. He was a psychologist with the army in World War II. After returning from the armed services, he served on the faculty of Ohio State University for seventeen years. His cognitive emphasis was undoubtedly influenced by the thinking of George Kelly, who was at the same university and wrote a major two-volume work on personal constructs, published in 1955. Since 1963 he has been at the University of Connecticut, where he directs the Clinical Psychology Training Program. He is a past president of the American Psychological Association. His work on locus of control has been highly influential and has generated over 600 studies since it was published in the late sixties.

His interest in generalized expectancies has also led him to construct an interpersonal trust scale.

Rotter published the main features of his theory in 1954 in *Social Learning and Clinical Psychology*. Other important works of Rotter's are *Applications of a Social Learning Theory of Personality* (Rotter, Chance and Phares, 1972); "Beliefs, Social Attitudes and Behavior," in *Cognition, Personality and Clinical Psychology* (Rotter, 1967); "Some Implications of a Social Learning Theory for the Practice of Psychotherapy," in *Learning Approaches to Therapeutic Behavior Change* (Rotter, 1970); and *Personality* (Rotter and Hochreich, 1975). Rotter's is essentially a field theory in that a personally meaningful cognitive field is the filter through which the environment exerts its influence on all behavior.

ALBERT ELLIS

Albert Ellis was born in Pittsburgh, Pennsylvania, in 1913. He received a Ph.D. in clinical psychology from Columbia University in 1947. He is known among psychologists primarily for his rational-emotive theory and therapy. Rational-emotive psychotherapy is highly popular. In a survey of over 800 psychologists regarding their therapeutic practice, Garfield and Kurtz (1976) found that rational-emotive psychotherapy was practiced more widely than client-centered therapy. Ellis is also known as a marriage and family counselor. He also considers himself to be a sexologist and has written several books for lay persons on sexuality. He is a popular speaker and has appeared on many radio and television talk programs. Dr. Ellis has founded two nonprofit institutes: the Institute for Rational Living and the Institute for Advanced Study in Rational Psychotherapy. He has written thirty-five books on topics relating to sex, marriage and family, and rational-emotive psychotherapy. Some of his most widely read books include *How to Live with a Neurotic*, 1957; *The Art and Science of Love*, 1960; *The Encyclopedia of Sexual Behavior*, edited by Ellis and Abarbanel. 1961; *Reason and Emotion in Psychotherapy*, 1962; *Sex and the Single Man*, 1963; *Is Objectivism a Religion?* 1968; *Growth Through Reason*, 1971; *How to Raise an Emotionally Healthy, Happy Child*, 1973; *Humanistic Psychotherapy*, 1973; *A Guide to Rational Living*, with Robert Harper, 1961; *New Guide to Rational Living*, with Robert Harper, 1975; *Sex and the Liberated Man*, 1976; *How to Live with and Without Anger*, 1977; *Overcoming Procrastination*, 1977; *The Intelligent Women's Guide to Dating and Mating*, 1979. An examination of the titles of this impressive list certainly reveals the breadth and scope of Ellis' interests.

WALTER MISCHEL

Walter Mischel was born in Vienna, Austria, in 1930. He received his B.A. from New York University, his M.A. in psychology from City College of New York, and his Ph.D. in psychology from Ohio State University. While at Ohio State University, he was influenced by both Julian Rotter and George Kelly, who have propounded influential cognitive theories. He has now joined several outstanding cognitive behavior theorists and therapists at Standford University. He has written several influential books: *Personality and Assessment*, 1968; *Introduction to Personality*, 3d ed., 1981; *Essentials of Psychology*, 1980. He has also written many journal articles dealing with his research on cognitive variables.

BANDURA'S OBSERVATIONAL LEARNING

A great deal of learning might be described as observational learning. We learn by observing the behavior of a model. Observational learning encompasses any type of *matching behavior*, such as imitation. Simply observing the behavior of the model appears to be sufficient to promote learning, according to Bandura and Walters (1963).

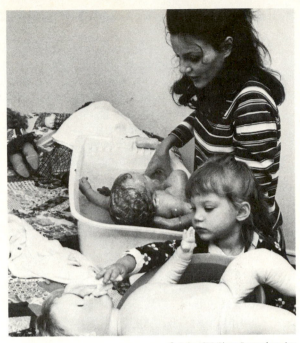

We model our models.

© Erika 1975/Photo Researchers, Inc.

But how can observational learning be related to the principle of reinforcement, which, it will be recalled, states that responses are learned only if they are reinforced? According to Bandura, learning may occur both as a consequence of reinforcement and through modeling or observation alone. Bandura (1969) has referred to observational learning as "no trial" learning because the observer learns without engaging in any overt activity.

In a new situation people learn what to do or what not do through observing the behaviors of those who seem to know how to act. If you approach a friend and pour out your worries about your new job, the friend might advise you to keep cool and observe what the others are doing. There is no question that much human learning— and even that of the higher animals—consists of matching the behavior of others. (Deutsch and Deutsch, 1966) Freud held that the child learns the behaviors appropriate to his or her sex through his or her emotional involvement with the parent of the same sex. All through life, we have models to copy. Success or failure in many aspects of living in a culture depends upon observational learning. The culture deviant—the criminal, the neurotic, the malingerer—may be one who has failed to conform to role expectations. Such failure may arise from inadequate modeling: having the wrong models or resisting the influence of models. Observational learning can be promoted as much by a deviant model as by a prosocial model (Walters and Llewellyn Thomas, 1963), and the absence of appropriate models can result in deficiencies of behavior. The person may simply be unequipped to be a contributing member of his or her society.

Reinforcement Versus Social Learning Mediated by Cognitive Symbols

Bandura stresses the social learning approach because he holds that most of our learning occurs in social contexts and through modeling. Certainly, learning can and does occur through trial and error, with the reinforcer selecting the correct behavior. Learning can and does occur through our own efforts, but the proportion of such learning is small compared to observational learning. We might even argue that direct learning through reinforcers would have jeopardized human survival long ago. Direct learning is usually very slow and requires appropriate occasions and conditions, which are not usually present when the learning is required. Furthermore, such learning is haphazard. Observing a model perform adaptive and coping behaviors leads to rapid learning and the avoidance of costly errors.

Observational learning requires the ability to engage in symbolic activity. (Bandura, 1977) We can form cognitive symbols, imaginal, conceptual, and verbal representations of events, people, and objects. These symbols mediate between situations and our reactions and actions. In other words, humans can picture or conceptualize a great many things, ranging from naming objects to highly abstract and complex events. Simply put, we can learn by forming cognitive representations of events going on around us and within us. We can learn by simply observing. The learning takes the form of images, concepts, and verbal representations. Watson (1925), the founder of behaviorism, conceived of thinking as subvocal speech. He literally reduced thinking to movements of the speech muscles. Modern cognitive behaviorists such as Bandura have moved the activity into the cognitive realm. They view thinking as *self-regulatory covert behavior*. This refers to forming cognitive symbols and arranging and rearranging them.

IS OBSERVATIONAL LEARNING SUFFICIENT?

Observational learning is highly complex and varied. There are many conditions that affect it. For one thing, the observer must (1) attend to relevant activities or models. The fact that models are reinforced or punished for behavior is a significant determinant of attention; thus, both the models' behavior and the outcomes of their behavior influence attention and learning. As a matter of fact, although learning may occur, its performance depends on whether or not the model was reinforced or punished for certain behavior. Learning through modeling also depends upon (2) the ability to retain what was observed, (3) capability of performing the skills involved, and (4) the motivation and incentive to perform the behavior. (Bandura and Walters, 1963)

Associative Learning

For Bandura cognitive processes play such a central role in human behavior that they operate even in relatively simple processes of associative learning.

It has long been known that ideas or events that occur together or in close temporal contiguity are linked, so that one becomes a reminder of the other. The behaviorists such as Pavlov and Watson found that stimuli may become linked to each other or to behavior in a similar manner. In Pavlovian conditioning, the conditioned stimulus is capable of eliciting the unconditioned response, or some form of anticipatory response. The linking process was assumed to take place automatically as a result of the pairing of the conditioned and unconditioned stimuli. Bandura argues against this mechanical linking even for animals, but especially in humans, who are capable of forming complex cognitive representations of events and their relationships.

Bandura points out that "people do not learn much, if anything, from repeated paired experiences unless they recognize that events are correlated." (1977, p. 67) He cites an experiment conducted by Chatterjee and Eriksen (1962) demonstrating that awareness is a determinant of conditioning. Conditioning did not take place as expected when awareness was controlled by instructions. As a matter of fact, many conditioning experiments with humans have used instructions to influence direction of attention or subjects' sets. This same procedure has been used to prove that extinction too is not a mechanical process but depends upon cognitive mediation. The investigators found that subjects who were informed that shock would follow particular words in a series of paired associates quickly evidenced changes in heart-rate activity to the key words. Subjects who were not informed of the correct plan, even though they received shocks for the same pairs as the other group, did not evidence autonomic conditioning in the same time period. Awareness of the plan of the experiment was the key factor in fostering the conditioning.

Cognitive mediation plays a remarkable role in eliminating fear and other avoidance behaviors. We can call upon our own experiences for examples. If students in a laboratory course learn that a poisonous snake is loose, fear and avoidance reactions will be very intense. But as soon as they are informed that the snake was caught, the fear ceases immediately.

Bandura summarizes the role of cognitive mediation in extinction as follows:

> The most striking evidence of cognitive control of anticipatory responses is provided by studies of the extinction of emotional reactions as a function of induced awareness. Affective reactions of people who are informed that predictive stimuli will no longer be followed by painful events are compared with those of people who are not told that the threat no longer exists. Induced awareness promptly eliminates fear arousal and avoidance behavior in the informed participants, while the uniformed lose their fear only gradually. [1977, p. 68; see also Bandura, 1969; Grings, 1973][1]

Cognitive mediational processes not only play a major determining role in classical conditioning and extinction, but also in operant conditioning. Knowledge of the nature of the reinforcer and the manner in which it is presented, the reinforcement schedule, greatly affects the rate of behavior. Skinner (1953) has proposed the view that operant learning is a mechanical linking of behaviors to environmental outcomes without any mediating cognitive symbolic activity. Working with rats and pigeons, he has demonstrated remarkable control of behavior through the use of various schedules of reinforcement. The behavior rate is greatly influenced by the schedule of reinforcement. Skinner has maintained that the same type of stimulus control can be achieved

---

[1]*Social Learning Theory; Principles of Behavior Modification.*

with human behavior, and he points out various schedules in real-life situations to support his argument.

An experiment by Kaufman, Baron, and Kopp (1966) investigated the role of cognitive factors in an operant procedure with humans. The subjects were to perform a simple manual task. The reinforcement was given on the average about once a minute. Because the reinforcement delivery varied, it was a variable interval schedule. Usually, this type of schedule leads to low but steady rates of responding in animals. One group, the variable interval group, was informed correctly about the actual schedule—that the reinforcer would occur about once a minute on the average so long as they were responding. The performance of this group was about sixty-five responses per minute. A second group, the fixed interval group, was told that the reinforcer would be given once a minute, but a response had to be made during that period in order for the reinforcer to be delivered. The rate of behavior was about six per minute. The variable ratio group, the third experimental group, was told that they must emit about 150 responses per minute in order to receive the reinforcer. The average for the variable ratio group was 259 per minute. It should be kept in mind that the three groups were actually reinforced according to the same variable interval schedule. The large differences were due to instructions.

Life Versus Symbolic Models

Bandura (1977) distinguishes between real-life and symbolic models. Under real-life models are included the agents of culture—parents, teachers, heroes, law enforcement authorities, sports stars. Real-life models are people with whom we are likely to have many direct interactions. Symbolic models include verbal material, pictorial presentation (films and television), and written material (books and magazines). Numerous studies demonstrate that both real-life and symbolic models influence the behavior of observers. What children see on television does, in fact, affect their behavior. (Murray, 1973) Bandura points out that the television productions may have greater influence than parental guidance because the direct portrayal of roles is more vivid than verbal instructions alone. The viewer of television and motion pictures is provided with life-like scenes.

Anyone who has ever watched a highly emotional film can recall the strong feelings that he or she felt. This common experience has been studied in controlled experiments, which demonstrated that even conditioned emotional responses can be produced by observational learning without a direct experience of the pain, fear, or sorrow the actors were portraying. Presented with the same cues given to the performers, the subjects made the same responses. (Bandura and Rosenthal, 1966) Thus, instrumental behaviors, positive and negative conditioned emotional responses, as well as cognitive symbols, may be acquired through observational learning; the learning may occur in the presence of real-life models or symbolic ones. Researchers studying the phenomena of observational learning have found that virtually every type of learning that occurs through direct experience is capable of being induced by observational learning. The reader should bear in mind the difference between learning through observation of a model and the subsequent performance of what is learned. Each process is influenced by a different set of variables.

VICARIOUS REINFORCEMENT

Vicarious learning means experiencing what another does by observation. *Vicarious reinforcement* means experiencing the benefits of reinforcement through observation of a model being reinforced or, in more recent studies by Bandura, seeing the models reinforcing themselves. The desirable consequences of the model's behavior often provide enough incentive to imitate performance.

Children will frequently follow the daring behavior of a leader who shows them how much fun he or she is having. The model's enthusiasm and delight, experienced vicariously, spur on the followers. Studies have indicated that both learning and performance are increased when the model experiences positive outcomes. The positive outcomes draw attention, a key factor in observational learning, to the model's instrumental behavior.

Behaviors that are not likely to occur can be fostered by observing a model receiving recognition or some other reinforcer. A person observing an interview in which the interviewee receives recognition for talking about personal matters would be more likely to engage in the same behavior. Behavior that does not have natural positive incentives may be increased by observing a model being reinforced for such behaviors. A student is more likely to study if a respected student is praised for studying. Therapeutic applications involve the use of models to demonstrate appropriate reactions and actions in certain troublesome situations. The observers are encouraged to engage in phobic, aggressive, or other dysfunctional behaviors. The model may teach the observer how to deal with the problem.

VICARIOUS PUNISHMENT

Vicarious punishment refers to experiencing the effects of punishment administered to models or by the models to themselves through observational learning.

Just as an observer may be stimulated to copy the reinforced behavior of a model, so also the behavior of a model that produces negative consequences can be lessened in the observer. We learn frequently from observing the mistakes of others. The effects of punishment have been studied by observing models punished for aggressive behavior. (Bandura, 1973) Children who saw aggressive behaviors punished evidenced much less aggression than the children who saw aggressive behaviors either rewarded or having no consequences.

Walters, Parke, and Cane (1965) found that observers were influenced by the outcomes of the models' transgressive behavior. If the models' transgressive behaviors were punished, the observers were less likely to imitate the behaviors than if the models' behaviors were rewarded or ignored. It should be noted that a violation of a rule or law that goes unpunished is assumed to constitute a reward. Rules and laws usually block

M. E. Warren/Photo Researchers, Inc.

We experience emotions by observing emotional behavior.

impulses that are rewarded through gratification. Again, we can see that vicarious experiences produce the same effects as direct experiences. We can learn fear, anger, affection, and many other positive and negative emotions vicariously.

What Types of Responses Are Acquired Through Observational Learning?

The specific responses that are subject to learning through imitation of a real-life or symbolic model are almost unlimited. The acquisition of aggressive responses has been studied most extensively, but dependency behavior, fear, sex-appropriate or-inappropriate behaviors, and others have also been studied. In general, behavior acquired through observational learning may be categorized under three headings: (1) the acquisition of new responses, such as the learning of aggressive responses from a model; (2) the strengthening or weakening of inhibitory responses, such as acquiring greater or less fear by observing the model's behavior in a fear situation; (3) stimulating already existing responses, such as practicing the piano longer after reading a biography of a great musician. (Bandura, 1977)

ACQUISITION OF NEW BEHAVIORS

Bandura and Walters (1963) cite many studies in which children exposed to a model behave more like the model as compared with a control group when presented with a test situation. In one experiment, the experimenter performed aggressive acts with a plastic doll—throwing the doll in the air, kicking it, hitting it with his fist, and pushing it over. When presented with a plastic doll shortly thereafter, the children who had witnessed the model's behavior performed many of the same behaviors. In the same test situation, children who had not witnessed the model's behavior did not engage in the aggressive acts.

Bandura and Walters (1963, Chap. 2) also cite studies that demonstrate that even generalized dispositions and tendencies, such as attitudes and personality traits, are the consequences of imitative learning. Children who were aggressive tended to have aggressive parents more frequently than children who were dependent in their orientations to problems. In various tasks children resembled parents. Undoubtedly, both observational learning and learning through reinforcement accounts for the similarities. Inherited constitutional dispositions may play a part as well. There may be a complementary or conflicting interaction between observational learning and the subsequent outcomes of the learned behavior. When new behavior is acquired through imitation, the consequences of performing the behavior may be either strengthened or weakened depending on whether such behavior is reinforced or punished. A boy may acquire dependent behaviors through observation of his father at home, but such behavior may be either punished or reinforced by his peers at school. Perhaps the disparity between what might be expected through observational learning and the behavior that actually occurs is due to the overriding influence of the reinforcement consequences of the learned behavior. (Liebert and Fernandez, 1970) For example, one daughter may be meticulous like her mother whereas the other daughter is careless. Both learned the mother's behavior through observation, but one daughter, the mother's favorite, was reinforced for imitative behavior whereas the other was ignored.

Self-regulation. A recent application of modeling involves the teaching of self-regulation and self-management techniques. Bandura (1977) attributes the development of self-regulation to observational learning, which promotes appropriate mediating cognitive strategies. Consider how cognitive strategies might be acquired through direct experience. We can perceive the consequences of our own reactions and actions and influence them by means of self-rewards and punishments. Furthermore, we can set goals and work out methods of attaining them. We can work out our own inducements and arrange the environment to promote our objectives. We can use both external and internal incentives as reinforcers. We can learn these same things by observing a model. We can learn problem-solving skills by observing models who demonstrate them and teach us how to go about solving any type of problem, including personal problems.

Meichenbaum (1974; 1978) has developed a promising procedure for modifying behavior by using models that not only demonstrated appropriate behaviors to children, but also engaged in verbal self-instructions regarding the appropriate methods to follow. The children were encouraged to copy the behaviors and the self-instructions of the models. These included action strategies, symbolic rehearsal of a plan of action, self-instructional guides for performance, and verbal self-rewards for successful performance of the observed behavior. In some cases, the model helped the observer carry out these activities.

Bandura (1977) points out that the approach used by Meichenbaum involves all component systems of behavior determinants: the environmental antecedents, the mediating cognitive processes, and the consequences of behavior. If a person relies on one component alone, as, for example, cognitive restructuring or controlling antecedent

© Thomas Hopker 1980/Woodfin Camp & Associates

Our own standards govern our behavior.

environmental stimuli or controlling the consequences of behavior, the outcome will be inconsistent or weak. A program of behavior change that involves all the determinants of behavior has a much greater probability of success than a partial approach. This is also true whether we are referring to behavior control by the professional behavior modifier or through our own self-regulatory systems. The main point is that observational learning alone can be used to teach self-regulatory skills, but a total approach, which is more effective, would include dealing with antecedent environmental stimuli as well as the consequences of behavior.

Bandura introduces the concept of *reciprocal determinism*, a view that Skinner has also espoused, to highlight the continual interaction that occurs between the person and the environment. The environment acts upon us, but we also act upon the environment. We can have considerable influence over our circumstances. Frequently, it is necessary to adjust or accommodate to the circumstances of our lives that cannot be controlled, but there are many conditions that we can change. We can accomplish this controlling power through increasing our knowledge and skills, as has so frequently been demonstrated in the history of civilization and in the lives of many individuals. To some extent, this concept helps to account for human freedom, but it does not completely do so. Having the appropriate knowledge and skills still requires their application. Not everyone uses what he or she knows and can do to best advantage.

Vicarious acquisition of standards.   We might question where we get the rules and principles to guide our own actions and reactions? Again we may arrive at them through our own direct experiences, which may involve reinforcements and punishments, or we may learn them from observing others and the consequences of their behaviors. In observing the behavior and behavior outcomes of others, we form hypotheses about the relationships between their behavior and outcomes. By this means, we formulate expectancies, which we may subsequently try out in actual situations. We can then evaluate them in terms of rewards or punishments (Mahoney, 1974). With many repetitions of testing our hypotheses and observing their outcomes we may form a generalized set for self-monitoring. This is an excellent means of profiting from mistakes.

An important aspect of self-regulatory systems is our set of standards. Studies have demonstrated that standard-setting is definitely influenced by observing a model rewarding or punishing his or her own behavior. Whether the standards for giving rewards or punishments are high or lenient influences the observer. Bandura, Grusec, and Menlove (1967) found that children copied high standards of adults if they both taught and practiced the high standards. The results were mixed when parents practiced high standards for themselves, but expected less from their children. Children who were given reinforcers for low-levels of performance by parents set lenient standards for themselves and rewarded themselves for low-levels of performance. We not only copy the behaviors of others, but also the standards and values that govern their behavior. This finding has many ramifications for therapy. Exposure to appropriate models can be a critical means of helping children to form prosocial and achievement-oriented values. Using models to inculcate middle-class standards among delinquents and criminals may open a whole new application to modeling techniques.

Bandura (1976) found that self-regulated reinforcement determines performance mainly through increasing motivation. We evaluate the efficacy of our own behavior by using standards of previous performance or by comparing our performance with the performance of others. As we have noted, a child may be taught and encouraged to set goals and standards and to evaluate his or her own behavior in terms of these standards. A model may perform a task at different degrees of proficiency and reward himself or herself for high or low standards of performance. Bandura and Kupers (1964) found experimental support for saying that children copied the performance standards and reinforcing practices of adults. If the adults accepted high standards of performance before rewarding themselves, the children followed the same pattern. The task consisted of a tossing game, and the rewards were pieces of candy. The candy was available, and the child could take it without any conditions. The children who observed the high standards followed exactly the rewarding procedure of the adults. The children who observed adults who set low standards for reinforcement also matched their behaviors. In the control group, the children set their own standards, but generally did not use the candy as rewards for performances although they ate the candy. There are many conditions for setting standards and rewarding or punishing our own conduct — the influence of peers, inconsistent standards, observing models that engage in disapproved behavior without receiving punishment, and many more.

INCREASING OR DECREASING INHIBITIONS

Bandura et al. (1969) demonstrated in an experiment dealing with snake phobias that observational techniques could actually lessen the snake phobia.

Subjects were divided into four groups, matched on fear of snakes. For one group, the live modeling group, the experimenter performed various activities with a live snake. He assisted the subjects in making some of the fear responses, such as touching the snake with gloves on. The second group, the symbolic modeling group, viewed a film that portrayed various scenes paralleling the live modeling performance. The subjects could work the projector, so that they could stop it or replay a scene. The members of the third group, the desensitization group, were presented with the same scenes verbally and were instructed to imagine them while they relaxed comfortably. The fourth group, the controls, were not exposed to any of the experimental conditions. The four groups were then tested on various approaches to a live snake. The three experimental groups showed a weakening of the snake phobia as compared with the control group, with the live modeling group showing the most approach responses. This experiment demonstrates that inhibitions can be weakened by observational techniques.

As we have noted, when a model helps the observer, both cognitively (by teaching self-instructions) and behaviorily (by helping the observer to control the antecedents and consequences of behavior), the prospects for behavior change are greatly enhanced — better than by any one of the procedures alone. Inhibitions and phobias are learned through imitation. Children will pick up the phobias of their parents through observation of their behavior. (Bandura and Menlove, 1968) A child might acquire a bug phobia or a phobia of storms simply by watching his or her mother's behavior in relation to the fear objects. The behavior of a leader can either strengthen or weaken the inhibitions of followers. If the leader performs a daring feat, his or her behavior will induce admirers to imitate him or her. Inhibitions related to sexual practices are often lessened in group situations. Those who might otherwise abstain from sexual intercourse may model their behavior after those who do participate in sexual activity, simply by observational imitation. The company we keep has much to do with the inhibitions we develop or lose. If a model engages in enjoyable but disapproved behavior without negative consequences, this may have a releasing effect in the observer who may then perform the same behavior. (Bandura, 1965)

RELEASING EXISTING RESPONSES

Bandura (1969) reports several experiments in which the model's behavior appeared to "set off" behavior in the observer. In his later writings, he refers to this function of modeling as *facilitating behavior*. The observer not only repeated some of the aggressive, dependent, or fear responses of the model, but also accomplished the same goals with his or her own behaviors. It frequently happens that those who imitate a model may exaggerate the model's behavior, as when religious fanatics carry out the precepts of their religion overscrupulously. Freud commented that he would hate to be a Freudian. He meant that his disciples were even more radical than he.

To sum up, as we attempt to adapt and cope with the circumstances of our lives, we must rely on observational learning. In real-life situations, behavior is seldom so neatly reinforced as in laboratory studies of animals, and mistakes may be fatal. We observe others, particularly those who are considered successful, to discover what should be done or avoided. To depend on natural reinforcements or punishments to guide us may subject us to many unnecessary hurts. Rather than being content to profit from our mistakes, we should try not to make them in the first place. From a practical standpoint, observational learning from the appropriate models can help us to avoid making costly errors.

Bandura has certainly been an able spokesman for a cognitive approach and has demonstrated the vast potential of observational learning.

ROTTER'S COGNITIVE LEARNING THEORY

Reinforcement Expectancies

You are with a group of people who are discussing a topic you know very well. You would like to participate, but you are afraid that you will be ignored. Why? You are afraid to participate in group settings because in the past you have encountered repeated failures in such settings; thus you have formed an *expectancy* of being ignored in a group context. The expectancy was *reinforced* when it was *confirmed*; that is, whenever you thought you had failed in group participation. In the present situation, your *freedom of movement* (Rotter, 1954) is restricted because you expect to be ignored and thus avoid participating in the group. If we asked a cognitive learning theorist such as Rotter "What is involved in learning?" his answer would be in part, "We learn a great number of expectancies about our world. Many of them help us to meet our needs and deal with our problems satisfactorily, but others cause us to restrict our participation, and to avoid many behaviors and situations that could enhance our lives." To say it simply, our reinforcement expectancies are our *hypotheses* about the probable outcomes of our behavior.

Where do the expectancies come from? As we have already noted, expectancies are based on attempts to satisfy needs; that is to say, they are based on the *acquired probabilities of obtaining reinforcements*. (Rotter, 1954) Expectancies should not be confused with expectations, which are our demands or aspirations based on needs and desires. A man who has failed frequently in his requests for favors may develop a generalized expectancy that he will be rejected by others. His generalized expectancy will produce perceptual distortion, so that he is unable to discriminate between situations in which his probability of success is high and those in which it is low. He might simply follow a fixed pattern of avoidance and not ask anyone for a favor. Many avoidances are based upon similar generalized expectancies. (Aronson and Carlsmith, 1962) An expectancy is based on past learning (Rotter and Hochreich, 1975) and is always subjective; it is logical from each person's own perspective although it may appear to be illogical to others.

Another condition that instigates generalized expectancies is an event that is novel or not adequately labeled. For example, a man may respond to a woman he meets for the first time with generalized expectancies that may be highly inappropriate. As he gets to know her, his expectancies will become more specifically related to her actual behavior. For instance, expectancies derived from experiences with teachers may be applied in a work setting to one's first encounter with a supervisor.

Reinforcement Value

Reinforcement value means the degree of worth one places on a goal. We have noted that the rate of occurrence of the reinforcement will influence the formation of expectancies. But the rate of hits and misses is not the only variable that must be taken into account in understanding learning and behavior, according to Rotter (1954); the *quality of the reinforcement*, the *reinforcement value*, is also a significant variable. If the reinforcement value of the goal object is strong, a person may be driven to perform behavior even when the expectancy of securing the goal object is limited. Much irrational behavior can be accounted for as the vain pursuit of highly valued goals. A man may give up almost everything to gain status and wealth. He may tie himself to his profession to the neglect of his health and family even when the attainment of these prized goals is highly unlikely. In such instances, we can see both the operation of modeling and the formation of false goal values. Admiring someone who is attaining the prized goals may stimulate imitative behavior. "If George can do it, why can't I?" Such thinking obviously overlooks many important variables: fortunate circumstances, individual differences in talent, the sheer operation of chance factors that might favor one over another who has the same drive and ability.

A major task is to harmonize our expectancies of success and our goal values. We have noted that the goal value may be so attractive that we place a high premium on its attainment. We may seek it even though the probability of attaining it is low. There is a constant matching of expectancy and goal value, and frequently we find that we must lower our standards and accept much less than we would like. Unfortunately, many people fail to harmonize their expectancy for success with the goal they select, and they experience torment.

Consider the goal of finding the perfect love object. There is no more alluring human ideal than to form an intimate relationship. The experiences we have had directly with romantic attachments or gained through vicarious observation are so tantalizing that many people set these as a major objective of life. A mediocre or actually unhappy marital situation is a far cry from this ideal; thus, many disgruntled people seek divorce and the possibility of another opportunity to find the perfect love object. We are forced to lower our goal values in many other areas of our lives, but we are unwilling to compromise with our ideal of a perfect mate.

From the standpoint of one who wishes to assess the behavior of others, it should be noted that people develop consistency in their value choices so that these become a part of the stable characteristics of personality (Rotter and Hochreich, 1975).

Minimal Goal Level

Rotter (1954) introduces the concept of *minimal goal level* to bring out another important aspect of reinforcement value. The minimal goal level is the *degree of reinforcement* along a continuum *that is acceptable* and below which is unacceptable. A student may set the grade of *A* in a course as his or her minimal goal level and consider anything below that unacceptable. The student might be disturbed if his or her report card has even one *B*. When minimal goal levels are set unrealistically, we are bound to experience needless frustration. Too often goals are valued on the basis of their appeal rather than on their feasibility. We choose the goals that are glamorous and idealistic: a perfect marriage; an exciting job; all-loving and faithful friends; perpetual peak experiences; not being frustrated, disappointed, hurt, or misunderstood. Furthermore, the minimal goal levels that some are willing to tolerate are also set uncompromisingly high; if we cannot have perfection (the most, the best, the flawless), then we feel cheated, deprived, and frustrated. Goals and minimal goal levels must constantly be examined and brought into line with the possibilities for gratification (reinforcement expectancies).

A curious thing often takes place with respect to unrealistic goals and unwillingness to lower minimal goal levels: a person may experience repeated failure (punishment), yet the goals are not altered. Sometimes in such instances the goal is actually intensified in value. (Mischel and Masters, 1966) The behavior that results from the intensified value of the goal may be highly irrational and maladaptive. Persistent goal frustration may result in generalized irritability, displaced hostility, regression, self-hate, apathy, depression, neurotic avoidance, and obsessive and compulsive behaviors.

The Psychological Situation

When Rotter states that perceiving precedes responding, he means that each individual responds to a subjectively meaningful world, a world as he or she interprets it. Perception is influenced by expectancies and the reinforcement value of the goals; thus, behavior depends upon *perception, expectancy*, and *reinforcement value*. (Rotter, 1954) In bringing about personality change, we can alter (1) our perception of particular events, (2) our expectancies, (3) the reinforcement value of goal objects, or (4) our behavior directly. Being a cognitive learning theorist, Rotter stresses the importance of subjective variables in producing change; thus, behavior will change if we alter our perceptions, expectancies, or goals and goal values. (Rotter, 1971) In brief, *the psychological situation* is Rotter's construct for a person's individualized view of the world.

NEEDS AND NEED POTENTIALS

Rotter has observed that behavior is directional in that the same goals may be repeatedly pursued by a person. It is possible to identify sets of behaviors that are directed toward a particular goal. Rotter refers to these behavior-goal units as *needs*.

Need potential refers to the strength of behaviors directed toward a goal. A need potential is a group of behaviors that have a common directional quality. For example, a need potential for physical comfort might lead a person to get enough sleep, to wear clothing appropriate for the weather, and to sit in a comfortable chair. Each of these behaviors could lead to the goal of physical comfort because the individual places high reinforcement value on the need for comfort, which is satisfied through the goals of being rested, maintaining a comfortable body temperature, and being in a physically comfortable position. It should be noted that the general goal or need for comfort is expressed in highly personal ways. In the same manner, the need for recognition might be personalized as need for academic recognition. Again, Rotter equates needs with behavior rather than distinguishing between needs and behavior.

Rotter and Hochreich (1975, pp. 101–102) have identified six general needs. Again, it should be recalled that these needs are defined in terms of directional behaviors. They are specified by reinforcers rather than being states within the organism; thus, they are operationally defined.

1. Recognition: the need to be acknowledged for our achievements.
2. Dominance: the need to be listened to and have influence over others.
3. Independence: the need to be self-reliant and to have control over our own decisions.
4. Protection-dependency: the need to be sheltered from harm and and to have support from others.
5. Love and affection: the need to be cared about and positively viewed by others.
6. Physical comfort: the need for both physical pleasure and freedom from discomfort or pain.

The reader may be aided in understanding Rotter's meaning of needs by recalling Murray's need-integrate construct, which refers to need and all its associated elements, as discussed in Chapter 4.

Rotter's View of the Unconscious

The unconscious in Rotter's theory may be thought of as expectancies that influence behavior but that are not in awareness. A long-standing yet unperceived expectancy of failure may be active in a situation and instigate inappropriate behavior — behavior that the person himself or herself does not understand. We may be aware only that we are behaving in an irrational or self-defeating manner, not of the expectancy that is determining this behavior. We may learn about our unconscious expectancies by letting our behavior reveal them.

We may also be unaware of our minimal goal levels and as a result suffer a host of unfavorable consequences. (Rotter, 1954) We may experience a profound sense of inferiority or of being a failure.

What we do not experience are the unrealistic goal levels that we have. Problems may also arise when the minimal goal levels are too low: the total pattern of striving and motivation may be generally depressed. Like knowledge of expectancies, knowledge of minimal goal levels may produce marked changes in the total personality, particularly if we make genuine efforts to alter our minimal goal levels to accord with our circumstances and abilities. An ability to change minimal goal levels should be cultivated as one of the major principles in the art of living. Being willing to identify these minimal goal levels along with acknowledging expectancies, is in itself a good first step; thus, making the unconscious conscious is an ideal that applies to the notions of minimal goal levels and expectancies.

Rotter's Research Topics

IMMEDIATE VERSUS POSTPONED REINFORCEMENT

Being able to forego immediate gratifications for the sake of potentially greater future satisfactions is certainly an important aspect of dealing with our needs. If we are able to tolerate frustration and tension as we work toward our goals, we are more likely actually to attain them. There are wide individual differences on the variable of delay of gratification. Expectancies can play a part in the ability to delay gratification: an untrusting environment encourages the preference for immediate satisfactions to long-term ones. The choice between a lesser but immediate reward and a potentially greater but postponed reward has been studied in relation to many personality and situation variables (for example, Bandura and Mischel, 1965; Klineberg, 1968; Mahrer, 1956). Many persons who are considered cultural deviants, such as criminals, neurotics, and psychopaths, seem unable to postpone gratification. Yet Rotter (1975) and his students have demonstrated that long-term expectancies can be promoted by providing the appropriate environmental conditions and that people can alter their own expectancies.

LOCUS OF CONTROL OF REINFORCEMENT

Rotter's theorizing has led to the investigation of another important adjustive and coping variable: whether or not people expect to have control over their reinforcements. This dimension is referred to as *internal or external locus of control.* (Rotter, 1966) We might think of locus of control as a measure of our sense of freedom. This dimension correlates with many behaviors. Rotter's construct of locus of control has been highly productive in generating research. Since the introduction of the I-E (internal-external) Scale in 1966, over 600 studies dealing with this dimension have been conducted. When subjects were divided according to internal or external locus of control of reinforcements, significant variations were discovered in such important behaviors as risk taking, quitting smoking, willingness to participate in civil rights movements, time needed to make difficult decisions, success in influencing the attitudes of others, changes in reinforcement expectancies following success or failure in tasks, and other behaviors favoring the internal locus of control subjects (for example, Davis and Davis, 1972). Because our total orientation to life is influenced by this variable, we should attempt to acquire a greater sense of control over our circumstances.

TRUST VERSUS MISTRUST

Rotter (1967) has developed a test that measures people's beliefs or expectancies of the trustworthiness of other people. He calls this test the Interpersonal Trust Scale. The test consists of forty items, to which the subject expresses degree of agreement or disagreement. Some sample items are these: People are more deceptive than ever before; people should be trusting in dealing with strangers until they prove themselves otherwise; the courts grant unbiased treatment to all; for the most part, appliance repair people are trustworthy; most people would steal if they could get by with it.

Rotter maintains that the test measures the reliability or credibility that a person assigns to the communications of others. An examination of the test items, however, reveals that the test appears to measure belief in the goodness of humans and willingness to accept the integrity of others in the absence of evidence. This latter meaning of trust resembles Erikson's meaning of a sense of trust, which refers to confidence in the goodness and trustworthiness of others in relation to ourselves. The test correlates with a number of important personality dimensions. The "high trusters" are not gullible or idealistic, but rather are willing to trust people until they receive indications to the contrary.

Summarizing the results of a large number of studies concerning the Interpersonal Trust Scale, Rotter (1980) draws some interesting conclusions: (1) High trusters trust without proof, but low trusters need proof in advance; (2) high trusters are more likable, better adjusted, and more likely to respect the rights of others; (3) high trusters are less likely to lie, cheat, or steal.

ELLIS' RATIONAL-EMOTIVE MODEL

The human species has been given the name *Homo sapiens*, which is Latin for "wise man." The characterization is appropriate because it stresses human cognitive abilities, which have been responsible for the great achievements of science and civilization. On an individual level, cognitive factors can play an extremely important role in the development and functioning of personality. Ellis (1958) has long stressed the role of cognitive theorizing and therapeutic applications. He has related cognitive structures with emotional and motivational processes. He points to *hidden unrealistic faulty verbalizations, "compounding" sentences, irrational thinking, inappropriate values*, and *unrealistic goals* (1974). Like Rotter, he has also placed much emphasis on faulty self-expectations. He refers to the unreasonable self-expectations in a quaint manner. He calls them "nutty shoulds" (1975). Ellis is one of the pioneers in the use of cognitive methods to gain control of affective states. Cognitive restructuring in its many varieties is becoming a highly popular therapeutic approach (see Beck, 1976; Burns, 1980, for further theoretical and methodological elaboration of cognitive therapy).

Kelly (1955) viewed all of us as lay scientists who attempt to comprehend our world by cognitively construing events. We form hypotheses and conceptual categories to make sense of our world.

Controlling Emotions Through Correct Reasoning

Ellis maintains that correct thinking is an excellent means of acquiring emotional control. Our cognitive constructs influence the types of affective states we experience. Emotional arousal depends on the types of information we receive and the interpretations that we derive from what we perceive. Ellis believes that it is possible to control unwanted emotional reactions by clear thinking. He says: "Clear thinking, we have insisted, leads to sane emoting. Stupidity, ignorance, and disturbance block straight thinking and result in serious degrees of over- or underemotionalizing." (1975, p. 38)

EMOTIONAL BEHAVIOR AND COGNITIVE CONTROL

When emotions are highly aroused, cognitive functioning is greatly impaired. We often speak of emotional behavior. The implication is that the controlling forces are emotions rather than cognitive self-regulating constructs. Emotional behavior is frequently unrealistic and maladaptive. During the height of an emotional episode, all efforts to suppress the emotion and impulsive behavior may fail. The time to control emotions is when reason can have the upper hand, that is, when emotions are not stirred up. We can learn and rehearse strategies for cognitive control. The significant terms are *learn* and *rehearse*. Like other cognitive theorists, Ellis maintains that we can learn effective cognitive strategies from various sources. We can work them out for ourselves by profiting from past mistakes or anticipate mistakes and prevent them. We can learn from direct experience or vicariously, as Bandura points out, by observing how others handle problem situations. Then we can rehearse self-instructions, or what Ellis terms *self-verbalizations*.

WHAT WE TELL OURSELVES

We have noted that Ellis stresses the role of self-verbalizations. Agreeing with Meichenbaum (1978), Ellis holds that we continually monitor our behavior. Furthermore, we utter favorable or unfavorable self-comments regarding the efficacy of our behaviors. This inner dialogue and continual self-evaluation directly influence emotional states.

Ellis repeatedly points out that many emotional experiences are generated by what we tell ourselves about the things that are happening. Self-criticism may occur frequently. A young man is turned down by the woman he asked for a date, and he becomes extremely depressed and self-deprecating. He may proceed to elaborate the criticism by telling himself many unflattering things. He might criticize himself for being unpopular, unattractive to women, inept, and worthless. His self-condemnation has gone far beyond the unfortunate rejection, even to the point of total self-condemnation. He has produced an extremely unpleasant emotional reaction by his own interpretation and elaboration of the event. Most of his inner dialogue had nothing to do with the actual event. Had he interpreted the situation differently, he would have experienced some emotional discomfort temporarily, but not the debilitating emotions associated with self-hatred.

COMPOUNDING SENTENCES

In the example of the young man who was turned down for a date, we can see the operation of what Ellis terms *compounding sentences*. The interpretation of the event was elaborated. His self-verbalizations introduced elements that were simply irrelevant to the event and probably not true. He allowed his unpleasant mood to arouse faulty interpretations that compounded the pain of the event. We have an example of a vicious circle, in which the faulty interpretation produced an aversive state, which, in turn, leads to further compounding irrational self-statements. These further aggravated the affective reaction. Here we see a similarity of Ellis' use of vicious circles and Horney's similar concept (1950). Taken in proper perspective, the situation was not atypical: everyone gets turned down by someone. The woman turned him down for a date. She did not tell him he was inferior, unlovable, and unacceptable to anyone.

DRAWING INVALID CONCLUSIONS

A woman who has few dates may tell a counselor that she is not popular. She then reveals that she has a poor opinion of herself. She may make still other derogatory statements about herself. Ellis would term this type of reasoning dysfunctional because it involves drawing invalid conclusions. In our effort to obtain an undistorted picture of ourselves and the events that take place in our lives, we often go too far and draw conclusions that simply do not follow from the given evidence. A premise may be valid (the woman may, in fact, not be popular), but the inferences she draws from this premise may be unwarranted. The result is not simply poor logic, but a highly disturbing and dysfunctional emotional state. Had she drawn the proper inferences, her reactions would have been totally different.

Common Errors of Thinking

Ellis (1962; 1971) specifies some common errors of thinking that cause faulty emotional reactions and lead to compounding sentences. Again, it should be recalled that emotions follow knowledge, and if a person's perception and interpretation of an event is incorrect, the emotional experience may be totally inappropriate. The emotional state is appropriate to the type of thinking a person is engaging in, but if the thinking is erroneous, the emotions that occur will be dysfunctional and may lead to irrational behavior. Correct thinking is essential for emotional control. Although our emotions depend upon our cognitive processes when emotions are intense, we may become so enmeshed in our problems that we cannot use reasoning to cope with them. Knowing some typical errors of thinking should enable us to guard against them.

OVERGENERALIZATION

A common error of thinking is to overgeneralize from single instances. We may conclude from a particularly painful mistake that we are a failure. We may reason incorrectly in this manner: "I did a stupid thing; therefore, I am a stupid person." This is an example of overgeneralization—drawing an unwarranted conclusion from a single occurrence. The tendency to generalize is more primitive than the ability to make fine discriminations. A mistake may be the result of lack of attention or inadequate skill, but it should not be taken as proof of lack of self-efficacy (Bandura, 1977), by which Bandura means self-confidence.

With respect to the tendency to overgeneralize, Dollard and Miller (1950) have noted that faulty verbal labeling can be its source. One of our most useful cognitive functions is the use of language symbols to name things. We name countless objects, events, experiences, people, emotions, and much more. If we name an event incorrectly, as by saying that a task is dreadful, we will react to the situation as the verbal label dictates. If we make a mistake and tell ourselves that it was stupid of us to act in such an irrational manner, we will experience intense negative feelings about ourselves. Dollard and Miller term this form of generalization *mediated generalization* because the language symbols serve as the cognitive mediators.

Language mediators play a significant role in forming proper discriminations as well. Humans have a great capacity to make fine discriminations and to assign verbal labels to designate specific things. This capacity enables us to cognize the events of our world in great detail as well as in patterned complexity.

In addition to cognizing our world, Ellis points out that we can assign a value to an event, according to a dimension of painfulness, worth, or personal responsibility. Naming events properly will guard against the tendency to overgeneralize or exaggerate their seriousness. How serious is the dented fender of our car? It depends upon our inner self-talk. If we "catastrophize" the event (a tendency that occurs among neurotics, Ellis believes), we will probably overgeneralize the meaning of the event. Ellis observes that the neurotic typically catastrophizes the ordinary events of everyday life. By this he means that they mislabel events and thereby overreact to ordinary stress experiences (1957).

EITHER-OR THINKING

Another common error of thinking is to dichotomize events into either-or classes. It is more difficult to make fine discriminations than simply to categorize events into discrete classes. The disappointed lover says, "If I cannot have all your love, I want none of it." The young dreamer says, "The world is either perfect, or it is worthless." The disgruntled student argues, "Because a college education does not solve all my problems, it is worthless." Perhaps our efforts at living would be made much easier if things could be neatly categorized, but they seldom are. There are degrees of truth, of desirability, of justice. Our evaluation processes need to reflect the dimensionality of things. Again, using appropriate verbal symbols to name events can help us to avoid either-or thinking.

INTERPRETATION RATHER THAN DESCRIPTION

Ellis distinguishes between *interpreting* and *reporting* our experiences. We may add elements to our perceptions of events that are irrelevant or unwarranted and thereby distort their meaning completely. The process of perception involves interpretation because incoming stimuli activate previous associations. But the cognitive elements we add may so distort the perception that it represents more an interpretation than a perception. A blue-collar worker may describe himself or herself as being *only* a laborer, a statement that connotes an unfavorable status. In this instance, the term *only* involves a value judgment; therefore, the worker's statement is an interpretation rather than a description of himself or herself. We might distinguish between objective reporting and subjective interpretation. The fact is that, as we have noted, all perception involves interpretation, but the question is a matter of degree of correspondence. When we interpret an event, our judgment is usually dictated by our values, our previous experiences, our expectations, and other cognitive variables. These variables may cause us to make serious mistakes in interpretation. Correct symbolization is essential for accurate perception and interpretation.

CORRELATION CONFUSED WITH CAUSATION

A common error of thinking is that two things that occur together—or one after the other—are related as cause and effect. Many superstitions are caused by accidental linking of unrelated events. Bad luck may follow a particular behavior or event, and then the bad luck is blamed on these occurrences. A person having a bad mood may blame the person he or she is with. Children from broken homes often blame themselves for the divorce. A survivor in an accident may experience a sense of guilt for the loss of his friend. (Bettelheim, 1967) A common form of correlational thinking is to blame ourselves for not having sufficient control of our circumstances to prevent or avoid problems. If we experience an unpleasant emotional state as the result of an unsolved problem, we may blame ourselves even though we actually had no control over the situation. In such instances, a person may have the unacknowledged assumption of always being in control of his or her circumstances and then blame himself or herself needlessly when things go wrong.

A notable example of the formation of superstitious thinking occurred during the Middle Ages, when people frequently became ill owing to contaminated food. The Jewish population in the area did not develop the illness because of their religious dietary requirements. Therefore, they were accused of causing the epidemics and, in some instances, were driven off or killed as punishment. Again, we are dealing with a common error of logical inference, but for Ellis (1962) such fallacious thinking has serious emotional and motivational consequences.

Logicians long ago delineated the various forms of illogical thinking and reasoning. Ellis and Harper (1975) relate them to personality and behavior malfunctioning. Like Bandura, Rotter, and Mischel, Ellis assigns a central role to cognitive processes in both normal and abnormal functioning.

Unexpressed Sentences

Ellis and Harper (1975) introduced the notion of *unexpressed sentences* to designate assumptions, values, or expectations of which we are not aware. The unexpressed sentences refer to beliefs and assumptions that a person holds but does not tell himself (or herself) or the therapist. They are not in the person's immediate awareness. A person may experience an intense emotion without knowing the cause. Likewise, a person who is troubled by his or her own behavior and reactions often cannot verbalize the reasons to himself/herself or to others. Freud spoke of unconscious determinants of behavior in such instances. Ellis views these instances as *lack of awareness of hidden assumptions*. The person's internal verbalizations are not complete. Our thinking and reasoning sequences are often abbreviated and incomplete. Take this statement: "I am angry because I did not get a good grade for this course." There are a number of unexpressed premises, which, if stated explicitly, might totally alter the person's reactions. For example, "I deserve only good grades in every course, but I did not receive a good grade in this one." "Whenever I do not get what I want, I get angry at someone else." "Anger is an appropriate way to respond to disappointment." "The only thing that matters in school is getting good grades." We may derive other inferences from the student's simple remark. An early cognitive psychologist, T. V. Moore (1939), described this type of reasoning as unacknowledged premises. Ellis and Harper (1975) refer to it as unexpressed sentences.

A person may be highly disturbed in his or her relationships with parents and may neither understand the reason nor be capable of controlling his or her reactions. The person's unrecognized internal sentence may be something like this: "My parents are really unfair because they treat me like a child." As we noted in the example of the poor grade, there are actually several unexpressed sentences in this situation. A strong habit of not being critical of parents may block the person's awareness of these unacknowledged and unexpressed assumptions.

In sensitive areas, our thinking and reasoning processes may be highly incomplete and distorted. (Ellis, 1973) The major task of *rational-emotive psychotherapy* is to bring to awareness the *hidden beliefs and assumptions* and to help the patient to counteract, dispute, or *challenge* them. Presumably, the irrationality of a person's thinking and reasoning can be clearly experienced, a condition that fosters change. The change process requires cognitive restructuring. (Ellis and Harper, 1975) The person comes to appreciate the irrationality of his or her expectations and works to modify them. Full awareness of the thinking process aids in bringing about behavior change. (Ellis, 1962)

We often respond automatically to situations without perceiving our underlying assumptions. Unexpressed internal sentences hinder self-management because we are reacting to, and acting upon, only partial or distorted information. Emotional overreaction is often due to this type of disordered cognition. (Ellis, 1974)

Another consequence of unacknowledged premises, assumptions, and beliefs is that our internal verbalizations do not reflect the actual state or problem we are describing. People who have serious emotional problems or even relatively normal people under stress may have difficulty revealing the actual problems and feelings they are experiencing. Clarification is a key aspect of therapies that attempt to foster insight. What the person tells himself (or herself) or the therapist is frequently an inadequate portrayal of the true conditions.

Unexpressed Assumptions and Beliefs

Ellis, like the other theorists we have considered, has taken a powerful postulate and developed it extensively. He has frequently noted that our emotions follow our cognitions. If we engage in dysfunctional cognitive activity, we will experience maladaptive emotional reactions that lead to faulty behavior. What we tell ourselves about ourselves and the events going on around and within us influences how we feel and behave. To quote Ellis and Harper: "you can considerably control your own destiny and live more effectively with your emotions by controlling your thinking and the things you tell yourself. There are certain irrational ideas which we must not only challenge, but we must work to counteract." (Ellis and Harper, 1975, Chap. 20)

If faulty behavior and emotions depend upon faulty thinking and reasoning, then we may ask about the sources of faulty thinking itself. What makes our thinking faulty? Ellis argues that one major cause is false beliefs and assumptions that are unrecognized. He attempts to identify some common faulty assumptions in his 1975 book. We should bear in mind that each person has his or her unique assumptions and beliefs, but some are quite common among middle-class Americans. Undoubtedly, assumptions and beliefs of people from other cultures and other times would be different. A rational approach to living requires that we become aware of these hidden cognitive constructs and that we counteract them.

TYPICAL UNRECOGNIZED BELIEFS AND ASSUMPTIONS

1. We should be loved and approved by almost every person we know and meet. Being disliked by others means we have a weakness or a flaw.
2. We should be highly competent, adequate, and successful in all possible respects if we are to think well of ourselves.
3. We have a right to expect that our friends demonstrate their loyalty and liking for us and that we should be angry or disappointed when they fall short of these expectations. People who are important to us should meet our perfectionistic ideals.
4. We are justified in thinking that it is awful or catastrophic when things are not what we would like them to be.
5. We are justified in believing that we are victims of external circumstances and that we cannot do much about our lot in life.

6. If something is potentially dangerous or troublesome, we should keep our thoughts constantly centered on the problem so that we can change it.

7. Because we cannot be good in everything, we should avoid certain of life's difficulties. We have many limitations as compared with the abilities of others.

8. Our past is the most important determiner of our present behavior. Whatever strongly affected our lives will forever be a problem and weakness. We cannot get over some things from the past.

9. Every one of our problems has a solution, and it is catastrophic if this solution is not found. Compromise and accepting less than we want are weaknesses. If we do not solve all our problems, we are to blame. [Adapted from Ellis and Harper, 1975, Chap. 20.][2]

Note: Ellis presents his system in a simplified (A-B-C-D) format in which:

A is the activating condition, the event, such as a dented fender, or the refusal of a date.

B is the person's belief system that enters into the interpretation of the significance of the event.

C is the consequences that result from the interpretive process, the dysfunctional behavior.

D is the therapeutic process of disputing the belief system.

MISCHEL'S COGNITIVE SOCIAL LEARNING VIEWS

We observe both consistencies and inconsistencies in behavior. Furthermore, there are wide differences among people in consistency of behavior. One person may be generally polite in many aspects of social encounters; another may be generally inconsiderate of others; still another may vary markedly in politeness. Even the polite person is not always equally polite and may actually be impolite with some people under certain conditions. There are three choices for those who wish to understand and predict behavior: (1) we may stress the role of situations in selecting behavior, or (2) we may assign the priority to personality variables in selecting behavior, or (3) we may look for complex interactions among the two sets of determinants. If we accept the *interactionist* position, it is necessary to identify in any individual case the instances when the situation may be dominant or when the personality variable may be dominant. Both sets of determinants for Mischel (1968; 1981), who subscribes to the interactionist approach, are (1) potentially highly varied, (2) extremely broad, and (3) unique to each person. Mischel holds that we are capable of making exceedingly fine discriminations among the stimuli in our environment and also capable of generating a multitude of adjustive and coping behaviors to deal with the diverse stimulus situations.

Mischel criticizes one-sided approaches to the formulation of personality models. The extreme behaviorists are typically *situationists* because they place most stress on environmental causes. For example, the *conditioned-reflex* model holds that all behavior consists of unlearned or conditioned reflexes. In either case, external stimuli activate behavior in machinelike fashion. The proponents of this view are termed stimulus-response (S-R) psychologists. By broadly defining the meaning of stimuli and also the

---

[2]*A New Guide to Rational Living.*

meaning of responses and by extending the meaning of stimuli and responses to psychological activity, they can account for much more of human behavior than the strict S-R approach of Watsonian behaviorism.

Another situationist approach is proposed by B. F. Skinner, who holds that reinforcers select and shape behaviors. This view holds that behavior is dependent upon a person's reinforcement history. Skinner believes that we behave differently in church from the way we behave at a football rally, because we have been reinforced for specific behaviors in each setting. Each situation selects specific behaviors although through the phenomena of generalization we may emit the same or similar behaviors to stimuli that are similar. Consistency in behavior results from generalization of stimuli and behaviors. Some people behave maladjustively because they have not been reinforced for appropriate behaviors.

At the other extreme are the adherents of the *personalistic* approach. This view holds that *internal personality dimensions are the major determinants of behavior.* Traits, dispositions, needs, or life-style determine the behaviors that occur. There are few representatives of such an extreme personalistic position, but Freud's character types and Adler's style of life would exemplify it. Sheldon's constitutional types would also fit this position.

It is assumed that we carry around in our heads strong dispositions or needs that select the type of behavior that occurs in a particular situation. This view tends to posit a great deal of consistency in a person's behavior across situations. The passive-dependent person manifests this tendency in a wide variety of situations. Passive-dependence may be such a central determinant of personality that it may be taken as a defining attribute of a person's identity. It would enter frequently into the total configuration of behavior in many aspects of the person's life. Allport (1961), who followed a trait approach, certainly makes allowance for situational variability as well as behavioral variability. He points out that, in order to know the operation of this trait, we would have to identify the situations that set off the dispositional core of the trait and the range of behavior that expresses the trait. Furthermore, the trait disposition is not always of equal intensity, and it is affected by other traits that are active. This more complex view of traits is not so radically different from Mischel's position. Mischel is more concrete in his specification of the machinery of person variables, however.

In his 1968 book, Mischel reviews the experimental literature dealing with consistency and predictability of behavior. He finds that many of the measuring devices (psychological tests that purport to demonstrate consistency in trait expression) are not good predictors of behavior in real-life situations. Furthermore, he did not find evidence that experts in clinical assessment distinguished themselves in making valid predictions. They did not perform better than we could do with demographic data such as class affiliation, age, sex, education, and income. Mischel argues that we need a better conceptualization of personality.

In the following statement Mischel presents his view of human nature:

> [He views] . . . the person as so complex and multifaceted as to defy easy classification and comparisons on any single or simple complex dimension, as multipli-influenced by a host of interacting determinants, as uniquely organized on the basis of prior experiences and

future experiences, and yet — as a rule — guided in systematic, potentially comprehensible ways that are open to study by the methods of science. [1977a, p. 253][3]

Although Mischel appreciates the highly complex and variable nature of human behavior and the pervasive influence of stimuli, he does propose several person variables that have an enduring role in determining behaviors. For example, he proposes that psychologists study a person's significant (1) cognitive and behavioral skills, (2) cognitive categories and constructs, (3) stimulus-outcome and behavior-outcome expectancies, (4) stimulus preferences and aversions, and (5) self-regulating strategies and plans. These variables interact with situational determinants in unique ways for each person and determine behaviors in complex ways. But the person variables can be assessed; and their interaction with situations and each other, discovered.

Cognitive Social Learning Person Variables

We have seen that Mischel rejects the postulation of broad underlying dimensions, basic factors, pervasive motives, or characteristic life-styles as the agents within personality that determine the directions of behavior. He holds that our broad repertoire of behavior is highly attuned to the multiplicity of situations that are unique to each of us. He is saying that we are capable of making fine discriminations among the many stimuli and situations that we encounter daily and are capable of generating a great variety of behavior. Mischel brings out this point in the following statement: "Humans are capable of great differentiation in their behavior, and they show extraordinary adaptiveness and discrimination as they cope with a continuously changing environment." (1977b, p. 335) A friend may elicit in us different behaviors at different times by verbal and other cues that convey a variety of messages to us. Even a slight change in a situation can produce marked changes in behavior, Mischel believes. He refers to these slight changes in stimulus conditions as *moderator variables* because they alter the nature of the behaviors that normally occur in the situation. We might respond quite differently to a male versus a female interviewer; in the morning versus in the evening; alone in the situation or with another; if the interviewer is young or older. Mischel proposes several cognitive variables that he holds can be assessed for each person. They account for the great variation in behavior frequently observed in experiments attempting to identify fixed dispositional determinants in the personality.

COGNITIVE AND BEHAVIORAL CONSTRUCTION COMPETENCIES

Mischel (1973b) refers to skills in knowing and behaving. In a particular situation, we must draw upon knowledge and skills to adapt or cope adequately. By *construction competencies*, Mischel refers to the creative use of our knowing capabilities and behavioral potentials. Consider a problem; the car will not start. The solution to this situation depends upon the knowledge and behavior we can generate. If we know something about the types of problems cars might have that relate to starting, we may generate

[3]"On the Future of Personality Measurement," *American Psychologist.*

the relevant knowledge to direct our behavior to get the car started. If we do not have the knowledge and skill to fix the car ourselves, we may resort to other solutions. Again, successful coping depends on the type of cognitions we generate. As a first step, we call a garage; then we have to work on getting to our destination and home again. We react to stimuli by generating a variety of cognitions and behavior patterns. We do not reel off automatic habits resulting from broad dispositions, but rather construct hypotheses and problem-directed behaviors. (Mischel, 1981)

We are continually interacting with situations. The situations produce cognitive activity and behavior, but our actions also alter the situations we encounter. If we lack appropriate cognitions and skills, we cannot cope with a problem. But knowledge and skills can be acquired through observational learning, through vicarious experiences with real-life or symbolic models, or through our own direct experiences. We can increase our cognitive—and skilled—generating capacity.

There are wide differences among people in cognition and behaviors. Tests are available to measure achievements and aptitudes. We are particularly interested in abilities associated with intelligence because they are enduring, stable, and predictive of other behaviors, according to Mischel (1973b). A person who has facility with language can employ this skill in many different situations. A person who knows how to be assertive can make use of this knowledge and skill in many human contacts. In attempting to predict what a person will do in a situation, we should assess the cognitive potential and the available skills of that person.

> The enormous differences between persons in the range and quality of the cognitive and behavioral patterns that they can generate is evident from even casual comparison of the construction potentials of any given individual with those, for example, of an Olympic athlete, a Nobel Prize winner, a retardate, an experienced forger, or a successful actor. [Mischel, 1973b, p. 266][4]

ENCODING STRATEGIES AND PERSONAL CONSTRUCTS

We need to know how a person interprets and categorizes stimulus inputs. We do not simply mirror events, but transform and process information in a personal manner. Mischel poses this question: "When people respond to the environment they are confronted with a potential flood of stimuli; how are these stimuli selected, perceived, processed, interpreted, and used by the individual?" (1977b, pp. 340–341) We select certain aspects of a situation and neglect others. We remember some things better than others. The impact that a stimulus has on our behavior depends on our selective attention, interpretation, and categorization of information. Psychologists should be interested in what people do cognitively, emotionally, and interpersonally, not merely in conditioned reflexes.

Mischel (1973b) views behavior in the broadest sense—as virtually anything a person experiences or does. If a person is aggressive, we would have to study not only the obvious expression in behavior but the intentions that motivated the aggressive behavior. Aggression stemming from hatred is totally different from that which results from an accidental hurtful act.

[4]"Toward a Cognitive Social Learning Reconceptualization of Personality," *Psychological Review*.

We tend to categorize events in terms of our personal constructs, which refer to our concepts and images. People use broad categories to group stimuli and to describe what they observe. Examples are race and political and class stereotypes. Such categories and constructs are unique and must be understood by the observer if the determinants of behavior are sought. An event that is construed one way by an observer may have a totally different meaning for the person having the experience. A failing grade may be interpreted as a major personal failure by the student who judges personal worth on the basis of achievement. In dealing with a person's encoding categories and personal constructs, we are dealing with the subjective nature of perception, interpretation, and categorization. Our images, concepts, and value assumptions greatly influence the manner of processing information and ultimately the types of behavior that occur in specific situations. As Mischel has pointed out, we are capable of making many fine discriminations and generating a wide diversity of behaviors, but both aspects of personality functioning become increasingly individualistic as a result of the existing constructs — concepts, images, assumptions, and attitudes.

Consider the influence of prejudice in perceptual and behavioral functions. Prejudice causes people to perceive behavior in a rigid manner. Individual differences are not considered; rather, only selected aspects of the behavior of certain people are perceived. In fact, the prejudice may be so pervasive that the perceptual process is seriously distorted, as when we perceive qualities that another does not have. The existing stereotypes not only distort information processing but also the behaviors that follow. Mischel holds that we act upon our constructs rather than upon the instigating stimuli. Our categories for interpreting information may be so broad and well-organized that they constitute a *cognitive style* such as repressors versus sensitizers, field dependence versus field independence, rigidity versus flexibility. Tests are available to assess the operation of such cognitive styles. (Mischel, 1981)

BEHAVIOR-OUTCOME AND STIMULUS-OUTCOME EXPECTANCIES

We have been dealing with Mischel's views on cognitive categorizing and abilities to generate behavior. Further constructs are necessary in order to deal with actual performance. We need to know a person's stimulus and behavior expectancies. We also need to know the value a person places on potential outcomes. Finally, we should also know how a person regulates his or her own behaviors that is, the self-generated values, standards, and strategies that govern behavior. Our expectancies refer to the possibilities we have available to us in a particular situation. *Expectancies* are our *hypotheses* about possible behaviors and their outcomes. Rather than following preconceived personality dimensions, the psychologist should look for the person's expectancies as a guide to predicting behavior in a particular situation. Mischel says, "We generate behavior in line with our expectancies even when they are not in line with the objective conditions in a situation." (1977b, p. 343) Within any situation, a person has an enormous number of behaviors that are possible; the one that is selected depends upon his or her expectancies about success and failure.

Such expectancies can be directly revealed by a person through verbal reports about beliefs concerning probabilities of outcomes. We can also learn about an individual's expectancies by directly observing behavior choices. There are also rating and ranking procedures that can be used to assess the priority of expectancies. We may understand expectancies as conditional relationships between behavior and outcome. The person reasons that if a particular behavior strategy is used, then a certain outcome is likely to occur. The "if-then" hypotheses include degrees of probability. We may be confident that a certain strategy will work and just as confident that a different one will not. We may, of course, miscalculate and make mistakes. Expectancies may be quite specific to a given situation, or they may be generalized. Mischel wishes to avoid what he believes is Rotter's overuse of generalized expectancy dimensions because they are similar to the fixed dispositions of the traditional personality theorists. Mischel and Staub (1965) found that presituational expectancies significantly affect the choice of behavior in situations in which we do not have much experience. New information can quickly alter existing expectancies, however. Mischel and Staub hold that highly specific expectancies typically become the major source of performance. Successful adaptation to an environment requires that one quickly learn the rules for effective behaviors. These are the expectancies that we acquire. If there is rigidity in structuring and interpreting events, we may not alter expectancies to match changing conditions. The maladapted individual does not learn the rules for appropriate conduct in his or her life situations. Those who wish to influence the behavior of others can promote more functional expectancies by means of modeling and instructional procedures. Some operant shaping procedures so frequently used with animals are highly inefficient with humans. (Mischel, 1981) We form our expectancies regarding not only the probable outcomes of our behaviors but also the meaning of stimuli and situations.

Mischel also considers stimulus-outcome expectancies. We learn by direct and observational experiences to make use of cues in our environment. We learn that certain events or cues predict other events or cues. We learn that stimuli predict outcomes for us. In other words, stimuli serve as signs that inform us about the possibilities (expectancies) we have in particular situations. Stimulus meanings are significant person variables. We learn to discern the meaning of subtle cues and cue changes and immediately construct behaviors to deal with the circumstances the cues signal. Subjects who experienced severe pain could be taught to identify the cues that signaled the onset of pain. If subjects learned to generate "happy thoughts" when confronted with stimuli that were highly painful, they could tolerate the pain much better. (Mischel, Ebbesen, and Zeiss, 1972)

We often make predictions from the social behavior of others. Frequently, we are not even aware of the cues that cause us to behave as we do or to make adjustments in our behavior. We learn numerous correlations between behavioral signs and outcomes. Mischel summarizes this point as follows: Just as correlational personality research yields a host of valid associations between behavioral "signs" from persons in one context and their behavior in other situations, so does the perceiver's learning history provide him with a vast repertoire of meaningful signs. [1973b, p. 271]

In the area of person perception (how people perceive other people), many variables have been identified—shifty eyes, tight lips, obese body-build, age, sex, and other features that are not so obvious that predict behaviors. Although such judgments may be correct in a small number of cases, the fact that they are predictive some of the time (intermittent reinforcement effects) is sufficient to retain them. Whereas the meaning of sign stimuli is typically personal, there are cultural signs that acquire widespread meaning for a particular group. Most people in our society know what to expect when they see a car with a flashing light following them.

Mischel stresses the specificity of expectancies with respect to both stimulus-outcomes and behavior-outcomes. (1981) Situations have specific meanings, and only slight changes in those situations are sufficient to alter their meaning. Behavior-outcome expectancies are dependent on highly specific conditions, and slight differences in the conditions are associated with different expectancies of success. A man may wait for just the right conditions to ask a woman for a date. He may pass up many cues because he is not certain of their meaning. His experience directs him to look for certain conditions that are predictive of success. Mischel points out that

> If expectancies are converted into global trait-like dispositions and extracted from their close interaction with situational conditions, they are likely to become just as useless as their many theoretical predecessors. On the other hand, if they are construed as relatively specific (and modifiable) ("if———, then———") hypotheses about contingencies, it becomes evident that they exert important effects on behavior. [1973b, p. 272][5]

SUBJECTIVE STIMULUS VALUES

Mischel (1973b) also introduces the construct of subjective stimulus value that Rotter and Hochreich (1975) found necessary to account for the determinants of an individual's behavior. The perceived value of events must be considered along with our hypotheses about success or failure. Perceived value may be extremely high, so that, even with a moderate or low expectancy of success, we may attempt to attain the prized goal. The value of reinforcers plays a significant determining function over behavior selection. Here we are dealing with preferences and aversions that serve as motivation for activating behaviors. Such motivations combine with expectancy probabilities in a highly individual manner. In a real sense, Mischel (as does Bandura) provides a place for reinforcers in his set of person variables. The *reinforcers* serve as *incentive* for the *performance* of certain behaviors in a situation rather than other possible behaviors. For Mischel, reinforcers are not strengtheners but inducements.

Stimulus choices can be measured. A person may indicate preferences verbally or in actual choice situations. Rating and ranking procedures can also be used to determine degree of stimulus values. Values and interests are among the most stable and enduring person variables. Often we can assess the strength of a preference by ascertaining what we are willing to pay for it. We can also identify what Mischel terms "high frequency" behavior, which occurs in particular situations. (Mischel, 1968) Such behaviors can be used to reinforce lower-probability behaviors, the Premack principle. (Premack, 1965) Play has a higher natural frequency of occurrence than work. Therefore, play can be used as a reinforcer (inducement) for work.

[5]"Toward a Cognitive Social Learning Reconceptualization of Personality," *Psychological Review*.

Goal value can be a major force in behavior.

Activities that have high goal value for an individual can serve as an incentive to promote instrumental behaviors directed toward attaining the desired goals. In such situations the goals appear to be reinforcers for the instrumental behaviors, but Mischel views the goal values as inducements rather than as strengtheners of behavior in the Skinnerian sense. The fact remains that highly valued activities can serve as motivators for performing lower valued activities.

Mischel (1968, 1973b) holds that stimulus value is a highly personal matter and that conditioned emotional responses may play an important part. Certain stimuli acquire emotion-evoking capacity through pleasurable or unpleasurable conditioning experiences. The specificity of anxiety can be discerned by having a person construct anxiety scenes in a hierarchical manner as Wolpe (1958) does. The therapist could not make up the hierarchy independent of the assistance of the subject.

Mischel stresses the idiosyncratic nature of reinforcement value, but there are certain common sources of reinforcement. Thousands of people attend sports events, eat the same foods, read the best-selling book, and listen to the same hit records. We should not push the individuality concept too far.

SELF-REGULATORY SYSTEMS AND PLANS

Our behavior is certainly affected by external consequences; yet we can influence our own behavior by setting goals, standards, rewarding consequences, and problem-solving strategies for ourselves. Just as others have the power to regulate our behavior by setting the rules for reinforcers to be given, so also we can set our own rules for self-reinforcement. Bandura (1974) considers the development of self-regulating systems an index of maturity. We can become more free of the controlling forces in our environment by being able to resist distractions that would cause us to deviate from our goals. We can avert the controlling power that others can exert by our own self-reinforcements and self-governing activities. Bandura argues further that we can acquire greater freedom by controlling our environment in more ways and by gaining control of ourselves as well. Bandura here is referring to the increase in freedom, which results from greater knowledge and skill.

We set our own criteria of performance and reward or punish ourselves accordingly. We formulate our own rules of behavior and strategies to apply them. Such rules specify the types of behaviors that are appropriate under certain conditions, the standards we must attain, and the consequences of reaching or failing to reach our standards. We have noted that even children will follow rules by which they regulate themselves. (Chatterjee and Erikson 1962) In an experiment, rules were acquired by observing models who reinforced themselves for high or low standards of performance. The children matched the model's reinforcement practices. (Mischel and Liebert, 1966) In the case of the children who observed models setting high standards for themselves, substantial demands were imposed by them on their own performance, and they followed complex conditions of self-reinforcement.

Mischel points out that working toward a long-term goal involves self-administered praise for attaining subgoals. Effort can be sustained through a long series of subgoals without any external reinforcement. In such instances, a person must provide his or her own reinforcers. (Meichenbaum and Goodman, 1971) Even the anticipation of positive or negative goals can produce emotional states that promote or hinder goal-directed behavior; thus, self-control can be aided by developing strategies for controlling or producing such states.

Important aspects of self-regulation, which Mischel points out have not been investigated sufficiently, are plans and intentions. Miller, Gallanter, and Pribram (1960) discussed the "planfulness" that can be built into a machine or a computer. The computer can be programmed to follow a highly complex series of instructions that include alternative sequencing based on the presence or absence of specific information. This is a simulation of human planning. We can form plans, metaplans, and subplans. In a metaplan, we establish a master plan that allows for alternative plans and subplans. We set a target, work out subgoals and steps along the way, provide alternative goals if something goes wrong, and set standards of performance evaluation. Cognitive psychologists are beginning to study the use of plans and intentions in human functioning. (Meichenbaum, 1978) Plans may be established in the form of self-contracts. (Mahoney, 1974) The various self-regulatory techniques and processes are highly useful functions that can be taught through modeling, instructional procedures, and direct experience.

Mischel (1973b) summarizes self-regulatory mechanisms as (1) setting rules that specify goals and performance standards, (2) establishing the consequences of achieving or failing to achieve these criteria, (3) devising self-instructions and cognitive stimulus transformations to achieve the self-control necessary for goal attainment, and (4) organizing rules and plans for the sequencing and termination of complex behavior.

APPLICATION TO THERAPY

Behavior Therapy

The major focus of this text is theories of personality. The major assumption of most of the theories we have been considering is that personality is something that exists and that its structure, functioning, and development can be known. The principal opposition to this view is maintained by the radical behaviorists such as Watson and Skinner, who challenged the value of inferring personality variables. It will be recalled that they seek to relate behavior to environmental events. Disordered behavior is viewed differently by those who attempt to infer personality variables intervening between stimuli and behavior as contrasted with those who relate behavior directly to environmental causes. In this discussion, it should be borne in mind that the moderate behaviorists, the cognitive and social learning theorists, resemble the traditional personality theorists in that they do accept personality variables intervening between environment and behavior. Their objections with the older theories of personality are related to definition and verification of such variables. They claim to base their inferences on the results of experimental research rather than on intuition or observations in therapy.

Traditional treatment of personality disorders is termed *psychotherapy*, which means *treatment of the psyche*. The psyche may be taken to mean personality; thus, psychotherapy deals with the treatment of personality disorders. Personality abnormalities may take many different forms. Any aspect of the personality may be involved. The personality may not have developed properly, or there may be repression and significant conflict that produce anxiety and disordered behavior. There may be deficiencies or exaggerations of traits, needs, and emotions. Intellectual impairment may be the primary problem. Lack of adequate motivation or having faulty values may be the aspect of personality that is the source of the disorder. The malfunctioning personality is assumed to be the cause of a particular behavior disturbance, the symptom. Furthermore, adequate treatment should focus on the personality disorder rather than on the disturbed behavior. If a conflict is the major problem and if inconsistent behaviors are the symptom, eliminating the conflict will relieve the symptom. The strict behavior therapist argues that the disordered behavior is the major problem and that its treatment will alter the person's circumstances directly. A shy person can be helped by being taught social skills and by learning to be comfortable in social situations. (Eysenck 1965; Zimbardo, 1977). If a boy does not fit in with his crowd because he does not know how to play baseball, teaching him such skills will change his circumstances.

The traditional psychotherapists have tended to use personality-change methods to treat personality. They have used such methods as free association, dream analysis, interpretation, reflection, empathic listening, probing of past traumas, uncovering of repression, promoting emotional experiencing, and self-discovery. These techniques are used to explore and treat the psyche. The same methods tend to be used for all personality problems. The behavior symptoms are interpreted according to a particular theory of personality. If the therapist follows Freud, he or she may look for early traumas that have been repressed or other hidden sources of anxiety. If Horney's views are followed, we may interpret symptoms as the product of an idealized self-image and the alienation process. If we follow Fromm, we may look for manifestations of an unproductive orientation. One thing is clear, according to the strict behaviorists: the symptoms are much more obvious than the causes are even if one accepts the distinction between symptoms and causes.

The strict behavior therapists, deriving their techniques from principles of classical and operant conditioning, believe that the total personality, even if we could know it, is seldom disordered; only specific portions or specific behaviors are. Nevertheless the behavior problem may have widespread effects. If we use an organic analogy, a toothache or sprained ankle can temporarily incapacitate a person. We may be unable to do our work; our social contacts may be disturbed; we may experience a depressed mood. Our total personality may be affected although the disorder is quite localized. Analogously, an argumentative person may drive away potential friends and create difficulties in all aspects of living. Reduce the intensity of the aggressive behavior, says the behavior therapist, and the person's total situation will improve. Being argumentative causes conditions that are frustrating, and these, in turn, may increase a person's tendency to be argumentative. Do something to lessen the disturbed behavior, and you make its further use unnecessary.

Those strict behaviorists who follow principles of classical conditioning point out that disordered behavior is frequently the result of faulty emotional conditioning. The inappropriate conditioned emotional reaction is elicited by a conditioned stimulus, a stimulus that acquires the capacity to produce the emotional reaction. The phobic person responds inappropriately to certain stimuli. His or her avoidance behaviors may be traced to the faulty emotional reaction. Reduce the phobic reaction, and the avoidance behaviors become unnecessary. This may be accomplished by extinction, flooding, counterconditioning, satiation, and other response-reducing or counteracting procedures. Another aspect of conditioning theory is the absence of appropriate behaviors that result from inadequate conditioning. In order to avoid certain potentially dangerous situations, a child should acquire conditioned emotional responses such as fear, anxiety, and aversion to certain stimuli. This could be accomplished by fostering the conditioned reactions to those stimuli.

We have already discussed operant reinforcement concepts and techniques in connection with our discussion of Skinner; thus, we only need mention here that both normal behavior and abnormal behavior are acquired and sustained by reinforcers. In this respect, the behavior therapist may be viewed as a behavior modifier who attempts to alter maladaptive behaviors and replace them with effective ones.

Behavior modifiers arrange contingencies to promote the acquisition of skills, such as those necessary to deal with problems of daily living. They may use positive reinforcers, negative reinforcers, extinction procedures, and even punishment to modify behavior. They use shaping procedures, discrimination learning techniques, schedules of reinforcement, and operant conditioning procedures.

Now we come to the cognitive and social learning theorists we have been considering in this chapter. They call themselves behaviorists as well, yet they accept the existence of personality variables and assign a key determining role to them. They hold such views as these: Situations are interpreted; behaviors are generated by cognitive abilities; expectancies and reinforcement value influence directional behavior; self-regulatory behavior (personal standards, values, and controls) greatly influences the quality and quantity of behavior. Mischel (1968) refers to such variables as person variables, a rather strange descriptive term for one who calls himself a behaviorist. Some would argue that the notion of person refers to a metaphysical entity: the homunculus view, the little man that pulls the strings, the person behind personality. In fairness to Mischel, it should be pointed out that he defines person variables operationally and measures them empirically. He is quite emphatic about person variables in the following statement: "While it would be bizarre to ignore the person in the psychology of personality, behavior often may be predicted and controlled efficaciously from knowledge about relevant stimulus conditions, especially when those conditions are powerful." (Mischel, 1973, p. 277) We will take up the issue of whether or not the cognitive and social learning theorists are really behaviorists in the critical evaluation section, but for now we will consider the application of their constructs and postulates to therapy. This is a new field referred to as *cognitive behavior therapy*. Actually, there are several types of cognitive behavior therapies.

Cognitive Behavior Therapies

Within the ranks of the behaviorists a radical shift has emerged during the 1970s in theoretical and therapeutic approach in the direction of stressing the role of cognitive variables in understanding and treating human behavior (Brewer, 1974). We have discussed the views of four major representatives of this movement: Bandura, Rotter, Ellis, and Mischel. They call themselves behaviorists and add some modifiers such as social learning, cognitive-expectancy, rational-emotive, and cognitive social-learning person. In this section thus far we have been discussing behavior therapy based on the behavior theories that assumed an empty organism approach. But the cognitive behavior theorists we have discussed have found it necessary to include in their theorizing cognitive processes and structures. They, too, have an applied side known as *cognitive behavior therapies*. They view cognitive processes as intervening between situation and behaviors. Stimuli or situations are interpreted and processed in unique ways by each individual. Emotional and motivational factors are also influenced by perceptual and other cognitive sets. (Ellis and Harper, 1975) Behavior does not proceed directly from stimuli, but is the result of a variety of cognitive variables. We have discussed such cognitive activities as expectancies, reinforcement value, and self-regulating functions that constitute determinants of behavior. We have seen that alternative behaviors are considered and evaluated, and short-term and long-term consequences are anticipated, depending on the cognitive skills of the person.

The proponents of cognitive behavior therapies do not accept a sharp distinction between what are traditionally termed behavioral approaches and therapies and the cognitive approaches (Meichenbaum, 1978). They argue that behavior therapies based on classical and operant conditioning approaches do, in fact, involve cognitive variables. Bandura (1977) has demonstrated that both classical and operant conditioning in humans are markedly influenced by cognitions about stimulus or response expectancies. One attaches meaning to certain stimuli because they are cues for anticipated consequences. Cognitive processes determine what is salient, what will be remembered, and what behaviors will occur. The components of behavior are interdependent. These include cognitive, affective, motivational, and environmental.

Strict behaviorists have attempted to relate behavior to environmental determinants without invoking unobservable person variables. But even one of the earliest behaviorists, E. C. Tolman (1949), began to introduce constructs that involved postulating intervening organismic variables in rats. Tolman said that he was using strict behavioral methods, but that he could explain his experimental findings only by inferring the existence of certain cognitive and conative variables. He found it necessary to introduce such variables as purpose, the formation and testing of hypotheses, the learning of cognitive maps, and place learning. Tolman used his observations of the rats' behaviors to arrive at these processes. The stimulus conditions alone could not account for what he observed in his experimental work. His views were in opposition to those of Clarke Hull (1943), who formulated a different set of intervening constructs based on a stimulus-response characterization of behavior. The controversy died down, but the issues were never resolved. Despite efforts of the strict behaviorists to deny any status to person variables, they have reappeared in the formulations of strict experimentalists, such as Bandura, Rotter, and Mischel, who feel that their formulations are in the behaviorist tradition.

COGNITIVE BEHAVIOR MODIFICATION PROCEDURES

Work with children. Cognitive behavior modification procedures have been used in studying problems in children associated with impulse control and aggressiveness. Such studies have demonstrated that self-control can be taught to children by means of a self-instructional training program. This program may include vicarious learning through observing a model demonstrating appropriate behavior and behavior strategies. This procedure is elaborated by encouraging the children to rehearse the behaviors and strategies first overtly and then covertly in imagination. (Alkus, 1977) The children are assisted with prompts, feedback, and social reinforcement. It should be noted that several approaches, each of which has demonstrated some validity in changing behavior, are utilized in a coordinated manner.

One of the objectives in working with children is to help them to "slow down"; to think before they act impulsively. Douglas et al. (1976) worked with hyperactive children who were exposed to a model who verbalized cognitive strategies. The children were asked to rehearse the strategies aloud and then to themselves. They were being taught problem-solving skills. They were to define first the problem and the various parts of it. Before acting on any given solution, they were to consider several possible alternatives. The model demonstrated the process of checking their possible solutions and correcting their errors as they proceeded. In addition, they were encouraged to stay with the problem until they had tried several alternative solutions. When the problem was solved, they were shown how to reward themselves. These various steps were designed to counteract their proneness to act impulsively and to shift attention quickly. The various activities involved in this study might be categorized as self-instructional activities.

Cognitive behavior approaches are also being used with children who are having problems with academic skills. Specific deficiencies are being identified in such areas as reading and writing, and appropriate remedial procedures are being tested. Children are taught problem-solving skills and methods of self-management. For example, children are taught to identify the nature of their problem, generate alternative solutions, collect information, recognize personal values, make a decision, and then verify that decision (Meichenbaum, 1978).

Meichenbaum (1978) has applauded the attempts to conduct comparative studies in which outcomes are related to particular strategies. For example, one group may concentrate on correcting errors while another group focuses on learning problem-solving skills. Furthermore, treatment efficacy should improve when specific deficits are matched to specific treatment procedures. We see the stress on empirical evaluation of methods rather than on universal application of a general treatment technique.

Metacognitive knowledge, experience, and skills. Behaviorists have had a great deal of difficulty with personality variables in general, but especially with those that were associated with the attributes of the self. We are referring to the general topic of self-awareness, which is sometimes termed *introspective ability*, *psychological mindedness*, or *self-reflection*. The cognitive behaviorists are making allowance in their theorizing for these crucial forms of cognition. The name that is given to them is *metacognition.* (Campione and Brown, 1977) Metacognition refers to cognition about cognition. We can know about our own processes of knowing. We can think about thinking and learn some things about ourselves in this regard.

John Flavell (1977), one of the leading experimentalists in this area, holds that we have metacognitions about three aspects of cognitive functioning: persons, tasks, and strategies. (1) We know things about our own cognitive strengths and weaknesses and how we compare with others. We may know that we are clumsy with tools but good with words or slow in certain subjects and bright in others. (2) We also have cognitions about the tasks we have to perform—whether they are difficult or easy for us; whether or not we are getting the information; whether or not we have the ability to solve a particular problem. The material may be organized or unorganized, familiar or unfamiliar, important or not important to us. We learn that some things come easier to us than others. (3) We know about the strategies that we can use. We learn many strategies in the course of solving the problems that confront us in growing up. We know how to test ourselves—how to monitor our own behavior so that we can detect errors and make adjustments. We learn how to interpret feedback information resulting from our own behaviors. We learn how to check and test behaviors without actually making overt attempts. We even learn how to learn, that is, to change strategies and approaches when certain cues are present. We might distinguish between what we know and how we know. The "how" refers to style or strategies of knowing. Many investigations have been directed to studying cognitive styles that refer to broad perceptual and interpretive sets.

We have metacognitive experiences when we learn about or experience our cognitive activities. As we perform cognitive tasks, we are often aware of our own feelings of success or failure. We may have thoughts that precede an activity such as worrying about how we might perform on a test. In addition, we may have metacognitive experiences during and after the test. These experiences may take the form of evaluations of our performance, and thus we may use such knowledge to change our behavior.

Metacognitive knowledge and experiences help us to acquire important skills. A person who *lacks metacognitive abilities* such as making use of feedback, altering strategies when the present one does not succeed, evaluating alternatives, working out self-regulatory approaches will encounter many difficulties in dealing with life's problems. These skills and other metacognitive processes can be taught by the use of models who teach self-instruction, guided self-imagery, rehearsal strategies, and new techniques that have not yet been developed. The possibilities for behavior change, by means of teaching cognitive and metacognitive skills, represent a challenging development in behavior therapy.

A variety of instructional aids can be adapted to teaching metacognitive skills to children. An excellent device is the use of video recordings, which can be prepared according to principles of cognitive behavior modification. Video recordings have the great advantage of being reproducible and used repeatedly. Cartoons, workbooks, posters, charts, and other teaching aids can be used to promote knowledge of metacognitive principles. The teacher, of course, can be a major source of instruction by modeling and rehearsing proper approaches such as self-monitoring, self-evaluation, pointing out causal relations between actions and outcomes. When a teacher says something such as, "You should always look over the headings and subheadings to get an overall picture of the material," she or he is teaching a metacognitive strategy. Teachers can demonstrate how to approach learning, problem solving, and memorizing.

Work with adults.   Cognitive behavior therapy with adults is not essentially different from that used with children except that different problems and specific methods appropriate to adults are employed. Again, the emphasis is upon the cognitive and metacognitive variables that play a part in the disturbed behavior. Cognitive change methods, like those used with children, include (1) modeling of appropriate behaviors and verbalizations by the model concerning coping strategies; (2) fostering rehearsal of self-instructions; (3) teaching self-monitoring and self-management skills; (4) promoting awareness of relationships between behaviors and outcomes (Foreyt & Rathjen, in press).

As we have noted, a current trend is to analyze the specific deficits rather than lumping people with a particular problem into the same category and using a general technique. Test anxiety has been dealt with by desensitization. Subjects have been taught deep relaxation techniques and, while relaxed, are presented with a series of anxiety scenes, embodying the person's problem area. These scenes are presented in a graded series — beginning with the least anxiety-promoting scene and progressing to the most. Sarason (in press) analyzed the basis of test anxiety and found that one of the major difficulties was an attentional deficit. Students who experience intense test anxiety engage in test-irrelevant behaviors such as thoughts about their feelings, worrying about what others are doing, concern about failure, focusing on bodily reactions. Spielberger (1976) found that cognitive behavior methods such as self-instruction, guided self-imagery, rehearsal of test-appropriate behaviors, and channeling attention on test-taking were more effective than desensitization alone. Novaco (1977) taught policemen intrapsychic and interpsychic skills for anger control. The policemen were shown how to control anger through self-instructional procedures, reinterpretation of feelings, and counteracting anger messages. They were also instructed, through modeling, how to express themselves in nonprovocative ways. These overt and covert techniques were rehearsed and role-played many times in the training sessions.

In cognitive behavior modification, the client is a collaborator. The change takes place in cognitive processes, and the individual must actively cooperate with the therapeutic procedures. The model's behavior must be rehearsed many times if cognitive change is to take place.

Bandura's interactional suggestion, namely all components of behavior — environment, cognition, emotion, and motivation — should be considered in a comprehensive program of change. Concentration on any one component is proving less effective than a total approach. Cognitive behavior is certainly a major component that has been previously neglected and offers great promise as part of a broader approach.

A great many specific techniques have been and are being developed for changing behavior. Such techniques are derived from principles of classical conditioning, from operant conditioning, and even from perceptual or cognitive learning. There is a host of new terms standing for new techniques: extinction, counterconditioning, deconditioning, aversion therapy or conditioning, reinforcement therapy, desensitization, satiation therapy, cognitive restructuring, guided self-imagery, self-management, self-instruction, observational learning, rational-emotive therapy, and others. The learning approach to personality study and change, although recent in origin, is already a strong competitor of the traditional psychotherapies. (Bandura 1977) Bad habits can be changed; sensitivities, reduced; new habits, engendered; irrational responses, eliminated; attitudes, altered.

CRITICAL EVALUATION

Maddi (1980) questions whether the cognitive social learning approaches are expressions of the spirit of behaviorism, which sought originally to remove the subjective determinants as causal factors. Personality variables, particularly verbal facility in humans, have always been troublesome for the behaviorists. The moderate behaviorists found that they could not do without mediational personality variables, but they attempted to define them in behavioristic language.

Maddi says:

> It is common to regard Bandura, Rotter, and Mischel as moderate behaviorists. But in them the notion of social learning has reached a kind of peak that virtually removes them from the behaviorist camp. This seems to me true for two reasons: (1) the assumption that learn-

ing can take place without the person emitting a response and receiving positive or negative reinforcement for it, and (2) the paramount importance in learning that is attributed to cognition (which is, after all, internal and not directly observable). [1980, p. 620]

He considers cognitive functions proposed by Bandura, such as rule-governed cognitive behavior, internal judgmental orientations, conceptual schemes, linguistic styles, and information processing strategies to be outside the behaviorist tradition. He concludes: "It goes without saying, at this point, that Bandura can only mean, when he calls himself a behaviorist, that he is still a rigorous scientist." [1980, p. 627]

The cognitive and social learning theorists have not only deviated significantly from the behavioristic tradition, but they have also borrowed liberally from the humanistic models that they claim to oppose. The following statement expresses this point clearly.

> Humanistic psychologists are often branded as "tender-minded" because they are purported to introduce concepts that are not objectively defined in terms of observable behavior. They are accused of bringing into psychology outmoded concepts such as self, free-choice, self-reflection, and other so-called mentalistic explanations that behaviorists claim explain nothing, but simply name or label behaviors which require explanation, (Walkenstein, 1977) On the other hand, it is quite fashionable to label one's ideas behavioristic. Paradoxically, some psychologists who call themselves behavioristic borrow quite liberally from humanistic concepts. This type of situation creates unnecessary confusion. The following statement of the ingredients of a model of man would be quite acceptable to most humanistic psychologists, but it is proposed as a behavioristic model by Mischel, who terms his model a *social cognitive behaviorism*.
>
> "My objective is a theoretical framework that recognizes the constructive (generative) nature of information processing, the active cognitive operations through which stimulus meanings may be transformed, the goal-directed self-regulation and planning through which the individual may avoid stimulus control, and the anticipatory quality of human expectations. Such a framework also holds that each person is potentially his or her own best assessor engaged in the evaluation and interpretation of behavior as well as in its enactment. But it also insists on attention to the intimate links between the qualities of the person and the specific psychological conditions in which they develop, are maintained, and change." [Mischel, 1976, p. 170][6] The acceptance of such processes by a behaviorist suggests that the humanistic models provide a more complete view of man than do the behavioristic models. [DiCaprio, 1980, p. 408][7]

Perhaps the cognitive and social learning theorists should call themselves humanistic behaviorists (as Bandura suggests), because they have taken over the major features of the humanistic tradition. (Bandura, 1977, pp. 206–207) To include in our model of humans such processes as self-reflection; personally established rules, standards, and goals; anticipation of the future by means of goals, plans, and intentions; reasoning abilities and other cognitive functions; and strategies to gain control of aspects of our environment and ourselves, certainly adds dimensions to traditional behavioristic models that involve a change of course. These alterations portray a radically different

---

[6]Quoted in Wondersman, Popper, and Rix (eds.), *Humanism and Behaviorism.*
[7]*Adjustment: Fulfilling Human Potentials.*

image of humans. But there is one important step missing that the cognitive and social learning models have not taken, namely, *the peculiar problems inherent in being human.*

Although Mischel (1973a) holds that there are some affinities between his ideas and the existentialists, in general the cognitive and social behaviorists have not dealt with the problems of human existence, the existential problems that result from their expanded image of humanity. We cannot separate what we conceive to be the nature of humans from problems and potentials for living. The ideals of living for a laboratory rat are surely different from those that we have. Because we are made the way we are, we must face certain problems and conflicts. Being human confronts us with existential problems: problems of living such as facing an unknown future, having to make binding decisions with only partial information, and living with the discrepancy between what is and what should be. No one ever accomplishes all he or she wishes and in just the manner desired. We must learn to tolerate these inconsistencies in our lives. Knowing what to expect in the future is a great help to us, but the ability to anticipate events is also the source of potential anxiety.

We may experience guilt for not doing enough with our lives and anxiety when we do attempt a course of action. We can wonder about the meaning of our lives, existential anxiety, and what will happen when we die, death anxiety. We can feel depressed because life does not have meaning for us, existential depression; or we can agonize about the imperfections in our lives. Self-reflection may help us to improve, but it also creates self-dissatisfaction. These problems render life for a human distinctly different from the life of lower species, and an adequate psychology of human nature must take them into account.

Given our distinctively human attributes, it would be desirable to know what constitutes ideal growth and living. Behavioristic models, even the cognitive and social learning versions, have not formally proposed ideals for humans, but we can infer them from their writings. Bandura speaks of improving self-efficacy, and Mischel refers to the many advantages of self-regulatory skills. Consider such ideals as being more rational and realistic in problem solving, increasing self-awareness, profiting more effectively from mistakes and learning to model the functional behavior of others, planning and setting goals more effectively, working out functional schedules and establishing priorities, increasing our degrees of freedom of choices by mastering skills and competencies, gaining control of our own circumstances and ourselves. These are ideals that humanistic psychologists and the cognitive and social learning theorists seem to have in common. What about other human attributes that have long been accepted by humanistic psychologists such as faith, hope, courage, commitment and involvements, and the ability to renew effort after failure? These have not yet been subjected to experimental investigation.

The cognitive and social learning theorists, as we have seen, have greatly broadened their conceptions of human nature. They have incorporated into their theorizing human attributes such as the cognitive variables and self-regulating strategies and plans that were cast out by the radical behaviorists. They have also conducted experiments that demonstrate that such processes can be manipulated, measured, and controlled. These are significant accomplishments, no matter what they call themselves, and there is high expectancy for a great deal more.

SUMMARY

1. This chapter summarizes the cognitive and social learning theories of Albert Bandura, Julian Rotter, Albert Ellis, and Walter Mischel.

2. Human abilities to cognize and interpret the world are so radically different from animal learning that we cannot apply the principles of animal learning to human learning. Much in human learning takes place in social context and through observation of models. Learning is cumulative for humans.

3. Like the traditional personality theorists, the cognitive and social learning theorists use personality variables as explanatory devices that are inferred from behavior. Unlike the traditional personality theorists who derive their constructs and postulates from their experiences in psychotherapy, these theorists derive their intervening variables from rigorous experimentation.

4. Simply observing the behavior of a model is sufficient to promote learning, according to Bandura. Observational learning has been referred to as no trial learning because the observer learns without engaging in any overt activity and without receiving reinforcement. Observational learning can be promoted as much by a deviant as by a prosocial model. Absence of appropriate models may cause deficiencies in learning.

5. Direct learning is usually very slow and requires appropriate occasions and conditions. Observing a model perform adaptive and coping behaviors leads to rapid learning and the avoidance of costly errors.

6. Cognitive symbols play an important mediational role in observational learning. Concepts, images, and verbal mediators serve as the basis of cognition.

7. Both the model's behavior and the outcomes of that behavior influence learning and performance of the observer. Cognitive processes play a part even in associative learning. Awareness is one of the determinants of conditioning and also influences extinction.

8. Learning through modeling requires attention, retention, the necessary skills, and inducement to perform what is learned.

9. Bandura holds that paired experiences, necessary in both classical and operant conditioning, are not sufficient for learning to occur in humans in most instances, but rather require, in addition, the awareness that the events are correlated. Extinction also depends on cognitive mediation.

10. Both real-life and symbolic models are effective in influencing behavior of observers. Even conditioned emotional responses can be produced by observational learning. Learning and performance are influenced by vicarious reinforcement and punishment of the model. The outcomes may be controlled by others or by the model's own efforts. Models may teach observers how to cope with a variety of situations by self-instructions, guided imagery, self-reinforcement for achieving certain goals, and other self-regulatory skills.

11. In general, three types of behaviors are acquired through observational learning: (a) the acquisition of new responses; for example, specific and generalized sets and expectations may be acquired through observational learning; self-regulation and self-management by means of cognitive and behavioral skills can also be modeled; (b) the strengthening or weakening of inhibitions; for example, models can help observers to weaken phobias and other avoidance behaviors by engaging in the sensitive or aversive behaviors; inhibitions may be strengthened by observing a model being punished for certain behaviors; (c) the stimulating of already-existing behaviors; for example, behavior may be facilitated by observing a model; in such instances, the observer's behavior may not be an exact copy and may even be more extreme that the model's.

12. Rotter proposes that we learn expectancies that are either confirmed or disconfirmed. Expectancies are our hypotheses about the probability of success or failure of specific behaviors. Expectancies determine our freedom of movement in seeking reinforcers. Expectations are demands or aspirations and are not the same as expectancies. Generalized expectancies are broad sets that we bring to new situations.

14. Reinforcement value also determines probability of behavior. It refers to the degree of worth a person places on a goal. A minimal goal level is the lowest degree of reinforcement that is acceptable.

15. The psychological situation for Rotter refers to the subjectively meaningful world, the perception of situations based on the individual psychological attributes. A need potential is a group of similar behaviors that have a common directional quality and are directed toward a particular goal. Rotter specifies six directional tendencies (needs): recognition, dominance, independence, protection-dependency, love and affection, and physical comfort. Expectancies, goal values, and minimal goal levels may operate outside a person's awareness. Such processes may be viewed as the unconscious for Rotter.

16. Rotter's research topics include internal and external locus of control, immediate versus postponed gratification, and the study of interpersonal trust.

17. Ellis stresses cognitive variables as key determinants of emotion and behavior and points to hidden unrealistic assumptions, faulty internal verbalizations, compounding sentences, irrational thinking, inappropriate values, and idealistic goals. Correct thinking leads to emotional control. Faulty thinking is the result of unacknowledged irrational assumptions. These must be challenged to produce change. Ellis delineates some common errors of thinking that cause faulty emotional reactions and maladaptive behavior. These are drawing invalid conclusions, overgeneralization (faulty labeling and catastrophizing), either-or thinking, interpretation rather than description, correlation confused with causation. Such errors in logical reasoning may be the source of emotional and behavioral disorders.

18. Mischel questions the validity of the extreme environmentalistic approach, represented by the extreme S-R and radical behaviorists, and the personalistic approach, represented by psychoanalytic theory. He proposes an interactionist approach. Mischel argues that human perception and behavior are finely attuned to the diverse stimuli and situations in our environment. He proposes several person variables that have an enduring role in processing stimuli and directing behavior. These are (a) cognitive and behavioral skills; (b) cognitive categories and constructs; (c) stimulus-outcome and behavior-outcome expectancies; (d) stimulus preferences and aversions; and (e) self-regulatory strategies, intentions, and plans. These variables interact with situational determinants and with one another. Such variables differ from the traditional personality determinants in that they are behaviorally defined and quantifiable.

19. Psychotherapy refers to the treatment of personality disorders, whereas behavior therapy focuses on the disordered behavior directly. The behavior therapists have tended to rely on principles of learning such as classical and operant conditioning and, more recently, on observational learning. Psychotherapy is usually based on a theory of personality that specifies the types of abnormalities that might occur and the ideal personality to be achieved. The moderate behaviorists have found it necessary to infer intervening cognitive variables. Their therapies involve changing such intervening variables as expectancies, goal values and minimal goal levels, perceptual and other cognitive sets, constructs and images, irrational thinking, values and standards, plans and intentions. Cognitive therapists also deal with metacognitive skills and experiences and teach them to those who are deficient. Metacognition refers to knowledge about self, especially about our abilities and skills.

20. Cognitive theorists and therapists call themselves behaviorists, but their constructs and postulates refer to intervening personality variables, which the strict behaviorists have rejected as explanatory devices. The cognitive and social learning theorists have also introduced variables such as self-regulatory systems, intentions, and plans that are the same as those proposed by the humanistic and existential psychologists whose views have been strongly rejected by the strict behaviorists. The notions of self and will are being brought back into psychology by these behaviorists, but they are defining them in objective terms and inferring them from rigorous experimentation. Although they have broadened the conception of humanness, they have not yet dealt with the existential problems associated with living as a human.

GLOSSARY (for Bandura)

Cognitive symbol: General term to cover cognitive representations, for example, images, concepts and words.

Covert rehearsal: Cognitive procedure such as self-instructions, which we practice under the guidance of a model.

Inhibition: Holding back; certain emotions such as fear and guilt block behavior; psychological process that restrains expression of behavior.

> **Strengthening inhibitions:** Increasing inner restraints resulting from observing a model being punished or administering punishment to self for certain behaviors.

> **Weakening inhibitions:** Weakening inner restraints resulting from observing a model being rewarded or rewarding self for certain behaviors. Not being punished for behavior that should be punished accomplishes the same result.

Model: A person who serves as an example for an observer.

> **Real-life model:** An actual person, hero, sports star, gang leader, whose behavior is copied by observers.

> **Symbolic models:** Media representations such as films, TV, pictures.

Modeling effect: The change in the observer (either in learning, performance, or both) resulting from observation of a model's behavior and the consequences.

Self-efficacy: Bandura's notion of having expectancies of success; a sense of personal power (self-confidence) similar to Rotter's internal locus of control.

Social learning theory: The view that most learning occurs in social settings; associated with Albert Bandura.

Vicarious experience: Having experiences that are similar to the observed experiences of another, for example, conditioned emotional responses experienced vicariously.

> **Vicarious reinforcement:** The elicitation of behavior or increase in performance following the observation of a model being rewarded for the same behaviors.

> **Vicarious punishment:** The cessation of behavior or decrease in performance following the observation of a model being punished for the same behaviors.

> **Facilitation of behavior:** Increased frequency of existing behavior as a result of observing a model performing the behavior.

GLOSSARY (for Rotter)

Behavior potential: The probability of an occurrence of a set of behaviors; determined by the psychological situation, reinforcement expectancy, and reinforcement value.

Directional tendencies: Behavior goal units used by Rotter to infer six directional tendencies defined as needs; these are: (1) recognition, (2) dominance, (3) independence, (4) protection dependency, (5) love and affection, and (6) physical comfort.

Freedom of movement: Behavior possibilities based on reinforcement expectancies.

Generalized expectancy: Broad hypotheses about behavior outcomes.

I-E scale: Rotter's scale to measure one's sense of freedom. Those who are high on I (internal locus of control) have a high sense of control over their reinforcers; those high on E (external locus of control) believe that their lives are controlled by external circumstances.

Minimal goal level: The lowest level of reinforcement that is acceptable.

Need potential: Strength of behavior directed toward a goal.

Psychological situation: Perception and interpretation of events.

Reinforcement expectancy: Hypotheses about the probable outcomes of behavior.

Reinforcement value: Degree of worth we place on a goal.

Research dimensions: Areas of research generated by Rotter's constructs.

> **Immediate versus postponed reinforcement:** Generalized expectancy

researched by Rotter attempting to identify personality variables associated with choice of immediate gratification versus ability to postpone gratification.

Trust Scale: Test developed by Rotter to measure our beliefs and expectancies of the trustworthiness of other people. The test appears to measure belief in the goodness of humans and willingness to accept the integrity of others in the absence of evidence.

GLOSSARY (for Ellis)

Cognitive control: Emphasis on the controlling power of cognitive variables.

Cognitive rehearsal: The practicing of cognitive strategies for controlling emotions related to specific disturbing situations during periods of calm when reason can have the upper hand.

Common errors of thinking: Forms of illogical thinking.

> **Drawing invalid conclusions:** Conclusions not justified by the evidence or the premises.
>
> **Overgeneralization:** Drawing an unwarranted general conclusion from a single occurrence.
>
> **Mediated generalization:** Generalization based on cognitive mediators, such as verbal labels, rather than similarity of stimulus properties, for example, labeling an event as dreadful.
>
> **Either-or thinking:** Dividing events into distinct categories rather than perceiving degrees of a dimension such as truth, value, justice, and so on.
>
> **Interpretation rather than description:** Using emotionally toned terms that carry value judgments to characterize events rather than direct reporting.
>
> **Correlation confused with causation:** Linking of unrelated events because they occur together or in close succession.

Compounding sentences: Self-verbalizations that involve interpreting events by adding elements that compound the severity of the situation.

Correct reasoning: Reasoning that follows the principles of logic and obeys the reality principle.

Rational-emotive theory: A theory associated with Ellis in which cognitive variables influence emotions and motivation.

Rational-emotive therapy: Therapy associated with Ellis, which stresses the control of dysfunctional emotions through correct thinking and challenging of irrational assumptions.

Self-verbalization: General term for inner dialogue; self-talk.

Unexpressed sentences: Refers to beliefs or assumptions that underlie behavior, but that the person does not reveal to himself (or herself) or others.

> **Hidden assumptions:** Unreasonable expectations that are not acknowledged by a person but influence behavior.
>
> **Challenging assumptions:** Becoming aware of hidden assumptions and questioning their validity. It is a key procedure in rational-emotive therapy.

GLOSSARY (for Mischel)

Approaches to personality: Options relating to the choice of the determinants of personality.

> **Situational approach:** Stress on environmental causes of behavior; espoused by strict or radical behaviorists.
>
> **Personalistic approach:** Stress on personality dimensions such as traits, needs, and dispositions as the major determinants of behavior; most typified by Freud's characterological approach and constitutional psychology.

Interactionist approach: Viewing behavior as a function of both situational and person variables.

Moderator variables: Slight changes in situations that alter the nature of the behavior that normally occurs, for example, speaking on the telephone differently alone or with another present.

Cognitive social learning theory: Theory of human psychological nature that emphasizes cognitive variables as determinants of behavior.

Cognitive social learning person variables: Cognitive variables proposed by Mischel.

    Cognitive and behavioral construction competencies: Creative use of our knowing capabilities and behavioral potentials.

Encoding strategies: Refers to personal perceptions and interpretations.

Personal constructs: Refers to ideational and imaginal representations.

Cognitive style : Refers to organized patterns of constructs that are characteristic of many people.

Behavior-outcome expectancies: Hypotheses about effectiveness of behavior.

Stimulus-outcome expectancies: Hypotheses about the meaning of situations and stimuli.

Subjective stimulus value: Value placed on goals or courses of action.

Self-regulatory systems and plans: Self-determined rules and standards of conduct. Self-management and self-control techniques.

GLOSSARY (General Terms for Cognitive Therapy)

Metacognitive: Knowledge, experience, and skills regarding cognition; knowing about knowing.

Personality and behavior change: Concepts and methods for altering personality variables (personal constructs, attitudes, intentions, and values) and behavior variables (phobias), compulsions, tics, and other abnormal behavior.

    Behavior modification: General term denoting behavior change; usually applied to operant conditioning procedures.

    Cognitive behavior modification: A general term that refers to altering cognitive operations.

    Behavior therapy: Treatment of abnormal behaviors.

Cognitive behavior therapy: View of behavior therapy in which cognitive variables are assumed to intervene between situation and behavior; changing behavior by modifying cognitive operations.

Cognitive mediational process: Intervening cognitive processes; images, concepts, and words.

Psychotherapy: Treatment of the psyche or personality, usually based on a theory of personality.

Self-instructional procedures: A cognitive behavioral method in which a person is taught appropriate self-instructions directly, or the self-instructions are modeled.

SUGGESTED READINGS

Mahoney, M. J. *Cognition and Behavior Modification.* Cambridge, Mass.: Ballinger, 1974.

    This book deals with an overview of the major concepts and techniques in self-management.

Ellis, A., and R. A. Harper, *A New Guide to Rational Living.* North Hollywood, Calif.: Wilshire, 1975.

    The authors present a popularized version of rational-emotive theory and applications of rational-emotive psychotherapy. It is an easy introduction to Ellis' thinking.

Rotter, J. B., and D. J. Hochreich, *Personality*. Glenview, Ill.: Scott, Foresman, 1975.

The authors present the latest statement of Rotter's cognitive theory and the supporting research.

Bandura, Albert. *Social Learning Theory*. Englewood Cliffs, N.J.: Prentice-Hall, 1977.

A rounding out of social learning theory and presentation of the current research in this area; a mature expression of social learning theory.

Meichenbaum, D. H. *Cognitive Behavior Modification*. Morristown, N.J.: General Learning Press, 1977.

A good introduction to the new field of cognitive behavior theory and therapy written by one of its major proponents and researchers.

Mischel, Walter. *Introduction to Personality*. 3rd ed. New York: Holt, Rinehart and Winston, 1981.

This popular textbook is an overview of the field of personality science. Mischel presents his cognitive person variables and argues for an interactionist approach to personality.

PERSONALITY THEORIES IN PERSPECTIVE

APPROACHES TO THE THEORIES

The student who has persisted in this long and arduous journey through fifteen complex systems of constructs and postulates concerning human nature has probably memorized a jumble of rather loosely organized ideas and terms. Having studied for tests, we have formed associations between the various theorists and the constructs and postulates that they have proposed. This is a good learning device for passing tests, and perhaps for a certain segment of readers this is as much as they expected from the course and the text. For the person who wishes to do more with the personality theories, there are some other options.

The Value of the Theories

One of the major premises of this book is that the theories of personality are guides to human nature. They are conceptual tools that can be functional for us. We have said that we are better off with the theories than without them. Their *value*, however, depends on our *purposes*. (1) If we are a counselor or a therapist, they can serve as guides to understanding and treating pathological personality and behavior. However, the theories vary considerably in their orientation and success. (2) The researcher might use a personality theory as a guide to suggest hypotheses that can be tested empirically. The theories of Freud, Rogers, Maslow, Bandura, and Rotter have been especially tantalizing to researchers. There are other theories that could be used for hypothesis-testing, but they have not attracted research interest. (3) We have noted that the theories were derived from the diagnostic and therapeutic efforts of therapists who were working with people who had personality and behavior problems; thus, they can serve as guides to living. Some of them are quite explicit about the nature of pathology and the goals of healthy living. The author has included sections for each of these topics for the theorists who have dealt with them. (4) Finally, the theories can aid us in understanding principles of personality and behavior. Each theory provides constructs and postulates that embody knowledge about the psychological nature of humans.

Surveying the various theories has taught us a great deal about ourselves and others. We should know some generalizations about developmental stages, learning and extinction, conflict and frustration, motivation and human aspirations, causes of abnormalities, and fulfillment. We have many constructs to describe features of personality such as traits, needs, motives, life-styles, perceptual and cognitive sets, expectancies, and a host of others. For each theorist a set of terms and propositions that stand for constructs and postulates should come to mind. We might think of Freud's division of the psyche into three warring components: the id, ego, and superego. The competition among these three components may be understood in terms of the oppositions of the pleasure, reality, and morality principles. We might think of Jung's constructs of persona, shadow, collective unconscious, complexes, and archetypes. We could go on to review Murray's various ideas on need, press, thema, and need-integrate. We could review Erikson's ego tasks and Horney's three orientations and major internal conflicts. There are so many theorists and terms and propositions that it would not be feasible to review them all here. The point of this discussion is that you have learned many things about human nature from the various theories.

The all-encompassing theory of human nature, if it is ever formulated, will surely have to take account of many of the constructs and postulates that our various theorists have proposed. For example, there is no doubt that reinforcement principles play an important part in the acquisition of behavior. There is no question that we experience conflict between our impulses and conscience, and between egoistic goals and the requirements of society. It is also probable that we have unconscious mental activities. Does it not seem plausible, as Freud pointed out, that at times a part of us works at cross-purposes with our conscious intentions? We can easily sense the struggle between pleasure, reality, and morality. We certainly can observe the defense mechanisms in others and, at times, in ourselves. It is probably true that an idea or belief can get into our unconscious and cause a lot of trouble for us. These notions and many others we have considered will have to be covered by the grand theory of personality.

The Eclectic Approach Versus the Single-Theory Approach

THE ECLECTIC APPROACH

We have noted repeatedly that the personality theories were meant to be functional. Many of them were formulated by therapists who had to deal daily with serious personality and behavior problems. Many of the theories were evolved from the data of the therapist's consulting room. Specialized techniques of investigation such as free association, dream analysis, interpretation, reflection, and other behavior-study techniques were invented to help the therapists learn about the nature of the problems that their patients or clients had. Some of the methods were primarily diagnostic in character in that they were used to identify the problems. Other methods were designed to treat the problems. In either case, it was necessary to conceptualize human nature from the standpoint of what it should be and what could go wrong. In most of the chapters, we have included a section dealing with views on abnormality and another section dealing with views on ideal personality and living, because most of the theorists dealt with these topics.

Although a theorist and his/her followers might claim universal application for the theory, the fact is that each theory applies best to specific problem areas. This point is one of the justifications for an *eclectic approach*, in which *theoretical concepts are matched with problem areas*. If a college sophomore drops out of school suddenly and joins a cultist group, one might refer to Erikson's idea of the psychosocial moratorium to explain this unexpected behavior. Erikson might also be consulted with respect to the remedies for resolving the identity crisis. We could explain the same behavior in Freudian, Rogerian, or Adlerian terms or within the framework of other theories, but Erikson dealt most directly with this problem. One might assume that he had direct experience with it.

If a person is suffering from a chronic and profound sense of inferiority, the obvious theorist to consult is Adler, who had most to say about this problem. He made the sense of inferiority one of the cornerstones of his theory. Other theorists have hardly made mention of it.

We have observed that the various therapists who have propounded personality theories have also tended to focus on a particular population. Freud treated upper-middle-class affluent women primarily suffering from hysterical and other severe neuroses. Rogers, on the other hand, worked primarily in a college setting when he formulated his personality theory and therapeutic methods. Rogers focused extensively on self-discovery and becoming more authentic. His college students were not suffering from the disabling symptoms of Victorian neuroses as much as from the life adjustment problems of late adolescence and young adulthood.

Fromm devoted more attention to loneliness and the role of love in human life than did any of the other theorists. Problems with loneliness and love are widespread and are found in people of all ages. Many theorists have referred to the need for love; Fromm has developed this theme as a cornerstone of his views. As a matter of fact, what one theorist simply mentions in passing as important in human nature, another makes the major focus of theorizing.

We noted in the first chapter that each theory has a *range of convenience*, by which is meant a *particular problem area* for which the theory is best suited and does its best work. Freud's theory is especially helpful in dealing with hidden sources of anxiety, the strange symptoms that seem to be related to past traumas. Freud found that he could account for the genesis of bizarre symptoms in terms of repression and unconscious conflicts. An overwhelming, painful experience during childhood, when the ego was too weak to cope with the stress, would be repressed and produce disturbing symptoms that the victim neither understood nor could dispell. Therapy required that the repressed material be uncovered and the problem worked through. No other theory is as complete as Freud's regarding the role of repression and unconscious conflict. The people with the types of symptoms with which Freud dealt responded better to his methods than they would have to Rogers' client-centered concepts and techniques. Some of the behavior therapists, however, claim that they can deal with the types of problems Freud worked with by means of principles and methods of classical and operant conditioning. (Eysenck, 1965; Wolpe, 1958)

THE SINGLE-THEORY APPROACH

Many people in the helping professions describe themselves as eclectic with respect to theoretical position. They mean, of course, that they use the contructs and postulates of many theories to treat the diverse problems they encounter, rather than adhering to a single theory. Actually, they may go on to indicate that they have leanings toward the psychodynamic or behavioral points of view, although they will borrow from other traditions.

Eclecticism, although valuable for dealing with certain problems, is not a viable alternative to a sound theory. Its use indicates that a comprehensive theory has not been devised.

Many therapists, however, do follow the rationale and methodology of a particular theoretical position. We have indicated that Rogers' client-centered therapy was very popular during the fifties and sixties, and still has many followers both inside and outside of psychology. Albert Ellis' rational-emotive therapy is currently enjoying increasing popularity and is one of the most widely used forms of therapy. Freud's psychoanalytic therapy is still widely practiced among psychiatrists, although there are indications that it is beginning to decline. The enrollment in schools of psychoanalytic therapy is dropping. Both Adler and Jung have a significant following here and abroad. Behavior modification and cognitive behavior modification procedures are receiving increased application, both in individual and in group settings. Behavior modification is becoming a widespread phenomenon in many settings in which behavior management is required.

There are some advantages in attempting to comprehend and treat behavior and personality phenomena with the constructs and postulates of a single theory. Most of the theories have fairly broad explanatory scope. The theorist has usually grasped the significance of a distinctive human theme and proposes broad applications of this theme. Skinner, for example, makes extensive use of the principle of reinforcement. No one would question that behavior is significantly influenced by its outcomes, but no theorist has made as extensive a use of this principle of behavior as Skinner. As we have noted, he finds a multitude of applications of the reinforcement principle. He translates into the language of *operant reinforcement* the traditional psychological variables such as striving and motivation. Even his unique contributions—shaping, discrimination learning, and schedules—involve the use of reinforcers. According to Skinner, abnormalities can be understood in reinforcement terms, and behavior modification can be accomplished by a program of environmental changes that involve the designed use of reinforcers. A person can become an expert in defining personality and behavioral phenomena in reinforcement terms.

In the same manner, Bandura has elaborated another basic type of human learning and has made extensive use of it, namely, the fact that we learn by observing. He has been able to demonstrate that virtually all human learning involves observation and cognitive processes. He has also found many therapeutic and educational applications of modeling principles. He has taken an important principle of human behavior and applied it to many significant aspects of life. A person who wishes to follow Bandura can do the same.

Rogers' phenomenological approach also embodies an important method of gaining knowledge about another person. We should attempt to perceive events from the perspective of the other person. By means of verbal reports and direct observations and perhaps our own similar experiences, we can gain insights into the point of view of another. Behavior can then be altered by helping the other person explore his or her unacknowledged feelings, motives, and interjected conditions of worth. Rogers' constructs and postulates center about this major phenomenological approach. We can follow his views concerning the causes of faulty development of the self and apply the client-centered methods to promote self-awareness and discovery. Again, it is a point of view that can have wide applications.

A theory usually contains several constructs and postulates that can be used in combination, thus increasing the explanatory scope. The use of a single construct or postulate of a theory does not take full advantage of the potential of the theory. Let us consider a simple example of the use of a principle taken from a theory and its modification and increased explanatory scope when used in conjunction with other principles taken from the same theory.

Adler's theory as an example.   As we have noted, Adler has proposed the principle that much of our behavior is a striving for power or superiority over others. We can certainly trace a great deal of behavior to this principle. It helps to explain the conduct of a pathological liar who repeatedly lies about such innocuous things as his achievements, personal attributes, and even trivial matters such as what he ate for supper. By lying, he experiences superiority over the person who is deceived. He says in effect: "I am superior to you because I am putting something over on you." What about the kleptomaniac, one who steals just to get away with it? Is this not a way of gaining superiority over others? What about the person who always tries to get an exemption, the one who thinks the rules simply do not apply to him or her? Is this not another way of achieving superiority by gaining privileged status?

If we consider our superiority strivings alone, we would certainly have a distorted view of humans, but Adler, it will be recalled, postulated an innate social disposition. This principle holds that there is in all humans an inborn potential to be socially responsive, but that this tendency requires a favorable loving climate to develop. Our social sentiments have a profound effect on the striving for superiority because they promote family and group living. The normal person strives for social ends and for self-improvement, whereas the person who is deficient in social interest strives for selfish ends, even at the expense of others. Adler's notion of guiding fictions and style of life are also relevant. Adler maintained that each child develops early in life characteristic ways of perceiving, evaluating, thinking, feeling, and acting that are enduring features of a person's identity. An important component of this style of life is a guiding goal of superiority, which is markedly influenced by the degree of social interest that the child has.

If you construe events within the framework of a single theory, you can become an expert in making use of the constructs and postulates. You can acquire facility in interpreting problems according to the views of the theory. As we have noted, the constructs and postulates are usually so broad that you can apply them to problems that really do not fit the theory very well. This is one of the limitations of a single-theory approach. Most of the personality theorists *overgeneralize the application of their major postulates.*

The All-Encompassing Theory

We have noted that each of the theorists has grasped an important truth about humans and has made extensive explanatory use of it. Some theories, such as Freud's and Jung's, are more comprehensive in their coverage of topics, but even these are by no means complete theories of the psychological nature of humans. A comprehensive theory would be a composite of several theories, because personality and behavior are so complex that one set of principles could not account for them. We might use the analogy of an automobile. It has an electrical system that operates according to the principles of electricity — volts, amperes, resistance — including knowledge of current distribution, fuses and switches, the battery, and the alternator. The automobile has a suspension system made up of springs, shocks, and tires. It has a fuel-injection system and combustion engine, which operate according to a set of principles different from the other systems. It also has a complex steering and braking system and a power train, each of which operates according to a unique set of principles. The smaller automobiles have serious problems with noise: vibrations, rattles, and roar. You must know principles of acoustics and noise control to remedy this problem. Another aspect of the smaller car is wind resistance and general stability. You must know principles of aerodynamics to construct a safe and efficient car.

In the same manner, personality involves a stimulus processing system, complex

Photo credits: upper left © Tom Burnside, 1967/Photo Researchers, Inc.; *upper right* © George E. Jones III 1977/Photo Researchers, Inc.; *lower* © George E. Jones III 1974/Photo Researchers, Inc.

The finished product is the result of many subsystems working together.

cognitive system, a motivational and emotional system, a self-system, and a complex output system. Furthermore, personality grows through maturation and learning. We need a theory to account for development. We also need a theory to deal with the many types of human learning. Surely, a set of principles is needed to account for the development and operation of the self. We might also include a theory of pathology, unless this can be accomplished within the framework of the other components. We would also want our grand theory to specify ideal personality and living. Furthermore, the theory would have to be flexible enough to account for the vast individual differences that we observe among humans. We are certainly a long way from such a grand theory.

Personal Application

You may have noted that each theory contains constructs and postulates that are universal and timeless. They will have different meanings at different periods in your life. Personal application should be a continuing venture. If you had read the same theories five years ago, they would have had a different meaning. If you reexamine them at another time in your life, they will have still another meaning, because they will be interpreted from the perspective of a different life-style. The theories can be useful only if their component constructs and postulates are personalized. The constructs and postulates are abstractions, but they were inferred from actual behaviors. They can acquire meaning for you if they are applied to your own behaviors in a personal way.

It seems valid to propose the hypothesis that a particular theory of personality applies more directly to us or our particular problems than do the other theories. We can gain insights about ourselves from studying that theory of personality which seems to make the most sense to us. Although the theories are presented in summary form in this text, you should be able to identify the theory that is most consonant with your views on life. The next step is to read an account of a disciple of the theorist rather than go directly to the original sources. Finally, you can obtain a simplified version presented by the theorist. You are then ready to delve into the thinking of your theorist by reading several of his or her major works.

We noted in the first chapter that we all have a personality theory. Actually, we have many images of people, whether we realize it or not. Such images profoundly influence our behavior. The image we have of a child makes a real difference in the thoughts, feelings, and expectations we have of the child. For example, a person who views children according to adult standards may view his or her child as being immature or emotionally disturbed. Unrealistic demands may be placed on the child. The problem is not the child, but rather the faulty image. A person who views a child as an "inferior adult" will impose many restrictions and demands and in general will attempt to shape the child's personality and behavior according to the requirements of his or her image of adult behavior. On the other hand, if we view the child as a growing person who has an inherent right to be himself or herself, we will behave very differently. Our image dictates a more permissive and democratic approach. We would define our roles as parent in such terms as counselor, growth facilitator, support person, and benevolent mentor.

Consider another example of the powerful effect of an image of a person. The traditional image of women greatly limited the roles that were considered acceptable for women. Proper roles were restricted to homemaker and mother. The acceptable image of women is changing and the roles which are now possible are increasing. It should be clear that our images of people and our personality theories in general are not academic curiosities; rather, these factors exert a powerful influence over our behavior. What we consider normal or abnormal, appropriate or inappropriate, desirable or undesirable behavior for various groups and ages depends on the images we have of them. The awareness that we harbor various images of people should alert us to the necessity of examining them. We may consider the possibility of changing our behavior by changing the images we have.

We have already noted that making more explicit our own personality theory and our many images of people can increase the scope of our understanding of people and ourselves. We can then make sense of more behavior and better comprehend the wide differences among people we encounter. One way to gain control of our own behavior is to know our personality theory and images of people and to change them. The theories proposed in this book should aid in this process.

BIBLIOGRAPHY

Adelson, J., and J. Redmond. "Personality Differences in the Capacity for Verbal Recall." *Journal of Abnormal Social Psychology.* 57:244–48, 1958.

Adler, Alfred (1912). "The Neurotic Character." Cited in H. L. Ansbacher and R. R. Ansbacher (eds.), *The Individual Psychology of Alfred Adler.* New York: Harper & Row, 1956.

———— (1913). "Individual-Psychological Treatment of Neurosis." Cited in H. L. Ansbacher and R. R. Ansbacher (eds.), *The Individual Psychology of Alfred Adler.* New York: Harper & Row, 1956.

————. *The Neurotic Constitution.* New York: Moffat, 1917.

————. *Practice and Theory of Individual Psychology.* New York: Harcourt Brace Jovanovich 1927.

————. *Problems of Neurosis.* London: Kegan Paul, 1929.

————. "Individual Psychology." In C. Murchinson, (ed.), *Psychologies of 1930.* Worcester, Mass.: Clark University Press, 1930, pp. 395–405.

————. *What Life Should Mean to You.* Boston: Little, Brown, 1931.

————. *Social Interest.* New York: Putnam, 1939.

————. *Understanding Human Nature.* New York: Fawcett, 1954.

————. *Social Interest: A Challenge to Mankind.* New York: Putnam, 1964.

Adorno, T. W., E. Frenkel-Brunswik, D. J. Levinson, and R. N. Sanford. *The Authoritarian Personality.* New York: Harper & Row, 1950.

Alkus, S. "Self-Regulation and Children's Task Performances: A Comparison of Self-instruction, Coping and Attribution Approaches". Unpublished doctoral dissertation, University of California, Los Angeles, 1977.

Allport, G. W. "Motivation in Personality: Reply to Mr. Bertocci." *Psychological Review,* 47:533–554, 1940.

————. *The Use of Personal Documents in Psychological Science.* New York: Social Science Research Council, Bulletin, 1942, 49.

————. "The Trend in Motivational Theory." *American Journal of Orthopsychiatry,* 23:107–119, 1953.

————. *Becoming.* New Haven: Yale University Press, 1955.

————. "The Open System in Personality Theory." *Journal of Abnormal Social Psychology,* 61:301–310, 1960.

————. *Pattern and Growth in Personality.* New York: Holt, Rinehart and Winston, 1961.

————. *Letters from Jenny.* New York: Harcourt, Brace, Jovanovich, 1965.

————. "Traits Revisited." *American Psychologist,* 21:1–10, 1966.

————. *The Person in Psychology: Selected Essays.* Boston: Beacon Press, 1968.

————, P. E. Vernon, and G. Lindzey, *Study of Values,* 3d ed. Boston: Houghton Mifflin, 1960.

Alper, T. G., V. S., Levin, and M. H. Klein, "Authoritarian vs. Humanistic Conscience." *Journal of Personality,* 32:313–333, 1964.

Altus, U. D. "Birth Order and its Sequelae." *Science* 151:44–49, 1966.

Anastasi, Anne. *Psychological Testing*, 4th ed. New York: Macmillan 1976.

Ansbacher, H. L., and R. R. Ansbacher, (eds.), *Individual Psychology of Alfred Adler*. New York Basic Books, 1956.

———— and ————, (eds.), *Superiority and Social Interest*. Evanston, Ill.: Northwestern University Press, 1964.

Arnold, M., "Perennial Problems in the Field of Emotion." In M. Arnold, (ed.), *Feelings and Emotions*. New York: Academic Press, 1970, pp. 169–185.

Aronson, E., and J. M. Carlsmith. "Performance Expectancy as a Determinant of Actual Performance." *Journal of Abnormal Social Psychology*, 65:178–182, 1962.

Atkinson, John W. *Motives in Fantasy, Action, and Society*. New York: Van Nostrand. 1958.

Atkinson, J., and N. T. Feather, (eds.), *A Theory of Achievement Motivation*. New York: Wiley, 1966.

Atkinson, J., and J. Raynor. *Personality, Motivation, and Achievement*. New York: Wiley, 1978.

Ayllon, T., and N. H. Azrin, "The Measurement and Reinforcement of Behavior of Psychotics." *Journal of the Experimental Analysis of Behavior*, 8:357–383, 1965.

————. "Reinforcement Sampling: A Technique for Increasing the Behavior of Mental Patients." *Journal of Applied Behavior Analysis*, 1:13–20, 1968.

Bandura, A. "Influence of Models' Reinforcement Contingencies on the Acquisition of Imitative Responses." *Journal of Personality and Social Psychology*, 1:589–595, 1965.

————. *Principles of Behavior Modification*. New York: Holt, Rinehart and Winston, 1969.

————. *Aggression: A Social Learning Analysis*. Englewood Cliffs, N.J.: Prentice-Hall, 1973.

————. "Behavior Theory and the Models of Man." *American Psychologist*, 29:859–869, 1974.

————. "Self-reinforcement: Theoretical and Methodological Considerations." *Behaviorism*, 4:135–155, 1976.

————. *Social Learning Theory*. Englewood Cliffs, N.J.: Prentice-Hall, 1977.

————, and R. H. Walters, *Social Learning and Personality Development* New York: Holt, Rinehart and Winston, 1963.

————, and C. J. Kupers, "The Transmission of Patterns of Self-reinforcement Through Modeling." *Journal of Abnormal and Social Psychology*, 69:1–9, 1964.

————, and W. Mischel, "Modification of Self-improved Delay of Reward Through Exposure to Live and Symbolic Models." *Journal of Personality and Social Psychology*. 2:698–705, 1965.

————, and T. L. Rosenthal. "Vicarious Classical Conditioning as a Function of Arousal Level." *Journal of Personality and Social Psychology*, 3:54–62, 1966.

————, J. E. Grusec, and F. L. Menlove, "Some Social Determinants of Self-Monitering Reinforcement Systems." *Journal of Personality and Social Psychology*, 5:449–455, 1967.

————, and F. L. Menlove. "Factors Determining Vicarious Extinction and Avoidance Behavior Through Symbolic Modeling." *Journal of Personality and Social Psychology*, 8:99–108, 1968.

————, E. B. Blanchard, and B. Ritter. "Relative Efficacy of Desensitization and Modeling Approaches for Inducing Behavioral, Affective, and Attitudinal Changes." *Journal of Personality and Social Psychology*, 13:173–198, 1969.

Bassett, J. E., E. B. Blanchard, and E. Koshland, "On Determining Reinforcement Stimuli: Armchair Versus Empirical Procedures." *Behavior Therapy*, 8:205–212, 1977.

Beck, Aaron T. *Cognitive Therapy and the Emotional Disorders*. New York: International Universities Press, 1976.

Benson, H., J. Beary, and M. Carol, "The Relaxation Response." *Psychiatry*, 37:37–46, 1974.

————, J. B. Kotch, K. D. Crassweller, and M. M. Greenwood. "Historical and Clinical Considerations of the Relaxation Response," *American Scientist*, 65:441–445, 1977.

Bergin, A. E. "The Evaluation of Theraputic Outcomes." In A. E. Bergin and S. C. Garfield (eds.),

Handbook of Psychotherapy and Behavior Change: An Empirical Analysis. New York: Wiley, 1971.

Berne, Eric. *Beyond Games and Scripts.* New York: Grove, 1976.

Bettelheim, Bruno. *The Empty Fortress.* New York: The Free Press, 1967.

Birney, R. C., H. Burdick, and R. C. Teevan, *Fear of Failure.* New York: Van Nostrand, 1969.

Blofeld, John. "The Background of the Book of Changes." In John Blofeld, (ed.), *I Ching.* New York: Dutton, 1965.

Bloomberg, M. "Creativity as It Relates to Field Independence and Mobility." *Journal of General Psychology*, 118:3–12, 1971.

Blum, R. H., J. Aron, T. Tutko, S. Feinglass, and J. Fort. "Drugs and High School Students." In Blum, R. H., et al., *Students and Drugs: College and High School Observations.* San Francisco: Jossey-Bass, 1969, pp. 321–348.

Bolen, Jean Shinoda, M.D. *The Tao of Psychology: Synchronicity and the Self.* New York: Harper & Row, 1979.

Boss, M. *Psychoanalysis and Daseinsanalysis.* New York: Basic Books, 1963.

Bowlby, J. *Maternal Care and Mental Health.* Geneva: World Health Organization Monograph, 1952.

———. *Attachment.* New York: Basic Books, 1969.

———. *Separation: Anxiety and Anger.* New York: Basic Books, 1973.

———. *Loss: Sadness and Depression.* New York: Basic Books, 1980.

Brady, J. U. "Ulcers in 'Executive' Monkeys." *Scientific American*, 199:95–103, October 1958.

Branden, Nathaniel. *The Psychology of Self-esteem.* New York: Bantam Books, 1969.

———. *The Disowned Self.* New York: Bantam Books, 1971.

Brandt, R. B. *Ethical Theory.* Englewood Cliffs, N.J.: Prentice-Hall, 1959.

Brewer, W. "There is no Convincing Evidence for Operant or Classical Conditioning in Adult Humans." In W. Weimer and D. Palermo (eds.), *Cognition and the Symbolic Processes.* New York: Halstead Press, 1974.

Bronfenbrenner, Uri. "Freudial Theories of Identification and Their Derivations." *Child Development*, 31:15–40, 1960.

Brophy, D. L. "Self, Role, and Satisfaction." *Genetic Psychological Monographs*, 59:236–308, 1959.

Brown, Barbara B. *Supermind: The Ultimate Energy.* New York: Harper & Row, 1980.

Bruner, J. S., and C. C. Goodman, "Value and Need as Organizing Factors in Perception." *Journal of Abnormal Social Psychology*, 42:33–44, 1947.

Burns, David D., M.D. *Feeling Good: The New Mood Therapy.* New York: William Morrow, 1980.

Buros, O. (ed.). *The Seventh Mental Measurements Yearbook.* Highland, N.J.: Gryphon Press, 1972.

Butler, J. M., and G. U. Haigh, "Changes in the Relationship Between Self-Concepts and Ideal-Concepts Consequent upon Client-Centered Counseling." In C. R. Rogers and R. F. Dymond (eds), *Psychotherapy and Personality Change.* Chicago: University of Chicago Press, 1954.

Campione, J., and A. Brown. "Memory and Metamemory Development in Educable Retarded Children." In R. Kail and J. Hagen (eds.), *Perspectives on the Development of Memory and Cognition.* New York: Erlbaum Associates, Halstead Press, 1977.

Carter, L. F., and M. Nixon, "An Investigation of the Relationship Between Four Criteria of Leadership Ability for Three Different Tasks." *Journal of Psychology*, 27:245–261, 1949.

Cattell, R. B. *Personality and Motivation: Structure and Measurement.* New York: Harcourt Brace Jovanovich, 1957.

Caudill, W., and H. Weinstein. "Maternal Care and Infant Behavior in Japan and America." *Psychiatry*, 32:12–43, 1969.

Chatterjee, B. B., and C. W. Eriksen. "Cognitive Factors in Heart Rate Conditioning." *Journal of Experimental Psychology*, 64:272–279, 1962.

Ciaccio, N. V. "A Test of Erikson's Theory of Ego Epigenesis." *Developmental Psychology*, 4:306–311, 1971.

Coan, R. W., "Measurable Components of Openness to Experience." *Journal of Consulting and Clinical Psychology*, 39:346, 1972.

Constantinople, Anna. "An Eriksonian Measure of Personality Development in College Students." *Developmental Psychology*, 1:357–372, July 1969.

Coopersmith, S. *The Antecedents of Self-esteem*. San Francisco: Freeman, 1967.

Crandall, V. C. "Differences in Parental Antecedents of External-Internal Control in Children and Young Adulthood." American Psychological Association Convention, 1973.

Crockett, H. J. "The Achievement Motive and Differential Occupational Mobility in the United States." *American Sociological Review*, 27:191–204, 1962.

Cronback, L. S. "The Two Disciplines of Scientific Psychology." *American Psychology*, 12:671–684, 1957.

Crutchfield, R. S. "The Creative Process." In M. Bloomberg, (ed.), *Creative Theory and Research*. New Haven: College and University Press, 1973, pp. 54–74.

Dahms, A. M. *Emotional Intimacy*. Boulder, Colo.: Pruett Publishing Company, 1972.

Danskin, D. G. "An Introduction to Kansas State University Students." In J. B. Warren, "Birth-Order and Social Behavior." *Psychological Bulletin*, 65:38–49, 1966.

Davis, W. L., and D. E. Davis. "Internal-External Control and Attribution of Responsibility for Success and Failure." *Journal of Personality*. 40:123–36, 1972.

Deci, E. L., "Intrinsic Motivation, Extrinsic Reinforcement, and Inequity." *Journal of Personality and Social Psychology*, 22:113–120, 1972.

Deutsch, J. A., and D. Deutsch, *Physiological Psychology*. Homeward, Ill.: Dorsey Press, 1966.

DiCaprio, Nicholas S. *Adjustment: Fulfilling Human Potentials*. Englewood Cliffs, N.J.: Prentice-Hall, 1980.

DiCarra, L. V. "Learning in the Autonomic Nervous System." In T. J. Teyler (ed.), *Altered States of Awareness*. San Francisco: Freeman, 1973.

Dinkmeyer, D. "The 'C' Group: Integrating Knowledge and Experience to Change Behavior. An Adlerian Approach to Consultation." *Journal of Consulting Psychology*. 3:63–71, 1971.

Dollard, J., and N. E. Miller, *Personality and Psychotherapy*. New York: McGraw-Hill, 1950.

Dreikurs, R., "Individual Psychology: The Adlerian Point of View." In J. M. Wepman, and R. W. Heine, (eds.), *Concepts of Personality*. Chicago: Aldine, 1963, pp. 234–256.

Douglas, V., P. Parry, P. Marton, and C. Garson. "Assessment of a Cognitive Training Program for Hyperactive Children." *Journal of Abnormal Child Psychology*, 4:389–410, 1976.

D'Zarilla, T. "Recall Efficiency and Mediating Cognitive Effects in 'Experimental Repression.' " *Journal of Personality and Social Psychology*, 37:253–256, 1965.

Edwards, Allen L. *Edwards Personal Preference Schedule Manual*, rev. New York: The Psychological Corporation. 1959.

Elkind, D. "Egocentrism in Adolescence." *Child Development* 38:1025–34, 1967.

Ellenberg, H. F. *Discovery of the Unconscious*. New York: Basic Books, 1970.

Ellis, A. *How to Live with a Neurotic*. New York: Crown, 1957.

———. "Rational Psychotherapy." *Journal of General Psychology*, 59:35–49, 1958.

———. *Reason and Emotion in Psychotherapy*. New York: Lyle Stuart, 1962.

———. *Growth Through Reason*. Palo Alto, Calif.: Science and Behavior Books, 1971.

————. *Humanistic Psychotherapy.* New York: McGraw-Hill, 1973.

————. "Rational-Emotive Theory." In A. Burton (ed.), *Operational Theories of Personality.* New York: Brunner/Mazel, 1974, pp. 308–344.

Ellis, A., and Robert A. Harper. *A New Guide to Rational Living.* Hollywood, Calif.: Wilshire, 1975.

Ellis, A. *Diagnostic and Statistical Manual of Mental Disorders,* 3d ed. Washington, D.C.: American Psychiatric Association, 1980.

Engel, B. T., and D. Shapiro, "The Use of Biofeedback Training in Enabling Patients to Control Autonomic Functions." In J. Segal (ed.), *Mental Health Program Reports—5.* Washington, D.C.: U.S. Government Printing Office, 1971.

Epstein, S. "Explorations in Personality Today and Tomorrow: A Tribute to Henray Murray." *American Psychologist,* 34:649–653, 1979.

Eriksen, C. W. "Discrimination and Learning Without Awareness: A Methodical Survey and Evaluation." *Psychological Review.* 67:279–300, 1960.

Erikson, E. H. *Childhood and Society,* 1st ed. New York: Norton, 1950.

————. "Ego Identity and the Psychosocial Moratorium." in H. Witmer and R. Kotinsk (eds.), *New Perspective for Research.* Washington, D.C.: U.S. Department of Health, Education and Welfare, 1956, pp. 1–23.

————. *Young Man Luther: A Study in Psychology Analysis and History.* New York: Norton, 1962.

————. *Childhood and Society,* 2d ed. New York: Norton, 1963.

————. *Insight and Responsibility: Lectures on the Ethical Implications of Psychoanalytic Insight.* New York: Norton, 1964.

————. *Youth and the Life Cycle.* In D. E. Hamachek (ed.), *The Self, Growth, Teaching, and Learning: Selected Reading.* Englewood Cliffs, N.J.: Prentice-Hall, 1965, pp. 325–334.

————. *Identity, Youth, and Crisis.* New York: Norton, 1968.

————. *Gandhi's Truth: On the Origins of Militant Nonviolence.* New York: Norton, 1969.

————. *Dimensions of a New Identity.* New York: Norton, 1974.

————. *Toys and Reasons.* New York: Norton, 1977.

Estes, W. K. "An Experimental Study of Punishment." *Psychological Monographs,* Whole No. 263, 57:3, 1944.

Ewen, Robert B. *An Introduction to Theories of Personality.* New York: Academic Press, 1980.

Eysenck, H. J. "The Effects of Psychotherapy: An Evaluation." *Journal of Consulting Psychology,* 16:319–324, 1952.

————. "The Effects of Psychotherapy." *International Journal of Psychiatry,* 1:99–142, 1965a.

————. *The Causes and Cures of Neurosis.* San Diego, Calif.: Knapp, 1965b.

————. *The Effects of Psychotherapy.* New York: International Science Press, 1966.

Eysenck, Michael W. "Extraversion, Arousal, and Retrieval from Semantic Memory." *Journal of Personality* 42:319–331, 1974.

Feldenkrais, Moshe. *Awareness Through Movement.* New York: Harper & Row, 1977.

Flavell, J. "Metacognitive Development." Paper presented at NATO Institute on Structural Process Theories of Complex Behavior. Banff, 1977.

Fordham, Frieda. *An Introduction to Jung's Psychology.* Great Britain: Pelican Books, 1966.

Forer, Lucille, and Henry Still. *The Birth Order Factor.* New York: Pocket Books, 1977.

Foreyt, J., and E. Rathjen. *Cognitive Behavior Therapy: Research and Application.* New York: Plenum Press, (in press).

Fox, J., R. R. Knapp, and W. B. Michael. "Assessment of Self-actualization of Psychiatric Patients: Validity of Personal Orientation Inventory." *Educational and Psychological Measurement,* 28:565–569, 1968.

Frankl, V. *The Doctor of the Soul*. New York: Knopf, 1955.

French, E. G. "Some Characteristics of Achievement Motivation." *Journal of Experimental Psychology*, 50:232–236, 1955.

French, E. G. and F. H. Thomas. "The Relation of Achievement to Problem-Solving Effectiveness." *Journal of Abnormal and Social Psychology*, 56:45–48. 1958.

Freud, Anna. *The Ego and the Mechanisms of Defense*, rev. ed. New York: International Universities Press, 1966.

Freud, S. *The Standard Edition of the Complete Psychological Works*. London: Hogarth Press, 1963.

——. "On Dreams" (1900). In *Standard Edition*, Vol. 5. London: Hogarth Press, 1953.

——. "Fragment of an Analysis of a Case of Hysteria" (1905). In *Standard Edition*, Vol. 7, London:Hogarth Press, 1953.

——. "On the History of the Psychoanalytic Movement. Papers on Metapsychology, and Other Works," (1914). In Standard Edition, Vol. 14. London: Hogarth Press, 1955.

——. "A Difficulty in the Path of Psycho-analysis" (1917a). In: *Standard Edition*, Vol. 17. London: Hogarth Press, 1955.

——. "On Transformation of Instincts with Special Reference to Anal Eroticism" (1917b). In *Standard Edition*, Vol. 17, London: Hogarth Press, 1955.

——. "Beyond the Pleasure Principle" (1920a). In *Standard Edition*, Vol. 18. London, Hogarth Press, 1955.

——. "Group Psychology and the Analysis of the Ego" (1920b). In *Standard Edition*, Vol 18. London: Hogarth Press, 1955.

——. "On Narcissism: An Introduction" (1904). In *Standard Edition*, Vol. 14. London: Hogarth Press, 1957.

——. "The Economic Problems of Masochism" (1924a). In *Standard Edition*, Vol. 19. London:Hogarth Press, 1957.

——. "The Dissolution of the Oedipus Complex" (1924b). In *Standard Edition*, Vol 19. London:Hogarth Press, 1957.

——. (1925a). "Some Character Types Met Within Psychoanalysis Work." In *Collected Papers*, Vol. 4(9). London: Hogarth Press, 1925.

——. (1925b). "Instincts and Their Vicissitudes." In *Collected Papers*, Vol 4(6). London: Hogarth Press, 1925.

——. "Inhibitions, Symptoms, and Anxiety" (1926). In *Standard Edition*, Vol. 20. London: Hogarth Press, 1959.

——. "The Future of an Illusion" (1927). In *Standard Edition*, Vol. 21. London: Hogarth Press, 1961.

——. "Civilization and Its Discontents" (1930). In *Standard Edition*, Vol. 21. London: Hogarth Press, 1961.

——. "Why War?" (1933). In *Standard Edition*, Vol. 22. London: Hogarth Press, 1964.

——. *The Problems of Anxiety*. New York: Norton, 1936.

——. *An Outline of Psychoanalysis*. New York: Norton, 1949.

Friedan, B. *The Femine Mystique*. New York: Dell, 1963.

Friedenberg, E. Z. *The Vanishing Adolescent*. New York: Dell, 1959.

Fromm, E. *Escape From Freedom*. New York: Holt, Rinehart, and Winston, 1941.

——. *Man for Himself*. New York: Holt, Rinehart, and Winston, 1947.

——. *The Sane Society*. New York: Holt, Rinehart, and Winston, 1955.

——. *The Art of Loving*. New York: Harper & Row, 1956.

——. *Sigmund Freud's Mission: An Analysis of His Personality and Influence*. New York: Harper & Row, 1959.

————. "Values, Psychology, and Human Existence." In J. C. Coleman, *Personality Dynamics and Effective Behavior*. Chicago: Scott, Foresman, 1960, pp. 522–527.

————. *The Heart of Man: Its Genius for Good and Evil*. New York: Harper & Row, 1964.

————. *The Crisis of Psychoanalysis*. New York: Holt, Rinehart and Winston, 1970.

————. *The Anatomy of Human Destructiveness*. New York: Holt, Rinehart and Winston, 1973.

————. *To Have or to Be?* New York: Harper & Row, 1976.

Fromm, E., and Michael Maccoby. *Social Character in a Mexican Village*. Englewood Cliffs, N.J.: Prentice-Hall, 1970.

Garai, J. C. "Sex Differences in Mental Health." *Genetic Psychological Monographs*, 81:123–142, 1970.

Garfield, Sol L., and Richard Kurtz. "Clinical Psychologists in the 1970s." *American Psychologist* 31(1):1–9, January 1976.

Gelfand, D. M. "The Influence of Self-Esteem on Rate of Verbal Conditioning and Social Matching Behavior." *Journal of Abnormal Social Psychology*, 65:259–265, 1962.

Gendlin, Eugene T. *Focusing*. New York: Everest House, 1978.

Gergen, K. J. *The Concept of Self*. New York: Holt, Rinehart, and Winston, 1971.

Ginott, H. G. *Between Parent and Child*. New York: Macmillan, 1965.

Glucksberg, S., and L. J. King, "Motivated Forgetting Mediated by Implicit Verbal Chaining: A Laboratory Analog of Repression." *Science*, 167:517–519, 1967.

Goffman, E. *The Presentation of Self in Everyday Life*. New York: Doubleday, 1959.

Goldiamond, I. "Self-control Procedures in Personal Behavior Problems." *Psychological Reports*. 17:851–858, 1965.

Goldman-Eisler, F. "Breastfeeding and Character Formation." In D. Kluckhohn, H. A. Murray, and D. M. Schneider, (eds.), *Personality In Nature, Society and Culture*. New York: Knopf, 1948, pp. 146–184.

Good, L. R., and K. C. Good. "An Objective Measure of the Motive to Avoid Failure." *Psychology*, 12:11–14, 1975.

Goodall, K. "Shapers at Work." *Psychology Today*, 6:53–63, 132–138, November 1972.

Gordon, T., and D. Cartwright. "The Effects of Psychotherapy upon Certain Attitudes Towards Others." in C. R. Rogers and Rosalind F. Dymond (eds.), *Psychotherapy and Personality Change: Co-ordinated Studies in the Client-Centered Approach*. Chicago: University of Chicago Press, 1954, pp. 167–195.

Gorer, G. "Man Has No 'Killer' Instinct." *New York Times Magazine*, November 27, 1966, pp. 47–57.

Greene, D. "Immediate and Subsequent Effects of Differential Reward Systems on Intrinsic Motivation in Public School Classrooms." Unpublished doctoral dissertation. Stanford University, California, 1974.

Greever, K. B., M. S. Tseng, and B. U. Friedland. "Development of Social Interest Index." *Journal of Consulting and Clinical Psychology*, 41:454–458, 1973.

Grings, W. W. "The Role of Consciousness and Cognition in Autonomic Behavior Change." In F. J. McGuigan and R. Schaunover (eds.), *The Psychophysiology of Thinking*. New York: Academic Press, 1973.

Grossack, M., T. Armstrong, and G. Lussieu, "Correlates of Self-Actualization." *Journal of Humanistic Psychology*, 6:37, 1966.

Gurman, A. S. "The Patient's Perception of Therapeutic Relationships." In A. S. Gurman and A. M. Razin (eds.), *Effective Psychotherapy: A Handbook of Research*. Oxford: Pergammon Press, 1977.

Hall, C. S., and G. Lindzey, *Theories of Personality*, 2d ed. New York: Wiley, 1970.

————. *Theories of Personality:* 3d ed. New York: Wiley, 1978.

Hall, D. T. and K. E. Nongaim. "An Examination of Maslow's Need Hierarchy in an Organizational Setting." *Organizational Behavior and Human Performance*, 3: 12–35, 1968.

Harlow, H. F. Learning to Love. San Francisco: Albion Publishing Company, 1971.

———. "Mice, Monkeys, Men and Motives." *Psychological Review*, 60:23–32, 1953.

———, and G. Griffin. "Induced Mental and Social Deficits in Rhesus Monkeys." In S. F. Osler and R. E. Cooke (eds.), *The Biosocial Basis of Mental Retardation*. Baltimore: The Johns Hopkins University Press, 1965.

Harmin, Merill, Howard Kirschenbaum, and Sidney B. Simon, *Clarifying Values Through Subject Matter: Applications for the Classroom*. Minneapolis: Winston Press, 1973.

Harris, F. R., M. M. Wolf, and D. M. Baer. "Effects of Adult Social Reinforcement on Child Behavior." In S. W. Bijou and D. M. Baer (eds.), *Child Development: Readings in Experimental Analysis*. New York: Appleton, 1967.

Hart, B. M., N. J. Reynolds, D. M. Baer, E. R. Brawley, and F. R. Harris. "Effect of Contingent and Non-Contingent Social Reinforcement on the Cooperative Play of a Preschool Child." *Journal of Applied Behavior Analysis*, 1:73–76, 1968.

Hess, E. H. "Imprinting in Birds." *Science*, 146:1129–1139, 1964.

Hilgard, E. R., and G. H. Bower, *Theories of Learning*. 4th ed. Englewood Cliffs, N.J.: Prentice-Hall, 1975.

Hirsch, S. J., and K. Keniston. "Psychosocial Issues in Talented College Dropouts." *Psychiatry*, 33:1–20, 1970.

Hobson, J. Allan. Cited in "Dream Experiences Tapped as Model of Psychosis." *Brain/Mind Bulletin*, 6(10):1–2, June 1, 1981.

Hoffman, M. "Moral Development." In P. H. Musson (ed.), *Carmichael's Manual of Child Psychology*. 3d ed. Vol. Z. New York: Wiley, 1970, pp. 261–359.

Holmes, D. S. "Repression or Interference? A Further Investigation." *Journal of Personality and Social Psychology*, 22:163–170. 1972.

———. and J. Schallow, "Reduced Recall After Ego Threat: Repression or Response Competition?" *Journal of Personality and Social Psychology*, 13:145–152, 1969.

Holt, J. *How Children Fail*. New York: Pitman, 1964.

Holt, R. R. "Individuality and Generalization in the Psychology of Personality." *Journal of Personality*, 30:377–404, 1962.

Honig, W., and J. Staddon, (eds.), *Handbook of Operant Behavior*. Englewood Cliffs, N.J.: Prentice-Hall, 1977.

Horner, Matina S. "Sex Differences in Achievement Motivation and Performance in Competitive and Non-Competitive Situations." Doctoral dissertation, University of Michigan, 1968. *Dissertation Abstracts International*, 1969, 30:407B (University Microfilms No. 69-12, 135). Cited here as Horner, 1968.

———. "A Psychological Barrier to Achievement in Women: The Motive to Avoid Success." In D. McClelland and R. Steele (eds.), *Human Motivation: A Book of Readings*. Morristown, N.J.: General Learning Press, 1973.

Horney, Karen. *The Neurotic Personality of Our Time*. New York: Norton, 1937.

———. *New Ways in Psychoanalysis*. New York: Norton, 1939.

———. *Self Analysis*. New York: Norton, 1942.

———. *Our Inner Conflicts*. New York: Norton, 1945.

———. *Neurosis and Human Growth*. New York: Norton, 1950.

———. *Feminine Psychology*. New York: Norton, 1967.

———. *The Adolescent Diaries of Karen Horney*. New York: Basic Books, 1980.

Huang, Al Chung-liang. *Embrace Tiger, Return to Mountain: The Essence of T'ai Chi*. Moab, Utah: Real People Press, 1973.

Hull, C. L. *Principles of Behavior*. New York: Appleton, 1943.

Hutt, M. L. "'Consecutive' and 'Adaptive' Testing With the Revised Stanford-Binet." *Journal of Consulting Psychology*, 11:93–103, 1947.

Jackson, D. N., S. A. Ahmed, and N. A. Heapy, "Is Achievement a Unitary Construct?" *Journal of Research in Personality*, 10:1–21, 1976.

Jenkins, W. O., and J. C. Stanley, "Partial Reinforcement: A Review and Critique." *Psychological Bulletin*, 47:193–234, 1950.

Johnson, H. E., and W. H. Garton, "Muscle Reeducation in Hemiplegia by Use of Electromyographic Device." *Archives of Physical Medicine and Rehabilitation*, 54:320–325, 1973.

Johnson, R. E. "Smoking and the Reduction of Cognitive Dissonance." *Journal of Personality and Social Psychology*. 9:260–265, 1968.

Jones, E. *Ingratiation*. New York: Appleton, 1964.

Jones, Landon. *Great Expectations: America and the Baby Boom Generation*. New York: Ballantine, 1981.

Jones, M. C. "A Laboratory Study of Fear: The Case of Peter." *Pedagog Seminar*, 31:308–315, 1924.

Jourard, S. M. *Personal Adjustment: An Approach Through the Study of Personality*. 2d ed. New York: Macmillan, 1963.

Jung, C. G. *Collected Papers on Analytical Psychology*. New York: Moffat, Yard, 1917.

———. *Studies on Word Association*. London: Heinemann, 1918.

———. "Freud and Jung—Contrasts." In *Modern Man in Search of a Soul*. New York: Harcourt Brace Jovanovich, 1933a.

———. *Psychological Types*. New York: Harcourt Brace Jovanovich 1933b.

———. "Two Essays on Analytical Psychology." In Sir Herbert Read et al., (eds.), R. F. C. Hull (translator, except Vol.2), *The Collected Works of C. G. Jung*, Vol. 17. Princeton, N.J.: Princeton University Press and London: Routledge and Kegan Paul, 1953.

———. *The Undiscovered Self*. New York: Mentor, 1958.

———. "The Archetypes and the Collective Unconscious." In *Collected Works*, Vol. 9, Part I. Princeton, N.J.: Princeton University Press, 1959a.

———. "Aion." In *Collected Works*, Vol. 9, Part II. Princeton, N.J.: Princeton University Press, 1959b.

———. "The Structure and Dynamics of the Psyche." In *Collected Works*, Vol. 8. Princeton, N.J.: Princeton University Press, 1960.

———. *Memories, Dreams, Reflections*. New York: Random House (Paperback Vintage Books), 1961/1965.

———. "Civilization in Transition." In *Collected Works*, Vol. 10. Princeton, N.J: Princeton University Press, 1964a.

———. *Man and His Symbols*. New York: Doubleday, 1964b.

———. "The Practice of Psychotherapy." In *Collected Works*, Vol. 16. Princeton, N.J.: Princeton University Press, 1966.

Kagan J. *Change and Continuity in Infancy*. New York: Wiley, 1971.

———. "The Emergence of Sex Differences." *School Review*, 80:217–227, 1972.

Kaplan, Louise J. *Oneness and Separateness: From Infant to Individual*. New York: Simon and Schuster, 1978.

Kaufman, A., A. Baron, and R. E. Kopp, "Some Effects of Instructions on Human Operant Behavior." *Psychonomic Monograph Supplements*, 1:243–250, 1966.

Kelley, H. H. "Attribution Theory in Social Psychology." In D. Levine (ed.), *Nebraska Symposium on Motivation*. Lincoln: University of Nebraska Press, 1967, pp. 192–238.

Kelly, G. A. *The Psychology of Personal Constructs*. New York: Norton, 1955.

Keniston, K. *The Uncommitted: Alienated Youth in American Society*. New York: Harcourt Brace Jovanovich, 1965.

Keys, A. B., Brozek, J., Henschel, A., Nickelson, O., and Taylor, H. L. *The Biology of Human Starvation*. Minneapolis: University of Minnesota Press, 1950.

Kierkegaard, S. *The Sickness unto Death*. Trans., W. Lowrie. New York: Doubleday, 1954.

Kinget, G. Marian. *On Being Human*. New York: Harcourt, Brace Jovanovich, 1975.

Kirschenbaum, H. *On Becoming Carl Rogers*. New York: Knopf, 1955.

Kline, P. *Fact and Fantasy in Freudian Theory*. London: Methuen, 1972.

Klineberg, S. L. "Future Time Perspective and the Preference for Delayed Reward." *Journal of Personality and Social Psychology*. 8:253–257, 1968.

Kohlberg, L. "Stage and Sequence: The Cognitive-Developmental Approach to Socialization." In D. A. Goslin (ed.), *Handbook of Socialization Theory and Research*. Chicago: Rand-McNally, 1969, pp. 347, 480.

Komaki, J., and Dore-Boyce, K. "Self-recording: Its Effects on Individuals High and Low in Motivation." *Behavior Therapy*, 9:65–72, 1978.

Korchin, S. J. *Modern Clinical Psychology*. New York: Basic Books, 1976.

Krumboltz, John D., and Krumboltz, Helen B. *Changing Children's Behavior*. Englewood Cliffs, N.J.: Prentice-Hall, 1972.

Laing, R. D. *The Politics of Experience*. New York: Pantheon Books, 1967.

Landy, Frank J., and Don A. Trumbo. *Psychology of Work Behavior*. Homewood, Ill.: The Dorsey Press, 1980.

Lang, P. J., and A. P. Lazovik, "Personality and Hypnotic Susceptibility." *Journal of Consulting Psychology*, 26:317–322, 1962.

Leboyer, F. *Birth Without Violence*. New York: Knopf, 1975.

Lefcourt, H. M. "The Function of the Illusions of Control and Freedom." *American Psychologist*, 28:417–425, 1973.

———. *Locus of Control: Current Trends in Theory and Research*. Hillsdale, N.J.: Lawrence Erlbaum Associates, 1976.

———. "Locus of Control and Coping with Life's Events." In Ervin Staub (ed.), *Personality: Basic Reports and Current Research*. Englewood Cliffs, N.J.: Prentice-Hall, 1980.

Levinson, Daniel J., et al. *The Seasons of a Man's Life*. New York: Knopf, 1978.

Levy, L. H. *Conceptions of Personality: Theories and Research*. New York: Random House, 1970.

Liebert, R. M. and L. E. Fernandez, "Effects of Various Consequences on Imitative Performance." *Child Development*. 41:847–52, 1970.

———, and Michael D. Spiegler. *Personality: Strategies for the Study of Man*, rev. ed. Homewood, Ill: The Dorsey Press, 1974.

Lifton, R. J. *History and Human Survival*. New York: Random House, 1970.

Lips, Hilary M., and Nina Lee Colwill, *The Psychology of Sex Differences*. Englewood Cliffs, N.J.: Prentice-Hall, 1978.

Loevinger, Jane. *Ego Development*. San Francisco: Jossey-Bass, 1976.

Lovass, O. I., G. Freitag, V. J. Gold, and I. C. Kassorla, "Experimental Studies in Childhood Schizophrenia: I. Analysis of Self-destructive Behavior." *Journal of Experimental Child Psychology*, 2:67–84, 1965.

Lowell, E. L. "The Effect of Need for Achievement on Learning and Speed of Performance." *Journal of Psychology*, 33:31–40, 1952.

Maccoby, E. E. "Sex Differences in Intellectual Functioning." In Maccoby, E. E. (ed.), *The Development of Sex Differences*. Stanford, Calif.: Stanford University Press, 1966.

———, and C. Jacklin, *The Psychology of Sex Differences*. Stanford, Calif.: Stanford University Press, 1974.

Maddi, S. "Humanistic Psychology: Allport and Murray." In J. Wepman and R. Heine (eds.), *Concepts of Personality*. Chicago: Aldine, 1963, pp. 162–205.

———. "Motivational Aspects of Creativity." *Journal of Personality*, 33:330–347, 1965.

————. *Personality Theories: A Comparative Analysis*, rev. ed. Homewood, Ill.: The Dorsey Press, 1972.

————. *Personality Theories: A Comparative Analysis*, 4th ed. Homewood, Ill.: The Dorsey Press, 1980.

Mahoney, J., and J. Harnett. "Self-actualization and Self-ideal Discrepancy." *Journal of Psychology*, 85:37–42, 1973.

Mahoney, M. J. *Cognition and Behavior Modification*. Cambridge, Mass.: Ballinger, 1974.

Mahrer, A. R. "The Role of Expectancy in Delayed Reinforcement." *Journal of Experimental Psychology*, 52:101–105, 1956.

Mann, George A., M.D. *The Dynamics of Addiction*. Minneapolis, Minn.: Johnson Institute, (no date).

Mann, H., M. Siegler, and H. Osmond, "Four Types of Personalities and Four Ways of Perceiving Time." *Psychology Today*, 6:76–84, 1972.

Marcia, J. E., "Development and Validation of Ego-Identity Status." *Journal of Personality and Social Psychology*, 3:551–558, 1966.

Marrow, A. J., D. G. Bowers, and S. E. Seashore. *Management by Participation*. New York: Harper & Row, 1967.

Maslow, A. H. "A Theory of Motivation." *Psychological Review*, 50:370–396, 1943.

————. *Motivation and Personality*. New York: Harper & Row, 1954.

————. "Deficiency Motivation and Growth Motivation." In M. R. Jones (ed.), *Nebraska Symposium on Motivation*. Lincoln: University of Nebraska Press, 1955.

————. *Toward A Psychology of Being*. Princeton, N.J.: Van Nostrand, 1962.

————. "Human Potentials and the Healthy Society." In H. Otto (ed.), *Human Potentials*. St. Louis: Warren H. Green, 1968a.

————. "Some Educational Implications of the Humanistic Psychologies." *Harvard Educational Review*, 38:685–696, 1968b.

————. *Toward a Psychology of Being*. 2d ed. Princeton: Van Nostrand, 1968c.

————. "A Theory of Metamotivation: The Biological Rooting of the Value-Life." *Psychology Today*, 2:38–39, 58–62, (July) 1968d.

————. "Toward a Humanistic Biology." *American Psychologist*, 24:724–735, 1969.

————. *Motivation and Personality*, 2d ed. New York: Harper & Row, 1970.

————. *The Farther Reaches of Human Nature*. New York: Viking, 1971.

Masters, Robert, and Jean Houston, *Listening to the Body*. New York: Delacorte, 1978.

Mathes, Eugene W. "Maslow's Hierarchy of Needs as a Guide for Living." *Journal of Humanistic Psychology*, 21(4), Fall 1981.

May, Rollo. *Man's Search for Himself*. New York: Norton, 1953.

————. *The Courage to Create*. New York: Bantam Books, 1975.

McClelland, D. *The Achieving Society*. Princeton: Van Nostrand, 1961.

————. "N Achievement and Enterpreneurship: A Longitudinal Study." *Journal of Personality and Social Psychology*, 1:389–392, 1965.

————. *Assessing Human Motivation*. New York: General Learning Press, 1971.

————. "Testing for Competence Rather Than for 'Intelligence'." *American Psychologist*, 28:1–14, 1973.

McKeachie, W. J., Y. Lin, and R. Milholland. "Student Affiliation Motives, Teacher Warmth, and Academic Achievement." *Journal of Personality and Social Psychology*. 4:457–61, 1966.

McReynolds, P. *Advances in Psychological Assessment*, Vol. 3. San Francisco: Jossey-Bass, 1975.

Medinnus, G. R., and F. J. Curtis. "The Relation Between Maternal Self-acceptance and Child Acceptance." *Journal of Counseling Psychology*, 27:542–544, 1963.

Meichenbaum, D. H. *Cognitive Behavior Modification*. Morristown, N.J.: General Learning Press, 1977.

————. *Cognitive Behavior Therapy*. New York: B. M. A. Audio Cassette Publications, 1978.

————, and J. Goodman. "Training Impulsive Children to Talk to Themselves: A Means of Developing Self-control." *Journal of Abnormal Psychology*, 77:115–126, 1971.

Mehrabian, A. *An Analysis of Personality Theories*. Englewood Cliffs, N.J.: Prentice-Hall, 1968.

Meltzoff, J., and M. Kornreich, *Research in Psychotherapy*. New York: Atherton, 1970.

Miller, G. A., E. Galanter, and K. H. Pribram, *Plans and the Structure of Behavior*. New York: Holt, Rinehart and Winston, 1960.

Miller, N. E., and Banuazizi, A. "Instrumental Learning by Curarized Rats of a Specific Visceral Response, Intestinal or Cardiac." *Journal of Comparative and Physiological Psychology*, 65:1–7, 1968.

Mischel, Harriet N., and Walter Mischel. *Essentials of Psychology*, 2nd ed., New York: Random House, 1980.

Mischel, W. *Personality and Assessment*. New York: Wiley, 1968.

————. "On the Empirical Dilemmas of Psychodynamic Approaches." *Journal of Abnormal Psychology*, 82:335–344, 1973a.

————. "Toward a Cognitive Social Learning Reconceptualization of Personality." *Psychological Review*, 80:252–283, 1973b.

————. Quoted in A. Wondersman, P. H. Popper, and D. F. Rix, (eds.), *Humanism And Behaviorism*. Elmsford, N.Y.: Pergamon, 1976.

————. "On the Future of Personality Measurement." *American Psychologist*, 32:253, 1977a.

————. "The Interaction of Person and Situation." In D. Magnusson and N. S. Endler, (eds.), *Personality at the Crossroads: Current Issues in Interactional Psychology*. Hillsdale, N.J.: Erlbaum, 1977b.

————. *Introduction to Personality*. 3d ed. New York: Holt, Rinehart and Winston, 1981.

————, and E. Staub. "Effects of Expectancy on Working and Waiting for Larger Rewards." *Journal of Personality and Social Psychology*, 4:211–214, 1965.

————. and J. E. Grusec. "The Model's Characteristics as Determinants of Social Learning." *Journal of Personality and Social Psychology*, 4:211–214, 1966.

————, and R. M. Liebert. "Effects of Discrepancies Between Observed and Imposed Reward Criteria on Their Acquisition and Transmission." *Journal of Personality and Social Psychology*, 3:390–396, 1966.

————, and J. C. Masters. "Effects of Probability of Reward Attainment on Responses to Frustration." *Journal of Personality and Social Psychology*. 3:390–396, 1966.

————, E. B. Ebbesen, and A. R. Zeiss, "Cognitive and Attentional Mechanisms in Delay of Gratification." *Journal of Personality and Social Psychology*, 21:204–218, 1972.

Misiak, H., and U. Sexton. *History of Psychology*. New York: Grune and Stratton, 1966.

Mitchell, K. M., J. D. Bozarth, and C. C. Krauft. "A Reappraisal of the Therapeutic Effectiveness of Accurate Empathy, Nonpossessive Warmth, and Genuineness." In D. S. Gurman and A. M. Razin (eds.), *Effective Psychotherapy: A Handbook of Research*. Elmsford, N.Y.: Pergamon, 1977.

Montagu, Ashley. *Touching: The Human Significance of the Skin*. New York: Columbia University Press, 1971.

————. *Touching: The Human Signficance of the Skin* 2d ed. New York: Harper & Row, 1978.

Montagu, Ashley, and Floyd Matson. *The Human Connection*. New York: McGraw-Hill, 1979.

Moore, T. V. *Cognitive Psychology*. Philadelphia: Lippincott, 1939.

Moustakas, C. E. *Loneliness and Love*. Englewood Cliffs, N.J.: Prentice-Hall, 1972.

Mowrer, O H. "Critique of Patterson's Client-Centered Counseling Article." *Counseling Psychologist*, 16:48–56, 1969.

Murray, H. A. *Explorations in Personality*. New York: Oxford, 1938.

———. "What Should Psychologists Do About Psychoanalysis?" *Journal of Abnormal Psychology*, 35:150–175, 1940.

———. *Thematic Aperception Test*. Cambridge, Mass.: Harvard University Press, 1943.

———. "Some Basic Psychological Assumptions and Conceptions." *Dialectica*, 5:266–292, 1951.

———. "Toward a Classification of Interaction." In T. Parsons, and E. A. Shils (eds.), *Towards a General Theory of Action*. Cambridge, Mass.: Harvard University Press, 1954, pp. 434–464.

———. "A Preparation for the Scaffold of a Comprehensive System." In S. Koch (ed.), *Psychology: A Study of a Science*. Vol. 3. New York: McGraw-Hill, 1959.

——— and MacKinnon, D. W. "Assessment of OSS Personnel." *Journal of Consulting Psychology*, 10:76–80, 1946.

——— and Kluckhohn, C. "Outline of a Conception of Personality." In C. Kluckhohn, H. A. Murray, and S. M. Schneider (eds.), *Personality in Nature, Society, Culture*. 2d ed. New York: Knopf, 1953.

Murray, J. P. "Television and Violence: Implications of the Surgeon General's Research Program." *American Psychologist*, Vol. 28:472–478, 1973.

Myers, I. S. *The Myers-Briggs Type Indicator*. Princeton, N.J.: Educational Testing Service, 1962.

Neilon, P. "Shirley's Babies After Fifteen Years." *Journal of Genetic Psychology*, 73:175–186, 1948.

Nordby, V. J., and C. S. Hall, *A Guide to Psychologists and Their Concepts*. San Francisco: Freeman, 1974.

Novaco, R. "A Stress Inoculation Approach to Anger Management in the Training of Law Enforcement Officers," *American Journal of Community Psychology*, 5:327–346, 1977.

Nowlis, P. P., and J. Kamiya. "The Control of Electroencephalographic Alpha Rhythms Through Auditory Feedback and the Associated Mental Activity." *Psychophysiology*, 5:476–484, 1970.

Oetzel, R. M. "Classified Summary of Research in Sex Differences." In E. E. Maccoby (ed.), *The Development of Sex Differences*. Stanford, Calif.: Stanford University Press, 1966, pp. 323–51.

Oppenheimer, R. J. "Analogy in Science." *American Psychologist*, 11:126–135, 1956.

Parloff, M. B., I. E. Waskow, and B. E. Wolf. "Research on Therapist Variables in Relation to Process and Outcome." In S. L. Garfield and A. E. Bergin (eds.), *Handbook of Psychotherapy and Behavior Change*. 2d ed. New York: Wiley, 1978.

Patterson, C. H. *Theories of Counseling and Psychotherapy*. New York: Harper & Row, 1973.

Pavlov, I. P. *Conditioned Reflexes*. London: Oxford, 1927.

Pawlik, K., and R. B. Cattell. "Third-Order Factors in Objective Personality Tests." *British Journal of Psychology*, 55:1–18, 1964.

Pearson, O. "Effects of Group Guidance Upon College Adjustment." Unpublished Doctoral Dissertation, University of Kentucky, 1966.

Peck, R. F., and R. J. Havighurst. *The Psychology of Character Development*. New York: Wiley, 1960.

Peele, Stanton, and Archie Brodsky. *Love and Addiction*. New York: New American Library, 1975.

Pervin, L. D. "Performance and Satisfaction as a Function of Individual-Environmental Fit." *Psychological Bulletin*, 69:56–68, 1968.

Peterson, D. R. "The Scope and Generality of Verbally Defined Personality Factors." *Psychological Review*, 72:48–59, 1965.

Piaget, J. *Play, Dreams, and Imitation*. New York: Norton, 1962.

Porter, L. W. "A Study of Perceived Satisfactions in Bottom and Middle Management Jobs." *Journal of Applied Psychology*, 45:1–10, 1961.

———, and E. E. Lawler. *Managerial Attitudes and Performance*. Homewood, Ill.: The Dorsey Press, 1968.

Premack, D. "Reinforcement Theory." In D. Levine (ed.), *Nebraska Symposium on Motivation*. Lincoln: University of Nebraska Press, 1965.

Putney, S., and G. J. Putney. *The Adjusted American: Normal Neuroses in the Individual and Society*. New York: Harper & Row, 1964.

Raimy, V. C. "Self-reference in Counseling Interviews." *Journal of Consulting Psychology*, 12:153–163, 1948.

Rappoport, J., and J. M. Chinsky. "Accurate Empathy: Confusion of a Construct." *Psychological Bulletin*, 77:400–404, 1972.

Raush, H. L., A. T. Dittman, and T. J. Taylor, "Person, Setting, and Change in Social Interaction." *Human Relations*, 12:361–378, 1959.

Redd, W. H. "Effects of Mixed Reinforcement Contingencies on Adults' Control of Children's Behavior." *Journal of Applied Behavioral Analysis*, 2:249–254, 1969.

Restak, Richard M. *The Brain: The Last Frontier*. New York: Doubleday, 1979.

Reynolds, Stanley G. *A Primer of Operant Conditioning*. Glenview, Ill.: Scott, Foresman, 1968.

Rheingold, H. L., J. L. Gewirtz, and H. W. Ross, "Social Conditioning of Vocalization in the Infant." *Journal of Comparative Physiological Psychology*, 52:68–73, 1959.

Riesman, D. *Faces in the Crowd*. New Haven: Yale University Press, 1952.

Rimm, D. C. "Behavior Therapy: Some General Comments and a Review of Selected Papers." In R. L. Spitzer and D. F. Klein (eds.), *Evaluation of Psychological Therapies*. Baltimore: Johns Hopkins University Press, 1976.

———, and J. C. Masters. *Behavior Therapy: Techniques and Empirical Findings*. 2d ed. New York: Academic Press, 1979.

Roazen, Paul. *Erik H. Erikson: The Power and Limits of a Vision*. New York: The Free Press, 1976.

Rogers, C. R. *Counseling and Psychotherapy*. Boston: Houghton Mifflin, 1942.

———. *Client-Centered Therapy*. Boston: Houghton Mifflin, 1951.

———. "A Theory of Therapy, Personality, and Interpersonal Relationships as Developed in the Client-Centered Framework." In S. Koch (ed.), *Psychology: A Study of Science*, Vol. 3. New York: McGraw-Hill, 1959.

———. *On Becoming a Person*. Boston: Houghton Mifflin, 1961.

———. "Actualizing Tendency in Relation to 'Motives' and Consciousness." In M. R. Jones (ed.), *Nebraska Symposium on Motivation*. Lincoln: University of Nebraska Press, 1963.

———, (ed.). *The Therapeutic Relationship and Its Impact: A Study of Psychotherapy With Schizophrenics*. Madison, Wis.: University of Wisconsin Press, 1967.

———. *Freedom to Learn*. Columbus, Ohio: Merrill, 1969.

Rogers, C. R. *Carl Rogers on Encounter Groups*. New York: Harper & Row, 1970.

———. "Toward a Modern Approach to Value: The Valuing Process in the Mature Person." In M. Bloomberg (ed.), *Creativity: Theory and Research*. New Haven: College and University Press, 1972.

———. "In Retrospect: Forty-six Years." *American Psychologist*, 29:115–123, 1974.

———. *Carl Rogers on Personal Power*. New York: Delacorte, 1977.

———. *A Way of Being*. Boston: Houghton Mifflin, 1980.

———, and R. F. Dymond. *Psychotherapy and Personality Change*. Chicago: University of Chicago Press, 1954.

Rogers, J. B. "External Control and Internal Control." *Psychology Today*, 5:37–42, 58–59, June 1971.

Rolf, Ida P. *Rolfing*. Santa Monica, Cal.: Dennis-Landman, 1977.

Rorbaugh, Joanna Bunker. *Women: Psychology's Puzzle*. New York: Basic Books, 1979.

Rosenbaum, M. "A Schedule for Assessing Self-control Behaviors: Preliminary Findings." *Behavior Therapy*, 11:109–121, 1980.

Rosenberg, L. A. "Idealization of Self and Social Adjustment." *Journal of Consulting Psychology*, 26:487, 1962.

Rosenzweig, S. "An Experimental Study of 'Repression' with Special Reference to Need-Perspective and Ego-Defense Reaction to Frustration." *Journal of Experimental Psychology*, 32:64–74, 1943.

Rotter, Julian B. *Social Learning and Clinical Psychology*. Englewood Cliffs, N.J.: Prentice-Hall, 1954.

——— . "Generalized Expectancies for Internal Versus External Control of Reinforcement." *Psychological Monographs*, 80, Whole No. 609, 1966, pp. 1–28.

——— . "Beliefs, Social Attitudes and Behavior: A Social Learning Analysis." In R. Jessor and S. Feshbach (eds.), *Cognition, Personality, and Clinical Psychology*. San Francisco: Jossey-Bass, 1967.

——— . "Some Implications of a Social Learning Theory for the Practice of Psychotherapy." In D. J. Levis (ed.), *Learning Approaches to Therapeutic Behavior Change*. Chicago: Aldine, 1970.

——— . "Generalized Expectancies for Interpersonal Trust." *American Psychologist*, 26:443–452, 1971.

——— . "Trust and Gullibility." *Psychology Today*, 14(5):35–42, 102, October 1980.

——— , June E. Chance, and E. Jerry Phares, *Applications of a Social Learning Theory of Personality*. New York: Holt, Rinehart and Winston. 1972.

——— , and D. J. Hochreich. *Personality*. Glenview, Ill.: Scott, Foresman, 1975.

Rubins, J. L. *Karen Horney: Gentle Rebel of Psychoanalysis*. New York: Dial, 1978.

Rudikoff, E. C. "A Comparative Study of the Changes in the Concepts of the Self, the Ordinary Person, and the Ideal in Eight Cases." In C. R. Rogers and R. F. Dymond (eds.), *Psychotherapy and Personality Change: Co-ordinated Studies in the Client-Centered Approach*. Chicago: University of Chicago Press, 1954.

Ryckman, R. M. *Theories of Personality*. Princeton, N.J.: Van Nostrand, 1978.

Sanford, John A. *The Invisible Partners: How the Male and Female in Each of Us Affects Our Relationships*. New York: Paulist Press, 1980.

Sarason, I. (ed.). *Test Anxiety: Theory, Research, and Applications*. San Francisco: L. Erlbaum, 1980.

Schachtel, E. G. "On Alienated Concepts of Identity." In E. Josephson and M. Josephson (eds.), *Man Alone: Alienation in Modern Society*. New York: Dell, 1962, pp. 73–83.

Schachter, S. *The Psychology of Affiliation: Experimental Studies of the Sources of Gregariousness*. Stanford, Calif.: Stanford University Press, 1959.

——— . "Birth-Order, Eminence, and Higher Education." *American Sociological Review*, 28:757–767, 1963.

——— . "Birth-Order and Sociometric Choice." *Journal of Abnormal Social Psychology*, 68:453–456, 1964.

Schiffman, M. *Gestalt Self Therapy*. Menlo Park, Cal.: Self Therapy Press, 1971.

Scott, W. A. "Social Desirability and Individual Conceptions of the Desirable." *Journal of Abnormal Social Psychology*, 67:547–585, 1963.

Sears, R. R., E. E. Maccoby, and H. Levin, *Patterns of Child Rearing*. Evanston, Ill.: Row, Peterson, 1957.

Seeman, J. "A Study of the Process of Non-Directive Therapy." *Journal of Consulting Psychology*, 13:157–168, 1949.

——— and N. J. Raskin, "Research Perspectives in Client-Centered Therapy." In O. H. Mowrer (ed.), *Psychotherapy*. New York: Ronald, 1953.

Shaver, P. "Questions Concerning Fear of Success and Its Conceptual Relatives." *Sex Roles*, 2:305–320, 1976.

Sheehy, Gail. *Passages*. New York: Dutton, 1976.

Sheerer, E. T. "An Analysis of the Relationship Between Acceptance of and Respect for Self and Acceptance of and Respect for Others in Ten Counseling Cases." *Journal of Consulting Psychology*, 13:169–175, 1949.

Sheldon, W. H., C. W. Dupertuis, and E. McDermott. *Atlas of Men: A Guide for Somatotyping the Adult Male at All Ages*. New York: Harper & Row, 1954.

Shirley, M. "The First Two Years." *Personality Manifestations*, Vol. 3. Minneapolis: University of Minnesota Press, 1933.

Shostrom, E. L. *Personal Orientation Inventory*. San Diego, Cal.: EdITS/Educational and Industrial Testing Service, 1963.

——. *Actualizing Therapy: Foundations for a Scientific Ethics*. San Diego, Cal.: EdITS/Educational and Industrial Testing Service, 1981.

Siegel, Ron K. In B. Van der Horst, "Cartographer of Consciousness." *OMNI*, (September) 1980, pp. 55–58.

Siegelman, M. "'Origins' of Extraversion-Introversion." *Journal of Psychology*, 69:85–91, 1968.

Silverman, L. H. "Psychoanalytic Theory: The Reports of My Death Are Greatly Exaggerated." *American Psychologist*, 31:621–637, 1976.

Simon, R. D. *Understanding Human Behavior in Health and Illness*. New York: Williams and Wilkins, 1977.

Simon, Sidney B. *Meeting Yourself Halfway*. Niles, Ill.: Argus Communications, 1974.

——, L. W. Howe, and H. Kirschenbaum. *Values Clarification: A Handbook of Practical Strategies for Teachers and Students*. New York: Hart, 1972.

Singer, J. L. *Daydreaming: An Introduction to the Experimental Study of Inner Experience*. New York: Random House, 1966.

Skinner, B. F. *The Behavior of Organisms*. New York: Appleton, 1938.

——. *Science and Human Behavior*. New York: Macmillan, 1953.

——. *Walden Two*. New York: Macmillan, 1948.

——. *Verbal Behavior*. New York: Appleton, 1957.

——. "Operant Behavior." *American Psychologist*, 18:503–515, 1963.

——. *The Technology of Teaching*. New York: Appleton, 1968.

——. *Beyond Freedom and Dignity*. New York: Knopf, 1971.

——. "Will Success Spoil B. F. Skinner?" (Interview Transcription), *Psychology Today*, 65:72–130, (November) 1972a.

——. *Cumulative Record: A Selection of Papers*, 3d ed. New York: Appleton, 1972b.

——. *Reflections on Behaviorism and Society*. Englewood Cliffs, N.J.: Prentice-Hall, 1978.

——. *Notebooks: B. F. Skinner*. Englewood Cliffs, N.J.: Prentice-Hall, 1981.

—— and C. Ferster, *Schedules of Reinforcement*. New York: Appleton, 1957.

Spielberger, C. Coping with Stress and Anxiety in the College Classroom. Paper presented to NATO Advanced Study Institute, Urbino, Italy, 1976.

Stampfl, T. G., and D. J. Levis. "Essentials of Implosive Therapy: A Learning-Theory Based Psychodynamic Behavioral Therapy." *Journal of Abnormal Psychology*, 72:496–503, 1967.

Staub, E. (ed.), *Personality: Basic Aspects and Current Research*. Englewood Cliffs, N.J.: Prentice-Hall, 1980.

Steers, R. M., and D. G. Spencer, "The Role of Achievement Motivation in Job Design." *Journal of Applied Psychology*, 62:472–479, 1977.

Steiner, Claude. *Scripts People Live By*. New York: Grove, 1974.

Stephenson, W. "The Significance of Q-Technique for the Study of Personality." In M. L. Reynort (ed.), *Feelings and Emotions: The Mooseheart Symposium*. New York: McGraw-Hill, 1950.

————. *The Study of Behavior: Q-Technique and Its Methodology*. Chicago: University of Chicago Press, 1953.

Stock, Dorothy. "An Investigation into the Interrelations Between Self-concept and Feelings Directed Toward Other Persons and Groups." *Journal of Consulting Psychology*, 13:176–180, 1949.

Suinn, R. M. "The Relationship Between Self-acceptance and Acceptance of Others: A Learning Theory Analysis." *Journal of Abnormal and Social Psychology*, 63:37–42, 1961.

Tatum, Jack. *They Call Me Assassin*. New York: Everest House, 1979.

Temerlin, M. K. "On Choice and Responsibility in a Humanistic Psychotherapy." In I. T. Severin (ed.), *Humanistic Viewpoints in Psychology*. New York: McGraw-Hill, 1965.

Thomas, A., and S. Chess, *The Dynamics of Psychological Development*. New York: Brunner/Mazel, 1980.

Thomas A., S. Chess, and H. G. Birch. "The Origin of Personality." *Scientific American*, 223:102–109, 1970.

Thompson, S. K., and P. M. Beutler. "The Priority of Cues in Sex Discrimination by Children and Adults." *Developmental Psychology*, 2:181–185, 1971.

Tolman, E. C. "There is More Than One Kind of Learning." *Psychological Review*, 56:144–155, 1949.

Tresemer, David W. "Success Avoidance and Gender Roles." (Doctoral Dissertation, Harvard University, 1974). *Dissertation Abstracts International*, 35:4263 B (University Microfilms No. 75-4933), 1975.

————. "Research on Fear of Success: Full Annotated Bibliography." Journal Supplement Abstract Service of the American Psychological Association. Ms. 1237, 1976.

Truax, C. B., and K. M. Mitchell, "Research on Certain Therapist Interpersonal Skills in Relation to Process and Outcome." In A. E. Bergin and S. L. Garfield (eds.), *Handbook of Psychotherapy and Behavior Change*. New York: Wiley, 1971.

Tuddenham, R. O. "Constancy of Personality Ratings over Two Decades." *Genetic Psychology Monographs*, 60:3–29, 1959.

Turner, R. H., and R. H. Vanderlippe, "Self-ideal Congruence as an Index of Adjustment." *Journal of Abnormal and Social Psychology*, 57:202–206, 1958.

Vaihinger, H. *The Philosophy of "As If."* New York: Harcourt Brace Jovanovich, 1925.

Vaillant, George E. *Adaptation to Life*. Boston: Little, Brown, 1977.

Vochell, E. L., D. W. Felker, and C. H. Miley, "Birth-Order Literature, 1967–1972." *Journal of Individual Psychology*, 29:39–53, 1973.

Wahba, M. A., and L. B. Bridwell, "Maslow Reconsidered: A Review of Research on the Need Hierarchy Theory." *Organizational Behavior and Human Performance*, 15:212–240, 1976.

Walkenstein, Eileen. *Don't Shrink to Fit: A Confrontation with Dehumanization in Psychiatry and Psychology*. New York: Grove, 1977.

Walters, R. H., and Thomas E. Llewellyn. "Enhancement of Punitiveness by Visual and Audio-visual Displays." *Canadian Journal of Psychology*, 16:244–255, 1963.

————, R. D. Parke, and V. A. Cane. "Timing of Punishment and the Observation of Consequences to Others as Determinants of Response Inhibition." *Journal of Experimental Child Psychology* 2:10–30, 1965.

Waterman, A. S., and C. K. Waterman. "Freshman Ego-Identity Status and Subsequent Academic Behavior: A Test of Marcia's Categorization System for Identity Status." *Developmental Psychology*, 6:179, 1972.

————, E. Kohutis, and J. Polone. "The Role of Expressive Writing in Ego Identity Formation." *Developmental Psychology*, 52:11–50, 1977.

Waterman, C. K., M. E. Buebel, and A. S. Waterman. "Relationship Between Resolution of the Identity Crisis and Outcomes of Previous Psychosocial Crises." *Proceedings of the Annual Convention of the APA*, 5:467–468, 1970.

Watson, J. B. *Behavior: An Introduction to Comparative Psychology*. New York: Holt, Rinehart and Winston, 1914.
——— . *Behaviorism*. New York: Norton, 1925.
Webb, W. B., and H. W. Agnew, Jr. *Sleep and Dreams*. Dubuque, Iowa: Wm. C. Brown, 1973.
Werner, H., and B. Kaplan. *Symbol Formation*. New York: Wiley, 1963.
Wessman, A. E., and D. F. Ricks. *Mood and Personality*. New York: Holt, Rinehart and Winston, 1960.
White, R. W. "Motivation Reconsidered: The Concept of Competence." *Psychological Review*, 66:297–333, 1959.
Wild, C. "Creativity and Adaptive Regression." *Journal of Personality and Social Psychology*. 2:161–169, 1965.
Williams, Juanita. *Psychology of Women: Behavior in a Biosocial Context*. New York: Norton, 1977.
Wilson, W. C., and W. S. Verplanck. "Some Observations on the Reinforcement of Verbal Operants." *American Journal of Psychology* 69:448–451, 1956.
Winterbottom, M. R. "The Relation of Childhood Training in Independence to Achievement Motivation." In D. C. McClelland et al., *The Achievement Motive*. New York: Irvington Publishers, 1953.
Wolitzy, D. "Cognitive Control and Cognitive Dissonance." *Journal of Personality and Social Psychology*. 5:486–496, 1967.
Wolpe, J. *Psychotherapy by Reciprocal Inhibition*. Stanford, Calif.: Stanford University Press, 1958.
Worchel, P. "Anxiety and Repression." *Journal of Abnormal and Social Psychology*, 51:701–705, 1955.
Worthen, R., and W. E. O'Connell. "Social Interest and Humor." *International Journal of Social Psychiatry*, 15:179–188, 1969.
Wylie, R. C. "The Present Status of Self Theory." In E. F. Borgatta and W. W. Lambert (eds.), *Handbook of Personality Theory and Research*. Chicago: Rand-McNally, 1968.
——— . *The Self-concept*. Vol. I, *A Review of Methodological Considerations and Measuring Instruments*, 1974; Vol. II, *Theory and Research on Selected Topics*, 1978. Lincoln: University of Nebraska Press.
Yankelovich, Daniel, *New Rules*. New York: Random House, 1981.
Zaccaria, J. S., and W. R. Weir, "A Comparison of Alcoholics and Selected Samples of Nonalcoholics in Terms of a Positive Concept of Mental Health." *Journal of Social Psychology*, 71:151–157, 1967.
Zeller, A. "An Experimental Analogue of Repression: II. The Effect of Individual Failure and Success on Memory Measured by Relearning." *Journal of Experimental Psychology*, 40:411–422, 1951.
Zimbardo, Philip G. *Shyness*. Reading, Mass.: Addison-Wesley, 1977.

INDEX